Complete Ancient Greek
Gavin Betts & Alan Henry

The authors wish to acknowledge the help of George Gellie, Deane Blackman and Peggy Molloy.

For UK order enquiries: please contact Bookpoint Ltd, 130 Milton Park, Abingdon, Oxon OX14 4SB. Telephone: +44 (0) 1235 827720. Fax: +44 (0) 1235 400454. Lines are open 09.00–17.00, Monday to Saturday, with a 24-hour message answering service. Details about our titles and how to order are available at www.teachyourself.com

For USA order enquiries: please contact McGraw-Hill Customer Services, PO Box 545, Blacklick, OH 43004-0545, USA. Telephone: 1-800-722-4726. Fax: 1-614-755-5645.

For Canada order enquiries: please contact McGraw-Hill Ryerson Ltd, 300 Water St, Whitby, Ontario L1N 9B6, Canada. Telephone: 905 430 5000. Fax: 905 430 5020.

Long renowned as the authoritative source for self-guided learning – with more than 50 million copies sold worldwide – the **Teach Yourself** series includes over 500 titles in the fields of languages, crafts, hobbies, business, computing and education.

British Library Cataloguing in Publication Data: a catalogue record for this title is available from the British Library.

Library of Congress Catalog Card Number: on file.

First published in UK 1989 as *Teach Yourself Ancient Greek* by Hodder Education, part of Hachette UK, 338 Euston Road, London NW1 3BH.

First published in US 1993 by The McGraw-Hill Companies, Inc.

This edition published 2010.

The **Teach Yourself** name is a registered trade mark of Hachette UK.

Typeset by MPS Limited, A Macmillan Company.

Printed in Great Britain for Hodder Education, an Hachette UK Company, 338 Euston Road, London NW1 3BH.

Hachette UK's policy is to use papers that are natural, renewable and recyclable products and made from wood grown in sustainable forests. The logging and manufacturing processes are expected to conform to the environmental regulations of the country of origin.

Impression number 10 9 8 7 6 5 4 3 2 1

Year 2014 2013 2012 2011 2010

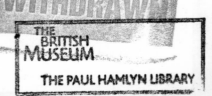

Contents

For the **Glossary of Grammatical Terms** and
Suggestions for Further Study see the Internet website
http://tyancientgreek.org

Credits

Front cover: © The Art Gallery Collection / Alamy

Back cover: © Jakub Semeniuk/iStockphoto.com, © Royalty-
Free/Corbis, © agencyby/iStockphoto.com, © Andy Cook/
iStockphoto.com, © Christopher Ewing/iStockphoto.com,
© zebicho – Fotolia.com, © Geoffrey Holman/iStockphoto.com,
© Photodisc/Getty Images, © James C. Pruitt/iStockphoto.com,
© Mohamed Saber – Fotolia.com

Meet the authors

Alan Henry and I worked together for over twenty years in the department of Classical Studies at Monash University, Melbourne, Australia. During that time we were engaged in teaching Ancient Greek from beginners' classes to fourth-year honours. We soon discovered that the beginners, who generally had no previous experience of learning another language, were handicapped by the elementary books available. Many of these had been written for use in schools when Greek was commonly taught, and as well as assuming a knowledge of traditional grammar they contained many sentences and passages of made-up Greek. Other elementary books were aimed at an adult audience but still suffered from the same fault. Sentences such as *the tree is neither beautiful nor useful* or *the gifts have loosened the sailor's tongue* seemed hardly likely to capture a reader's interest. To avoid this we wondered if real Greek from ancient authors could be found, authentic texts that beginners could understand and that would serve both as examples of grammar and as reading exercises. We might need to adapt some pieces, but this could be kept to a minimum. The present volume is the result. Many proverbs and pithy sayings have been included, as well as stories about famous figures such as Diogenes, the eccentric philosopher who lived in a tub. These lead on to passages from the great authors such as Aeschylus, Euripides, Demosthenes and others, and the book concludes with four pieces from the poet who dominated Greek literature – Homer.

Gavin Betts

Only got a minute?

A modern translation of an ancient classic such as Homer's *Iliad* often puzzles readers with the difference between the work's overall conception and the flatness of the English. The work's true merit may flicker dimly through the translation's mundane prose or clumsy verse but any subtlety is missing. Instead of a literary masterpiece we are often left with a hotchpotch of banal words and awkward expressions. Take this version of the first lines of the Iliad:

> *The Wrath of Achilles is my theme, that fatal wrath which, in fulfilment of the will of Zeus, brought the Achaeans so much suffering and sent the gallant souls of many noblemen to Hades, leaving their bodies as carrion for the dogs and passing birds. Let us begin, goddess of song, with the angry parting that took place between Agamemnon King of Men and the great Achilles son of Peleus. Which of the gods was it that made them quarrel?* (translated E.V.Rieu, Penguin Books 1950)

Can this really represent the work of a poet who has been universally admired for millennia? Or is it a TV announcer introducing a guest singer, whom he flatters with the trite phrase *goddess of song*?

Compare the eighteenth-century translation of Alexander Pope:

Achilles' wrath, to Greece the direful spring
Of woes unnumber'd, heavenly goddess, sing!

That wrath which hurl'd to Pluto's gloomy reign
The souls of mighty chiefs untimely slain;
Whose limbs unburied on the naked shore,
Devouring dogs and hungry vultures tore:
Since great Achilles and Atrides strove,
Such was the sovereign doom, and such the will of Jove!
Declare, O Muse! in what ill-fated hour
Sprung the fierce strife, from what offended power?

Here we have genuine poetry. Only when the translator himself is a real poet can the result give some idea of the original but even then its true spirit is lost and, as here, the translator's own style and personality inevitably intrudes. There is no substitute for getting back to the author's actual words. To understand and appreciate the masterpieces of ancient Greek literature we must go back to the original Greek.

This book is for complete beginners. At an early stage they are presented with original sentences and extracts from Greek authors. Made-up Greek, a feature of many introductory courses, is kept to an absolute minimum. Readers are introduced to the great writers of Greek literature such as Homer, Aeschylus, Euripides, Plato and others. After completing the book they will be able to continue further in these and other authors.

The book is accompanied by a web site with extra material (tyancientgreek.org).

5 Only got five minutes?

Even a sheep bites an unlucky man.

Diogenes was once begging alms from a statue. When he was asked why he was doing this, he said, 'I am practising failure.'

An army of deer led by a lion is more frightening than an army of lions led by a deer.

When a garrulous barber asked the Spartan king Archelaus, 'How am I to cut your hair, O King?' Archelaus said, 'In silence.'

That the Greeks had a talent for wit is evident in many sentences and passages included in the reading exercises of this book. However, the Greek genius went far deeper than amusing proverbs and stories. In most literary genres our western traditions began with them. For example, the Greeks invented the different forms of drama that we still enjoy today. Both tragedy and comedy began in Greece in the sixth and fifth centuries BC.

Tragedy developed from a ritual in honour of the god Dionysus in which formal choral songs were presented to an audience by a group of dancers with a single actor speaking at intervals to its leaders. When a second and third actor were introduced it became possible to depict conflict and action on stage. The three leading exponents, Aeschylus, Sophocles and Euripides (all fifth century BC), used tragedy to present social and moral problems through the conflicting interests of the individuals represented. Their surviving plays and those of their Roman imitator, Seneca, were the models used in the Renaissance to revive tragedy as a genre.

The earliest surviving writer of comedy was the Athenian Aristophanes, whose plays span the first two phases of comedy. The strong political and social criticism of Old Comedy (fifth century BC) was followed by the less vehement Middle Comedy (early and middle fourth century BC), but it was the third stage, New Comedy (late fourth century BC), that remained the favourite form up to the end of the ancient world. The plays of its most successful authors, in particular Menander, were adapted by Roman playwrights, who supplied prototypes for Shakespeare, Molière and others. The basic plot of New Comedy, that of two ill-starred lovers who are finally united, lives on today in countless television melodramas.

But it is not in cultural matters alone that western civilization is built on Greek foundations. The scientific examination and treatment of human maladies and diseases had a long history in Greece and what survived of ancient medical writings was taken up and built upon in Renaissance Europe. Democracy first appeared and developed in city states such as Athens. Their experience has been studied in modern times and has influenced the way in which constitutions have been drawn up and governments established.

What we have of Greek literature, political theory and science has many claims on our attention. This book introduces readers to ancient Greek and takes them through passages from the tragedians, Plato, Demosthenes and others. It is directed to adults and does not contain the usual stodgy made-up Greek of the type 'Granny ate five small fish on the Acropolis'. The many poems and stories, all taken from ancient authors, provide entertaining reading as well as instruction in language matters. A website (tyancientgreek.org) gives the reader extra material.

10 Only got ten minutes?

The Greeks had a word for it was an expression current some years ago and it carried the implication that the ancient Greeks were more adept than we are today at putting a name to concepts or to phenomena not easily named or classified.

The truth of this lies in the vast number of Greek words that have been taken into English. *Acme, analysis, automaton, genesis, dogma, crisis, chaos, character, psyche* and many others have all been borrowed from ancient Greek without any change. Others such as *anthology, arithmetic, polygamy* have been slightly altered. Many of these words have been in English for centuries but so ingrained is our habit of turning to Greek for lexical needs that we make up new words from Greek elements. An example is *cosmonaut*, formed from the Greek **kosmos** *universe* and **nautes** *sailor*.

However, our debt to the civilization of the Greeks goes much deeper than words and the concepts that lie behind them. It was the Greeks who began most of the literary genres with which we are familiar today. Herodotus (died c.425 BC) was declared even in antiquity to be the father of history. Drama, both tragedy and comedy, was first produced in Greek of the sixth and fifth century BC. Epic and lyric poetry go back even earlier with Homer, Archilochus, Sappho and others. The first biography is that of the Persian, Cyrus the Great, written by a Greek, Xenophon. The idea of using prose to tell a long story led to the novel, which writers such as Longus, the author of *Daphnis and Chloe*, employed to recount the wildly romantic adventures and final reunion of two lovers. Their initiative was taken up over a millennium later when the modern novel began.

In science too the Greeks were innovators. In none of the older civilizations, such as those of India and China, do we find societies that encouraged, or even allowed, an examination of the world and human life untrammelled by superstitions or political fiats. It is to the Greeks that we owe the spirit of free inquiry. They alone turned from traditional beliefs and began an investigation into natural phenomena. The explanations they gave were based on observation.

In medicine this frame of mind led to doctors diagnosing health problems rather than imagining them to be the result of supernatural interference. Surgical techniques were developed, but efforts were also directed towards a proper understanding of the workings of the human body. One such theory was that diseases and physical infirmities were caused by an imbalance of four bodily fluids – blood, phlegm, yellow bile and black bile. In later ages this remained current long enough to give us the English *sanguine*, *phlegmatic* and *melancholic,* each describing a condition caused by an excess of blood, phlegm and black bile respectively. Galen (second century AD), perhaps the greatest of Greek doctors, continued to be studied during the Renaissance, and with his surviving writings and those of other ancient doctors modern medicine began.

The inquiries into the nature of the physical world that started in the sixth century BC represented a deliberate renunciation of the old myths that saw divine activity everywhere. These culminated with Leucippus and Democritus, who postulated that matter was formed of small indivisible particles, to which they gave the name of atoms, and so anticipated the findings of modern physics.

At the same time the Athenian Socrates began investigating society and the behaviour of the individual within it. In this he was followed by Plato, who, with his younger contemporary Aristotle, set up a field of study which still exists and which we call philosophy. The schools of thought they established were supplemented by others, of which the most influential were the Stoics and Epicureans.

However, it is in the organization of society that we owe most to ancient Greece. It was in Greece that democracy first appeared and flourished. Herodotus in a famous passage declared that the fairest claim of democracy was equality before the law and that it avoided the excesses of despotism; those holding office were held accountable for their actions, and all matters were referred to the people. When he wrote, the most prominent example of the democratic system was Athens, where elaborate checks and controls also ensured that citizens participated in both decision-making and administration. The Athenian model has often been studied and imitated in modern times.

In cultural, scientific and civic matters the debt we owe to the Greeks is enormous. It is no exaggeration to say that western civilisation began with them.

This book takes a wholly adult approach. It does not contain the mass of artificial Greek, once a standard feature of school text-books, that still appears in many books of self-instruction in the language. No prior knowledge of the language is assumed. Genuine Greek is introduced at an early stage. A web-site (tyancientgreek. org) provides a glossary of grammatical terms, suggestions for further study, extra reading and exercises.

Introduction

How to use this book

ἀρχὴ ἥμισυ παντός *a [good] beginning is half the whole*

On one occasion when giving a speech, Hiero, a Greek ruler in ancient Sicily, was interrupted by complaints about his bad breath. This revelation of what must have been a chronic problem distressed him considerably, and on returning home he reproached his wife for not having told him of it. She indignantly justified herself by saying that she had thought that all adult males smelt as he did. To depend on a virtuous spouse to correct such faults has obvious dangers. If you are relying solely on this book to begin the study of ancient Greek, there are similar pitfalls. Apart from the key, you will have few checks on your progress, and it will be essential to follow up any doubt, however small, about meanings of words and points of grammar. To be able to do this you must make yourself completely familiar with the arrangement of the book's contents.

We assume that you are acquainted with the basics of traditional English grammar, as this is the framework we use to explain the structure of Greek. You should be familiar with the **parts of speech** (*adjective, adverb, article, conjunction, interjection, noun, preposition, pronoun, verb*) and with the meaning of such terms as *finite, transitive/intransitive, clause, phrase, subject, object,* etc. If these are new to you, you should consult the *Glossary of grammatical terms* on the website **tyancientgreek.org,** or one of the many elementary books on the subject.

The main part of the book consists of twenty-five units. Each consists of either two or three sections. The first is taken up with grammar, the second contains sentences and passages of Greek for reading, while the third section (except in the first unit) is a longer Greek passage for additional reading.

The grammatical sections, which are headed **.1**, are carefully graded over the course of the book in order to set out the basic features of Greek grammar in a systematic and easily digestible way. Each should be mastered before tackling the next. Very often a particular section cannot be understood without a knowledge of what has gone before.

Grammar as a whole can be divided into two parts, one involving the forms which a word can take (e.g. those of a first declension feminine noun, 2.1/2), the other dealing with the ways in which these forms are used to make up phrases and sentences (e.g. the uses of the dative case, 2.1/3*e*). The former we must learn by heart. The latter we can only fully understand when, after learning a general rule, we see, and are able to understand, examples of it in use. Because of the importance of such examples the sentences given to illustrate grammatical rules are nearly always original Greek, and every effort should be made to understand them fully. By reading them carefully every time you revise a unit you will not only come to understand the grammatical point involved but also extend your vocabulary.

To work through the reading exercises with one finger in the corresponding page of the key is **not** recommended, although you should make full use of any help provided by the notes. It is only by analyzing the forms of words and patiently working out the construction of clauses and sentences that you will make progress. A full translation of an exercise should be written out and then compared with the key. When you discover you have made a mistake, you must meticulously hunt out the point of grammar concerned and see how you came to be wrong. To help you do this many cross references have been supplied in all parts of the book (a reference of the form 22.1/2 is for the **grammatical** section (.1) of a unit, but one such as 22.2.2 is to the **reading** section (.2)). Your final step should be to read through the Greek aloud until you are able to translate it without reference to your own version or the key. This will familiarize you with the construction employed and any new vocabulary. Some rote learning of new words is, of course, inevitable. If, however, you go to the trouble of actually memorizing some of the many famous phrases and verse passages contained in the reading you will find your grasp on the language extending itself in an enjoyable and rewarding fashion.

Appendices 1–7 give grammatical tables and other information to supplement particular units. **Appendix 8** is on accentuation and should be consulted regularly and mastered over the course of the whole book. **Appendix 9** is added to show how Greek verse was constructed; a knowledge of metre is not necessary for understanding Greek verse but obviously adds to our enjoyment of it.

The section **Principal parts of verbs** complements the vocabulary with information about verbs whose present stem is either not used, or not used in a regular way, to provide the stems of other tenses.

For ease of reference to grammatical points an index is provided.

The Glossary of Grammatical Terms, Suggestions for Further Study, as well as extra reading, revision exercises, and other material will be found on the website **http://tyancientgreek.org**.

Abbreviations

a. or acc.	accusative	cap.	capital
absol.	absolute	cf.	compare
act.	active	compar.	comparative
adj.	adjective, adjectival	conj.	conjunction
adv.	adverb, adverbial	dat.	dative
aor.	aorist	ex.	example
c.	about, approximately	f. or f	feminine

f.	following	pass.	passive
fut.	future	pers.	person
gen.	genitive	perf.	perfect
imp.	imperative	pl.	plural
impers.	impersonal	plpf.	pluperfect
impf.	imperfect	poet.	poetical
ind.	indicative	poss.	possessive
indecl.	indeclinable	pple.	participle
indef.	indefinite	prep.	preposition
indir.	indirect	pres.	present
inf.	infinitive	pron.	pronoun
interrog.	interrogative	refl.	reflexive
intr.	intransitive	rel.	relative
l.	line	s.	singular
lit.	literally	*sc.*	namely
ll.	lines	subj.	subjunctive
m. or m	masculine	supl.	superlative
mid.	middle	tr.	transitive
n. or n	neuter	trans.	translate
n. or nom.	nominative	v. or voc.	vocative
opt.	optative	viz	that is to say

Round brackets ( ) contain explanatory material or a literal translation; in the vocabulary round brackets are also used to indicate alternative forms.

Square brackets [ ] are used in translations for words which are required by English idiom but have no equivalent in the Greek original; not all such words are marked in this way. Square brackets are also used to supply missing words.

+ means *in conjunction with, compounded with,* or *followed by.*

< means *is derived from.*

> means *produce(s).*

* marks a word which cannot stand first in a clause or phrase.

\# indicates that the following sentence or passage is verse; in the vocabulary this sign indicates that the word to which it is attached is poetical.

† is explained in the introductory note to the vocabulary.

Unit 1

....

1.1 Grammar

1.1/1 The Greek alphabet and its pronunciation

The Greek alphabet consists of twenty-four letters, each with its traditional name. Today it is used in both upper and lower case but in antiquity it existed only in different varieties of capitals. The pronunciation given below does not in every case reflect what we know of the language of fourth century Athens (the type of Greek described here – see 1.3); because we learn ancient Greek for the purpose of reading, not of communication, we do not need to be as careful about its pronunciation as we would be with a modern language.

	Name	Pronunciation
A α	alpha (ἄλφα)	*a* (see below)
B β	bēta (βῆτα)	*b*
Γ γ	gamma (γάμμα)	*g* (as in *game*, never as in *gesture*, but as *n* in *ink* before κ, ξ, χ or another γ; see below)
Δ δ	delta (δέλτα)	*d*
E ε	epsilon (ἒ ψῑλόν)	short *e* (as in *met*)
Z ζ	zēta (ζῆτα)	*sd* (as in *wisdom*, but represented in English as *z*)
H η	ēta (ἦτα)	long *e* (like *ai* in *fairy*)
Θ θ	thēta (θῆτα)	*th* (as in *thing*; see below)
I ι	iōta (ἰῶτα)	*i* (see below)
K κ	kappa (κάππα)	*k* (but represented in English as *c*)
Λ λ	lambda (λάμβδα)	*l*
M μ	mū (μῦ)	*m*
N ν	nū (νῦ)	*n*
Ξ ξ	xī (ξεῖ)	*x* (as in *axe*)
O ο	omicron (ὂ μικρόν)	short *o* (as in *lot*)
Π π	pī (πεῖ)	*p*
P ρ	rhō (ῥῶ)	*r*

Σ σ, ς	sigma (σίγμα)	s (as in *sign*)
Τ τ	tau (ταῦ)	t
Υ υ	upsīlon (ὖ ψῑλόν)	u (but represented in English as y except in diphthongs, e.g. *hypothesis, autopsy*)
Φ φ	phī (φεῖ)	ph (see below)
Χ χ	chī (χεῖ)	ch (see below)
Ψ ψ	psī (ψεῖ)	ps (as in *maps*)
Ω ω	ōmega (ὦ μέγα)	long o (like *oa* in *broad*)

When initial or medial, sigma takes the form σ but when final it is written ς. Examples are σύστασις *composition*, Σωσιγένης *Sosigenes*. There is only one upper-case sigma (Σ).

In Greek words taken into English and in transcriptions of Greek proper names Greek letters are normally represented by their phonetic equivalent except where indicated above (and in some diphthongs – see note 2).

Consonants

The normal English pronunciation is recommended where no example is given. To distinguish between κ and χ the latter is pronounced as the *ch* in the Scottish pronunciation of *loch*. The letters ζ, ξ, ψ are double consonants and the equivalents of σδ, κσ, πσ respectively, for which they must always be used: e.g. when σ is added to the stem γῦπ- we must write γῦψ, never γῦπς (5.1/1). The letters θ, φ, χ are **not** double consonants; the pronunciation given above is that normally used today but in the Greek of our period they were pronounced as *t, p, k* with an accompanying emission of breath (i.e. something like these consonants in English when initial. Compare the difference between the English and French pronunciation of the *P* in *Paris*).

Examples of the second pronunciation of γ are: σπόγγος (spóngos) *sponge*, Σφίγξ (Sphinx) *Sphinx*, ἔλεγχος (élenchos) *scrutiny*.

Vowels

All Greek vowels have a long and short pronunciation. These pronunciations have separate symbols in the case of ε/η and ο/ω.

The other vowels have both values but only one symbol. In works of reference, but not in normal printed texts, the two values of these vowels are distinguished by marking the long form with a bar above (macron), ᾱ, ῑ, ῡ. They are pronounced:

ᾱ as in *father*
α (i.e. short *a*) as in a shortened version of ᾱ, like *u* in *but*, never as in *sat* (this sound did not exist in Greek).
ῑ as *ee* in *need*
ι as *i* in *sit* (or, more accurately, as in French *petit*).
ῡ as in French *sûr*
υ as in French *tu*

Diphthongs

Greek had two types of diphthongs:

(i) where both elements are written normally and pronounced as follows:

αι as *ai* in *aisle*	οι as *oi* in *oil*
αυ as *ow* in *cow*	ου as *oo* in *cool*
ει as *ei* in *rein*	υι as *we*
ευ/ηυ as *eu* in *feud*	

When any of these combinations is not to be taken as a diphthong, the second element is marked with a diaeresis (¨): βοΐ (bo-í), Λαΐς (La-ís).

(ii) where the long vowels ᾱ, η, ω are combined with an iota. This iota is placed **below** the vowel (**iota subscript**), not after it: ᾳ, ῃ, ῳ.[1] For convenience these diphthongs are always pronounced as simple ᾱ, η, ω.

Breathings

Every word beginning with a vowel or diphthong has a rough (ʽ) or smooth (ʼ) breathing. A rough breathing denotes an initial *h*; a

---

[1] The iota is, however, placed **after** the long vowel when the latter is in upper case. The only common example is Ἀιδης *Hades*.

smooth breathing (which is something of a superfluity) the absence of initial *h*: ἡμέρᾱ (hēmérā) *day*, ἀγαθός (agathós) *good*. A breathing is placed over the second element of a category (i) diphthong: αἴνιγμα (aínigma) *riddle*; Αἰσχύλος (Aischúlos) *Aeschylus*; but when an initial vowel which does not form part of a diphthong is in upper case the breathing is placed in front: Ὅμηρος (Hómēros) *Homer*. Words beginning with υ always have a rough breathing ὗς (hūs) *pig*; ὕψος (húpsos) *height*. Initial ρ is also always given a rough breathing because it was pronounced *rh*: ῥυθμός (rhuthmós) *rhythm*.

Notes

1 In the grammar and reference sections long α, ι, υ are marked ᾱ, ῑ, ῡ, except in the case of ᾳ, ᾷ, ῗ, ῧ, because iota subscript appears only under long vowels and in the other three cases the circumflex accent (see next subsection) shows that the vowel must be long.

2 The traditional spelling and pronunciation of Greek proper names, and also the form taken by Greek derivatives in English, almost always reflect the Roman system of transliteration: Αἰσχύλος (Aischúlos) *Aéschylus*; Οἰδίπους (Oidípous) *Oédipus*; καταστροφή (katastrophé) *catástrophe*.

3 For marks of punctuation Greek uses the full stop and comma as in English but for colon and semicolon there is only one sign, which is a dot towards the top of the line (·). Our semicolon is used as a question mark in Greek (;). Inverted commas and the exclamation mark are not normally used. A capital letter is used at the beginning of a paragraph but not with each new sentence.

1.1/2 Accents

We owe the idea of visually indicating word accent to Aristophanes of Byzantium (not to be confused with the Athenian comic poet), an altruistic scholar of around 200 BC who wished to help foreigners to pronounce Greek correctly. Since the Renaissance, accents have always been employed in printed texts. While not of crucial importance in reading Greek, they are useful in distinguishing certain words and present little difficulty if correctly approached.

Accent in classical Greek was one of **pitch**, not of stress as in English. An English-speaker, when told that ἄνθρωπος *human being* is accented on its first syllable, would naturally pronounce that syllable with a heavier emphasis. A Greek, however, instead of emphasising the α, would have pronounced it at a higher pitch and so given the word what we should consider a somewhat sing-song effect. We do, of course, use pitch in spoken English, but in a totally different way. In the question *you're going to Athens?* the last word has a rising pitch, but in the statement *you're going to Athens* it has a falling pitch.

Classical Greek has three accents:
    ΄ **acute**, indicating rising pitch
    ` **grave**, indicating falling pitch
    ˆ **circumflex**, indicating a combined rising and falling pitch (the sign, originally ^, is a combination of an acute and a grave). Because the time taken by this operation was necessarily longer than that indicated by an acute or a grave, it can occur only with long vowels and diphthongs, and only on these do we find a circumflex.

The basic features of Greek accentuation are:

(a) nearly every word has an accent, which can be on the final syllable (ποταμός *river*), or the second syllable from the end (ἵππος *horse*), or on the third syllable from the end (ἱπποπόταμος *hippopotamus*). In forms of verbs the position of the accent is nearly always determined by the length of the final syllable (see **Appendix 8**, *b*); with other words whose form can change the accent is generally fixed.

(b) an acute or grave accent can stand on a diphthong or long or short vowel, but a circumflex only on a long vowel or diphthong.

(c) an acute can stand on the end syllable of a word (πειρᾱτής *pirate*), on the second from the end (μοναρχίᾱ *monarchy*), or on the third from the end (ἀκρόπολις *acropolis*).

(d) a grave can stand only on a final syllable, where it automatically replaces an acute when another word follows (ὁ πειρᾶτὴς ἀπάγει τὸν ἱπποπόταμον *the pirate is leading away the hippopotamus*). A final acute is retained, however, before a mark of punctuation (ὦ ποιητά, ἢ πῖθι ἢ ἄπιθι *O poet, either drink or go away*) or when a word so accented is quoted. (For the effect of enclitics see **Appendix 8, *d***).

(e) a circumflex can stand on a final syllable (τῶν ποταμῶν *of the rivers*) and, within certain limitations, on the second from the end (Μυκῆναι *Mycenae*).

The rules for accents are given in **Appendix 8**. These should be referred to and gradually mastered in the course of studying this book. For purposes of pronouncing Greek words, each of the three accents should be treated alike and given a simple stress accent as in English. The old British (and Dutch) habit of imposing the Latin system of accentuation on Greek is to be avoided. This system has prevailed in our pronunciation of nearly all Greek proper names in English. We say *Eurípides* (Εὐρῑπίδης), *Sócrates* (Σωκράτης), *Epidaúrus* (Ἐπίδαυρος) because the Romans, not unreasonably, adapted them in this way to their own language (cf. second note to last subsection). A Roman, however, who did the same in actually speaking Greek (as every educated Roman could), would have been disowned by his friends as an embarrassing ignoramus.

Insight

Our earliest evidence for the Greek alphabet as we know it dates from the eighth century BC. This was adapted from a script used by the Phoenicians, a Semitic people living on the coast of modern Syria and Lebanon. The novelty of the Greek alphabet was the introduction of letters representing vowels, which had been lacking in its Phoenician precursor. To this day it has remained the instrument for writing Greek. The adapted form used by the Romans has always been used in Western Europe, while another derivative, the Cyrillic alphabet, is used in Russia and other countries where the dominant religion is Orthodox Christianity.

1.2 Exercise

1 Read aloud and transliterate the following names of famous writers: Ἀριστοτέλης, Ἀριστοφάνης, Δημοσθένης, Ἡρόδοτος, Θεόκριτος, Καλλίμαχος, Πίνδαρος, Πλάτων.

2 Read aloud and transliterate the following words and then look up their meaning in the vocabulary:

ἀκμή, ἀνάθεμα, ἀνάλῡσις, ἀντίθεσις, ἄσβεστος, αὐτόματον, ἀφασίᾱ, βάθος, γένεσις, διάγνωσις, δόγμα, δρᾶμα, ζώνη, ἦθος, ἠχώ, ἰδέᾱ, κῑνημα, κλῖμαξ, κόσμος, κρίσις, κῶλον, μέτρον, μίασμα, νέκταρ, νέμεσις, ὀρχήστρᾱ, πάθος, σκηνή, στίγμα, ὕβρις, ὑπόθεσις, χάος, χαρακτήρ, ψῡχή.

3 For practice with capitals read aloud and identify the following proper names (accents are not used when a word is put in upper case):
(*a*) ΑΓΑΜΕΜΝΩΝ, ΑΧΙΛΛΕΥΣ, ΕΚΤΩΡ, ΕΛΕΝΗ, ΟΔΥΣΣΕΥΣ, ΠΑΤΡΟΚΛΟΣ, ΠΗΝΕΛΟΠΕΙΑ.
(*b*) ΑΘΗΝΑΙ, ΑΡΓΟΣ, ΘΗΒΑΙ, ΚΟΡΙΝΘΟΣ, ΣΠΑΡΤΗ, ΚΡΗΤΗ, ΡΟΔΟΣ, ΣΑΜΟΣ.

1.3 Excursus – The different forms of Greek

Greek is a member of the Indo-European family of languages, as are English, French, German and most European languages. The original Indo-European speakers lived in what is now western Russia but migration began at an early date, possibly soon after 3000 BC. The groups which we would now call Greek originally came to Greece at different times during the period 2000–1000 BC. They have lived there ever since and preserved their identity despite invasions and long periods of foreign domination. Greek communities also existed, in some cases for over 2,500 years, in other Mediterranean countries and in Asia Minor.

The earliest records in Greek date from about 1300 BC and are written on clay tablets in a syllabic script called Linear B, which is totally different from the Greek alphabet familiar to us. On the latter see above.

It is possible that Greek had already split into dialects early in the second millenium BC. Certainly there is unmistakable evidence of different dialects in the oldest works of Greek literature, the *Iliad* and the *Odyssey* of Homer (25.1/1), which must have been composed before 700 BC (their exact date and manner of composition are matters of dispute). From then up to the time of Alexander the Great (died 323 BC) a large quantity of Greek texts survives and proves the existence of five major dialect groups, which show, in some cases, considerable differences from each other. By no means all dialects served as vehicles of literature and we need only concern ourselves with those which were so used. From an early stage Greek literature was clearly divided into different genres (epic, elegiac poetry, choral lyric, etc.), and often a particular dialect became so intimately associated with a literary genre that a tradition was established which sometimes lasted long after the dialect had ceased to be spoken. Some of these associations are mentioned in the following list:

Ionic – the language of the Aegean islands (except those on the southern fringe and Lesbos to the north) and the central area of the west coast of Asia Minor. The latter contained the most important Ionic settlements and it was there that Greek cultural and intellectual life began with Homer and the earliest philosophers. Poets of the 7th and 6th centuries BC established Ionic as the dialect of elegiac and iambic poetry. It was also the original dialect for literary prose and was used by Herodotus (a Dorian by birth) for his *Histories* (4.2.9).

Aeolic – the language of Lesbos and the adjoining Asia Minor coast. It was used by the most famous poetess of antiquity, Sappho (early 6th century BC), and her male contemporary, Alcaeus, for personal lyric poetry. Their initiative was not continued.

Homeric dialect – the language of Homer's *Iliad* and *Odyssey*. This was an artificial dialect which was never the language of a particular area or group, but had been developed over a long period by generations of poets. It was basically an older form of Ionic but with elements from other dialects, chiefly Aeolic. Homer's position as the greatest Greek poet was never disputed in antiquity, and epics which reproduced his language were still being written in the 5th century AD. The Ionic of Elegy, which survived even longer, generally had a Homeric flavour.

Doric – the language of the Peloponnesus (except the central and north-west area), Crete, and other parts of the Greek world. Choral poetry, which was sung by dancing choirs, was originally the creation of Dorians and even when written by non-Doric speakers was always given at least a Doric flavour.

Attic – the language of Athens (historically an offshoot of Ionic). With the rapid political expansion and cultural development of Athens after the final defeat of the Persians by the Greeks (479 BC) Attic became firmly established as a literary dialect despite its late start when compared with Ionic and Aeolic. By the beginning of the 4th century BC Athens had become the main cultural centre of Greece. This was in no small measure brought about by the literary masterpieces that had been written and were still being written by Athenians in their own dialect. The Attic of the early and middle period of the 4th century BC, as exemplified in Plato's dialogues and Demosthenes' speeches, has always been taken as the most satisfactory form of Greek for beginners and is the type described in this book. Attic is the language of Tragedy and Comedy (except for their choral odes, which have a tinge of Doric). By the end of the 5th century BC it had superseded Ionic as the language of prose.

The conquests of Alexander had important political and linguistic consequences for the Greek world, which he enlarged considerably. Greek culture and civilisation were extended over all lands bordering on the eastern Mediterranean and a lingua franca emerged which, with a few exceptions, gradually replaced the older dialects even in Greece itself. This new language was basically a development of Attic and was called ἡ κοινὴ διάλεκτος *the common dialect* (in English the **koine**). It was the language of the Greek man in the street and for that reason was used by the writers of the New Testament, who wanted to reach as wide an audience as possible. Educated classes, imbued with the prestige of Classical Attic, regarded it as a debased form of Greek, but the koine, apart from the few survivors of the older dialects, had, by the first century of our era, become the living form of the language and is the ancestor of **Modern Greek**.

The latter cannot, of course, be understood simply with a knowledge of 4th century Attic or the koine, but, because of the conservative nature of Greek, which we see at all periods, the changes that have occurred over a period of 2400 years are fewer than those which distinguish Modern English from Anglo-Saxon.

Unit 2

For *this and all subsequent units extra reading will be found at the Internet website* **http://tyancientgreek.org**

2.1 Grammar

2.1/1 Nouns in Greek

In English the gender of a noun is determined by its meaning; *man* is masculine, *woman* is feminine, *car* is neuter, and when referring to these we would say *he, she, it* respectively. In Greek, however, the gender of a noun is often arbitrary and does not necessarily indicate anything about what it denotes. While, for example, γυνή *woman* is feminine and ἀνήρ *man* is masculine, χώρᾱ *land* is feminine, and λόγος *speech* is masculine, though δῶρον *gift* is, understandably, neuter. More often than not we cannot see why a particular noun has a particular gender. It is, however, generally possible to tell the gender of a noun by its ending in the nominative and genitive singular, and it is also according to these endings that Greek nouns are grouped into three classes, which are called **declensions**. Each declension has a distinctive set of endings which indicate both case and number, just as in English we have *child, child's, children, children's,* though Greek distinguishes more cases. To go through the list of all possible forms of a noun is to **decline** it.

2.1/2 First declension (feminine nouns) and the feminine definite article

Most first declension nouns are feminine (the few masculines are declined slightly differently – 3.1/2). The feminines end in -η or -α. Those in -α change alpha to eta in the genitive and dative singular unless the alpha is preceded by a vowel or ρ. All first declension nouns have the same endings in the plural. The feminine form of the definite article is declined in the same way as the feminines in -η.

Nominative	ἡ	τῑμ-ή	χώρ-ᾱ	θάλαττ-α
	the	honour	country	sea
Vocative	——	τῑμ-ή	χώρ-ᾱ	θάλαττ-α
Accusative	τήν	τῑμ-ήν	χώρ-ᾱν	θάλαττ-αν
Genitive	τῆς	τῑμ-ῆς	χώρ-ᾱς	θαλάττ-ης
Dative	τῇ	τῑμ-ῇ	χώρ-ᾳ	θαλάττ-ῃ

PLURAL

Nominative	αἱ	τῑμ-αί	χῶρ-αι	θάλαττ-αι
Vocative	——	τῑμ-αί	χῶρ-αι	θάλαττ-αι
Accusative	τᾱς	τῑμ-ᾱς	χώρ-ᾱς	θαλάττ-ᾱς
Genitive	τῶν	τῑμ-ῶν	χωρ-ῶν	θαλαττ-ῶν
Dative	ταῖς	τῑμ-αῖς	χώρ-αις	θαλάττ-αις

Notes

1 The definite article must agree with the noun it qualifies in number, gender, and case: τῶν τῑμῶν *of the honours*, τᾱς χώρᾱς *the countries* (accusative). Contexts where it is used in Greek but not in English are:

(i) with abstract nouns, ἡ ἀλήθεια *truth*

(ii) with nouns (usually plural) indicating a general class, αἱ κόραι *girls* (as a class)

(iii) optionally with proper nouns, with no differences in sense: ἡ Σικελίᾱ or Σικελίᾱ *Sicily*, ἡ Ἀφροδίτη or Ἀφροδίτη *Aphrodite*.

In translating a common noun in the singular without the definite article, *a* should be supplied in English: ἡ νίκη *the victory*, but νίκη *a victory*.

2 The final alpha of most nouns ending in -έα, -ία, -ρα is long.

3 Here (and in the second declension) when the final syllable bears an acute in the nominative, as in τῑμή, the accent becomes a circumflex in the genitive and dative (for the technical terms see **Appendix 8**).

4 In the genitive plural all first declension nouns have a circumflex on their final syllable.

2.1/3 Basic uses of cases

In English the only case ending in nouns is that of the genitive (as in *girl's, men's,* etc.). Elsewhere, the function of a noun is shown by its position (the difference in meaning between *the traffic warden hit the driver* and *the driver hit the traffic warden* depends solely on the word order) or by a preposition: *the traffic warden was hit by a car* (here the part played by the car is indicated by the preposition *by*). In Greek, however, the function of a noun is indicated by its **case ending**:

(a) The subject of a clause must be put in the **nominative**.

(b) When we address a person the **vocative** is used; this is normally preceded by ὦ *O* and followed by a mark of punctuation. For the sake of completeness the vocative is given for such nouns as τῑμή but these forms rarely occur.

(c) The direct object of a verb must be put in the **accusative**.

(d) The **genitive** can express possession: *Cleon's horse* (in English we can also say the *horse of Cleon*). Another common use of the genitive in Greek is to express separation (20.1/4).

(e) With nouns denoting living things the **dative** expresses the indirect object after verbs of saying, giving and the like (23.1/2*a*). In *Socrates gave a drachma to Xanthippe* the direct object is *drachma* (answering the question *gave what?*), which would be put into the accusative δραχμήν; the indirect object is *Xanthippe* (*gave to whom?*), which would be τῇ Ξανθίππῃ with no preposition (we may also say in English *Socrates gave Xanthippe a drachma*). The dative has other uses with nouns denoting living things and can nearly always be translated by *to* or *for*. With inanimate nouns (*Athens, arrow, boat*) different uses are possible and will be treated separately.

The accusative, genitive, and dative, are, for convenience of reference, called the **oblique cases**. They are the cases used after **prepositions**, which perform the same function in Greek as in English, i.e. they define the relation between the word they govern and the rest of the clause in which they are used. In Greek the word governed is always a noun (or noun-equivalent, see 5.1/3) or pronoun (Greek does not say *before now* because *now* is an adverb). With prepositions indicating **motion** and **rest** a pattern can be seen in the case required:

(f) Prepositions indicating **motion towards** govern the accusative, e.g. εἰς τὴν χώραν *into the country,* πρὸς τὴν οἰκίαν *towards the house.*

(g) Prepositions indicating **motion away from** govern the genitive, e.g. ἀπὸ τῆς μάχης *from the battle,* ἐκ Σικελίᾱς *out of Sicily.*

(h) Prepositions indicating **rest** or **fixed position** govern the dative, e.g. ἐν τῇ θαλάττῃ *in the sea.*

All the above prepositions, except πρός (cf. παρά 3.1/5), take only the case shown.

2.1/4 Verbs in Greek

A finite form of a Greek verb (i.e. one that can function as the verb of a clause) is defined in terms of person, number, tense, mood, and voice. **Person** and **number** are determined by the subject of the verb: a finite verb must agree with its subject in person and number (just as in English we cannot say *we is*). First person is the person(s) speaking, i.e. *I* or *we*; second person is the person(s) spoken to, i.e. *you*; third person is the person(s) or thing(s) spoken about, which can be a pronoun (*he, she, it, they*) or a noun. The concept of number is the same as with nouns. **Tense** indicates the time in which the action of the verb takes place. **Mood** tells us something about the nature of the verb's action in a particular context; at the moment we are only concerned with the **indicative** mood, which is used to express facts. **Voice** shows the relation of the subject to the verb. We shall first deal with the **active**, which is the voice used when the subject is the doer of the action.

Auxiliary verbs (*shall/will, have, be* etc.) are used to form most tenses of an English verb (*I shall teach, he has taught, we will be taught*), but in Greek are found only in certain passive forms. Elsewhere, the person, number, tense and voice (and also mood – 14.1/1) are shown by the stem and ending. For example, we can tell by the stem and ending that λῡσουσι is third person plural future indicative active of the verb λῡω *I loosen,* and therefore means *they will loosen.* It is superfluous to add the Greek for *they* (unless for emphasis), as this is part of the information conveyed by the ending.

Verbs in Greek belong to one of two groups (called **conjugations**). These are distinguished by the ending of the first person singular present indicative active, the form in which Greek verbs are customarily cited[1] (contrast the convention in English of referring to a verb by its present infinitive active). Those in -ω (e.g. λύω) are by far the larger class; the other consists of verbs in -μι, e.g. εἰμί *I am* (3.1/6), δίδωμι *give* (18.1/2).

2.1/5 Present and future indicative active of -ω verbs (and corresponding infinitives)

The present indicative active is formed by taking the present stem (λῡ- i.e. λύω minus ω) and adding the endings given below. For the future indicative active we make up the future stem by adding sigma to that of the present (i.e. λῡ + σ > λῡσ-) and we then apply the same endings. These stems are also used for the infinitives.

		PRESENT		FUTURE	
SINGULAR	1	λύ-ω	*I loosen*	λύσ-ω	*I shall loosen*
	2	λύ-εις	*you* (s.) *loosen*	λύσ-εις	*you* (s.) *will loosen*
	3	λύ-ει	*he, she, it loosens*	λύσ-ει	*he, she, it will loosen*
PLURAL	1	λύ-ομεν	*we loosen*	λύσ-ομεν	*we shall loosen*
	2	λύ-ετε	*you* (pl.) *loosen*	λύσ-ετε	*you* (pl.) *will loosen*
	3	λύ-ουσι(ν)	*they loosen*	λύσ-ουσι(ν)	*they will loosen*
INFINITIVE		λύ-ειν	*to loosen*	λύσ-ειν	*to be going to loosen*

Notes

1 In English we have different forms of the present tense, *I loosen, I am loosening, I do loosen* and so on. There are distinctions in usage between these forms, but as Greek has only one we must decide from the context which English form we should use to

---

[1]A sub-category called deponents is slightly different – 8.1/2.

translate a Greek verb in the present tense. In one context λύουσι might mean *they loosen,* in another *they are loosening* or *do they loosen.* Likewise, λύσω can also mean *I shall be loosening.*

2 The Greek second person singular is always used when addressing one person, the plural when addressing more than one person. Greek has a distinction here which we no longer have in English. Greek does not, however, have familiar and polite forms of the second person as in French, German, and other languages. A slave and master would have addressed each other in the second person singular.

3 It will be noticed that in each form the stem is followed by an o- or e- sound. This indicates the presence of the so-called **thematic vowel** (o or ε), which is most clearly seen in the first and second persons plural. The same pattern, which marks these tenses as **thematic**, is repeated in the imperfect (4.1/1).

4 The final ν shown in brackets in the ending of the third person plural is called the movable ν. In prose it is used (without brackets) only when a word with this ending is followed by a word beginning with a vowel or diphthong or stands at the end of a clause (its use in verse is freer). It occurs here and in a few other endings.

5 To form the future of πέμπω *send,* the final π of the present stem is combined with σ to give πέμψ-ω *I will send.* Other final consonants in present stems will be treated at 6.1/4 and 11.1/3.

2.1/6 Word order and elision

(*a*) Although the order of words within a Greek sentence may often be similar to that of English, Greek word order is generally much less predictable. As mentioned in 2.1/3, there is a close link in English between the order in which words occur and their function. In Greek, however, where the grammatical function of a word is determined by its form, not by its position, word order can be varied much more than in English. This is mainly done to emphasize a particular word or phrase. If in the English sentence *Aphrodite is beautiful* we wished to emphasize *beautiful* we would, in speech, articulate it with greater weight (in writing we could underline it or put it in italics). In Greek the emphasis would be conveyed by a change in the word order; ἡ Ἀφροδίτη ἐστὶ καλή would become καλή ἐστιν ἡ Ἀφροδίτη. These differences will be indicated as they occur. Emphasis apart, two further points regarding word order should be noted here:

(i) Adverbs nearly always precede the word they modify, ταχέως τρέχει *he runs* (τρέχει) *quickly* (ταχέως). This particularly applies to the negative οὐ(κ) *not*, οὐκ ἔχω ... *I do not have* ... (οὐκ is the form used before vowels and diphthongs with a smooth breathing; it becomes οὐχ if the following vowel or diphthong has a rough breathing, e.g. οὐχ ὕει *it is not raining*).

(ii) Just as in English we can say *the land of Aphrodite* or *Aphrodite's land,* so in Greek we have ἡ χώρᾱ τῆς Ἀφροδίτης and ἡ τῆς Ἀφροδίτης χώρᾱ (note that the article of χώρᾱ must be retained in the latter).

(*b*) The Greeks disliked the juxtaposition of a final vowel and an initial vowel (e.g. ἀπὸ Ἀθηνῶν *from Athens*). Although tolerated in prose, this is almost totally absent from most forms of verse. In the case of final short vowels (except υ) it is avoided by eliding (i.e. dropping and not pronouncing) α, ε, ι, o before a word beginning with a vowel or diphthong, e.g. ἀπ᾽ οἰκίᾱς (= ἀπὸ οἰκίᾱς) *from a house*; παρ᾽ Ἀφροδίτην (= παρὰ Ἀ.) *to Aphrodite*. When the vowel following κ, π, or τ is elided before a word beginning with a rough breathing, these consonants become χ, φ, θ, respectively, e.g. ὑφ᾽ Ἑλένης (= ὑπὸ Ἑ.) *by Helen*. Elision is marked by an apostrophe as shown. It is not always applied in prose texts.[2]

....

Insight

Place names usually remain despite invasion and changes in population. This has occurred in Asia Minor where some cities of what is now modern Turkey preserve a disguised version of their former Greek name. Both Isnik and Izmir were settled by the Greeks in the early part of the first millennium BC. The Turkish incursion began soon after

---

[2]The final αι of verbal endings can be elided in poetry, and occasionally even in prose (example at 21.2.2(xi)).

AD 1000 and the cities now bear no trace of their origins except for a few ruins and a mangled form of their ancient names, which were Νικαία and Σμύρνα. The modern versions go back to the phrases εἰς Νικαίαν and εἰς Σμύρνα i.e. *to Nicaea, to Smyrna*. Presumably the first Turks in the area mistook a direction to a city ([*the road*] **to Nicaea/Smyrna**) for the name of a city itself and instead to saying *Nicaea* or Smyrna fell into the habit of saying *to Nicaea* or *to Smyrna*. The words were adapted to Turkish by dropping the last element of the Greek names. For εἰς + acc. see 2.1/3f.

2.2 Greek reading

The *Odyssey* describes the return of the Greek hero Odysseus (in English we sometimes use the Latin form of his name *Ulysses*) to his homeland, Ithaca, after the sack of Troy. At a later stage we shall read some of the original, but now we shall start with a simplified version of Odysseus's landing at Scheria, probably to be identified with the modern Corfu. The scene occurs in the sixth book of the Odyssey.

In reading Greek the following steps should be followed:

(a) *Look up each word in the vocabulary and parse it (i.e. define it grammatically; this is particularly necessary with words which vary in form).*

(b) *Mark all finite verbs as this will indicate the number of clauses.*

(c) *By observing punctuation and conjunctions used to join clauses, work out where each clause begins and ends.*

(d) *Take each clause separately and see how each word relates to the finite verb of its clause (subject, object, part of an adverbial phrase etc.).*

(e) *See from the conjunctions how the clauses are related to each other and work out the overall meaning of the sentence.*

An analysis of sentence 13 will be found in the key

1 ὁ Ὀδυσσεὺς ἀπὸ τῆς Τροίας ἥκει, ἀλλὰ ὁ Ποσειδῶν ἐν τῇ Σχερίᾳ τὴν ναῦν (*ship*) διαφθείρει.

2 ὁ Ὀδυσσεὺς ἐκ τῆς θαλάττης φεύγει καὶ ὑπὸ ἐλάᾳ ἑαυτὸν (*himself* acc.) κρύπτει πρὸς τῇ ἀκτῇ.

3 ὄναρ ἡ Ἀθηνᾶ τῇ βασιλείᾳ Ναυσικάᾳ λέγει ὅτι δεῖ (*it is necessary*) τὴν στολὴν ἐν τῇ ἀκτῇ πλύνειν.

4 ἅμα τῇ ἡμέρᾳ ἡ Ναυσικάα τὴν στολὴν ἐκ τῆς οἰκίας ἐν ἁμάξῃ πρὸς τὴν θάλατταν φέρει.

5 ἐν τῇ ἁμάξῃ ἐστὶ (*there is*) καὶ (*also*) ἐδωδὴ τῇ Ναυσικάᾳ καὶ ταῖς ἑταίραις.

6 αἱ κόραι τάχα πλύνουσι τὴν στολὴν πρὸς τῇ ἐλάᾳ οὗ ὁ Ὀδυσσεὺς καθεύδει.

7 ἔπειτα αἱ κόραι τὴν στολὴν ἐπὶ τὴν ἀκτὴν ἐπιβάλλουσιν.

8 λούουσιν ἑαυτὰς (*themselves*) καὶ τὴν ἐδωδὴν ἐσθίουσιν ἣν (*which*) ἐν τῇ ἁμάξῃ ἔχουσιν.

9 ἕως (*while*) ἐν τῇ ἀκτῇ παίζουσιν, ἡ Ναυσικάα σφαῖραν ῥίπτει ἀλλ᾽ ἡ σφαῖρα εἰς δίνην πίπτει.

10 αἱ τῶν κορῶν βοαὶ τὸν Ὀδυσσέα (acc.) ἐγείρουσι καὶ ἐκπλήττουσιν.

11 ὁ Ὀδυσσεὺς θαυμάζει ποῖ τῆς γῆς ἥκει, καὶ ἀπὸ τῆς ἐλάας ἐξαίφνης ἕρπει.

12 τὴν Ναυσικάαν καὶ τὰς ἑταίρας ἐκπλήττει.

13 ἀλλ᾽ ἡ Ναυσικάα ἐν τῇ ἀκτῇ ἀναμένει διότι ἡ Ἀθηνᾶ τὴν ἀνδρείαν εἰς τὴν καρδίαν εἰσβάλλει.

14 ὁ Ὀδυσσεὺς τῇ Ναυσικάᾳ λέγει ὅτι ἀπὸ τῆς Ὠγυγίας ἥκει.

15 ἡ Ναυσικάα ταῖς ἑταίραις λέγει ὅτι δεῖ τῷ Ὀδυσσεῖ (dat.) ἐδωδὴν καὶ στολὴν παρέχειν.

16 τὸν Ὀδυσσέα πρὸς τὴν τοῦ πατρὸς (*of her father*) οἰκίαν ἄγειν ἐθέλει ἀλλὰ τὴν τῶν πολιτῶν (*of the citizens*) αἰτίαν δειμαίνει εἰ βλέπουσιν αὐτὴν (*her*) μετὰ τοῦ Ὀδυσσέως (gen.).

17 ὥστε ἡ Ναυσικάα καὶ αἱ κόραι τὴν στολὴν πάλιν ἐν τῇ ἁμάξῃ πρὸς τὴν οἰκίαν φέρουσιν, ἀλλ᾽ ὁ Ὀδυσσεὺς ἐκτὸς ἀναμένει.

Notes

1 ὁ nom. s. m. of the definite article (3.1/1); Ὀδυσσεύς 3rd declension (11.1/4); ἥκει *has come* (the subject is ὁ Ὀδυσσεύς) the present tense of this verb is to be translated by the perfect tense in English; τὴν ναῦν lit. *the ship,* but we would translate *his ship*; Greek normally does not indicate possession if this is obvious from the context (9.1/5; cf. sentences 4, 5, 12, 13, 15, 16).

2 ὑπὸ ἐλάᾳ *beneath an olive-tree*; as Greek does not have an indefinite article (*a, an* in English) this must be supplied in our translation; cf. below ἐν ἁμάξῃ (4) and σφαῖραν (9).

5 The datives τῇ Ναυσικάᾳ and ταῖς ἑταίραις are to be translated *for ...*

7 ἐπὶ ... ἐπιβάλλουσιν the repetition of ἐπί as a verbal prefix cannot be reproduced in English and we would simply say *they throw ... on to the shore.*

9 ἀλλ᾽ = ἀλλά (2.1/6*b*).

10 τόν acc. s. m. of the definite article; ἐκπλήττουσιν *sc. him* (Odysseus; because the object of the second verb is the same as that of the first, no pronoun is needed in Greek).

13 εἰς ... εἰσβάλλει for the repetition of εἰς cf. note on 7.

15 τῷ dat. s. m. of the definite article.

16 τοῦ gen. s. m. of the definite article.

2.2/1 Vocabulary

Individual vocabularies are provided for Units 2–9. Personal names whose English form is a simple transliteration of the Greek, or close to it (e.g. Σωκράτης *Socrates*), are not included, but will be found in the main vocabulary. The meaning given to each word is that appropriate to its use in the preceding reading; for a fuller range of meanings the main vocabulary should be consulted. Words already given in a grammatical table (or earlier vocabulary) are not repeated, except where a different meaning is involved.

It is normal practice in Greek dictionaries and lists of Greek words to give the nominative singular of a noun, its genitive (usually in abbreviated form) and the appropriate nominative singular form of the article; this information establishes both its declension and gender, e.g. θάλαττα, -ης, ἡ (note that the accent in the genitive – here θαλάττης – is not always on the same syllable as in the nominative; see **Appendix 8**, *a*). Verbs are cited in the first person singular present indicative, e.g. κρύπτω.

ἄγω   *lead, bring*
Ἀθηνᾶ, -ᾶς,[3] ἡ   (the goddess)
  Athena
αἰτίᾱ, -ᾱς, ἡ   *blame, censure*
ἀκτή, -ῆς, ἡ   *shore, coast*
ἀλλά (conj.)   *but*
ἅμα see ἡμέρα
ἅμαξα, -ης, ἡ   *wagon*
ἀναμένω   *wait, stay*
ἀνδρείᾱ, -ᾱς, ἡ   *courage*
βασίλεια, -ᾱς, ἡ   *princess*
βλέπω   *see*

βοή, -ῆς, ἡ   *shout*
γῆ, -ῆς, ἡ   *land, earth, world*
δειμαίνω (+acc.)   *be afraid of,*
  fear
διαφθείρω   *destroy*
δίνη, -ης, ἡ   *whirlpool*
διότι (conj.)   *because*
ἐγείρω   *awaken, arouse*
ἐδωδή, -ῆς, ἡ   *food*
ἐθέλω   *be willing, wish*
εἰ (conj.)   *if*
εἰς (prep.+acc.)   *into*

---

[3] Ἀθηνᾶ, originally Ἀθηνάᾱ, has its genitive in -ᾶς (not -ῆς); cf. ἐλάᾱ, -ᾶς below.

εἰσβάλλω *throw into, put into*
ἐκ (prep.+gen.) *out of*
ἐκπλήττω *strike with panic,*
  frighten
ἐκτός (adv.) *outside*
ἐλάᾱ, -ᾱς, ἡ *olive-tree*
ἐν (prep.+dat.) *in, on*
ἐξαίφνης (adv.) *suddenly*
ἔπειτα (adv.) *then, next*
ἐπί (prep.+acc.) *on to*
ἐπιβάλλω *throw upon*
ἕρπω *creep, crawl*
ἐσθίω *eat*
ἑταίρᾱ, -ᾱς, ἡ *companion*
  (female)
ἔχω *have*
ἥκω *have come*
ἡμέρᾱ, -ᾱς, ἡ *day*
ἅμα τῇ ἡμέρᾳ *at day-break*
  or dawn
θαυμάζω *wonder*
καθεύδω *sleep*
καί (conj.) *and*
καρδίᾱ, -ᾱς, ἡ *heart*
κόρη, -ης, ἡ *girl*
κρύπτω *hide*
λέγω *say, speak*
λούω *wash* (the body)
μετά (prep.+gen.) *along with,*
  (in company) with

οἰκίᾱ, -ᾱς, ἡ *house*
ὄναρ (adv.) *in a dream*
ὅτι (conj.) *that*
οὗ (conj.) *where*
παίζω *play*
πάλιν (adv.) *back*
παρέχω *provide* (something to
  somebody)
πίπτω *fall*
πλύνω *wash* (clothes)
ποῖ (interrog. adv.) *(to)*
  where?
  ποῖ τῆς γῆς *where in the*
  world
πρός (prep.) (+acc.) *towards,*
  to
  (+dat.) *near, beside*
ῥίπτω *throw*
στολή, -ῆς, ἡ *clothes*
σφαῖρα, -ᾱς, ἡ *ball*
Σχερίᾱ, -ᾱς, ἡ *Scheria*, the
  land of the Phaeacians
τάχα (adv.) *quickly*
Τροίᾱ, -ᾱς, ἡ *Troy*
ὑπό (prep.+dat.) *beneath*
φέρω *carry, bring, take*
φεύγω *flee, run away*
Ὠγυγίᾱ, -ᾱς, ἡ *Ogygia*, the
  island of Calypso
ὥστε (conj.) *consequently, so*

Main points

- Nouns in Greek have gender (masculine, feminine, neuter)

- Most first declension nouns are feminine

- The endings of a noun change to indicate its number and case

- The definite article must agree with its noun in number, gender and case

- The case of a noun shows how it relates to the other words in its clause

- Verb endings indicate when an action occurs

- Verb endings also indicate whether the subject is singular or plural and whether it is first person (*I, we*), second person (*you* singular or plural), or third person (*he, she, it, they*), or a noun such as *Pericles, slave, cart*

- When the subject is a pronoun, it is usually omitted

- The present tense describes something happening in the present, the future tense describes something that will happen in the future

- Word order in Greek is more flexible than in English

- Elision can occur when a word ending with a vowel is followed by a word beginning with a vowel or diphthong

Unit 3

....

3.1 Grammar

3.1/1 Second declension and the masculine and neuter definite article

The second declension is divided into two groups: nouns whose nominative singular ends in -ος, which, with a few exceptions, are masculine, and those whose nominative singular ends in -ον, which are all neuter. Both groups have identical endings except for the nominative, vocative, and accusative. For these cases second declension neuter nouns observe the rule which holds for all neuter nouns in Greek:

The vocative and accusative of all neuter nouns are the same as the nominative, both in the singular and in the plural. In the plural the nominative, vocative, and accusative of all neuter nouns end in -α (for an apparent exception see 6.1/1*c*).

	ὁ ἵππος *the horse*				τὸ δῶρον *the gift*			
	SINGULAR		PLURAL		SINGULAR		PLURAL	
Nom.	ὁ	ἵππ-ος	οἱ	ἵππ-οι	τὸ	δῶρ-ον	τὰ	δῶρ-α
Voc.	—	ἵππ-ε	—	ἵππ-οι	—	δῶρ-ον	—	δῶρ-α
Acc.	τὸν	ἵππ-ον	τοὺς	ἵππ-ους	τὸ	δῶρ-ον	τὰ	δῶρ-α
Gen.	τοῦ	ἵππ-ου	τῶν	ἵππ-ων	τοῦ	δώρ-ου	τῶν	δώρ-ων
Dat.	τῷ	ἵππ-ῳ	τοῖς	ἵππ-οις	τῷ	δώρ-ῳ	τοῖς	δώρ-οις

Notes

1 Feminine nouns of the second declension are declined in exactly the same way as masculines but they require the feminine form of the definite article (and of adjectives; see below 3.1/3): ἡ νῆσος *the island,* τῆς νόσου *of the disease.* Only rarely can they be recognized as feminine by their meaning, e.g. ἡ παρθένος *the girl.*

2 A finite verb which has a plural **neuter** noun as its subject is almost always *singular*: τὰ δῶρά ἐστιν ἐν τῇ οἰκίᾳ *the gifts are in the house* (ἐστί is the 3rd s. pres. ind. of εἰμί *I am* – see below 3.1/6). This curious idiom, which has not been satisfactorily explained, even applies when the neuter noun denotes human beings: τὰ ἀνδράποδα οὐκ ἔστιν ἐν τῇ ἀγορᾷ *the captives are not in the market place.*

3 In poetry an expanded form of the dative plural of both first and second declensions, -αισι(ν) -οισι(ν), often occurs, e.g. τῑμαῖσι(ν), ἵπποισι(ν) (on the movable ν see 2.1/5 note 4).

3.1/2 First declension (masculine nouns)

These nouns have borrowed the -ς of the nominative singular and the -ου ending of the genitive singular from second declension masculines. They are subdivided into those ending in -ᾱς (always preceded by ε, ι or ρ) and those in -ης.

	νεᾱνίᾱς *young man*		κριτής *judge*	
	SINGULAR	PLURAL	SINGULAR	PLURAL
Nom.	νεᾱνί-ᾱς	νεᾱνί-αι	κριτ-ής	κριτ-αί
Voc.	νεᾱνί-ᾱ	νεᾱνί-αι	κριτ-ά	κριτ-αί
Acc.	νεᾱνί-ᾱν	νεᾱνί-ᾱς	κριτ-ήν	κριτ-ᾱς
Gen.	νεᾱνί-ου	νεᾱνι-ῶν	κριτ-οῦ	κριτ-ῶν
Dat.	νεᾱνί-ᾳ	νεᾱνί-αις	κριτ-ῇ	κριτ-αῖς

Notes

1 Most nouns in this class involve male occupations; cf. also ναύτης *sailor*, στρατιώτης *soldier*.

2 When used with these nouns the definite article (and adjectives) must be masculine.

3 Nouns in -της (as well as compounds and names of peoples) have a vocative singular in -α (not -ᾱ). All other nouns in -ης of this declension have a vocative in -η, e.g. ὦ Ἑρμῆ *O Hermes!* Contrast third declension proper names such as Σωκράτης (6.1/1c).

4 The patronymic suffixes -ίδης, -ιάδης are added to the stem of proper names to mean *son of* (Κρονίδης *son of* Κρόνος). In many names these suffixes have lost their original force: Θουκυδίδης *Thucydides,* Ἀλκιβιάδης *Alcibiades.*

3.1/3 First and second declension adjectives

Adjectives in English, apart from *this* (pl. *these*) and *that* (pl. *those*), are invariable in form. In Greek, however, adjectives must agree with the nouns they qualify (i.e. go with and describe) in case, number and gender, and consequently they are declined in the same way as nouns, e.g. ὁ κακὸς νόμος *the wicked law,* τὴν καλὴν νίκην *the fine victory* (acc.), λόγων δεινῶν *of clever speeches.*

The majority of Greek adjectives have their feminine form declined according to the first declension but their masculine and neuter according to the second or third. This latter feature allows us to classify them into first and second declension adjectives and first and third declension adjectives (10.1/3). First and second declension adjectives have, therefore, a feminine in -η (or -ᾱ, when preceded by ε, ι, ρ), a masculine in -ος and a neuter in -ον. καλός *handsome, beautiful, fine* is declined:

	SINGULAR			PLURAL		
	M.	F.	N.	M.	F.	N.
Nom.	καλ-ός	καλ-ή	καλ-όν	καλ-οί	καλ-αί	καλ-ά
Voc.	καλ-έ	καλ-ή	καλ-όν	καλ-οί	καλ-αί	καλ-ά
Acc.	καλ-όν	καλ-ήν	καλ-όν	καλ-ούς	καλ-ᾱς	καλ-ά
Gen.	καλ-οῦ	καλ-ῆς	καλ-οῦ	καλ-ῶν	καλ-ῶν	καλ-ῶν
Dat.	καλ-ῷ	καλ-ῇ	καλ-ῷ	καλ-οῖς	καλ-αῖς	καλ-οῖς

δίκαιος *just* and αἰσχρός *ugly, disgraceful* are declined as follows in the singular:

	M.	F.	N.	M.	F.	N.
Nom.	δίκαι-ος	δικαί-ᾱ	δίκαι-ον	αἰσχρ-ός	αἰσχρ-ά	αἰσχρ-όν
Voc.	δίκαι-ε	δικαί-ᾱ	δίκαι-ον	αἰσχρ-έ	αἰσχρ-ά	αἰσχρ-όν
Acc.	δίκαι-ον	δικαί-ᾱν	δίκαι-ον	αἰσχρ-όν	αἰσχρ-άν	αἰσχρ-όν
Gen.	δικαί-ου	δικαί-ᾱς	δικαί-ου	αἰσχρ-οῦ	αἰσχρ-ᾶς	αἰσχρ-οῦ
Dat.	δικαί-ῳ	δικαί-ᾳ	δικαί-ῳ	αἰσχρ-ῷ	αἰσχρ-ᾷ	αἰσχρ-ῷ

The plural is the same as for καλός.[1]

The way in which these adjectives are given in the vocabulary (and in dictionaries) is καλός, -ή, -όν; δίκαιος, -ᾱ, -ον; αἰσχρός, -ᾱ́, -όν.

Some adjectives, however, have no separate feminine (the so-called **two termination** adjectives) but employ the -ος forms for masculine and feminine alike. These are nearly all compounds, e.g. εὔλογος *reasonable* (εὖ + λόγος *reason*), ἔμπειρος *experienced* (ἐν + πεῖρα *experience*). Many have the negative ἀ- (or ἀν- before a vowel; cf. English *in-, un-*) e.g. ἄλογος *irrational* (ἀ + λόγος *reason*); ἀνάξιος *unworthy* (ἀν + ἄξιος *worthy*). These adjectives are cited in the form εὔλογος, -ον; ἔμπειρος, -ον. Examples of them in agreement with feminine nouns are: ἡ ἄδικος νῑ́κη *the unjust victory*, αἱ ἔμπειροι Μοῦσαι *the experienced Muses*.

Two important adjectives, πολύς *much* (pl. *many*), and μέγας *great, big*, show irregularities in the masculine and neuter nominative and accusative singular. Otherwise they are declined exactly as if their nominative singular masculine were πολλ-ός and μεγάλ-ος. So in the singular we find:

	M.	F.	N.	M.	F.	N.
Nom.	**πολύς**	πολλ-ή	**πολύ**	**μέγας**	μεγάλ-η	**μέγα**
Voc.	—	—	—	μεγάλ-ε	μεγάλ-η	**μέγα**
Acc.	**πολύν**	πολλ-ήν	**πολύ**	**μέγαν**	μεγάλ-ην	**μέγα**
Gen.	πολλ-οῦ	πολλ-ῆς	πολλ-οῦ	μεγάλ-ου	μεγάλ-ης	μεγάλ-ου
Dat.	πολλ-ῷ	πολλ-ῇ	πολλ-ῷ	μεγάλ-ῳ	μεγάλ-ῃ	μεγάλ-ῳ

The plural is entirely regular.

Position of adjectives

(*a*) Where the definite article is absent, the adjective may appear either before or after its noun: εἰς οἰκίᾱν καλήν *into a beautiful house*, περὶ δεινοῦ λόγου *concerning a clever speech*.

---

[1] The accent in the genitive plural feminine follows that of the masculine: δικαίων, not δικαιῶν which we would have expected on the analogy of first declension nouns (2.1/2 note 4).

(b) When a noun is used with the definite article we have several possibilities. An adjective used as a simple attribute may occupy the same position as in English: ὁ δίκαιος νεᾱνίᾱς *the just young man*. But note that Greek may achieve exactly the same effect by writing ὁ νεᾱνίᾱς ὁ δίκαιος with the article repeated. Both these positions are called **attributive**. Totally different, however, is the case where the adjective appears outside of the article-noun complex, ὁ νεᾱνίᾱς δίκαιος or δίκαιος ὁ νεᾱνίᾱς. In both these positions the adjective is considered as functioning as a predicate, and the meaning is *the young man is just* (on the omission of ἐστί see below 3.1/6). Greek makes great use of this **predicative** position and can have a simple sentence where English would require a complex one. So whereas οἰκίᾱν ἔχει καλήν means *he has a beautiful house*, τὴν οἰκίᾱν ἔχει καλήν or καλὴν ἔχει τὴν οἰκίᾱν means *the house which he has is beautiful, it is a beautiful house which he has* (lit. *beautiful the house he has*).

3.1/4 Adverbs

Most adverbs are formed from adjectives by adding -ως to the stem. In effect this means changing the final ν of the gen. pl. m. of the adjective to ς, e.g. δίκαιος (gen. pl. m. δικαίων) *just,* adv. δικαίως *justly*; ἄδικος (gen. pl. m. ἀδίκων) *unjust*, adv. ἀδίκως *unjustly*.

Unlike in English, adverbs are nearly always placed immediately **before** the word they modify (2.1/6a(i)); κακῶς καθεύδουσιν *they sleep badly*. This is frequently a valuable clue in reading Greek.

3.1/5 Prepositions

We have already seen some prepositions which indicate motion or rest (2.1/3f, g, h). Many prepositions govern both the accusative and genitive, some the accusative, genitive and dative. There are always differences of meaning involved, e.g. παρά +acc. = *to (wards)*; +gen. = *from*; +dat. = *at, beside* (παρά is used for persons, not places, e.g. παρὰ ἐμοί lit. *beside me*, i.e. *at my house*, cf. Fr. *chez moi*). The following are particularly common:

(a) with accusative: διά *on account of*
                       μετά *after*
                       περί *around* (time, place, or number)

(*b*) with genitive:

ἀντί	*instead of*
διά	*through, by means of*
μετά	*(in company) with*
ὑπέρ	*on behalf of*
περί	*concerning*

Common idiomatic phrases involving παρά and another preposition κατά are: κατὰ γῆν καὶ κατὰ θάλατταν *by land and sea*; κατὰ/παρὰ τοὺς νόμους *according to/contrary to the laws*.

3.1/6 Present indicative and infinitive of εἰμί I am

This verb is irregular in Greek as is its equivalent in other languages. It has little in common with other -μι verbs (18.1/1).

SINGULAR				PLURAL		
	1	εἰμί	*I am*		ἐσμέν	*we are*
	2	εἶ	*you* (s.) *are*		ἐστέ	*you* (pl.) *are*
	3	ἐστί(ν)	*he, she, it is*		εἰσί(ν)	*they are*
INFINITIVE		εἶναι	*to be*			

All the above forms are enclitic (see **Appendix 8,** *d*) except εἶ and εἶναι.

εἰμί **never** governs an accusative because it does not express an action inflicted by a subject on an object. What is said about the subject in clauses such as *I am Aphrodite, wisdom is a skill, the girls are beautiful* is put into the **nominative**: εἰμὶ Ἀφροδίτη, ἡ σοφίᾱ τέχνη ἐστίν, αἱ κόραι εἰσὶ καλαί. In clauses of this nature the appropriate form of εἰμί (usually ἐστί or εἰσί) is often omitted (cf. above 3.1/3*b*): ἀθάνατος ἡ ψῡχή *the soul [is] immortal*; ἄνθρωπος μέτρον ἁπάντων *a man [is] the measure of all things*. Sometimes the context requires that ἐστί and εἰσί should be translated by *there is* and *there are* respectively; κόραι ἐν τῇ ἀγορᾷ εἰσιν *there are girls in the agora* (we would not normally say in English *girls are in the agora*).

Insight

The Greeks practised reciprocal entertainment but this meant more than simply returning a dinner party. Many citizens of a Greek city would have had cause to visit another city in Greece or abroad. Nowhere was there anything but the meanest lodging facilities and a traveller would generally stay with a friend or acquaintance according to a pre-arranged agreement. When the latter came to the traveller's own city this hospitality would be returned. Each party was called a ξένος, which consequently could mean both *host* and *guest*. However, as a ξένος was always a person from a city other than one's own, the word acquired the further meaning of *stranger*. ξένος is declined like ἵππος (3.1/1)

3.2 Greek reading

An analysis of sentence 10 will be found in the key.

Proverbs and short quotations

By the end of antiquity the Greeks had accumulated an enormous number of proverbs and pithy sayings. Some have no identifiable origin, others are quotations, generally from poets. The following, and those included in future exercises, are nearly always in their original form.

1 οὐκ εἰσὶν οἱ παμπλούσιοι (*the very rich*) ἀγαθοί.

2 ἐρημία μεγάλη ἐστὶν ἡ μεγάλη πόλις (*city*).

3 ἡ πενία τὰς τέχνας ἐγείρει.

4 νεκρὸς οὐ δάκνει.

5 In these shorter sayings supply εἰσί in (*i*), ἐστί in the rest: (*i*) πολλοὶ τραπέζης, οὐκ ἀληθείας, φίλοι. (*ii*) ἡ εὐτυχία πολύφιλος. (*iii*) ὁ ἄνθρωπος πολιτικὸν ζῷον. (*iv*) ἀθάνατος ὁ θάνατος. (*v*) οὐ σχολὴ δούλοις. (*vi*) χωρὶς ὑγιείας ἄβιος βίος. (*vii*) νόσος φιλίας ἡ κολακεία. (*viii*) κακὸς ἀνὴρ (*man*) μακρόβιος.

30

6# τὰ μεγάλα δῶρα τῆς Τύχης ἔχει φόβον.

7# κακὸν φέρουσι καρπὸν οἱ κακοὶ φίλοι.

8# αὐθαίρετος λύπη ἐστὶν ἡ τέκνων σπορά.

9 δῶρα θεοὺς πείθει.

10 οὔτε συμπόσιον χωρὶς ὁμιλίας οὔτε πλοῦτος χωρὶς ἀρετῆς ἡδονὴν ἔχει.

11 ὁ ἀνεξέταστος βίος οὐ βιωτὸς ἀνθρώπῳ.

12 **A fable of Aesop**
Aesop was a slave on the island of Samos in the early sixth century BC who composed animal fables. These were at first transmitted orally and became widely known. The collection that survives under Aesop's name seems to have been put into its present form early in the Christian era. The following is an adaptation.

(*i*) πολλοὶ βάτραχοι ἀγγέλους πέμπουσι πρὸς τὸν Κρονίδην διότι μονάρχου χρῄζουσιν.

(*ii*) οἱ ἄγγελοι τῷ Κρονίδῃ ὑπὲρ τῶν βατράχων λέγουσιν· ὦ δίκαιε Κρονίδη, δεσπότης εἶ τῶν θεῶν. ἆρα ἐθέλεις τοῖς βατράχοις δεσπότην παρέχειν;

(*iii*) ὁ Κρονίδης σφόδρα θαυμάζει καὶ μέγα ξύλον εἰς τὴν τῶν βατράχων λίμνην ῥίπτει.

(*iv*) τὸ ξύλον ἐκπλήττει τοὺς βατράχους καὶ ταχέως ἀποτρέχουσιν, ἀλλὰ ὑποπτεύειν ἄρχουσιν ἐπεὶ τὸ ξύλον ἐστὶν ἀκίνητον.

(*v*) ὕστερον τῷ ξύλῳ ἄνευ φόβου ἐπιβαίνουσι καὶ λέγουσιν· ὦ ξένε, ἆρα θεὸς εἶ ἢ ἄνθρωπος ἢ ζῷον;

(*vi*) ἐπεὶ οὐ λέγει οὐδέν, νομίζουσιν ἀνάξιον εἶναι εἰ τοιοῦτον δεσπότην ἔχουσι καὶ ἀγγέλους πάλιν πρὸς τὸν Κρονίδην πέμπουσιν περὶ νέου μονάρχου.

(*vii*) οἱ ἄγγελοι τῷ Κρονίδῃ λέγουσιν· ὦ δέσποτα, δεῖ ἄλλον μόναρχον τοῖς βατράχοις πέμπειν ἐπεὶ ὁ πρῶτός ἐστιν ἀκίνητος καὶ ἀργός.

(*viii*) ὁ τῶν θεῶν δεσπότης ἐν ὀργῇ ἔχει τοὺς βατράχους καὶ μεγάλην ὕδραν πέμπει.

(*ix*)   ἡ ὕδρα ἐστὶν ἀπαραίτητος καὶ τοὺς βατράχους ἐσθίει.

(*x*)   ὁ μῦθος σαφηνίζει ὅτι δεῖ τοὺς ἀργοὺς δεσπότας φέρειν ἐπεὶ
         οἱ δραστήριοι δεσπόται ταλαιπωρίας πολλάκις φέρουσιν.

Notes

2   ἡ μεγάλη πόλις the article indicates a general class (2.1/2 note 1);
        in English we would say *a large city.*

3   With neither noun would we use an article in English (2.1/2
        note 1). The same applies in 5 (*ii*), (*iii*), (*iv*), and 7.

6   # indicates that the sentence (or passage) is in verse. Poets often
        vary normal prose usage (but not in 6, 7, 8). Here (and in 9) a
        neuter plural subject is followed by a singular verb (3.1/1 note 2).

12 (*ii*)A question which does not involve an interrogative word
        (*who? how?*, etc.) may be introduced by ἆρα (10.1/2), which
        has no English equivalent; in such cases, we normally reverse
        subject and verb (*are you a sailor?* ἆρα ναύτης εἶ;).

        (*iv*)   ἄρχουσιν here *begin.*

        (*v*)   τῷ ξύλῳ ... ἐπιβαίνουσι *they step on to the log,* ἐπιβαίνω
                 here takes the dative (cf. 13.1/2*b*).

        (*vi*)   Certain compound negatives (here οὐδέν) **reinforce** a
                 preceding simple negative (οὐ) and the meaning here is *it
                 says nothing at all* (see 7.1/6); ἀνάξιον (neuter) εἶναι εἰ ...
                 lit. [*it*] *to be unworthy if ...,* i.e. *that it is despicable that ...*

        (*viii*) ἐν ὀργῇ ἔχει lit. *has in anger,* i.e. *is angry with.*

        (*x*)   Note the pun on the two meanings of φέρω, *endure* and
                 bring.

3.2/1 Vocabulary

ἄβιος, -ον *unlivable, intolerable*
ἀγαθός, -ή, -όν   *good*
ἄγγελος, -ου, ὁ   *messenger*
ἀθάνατος, -ον   *immortal*
ἀκίνητος, -ον   *motionless*
ἀλήθεια, -ᾱς, ἡ   *truth*
ἄλλος, -η, -ον   *other, another*

ἀνάξιος, -ον   *unworthy*
ἀνεξέταστος, -ον   *without enquiry*
ἄνευ (prep.+gen.)   *without*
ἄνθρωπος, -ου, ὁ   *man, human
being*
ἀπαραίτητος, -ον   *unmoved by
prayer, pitiless*

ἀποτρέχω   run away
ἆρα (interrog. particle) see note
   to 12 (*ii*)
ἀργός, -όν   lazy, idle
ἀρετή, -ῆς, ἡ   excellence, virtue
ἄρχω   begin
αὐθαίρετος, -ον   self-chosen,
   self-inflicted
βάτραχος, -ου, ὁ   frog
βίος, -ου, ὁ   life
βιωτός, -όν   worth living
δάκνω   bite
δεσπότης, -ου, ὁ   master
δοῦλος, -ου, ὁ   slave
δραστήριος, -ον   active
δῶρον, -ου, τό   gift
ἐπεί (conj.)   since
ἐπιβαίνω (+dat.)   step on to
ἐρημίᾱ, -ᾱς, ἡ   desert, wilderness
εὐτυχίᾱ, -ᾱς, ἡ   good fortune
ζῷον, -ου, τό   living being, animal
ἤ (conj.)   or
ἡδονή, -ῆς, ἡ   pleasure
θάνατος, -ου, ὁ   death
θεός, -οῦ, ὁ   god
κακός, -ή, -όν   bad, evil
καρπός, -οῦ, ὁ   fruit
κολακείᾱ, -ᾱς, ἡ   flattery
Κρονίδης, -ου, ὁ   son of Cronos
   (i.e. Zeus)
λίμνη, -ης, ἡ   pool, marsh
λύπη, -ης, ἡ   grief
μακρόβιος, -ον   long-lived
μόναρχος, -ου, ὁ   monarch
μῦθος, -ου, ὁ   story, fable
νεκρός, -οῦ, ὁ   corpse
νέος, -ᾱ, -ον   new
νομίζω   think, consider
νόσος, -ου, ἡ   disease
ξένος, -ου, ὁ   stranger

ξύλον, -ου, τό   log
ὁμῑλίᾱ, -ᾱς, ἡ   company
ὀργή, -ῆς, ἡ   anger;
   ἐν ὀργῇ ἔχειν (+acc.)   be
   angry with
οὐ (οὐκ, οὐχ)   no(t) (see 2.1/6*a*)
οὐδέν (neuter pron.)   nothing
οὔτε ... οὔτε   neither ... nor
παμπλούσιος, -ον   very rich
πείθω   persuade
πέμπω   send
πενίᾱ, -ᾱς, ἡ   poverty
πλοῦτος, -ου, ὁ   wealth
πολῑτικός, -ή, -όν   political
πολλάκις (adv.)   often
πολύφιλος, -ον   having many
   friends
πρῶτος, -η, -ον   first
σαφηνίζω   make clear
σπορά̄, -ᾱς, ἡ   sowing, begetting
συμπόσιον, -ου, τό   drinking party
σφόδρα (adv.)   very much,
   exceedingly
σχολή, -ῆς, ἡ   leisure, rest
ταλαιπωρίᾱ, -ᾱς, ἡ   hardship,
   distress
ταχέως (adv.)   quickly
τέκνον, -ου, τό   child
τέχνη, -ης, ἡ   art, craft, skill
τοιοῦτος (adj. 21.1/3)   of such
   a kind, such
τράπεζα, -ης, ἡ   table
Τύχη, -ης, ἡ   Fortune, Chance
ὑγίεια, -ᾱς, ἡ   health
ὕδρᾱ, -ᾱς, ἡ   hydra, water-
   serpent
ὑποπτεύω   suspect, be suspicious
ὕστερον (adv.)   later, afterwards
φέρω   bear, bring
φιλίᾱ, -ᾱς, ἡ   friendship

φίλος, -η, -ον *dear, friendly*; as
   a noun *friend*

φόβος, -ου, ὁ *fear*

χρῄζω (+gen.) *be in need of, desire*

χωρίς (prep.+gen.) *without, apart from*

Main points

- Second declension nouns are divided into two main classes, masculine and neuter

- The few feminine nouns of the second declension are declined like the masculine

- Neuter nouns have the same ending in the n.v.a. (the plural n.v.a. ending is -α)

- First declension masculine nouns have -ς in the nom. s. and -ου in the gen. s.

- First and second declension adjectives decline as first and second declension nouns

- An adjective must agree with its noun in **number, gender** and **case**; this does not mean that it will necessarily have the same ending as its noun

- There is a distinction between the **attributive** and **predicative** use of adjectives

- Most adverbs end in -ως

- Adverbs are normally placed immediately before the word they qualify

- Some prepositions take different cases according to the meaning required

- The irregular εἰμί never governs an accusative and is often omitted

....

For this and every third subsequent unit a revision exercise will be found at the Internet website **http://tyancientgreek.org**

4.1 Grammar

4.1/1 Imperfect indicative active and weak aorist indicative active and infinitive active of -ω verbs

Both the imperfect and the aorist (in the indicative) have reference to the past. The aorist has other moods, which we shall treat later, but the imperfect exists only in the indicative.

The term **weak** aorist is used to distinguish the formation of this tense in λύω (and most other -ω verbs) from that in a minority of -ω verbs which have a **strong** aorist (7.1/1). There is no difference in meaning. The weak aorist is so named because its stem requires a suffix (σ added to the present stem), whereas the stem of the strong aorist resembles that of the imperfect in having no suffix. The concept of verbal strength as shown in the presence (weak) or absence (strong) of suffixes is a somewhat whimsical notion of nineteenth-century grammarians.

The aorist stem of λύω is λῡσ- (the same as for the future), while the imperfect simply uses that of the present, λῡ-. The **augment** is prefixed to the stem in the indicative of both. This, in λύω and other verbs beginning with a consonant, consists of the vowel ἐ, giving us ἐλῡ- (imperfect), ἐλῡσ- (aorist). The two sets of endings have similarities but the vowel immediately following the stem in the aorist is α in five of the six forms, whereas in this position in the imperfect we have the same pattern of o- and e- sounds as in the present (cf. 2.1/5 note 3):

		IMPERFECT	AORIST
SINGULAR	1	ἔλῡ-ον *I was loosening, used to loosen*	ἔλῡσ-α *I loosened*
	2	ἔλῡ-ες	ἔλῡσ-ας
	3	ἔλῡ-ε(ν)	ἔλῡσ-ε(ν)

		IMPERFECT	AORIST
PLURAL	1	ἐλύ-ομεν	ἐλύσ-αμεν
	2	ἐλύ-ετε	ἐλύσ-ατε
	3	ἔλῡ-ον	ἔλῡσ-αν
INFINITIVE		____	λῦσ-αι

The imperfect and the aorist indicative both represent actions which occurred in the past, but, whereas the aorist simply tells us that an action took place, e.g. τοὺς νεᾱνίᾱς ἐπαιδεύσαμεν *we educated the young men*, the imperfect tells us that an action was continuous or repeated, e.g. τοὺς νεᾱνίᾱς ἐπαιδεύομεν *we were educating/used to educate the young men* (the choice between continuous action *were educating* and habitual action *used to educate* will depend on the context).[1] In other words, while the aorist indicative views a past action as a simple event, the imperfect indicative views it as a process, either continuous or interrupted (repeated or habitual). The difference between the two usually depends on our perception of the nature of the action or event described. We may, in a particular context, see it simply as something that happened in the past (*it rained last summer*). In another context we may see the same event as something continuous (*it was raining last summer when Socrates visited us*) or repeated (*last summer it used to rain every time I went to the Acropolis*). Naturally, many past actions and events are not normally viewed in more than one way (*Pericles died during the plague*). The term covering distinctions of this sort is **aspect**. We say that, although both these tenses of the indicative describe something that happened in the past, the aorist indicative expresses a momentary aspect, the imperfect a continuous or habitual aspect.

This distinction in the indicative between the imperfect and the aorist also applies in the **infinitive** between the **present** and **aorist**, although there is no specific time reference (but see 8.1/3a and 21.1/1 note). The present infinitive is used for an action which is seen as going on, in the process of happening or being repeated. The aorist infinitive is used for an action which is seen simply as an event. Often both are to be translated in English simply by a present

---

[1] The imperfect has two other meanings, which are less common: *began to* (*I began to educate* etc. **inceptive** imperfect) and *tried to* (*I tried to educate* etc. **conative** imperfect).

infinitive: ὁ Ἱππόλυτος τὸν Γλαῦκον ἐκέλευσεν αἰὲν ἀριστεύειν *Hippolytus ordered Glaucus to be always best* (ἀριστεύειν *to be best* present infinitive, because the action is seen as one which is going on and continuing); ἡ Ξανθίππη τὸν δοῦλον ἐκέλευσε κροῦσαι τὴν θύραν *Xanthippe ordered the slave to knock [on] the door* (κροῦσαι aorist infinitive, because Xanthippe envisages a simple (single) act; the present infinitive κρούειν would imply a continual action and require the translation *to keep knocking*).

The imperfect has no infinitive because the present infinitive covers the meaning it would have had (i.e. *to be loosening* in a past context). For similar reasons the imperfect has no moods other than the indicative.

Notes

1 The augment is prefixed to the indicative forms of the three **historic** tenses (the tenses whose indicative describes something in the past, viz imperfect, aorist, pluperfect (16.1/2)); it does **not** occur in the four **primary** tenses (the tenses whose indicative describes something in the present or future, viz present, future, perfect (15.1/1), and future perfect (16.1/4 note 2)). There is also a formal difference between the two categories in the 3rd pl. ind. act. ending. In historic tenses this has a final -ν (e.g. ἔλῦον, ἔλῦσαν), but in primary tenses ends in -σι(ν) (e.g. λῡ́ουσι(ν), λῡ́σουσι(ν)).

2 There are two types of augment:
   (i) the **syllabic** augment, as described above, where a verb begins with a consonant. An initial ρ is doubled: ῥῑ́πτω *throw*, impf. ἔρρῑπτον. This augment is so called because it adds a syllable to the forms where it is used.
   (ii) the **temporal** augment. This variety of the augment is called temporal (Latin **tempus** *time*) because it increases the time taken to pronounce (i.e. it lengthens) an initial vowel according to the following table. Note that α is lengthened to η and that ι, when the second element of a diphthong, becomes subscript. As ι and υ (unlike ε/η and ο/ω) can represent both long and short vowels the temporal augment does not affect the spelling of verbs beginning with them.

α > η	αι > ῃ
ε > η	αυ > ηυ
ι > ῑ	ει > ῃ
o > ω	ευ > ηυ
υ > ῡ	οι > ῳ

η and ω remain unchanged

Examples are: ἀκούω *hear*, aor ἤκουσα; ἐλπίζω *hope*, impf. ἤλπιζον; οἰκτίρω *pity*, impf. ᾤκτῑρον; ὠδίνω *be in labour*, impf. ὤδῑνον (for other examples see **Principal parts of verbs**). A few verbs with initial ε take ει not η, e.g. ἔχω has impf. εἶχον. ει and ευ are often not changed, e.g. εὑρίσκω *find*, impf. εὕρισκον or ηὕρισκον.

3 The endings of the lst s. and 3rd pl. of the imperfect indicative active are the same. The context of a particular form will always make clear which person is meant.

4 Like its present, the imperfect of εἰμί is irregular: ἦ or ἦν, ἦσθα, ἦν, ἦμεν, ἦτε, ἦσαν. This is the only past tense of εἰμί because the act of being was regarded as necessarily extending over a period of time. For all forms of εἰμί see **Appendix 3**.

4.1/2 First and second person pronouns, and αὐτόν, -ήν, -ό

As in English, so in Greek we have pronouns of the first and second persons. These are declined as follows:

	First Person		**Second Person**	
	SINGULAR			
Nom.	ἐγώ	*I*	σύ (also voc.)	*you* (s.)
Acc.	ἐμέ, με	*me*	σέ, σε	*you*
Gen.	ἐμοῦ, μου	*of me*	σοῦ, σου	*of you*
Dat.	ἐμοί, μοι	*to/for me*	σοί, σοι	*to/for you*
	PLURAL			
Nom.	ἡμεῖς	*we*	ὑμεῖς (also voc.)	*you* (pl.)
Acc.	ἡμᾶς	*us*	ὑμᾶς	*you*
Gen.	ἡμῶν	*of us*	ὑμῶν	*of you*
Dat.	ἡμῖν	*to/for us*	ὑμῖν	*to/for you*

The unaccented forms με, μου, μοι, σε, σου, σοι are unemphatic and enclitic (**Appendix 8**, *d*): διώκει με ἡ Ἀσπασίᾱ *Aspasia is chasing me*. The other forms are emphatic: οὐ σέ, ἀλλὰ ἐμὲ διώκει ἡ Ἀσπασίᾱ *it's me, not you, that Aspasia is chasing* (lit. *Aspasia is chasing not you but me*). With prepositions the emphatic forms are used, e.g. μετὰ σοῦ *with you*, except for πρός: πρός με *towards me*. Since the endings of verbs indicate the person involved, the nominative forms will occur only where emphasis is required.

Likewise, in the third person there is no need in Greek for an unemphatic form of the pronoun in the nominative since this too is supplied by the personal endings of the verb: λέγει *he/she/it speaks* (the gender of the subject will be clear from the context). The oblique cases (2.1/3), however, are supplied by αὐτόν, -ήν, -ό *him, her, it* (the nominative has another meaning – 9.1/3), which is declined exactly like the corresponding forms of καλός (3.1/3) except that the neuter accusative singular is αὐτό: ἡ Ἀσπασίᾱ ἐχθὲς ἐδίωκεν αὐτόν *Aspasia was chasing him yesterday*. In the plural, whereas English has only one form (*them*), Greek distinguishes between the genders: m. αὐτούς, f. αὐτᾱς, n. αὐτά etc. (for the emphatic third person pronouns, see 9.1/1).

Note

The possessive genitive of the **unemphatic** personal pronoun is placed after the noun which it qualifies, εἰς τὴν οἰκίᾱν μου *into my house* (lit. *into the house of me*); ἐκ τῆς οἰκίᾱς αὐτῶν *from their house* (lit. *from the house of them*). For the position of the genitive of the **emphatic** personal pronouns see 9.1/5*b*.

4.1/3 Connecting particles

A fundamental feature of Greek is the ubiquitous occurrence of particles. These are short, indeclinable words, many of which are **postpositive**, i.e. they cannot occur as first word in the phrase or sentence where they are used (these we shall mark here and in the vocabulary with an asterisk). Those such as καί *and* and ἀλλά *but*, which are not postpositive, are also called conjunctions.

Particles have two basic functions:

(a) to act as connectives linking grammatical elements of equal weight (words with words, phrases with phrases, sentences with sentences).

(b) to add shades of tone, colour, or emphasis to individual words, phrases, or sentences, which in English would simply be conveyed by a variation in the tone or emphasis of the voice.

Here we will concentrate mainly on connectives. Other particles will be explained as they occur in the reading and at 13.1/3.

With very few well-defined exceptions, every sentence in Greek is connected to the preceding sentence by a connecting particle. The commonest of these is δέ* *and,* which is regularly used to connect a string of sentences where in English we would avoid any connecting word at all. In English it would be considered very bad style to begin sentence after sentence with *and*, but in Greek it is totally natural and acceptable. δέ* is also translatable as *but*, but when so used it denotes only a slight contrast: ὁ Ἀχιλλεὺς ἦν ἐν τῇ σκηνῇ· ὁ δὲ Πάτροκλος ἔφερεν οἶνον *Achilles was in the tent but* (or *and*) *Patroclus was bringing wine.* A strongly contrasting *but* is expressed by ἀλλά, e.g. οὐ βραδέως ἀλλὰ ταχέως οἱ βάρβαροι ἡμᾶς ἐδίωκον *the barbarians were chasing us not slowly but quickly.* Note also γάρ* *for, as,* which introduces the **reason** for what goes before, οὐ μένομεν· οἱ γὰρ βάρβαροι ἡμᾶς διώκουσιν *we are not staying as the barbarians are chasing us.* Similarly οὖν* *therefore, so,* introduces the **result** of what goes before, οἱ βάρβαροι ἡμᾶς διώκουσιν· ταχέως οὖν τρέχομεν *the barbarians are chasing us; therefore we are running quickly.*

καί *and* is frequently used as a simple conjunction connecting words, clauses or sentences, ἡμεῖς καὶ ὑμεῖς *you and we* (Greek gives precedence to the lst person, English is more polite). καί ... καί is used to express *both ... and* καὶ ἡ Ἀφροδίτη καὶ ὁ Διόνῡσος *both Aphrodite and Dionysos,* and the same sense can also be conveyed by τε* ... καί, but since τε* is postpositive (and enclitic; see **Appendix 8**, *d*), the above phrase would become ἥ τε Ἀφροδίτη καὶ ὁ Διόνῡσος. Less commonly τε* is used by itself as the equivalent of δέ or καί to connect a sentence to a preceding sentence.

καί may also be used **adverbially** in the sense *also, even, actually*, καὶ σύ, τέκνον *even you* (or *you too*), *[my] child*; τὸν βάρβαρον καὶ ἐδιώκομεν *we were actually chasing the barbarian*. In this usage καί stands immediately before the word it modifies. The negative of adverbial καί is οὐδέ, *not even*, e.g. οὐδὲ ὁ οἶνος ἀγαθός *not even the wine [is] good*. (As a conjunction οὐδέ also means *nor, and ... not*).

One of the most important combinations of particles is that of μέν* followed at a distance by δέ*. μέν*, however, does **not** connect its own word group with anything preceding. For convenience, it is normally translated in dictionaries by *on the one hand*, which is somewhat too emphatic since μέν* simply introduces the first of a parallel pair of balanced or contrasted items. When we see μέν* we know to look ahead to find the corresponding δέ*. This tendency to place words in a formally balanced structure is fundamental to Greek. Any page of a Greek author will contain at least one μέν* ... δέ*.

We may think of the pair as meaning *on the one hand ... and/but on the other hand,* but in most cases such a translation would be heavy or clumsy. Thus Σωκράτης μὲν λέγει ἐν τῇ ἀγορᾷ, ἐγὼ δὲ βαδίζω μετὰ τῆς Ἀσπασίας should not be translated by *Socrates on the one hand is speaking in the agora, but I on the other hand am walking with Aspasia* but by *Socrates is speaking ... but I am walking ...* or *whereas Socrates is speaking ... I am walking ...*

The two elements balanced by μέν* ... δέ* must always be structurally parallel and the words they follow must be of equal grammatical weight. These can be nouns and pronouns (as above), or adverbs, e.g. εὖ μὲν λέγει, κακῶς δὲ πράττει *he speaks **well** but acts **badly**,* or verbs e.g. λέγει μὲν εὖ, πράττει δὲ κακῶς *he **speaks** well but **acts** badly*; here the change in the elements contrasted has meant that the adverbs εὖ and κακῶς have been placed after the words they qualify (cf. 2.1/6a). Other parts of speech can also be contrasted in this way.

Insight

Divine powers and certain natural phenomena were always to be treated with caution, and when they had a name that might be offensive or bode ill the Greeks sometimes avoided using it by changing the name in some way or by substituting a different word. The dreaded avengers of crime, the Ἐρινύες, provide an example of the latter. They were given the name of Εὐμενίδες lit. *the kindly ones*. The former practice is shown with the Persian name for the Black Sea axšaēna (lit. *dark-coloured*), which was taken over by the Greeks as ἄξενος. As this in Greek would mean *not-stranger-[accepting]*, i.e. *inhospitable* the word was changed to Εὔξενος lit. *good-at-stranger-[accepting]*, i.e. *hospitable* (on ξένος see Insight, Unit 3). In a similar spirit the normal word for *left* ἀριστερός was often replaced with εὐώνυμος lit. *well-omened* precisely because the left side was regarded as ill-omened.

The prefix in Εὐμενίδες, Εὔξενος and εὐώνυμος is the adverb εὖ *well*, *kindly*, which can also function as an independent word; the α in ἄξενος is the negative prefix that occurs in such English derivatives as *amorphous* (*not-shape [having]*), *agnostic* (*not-belief [having]*).

4.2 Greek reading

An analysis of sentence 5 will be found in the key.

1 αἰ μὲν ἡδοναὶ θνηταί, αἱ δ᾽ ἀρεταὶ ἀθάνατοι.

2 ἄρτον οὐκ εἶχεν ὁ πτωχὸς καὶ τυρὸν ἠγόραζεν.

3 μισθὸς ἀρετῆς ἔπαινος, κακίας δὲ ψόγος.

4# δεινοὶ πλέκειν τοι μηχανὰς Αἰγύπτιοι.

5 τοῖς μὲν δούλοις ἡ ἀνάγκη νόμος, τοῖς δὲ ἐλευθέροις ἀνθρώποις ὁ νόμος ἀνάγκη.

6 πάλαι ποτ᾽ ἦσαν ἄλκιμοι Μιλήσιοι.

7 ἀετὸς μυίας οὐ θηρεύει.

8 Futility
(*i*) εἰς οὐρανὸν πτύεις. (*ii*) ἐξ ἄμμου σχοινίον πλέκεις. (*iii*) θάλατταν σπείρεις. (*iv*) ἵππον εἰς πεδίον διδάσκεις τρέχειν.

(v) κατόπιν ἑορτῆς ἥκεις. (vi) νεκρὸν μαστίζεις. (vii) ὄνον κείρεις.
(viii) πρὸ τῆς νίκης τὸ ἐγκώμιον ᾄδεις. (ix) πρὸς κέντρα λακτίζεις.
(x) τὰς μηχανὰς μετὰ τὸν πόλεμον κομίζεις.

9 The fall of Croesus

Herodotus (fifth century BC) is the earliest surviving Greek
historian and has been called the father of history. The subject of
his work is the rise of the Persian empire and its fateful clash with
the Greek world which culminated in the unsuccessful invasion
of Greece in 480–479 BC. The following passage is based on
Herodotus' description of the subjugation of Lydia (see map at
end of Introduction), which brought the Persians into contact
with the Greeks of the Asia Minor coast.

ὁ δὲ Κροῖσος ὁ τῶν Λυδῶν βασιλεὺς (king) τὴν τῶν Περσῶν ἀρχὴν
διαφθείρειν ἤθελεν· κατὰ γὰρ τὸ ἐν Δελφοῖς χρηστήριον ἀρχὴν
μεγάλην ἔμελλε παῦσαι. ἀλλὰ τέλος τὴν μὲν ἑαυτοῦ (his own)
ἀρχὴν ἔπαυσεν, τὴν δὲ τῶν Περσῶν οὔ. μετὰ δὲ τὴν τῶν Περσῶν
νίκην ὁ Κῦρος ὁ τῶν Περσῶν βασιλεὺς τὸν Κροῖσον ἐπὶ πυρὰν 5
μεγάλην ἀνεβίβασεν (made ... go up). ὁ δὲ Κροῖσος τοὺς λόγους
τοὺς τοῦ Σόλωνος (of Solon) τοῦ Ἀθηναίου ἐφρόντιζεν· οὐδεὶς
(no-one) τῶν ἀνθρώπων ὄλβιος πρὸ τοῦ θανάτου. ἥσυχος οὖν
ἔμενε τὴν τελευτήν· ἀλλὰ ὁ Κῦρος, διότι ὁ Κροῖσος καὶ ὅσιος ἦν
καὶ ἀγαθός, ἐκέλευσε μὲν τοὺς στρατιώτας ἀπὸ τῆς πυρᾶς αὐτὸν 10
καταβιβάσαι (to bring down), ἔλεξε (spoke) δὲ ὧδε· ὦ Κροῖσε,
τίς (who?) σε ἀνθρώπων ἔπεισε (persuaded) πολέμιον ἀντὶ φίλου
ἐπὶ τὴν γῆν μου στρατεῦσαι; ὁ δὲ Κροῖσος, ὦ Κῦρε, ἔφη (said),
ἐγὼ μὲν ἐπὶ σὲ ἐστράτευσα, ὁ δὲ θεὸς ὁ ἐν Δελφοῖς ἔπεισέ με
στρατεῦσαι. οὐ γὰρ εἰμι ἀνόητος οὐδὲ ἐθέλω τὸν πόλεμον ἔχειν 15
ἀντὶ τῆς εἰρήνης. ἐν μὲν γὰρ τῇ εἰρήνῃ οἱ νεανίαι τοὺς γεραιοὺς
(the old) θάπτουσιν, ἐν δὲ τῷ πολέμῳ οἱ γεραιοὶ τοὺς νεανίας.
ἀλλὰ τοῦτο (lit. this thing) φίλον ἦν τοῖς θεοῖς. ὁ οὖν Κῦρος αὐτὸν
ἔλυσε καὶ ἐγγὺς καθεῖσεν (made ... sit). ὁ δὲ Κροῖσος αὖθις
ἔλεξεν· ὦ Κῦρε, τί (what?) πράττουσιν οἱ στρατιῶταί σου; τὴν 20
πόλιν (city) σου, ἔφη ὁ Κῦρος, ἁρπάζουσι καὶ τὸν πλοῦτόν σου
ἐκφέρουσιν. οὐχ ἁρπάζουσι τὴν πόλιν μου, ἔφη ὁ Κροῖσος, οὐδὲ
τὸν πλοῦτον· οὐδὲν (nothing) γὰρ ἐμοί ἐστιν. ἀλλὰ σὲ ἄγουσί τε
καὶ φέρουσιν. μετὰ δὲ τοῦτο φίλος ἦν αὐτῷ. τὴν γὰρ σοφίαν αὐτοῦ
ἐν τιμῇ εἶχεν ὁ Κῦρος. 25

Notes

1 The appropriate part of εἰμί is to be supplied (also in 3, 4, 5).

2 Cheese (τῡρός) would have been something of a luxury to the poor.

3 Take μισθός with the genitives ἀρετῆς and κακίας; normal prose usage would require ὁ μισθός but the definite article is often omitted in proverbs and in verse.

4 τοι is a particle conveying emphasis, commonly employed in proverbs; it is not to be translated, since in English we would convey the emphasis by tone of voice; μηχανάς here used metaphorically *devices, ways and means* (in 8(x) below the word is used concretely).

6 Miletus, the city of the Μιλήσιοι, flourished in the seventh and sixth centuries BC; in later times it became symbolic of past greatness; Μιλήσιοι does not have an article as this is optional with proper nouns (2.1/2 note 1(iii)).

8 (x) μηχαναί are here *engines of war* (siege weapons and the like).

9 *l.*1 δέ connects this passage with what precedes in the original and need not be translated. *l.*2 Δελφοί is a plural place name. There are many such names in Greek (Ἀθῆναι *Athens*, Θῆβαι *Thebes*). *l.*3 ἔμελλε *was destined to, was going to. ll.*7ff. Solon was an Athenian statesman who had visited Croesus and, in conversation with him, had enunciated the very Greek sentiment *Call no man happy before he dies* (only then can a true and full judgement be made); ἐφρόντιζεν *began to ponder* inceptive imperfect (4.1/1 footnote); οὐδεὶς ... θανάτου are Solon's actual words (inverted commas are not normally used in printing Greek – 1.1/1 note 3). *l.*8 ἥσυχος translate by an adverb *quietly* (Greek often uses an adjective where English would have an adverb). *ll.*12f. Take τίς ... ἀνθρώπων together; take πολέμιον with σε, *[as an] enemy* (Greek does not here need an equivalent to the English *as*). *l.*18 τοῦτο refers to what has happened to Croesus; φίλον +dat. *dear to, pleasing to. l.*22 οὐχ 2.1/6a(i). *ll.*23f. ἄγουσί τε καὶ φέρουσιν lit. *are both driving and carrying,* i.e. *are plundering and carrying off*

44

(a set expression; the τε need not be translated) but here translate
simply by *plunder*.

4.2/1 Vocabulary

ἀγοράζω   *buy*
ἄγω καὶ φέρω   *plunder*
ᾄδω   *sing*
ἀετός, -οῦ, ὁ   *eagle*
Ἀθηναῖος, -ᾱ, -ον   *Athenian*
Αἰγύπτιος, -ᾱ, -ον   *Egyptian*
ἄλκιμος, -ον   *brave*
ἄμμος, -ου, ἡ   *sand*
ἀνάγκη, -ης, ἡ   *necessity*
ἀνόητος -ον   *foolish*
ἀντί (prep.+gen.)   *instead of*
ἀπό (prep.+gen.)   *from, away
   from*
ἁρπάζω   *seize, plunder, snatch*
ἄρτος, -ου, ὁ   *bread*
ἀρχή, -ῆς, ἡ   *empire*
αὖθις (adv.)   *again*
γάρ* (connecting particle)
   for, as
δεινός, -ή, -όν   *clever at* (+inf.)
Δελφοί, -ῶν, οἱ   *Delphi*
διδάσκω   *teach*
ἐγγύς (adv.)   *near, nearby*
ἐγκώμιον, -ου, τό   *victory-song*
ἐθέλω   *am willing, wish*
εἰρήνη, -ης, ἡ   *peace*
ἐκφέρω   *carry out*
ἐλεύθερος, -ᾱ, -ον   *free*
ἐξ = ἐκ
ἑορτή, -ῆς, ἡ   *feast,*
ἔπαινος, -ου, ὁ   *praise*
ἐπί (prep.+acc.)   *on to, to,
   against*
ἥσυχος, -η, -ον   *quiet, peaceful*
θάπτω   *bury*

θηρεύω   *hunt*
θνητός, -ή, -όν   *mortal*
ἵππος, -ου, ὁ   *horse*
κακίᾱ, -ᾱς, ἡ   *wickedness*
κατά (prep.+acc.)   *according to*
κατόπιν (+gen.)   *after*
κείρω   *cut* (the hair), *shear*
κελεύω   *order*
κέντρον, -ου, τό   *goad*
κομίζω   *bring*
λακτίζω   *kick*
λόγος, -ου, ὁ   *word*
Λῡδός, -οῦ, ὁ   *Lydian*
μαστίζω   *whip, flog*
μέλλω   *be destined to*
μένω   *wait (for)*
μετά (prep.+acc.)   *after*
μηχανή, -ῆς, ἡ   *engine of war;
   device*
Μῑλήσιος, -ᾱ, -ον   *of Miletus,
   Milesian*
μισθός, -οῦ, ὁ   *pay, reward*
μυῖα, -ᾱς, ἡ   *fly*
νίκη, -ης, ἡ   *victory*
νόμος, -ου, ὁ   *law*
ὄλβιος, -ᾱ, -ον   *happy*
ὄνος, -ου, ὁ/ἡ   *ass*
ὅσιος, -ᾱ, -ον   *pious, devout*
οὐδέ (conj.)   *and not, nor*
οὖν* (particle)   *therefore, so,
   then*
οὐρανός, -οῦ, ὁ   *sky*
πάλαι (adv.)   *long ago*
παύω (tr.)   *stop, put an end to*
πεδίον, -ου, τό   *plain*

Πέρσης, -ου, ὁ   *Persian*
πλέκω   *plait; devise, contrive*
πολέμιος, -ᾱ, -ον   *hostile, enemy*
πόλεμος, -ου, ὁ   *war*
ποτέ*   *once*
πράττω   *do*
πρό (prep.+gen.)   *before*
πτύω   *spit*
πτωχός, -οῦ, ὁ   *beggar*
πυρά, -ᾶς, ἡ   *funeral pyre*
σοφίᾱ, -ᾱς, ἡ   *wisdom*
σπείρω   *sow* (with seed)
στρατεύω   *make an expedition*

στρατιώτης, -ου, ὁ   *soldier*
σχοινίον, -ου, τό   *little rope*
τε* ... καί/τε*   *both ... and*
τελευτή, -ῆς, ἡ   *end, death*
τέλος (adv.)   *in the end, finally*
τῑμή, -ῆς, ἡ   *respect*
τοι*   see note on 4.2.4
τρέχω   *run*
τῡρός, -οῦ, ὁ   *cheese*
φροντίζω   *think about, ponder*
χρηστήριον, -ου, τό   *oracle*
ψόγος, -ου, ὁ   *blame*
ὧδε (adv.)   *thus, as follows*

Main points

- The imperfect tense is used for a continuous or repeated past action

- The aorist simply indicates that an action happened in the past

- Both the aorist indicative and the imperfect add an augment to their stem

- The initial letter or letters of a verb determine whether it takes a syllabic or temporal augment

- The nominative of first and second person pronouns is only used for emphasis

- αὐτόν exists only as a third person pronoun in the acc. gen. dat. (s. and pl.)

- Particles are short, indeclinable words that either act as connectives or convey a particular nuance

Unit 5

....

5.1 Grammar

5.1/1 Third declension – consonant stem nouns (1)

The third declension contains nouns of all three genders. They are divided into two classes, those with stems ending in a consonant and those with stems ending in a vowel or diphthong. Within the various sub-groups of each class masculine and feminine nouns have the same case endings but neuters always follow the rule previously given (3.1/1) for the nominative, vocative and accusative (not every sub-group has each gender). The gender of a third declension noun is only sometimes predictable from its ending.

With all consonant stem nouns we discover the stem by subtracting -ος from the genitive singular (e.g. γύψ *vulture*, gen. γῡπός, stem γῡπ-) and the other case endings are added to this. As the stem is modified, occasionally beyond recognition, in the nominative singular, both nominative and genitive singular must be learnt.

(*a*) *Stems in* κ, γ, χ *(palatals),* π, β, φ *(labials), and* τ, δ, θ *(dentals)*
The declension of regular masculine and feminine nouns with stems ending in these consonants is given below. Masculine and feminine nouns in these sub-groups have a nominative singular in ς, which combines with, or replaces, the final consonant of the stem as follows:

κ/γ/χ + σ > ξ; π/β/φ + σ > ψ; τ/δ/θ + σ > σ

The same changes occur before the dative plural ending -σι (which can take a movable ν; cf. 2.1/5 note 4); they also occur in verbs with similar stems (6.1/4).

	φύλαξ (m)	γύψ (m)	ἔρως (m)	πατρίς (f)
	guard	*vulture*	*love*	*native land*
stem	φυλακ-	γῡπ-	ἐρωτ-	πατριδ-

N.V.	φύλαξ	γύψ	ἔρως	πατρίς (voc. πατρί)
Acc.	φύλακ-α	γῦπ-α	ἔρωτ-α	πατρίδ-α
Gen.	φύλακ-ος	γῦπ-ός	ἔρωτ-ος	πατρίδ-ος
Dat.	φύλακ-ι	γῦπ-ί	ἔρωτ-ι	πατρίδ-ι
PLURAL				
N.V.	φύλακ-ες	γῦπ-ες	ἔρωτ-ες	πατρίδ-ες
Acc.	φύλακ-ας	γῦπ-ας	ἔρωτ-ας	πατρίδ-ας
Gen.	φυλάκ-ων	γῦπ-ῶν	ἐρώτ-ων	πατρίδ-ων
Dat.	φύλαξι(ν)	γῦψί(ν)	ἔρω-σι(ν)	πατρί-σι(ν)

Within these sub-groups the only neuters are those with a τ stem. The vast majority of these have a nominative singular in -μα and a genitive in -ματος. Of the others some have a sigma in the nominative singular (as κέρας), some do not (e.g. ἧπαρ, ἥπατος *liver*).

	σῶμα (n) *body*		κέρας (n) *horn*	
stem	σωματ-		κερᾱτ-	
	SINGULAR	PLURAL	SINGULAR	PLURAL
N.V.	σῶμα	σώματ-α	κέρας	κέρᾱτ-α
Acc.	σῶμα	σώματ-α	κέρας	κέρᾱτ-α
Gen.	σώματ-ος	σωμάτ-ων	κέρᾱτ-ος	κερᾱ́τ-ων
Dat.	σώματ-ι	σώμα-σι(ν)	κέρᾱτ-ι	κέρᾱ-σι(ν)

(b) Stems in ντ (all masculine)

These have a nominative singular in -ᾱς or -ων. Unlike nouns of the preceding sub-groups (except πατρίς), they have a separate vocative singular, which is formed by dropping τ from the stem. Their dative plural has the change ντ + σ > σ, with lengthening of the preceding α and o to ᾱ and ου (not ω) respectively. This lengthening occurs to compensate for the reduction of three consonants to one.

	γίγᾱς (m) *giant*		λέων (m) *lion*	
stem	γιγαντ-		λεοντ-	
	SINGULAR	PLURAL	SINGULAR	PLURAL
Nom.	γίγᾱς	γίγαντ-ες	λέων	λέοντ-ες
Voc.	γίγαν	γίγαντ-ες	λέον	λέοντ-ες
Acc.	γίγαντ-α	γίγαντ-ας	λέοντ-α	λέοντ-ας
Gen.	γίγαντ-ος	γιγάντ-ων	λέοντ-ος	λεόντ-ων
Dat.	γίγαντ-ι	γίγᾱσι(ν)	λέοντ-ι	λέουσι(ν)

Notes

1 Some nouns with these stems are slightly irregular, mostly in the nominative singular. The most common are:

γόνυ	γόνατος (n)	*knee*
γυνή	γυναικός (f)	*woman* (voc. s. γύναι)
θρίξ	τριχός (f)	*hair* (dat. pl. θριξί(ν)
νύξ	νυκτός (f)	*night* (dat. pl. νυξί(ν))
ὀδούς	ὀδόντος (m)	*tooth*
οὖς	ὠτός (n)	*ear*
παῖς	παιδός (m or f)	*child* (voc. sing. παῖ)
πούς	ποδός (m)	*foot*
ὕδωρ	ὕδατος (n)	*water*

2 Stems in ιδ which are **not** accented on the ι have -ιν, not -ιδα, in the acc. s., e.g. ἔρις, ἔριδος (f) *strife*, acc. ἔριν. This also applies to χάρις, χάριτος (f) *favour*, acc. χάριν and ὄρνῑς, ὄρνῑθος (m. or f.) *bird*, acc. ὄρνιν.

3 Third declension monosyllables are accented on their ending in the genitive and dative, both singular and plural (see γύψ above).

5.1/2 Contracted verbs

Unlike verbs with stems ending in ι and υ (ἐσθίω *eat*, λύω *loosen*), verbs whose stems end in α, ε and o contract their stem vowel with the initial vowel of the endings in the present and imperfect. A consonantal suffix is used to form the stem of the other tenses (e.g. σ in the future and aorist – see note 2). Examples of contracted verbs are: τῑμά-ω *honour*, ποιέ-ω *do, make*, δηλό-ω *make clear, show*. Since all three types contract their stem vowels and the -ω of the lst s. pres. ind. act. to -ῶ (τῑμῶ, ποιῶ, δηλῶ), these verbs are always cited in vocabulary lists in their **uncontracted** form to make identification immediately obvious. For the rules governing the accentuation of contracted verbs see **Appendix 8**, *b*(i). Paradigms for the three types are given in **Appendix 2**. As the endings involved are the same as for λύω, it is the rules for contraction which are our principal concern here:

(a) **Stems in α** (*model* τῑμάω)

α + an e-sound *(ε, η)* > ᾱ: ἐτῑμᾱ *(ἐτίμα-ε)*

α + an o-sound *(ο, ου, ω)* > ω: τῑμῶσι *(τῑμά-ουσι)*; τῑμῶμεν *(τῑμά-ομεν)*

α + an ι- diphthong *(ει, η, οι)* obeys the above rules but retains the iota as a subscript in the contracted form: τῑμᾷ *(τῑμά-ει)*

The combinations of α + η/ῃ/οι occur in forms not yet treated.

(b) **Stems in ε** (*model* ποιέω)

ε + ε > ει: ποιεῖτε (ποιέ-ετε)

ε + ο > ου: ἐποίουν (ἐποίε-ον)

ε disappears before a long vowel or diphthong: ποιῶ (ποιέ-ω); ποιοῦσι (ποιέ-ουσι).

(c) **Stems in ο** (*model* δηλόω)

ο + ε/ο/ου > ου: ἐδήλου (ἐδήλο-ε); δηλοῦμεν (δηλό-ομεν); δηλοῦσι (δηλό-ουσι)

ο + η/ω > ω: δηλῶ (δηλό-ω)

ο + an ι-diphthong (ει, οι, η) > οι: δηλοῖ (δηλό-ει)

The combinations ο + η/οι/ῃ occur in forms not yet treated.

The above contractions, which cover all forms of contracted verbs, also occur in other parts of speech, e.g. the noun νοῦς (< νόος; 6.1/2). Contraction was a regular feature of Attic Greek but was not as rigorously applied in other dialects.

Notes

1 The present infinitives of α- and o-stems contract to -ᾶν and -ουν respectively, **not** -ᾷν and -οιν. This is because the -ειν of the pres. inf. act. of uncontracted -ω verbs (e.g. λύ-ειν) is itself a contraction of ε + εν. With -αω and -οω verbs we therefore have the double contractions α + ε + εν > ᾱ + εν > ᾶν; ο + ε + εν > ου + εν > ουν, which give us τῑμᾶν, δηλοῦν.

2 All tenses other than the present and imperfect are formed by lengthening the stem vowel and proceeding exactly as with uncontracted verbs (α > η (except after ε, ι, ρ where we have α > ᾱ); ε > η; ο > ω). The fut. ind. act. of the model verbs is τῑμήσω, ποιήσω, δηλώσω and the aor. ind. act. ἐτίμησα, ἐποίησα, ἐδήλωσα. However, γελάω *laugh* does not lengthen its α: fut. γελάσομαι (8.1/1 note l) aor. ἐγέλασα. Likewise, καλέω *call* and τελέω *complete* do not lengthen their ε in the aorist: ἐκάλεσα, ἐτέλεσα; their future is, rather confusingly, the same as their present, καλῶ, τελῶ, because the expected καλέσω, τελέσω lost the intervocalic σ and contraction resulted (cf. 6.1/1*c*).

3 A contracted future also occurs in most verbs in -ίζω (6.1/4*b*) and all verbs with stems in λ, μ, ν, ρ (11.1/3). Nearly all such futures have a stem in ε (i.e. the contraction is -ῶ, -εῖς, -εῖ, etc., exactly as the present of ποιέω). A few have a stem in α, as ἐλαύνω *drive,* fut. stem ἐλα- giving ἐλῶ, ἐλᾷς, ἐλᾷ, etc., exactly as the present of τῑμάω.

4 ζάω *be alive* contracts to η where other -άω verbs have ᾱ: pres. ind. act. ζῶ, ζῇς, ζῇ, ζῶμεν, ζῆτε, ζῶσι(ν), inf. ζῆν; impf. ind. act. ἔζων, ἔζης, ἔζη, ἐζῶμεν, ἐζῆτε, ἔζων. So also πεινάω *be hungry* and διψάω *be thirsty.*

5 Most disyllabic verbs in -εω (as δέω *need,* πλέω *sail,* πνέω *breathe,* ῥέω *flow*) contract only when ε is followed by ε. The pres. ind. act. of πλέω is πλέω, πλεῖς, πλεῖ, πλέομεν, πλεῖτε, πλέουσι(ν); impf. ἔπλεον, ἔπλεις, ἔπλει, ἐπλέομεν, ἐπλεῖτε, ἔπλεον. The 3rd s. act. of δέω *need,* pres. δεῖ, impf. ἔδει, is used impersonally in the sense of *it is/was necessary* (examples have already occurred in the reading exercises). It is construed with the **accusative** of the person involved and an infinitive: δεῖ με ἐν τῇ οἰκίᾳ μένειν, *it is necessary for me to remain in the house,* i.e. *I must remain ...*

6 There is **no** movable ν in the 3rd s. of the impf. ind. act. of contracted verbs.

5.1/3 Further uses of the definite article

In English we can, to a limited degree, use the definite article with an adjective to form a noun-equivalent: *only the good die young; only the brave deserve the fair.* In Greek, however, the definite article can be used to create a noun-equivalent out of virtually any part of speech (adjective, adverb, prepositional phrase, infinitive) to which it is prefixed: ὁ σοφός *the wise [man]*; ἡ σοφή *the wise [woman]*; οἱ τότε *the then [men]* i.e. *the men of that time*; οἱ νῦν *the now [men]* i.e. *the men of today*; οἱ ἐν τῇ οἰκίᾳ *the [men] in the house* (the last three examples can also mean *the [people]* ..., as Greek uses the masculine article to refer to mixed groups). The neuter singular article is used with adjectives to express abstractions: τὸ καλόν *beauty*, τὸ αἰσχρόν *ugliness*. When prefixed to an infinitive (**articular infinitive**, i.e. article + infinitive) it forms an equivalent of verbal nouns in English: τὸ λέγειν *the [act of] speaking, speech*; τὸ φεύγειν *the [act of] fleeing, flight*. Each of these noun-equivalents functions exactly like any normal noun, and the case of the article (and of an accompanying adjective) varies according to a particular context: φέρω τὸν κακόν *I am carrying the cowardly [man]*; περὶ τοῦ παιδεύειν ἔλεγεν *he was speaking about the [act of] educating* i.e. *about education*; ἐδιώκομεν τοὺς ἐν τῇ νήσῳ *we were chasing the [men] in the island*.

Another very common type of noun-phrase consists of the neuter plural of the definite article followed by a genitive. Here the article may be translated in a wide variety of ways. Thus τὰ τῶν Ἀθηναίων (lit. *the [things] of the Athenians*) can mean *the property/situation/condition/fortunes/interests*, etc., *of the Athenians*; τὰ ἐν τῇ Ῥώμῃ *the things/events/circumstances*, etc. *in Rome*. The context must determine the most appropriate rendering.

The article can also be used as a third person pronoun when combined with the particles μέν* ... δέ; ὁ μέν ... ὁ δέ *the one ... the other* (*one man ... another*); οἱ μέν ... οἱ δέ *some ... others*: ὁ μέν διώκει τὴν δόξαν, ὁ δὲ τὸ ἀργύριον *one man chases fame, another money*; οἱ μέν ἀπέθνησκον, οἱ δὲ ἔφευγον *some were dying, others running away*. ὁ δέ *but/and he* (and οἱ δέ etc.) when used by itself refers to someone mentioned in the preceding sentence other than its subject: ὁ Σωκράτης ἐκέλευσε τὴν Ξανθίππην κροῦσαι τὴν μυῖαν· ἡ δὲ οὐκ ἤθελεν *Socrates ordered Xanthippe to swat the fly but she refused* (lit. *was not willing*). This use of the article is a survival from an earlier stage in Greek when it was employed solely as a third person pronoun (cf. 25.1/3*a*)

We have already met three usages of the article in Greek where there is no corresponding article in English (2.1/2 note 1). There is also

52

one important instance where the reverse holds true, viz where the noun or adjective is predicative. Thus, when Thucydides (6.2.11) is telling us that originally the Athenians called the Acropolis simply 'the polis', he writes καλεῖται (3rd s. pres. ind. passive) ἡ Ἀκρόπολις ἔτι πόλις *the Acropolis is still called 'the polis'*, but there is no article with πόλις. In such sentences, therefore, there should be no doubt as to which word is the subject and which is the complement.

Notes

1 Adjectives without the definite article can also be used as nouns but they then have an indefinite sense: ἐν τῷ πολέμῳ πολλοὶ κακὰ ἔφερον *in the war many [people] were suffering hardships* (lit. *bad things*). When used indefinitely in the singular an adjective is normally accompanied by the indefinite pronoun τις (10.1/1).

2 In expressions such as Ἀλκιβιάδης ὁ Κλεινίου *Alcibiades, [son] of Cleinias* the article is followed by the genitive and the word for son or daughter is omitted (cf. 23.1/1a). As Greeks, both male and female, had only one name, the name of a person's father is often given in this way to achieve greater precision.

Insight

The only Greek god who had a name with cognates in other Indo-European languages (cf. 1.3) and so could, in a sense, claim to be genuinely Greek was Zeus (Ζεύς; cf. Sanskrit *Dyaus*), whom Homer calls ἄναξ ἀνδρῶν τε θεῶν τε (*ruler of gods and men*). The many other divinities worshipped, or at least acknowledged, by the Greeks seem to have been adopted from other cultures. However, they were all brought into some relationship with Zeus so as to form a family unit. The most recent newcomer of any importance was Dionysus (Διόνῡσος), the god of wine, who was transformed into one of Zeus' many children born, so to speak, out of wedlock. In historic times, after the Greek pantheon had been established, a foreign god was simply equated with a Greek divinity whose functions were similar. In this way Ammon, the chief god of the Egyptians, was identified with Zeus.

5.2 Greek reading

1 ὁ χρόνος παιδεύει τοὺς σοφούς.

2 πόλλ᾽ ἔχει σιωπὴ καλά.

3# πόλλ᾽ ἔστιν ἀνθρώποισιν, ὦ ξένοι, κακά.

4# οὐ δεῖ φέρειν τὰ πρόσθεν ἐν μνήμῃ κακά.

5 Supply ἐστί in the following: (*i*) καλὸν ἡσυχία. (*ii*) χαλεπὰ τὰ καλά. (*iii*) μέτρον ἄριστον. (*iv*) μέγα βιβλίον μέγα κακόν. (*v*) κοινὰ τὰ τῶν φίλων. (*vi*) κοινὸς Ἑρμῆς. (*vii*) μικρὸν κακὸν μέγα ἀγαθόν. (*viii*) ἄλλα ἄλλοις καλά. (*ix*) ἡ γλῶττα πολλῶν αἰτία κακῶν. (*x*) χαλεπὸν τὸ ποιεῖν, τὸ δὲ κελεῦσαι ῥάδιον. (*xi*)# κακὸν τὸ μεθύειν πημονῆς λυτήριον. (*xii*) παθήματα μαθήματα. (*xiii*) κακοῦ κόρακος κακὸν ᾠόν. (*xiv*) πιστὸν γῆ, ἄπιστον θάλαττα. (*xv*) κἂν μύρμηκι χολή.

6 (*i*) δεῖ γαμεῖν ἐκ τῶν ὁμοίων. (*ii*) μῶρος μῶρα λέγει. (*iii*) ἔξω πηλοῦ τὸν πόδα ἔχεις. (*iv*) ζεῖ χύτρα, ζῇ φιλία. (*v*) λέοντα ξυρεῖς. (*vi*) πρὸς σῆμα μητρυιᾶς κλαίεις.

7# φεῦ φεῦ, τὰ μεγάλα μεγάλα καὶ πάσχει κακά.

8# ὄνου χρείαν ἐλέγχει τραχύτης ὁδοῦ.

9# ἄνθρωπός ἐστι πνεῦμα καὶ σκιὰ μόνον.

10# τύχη τέχνην ὤρθωσεν, οὐ τέχνη τύχην.

11# πολλῶν τὰ χρήματ᾽ αἴτι᾽ ἀνθρώποις κακῶν.

12# γύναι, γυναιξὶ κόσμον ἡ σιγὴ φέρει.

13# καλὸν δὲ καὶ γέροντι μανθάνειν σοφά.

14 οἱ Ἀθηναῖοι Θουκυδίδην τὸν Ὀλόρου ἔπεμψαν πρὸς τὸν στρατηγὸν τῶν ἐν Θρᾴκῃ.

15 οὔτε παρὰ νεκροῦ ὁμιλίαν οὔτε παρὰ φιλαργύρου χάριν δεῖ ζητεῖν.

16# ἱκανὸν τὸ νικᾶν ἐστι τοῖς ἐλευθεροῖς.

17# κἂν τοῖς ἀγροίκοις ἐστὶ παιδείας ἔρως.

18 ὁ λύκος τὴν τρίχα, οὐ τὴν γνώμην, ἀλλάττει.

19# τὰ χρήματ᾽ ἀνθρώποισιν εὑρίσκει φίλους.

20 φαῦλος κριτὴς καλοῦ πράγματος ὄχλος.

21 The Egyptians and their crocodiles (from Herodotus)
τοῖς μὲν οὖν τῶν Αἰγυπτίων ἱεροί εἰσιν οἱ κροκόδιλοι, τοῖς δ᾽ οὔ, ἀλλ᾽ ἅτε πολεμίους περιέπουσιν. οἱ δὲ περί τε Θήβας καὶ τὴν Μοίρεως (of Moeris) λίμνην σφόδρα νομίζουσιν αὐτοὺς εἶναι ἱερούς. ἕνα (one) δὲ ἑκάτεροι τρέφουσι κροκόδιλον καὶ διδάσκουσιν, ἀρτήματα δὲ λίθινα χυτὰ εἰς τὰ ὦτα ἐμβάλλουσι 5 καὶ ἀμφιδέας περὶ τοὺς ἐμπροσθίους πόδας καὶ σιτία ἀπότακτα παρέχουσι καὶ ἱερεῖα. ἕως μὲν οὖν ζῶσιν οἱ κροκόδιλοι μάλ᾽ εὖ πάσχουσιν, μετὰ δὲ τὸν θάνατον ταριχεύουσιν αὐτοὺς οἱ Αἰγύπτιοι καὶ θάπτουσιν ἐν ἱεραῖς θήκαις. ἀλλ᾽ οἱ περὶ Ἐλεφαντίνην πόλιν (city) καὶ ἐσθίουσιν αὐτούς· οὐ γὰρ 10 νομίζουσιν ἱερούς εἶναι.

Notes

2 πόλλ᾽ = πολλά (also in 3) 2.1/6*b*.

3 ἀνθρώποισιν dat. pl.; -οισιν is the longer form of the ending (3.1/1 note 3).

4 Take τὰ πρόσθεν ... κακά together and ἐν μνήμῃ with φέρειν; dislocations of this sort are common in verse.

5 (*i*) καλόν is neuter because the meaning is *a fair [thing]*; we would have expected the definite article with ἡσυχία (2.1/2 note 1) – see note on 4.2.3. (*iv*) here, and in some of the following proverbs, it is necessary to decide which is subject and which is predicate, i.e. *is a big book a big evil?* or *is a big evil a big book?* Obviously the former is what is meant. (*vi*) An appeal to share in the luck that another is enjoying (e.g. in finding a coin in the street); Hermes, as god of luck, shares, or should share, his blessings equally. (*viii*) ἄλλα ἄλλοις ... lit. *other [things] ... to other [people]*, i.e. *different [things] ... to different people.* (*xiv*) πιστόν, ἄπιστον cf. καλόν in (*i*). (*xv*) κἄν = καὶ ἐν (crasis 11.1/5); καί here means *even* (4.1/3).

6 (*iv*) ζεῖ < ζέω *boil*, ζῆ < ζάω *live* (the latter is irregular – 5.1/2 note 4).

7 Prose order would be τὰ μεγάλα καὶ πάσχει μεγάλα κακά; καὶ is here adverbial *also* (4.1/3); take the second μεγάλα with κακά.

10 Translate ὤρθωσεν by a present; the aorist is often used to express general truths, particularly in proverbs (so-called **gnomic aorist**; cf. *faint heart never won fair lady*).

11 Supply ἐστί (and also in 13 and 20); χρήματ᾽ αἰτί᾽ both have an elided α; the plural of χρῆμα *thing* here means *money* (a very common use).

13 δέ cf. note on 4.2.9 (there are many examples of such connectives at the beginning of verse and prose extracts in subsequent reading exercises); καί *even* 4.1/3.

14 τὸν Ὀλόρου 5.1/3 note 2.

17 κἄν see above on 5 (*xv*).

19 χρήματ(α) see on 11; ἀνθρώποισιν see note on 3.

20 Only the sense can indicate which noun is subject and which predicate (cf. note on 5(*iv*)).

21 *ll.*1f. τοῖς μὲν ... τοῖς δέ *for some ... for others* (5.1/3); οὖν connects this passage with what goes before in the original context (cf. 13 above); ἄτε πολεμίους *as enemies*; Θῆβαι *Thebes* not to be confused with the city of the same name in Greece. *l.*4 Take ἕνα (m. acc. of εἷς (7.1/5)) with κροκόδιλον; ἑκάτεροι *each of the two* (i.e. those around Thebes and those around the swamp of Moeris). *l.7* οὖν *therefore, so* shows that what follows is a consequence of what was said in the previous sentence, while μέν functions with the δέ of the next line to contrast ἕως ζῶσιν ... with μετὰ τὸν θάνατον ...

5.2/1 Vocabulary

ἄγροικος, -ον *from the country, rustic, boorish*
αἰτίᾱ, -ᾱς, ἡ *cause*
ἀλλάττω *change* (tr.)
ἀμφιδέᾱ, -ᾱς, ἡ *bracelet, anklet*
ἄπιστος, -ον *untrustworthy*
ἀπότακτος, -ον *set apart for special use*
ἄριστος, -η, -ον *best*
ἄρτημα, -ατος, τό *ear-ring*
ἄτε (particle) *as if, as*
βιβλίον, -ου, τό *book*
γαμέω *marry*
γέρων, -οντος, ὁ *old man*
γλῶττα, -ης, ἡ *tongue*
γνώμη, -ης, ἡ *mind*
γυνή, -αικός, ἡ *woman*
διδάσκω *teach, train*
ἑκάτερος, -ᾱ -ον *each* (of two)
ἐλέγχω *test*
Ἐλεφαντίνη, -ης, ἡ *Elephantine* (city in Egypt)
ἐμβάλλω *put in*
ἐμπρόσθιος, -ον *(in) front*
ἔξω (+gen.) *outside*
εὖ (adv.) *well*
εὑρίσκω *find; get*
ἕως (conj.) *while*
ζάω *be alive, live, pass one's life*
ζέω *boil*
ζητέω *look for, seek* (+acc.)

ἡσυχίᾱ, -ᾱς, ἡ *peace, quiet*
Θῆβαι, -ῶν, αἱ *Thebes* (city in Egypt)
θήκη, -ης, ἡ *tomb*
Θρᾴκη, -ης, ἡ *Thrace*
θρίξ, τριχός, ἡ *hair*
ἱερεῖα, -ων, τά *offerings*
ἱερός, -ᾱ́, -όν *sacred, holy*
ἱκανός, -ή, -όν *sufficient*
κλαίω *weep*
κοινός, -ή, -όν *common, shared*
κόραξ, -ακος, ὁ *crow*
κόσμος, -ου, ὁ *decoration*
κροκόδῑλος, -ου, ὁ *crocodile*
λίθινος, -η, -ον (χυτός) *made of glass*
λύκος, -ου, ὁ *wolf*
λυτήριον, -ου, τό *remedy*
μάθημα, -ατος, τό *lesson*
μάλα (adv.) *very*
μανθάνω *learn*
μεθύω *be drunk*
μέτρον, -ου, τό *measure, due measure, moderation*
μητρυιά, -ᾱς, ἡ *step-mother*
μικρός, -ᾱ́, -όν *small,*
μνήμη, -ης, ἡ *memory*
μόνον (adv.) *only, merely*
μύρμηξ, -ηκος, ὁ *ant*
μῶρος, -ᾱ, -ον, *stupid, foolish*
νικάω *win*

ξυρέω *shave*
ὁδός, -οῦ, ἡ *road*
ὅμοιος, -ᾱ, -ον *like*
ὀρθόω *guide*
οὖς, ὠτός, τό *ear*
ὄχλος, -ου, ὁ *crowd, mob*
πάθημα -ατος, τό *suffering, misfortune*
παιδείᾱ, -ᾱς, ἡ *education, culture*
παιδεύω *teach, educate*
παρά (prep.) (+gen.) *from*
πάσχω *suffer;* εὖ πάσχω *be well treated*
περί (prep.) (+acc.) *around*
περιέπω *treat*
πηλός, -οῦ, ὁ *mud*
πημονή, -ῆς, ἡ *woe, misery*
πιστός, -ή, -όν *trustworthy*
πνεῦμα, -ατος, τό *breath*
ποιέω *make, do*
πολέμιος, -ᾱ, -ον *hostile, enemy*
πούς, ποδός, ὁ, *foot*
πρᾱγμα, -ατος, τό *thing, matter*
πρός (prep.) (+acc.) *to, towards; on, at*
πρόσθεν(adv.) *previously*
ῥᾴδιος, -ᾱ, -ον *easy*

σῆμα, -ατος, τό *tomb*
σῑγή, -ῆς, ἡ *silence*
σῑτία, -ων, τά *provisions, food*
σιωπή, -ῆς, ἡ *silence*
σκιά, -ᾶς, ἡ *shadow*
σοφός, -ή, -όν *wise, clever*
στρατηγός, -οῦ, ὁ *general, commander*
ταριχεύω *embalm, mummify*
τραχύτης, -ητος, ἡ *roughness*
τρέφω *rear*
φαῦλος, -ον (also -η, -ον) *poor, inadequate*
φεῦ (interjection) *alas!*
φιλάργυρος, -ον *avaricious, miserly*
χαλεπός, -ή, -όν *difficult, hard*
χάρις, -ιτος (acc. χάριν), ἡ *favour*
χολή, -ῆς, ἡ *bile; anger*
χρείᾱ, -ᾱς, ἡ *use, serviceability*
χρῆμα, -ατος, τό *thing;* (pl.) *money*
χρόνος, -ου, ὁ *time*
χυτός, -ή, όν *melted* (with λίθινος, *made of glass*)
χύτρᾱ, -ᾱς, ἡ *pot*
ᾠόν, -οῦ, τό *egg*

Main points

- The third declension contains masculine, feminine and neuter nouns; in most subgroups the genitive singular must be learnt to discover a noun's stem

- The third declension has consonant stems in palatals, labials and dentals (including -ντ)

- Contracted verbs end in -άω, -έω, -όω

- The definite article is used to turn an adjective, infinitive or phrase into a noun-equivalent

- ὁ μὲν ... ὁ δέ means *the one ... the other*

Unit 6

6.1 Grammar

6.1/1 Third declension – consonant stem nouns (2)

(a) *Stems in ν (masculine and, rarely, feminine)*
These stems nearly all have a nominative singular in -ην or -ων with
a genitive -ενος/-ηνος or -ονος/-ωνος. There is no rule to determine
whether a particular word has a long or short vowel in its stem.
Those with a short vowel do not lengthen it in the dative plural
because here we have ν + σ > σ, not ντ + σ > σ (cf. 5.1/1*b*).

	λιμήν (m) *harbour*	μήν (m) *month*	δαίμων (m or f) *divine being*	ἀγών (m) *contest*
stem	λιμεν-	μην-	δαιμον-	ἀγων-
SINGULAR				
Nom.	λιμήν	μήν	δαίμων	ἀγών
Voc.	λιμήν	μήν	δαῖμον	ἀγών
Acc.	λιμέν-α	μῆν-α	δαίμον-α	ἀγῶν-α
Gen.	λιμέν-ος	μην-ός	δαίμον-ος	ἀγῶν-ος
Dat.	λιμέν-ι	μην-ί	δαίμον-ι	ἀγῶν-ι
PLURAL				
N.V.	λιμέν-ες	μῆν-ες	δαίμον-ες	ἀγῶν-ες
Acc.	λιμέν-ας	μῆν-ας	δαίμον-ας	ἀγῶν-ας
Gen.	λιμέν-ων	μην-ῶν	δαιμόν-ων	ἀγών-ων
Dat.	λιμέ-σι(ν)	μη-σί(ν)	δαίμο-σι(ν)	ἀγῶ-σι(ν)

Notes

1 There are a few such nouns in -ῑς, -ῑνος, e.g. ῥίς, ῥῑνός (f) *nose*;
δελφίς, -ῖνος (m) *dolphin*.

2 The vocative singular of ν-stems is the same as the nominative when
the nominative is accented on the final syllable (so λιμήν, but δαῖμον).

3 κύων, κυνός (m or f) *dog* has an irregular stem κυν-.

(b) Stems in ρ (*mainly masculine*)

The majority have a nom. s. -ηρ, gen. -ηρος or nom. s. -ωρ, gen. -ορος. Four nouns with a nom. s. in -ηρ form a special sub-group and are declined alike: πατήρ *father*, μήτηρ *mother*, θυγάτηρ *daughter*, γαστήρ (f) *stomach*. Also given below is the slightly irregular ἀνήρ *man, male*. Of these nouns only those in -ηρ, -ηρος do not have a distinct vocative singular (σῶτερ from σωτήρ, -ῆρος (m) *saviour* is an exception).

	θήρ (m) *wild beast*	ῥήτωρ (m) *speaker*	πατήρ (m) *father*	ἀνήρ (m) *man*
stem	θηρ-	ῥητορ-	πατ(ε)ρ-	ἀνδρ-
SINGULAR				
Nom.	θήρ	ῥήτωρ	πατήρ	ἀνήρ
Voc.	θήρ	ῥῆτορ	πάτερ	ἄνερ
Acc.	θήρ-α	ῥήτορ-α	πατέρ-α	ἄνδρ-α
Gen.	θηρ-ός	ῥήτορ-ος	πατρ-ός	ἀνδρ-ός
Dat.	θηρ-ί	ῥήτορ-ι	πατρ-ί	ἀνδρ-ί
PLURAL				
N.V.	θῆρες	ῥήτορ-ες	πατέρ-ες	ἄνδρ-ες
Acc.	θῆρ-ας	ῥήτορ-ας	πατέρ-ας	ἄνδρ-ας
Gen.	θηρ-ῶν	ῥητόρ-ων	πατέρ-ων	ἀνδρ-ῶν
Dat.	θηρ-σί(ν)	ῥήτορ-σι(ν)	πατρά-σι(ν)	ἀνδράσι(ν)

A few nouns with stems in ρ do not have a nom. sing. in -ηρ/-ωρ. Of these, χείρ, χειρός (f) *hand* (stem χειρ-) can also have a stem χερ- , which is the more usual in the dat. pl., viz χερσί(ν); ἔαρ (n) (the season of) *spring* has gen. ἦρος, dat. ἦρι; πῦρ (n) *fire* has gen. πυρός, dat. πυρί (see also 13.1/1c).

(c) Stems in εϛ (*neuters in -οϛ, masculine proper names in -ηϛ*)

Neuters in -οϛ, as γένος, γένους *race, clan* (stem γενεϛ-), form a large class. They appear to be irregular because they were affected by a sound change at an earlier stage of Greek whereby intervocalic sigma was lost and in Attic the two previously separated vowels were contracted (in Homeric Greek and other dialects the uncontracted forms survived).

	SINGULAR		PLURAL	
N.V.	γένος		γένη	(<γένε(σ)-α)
Acc.	γένος		γένη	
Gen.	γένους	(<γένε(σ)-ος)	γενῶν	(<γενέ(σ)-ων)
Dat.	γένει	(<γένε(σ)-ι)	γένεσι (ν)	(<γένε(σ)-σι)

Many masculine proper names are compounds with a stem in ες because their second element is a neuter noun of this type, e.g. Διογένης (γένος), Σωκράτης (κράτος), Ἀριστοτέλης (τέλος). These must be distinguished from first declension masculine proper names in -ης (see 3.1/2 notes 3 and 4). A complication arises with proper names containing the neuter κλέος *fame* as their second element (e.g. Περικλῆς, Ἡρακλῆς, Θεμιστοκλῆς) since a further contraction is made in the nom. voc. and dat. with the additional ε in the stem (κλεεσ-). Compare the declensions of Σωκράτης and Περικλῆς:

Nom.	Σωκράτης		Περικλῆς	(<κλέης)
Voc.	Σώκρατες		Περίκλεις	(<κλεες)
Acc.	Σωκράτη	(<-ε(σ)α)	Περικλέᾱ	(<κλέε(σ)α)
Gen.	Σωκράτους	(<-ε(σ)ος)	Περικλέους	(<-κλέε(σ)ος)
Dat.	Σωκράτει	(<-ε(σ)ι)	Περικλεῖ	(<-κλέε(σ)ι)

The acc. Περικλέᾱ has a final ᾱ (not η as in γένη) because of the preceding ε (cf. ἀργυρᾶ < -εᾱ, 6.1/2). One noun in -ης which belongs here but is not a masculine proper noun is τριήρης (f) *trireme* (singular as for Σωκράτης, plural n.v.a. τριήρεις, gen. τριήρων, dat. τριήρεσι(ν)).

6.1/2 Second declension contracted nouns and first and second declension contracted adjectives

The few second declension masculine nouns in -οος and neuters in -εον are contracted in Attic according to the rules given for contracted verbs (5.1/2; on ε + α, which does not occur in verbs, see below). The uncontracted forms, which are regular, occur in other dialects. Examples are:

| | νόος *mind* | | ὀστέον *bone* | |
	Contracted (Attic)	Uncontracted (non-Attic)	Contracted (Attic)	Uncontracted (non-Attic)
SINGULAR				
Nom.	νοῦς	νό-ος	ὀστοῦν	ὀστέ-ον
Voc.	νοῦ	νό-ε	ὀστοῦν	ὀστέ-ον
Acc.	νοῦν	νό-ον	ὀστοῦν	ὀστέ-ον
Gen.	νοῦ	νό-ου	ὀστοῦ	ὀστέ-ου
Dat.	νῷ	νό-ῳ	ὀστῷ	ὀστέ-ῳ
PLURAL				
Nom.	νοῖ	νό-οι	ὀστᾶ	ὀστέ-α
Voc.	νοῖ	νό-οι	ὀστᾶ	ὀστέ-α
Acc.	νοῦς	νό-ους	ὀστᾶ	ὀστέ-α
Gen.	νῶν	νό-ων	ὀστῶν	ὀστέ-ων
Dat.	νοῖς	νό-οις	ὀστοῖς	ὀστέ-οις

In the nom. voc. acc. pl. of neuters ε + ᾰ produces ᾱ on the analogy of the α-ending of normal second declension neuters (cf. χρῡσᾶ below).

Like νοῦς are declined ῥοῦς *stream*, πλοῦς *voyage*, and compounds of the latter such as περίπλους *circumnavigation*.

Most first and second declension contracted adjectives are formed with -εος, -εα, -εον, e.g. χρῡσοῦς (< χρύσεος) *golden*, which is declined:

SINGULAR	**M.**		**F.**		**N.**	
N.V.	χρῡσοῦς	(-εος)	χρῡσῆ	(-έᾱ)	χρῡσοῦν	(-εον)
Acc.	χρῡσοῦν	(-εον)	χρῡσῆν	(-έᾱν)	χρῡσοῦν	(-εον)
Gen.	χρῡσοῦ	(-έου)	χρῡσῆς	(-έᾱς)	χρῡσοῦ	(-έου)
Dat.	χρῡσῷ	(-έῳ)	χρῡσῇ	(-έᾳ)	χρῡσῷ	(-έῳ)

PLURAL						
N.V.	χρῡσοῖ	(-εοι)	χρῡσαῖ	(-εαι)	χρῡσᾶ	(-εα)
Acc.	χρῡσοῦς	(-έους)	χρῡσᾶς	(-έᾱς)	χρῡσᾶ	(-εα)
Gen.	χρῡσῶν	(-έων)	χρῡσῶν	(-έων)	χρῡσῶν	(-έων)
Dat.	χρῡσοῖς	(-έοις)	χρῡσαῖς	(-έαις)	χρῡσοῖς	(-έοις)

In the feminine singular ε + ᾱ > η, except where ε is preceded by ε, ι, or ρ, e.g. ἀργυροῦς (-εος), -ᾶ (-έᾱ), -οῦν, (-εον) *[made of] silver*, whose feminine singular is: nom. ἀργυρᾶ, acc. ἀργυρᾶν, gen. ἀργυρᾶς, dat. ἀργυρᾷ (here ε + ᾱ > ᾱ).

ἁπλοῦς, -ῆ, -οῦν *simple* is contracted from ἁπλόος but follows χρῦσοῦς completely, even in the feminine.

6.1/3 Compound verbs formed with prepositional prefixes

Many verbs form compounds by prefixing one, or sometimes more than one, preposition (e.g. ἐπιβαίνω, 3.2.12(*v*)). When certain sounds are brought together a change is necessary:

(*a*) With the exception of περί and πρό, prepositions ending in a vowel drop this vowel (by elision) when compounded with a verb which begins with a vowel or diphthong: ἀπάγω (ἀπό+ἄγω) *lead away*, παρέχω (παρά+ἔχω) *provide*, but προάγω *lead forward*, περιάγω *lead round*.

(*b*) When, owing to the elision of the final vowel of the preposition, π, τ, or κ are brought into contact with an initial aspirated vowel or diphthong, these consonants must themselves adopt their aspirated forms, φ, θ and χ: ἀφαιρέω (ἀπό+αἱρέω) *take away*; καθαιρέω (κατά+αἱρέω) *destroy*.

(*c*) When compounded with a verb beginning with a vowel or diphthong, ἐκ becomes ἐξ: ἐξάγω (ἐκ+ἄγω) *lead out*; ἐξαιρέω (ἐκ+αἱρέω) *take out*.

(*d*) When compounded with a verb beginning with a consonant, the ν of ἐν and σύν is assimilated as follows:

> ν before π, β, φ, ψ and μ becomes μ: συμβουλεύω (συν+βουλεύω) *advise*
> ν before γ, κ, χ, and ξ becomes nasal γ: ἐγγράφω (ἐν+γράφω) *write in/on*
> ν before λ becomes λ: συλλαμβάνω (συν+λαμβάνω) *gather together*
> ν of σύν is dropped before σ: συστρατεύω (συν+στρατεύω) *join in an expedition*.

(e) When a verb compounded with a preposition is used in a tense which requires the augment, the augment comes between the preposition and the verb, **not** in front of the preposition: προσ-έ-βαλλον (<προσβάλλω) *I was attacking*. If the insertion of the augment results in the clash of two vowels, e.g. κατα + έ-γίγνωσκον the same process as in (a) above will apply: so κατεγίγνωσκον (<καταγιγνώσκω) *I was condemning*. In these circumstances πρό normally contracts with the augment προὔβαλλον[1] (<προβάλλω; the expected form would be προέβαλλον as πρό is not elided (see (a) above)) *I was putting forward*; προὔπεμπον (<προπέμπω) *I was escorting* (the contracted diphthong is generally indicated by a sign identical with a smooth breathing (11.1/5b)).

(f) The assimilation of ἐν and σύν described in (d) is blocked by the syllabic augment in the augmented tenses; thus συμβουλεύω but συνεβούλευον.

Notes

1 The meaning of a compound verb is not always predictable from its constituent parts (cf. παρέχω [above (a)]). Prepositions may retain their normal meanings (as ἀπάγω, ἐγγράφω) but some have acquired a special sense, e.g. μεταγιγνώσκω *change one's mind* (from γιγνώσκω *know*) where μετα- conveys the idea of change.

2 In the augmented tenses of compound verbs the accent never goes further back than the augment, even when the last syllable is short: παρεῖχον *they were providing*; παρῆσαν *they were present*; cf. **Appendix 8** b(vi).

3 Greek has a few compound verbs which contain no prepositional element: οἰκοδομέω *build a house* (οἶκος *house*); ναυμαχέω *fight with ships* (ναῦς *ship*). These compounds are augmented at the beginning, **not** between the two elements (ᾠκοδόμησα, ἐναυμάχησα).

---

[1] On this type of contraction, which is called crasis, see 11.1/5.

6.1/4 -ω verbs with stems in palatals, labials, dentals

The sound changes shown by nouns with these stems (5.1/l) also occur in the corresponding verbs when σ is added to form the future or weak aorist. Some resemble λύω in having a simple present stem to which this σ can be attached. Others, far more numerous, have a suffix in their present stem which is not kept elsewhere.

(*a*) *Verbs with no suffix in the present stem*

πλέκω	plait	fut.	πλέξω	aor.	ἔπλεξα
πέμπω	send	fut.	πέμψω	aor.	ἔπεμψα
πείθω	persuade	fut.	πείσω	aor.	ἔπεισα

(*b*) *Verbs with a suffix in the present stem*

At a very early stage in its development Greek possessed a consonant which was pronounced as the *y* in the English *yes*. This sound no longer existed in the form Greek had taken by the time of the introduction of the alphabet. It had occurred in words inherited from Indo-European (1.3) and had also served as a suffix to form the present stem of many -ω verbs whose primitive or original stem ended in a consonant. In this function it combined with the preceding consonant. The combinations which concern us here are κ/γ/χ + *y* > ττ; π/β/φ +*y* > πτ; τ/δ/θ + *y* > ζ. As this suffix (and others – see below) was only used to form the present stem, the future and weak aorist are formed by applying σ to the original stem. Examples are (the original stem is given in brackets):

PALATALS

| φυλάττω | guard | (φυλακ-) | fut. | φυλάξω | aor. | ἐφύλαξα |
| ἀλλάττω | change | (ἀλλαγ-) | fut. | ἀλλάξω | aor. | ἤλλαξα |

LABIALS

κόπτω	cut	(κοπ-)	fut.	κόψω	aor.	ἔκοψα
βλάπτω	harm	(βλαβ-)	fut.	βλάψω	aor.	ἔβλαψα
κρύπτω	hide	(κρυφ-)	fut.	κρύψω	aor.	ἔκρυψα

DENTALS

| φράζω | tell | (φραδ-) | fut. | φράσω | aor. | ἔφρασα |

The original stem can be seen in cognate words (e.g. φυλακή *act of guarding*, βλάβη *damage*). It need not be memorised as these verbs follow the above patterns. An exception is a few verbs in -ζω which are palatals, not dentals, as e.g. σφάζω *slaughter* (σφαγ-) fut. σφάξω, aor. ἔσφαξα (cf. σφαγή *[act of] slaughtering*).

All dental-stem verbs in -ίζω of more than two syllables have a future in -ιέω (originally -ιέσω; cf. 5.1/2 note 3), which always contracts to -ιῶ: νομίζω *think*, fut. νομιῶ, νομιεῖς, νομιεῖ, etc., but κτίζω *found, build*, fut. κτίσω. A few verbs in -ίζω are palatals: μαστίζω *whip* (stem μαστιγ-), fut. μαστίξω, aor. ἐμάστιξα.

Of the other present stem suffixes belonging here we may mention σκ (as in διδάσκω (<διδαχ + σκ-ω) *teach*, fut. διδάξω, etc.) and αν. The latter is often accompanied by a nasal infix (i.e. a nasal inserted before the final consonant of the root); neither αν nor the infix occur outside the present stem, e.g. λαμβάνω *take*, aor. stem λαβ- (in λα-μ-β-άν-ω the nasal infix takes the form of the labial nasal μ before the following labial; cf. μα-ν-θ-άν-ω *learn*, aor. stem μαθ-; λα-γ-χ-άν-ω *obtain*, aor. stem λαχ-; see 7.1/1).

Insight

The chief Greek gods lived on Mt Olympus in northern Greece. Zeus (Ζεύς), the divine ruler (see Insight, Unit 5), had a wife, Hera (Ἥρα), with whom he lived in a state of constant tension because of his affairs with mortal women. They had two sons, Hephaestus (Ἥφαιστος), the divine blacksmith, and Ares (Ἄρης), the god of war. Zeus' brother Poseidon (Ποσειδῶν) ruled over the seas. His other brother, Hades (Ἅιδης), was absent from Mt Olympus because his duties as king of the dead required his permanent residence in the Underworld. Zeus had other children but not by Hera: Athena (Ἀθηνᾶ), goddess of warfare and of crafts; Apollo (Ἀπόλλων), patron of music and poetry; Dionysus (Διόνῡσος), god of wine; Hermes (Ἑρμῆς), the divine messenger; Artemis (Ἄρτεμις), goddess of nature. More distant relatives were Aphrodite (Ἀφροδίτη), goddess of love and procreation, and Demeter (Δημήτηρ), goddess of agriculture.

6.2 Greek reading

1 *As well as translating the following give the 1st s. present indicative of each verb:*
(*i*) οἱ φύλακες τοὺς Πέρσας ἐφύλαξαν. (*ii*) ἆρα ἔκρυψας τὸν χρυσοῦν ἵππον; (*iii*) οἱ Ἀθηναῖοι καὶ οἱ Λακεδαιμόνιοι συνεστράτευσαν. (*iv*) πολλὰ ἐν τῇ πέτρᾳ ἐνέγραψεν. (*v*) οἱ δαίμονες πολλὰ καὶ μεγάλα πράξουσιν. (*vi*) ὁ Σωκράτης ἡμᾶς ἐδίδαξεν. (*vii*) τὴν οἰκίαν τοῦ Περικλέους ἔβλαψαν. (*viii*) ἐν τῷ λιμένι ἐναυμαχήσαμεν.

2# κάτοπτρον εἴδους χαλκός ἐστ᾽, οἶνος δὲ νοῦ.

3# χεὶρ χεῖρα νίπτει, δάκτυλοι δὲ δακτύλους.

4 ἡ μὲν φωνή ἐστιν ἀργυρᾶ, ἡ δὲ σιγὴ χρυσῆ.

5# ὦ δαῖμον, ὡς οὐκ ἔστ᾽ ἀποστροφὴ βροτοῖς
τῶν ἐμφύτων τε καὶ θεηλάτων κακῶν.

6 Further futility
(*i*) εἰς ὕδωρ γράφεις. (*ii*) εἰς ψάμμον οἰκοδομεῖς. (*iii*) γλαῦκ᾽ Ἀθήναζε (*sc.* φέρεις). (*iv*) κύματα μετρεῖς. (*v*) ὄρνιθος γάλα ζητεῖς. (*vi*) σίδηρον πλεῖν διδάσκεις. (*vii*) ἡλίῳ φῶς δανείζεις. (*viii*) βατράχοις οἰνοχοεῖς. (*ix*) τὸν ἀέρα τύπτεις. (*x*) ἐλέφαντα ἐκ μυίας ποιεῖ.

7 Other short proverbs and aphorisms
(*i*) ψυχῆς μέγας χαλινός ἐστιν ὁ νοῦς. (*ii*) Ἕλληνες ἀεὶ παῖδες, γέρων δὲ Ἕλλην οὐκ ἔστιν. (*iii*)# εἰσὶ μητρὶ παῖδες ἄγκυραι βίου. (*iv*) οἴκοι λέοντες, ἐν μάχῃ δ᾽ ἀλώπεκες. (*v*) νοῦς ὁρᾷ καὶ νοῦς ἀκούει. (*vi*) μακραὶ τυράννων χεῖρες. (*vii*) ψεύδεσιν Ἄρης φίλος. (*viii*) Ἑλλὰς Ἑλλάδος αἱ Ἀθῆναι. (*ix*) τέττιγι μέλιτταν συγκρίνεις. (*x*) χαλεπὸν θυγάτηρ κτῆμα.

8 τὸ μὲν πῦρ ὁ ἄνεμος, τὸν δὲ ἔρωτα ἡ συνήθεια ἐκκαίει.

9 κατὰ τὸν Σωκράτη οὐδεὶς ἑκουσίως ἁμαρτάνει.

10 οὐ μετανοεῖν ἀλλὰ προνοεῖν χρὴ τὸν ἄνδρα τὸν σοφόν.

11 The siege of Melos

Thucydides, the other great historian of the fifth century BC, wrote a history of the Peloponnesian war, which was fought between Athens and Sparta (the major power in the Peloponnese) from 431 BC to 404 BC, when Athens fell. Melos was an island in the southern Aegean whose desire to stay neutral was brutally suppressed by the Athenians.

καὶ οἱ μὲν Ἀθηναίων πρέσβεις (*ambassadors*) ἀνεχώρησαν εἰς
τὸ στράτευμα, οἱ δὲ στρατηγοὶ περιετείχισαν τοὺς Μηλίους.
καὶ ὕστερον φυλακὴ μὲν ὀλίγη τῶν συμμάχων ἐκεῖ παρέμενε
καὶ ἐπολιόρκει τὸ χωρίον, οἱ δὲ ἄλλοι στρατιῶται καὶ κατὰ
γῆν καὶ κατὰ θάλατταν ἀνεχώρησαν. ἔπειτα δὲ οἱ Μήλιοι τὸ   5
περιτείχισμα ἀνέσπασαν τῶν Ἀθηναίων, ἐπειδὴ παρῆσαν
οὐ πολλοὶ τῶν φυλάκων. ἀλλὰ στρατιὰν ὕστερον ἐκ τῶν
Ἀθηνῶν ἄλλην ἐξέπεμψαν οἱ Ἀθηναῖοι, καὶ κατὰ κράτος ἤδη
ἐπολιόρκουν. προδοσία δὲ ἦν ἐν τοῖς Μηλίοις καὶ συνεχώρησαν
τοῖς Ἀθηναίοις. οἱ δὲ ἔσφαξαν Μηλίων τοὺς ἄνδρας, παῖδας δὲ   10
καὶ γυναῖκας ἠνδραπόδισαν. καὶ ὕστερον ἀποίκους πολλοὺς
ἐξέπεμψαν καὶ τὸ χωρίον ᾤκισαν.

Notes

1 (*v*) πολλὰ καὶ μεγάλα lit. *many and great [things]* but translate
many great [things]; when πολύς in the plural is combined with
another adjective καί is regularly inserted between the two.

2 Greek mirrors were made of polished bronze or silver.

5 Take ἀποστροφή with the genitives in the next line. *l*.2 Take
κακῶν as a noun and ἐμφύτων and θεηλάτων as adjectives; καί
can be translated here by *and* or *or* because the evils are not
necessarily both *innate* and *sent by the gods*.

6 (*iii*) The Acropolis at Athens was notorious as a haunt of small
brown owls, the bird which was adopted as the Athenian
emblem.

7 (*ii*) This remark of an Egyptian priest to the Athenian statesman Solon implicitly contrasts the age of Greek civilisation with that of the Egyptians. (*iv*) A phrase of abuse, not a sentence; foxes were symbolic of a low cunning devoid of courage. (*viii*) The Athenians liked to regard themselves as the quintessence of Greekness. (*x*) The patriarchal nature of most Greek societies meant that sons were more highly valued than daughters.

11 *ll*.3f. Translate the imperfects παρέμενε and ἐπολιόρκει by *stayed* and *besieged* (Greek prefers to regard both events as extending over a period of time rather than as single actions – 4.1/1). *l*.8 ἐξέπεμψαν < ἐκπέμπω (6.1/3); κατὰ κράτος lit. *in accordance with [their full] strength*, i.e. *energetically*. *ll*.10f. παῖδας καὶ γυναῖκας the regular order in Greek for *women and children*; ἠνδραπόδισαν < ἀνδραποδίζω (4.1/1 note 2(ii)).

6.2/1 Vocabulary

ἄγκῡρα, -ᾱς, ἡ *anchor*
ἀεί (adv.) *always*
ἀήρ, -έρος, ὁ *air*
Ἀθήναζε (adv.) *to Athens*
Ἀθῆναι, -ῶν, αἱ *Athens*
ἀκούω *hear*
ἀλώπηξ, -εκος, ἡ *fox*
ἁμαρτάνω *err, do wrong*
ἀνασπάω *pull down*
ἀναχωρέω *withdraw, retreat, retire*
ἀνδραποδίζω *enslave*
ἄνεμος, -ου, ὁ *wind*
ἀνήρ, ἀνδρός, ὁ *man*
ἄποικος, -ου, ὁ *settler, colonist*
ἀποστροφή, -ῆς, ἡ *turning away from, escape*
ἀργυροῦς, -ᾶ, -οῦν *made of silver, silver*
Ἄρης, -ου ὁ, *Ares* (god of war)

βλάπτω *damage*
βροτός, -οῦ, ὁ *mortal man*
γάλα, -ακτος, τό *milk*
γλαῦξ, γαυκός, ἡ *owl*
γράφω *write*
δαίμων, -ονος, ὁ *god*
δάκτυλος, -ου, ὁ *finger*
δανείζω *lend*
ἐγγράφω *write in/on, inscribe*
εἶδος, -ους, τό *appearance*
ἐκεῖ (adv.) *there*
ἐκκαίω *kindle*
ἑκουσίως (adv.) *willingly*
ἐκπέμπω *send out*
ἐλέφᾱς, -αντος, ὁ *elephant*
Ἑλλάς, -άδος, ἡ *Greece*
Ἕλλην, -ηνος, ὁ (*a*) *Greek*
ἔμφυτος, -ον *inborn, innate*
ἐπειδή (conj.) *when*

ἤδη (adv.)   now
ἥλιος, -ου, ὁ   sun
θεήλατος, -ον   sent by the gods
θυγάτηρ, -τρός, ἡ   daughter
κάτοπτρον, -ου, τό   mirror
κράτος -ους, τό   strength, power
κτῆμα, -ατος, τό   (a) possession
κῦμα, -ατος, τό   wave
Λακεδαιμόνιος, -ου, ὁ
    Lacedaemonian, Spartan
μακρός, -ά, -όν   long
μάχη, -ης, ἡ   battle, fight
μέλιττα, -ης, ἡ   bee
μετανοέω   think afterwards,
    change one's mind, repent
μετρέω   measure
Μήλιοι, -ων, οἱ   Melians
μήτηρ, -τρός, ἡ   mother
ναυμαχέω   fight a sea battle
νίπτω   wash
οἰκίζω   colonise
οἰκοδομέω   build a house
οἴκοι (adv.)   at home
οἶνος, -ου, ὁ   wine
οἰνοχοέω   pour wine
ὀλίγος, -η, -ον   small
ὁράω   see
ὄρνῑς, -ῑθος, ὁ/ἡ   bird
οὐδείς   no one (7.1/5a)
παῖς, παιδός, ὁ/ἡ   child
παραμένω   remain
πάρειμι (παρά+εἰμί)   be present
περιτειχίζω   build a wall round
περιτείχισμα, -ατος, τό
    blockading wall
πέτρᾱ, -ᾱς, ἡ   rock
πλέω   sail

πολιορκέω   besiege
προδοσίᾱ, -ᾱς, ἡ   treachery
προνοέω   think beforehand
πῦρ, πυρός, τό   fire
σίδηρος, -ου, ὁ   iron
στράτευμα, -ατος, τό   army
στρατιᾱ́, -ᾶς, ἡ   army
συγκρῑ́νω   compare (something
    with something, acc. and dat.)
συγχωρέω   yield to (+dat.)
σύμμαχος, -ου, ὁ ally
συνήθεια, -ᾱς, ἡ   acquaintance,
    intimacy
συστρατεύω   join an
    expedition, fight alongside
σφάζω   slaughter
τέττιξ, -ῑγος, ὁ   cicada,
    grasshopper
τύπτω   hit, beat
τύραννος, -ου, ὁ   absolute
    ruler; tyrant
ὕδωρ, -ατος, τό   water
φυλακή, -ῆς, ἡ guard,   garrison
φύλαξ, -ακος, ὁ   (a) guard
φυλάττω   guard
φωνή, -ῆς, ἡ   voice, speech
φῶς, φωτός, τό   light
χαλινός, -οῦ, ὁ   bit (for a
    horse's bridle)
χαλκός, -οῦ, ὁ   bronze
χείρ, χειρός, ἡ   hand
χρή   it is necessary
χωρίον, -ου, τό   place
ψάμμος, -ου, ἡ   sand
ψεῦδος, -ους, τό   falsehood, lie
ψῡχή, -ῆς, ἡ   soul
ὡς (exclamatory adv.)   how ...!

Main points

- The third declension also has consonant stems in ν, ρ and -ες

- The final two vowels of second declension nouns in -οος (m) and -εον (n) are contracted, e.g. νόος > νοῦς and ὀστέον > ὀστοῦν

- A few first and second declension adjectives also show contraction, e.g. χρύσεος > χρυσοῦς

- The final sound of a preposition used to form a compound verb is sometimes omitted or changed according to fixed rules

- Verbs with a prepositional prefix insert the augment after the preposition

- -ω verbs with a palatal, labial or dental stem sometimes have a suffix in the present tense that hides their true stem

Unit 7

··

7.1 Grammar

7.1/1 Strong aorist indicative and infinitive active of -ω verbs

We have seen at 4.1/1 that -ω verbs have either a weak or a strong aorist and that the distinction between the two is solely one of form. The indicative of the strong aorist has the same endings as the imperfect; the infinitive has the same ending as the present (as do all parts other than the indicative). As the strong aorist takes no suffix its stem must necessarily undergo some internal modification to differentiate it from that of the present. Any suffix attached to the latter is dropped (cf. 6.1/4*b*), and ει is reduced to ι, and ευ to υ. Some strong aorist stems are simply irregular and must be learnt.

The following list of the most common verbs with a strong aorist shows examples of each type. The present infinitive and the imperfect indicative are included for comparison.

PRESENT INDICATIVE	IMPERFECT INDICATIVE	AORIST INDICATIVE	PRESENT INFINITIVE	AORIST INFINITIVE
ἄγω *lead, bring*	ἦγον	ἤγαγον	ἄγειν	ἀγαγεῖν
αἱρέω *take, capture*	ᾕρουν	εἷλον (stem ἑλ-)	αἱρεῖν	ἑλεῖν
βάλλω *throw*	ἔβαλλον	ἔβαλον	βάλλειν	βαλεῖν
εὑρίσκω *find*	εὕρισκον (or ηὕ-)	εὗρον (or ηὗ-)	εὑρίσκειν	εὑρεῖν
ἔχω *have*	εἶχον	ἔσχον	ἔχειν	σχεῖν
λαγχάνω *obtain*	ἐλάγχανον	ἔλαχον	λαγχάνειν	λαχεῖν
λαμβάνω *take*	ἐλάμβανον	ἔλαβον	λαμβάνειν	λαβεῖν
λέγω *say*	ἔλεγον	εἶπον (stem εἰπ-)	λέγειν	εἰπεῖν
λείπω *leave*	ἔλειπον	ἔλιπον	λείπειν	λιπεῖν
μανθάνω *learn*	ἐμάνθανον	ἔμαθον	μανθάνειν	μαθεῖν

PRESENT INDICATIVE	IMPERFECT INDICATIVE	AORIST INDICATIVE	PRESENT INFINITIVE	AORIST INFINITIVE
ὁράω *see*	ἑώρων	εἶδον (stem ἰδ-)	ὁρᾶν	ἰδεῖν
πάσχω *suffer*	ἔπασχον	ἔπαθον	πάσχειν	παθεῖν
πίπτω *fall*	ἔπῑπτον	ἔπεσον	πίπτειν	πεσεῖν
τυγχάνω *happen*	ἐτύγχανον	ἔτυχον	τυγχάνειν	τυχεῖν
φέρω *carry*	ἔφερον	ἤνεγκον	φέρειν	ἐνεγκεῖν
φεύγω *flee*	ἔφευγον	ἔφυγον	φεύγειν	φυγεῖν

Notes

1 The ending of the strong aorist infinitive active always has a circumflex accent.

2 The aorists of αἱρέω, λέγω, ὁράω, φέρω come from roots entirely different from their presents (cf. English *go/went*). The unaugmented aorist stems of the first three (ἑλ-, εἰπ-, ἰδ-) require particular attention. εἶπον and ἤνεγκον quite irregularly take the **weak** aorist endings in the 2nd. s. and pl.: εἶπας, εἴπατε; ἤνεγκας, ἠνέγκατε. We may sympathize with the Greeks who found εἶπον too complicated and gave λέγω a regular weak aorist ἔλεξα (good Attic but not as common). The strong aorist ἦλθον *I came/went* likewise has a present tense from another root. This verb is peculiar in having an active aorist but a deponent present (ἔρχομαι 8.1/2).

3 By this stage you should be confident enough to consult the table of **Principal parts of verbs**, which sets out the principal parts of important verbs that have some irregularity. A normal transitive verb in Greek has six principal parts and from these all possible forms can be deduced (see next note for the only exceptions). These parts are:
  (i) lst s. present indicative active (λύω; 2.1/5)
  (ii) lst s. future indicative active (λύσω; 2.1/5)
  (iii) lst s. aorist indicative active (ἔλῡσα; 4.1/1; for strong aorist see above)
  (iv) lst s. perfect indicative active (λέλυκα; 15.1/1)
  (v) lst s. perfect indicative middle and passive (λέλυμαι; 16.1/3)
  (vi) lst s. aorist indicative passive (ἐλύθην; 11.1/1).

This list is not as formidable as it might seem at first sight as some verbs do not exist in every possible part, while many (such as λύω) are completely regular and all their principal parts can be deduced from their present stem. Do not, at this stage, try to digest the **Principal parts of verbs** (in any case, we have not yet dealt with principal parts (iv) – (vi)), but familiarize yourself with its arrangement and get into the habit of using it. When individual principal parts are wildly irregular (e.g. εἶπον), they are given separate entries in the **Vocabulary**.

4 A few verbs have an imperfect which cannot be predicted from their present stem. Thus ὁράω > ἑώρων, with both syllabic and temporal augment; ἔχω > εἶχον (the original form of ἔχω was σέχω with an imperfect ἔσεχον, which lost its intervocalic sigma (6.1/1c) and then contracted ε+ε to ει (5.1/2b)).

7.1/2 φημί *say* (see also **Appendix 3**)

This irregular -μι verb (2.1/4) is inflected as follows in the present and imperfect:

		PRESENT	IMPERFECT
SINGULAR	1	φημί	ἔφην
	2	φῄς	ἔφησθα or ἔφης
	3	φησί (ν)	ἔφη
PLURAL	1	φαμέν	ἔφαμεν
	2	φατέ	ἔφατε
	3	φασί (ν)	ἔφασαν
INFINITIVE		φάναι	

Notes

1 All the forms of the present indicative are enclitic (**Appendix 8d**) except the second person singular (cf. εἰμί, 3.1/6).

2 The imperfect regularly has an aorist meaning, *I said*.

3 φημί, not λέγω, is commonly used in the direct quotation of conversations (i.e. **direct speech** – see next subsection). When so used, φημί does not appear until after the beginning of the quotation: δοκεῖς, ἔφη, ὦ Σώκρατες, εὖ λέγειν *'You seem'*, *he said*, *'to be speaking well, Socrates.'*

4 The φη/φα alternation in the forms of this verb is explained at 19.1/1.

7.1/3 Indirect speech

When we wish to report what someone has said (or thought, etc.) we may do this in one of two ways. We may either give his exact words (cf. 7.1/2 note 3): *"Justice is the advantage of the stronger," said Thrasymachus*; or we may grammatically subordinate the speaker's words to a verb of saying (or thinking, etc.): *Thrasymachus said that justice was the advantage of the stronger.* The first form is called **direct speech**, the second **indirect** (or **reported**) **speech**.

Since speech may be conveniently divided into statement, question and command, we therefore have three corresponding forms of indirect speech:

(a) Indirect statement: *He said that he was happy.* (Direct *I am happy.*)

(b) Indirect question: *We asked if he was happy.* (Direct *Are you happy?*)

(c) Indirect command: *I ordered him to cheer up.* (Direct *Cheer up!*)

These examples show the adjustments in pronouns that are nearly always necessary in English. Greek does the same but does not, as we shall see, make the **tense** adjustments required by English in (*a*) and (*b*).

7.1/4 Indirect command

For this construction Greek, like English, uses an infinitive after a verb of ordering: ἐκέλευσε τὸν παῖδα τὰ γράμματα μαθεῖν *he ordered the boy to learn [his] letters.* If the infinitive is negated, the negative μή, not οὐ, is used: ὁ νόμος ἡμᾶς κελεύει μὴ ἀδικεῖν *the law orders us not to do wrong.*

The two adverbs of negation, μή and οὐ, are always to be translated by *no/not* but have quite distinct uses (see 7.1/6). The rule here is that μή is always used to negate an infinitive except in indirect statement (8.1/3).

The tense of the infinitive is a matter of aspect (4.1/1). In the above examples μαθεῖν simply conveys that the learning is to be done, whereas ἀδικεῖν indicates that we are not to do wrong on any occasion.

7.1/5 Numerals (see also Appendix 7)

There are three types of numeral:

(a) **Cardinals** (in English *one, two, three, four*, etc.)
In Greek, as in English, these function as adjectives. The numbers *one* to *four* are declined as follows:

	εἷς *one*			δύο *two*
	M.	F.	N.	M.F.N.
Nom.	εἷς	μία	ἕν	δύο
Acc.	ἕνα	μίαν	ἕν	δύο
Gen.	ἑνός	μιᾶς	ἑνός	δυοῖν
Dat.	ἑνί	μιᾷ	ἑνί	δυοῖν

	τρεῖς *three*		τέτταρες *four*	
	M. & F.	N.	M. & F.	N.
Nom.	τρεῖς	τρία	τέτταρες	τέτταρα
Acc.	τρεῖς	τρία	τέτταρας	τέτταρα
Gen.	τριῶν	τριῶν	τεττάρων	τεττάρων
Dat.	τρισί(ν)	τρισί(ν)	τέτταρσι(ν)	τέτταρσι(ν)

So, e.g. ἐκ μιᾶς νήσου *out of one island*, εἰς τέτταρας οἰκίας *into four houses*.

The numbers *five* to *one hundred* are indeclinable (i.e. have no variable inflections), except when they contain any of the numbers *one* to *four* (e.g. εἴκοσι τέτταρες *twenty-four*, where τέτταρες would alter its ending as required: εἴκοσι τέτταρα ἔργα *twenty-four tasks*). The words for *two hundred*, *three hundred*, etc. follow the plural of καλός (3.1/3): so διᾱκόσιοι, -αι, -α, *two hundred*; τρισχίλιοι, -αι, -α *three thousand*.

(*b*) **Ordinals** (in English, *first, second, third,* etc.)
These also are first and second declension adjectives (3.1/3), e.g. ἡ πρώτη γυνή *the first woman.*

(*c*) **Numeral adverbs** (in English, *once, twice, three times,* etc.)
All except ἅπαξ *once,* δίς *twice,* τρίς *three times,* end in -άκις (cf. πολλάκις *often,* lit. *many times*).

Notes

1 Like εἷς is declined the pronoun οὐδείς (< οὐδέ + εἷς *not even one*), οὐδεμία, οὐδέν, gen. οὐδενός, οὐδεμιᾶς, οὐδενός *no-one, nobody, none.* The neuter οὐδέν means *nothing,* but is often used adverbially in the sense *in no respect, not at all* (20.1/5). οὐδείς can also be used as an adjective meaning *no,* e.g. οὐδεμία γυνή *no woman.*

2 Compound numbers over twenty are expressed by putting the smaller number first with καί (δύο καὶ εἴκοσι *two and twenty*), or the larger number first without καί (εἴκοσι δύο *twenty-two*).

7.1/6 Negatives

Unlike English, Greek has two negatives οὐ (οὐκ, οὐχ, 2.1/6*a*(i)) and μή, and although we translate both by *not* their uses are quite distinct. These involve many constructions not yet described (for a summary see 24.1/2). We may, however, note:

(*a*) οὐ is used to negate statements and so is the negative used with a verb in the indicative in main clauses (examples at 3.2.1, 3.2.4 etc.)

(*b*) μή is the negative used with infinitives except in indirect statement (see above 7.1/4 and 8.1/3*a*).

(*c*) For every compound of οὐ (e.g. οὐδέ, οὐδείς) there is a corresponding compound of μή (e.g. μηδέ, μηδείς). The latter are used, where appropriate, in constructions otherwise requiring μή.

We have already seen at 3.2.12(*vi*) (see note) that the compound negative οὐδείς reinforces a simple preceding negative (οὐ λέγει οὐδέν *he says nothing*). However, when the order is reversed and a compound negative precedes a simple negative the two cancel each other to give a strong affirmative: οὐδεὶς οὐκ ἔπαθεν *no-one did not suffer*, i.e. *everyone suffered*.

7.1/7 Phrases expressing time and space

Many temporal phrases in English contain a preposition, e.g. *on Wednesday, for six days* (but cf. *I will see you next week*). In three types of temporal phrase of this sort Greek simply uses a particular case, provided that the noun involved signifies some period, point, or division of time (*dawn, day, winter, year*, etc.):

(*a*) **Time how long** is expressed by the **accusative:**

ἐννέα ἔτη οἱ Ἀχαιοὶ πρὸ τῆς Τροίας ἐστρατοπέδευον. *For nine years the Achaeans were encamped before Troy.*

(*b*) **Time when** is expressed by the **dative:**

δεκάτῳ ἔτει ἱερὸν Ἴλιον ἐπόρθησαν. *In the tenth year they sacked holy Ilium* (the definite article is generally omitted before ordinal numerals in this construction).

(*c*) **Time within which** is expressed by the **genitive:**

τριῶν ἡμερῶν ἔπλευσε Μενέλαος εἰς τὴν Ἑλλάδα. *Within three days Menelaus sailed to Greece.*
εἴκοσι ἐτῶν Ὀδυσσεὺς τὴν Ἰθάκην οὐκ εἶδεν. *For (i.e. within the space of) twenty years Odysseus did not see Ithaca.*
τέλος εἰς τὴν πατρίδα νυκτὸς ἐνόστησεν. *Finally he returned to [his] native land by night.*

With nouns which do not indicate a period, point, or division of time (e.g. *war* as in *during the war*) a preposition is generally used (e.g. διά + gen.).

(*d*) **Spatial extent** is expressed by the **accusative** (this use is similar to (*a*) above):

> ἀπέχει τῆς Τροίας ἡ Ἰθάκη πολλοὺς σταδίους. *Ithaca is many stades distant from Troy.*
> οἱ στρατιῶται διὰ τοῦ πεδίου ἐβάδισαν σταθμοὺς τέτταρας. *The soldiers walked four stages through the plain.*

Insight

The normal terms for a divine being were θεός *god* and θεά *goddess*, which were applied to important figures of Greek religion such as Zeus, Hera, Athena, etc. Another word, δαίμων, was used of supernatural powers or spirits who were conceived as influencing the lives of individuals but who could not be more closely identified. Δαίμονες (6.1/2) were powers for good or bad; a person could be εὐδαίμων *having a good daimon* and so be *happy, fortunate* or κακόδαιμων *having a bad daimon* and so be *unfortunate, unlucky*. Whether a person's δαίμων was good or bad, or indulged in both tendencies, was a matter of chance. When with the advent of Christianity the Devil became the ultimate source of all misfortune it was natural that the δαίμονες of the old religion were reviled and rejected, and as **demons** they became the Devil's instruments.

The use of the adverb εὖ as a prefix we have already met (Insight, Unit 4); its opposite is κακο-, the stem of the adjective κακός *bad*. Greek has many pairs of compounds similar to the above, e.g. εὐμενής *well-disposed*, δυσμενής *hostile*. On the declension of these adjectives see 10.1/4.

7.2 Greek reading

1 ἡ παροιμία ἡμᾶς κελεύει μὴ κινεῖν ἀκίνητα.

2# εὑρεῖν τὸ δίκαιον πανταχῶς οὐ ῥᾴδιον.

3 ὁ δὲ Ἰσχόμαχος εἶπεν, ὦ Σώκρατες, χειμῶνος μὲν τὴν οἰκίαν δεῖ εὐήλιον εἶναι, τοῦ δὲ θέρους εὔσκιον.

4 οὐκ ἔχομεν οὔτε ὅπλα οὔτε ἵππους.

5# οὐδὲν ἕρπει ψεῦδος εἰς μῆκος χρόνου.

6 μίαν μὲν οὖν ἡμέραν οἱ Ἀθηναῖοι αὐτοῦ ἐστρατοπέδευσαν· τῇ δὲ ὑστεραίᾳ Ἀλκιβιάδης ἐκκλησίαν ἐποίησε καὶ ἐκέλευσεν αὐτοὺς καὶ ναυμαχεῖν καὶ πεζομαχεῖν καὶ τειχομαχεῖν. οὐ γὰρ ἔστιν, ἔφη, χρήματα ἡμῖν, τοῖς δὲ πολεμίοις ἄφθονα.

7 οὐδεὶς ἀνθρώπων οὐκ ἀποθνῄσκει.

8 Proverbs
(*i*) μία χελιδὼν ἔαρ οὐ ποιεῖ. (*ii*) δὶς παῖδες οἱ γέροντες. (*iii*) ἐν δυοῖν τρία βλέπεις. (*iv*) εἷς ἀνὴρ οὐδεὶς ἀνήρ. (*v*) μία ἡμέρα σοφὸν οὐ ποιεῖ. (*vi*) ἡ γλῶττα πολλοὺς εἰς ὄλεθρον ἤγαγεν. (*vii*) ἐν πολέμῳ οὐκ ἔνεστι δὶς ἁμαρτεῖν. (*viii*) ἐξ ὀνύχων τὸν λέοντα ἔνεστι μαθεῖν.

9 ὁ Κῦρος ἦλθε διὰ τῆς Λυδίας σταθμοὺς τρεῖς παρασάγγας δύο καὶ εἴκοσι ἐπὶ τὸν Μαίανδρον ποταμόν. τὸ δὲ εὖρος αὐτοῦ ἦν δύο πλέθρα.

10 ὁ κόσμος σκηνή, ὁ βίος πάροδος· ἦλθες, εἶδες, ἀπῆλθες.

11 εἶπέ τις (*someone*) τῷ Σωκράτει, κακῶς ὁ Μεγακλῆς σε λέγει· ὁ δὲ, καλῶς γάρ, ἔφη, λέγειν οὐκ ἔμαθεν.

12 A Sea Battle
Thucydides did not finish his history of the Peloponnesian war but his account was taken up and completed by Xenophon, a versatile writer whose life straddled the fifth and fourth centuries BC. The battle described by him below took place in 406 BC.

εἶχε δὲ τὸ δεξιὸν κέρας τῶν Πελοποννησίων Καλλικρατίδας. Ἕρμων δὲ ὁ κυβερνήτης, καλόν ἐστιν, ἔφη, ἀποπλεῦσαι· αἱ γὰρ τριήρεις τῶν Ἀθηναίων μάλα ἰσχυραί εἰσιν. ἀλλὰ Καλλικρατίδας, αἰσχρόν ἐστιν, ἔφη, τὸ φεύγειν. ἐναυμάχησαν δὲ αἱ τριήρεις χρόνον πολύν, πρῶτον μὲν ἀθρόαι, ἔπειτα δὲ σποράδες. ἐπεὶ 5 δὲ Καλλικρατίδας τε ἀπέπεσεν εἰς τὴν θάλατταν καὶ ἀπέθανε καὶ Πρωτόμαχος ὁ Ἀθηναῖος καὶ οἱ μετ᾽ αὐτοῦ τῷ δεξιῷ τὸ

εὐώνυμον ἐνίκησαν, ἐντεῦθεν φυγῇ ἦν τῶν Πελοποννησίων εἴς
τε Χίον καὶ Φώκαιαν· οἱ δὲ Ἀθηναῖοι πάλιν εἰς τὰς Ἀργινούσας
κατέπλευσαν. τῶν μὲν οὖν Ἀθηναίων τριήρεις πέντε καὶ 10
εἴκοσι κατέδυσαν οἱ Λακεδαιμόνιοι, τῶν δὲ Πελοποννησίων
Λακωνικὰς μὲν ἐννέα οἱ Ἀθηναῖοι, τῶν δὲ ἄλλων συμμάχων ὡς
ἑξήκοντα.

13 A troublesome visitor

In Athenian courts litigants were obliged to conduct their
own cases, but they could use speeches written for them by
professional writers. The following comes from such a speech
composed by Lysias some time after 394 BC for a middle-aged
homosexual defending himself against a charge of assault
brought against him by a fellow Athenian, Simon, who was
his rival for the affection of a young slave.

ἐπεὶ γὰρ ἐπὶ τὴν οἰκίαν μου τῆς νυκτὸς ἦλθεν ὁ Σίμων, ἐξέκοψε
τὰς θύρας καὶ εἰσῆλθεν εἰς τὴν γυναικωνῖτιν, οὗ ἦσαν ἥ τ᾽
ἀδελφή μου καὶ αἱ ἀδελφιδαῖ. πρῶτον μὲν οὖν οἱ ἐν τῇ οἰκίᾳ
ἐκέλευσαν αὐτὸν ἀπελθεῖν, ὁ δ᾽ οὐκ ἤθελεν. ἔπειτα δὲ
ἐξέωσαν βίᾳ. ἀλλ᾽ ἐξηῦρεν οὗ ἐδειπνοῦμεν καὶ πρᾶγμα σφόδρα 5
ἄτοπον καὶ ἄπιστον ἐποίησεν. ἐξεκάλεσε γάρ με ἔνδοθεν, καὶ
ἐπειδὴ τάχιστα ἐξῆλθον, εὐθύς με τύπτειν ἐπεχείρησεν· ἐπειδὴ
δὲ αὐτὸν ἀπέωσα, ἔβαλλέ με λίθοις καὶ ἐμοῦ μὲν ἁμαρτάνει,
Ἀριστόκριτον δὲ ἔβαλε λίθῳ καὶ συντρίβει τὸ μέτωπον.

Notes

2 Supply ἐστί; τὸ δίκαιον (*what is*) *right* (5.1/3)

3 χειμῶνος, τοῦ θέρους the definite article can be omitted in such
expressions; τὴν οἰκίᾱν indicates a general class (hence the
definite article, 2.1/2 note 1) – trans. *a house*.

5 οὐδέν is here an adjective with ψεῦδος; trans. *no falsehood*
(cf. οὐδείς in 8(*iv*)).

6 *l*.1 αὐτοῦ adv. *there, in that place* (**not** the gen. sing. m. or n. of
αὐτός). *ll*.3f. οὐ ... ἔστιν ... ἡμῖν lit. *there is not to us*, i.e. *we do
not have*.

8 (*vi*) The aorist is gnomic and should be translated by a present (see note on 5.2.10).

9 παρασάγγας δύο καὶ εἴκοσι (*22 parasangs*) is in apposition to σταθμοὺς τρεῖς (*three days' march*) and explains how far Cyrus marched in three days; αὐτοῦ gen. sing. m. of αὐτός (referring back to τὸν Μαίανδρον).

10 Gnomic aorists (see note on 8 above).

11 κακῶς λέγω + acc. *speak ill of, malign, abuse*; ὁ δέ *and he* (i.e. Socrates) 5.1/3; γάρ Socrates' reply sarcastically explains M's action and in English would be introduced by *yes, for he* ... (see 24.1/1) or *well, he* ...; καλῶς λέγω can mean either *speak well of* or *speak properly* (κακῶς λέγω by itself can also mean *speak badly*) – Socrates is punning on the two senses.

12 *l*.1 εἶχε *had* i.e. *commanded*; the first δέ connects this sentence with the preceding one in the original context and need not be translated (cf. the beginning of 4.2.9); Καλλικρατίδας (nom. s.; = Attic -ίδης – 3.1/2 note 4) was a Spartan and his name has the non-Attic (and non-Ionic) form of the patronymic suffix. *l*.3 τριήρεις 6.1/1c. *ll*.5ff. σποράδες nom. pl. f. (this is a third declension adj., 10.1/4a) *scattered* (agreeing with τριήρεις); Καλλικρατίδας τε ... καὶ Πρωτόμαχος ... lit. *both Callicratidas ... and Protomachus* ... Greek is fond of linking clauses with particles such as τε ... καί (cf. 4.1/3 and ἄγουσί τε καὶ φέρουσιν in *ll*.23f. of 4.2.9) but in English we would not translate τε; notice that between this τε ... καί another καί occurs to join ἀπέπεσεν (< ἀποπίπτω) and ἀπέθανε (< ἀποθνήσκω) but it is the second καί which picks up τε because the two elements, which must be parallel, are *Callicratidas* and *Protomachus and those with him*; τῷ δεξιῷ *with their right [wing]* dat. of instrument (11.1/2). *l*.12 ἄλλων cannot here be translated *other* because the allies referred to are allies of the Spartans; the meaning is *of their allies as well* (cf. Ἀθῆναι καὶ αἱ ἄλλαι νῆσοι *Athens and the islands as well* **not** *Athens and the other islands* because Athens is not an island); ὡς here *about* (22.1/1a(vii)).

13 *ll.*2ff. τὰς θύρας i.e. the two leaves of the door at the house entrance; γυναικωνῖτιν in an Athenian house the women had separate quarters; ἤ τ᾽ ... καί the τε need not be translated (cf. *l.*6 of previous passage); μέν is balanced by δέ (*l.*4) after ἔπειτα, and οὖν connects this sentence with the previous one (neither word would have an equivalent in idiomatic English). *l.*5 ἐξέωσαν < ἐξωθέω (the temporal augment in the aorist of this verb is irregular, cf. 4.1/1 note 2(ii). *ll.*8f. ἀπέωσα < ἀπωθέω; ἔβαλλε *started to pelt* inceptive use of the imperfect (4.1/1 footnote); λίθοις *with stones* (dat. of instrument, 11.1/2); ἁμαρτάνει ... συντρίβει Greek often uses the present tense in narrative for vividness (vivid present); translate with the English simple past (*missed... gashed*); take ἐμοῦ (*l.*8) with ἁμαρτάνει *missed me* (ἁμαρτάνω is followed by the gen., 13.1/2*a*(iv)).

7.2/1 Vocabulary

ἀδελφή, -ῆς, ἡ *sister*
ἀδελφιδῆ, -ῆς, ἡ *niece*
ἀθρόος, -ᾱ, -ον *all together, all at once, in a body*
αἰσχρός, -ά, -όν *shameful, disgraceful*
ἀκίνητος, -ον *motionless, immovable*
ἁμαρτάνω *make a mistake;* (+gen.) *miss*
ἀπέθανον aor. of ἀποθνήσκω *die, be killed*
ἀπῆλθον aor. of ἀπέρχομαι *go away, depart*
ἀποπίπτω (aor. ἀπέπεσον) *fall overboard*
ἄπιστος, -ον *incredible*
ἀποπλέω (aor. ἀπέπλευσα) *sail away*
ἀπωθέω (aor. ἀπέωσα) *push away*
Ἀργινοῦσαι, -ῶν, αἱ *Arginousae (islands)*

ἄτοπος, -ον *extraordinary*
αὐτοῦ (adv.) *there, in that place*
ἄφθονος, -ον *abundant, plentiful*
βάλλω *pelt*
βίᾱ, -ᾱς, ἡ *force, violence*
βίος, -ου, ὁ *life*
γυναικωνῖτις, -ιδος, ἡ *women's apartments*
δειπνέω *dine*
δεξιός, -ά, -όν *on the right hand*
διά (prep.+gen.) *through, across*
δίκαιος, -ᾱ, -ον *just*
δίς (adv.) *twice*
ἔαρ, ἦρος, τό *(the season of) spring*
εἶδον aor. of ὁράω *see, look at*
εἴκοσι(ν) (indecl. adj.) *twenty*
εἶπον aor. of λέγω *say*
εἰσῆλθον aor. of εἰσέρχομαι *enter*
ἐκκαλέω *call* (someone) *out*
ἐκκλησίᾱ, -ᾱς, ἡ *assembly*
ἐκκόπτω *knock out*

ἔνδοθεν (adv.)   *from inside*
ἔνεστι (impers.)   *it is possible*
ἐννέα (indecl. adj.)   *nine*
ἐντεῦθεν (adv.)   *thereupon*
ἐξευρίσκω   *find out, discover*
ἐξήκοντα (indecl. adj.)   *sixty*
ἐξῆλθον aor. of ἐξέρχομαι
    come out
ἐξωθέω (aor. ἐξέωσα)   *push out*
ἐπεί (conj.)   *when*
ἐπειδὴ τάχιστα   *as soon as*
ἐπί (prep.+acc.)   *to*
ἐπιχειρέω   *attempt, take in hand*
ἔρπω   *spread*
εὐήλιος, -ον   *sunny, with a
    sunny aspect*
εὐθύς (adv.)   *at once,
    straightaway*
εὖρος, -ους, τό   *breadth*
εὔσκιος, -ον   *well-shaded*
εὐώνυμος, -ον   *left, on the left
    hand*
ἤγαγον aor. of ἄγω   *lead, bring*
ἦλθον aor. of ἔρχομαι   *go, come*
θέρος, -ους, τό   *summer*
θύρᾱ, -ᾱς, ἡ   *door*
ἰσχῡρός, -ά, -όν   *powerful, strong*
κακῶς/καλῶς (+acc.) λέγω *speak
    ill/well (of)* (see note on 11)
καταδύω   *make to sink, sink* (tr.)
καταπλέω   *sail back*
κέρας, -ατος, τό   *wing of a fleet*
κῑνέω   *move*
κόσμος, -ου, ὁ   *world*
κυβερνήτης, -ου, ὁ   *helmsman*
Λακωνικός, -ή, -όν   *Laconian,
    Spartan*
λίθος, -ου, ὁ   *stone*
Λῡδίᾱ, -ᾱς, ἡ   Lydia (territory
    in west of Asia Minor)

Μαίανδρος, -ου, ὁ   *Maeander*
    (river in Phrygia)
μέτωπον, -ου, τό   *forehead*
μῆκος, -ους, τό   *length*
νύξ, νυκτός, ἡ   *night*
ὄλεθρος, -ου, ὁ   *destruction*
ὄνυξ, -υχος, ὁ   *claw*
ὅπλα, -ων, τά   *weapons, arms*
οὗ (conj.)   *where*
πανταχῶς (adv.)   *in all ways,
    altogether*
παρασάγγης, -ου, ὁ   *parasang*
    (a Persian measure of
    distance of about 30 stades
    [= c. 6 km.])
πάροδος, -ου, ὁ   *passage,
    entrance*
παροιμίᾱ, -ᾱς, ἡ   *proverb*
πεζομαχέω   *fight on land*
Πελοποννήσιοι, -ων, οἱ
    Peloponnesians
πέντε (indecl. adj.)   *five*
πλέθρον, -ου, τό   *plethron*
    (c. 30 metres)
ποταμός, -οῦ, ὁ   *river*
σκηνή, -ῆς, ἡ   *stage* (in
    theatre)
σποράς, -άδος (adj.)
    scattered
σταθμός, -οῦ, ὁ   *day's march*
στρατοπεδεύω   *make camp,
    encamp*
συντρίβω   *smash, gash*
τειχομαχέω   *fight against
    walls/fortifications*
τριήρης, -ους, ἡ   *trireme*
ὑστεραῖος, -ᾱ, -ον   *following,
    next;* τῇ ὑστεραίᾱ   *on the
    following day*
φυγή, -ῆς, ἡ   *flight*

Φώκαια, -ᾱς, ἡ *Phocaea* (city in Asia Minor)

χειμών, -ῶνος, ὁ *winter*

χελῑδών, -όνος, ἡ *swallow*

Χίος, -ου, ἡ *Chios* (island and city in the Aegean Sea)

Main points

- The distinction between the weak and strong aorist is one of form, **not** of meaning

- The strong aorist has no suffix; its endings in the indicative are the same as those of the imperfect and its infinitive ending is the same as that of the present

- φημί *say* is an irregular -μι verb

- Direct and indirect speech can have one of three forms: statement, question or command

- Indirect command is expressed by an infinitive (negative μή)

- Cardinal numbers for 1–4, 200–900, 1000+ are declined; the other cardinals are not

- Ordinal numbers (πρῶτος, δεύτερος, etc.) are first and second declension adjectives

- ἅπαξ (*once*), δίς (*twice*), etc. are numeral adverbs

- Greek has two negatives οὐ and μή; these have separate uses and are not interchangeable

- **Time how long** and **spatial extent** are expressed by the accusative, **time when** is expressed by the dative, **time within which** by the genitive

Unit 8

8.1 Grammar

8.1/1 Middle and passive voices

In a clause where the verb is active the subject is the doer (*the man bit the dog; Alcibiades is running through the agora*). There may or may not be an object, depending on whether the verb is transitive or intransitive. In a clause with a passive verb the subject is the sufferer (*the dog was bitten by the man; the Athenians were defeated in Sicily*). The agent or instrument (11.1/2) may or may not be specified. The active and passive voices are used in Greek in much the same way as in English. Greek, however, has a third voice, the **middle**. This has no English equivalent because the meanings it conveys are expressed in English in different ways. These meanings are:

(a) to do something to oneself, e.g. λούομαι *I wash myself, I wash* (intr.); παύομαι *I stop myself, I cease, stop* (intr.)

(b) to do something for oneself, for one's own advantage, e.g. κομίζω (act.) *carry, convey*, κομίζομαι (mid.) *I convey for myself, recover*:

 ἑκατὸν δραχμὰς ἐκομίσατο. *He recovered a hundred drachmas.*

(c) to cause something to be done (one's own advantage is always involved):

 διδάσκομαι τοὺς παῖδας τὴν τῶν Ἑλλήνων γλῶτταν. *I am having [my] children taught the language of the Greeks.*

Of these three uses (*a*) is restricted to verbs with an appropriate meaning, (*b*) is very common, (*c*) is somewhat rare. Very often a verb when used in the middle voice in sense (*b*) acquires a special meaning, e.g. λύω *loosen, free*, λύομαι (mid.) *free (someone) for one's own advantage, ransom*; αἱρέω *take, seize*, αἱρέομαι *take for oneself, choose*.

As will be seen in **Appendix 1**, the forms of the middle and passive indicative are identical in the present and imperfect (and also in the perfect and pluperfect – 16.1/3). This does not create ambiguity as the context of a particular verb normally shows its voice. The future and aorist passive differ in form from the middle and will be treated separately in 11.1/1. With regard to the forms of the indicative of the present middle and passive, the imperfect middle and passive, the future middle and the aorist middle, which can now be learnt (see **Appendices**), we should note that:

(d) in each tense the stem is the same as for the active, and the link vowel between the stem and the ending proper (which is more easily distinguishable in these forms) is o/ε in the present, imperfect (and strong aorist) and future, but α in the weak aorist (on -ω of the 2nd s., see below).

(e) in each tense the 2nd s. ending has undergone contraction. The present and future ending was originally -εσαι, the imperfect -εσο and the aorist -ασο. With the loss of intervocalic σ (cf. 6.1/1(*c*)) these became η (or ει), ου, ω respectively (we have already met the second and third contractions with contracted verbs – 5.1/2).

(f) when allowance has been made for the 2nd s., the endings, except for the lst pl. and 2nd pl. which do not vary, fall into two classes. For the primary tenses they are -μαι, -σαι, -ται, -νται and for the historic -μην, -σο, -το, -ντο (cf. 4.1/1 note 1).

(g) the endings of the strong aorist indicative middle are the same as those of the imperfect: αἰσθάνομαι *perceive,* impf. ἠσθανόμην, aor. ἠσθόμην; and the infinitive ending of the strong aorist is the same as that of the present: αἰσθάνεσθαι (pres.), αἰσθέσθαι (aor.).

Notes

1 Many common verbs have, for no perceptible reason, their future in the middle voice, not the active, e.g. ἀκούω *hear,* ἀκούσομαι; βοάω, βοήσομαι *shout*; διώκω *pursue*, διώξομαι; μανθάνω *learn*, μαθήσομαι. These are verbs which would not otherwise have had reason to be used in the middle. For other examples see **Principal parts of verbs.**

2 εἰμί *be* also has a future middle, which is formed with the stem ἐσ-: ἔσομαι, ἔσει (-ῃ), ἔσται, ἐσόμεθα, ἔσεσθε, ἔσονται. The original form of the 3rd s., ἔσεται, occurs in dialects other than Attic.

3 Contracted verbs form their present and imperfect middle/passive according to the rules given at 5.1/2 (see **Appendix 2**).

4 In Indo-European (1.3) there were only active and middle voices. In Greek the passive use of the middle led to the development of separate forms in the future and aorist, but even in Attic we occasionally meet the future middle used in a passive sense.

8.1/2 Deponent verbs

A linguistic peculiarity for which English offers no parallel is deponent verbs, which are **middle or passive in form** but **active in meaning.** They may be transitive (as κτάομαι *acquire*) or intransitive (as πορεύομαι *march*). In some cases the meaning of a deponent exemplifies one of the uses of the middle voice (κτάομαι originally meant *procure for oneself*), but elsewhere (as ἕπομαι *follow*) no explanation seems possible, although these verbs are among the most commonly used in Greek.

As we have seen in the previous subsection, the forms of the middle and passive voices differ only in the future and aorist. This divergence allows a classification of deponents into two groups:

(a) **middle deponents,** whose future and aorist are middle in form, as αἰνίττομαι *speak in riddles,* fut. αἰνίξομαι, aor. ᾐνιξάμην. This is the larger group.

(b) **passive deponents,** whose aorist is passive in form. Nearly all passive deponents, however, have a middle, not passive, future. For the aorist passive and examples of passive deponents see 11.1/1.

Examples of deponents in use are: ἀπὸ τῶν Ἀθηνῶν ἔρχονται *they are coming from Athens* (ἔρχομαι *come, go*; for the aorist of this verb see 7.1/1 note 2); τὸ ἆθλον δέχομαι *I accept the prize* (δέχομαι *accept, receive*).

A very common deponent is γίγνομαι, which has the basic meanings *be born, become, happen*. In many contexts, however, English requires a more specific word: ἀνὴρ ἀγαθὸς ἐγένετο *he showed himself a brave man* (lit. *he became a brave man*); νὺξ ἐγένετο *night fell*.

8.1/3 Indirect statement

In English we can say, with the same meaning, *he considers that I am clever* or *he considers me to be clever*. Both constructions, a noun clause introduced by *that* or an infinitive phrase without *that*, have their equivalents in Greek, but, unlike English, Greek shows a distinct preference for the infinitive construction after most verbs of **saying, thinking** and the like, e.g. νομίζω, οἴομαι both *think, consider*; φάσκω *state, declare*; ἡγέομαι *consider*; the first three are used almost exclusively with the infinitive construction. For verbs of **knowing** and **perceiving**, see 15.1/2*a*.

(*a*) *Infinitive construction*
In this form there is no introductory word (like ὅτι *that* in the other construction – see below (*b*)) and the finite verb of the original statement is changed to the infinitive of the same tense (the present infinitive represents both the present and the imperfect indicative of the direct form). If the subject of the finite verb of the original direct statement is the same as the subject of the verb of saying or thinking that introduces the indirect statement, it remains in the nominative, as do any words agreeing with it (**nominative and infinitive**). Such sentences are of the type *Xerxes said that he was master*. Since in the original direct statement (δεσπότης εἰμί *I am master*) there is no need to state the subject explicitly (except for emphasis: ἐγώ εἰμι δεσπότης *I am master*), so too the subject of the infinitive is normally not expressed: Ξέρξης ἔφη δεσπότης εἶναι. When the two subjects are not identical, the subject of the infinitive is put into the accusative (**accusative and infinitive**): ὁ σατράπης ἔφη Ξέρξην εἶναι δεσπότην *the satrap said that Xerxes was master* (lit. *Xerxes to be master*; original Ξέρξης ἐστὶ δεσπότης *Xerxes is master*). If the direct statement was negated, the same negative, οὐ (see 7.1/6), will appear with the infinitive. Further examples are:

> ἡ Ἀσπασίᾱ νομίζει καλὴ εἶναι. *Aspasia thinks that she is beautiful* (original καλή εἰμι I am *beautiful*).

ὁ Περικλῆς ἐνόμιζε τὴν Ἀσπασίᾱν καλὴν εἶναι. *Pericles used to think that Aspasia was beautiful* (original ἡ Ἀσπασίᾱ ἐστὶ καλή. *Aspasia is beautiful*).

ἡγοῦμαι τὴν Ἀσπασίᾱν οὐκ εἶναι αἰσχράν. *I consider that Aspasia is not ugly* (original ἡ Ἀσπασίᾱ οὐκ ἔστιν αἰσχρά. *Aspasia is not ugly*).

ὁ Σωκράτης ἔφη τὴν γυναῖκα χιτῶνα κτήσεσθαι. *Socrates said [his] wife would get a chiton* (original ἡ γυνὴ χιτῶνα κτήσεται (lit. *the wife will get a chiton*).

ὑποπτεύω τὴν Ξανθίππην πέντε χιτῶνας ἐχθὲς κτήσασθαι. *I suspect that Xanthippe got five chitons yesterday* (original ἡ Ξανθίππη πέντε χιτῶνας ἐχθὲς ἐκτήσατο *Xanthippe got five chitons yesterday*).

Notes

1 It is only in this construction that the distinction between the present and aorist infinitives is one of time, **not** aspect (cf. 4.1/1). In the last example κτήσασθαι means literally *to have got*. If we were to substitute the present infinitive κτᾶσθαι *to be getting* (and eliminate ἐχθές) the meaning would be *I suspect that Xanthippe is getting...* (original ἡ Ξανθίππη κτᾶται ...).

2 Since, in the accusative and infinitive construction, the infinitive of a transitive verb has both its subject and its object in the accusative, there is obviously a possibility of ambiguity. When confronted with σέ φημι Ῥωμαίους νῑκήσειν (the reply of the Delphic priestess to Pyrrhus of Epirus) one might well wonder whether the meaning was *I say that you will conquer the Romans* or *I say that the Romans will conquer you*. Normal Greeks left such equivocation to oracles.

3 φημί tends to occupy an unemphatic position and so, unlike in English, does not precede the indirect statement which it reports: Πέρσης ἔφη εἶναι *he said he was a Persian* (cf. 7.1/2 note 3).

4 οὔ φημι means *I say that ... not, I deny*: οὐκ ἔφη Πέρσης εἶναι *he denied he was a Persian*; it **never** means *I do not say that...*, which would require a different verb, e.g. οὐ λέγω ὅτι ... (on ὅτι see (*b*) below).

5 Verbs of **hoping** (ἐλπίζω), **promising** (ὑπισχνέομαι), **swearing** (ὄμνῡμι 20.1/1), **threatening** (ἀπειλέω) and the like regularly take the infinitive construction. When these verbs have a future reference, as they generally do, they can be construed with the future infinitive (a present or aorist infinitive is also possible): ἐλπίζω νῑκήσειν ἐν τῇ μάχῃ *I hope to conquer in the battle.* For a negative hope of this sort the negative μή, not οὐ, is used because the original is really not a statement but a wish (wishes are always negated by μή – 21.1/1): ἐλπίζω τοὺς Λακεδαιμονίους μὴ καύσειν τὸν ἐμὸν ἀγρόν *I hope the Spartans won't burn my farm* (original *may the Spartans not burn my farm!*). This use of μή is extended to verbs of promising, swearing and threatening.

(b) *Construction with finite verb*

Indirect statements in Greek may also be expressed by a noun-clause introduced by ὅτι or ὡς, *that.* Insofar as these two conjunctions can be differentiated, ὅτι is used to introduce a fact, whereas ὡς tends to convey the suggestion that the reporter considers the statement as a mere opinion, an allegation, or as untrue. As in the infinitive construction, the tense of the direct speech is retained in the indirect form even after a main verb which is in the past; in such cases we make a tense adjustment in English (see the second, third and fourth examples below).

This is the regular construction after λέγω *say* (but see note 1) and certain other verbs. Examples are:

λέγει ὡς ὑβριστής εἰμι. *He claims that I am insolent.*
εἶπον ὅτι ὁ Κῦρος διώκει. *They said that Cyrus was pursuing* (original *Cyrus is pursuing*).
ἀπεκρίναντο ὅτι στρατὸν πέμψουσιν. *They replied that they would send an army* (original *we will send an army*).
εἴπομεν ὅτι ὁ Περικλῆς ταῦτα οὐ ποιήσει. *We said that Pericles would not do this* (original *Pericles will not do this*).

Notes

1 For the impersonal English construction *it is said that* ... Greek uses a personal construction with the infinitive: ὁ Σωκράτης λέγεται τοὺς νέους βλάψαι *it is said that Socrates harmed the young* (lit. *Socrates is said to have harmed ...*).

2 Occasionally even a **direct** quote is introduced by ὅτι: εἶπον ὅτι ἑτοῖμοί ἐσμεν *they said, 'We are ready'*.

3 For the change of mood which may occur after a historic main verb see 14.1/4*d*.

8.1/4 Third declension nouns – stems in ι and υ

These stems differ from those in consonants (5.1/1, 6.1/1) in having ν, not α, as the acc. s. ending for masculine and feminine nouns.

Stems in ι consist of a large number of feminines (including many abstract nouns, mostly in -σις, e.g. φύσις *nature*), a few masculines, but no neuters in normal use. All are declined alike, with the odd anomaly that the original ι of the stem has been lost in most forms. The -εως of the gen. s. was originally -ηος (as occurs in Homer); the quantity of the two vowels was interchanged but the original accent was retained, i.e. πόληος > πόλεως. This accent was extended by analogy to the genitive plural.

Masculine and feminine υ stems are divided into two sub-groups, both very small. The declension of the first (πῆχυς) is very close to πόλις, of the second (ἰχθύς) to consonantal stems. ἄστυ, the only neuter, follows πῆχυς in the genitive and dative.

	πόλις (f) *city*	πῆχυς (m) *forearm*	ἄστυ (n) *city*	ἰχθύς (m) *fish*
SINGULAR				
Nom.	πόλις	πῆχυς	ἄστυ	ἰχθύς
Voc.	πόλι	πῆχυ	ἄστυ	ἰχθύ
Acc.	πόλιν	πῆχυν	ἄστυ	ἰχθύν
Gen.	πόλεως	πήχεως	ἄστεως	ἰχθύος
Dat.	πόλει	πήχει	ἄστει	ἰχθύϊ
PLURAL				
N.V.	πόλεις	πήχεις	ἄστη (<εα)	ἰχθύες
Acc.	πόλεις	πήχεις	ἄστη (<εα)	ἰχθῦς
Gen.	πόλεων	πήχεων	ἄστεων	ἰχθύων
Dat.	πόλεσι(ν)	πήχεσι(ν)	ἄστεσι(ν)	ἰχθύσι(ν)

The normal word for *city* is πόλις. ἄστυ means *city, town* as opposed to the country.

Note

πρέσβυς, which follows πῆχυς, is a poetical word for *old man* (prose uses γέρων or πρεσβύτης). Its plural πρέσβεις, however, is the normal prose word for *ambassadors* (the singular *ambassador* is supplied by πρεσβευτής).

Insight

During the Renaissance when the study of ancient Greek literature and culture was revived in Western Europe many Greek words were taken into English either directly or through the medium of Latin. Some were changed slightly, some not at all (see the list in 1.2.2). In some cases a group of related words was taken over, e.g. *crisis, critic, critical, criterion* (all derived from κρίνω *judge*). Occasionally the meaning of an English derivative has evolved. Κλῖμαξ means *ladder* whereas our *climax* is used in the metaphorical sense of *culmination*. Greek vocabulary continues to enter the language today. A *cosmonaut* is *a sailor* (ναύτης) *in the universe* (κόσμος).

8.2 Greek reading

1 ὁ θεὸς καὶ ἡ φύσις οὐδὲν μάτην ποιοῦσιν.

2# φύσιν πονηρὰν μεταβαλεῖν οὐ ῥᾴδιον.

3# πόλεις ὅλας ἠφάνισε διαβολὴ κακή.

4 Ἰησοῦς Χριστὸς Θεοῦ Υἱὸς Σωτήρ (*the name of an early Christian symbol is concealed in the initial letters of this formula*).

5 ὁ χρυσὸς οὐ μιαίνεται.

6 οἴεσθε ἄλλους τὴν Ἑλλάδα σώσειν, ὑμεῖς δ᾽ ἀποδράσεσθαι;

7 ἐκ τοῦ ἐσορᾶν γίγνεται ἀνθρώποις ἐρᾶν.

8# ἀρετῆς βέβαιαί εἰσιν αἱ κτήσεις μόνης.

9# φεῦ φεῦ, παλαιὸς αἶνος ὡς καλῶς ἔχει·
γέροντες οὐδέν ἐσμεν ἄλλο πλὴν ψόφος
καὶ σχῆμ᾽, ὀνείρων δ᾽ ἕρπομεν μιμήματα,
νοῦς δ᾽ οὐκ ἔνεστιν, οἰόμεσθα δ᾽ εὖ φρονεῖν.

10 ἐλέφας μῦν οὐ δάκνει.

11 ἀταλαίπωρος τοῖς πολλοῖς ἡ ζήτησις τῆς ἀληθείας καὶ ἐπὶ τὰ
ἕτοιμα μᾶλλον τρέπονται.

12 οἱ Λακεδαιμόνιοι κήρυκα ἔπεμψαν καὶ τοὺς νεκροὺς
διεκομίσαντο.

13 διὰ τὸ θαυμάζειν οἱ ἄνθρωποι καὶ νῦν καὶ τὸ πρῶτον ἤρξαντο
φιλοσοφεῖν.

14 ὤδινεν ὄρος, εἶτα μῦν ἔτεκεν.

15# πολλῶν ὁ λιμὸς γίγνεται διδάσκαλος.

16 οἱ Σκύθαι οὐ λούονται ὕδατι.

17 A Greek translation of the Old Testament was prepared at
Alexandria in the third century BC. Legend tells us that the
version acquired its name of *Septuagint* (Latin **septuaginta**
seventy) from the number of those involved, of whom
thirty knew Greek but not Hebrew, thirty Hebrew but not
Greek, while the remaining ten were administrators with no
knowledge of either. This calumny probably arose from the
colloquial nature of its language. The following are well-
known passages.

(*i*) ἐν ἀρχῇ ἐποίησεν ὁ θεὸς τὸν οὐρανὸν καὶ τὴν γῆν. ἡ δὲ γῆ ἦν
ἀόρατος καὶ ἀκατασκεύαστος, καὶ σκότος ἐπάνω τῆς ἀβύσσου,
καὶ πνεῦμα τοῦ θεοῦ ἐπεφέρετο ἐπάνω τοῦ ὕδατος. καὶ εἶπεν ὁ
θεός, γεννηθήτω (lit. *let ... be born*) φῶς. καὶ ἐγένετο φῶς. καὶ

εἶδεν ὁ θεὸς τὸ φῶς ὅτι καλόν. καὶ διεχώρισεν ὁ θεὸς ἀνὰ μέσον 5
τοῦ φωτὸς καὶ ἀνὰ μέσον τοῦ σκότους. καὶ ἐκάλεσεν ὁ θεὸς τὸ
φῶς ἡμέραν καὶ τὸ σκότος ἐκάλεσεν νύκτα.

(*ii*) ἐπέστρεψα καὶ εἶδον ὑπὸ τὸν ἥλιον ὅτι οὐ τοῖς κούφοις ὁ
δρόμος, καὶ οὐ τοῖς δυνατοῖς ὁ πόλεμος, καὶ οὐ τοῖς σοφοῖς ἄρτος,
καὶ οὐ τοῖς συνετοῖς πλοῦτος.

18 Crime does not pay

Hegestratus, a rascally owner-captain, had hired his ship to
an Athenian who wished to import grain from Syracuse. After
the grain had been loaded, Hegestratus, with Zenothemis, an
accomplice in crime, went round Syracuse borrowing money
against the cargo as though it were his. This type of loan
(bottomry) was made to enable merchants to cover costs of
transportation by sea, and was not recoverable if the ship
sank.

Ζηνόθεμις δ᾽ ἀδίκημα κακὸν μεθ᾽ Ἡγεστράτου συνεσκευάσατο.
χρήματα γὰρ ἐν ταῖς Συρακούσαις ἐδανείζοντο. ὡς δὲ ἐλάμβανον
τὰ χρήματα, οἴκαδε ἀπέστελλον εἰς τὴν Μασσαλίαν, καὶ οὐδὲν
εἰς τὸ πλοῖον εἰσέφερον. ἐπειδὴ δὲ ἦσαν αἱ συγγραφαὶ ἀποδοῦναι
(*to repay*) τὰ χρήματα μετὰ τὸν τοῦ πλοίου κατάπλουν, καταδῦσαι 5
ἐβουλεύσαντο τὸ πλοῖον· ἐβούλοντο γὰρ τοὺς δανειστὰς
ἀποστερῆσαι. ὁ μὲν οὖν Ἡγέστρατος, ὡς ἀπὸ τῆς γῆς ἀπῆραν
δυοῖν ἢ τριῶν ἡμερῶν πλοῦν, τῆς νυκτὸς διέκοπτε τοῦ πλοίου τὸ
ἔδαφος, ὁ δὲ Ζηνόθεμις ἄνω μετὰ τῶν ἄλλων ἐπιβατῶν διέτριβεν.
ἀλλὰ ἐπεὶ ψόφος ἐγένετο, αἰσθάνονται οἱ ἐν τῷ πλοίῳ ὅτι κακόν 10
τι (*some mischief*) κάτω γίγνεται, καὶ βοηθοῦσιν. ὡς δ᾽ ἡλίσκετο
ὁ Ἡγέστρατος καὶ κακῶς πείσεσθαι ὑπελάμβανε, φεύγει καὶ
πηδᾷ εἰς τὴν θάλατταν. οὕτως οὖν, ὥσπερ ἄξιος ἦν, κακὸς κακῶς
ἀπέθανεν.

Notes

2 ῥᾴδιον (*sc.* ἐστί) *it is easy* – when impersonal expressions involve
an adjective the neuter singular form is used.

3 ἠφάνισε < ἀφανίζω (4.1/1 note 2(ii)), the aorist is gnomic (see
note on 5.2.10).

96

6 ἄλλους ... σώσειν acc. and inf., ὑμεῖς ... ἀποδράσεσθαι nom. and inf.; ἀποδράσεσθαι < ἀποδιδράσκω, which has a middle future (8.1/1 note 1).

7 ἐρᾶν is the subject of γίγνεται.

8 κτήσεις should be translated by a singular.

9 *l*.1 *how right the old saying is* (ὡς is exclamatory, 22.1/1*a*(ii)); Greek uses ἔχω + an adverb (here καλῶς) to express a state where English has the verb *to be* + an adjective. *l*.3 μιμήματα is in apposition to the understood subject of ἕρπομεν *we crawl [along] [as] copies* ... *l*.4 -μεσθα (in οἰόμεσθα) is an alternative ending used in verse for -μεθα (1st pl.) of the middle and passive; εὖ φρονεῖν *think rightly* i.e. *be sane, be of right mind*.

11 τοῖς πολλοῖς lit. *for the many*, i.e. *for the majority, for most people*; τρέπονται lit. *they turn themselves* (use (*a*) of the middle in 8.1/1). Whereas the English verb *turn* can be either transitive (*I turned my car towards him*) or intransitive (*I turned towards him*), τρέπω in the active is transitive only (i.e. must be always followed by an object), and the middle (τρέπομαι lit. *I turn myself*, i.e. *I turn*) is employed for the intransitive use of the English *turn*. Here we would translate *they turn*.

12 διεκομίσαντο could represent use (*b*) or (*c*) as given in 8.1/1.

14 ὤδῑνεν impf. (or aor.) of ὠδῑνω (4.1/1 note 2(ii)).

16 λούονται *wash*; just as with τρέπω and *turn* (above 11), λούω is transitive only, whereas *wash* in English can be transitive (*I washed the baby five times*) or intransitive (*I washed five times*).

17 (*i*) *l*.1 ἐν ἀρχῇ the absence of the article gives the phrase a poetical ring. *ll*.5f. εἶδεν ... τὸ φῶς ὅτι καλόν lit. *saw the light that [it was] beautiful*. i.e. *saw that the light was* ...; ἀνὰ μέσον (+ gen. *between*) need only be translated once.

(*ii*) ἐπέστρεψα *I turned* (unlike τρέπω this verb can be either transitive or intransitive in the active mood) – the author, who was of a rather pessimistic nature, *turned* from one depressing observation to another; ὑπὸ τὸν ἥλιον i.e. here on earth.

18 *l*.1 συνεσκευάσατο < συσκευάζομαι (6.1/3). *ll*.2ff. ὡς *when, as* as also in *ll*.7 and 11 below (22.1/1*b*(iv)); ἐλάμβανον ... ἀπέστελλον ... εἰσέφερον the imperfect indicates that they did these things on several occasions. *l*.4 αἱ συγγραφαί *the contracts* – the infinitive phrase beginning with ἀποδοῦναι defines them. *ll*.7f. ἀπῆραν < ἀπαίρω *sail away*; πλοῦν acc. of extent (7.1/7*d*); διέκοπτε *began to cut through*; (inceptive imperfect, 4.1/1 footnote). *ll*.10ff. αἰσθάνονται ... γίγνεται ... βοηθοῦσιν vivid presents (cf. note on 7.2.13 *ll*.8f.); ἡλίσκετο ... ὑπελάμβανε imperfect because these two actions were going on when Hegestratus escaped; the two following verbs are in the vivid present, which is more commonly used in main clauses than in subordinate clauses.

8.2/1 Vocabulary

ἄβυσσος, -ου, ἡ *abyss*
ἀδίκημα, -ατος, τό *crime, wrong*
αἶνος, -ου, ὁ *tale, story*
αἰσθάνομαι *perceive, notice, realise*
ἀκατασκεύαστος, -ον *unformed*
ἁλίσκομαι *be caught*
ἀνὰ μέσον see note on 8.2.17(*i*)
ἄνω (adv.) *above, up above*
ἄξιος, -ᾱ, -ον *deserving*
ἀόρᾱτος, -ον *unseen, invisible*
ἀπαίρω (aor. ἀπῆρα) *sail away, depart*
ἀποδιδράσκω (fut. -δράσομαι) *run away, escape*
ἀποστέλλω *send, send away*
ἀποστερέω *rob, defraud*
ἄρχομαι (mid.) *begin* (of something continued by oneself)
ἀταλαίπωρος, -ον *without taking pains, not painstaking*

ἀφανίζω *make unseen, wipe out, destroy*
βέβαιος, -ᾱ, -ον *secure*
βοηθέω *(run to) help*
βουλεύω *plan, resolve*; (mid.) *plot*
βούλομαι *wish, want*
γίγνομαι *become, be, happen, take place*
δανείζω *lend*; (mid.) *borrow*
δανειστής, -οῦ, ὁ *creditor*
διά (prep.+acc.) *because of, on account of*
διαβολή, -ῆς, ἡ *slander*
διακομίζομαι (mid.) *carry across*
διακόπτω *cut through*
διατρίβω *pass* (time)
διαχωρίζω *separate, divide*
διδάσκαλος, -ου, ὁ *teacher*
δρόμος, -ου, ὁ *race*
δυνατός, -ή, -όν *strong*

ἔδαφος, -ους, τό *bottom*
εἰσφέρω *bring/carry into*
εἶτα (adv.) *then, next*
ἔνειμι *be in*
ἐπάνω (+gen.) *upon*
ἐπιβάτης, -ου, ὁ *passenger*
ἐπιστρέφω *turn about*
ἐπιφέρομαι *move* (intr.)
ἐράω *love, desire passionately*
ἐσοράω (= εἰσοράω) *behold, look at*
ἕτοιμος, -η, -ον *ready, ready to hand*
ζήτησις, -εως, ἡ *search, inquiry*
Ἰησοῦς, -οῦ, ὁ *Jesus*
καλέω *call, name*
καλῶς ἔχω *be right*
κατάπλους, -ου, ὁ *arrival in port*
κάτω (adv.) *below, down*
κῆρυξ, -υκος, ὁ *herald*
κοῦφος, -η, -ον *light, nimble*
κτῆσις, -εως, ἡ *possession*
λαμβάνω *take, get*
λῑμός, -οῦ, ὁ *hunger, famine*
λούω *wash* (the body); (mid.) *wash oneself*
μᾶλλον *rather*
Μασσαλίᾱ, -ᾱς, ἡ *Marseilles*
μάτην (adv.) *in vain; without reason*
μεταβάλλω *change, alter* (tr. and intr.)
μιαίνω *stain, pollute*
μίμημα, -ατος, τό *imitation*
μόνος, -η, -ον *alone, only*
μῦς, μυός, ὁ *mouse*
νῦν (adv.) *now*
οἴκαδε (adv.) *homewards*
οἴομαι (also οἶμαι) *think*
ὅλος, -η, -ον *whole, complete*

ὄνειρος, -ου, ὁ *dream*
ὄρος, -ους, τό *mountain*
οὕτως (adv.) *thus, in this way*
παλαιός, -ά, -όν *ancient, (of) old*
πάσχω (fut. πείσεσθαι) *experience, be treated*
πηδάω *leap, jump*
πλήν (adv.) *but, except*
πλοῖον, -ου, τό *vessel, ship*
πλοῦς, -οῦ, ὁ *sailing, voyage*
πόλις, -εως, ἡ *city, city-state*
πονηρός, -ά, -όν *wicked, bad*
σκότος, -ους, τό *darkness*
Σκύθης, -ου, ὁ *(a) Scythian*
συγγραφαί, -ῶν, αἱ *contract, bond*
συνετός, -ή, -όν *intelligent*
Συρᾱκοῦσαι, -ῶν, αἱ *Syracuse*
συσκευάζομαι *contrive, concoct*
σχῆμα, -ατος, τό *form, shape, appearance*
σῴζω *save, keep safe*
σωτήρ, -ῆρος, ὁ *saviour*
τίκτω (aor. ἔτεκον) *give birth to*
τρέπομαι *see note on 8.2.11*
υἱός, -οῦ, ὁ *son*
ὑπό (prep.+acc.) *under*
ὑπολαμβάνω *assume*
φιλοσοφέω *pursue/study philosophy*
φρονέω *think;* εὖ φρονέω *be sane*
φύσις, -εως, ἡ *nature/Nature*
χρῡσός, -οῦ, ὁ *gold*
ψόφος, -ου, ὁ *noise*
ὠδίνω *be in labour* (of childbirth)
ὡς *see notes to 8.2.9 and 18*
ὥσπερ (conj.) *as*

Main points

- With the passive voice the subject is the sufferer

- The middle voice means *to do something to/for oneself* or *to cause something to be done*

- The endings of the middle and passive voices are the same except in aorist and future

- Deponent verbs are middle or passive in form but active in meaning

- Indirect statement is expressed by either the infinitive construction or the finite verb construction

- Third declension also contains nouns in ι and υ (πόλις, πῆχυς, ἄστυ, ἰχθύς)

Unit 9

9.1 Grammar

9.1/1 Demonstrative Pronouns

Demonstratives in Greek draw our attention to persons and things and are used not only as pronouns but also as adjectives. The English *this* and *that* have similar functions although their use as pronouns is restricted; *this* in *this temple* is an adjective, *that* in *I do not like that* is a pronoun. Greek has three demonstratives, each with a special shade of meaning. The basic differences between them when used as adjectives are:

ὅδε *this near me* (the speaker); normally to be translated *this*
οὗτος *this* or *that near you* (the person spoken to); normally to be translated *this* or *that*
ἐκεῖνος *that over there* (i.e. away from both speaker and person spoken to); normally to be translated *that*.

When used as pronouns ὅδε will literally mean *this man near me*, οὗτος *this* or *that man near you*, ἐκεῖνος *that man over there*, but the first can generally be translated by *this man*, the third by *that man*, while the translation of οὗτος by *this man* or *that man* will depend on the context.

ὅδε is simply a compound of the definite article and -δε. In this combination even the unaccented forms of the article bear an accent: ὅδε, ἥδε, οἵδε, αἵδε (cf. 2.1/2; 3.1/1). ἐκεῖνος is declined as a first and second declension adjective (3.1/3), except that the neuter nom. and acc. s. is ἐκεῖνο (for other words with this ending -o see 9.1/3). οὗτος is similarly declined but the first syllable undergoes changes according to the following rules:

(a) an initial vowel with a rough breathing occurs in the same forms as in the definite article (2.1/2, 3.1/1)

(b) an initial τ occurs in the same forms as in the definite article

(c) where the ending contains α or η the diphthong of the first syllable changes from ου to αυ.

	SINGULAR			PLURAL		
	M.	F.	N.	M.	F.	N.
Nom.	οὗτος	αὕτη	τοῦτο	οὗτοι	αὗται	ταῦτα
Acc.	τοῦτον	ταύτην	τοῦτο	τούτους	ταύτᾱς	ταῦτα
Gen.	τούτου	ταύτης	τούτου	τούτων	τούτων	τούτων
Dat.	τούτῳ	ταύτῃ	τούτῳ	τούτοις	ταύταις	τούτοις

In prose, when a demonstrative is used as an adjective, the noun which it qualifies must retain the definite article and the demonstrative must appear in the predicative position (3.1/3*b*): ἐκεῖνος ὁ νεᾱνίᾱς *that young man*; ἡ γυνὴ ἥδε *this woman*.

Notes

1 In certain contexts οὗτος refers to what precedes, ὅδε to what follows: ταῦτα ἔλεξεν *he said this* (as already reported), but τάδε ἔλεξεν *he spoke as follows*.

2 ἐκεῖνος ... οὗτος can mean *the former ... the latter.*

9.1/2 The relative pronoun ὅς and adjectival clauses

Adjectival clauses qualify nouns or pronouns, and so perform the same function as adjectives. They are introduced by a relative pronoun, which in English is *who, which* etc.

> *I am the man **who** dedicated a bronze tripod at Delphi.*
> *The tripod **which** you dedicated is inferior.*

An adjectival clause normally has an antecedent, i.e. a noun or pronoun to which the clause refers and which it qualifies (in the above examples *man* and *tripod*). In English the forms of the relative pronoun are not interchangeable but are influenced by the antecedent (*the man which* or *the tripod who* are clearly impossible).

Further, we cannot say *I know the man whom visited Delos* because, although *man*, the antecedent of the adjectival clause, is the object of *know* (and so would be in the accusative in Greek), the relative pronoun is the subject of the clause it introduces and must take the nominative form *who*, not the accusative form *whom*. The same holds for Greek, where the rule is **a relative pronoun takes its number and gender from its antecedent but its case from the function it performs in its own clause** (but see note 2 below). Greek cannot, moreover, omit the relative pronoun as we so often do in English (*the man Apollo cursed cannot come into my house*; Greek must say *the man whom ...*).

The normal relative pronoun in Greek is ὅς, which is declined as a first and second declension adjective (3.1/3) except that the neuter s. nom. and acc. is ὅ without ν (for other words with this ending see 9.1/3):

	SINGULAR			PLURAL		
	M.	F.	N.	M.	F.	N.
Nom.	ὅς	ἥ	ὅ	οἵ	αἵ	ἅ
Acc.	ὅν	ἥν	ὅ	οὕς	ἅς	ἅ
Gen.	οὗ	ἧς	οὗ	ὧν	ὧν	ὧν
Dat.	ᾧ	ᾗ	ᾧ	οἷς	αἷς	οἷς

Unlike *who*, *which* etc. in English, which can also be used as interrogatives (*which is your tripod?*), the Greek relative pronoun has no other functions in prose. Examples of adjectival clauses are:

Θάνατον εἰσορῶ ὃς Ἄλκηστιν εἰς Ἅιδου δόμον μέλλει κατάξειν. *I see Death who is going to* (μέλλει) *take Alcestis down to the house of Hades.*

ὁρᾷς τὸν μόρον τοῦ Ἀκταίωνος ὃν οἱ κύνες οὓς ἐθρέψατο διεσπάσαντο. *You know* (lit. *see*) *the fate of Actaeon whom the dogs whom he [had] reared tore apart.*

οἱ στρατιῶται οἷς ταῦτα εἶπε Ξενοφῶν ἐπανῆλθον πρὸς τοὺς Πέρσας. *The soldiers to whom Xenophon said this* (lit. *these things*) *returned to the Persians.*

Notes

1 The antecedent of an adjectival clause, if a pronoun, is often omitted: ὃν οἱ θεοὶ φιλοῦσιν ἀποθνῄσκει νέος *[he] whom the gods love dies young.*

2 Contrary to the rule given above, the Greek relative pronoun is often put into the same case as its antecedent. This quite illogical attraction is most frequent when a relative pronoun in the accusative case has an antecedent in the genitive or dative: ἤγαγεν στρατὸν ἀπὸ τῶν πόλεων ὧν (for ἃς) ἔπεισεν *he led an army from the cities which he had persuaded.* Sometimes the antecedent, if a pronoun, is omitted (cf. note l); ἐπαινῶ σε ἐφ' οἷς (for ἐπὶ τούτοις ἃ) λέγεις *I praise you for what you are saying.*

3 Sometimes when both the relative and its antecedent are in the accusative the latter is put into the adjectival clause: οὐκ ἀπεκρύπτετο ἣν εἶχε γνώμην *he did not conceal the opinion which he had* (= τὴν γνώμην ἣν εἶχε); here the relative is used as an adjective.

9.1/3 αὐτός *and its uses*

For the terms **attributive position** *and* **predicative position** *see 3.1/3b.*

αὐτός is a pronoun which, like demonstratives (9.1/1), is also used as an adjective. αὐτός is declined like καλός (3.1/3) except that in the neuter its nom. and acc. s. is αὐτό (the expected αὐτόν only occurs in ταὐτόν – see below). The -o ending for the nom. and acc. neuter singular also occurs in the definite article (τό), the relative pronoun (ὅ), τοῦτο, ἐκεῖνο (9.1/1), and ἄλλο *other.* αὐτός is used in three ways:

(*a*) as an **emphasizing adjective** meaning *self.* Greek has no separate words corresponding to the English emphatic *myself, yourself* etc. (as opposed to the **reflexive** *myself, yourself* etc., see 9.1/4) and instead uses αὐτός for all persons. When used with a noun it stands in the **predicative** position: αὐτὸς ὁ ἀνήρ *the man himself,* περὶ τῆς γυναικὸς αὐτῆς *concerning the woman herself.* αὐτός can also be used by itself in the nominative and agree with the understood subject: αὐτὸς ἥκεις *you yourself have come.*

Two idioms involving this use of αὐτός are:

(i) with ordinal numbers: πρεσβευτὴς ἦλθε δέκατος αὐτός *he came as ambassador with nine others* (lit. *himself the tenth*).

(ii) with a dative to express the idea of accompaniment (23.1/2*k*), especially in connection with the loss or destruction of something; τῶν τριήρων μίαν κατέδυσαν αὐτοῖς ἀνδράσιν *they sank one of the triremes crew and all* (lit. *[with] men themselves*).

(*b*)ὁ αὐτός means *the same.* In the **attributive** position (i.e. between the article and the noun) αὐτός **always** has this meaning: τοὺς αὐτοὺς δεσπότᾱς εἴχομεν, *we had the same masters*; ἐγὼ μὲν ὁ αὐτός εἰμι, ὑμεῖς δὲ μεταβάλλετε, *I am the same, [it is] you [who] change. The same as* is expressed either by ὁ αὐτὸς καί or, more commonly, by ὁ αὐτός and the dative:

τὰ αὐτὰ φρονεῖ ἐμοί. *He thinks the same as I do.*
τὰ αὐτὰ καὶ ὁ Ἀλκιβιάδης πείθουσιν. *They give the same advice as Alcibiades* (lit. *they persuade the same [things] ...*).

In this use αὐτός may coalesce with those parts of the article ending in a vowel (**crasis** – 11.1/5), and where this is possible both contracted and uncontracted forms are found in normal use. The following table shows all possible variations.

	SINGULAR		
	M.	**F.**	**N.**
Nom.	ὁ αὐτός, αὐτός	ἡ αὐτή, αὐτή	τὸ αὐτό, ταὐτό, ταὐτόν
Acc.	τὸν αὐτόν	τὴν αὐτήν	τὸ αὐτό, ταὐτό, ταὐτόν
Gen.	τοῦ αὐτοῦ, ταὐτοῦ	τῆς αὐτῆς	τοῦ αὐτοῦ, ταὐτοῦ
Dat.	τῷ αὐτῷ, ταὐτῷ	τῇ αὐτῇ, ταὐτῇ	τῷ αὐτῷ, ταὐτῷ
	PLURAL		
Nom.	οἱ αὐτοί, αὐτοί	αἱ αὐταί, αὐταί	τὰ αὐτά, ταὐτά
Acc.	τοὺς αὐτούς	τὰς αὐτάς	τὰ αὐτά, ταὐτά
Gen.	τῶν αὐτῶν	τῶν αὐτῶν	τῶν αὐτῶν
Dat.	τοῖς αὐτοῖς	ταῖς αὐταῖς	τοῖς αὐτοῖς

The alternative neuter in -ov occurs only in the contracted form.

The shorter forms bear a confusing resemblance to the corresponding parts of οὗτος, e.g. αὐτή *the same woman,* αὕτη *this/that woman;* ταὐτά *the same things,* ταῦτα *these/those things.* The accent will always show which word is involved.

(*c*) The **oblique cases** (2.1/3) of αὐτός are used to **express the personal pronoun of the third person,** *him, her, it, them* (4.1/2). In this use αὐτόν, αὐτήν etc. are unemphatic and postpositive (just as are με, σε, etc., cf. 4.1/2): ἐκέλευσεν αὐτὴν μένειν *they ordered her to remain.* As an **emphatic** third person pronoun, Greek uses the demonstratives οὗτος or ἐκεῖνος:

> οὗτος μὲν τοὺς Ἀθηναίους φιλεῖ, αὕτη δὲ τοὺς Λακεδαιμονίους. *He likes the Athenians, but* **she** *likes the Spartans;*
> ἐκεῖνον φιλοῦμεν. *We like* **him.**

Greek has no word which functions as an unemphatic third person pronoun in the nominative since the verbal inflections themselves already indicate the person involved.

To illustrate all three principal uses of αὐτός learn the following sentence:

> ὁ στρατηγὸς αὐτὸς τῷ αὐτῷ ξίφει αὐτοὺς ἔσφαξεν. *The general himself killed them with the same sword*

9.1/4 Reflexive and reciprocal pronouns

(*a*) A **reflexive pronoun** is one which refers back to the subject of a sentence or clause, as in the sentence *he killed himself.* In English all reflexive pronouns end in *-self* (*myself, yourself, himself, themselves,* etc.) and are to be carefully distinguished from the emphatic adjectives of the same form, e.g. *he himself killed the soldier.*

In the singular the reflexives of the first and second persons are formed by joining the stems of the personal pronouns (4.1/2) to the appropriate parts of αὐτός; in the plural the two components are written and declined separately. The normal third person reflexive is formed from the stem of the indirect third person reflexive ἑ (see below) and αὐτός. Reflexive pronouns can occur only in the oblique cases and the possibility of a neuter exists only in the direct third person forms.

	First Person		Second Person	
	M.	F.	M.	F.
	SINGULAR			
Acc.	ἐμαυτόν	ἐμαυτήν	σεαυτόν, σαυτόν	σεαυτήν, σαυτήν
Gen.	ἐμαυτοῦ	ἐμαυτῆς	σεαυτοῦ, σαυτοῦ	σεαυτῆς, σαυτῆς
Dat.	ἐμαυτῷ	ἐμαυτῇ	σεαυτῷ, σαυτῷ	σεαυτῇ, σαυτῇ
	PLURAL			
Acc.	ἡμᾶς αὐτούς	ἡμᾶς αὐτάς	ὑμᾶς αὐτούς	ὑμᾶς αὐτάς
Gen.	ἡμῶν αὐτῶν	ἡμῶν αὐτῶν	ὑμῶν αὐτῶν	ὑμῶν αὐτῶν
Dat.	ἡμῖν αὐτοῖς	ἡμῖν αὐταῖς	ὑμῖν αὐτοῖς	ὑμῖν αὐταῖς

	Third Person Direct			Indirect
	M.	F.	N.	M. & F.
	SINGULAR			
Acc.	ἑαυτόν, αὑτόν	ἑαυτήν, αὑτήν	ἑαυτό, αὑτό	ἑ
Gen.	ἑαυτοῦ, αὑτοῦ	ἑαυτῆς, αὑτῆς	ἑαυτοῦ, αὑτοῦ	οὗ
Dat.	ἑαυτῷ, αὑτῷ	ἑαυτῇ, αὑτῇ	ἑαυτῷ, αὑτῷ	οἷ
	PLURAL			
Acc.	ἑαυτούς, αὑτούς	ἑαυτάς, αὑτάς	ἑαυτά, αὑτά	σφᾶς
Gen.	ἑαυτῶν, αὑτῶν	ἑαυτῶν, αὑτῶν	ἑαυτῶν, αὑτῶν	σφῶν
Dat.	ἑαυτοῖς, αὑτοῖς	ἑαυταῖς, αὑταῖς	ἑαυτοῖς, αὑτοῖς	σφίσι(ν)

The contracted forms of the second and third person reflexives are more common than the uncontracted ones; ἑ, οὗ and οἷ are usually enclitic.

Examples of these pronouns in use are

βούλομαι ἐμαυτὸν μὲν ἀποκτείνειν, ὑμᾶς δ' οὔ. *I want to kill myself, not you.*

ἑαυτοὺς μὲν φιλοῦσιν οἱ κακοί, τοὺς δ' ἄλλους οἱ ἀγαθοί. *Wicked people love themselves, good people [love] others.*

ὁρᾷς σαυτὸν ἐν τῷ κατόπτρῳ. *You see yourself in the mirror.*

The third person **direct** reflexive is used as above. The third person **indirect** reflexive is used only in subordinate constructions referring back to the subject of the main clause: κελεύουσιν ἡμᾶς κοινῇ μετὰ σφῶν πολεμεῖν *they urge us to make war in common with them* (ἡμᾶς is the subject of the infinitive πολεμεῖν but σφῶν refers back to the subject of the main verb, κελεύουσιν). Direct reflexive forms are, however, often substituted: Ὀρέστης ἔπεισεν τοὺς Ἀθηναίους ἑαυτὸν κατάγειν *Orestes persuaded the Athenians to restore him(self)*.

(*b*) For **reciprocal** action the reflexive pronoun can be used: ἡμῖν αὐτοῖς διαλεξόμεθα *we shall converse with ourselves*, i.e. *each other*. Greek does, however, have a special reciprocal pronoun which was formed by doubling the stem of ἄλλος *other*: ἀλλήλους, ἀλλήλᾱς, ἄλληλα *one another, each other*. It is declined like καλός (3.1/3) except that its meaning excludes a nominative case and a singular number. With ἀλλήλους no ambiguity is possible: ἀλλήλους σφάζουσιν *they are killing each other*. It is used for all three persons.

9.1/5 Possessive adjectives and pronouns

Possessive adjectives are of two types in English, attributive (*my, your, his, her, its; our, your, their*, which occur in phrases such as *my house*) and predicative (*mine, yours, his, hers; ours, yours, theirs*, which occur in clauses such as *the house is mine*). Greek has similar possessive adjectives for the first and second persons only, and these may be used either attributively or predicatively. For the third person it uses the genitive of the personal and demonstrative pronouns. Significantly, however, where the context leaves no doubt as to who the possessor is and there is no need for emphasis, the definite article alone suffices in Greek: ὠφέλησα τόν πατέρα *I helped my father*; εὖ ἐποίησε τὴν πόλιν *he benefited his city* (cf. note on 2.2.1). In these cases no personal pronoun or possessive adjective is employed. In cases where it is desirable to clarify the reference, Greek proceeds as follows:

(*a*) Where no emphasis is intended the genitive of the unemphatic personal pronouns (μου, σου, αὐτοῦ, αὐτῆς; ἡμῶν, ὑμῶν, αὐτῶν) is employed in the **predicative** position:

φιλεῖ τὴν μητέρα μου. *He loves my mother* (lit. *the mother of me*).

εἰς τὴν οἰκίαν αὐτοῦ εἰσήλθομεν. *We entered his house (the house of him).*
θαυμάζω τὸ κάλλος αὐτῆς. *I admire her beauty (the beauty of her).*

(b) Where some degree of emphasis is desired:

   (i) For the first and second persons Greek uses the adjectives ἐμός, -ή, -όν (*my, mine*); σός, σή, σόν (*your* when referring to one person); ἡμέτερος, -ᾱ, -ον (*our*); ὑμέτερος, -ᾱ, -ον (*your* when referring to more than one person), in the **attributive** position:

   εἰς τὰς ὑμετέρᾱς οἰκίᾱς ἦλθον. *They went into your houses.*
   ὁ σός, Αἰσχίνη, κοινωνός, οὐχ ὁ ἐμός. *Your partner, Aeschines, not mine.*

   Note carefully that Greek requires both the definite article and the possessive adjective.[1]

   (ii) For the third person Greek uses the genitive of a demonstrative pronoun, e.g. τούτου *of this/that man*; ἐκείνης *of that woman,* again in the **attributive** position:

   περὶ τῶν τούτου λόγων. *Concerning his words.*
   ἀφικνοῦνται παρ᾽ Ἀριαῖον καὶ τὴν ἐκείνου στρατιάν. *They come up to Ariaeus and his army.*

(c) When a **reflexive** sense is involved (i.e. when the reference is to the subject of the clause to which the noun-group containing the possessive belongs), the genitive of the reflexive pronouns is used, again in the **attributive** position:

   τὸν ἐμαυτοῦ ἀδελφὸν ἔπεμψα. *I sent my own brother.*
   τὴν ἑαυτοῦ γυναῖκα ὑβρίζει. *He misuses his own wife.*
   ἀγαπῶσι τοὺς ἑαυτῶν ἵππους. *They love their own horses.*

---

[1] But contrast ὁ ἐμὸς δοῦλος *my slave* and ἐμὸς ὁ δοῦλος (or ὁ δοῦλος ἐμὸς) *the slave [is] mine* (predicative). The latter has no article immediately before the possessive.

In less emphatic contexts, however, the ordinary first and second person possessives, ἐμός, σός, ἡμέτερος, ὑμέτερος (above b(i)), may also be used:

τοὺς ὑμετέρους παῖδας ἀγαπᾶτε. *You love your children.*

Insight

Istanbul affords the most curious example of the survival of a Greek place name in modern Turkey (cf. Insight, Unit 2). The city began as a Greek colony in the seventh century BC with the name of Byzantium (Βυζάντιον) but was refounded in AD 330 by Constantine the Great to be the eastern capital of the now divided Roman empire. To perpetuate his memory he changed its name to Κωνσταντινουπόλις (Constantinople) *the city of Constantine.* When the western Roman empire fell in the fifth century its eastern counterpart continued and its capital, Constantinople was popularly called ἡ Πόλις i.e. **the** city *par excellence.* When it eventually fell to the Turks in 1453 it was known amongst them as Istanbul, which was an adaptation of the Greek phrase εἰς τὴν Πόλιν lit. *to the City.* The name has remained ever since. For πόλις see 8.1/4.

9.2 Greek reading

1# καλὸν τὸ θνήσκειν οἷς ὕβριν τὸ ζῆν φέρει.

2 ὁ σοφὸς ἐν αὐτῷ περιφέρει τὴν οὐσίαν.

3# καρτερὸς ἐν πολέμοις Τιμόκριτος οὗ τόδε σῆμα·
    Ἄρης δ᾽ οὐκ ἀγαθῶν φείδεται, ἀλλὰ κακῶν.

4 ὁ Κλέων οὐκ ἔφη αὐτὸς ἀλλ᾽ ἐκεῖνον στρατηγεῖν.

5 οἱ αὐτοὶ περὶ τῶν αὐτῶν τοῖς αὐτοῖς τὰ αὐτά (*sc.* λέγουσιν).

6 τὸ ἐμὸν ἐμοὶ λέγεις ὄναρ.

7 ἔπειτα ἐκεῖνος ὁ ἀνὴρ εἶπεν, ἀλλ᾽ εἰ ἄλλου δεῖ πρὸς τούτοις οἷς
λέγει Ξενοφῶν, αὐτίκα ἔξεστι ποιεῖν. μετὰ δὲ ταῦτα Ξενοφῶν εἶπε
τάδε· δῆλον ὅτι πορεύεσθαι ἡμᾶς δεῖ ὅπου ἕξομεν τὰ ἐπιτήδεια·
ἀκούω δὲ κώμας εἶναι καλὰς αἳ εἴκοσι στάδια ἀπέχουσιν.

8 ὁ φίλος ἐστὶν ἄλλος αὐτός.

9 φιλοσοφίαν πρῶτος ὠνόμασε Πυθαγόρας καὶ ἑαυτὸν φιλόσοφον.

10 παραβαλεῖν δεῖ αὐτοὺς παρ᾽ ἀλλήλους· οὕτω γὰρ σκεψόμεθα εἰ
διοίσουσιν ἀλλήλων.

11 ἀπίστως ἔχουσι πρὸς αὐτοὺς οἱ Ἕλληνες.

12 The Persian empire was founded in the sixth century BC by
Cyrus the Great (died 530 BC). His achievements were such that
in the following century Xenophon (7.2.12) wrote an account
of his life (the earliest surviving biography). The following is an
extract.

μετὰ δὲ δεῖπνον ἐπήρετο ὁ Κῦρος, ὦ Τιγράνη, ποῦ δὴ ἐκεῖνός ἐστιν
ὁ ἀνὴρ ὃς συνεθήρα ἡμῖν; σὺ γάρ μοι μάλα ἐδόκεις θαυμάζειν
αὐτόν. ἐφόνευσεν αὐτόν, ἔφη, οὗτος ὁ ἐμὸς πατήρ. διαφθείρειν
γὰρ αὐτὸν ἔφη ἐμέ. καίτοι, ὦ Κῦρε, καλὸς κἀγαθὸς ἐκεῖνος
ἦν· ὅτε γὰρ ἀποθνήσκειν ἔμελλε προσεκάλεσέ με καὶ εἶπε, οὐ 5
δεῖ σέ, ὦ Τιγράνη, χαλεπαίνειν ὅτι ὁ σὸς πατὴρ ἀποκτείνει με·
οὐ γὰρ διὰ κακόνοιαν τοῦτο ποιεῖ, ἀλλὰ δι᾽ ἄγνοιαν· ἃ δὲ δι᾽
ἄγνοιαν οἱ ἄνθρωποι ἐξαμαρτάνουσιν, ἀκούσια ταῦτ᾽ ἔγωγε
νομίζω.

13 Δημοσθένης δέ, ὃς ἑώρα τοὺς Λακεδαιμονίους μέλλειν
προσβάλλειν πλοίοις τε ἅμα καὶ πεζῷ, παρεσκευάζετο καὶ αὐτός,
καὶ τὰς τριήρεις αἳ περιῆσαν αὐτῷ ἀνέσπασε ὑπὸ τὸ τείχισμα,
καὶ τοὺς ναύτας ἐξ αὐτῶν ὥπλισεν ἀσπίσι φαύλαις καὶ οἰσυΐναις
ταῖς πολλαῖς· οὐ γὰρ ἦν ὅπλα ἐν χωρίῳ ἐρήμῳ πορίσασθαι, 5
ἀλλὰ καὶ ταῦτα ἐκ λῃστρικῆς Μεσσηνίων τριακοντέρου καὶ
κέλητος ἔλαβον, οἳ παρεγίγνοντο. ὁπλῖταί τε τῶν Μεσσηνίων
τούτων ὡς τετταράκοντα ἐγένοντο. τοὺς μὲν οὖν πολλοὺς τῶν
στρατιωτῶν ἐπὶ τὰ ἐχυρὰ τοῦ χωρίου πρὸς τὴν ἤπειρον ἔταξε,

αὐτὸς δὲ ἀπελέξατο ἑξήκοντα ὁπλίτας καὶ τοξότας ὀλίγους καὶ 10
ἐχώρει ἔξω τοῦ τείχους ἐπὶ τὴν θάλατταν, ᾗ μάλιστα ἐκείνους
προσεδέχετο πειράσεσθαι ἀποβαίνειν. κατὰ τοῦτο οὖν πρὸς
αὐτὴν τὴν θάλατταν ἔταξε τοὺς ὁπλίτας.

Notes

1 τὸ θνῄσκειν (supply ἐστί) and τὸ ζῆν are both articular infinitives
(5.1/3); understand τούτοις as the antecedent of οἷς.

3 Translate πολέμοις by a singular; supply ἦν with Τῑμόκριτος
and ἐστί with σῆμα. *l*.2 φείδεται *is sparing of, spares* takes the
genitive (cf. 13.1/2).

4 οὐκ ἔφη 8.1/3*a* note 4; after ἔφη we have a combination of a
nominative (αὐτός) + infinitive and accusative (ἐκεῖνον) +
infinitive (8.1/3*a*).

7 *l*.1 δεῖ + gen. *there is need of* (21.1/4*b* and note 3); both ἄλλου
(*another thing*) and τούτοις (*those things*) are neuter; οἷς (= ἅ)
has been attracted into the case of its antecedent (τούτοις) – 9.1/2
note 2. *l*.2 ἔξεστι an impersonal verb (cf. δεῖ, χρή) meaning *it
is possible* (21.1/4*a*). *l*.3 δῆλον supply ἐστί, [*it is*] *clear*; ἕξομεν
(note rough breathing) fut. of ἔχω.

10 As this sentence comes from a conversation we can supply ἡμᾶς
(*us* i.e. the speaker and his audience) with δεῖ.

11 ἀπίστως ἔχουσι = ἄπιστοί εἰσι (cf. note on 8.2.9).

12 *l*.1 ἐπήρετο < ἐπερωτάω. *ll*.3f. οὗτος ὁ ἐμὸς πατήρ *my father
here*; we must tell from the context that αὐτόν is the subject of
διαφθείρειν and ἐμέ its object. *l*.4 καλὸς κἀγαθός (= καὶ ἀγαθός)
a set expression meaning *fine fellow, gentleman* (cf.13.3(ii) *l*.14).
ll.5f. οὐ δεῖ σέ ... i.e. *you must not* ... *ll*.7f. The relative clause ἅ
... precedes its antecedent ταῦτ᾽(α); νομίζω here has the acc. and
inf. construction (8.1/3*a*) but the inf. εἶναι is understood.

13 *l*.2 πλοίοις ... πεζῷ dat. of instrument (11.1/2) lit. *with both ships
and infantry at the same time* (ἅμα, which is here an adverb).

l.3 αὐτῷ (*to/for him*) is dative with περιῆσαν (< περίειμι). *ll*.4f.
ἀσπίσι ... πολλαῖς lit. *with shields* (dat. of instrument – see
above) *inferior and the many made of wickerwork*, i.e *inferior
shields mostly made of wickerwork* (οἱ πολλοί can mean *the
majority* as it does in *l*.8); ἦν = ἐξῆν *it was possible* (ἔστι used
in the sense of the impersonal ἔξεστι (21.1/4*a*) is common).
ll.6f. Μεσσηνίων, which is to be taken with both τριακοντέρου
and κέλητος in the sense *belonging to [some] Messenians*, is
the antecedent of οἵ. *l*.9 τὰ ἐχυρά *the strong [points]*; πρός
towards, i.e. *facing*. *l*.11 ᾗ is here the relative adverb *where*,
not the relative pronoun; ἐκείνους i.e. the enemy. *l*.12 κατὰ
τοῦτο *at this [point]* (κατά is used here of *place where*); πρὸς
... τὴν θάλατταν Greek regularly uses prepositions appropriate
to **motion towards** (πρός + acc., εἰς etc.) with verbs logically
requiring a preposition indicating **position at**, when some
previous motion is to be understood (Demosthenes must have
moved his troops **to** the seaside before drawing them up there).
Consequently πρὸς ... τὴν θάλατταν must be translated *by the
sea*. This **pregnant** use of prepositions is so termed because the
idea of motion towards is implied by (i.e. contained within)
the preposition.

9.2/1 Vocabulary

ἀγαθός, -ή, -όν *brave*
ἄγνοια, -ᾱς, ἡ *ignorance*
ἀκούσιος, -ον *against the will,
   involuntary*
ἀλλήλους, -ᾱς, -α (reciprocal
   pron.) *each other, one
   another* (9.1/4*b*)
ἅμα (adv.) *at the same time*
ἀνασπάω (aor. -έσπασα)
   haul up
ἀπέχω *be distant*
ἀπίστως ἔχω *be mistrustful*
ἀποβαίνω *land*
ἀποκτείνω *kill*
ἀπολέγομαι *pick out*
ἀσπίς, -ίδος, ἡ *shield*

αὐτίκα (adv.) *at once,
   immediately*
δεῖ (impers.) *it is necessary
   (+acc. and infin.); there is a
   need of* (+ gen.)
δεῖπνον, -ου, τό *dinner*
δή* (particle) *indeed, certainly*
δῆλος, -η, -ον *clear, obvious*
διαφέρω (fut. διοίσω) *differ
   from* (+gen.)
διαφθείρω *corrupt*
δοκέω *seem*
ἔγωγε (= ἐγώ + γε, 13.1/3*b*) *I
   at least; I for my part*
εἴκοσι(ν) (indecl. adj.) *twenty*
ἔλαβον aor. of λαμβάνω *take*

ἐξαμαρτάνω   *do wrong*
ἔξεστι (impers.)   *it is possible*
ἐπερωτάω (aor. ἐπηρόμην)   *ask (a question)*
ἐπιτήδεια, -ων, τά   *necessities of life, provisions*
ἔρημος, -ον   *empty, deserted*
ἐχυρός, -ά, -όν   *strong, secure*
ἑώρα   3rd s. impf. of ὁράω   *see*
ᾗ (adv.)   *where*
ἤπειρος, -ου, ἡ   *mainland*
θνήσκω   *die*
καίτοι (particle)   *and yet, however*
κακόνοια, -ᾱς, ἡ   *malice*
κακός, -ή, -όν   *cowardly*
καλὸς κἀγαθός   see note on 12
καρτερός, -ά, -όν   *strong, mighty*
κέλης, -ητος, ὁ   *fast-sailing ship, pinnacle*
κώμη, -ης, ἡ   *village*
ληστρικός, -ή, -όν   *belonging to pirates*
μάλιστα   *especially*
μέλλω   *be about to*
Μεσσήνιος, -ᾱ, -ον   *Messenian*
ναύτης, -ου, ὁ   *sailor*
οἰσύϊνος, -η, -ον   *made of osier/ wickerwork*
ὄναρ, τό (nom. and acc. only)   *dream*
ὀνομάζω   *call, name*
ὁπλίζω   *equip, arm*
ὁπλίτης, -ου, ὁ   *hoplite*
ὅπου (relative adv.)   *where*
ὅτε (conj.)   *when*
οὐσίᾱ, -ᾱς, ἡ   *property, substance*
οὕτω another form of οὕτως
παραβάλλω   *compare*
παραγίγνομαι   *be present*

παρασκευάζω   *prepare, equip*; (mid.) *make one's preparations*
πεζός, -ή, -όν   *on foot*; πεζοί *infantry*
πειράομαι   *try*
περίειμι   *survive, remain*
περιφέρω   *carry round*
πορεύομαι   *march, journey*
πορίζομαι   *procure*
πρός (prep.+dat.)   *in addition to*
προσβάλλω   *attack*
προσδέχομαι   *expect*
προσκαλέω   *summon*
ποῦ; (adv.)   *where?*
σκέπτομαι   *examine, consider*
στάδιον, -ου, τό   *stade (c. 200 metres)*
στρατηγέω   *be general*
συνθηράω   *hunt with* (+ dat.)
τάττω   *station, draw up, post*
τείχισμα, -ατος, τό   *fort*
τεῖχος, -ους, τό   *wall*
τετταράκοντα (indecl. numeral)   *forty*
τοξότης, -ου, ὁ   *archer*
τριᾱκόντερος, -ου, ἡ   *thirty-oared ship*
ὕβρις, -εως, ἡ   *insult, humiliation*
φαῦλος, -ον (also -η, -ον)   *cheap, of poor quality*
φείδομαι   *spare* (+ gen.)
φιλοσοφίᾱ, -ᾱς, ἡ   *philosophy*
φιλόσοφος, -ου, ὁ   *philosopher*
φονεύω   *murder, slay*
χαλεπαίνω   *be angry*
χωρέω   *go*
ὡς (adv.+numerals)   *about, nearly*

Main points

- The demonstrative pronoun ὅδε follows ὁ; ἐκεῖνος is declined as a first and second declension adjective except for ἐκεῖνο (n.v.a. singular); οὗτος is irregular

- Adjectival clauses are introduced by the relative pronoun ὅς

- ὅς normally takes its case from the clause it introduces

- The meaning of αὐτός depends on its context

- Reflexive and reciprocal pronouns (ἐμαυτόν etc.) refer back to the subject

- Possessive adjectives (ἐμός etc.) and pronouns (μου etc.) are not used as much as in English

Unit 10

10.1 Grammar

10.1/1 Interrogative τίς and indefinite τις

The interrogative and indefinite pronouns belong to the third declension and have identical forms except for the accent. The interrogative pronoun τίς *who?*, τί *what?* is easily identifiable, since it always retains an acute accent on the first syllable (see **Appendix 8**, note 2). The indefinite pronoun τις *someone, anyone*, τι *something, anything*, is enclitic and postpositive.

		Interrogative		Indefinite	
		M. & F.	N.	M. & F.	N.
SINGULAR	Nom.	τίς	τί	τις	τι
	Acc.	τίνα	τί	τινά	τι
	Gen.	τίνος, τοῦ	τίνος, τοῦ	τινός, του	τινός, του
	Dat.	τίνι, τῷ	τίνι, τῷ	τινί, τῳ	τινί, τῳ
PLURAL	Nom.	τίνες	τίνα	τινές	τινά
	Acc.	τίνας	τίνα	τινάς	τινά
	Gen.	τίνων	τίνων	τινῶν	τινῶν
	Dat.	τίσι(ν)	τίσι(ν)	τισί(ν)	τισί(ν)

In the genitive and dative singular the shorter forms coincide with the corresponding masculine and neuter forms of the definite article (3.1/1; the indefinite forms have no accent). Both the interrogative and the indefinite pronouns may also be used as adjectives: τίς (τίς ἀνὴρ) τοῦτο ἐποίησεν; *who (what man) did this?* λέγει τις τοῦτο *someone says this*; κλέπτης τις τοῦτο ἐποίησεν *some thief did this*. Used in this way, indefinite τις is often little more than the equivalent of the English indefinite article.

Notes

1 The acc. sing. neuter τί (or, more fully, διὰ τί, lit. *on account of what?*) means *why* (cf. 20.1/5).

2 ἄττα, which is **not** enclitic, sometimes replaces the indefinite neuter pl. τινά.

10.1/2 Questions, direct and indirect

(a) Direct questions

Direct questions are those which are directly asked of someone else. In Greek, as in English, they are, where appropriate, introduced by an interrogative pronoun or adjective (10.1/1) or adverb (e.g. πότε *when?*). Where there is no interrogative word and English uses inversion (*are you sick?*) Greek, as we have seen (e.g. 3.2.12(*ii*)), uses the interrogative particle ἆρα (ἆρα νοσεῖς;), which has no English equivalent. However, a question of this sort may simply be indicated by a different tone of voice without ἆρα: ταῦτα εἶπας; *you said this?* (lit. *these things*).

This latter type of direct question may also be framed in such a way as to invite (but not necessarily receive) a negative answer: *you didn't say this, did you?* or *surely you didn't say this?* In Greek such a question is prefixed with μῶν (<μὴ οὖν) or μή: μῶν (or μή) ταῦτα εἶπας; We may also invite a positive answer by saying *you did say this, didn't you?* or *surely you said this?* In Greek we begin with ἆρα οὐ (ἆρ᾽ οὐ) or οὐ: ἆρα οὐ ταῦτα εἶπας;

For alternative questions Greek uses as an introductory word for which English has no equivalent, πότερον or πότερα (there is no distinction between the two[1]): πότερον ταῦτα εἶπας ἢ ἐκεῖνα; *did you say this or that?* (lit. *these things or those things*). As with ἆρα, the introductory word can be omitted.

(b) Indirect questions

Indirect questions are another form of indirect speech (7.1/3) and are expressed in Greek by a subordinate clause, just as in English: ἐρωτᾷ εἰ Περικλῆς πρὸς τὸν Πειραιᾶ ἦλθεν *he is asking if Pericles went to Piraeus* (direct question: ἆρα Περικλῆς πρὸς τὸν Πειραιᾶ ἦλθεν; *did Pericles go to Piraeus?*).

---

[1] They are respectively the n. acc. s. and n. acc. pl. of πότερος *which (of two)?* The accusative is here used adverbially (20.1/5).

The Greek interrogative pronouns, adjectives and adverbs, which, where appropriate, introduce questions, can have a direct form (τίς, πότε, ποῦ, etc.) or an indirect form:

DIRECT	INDIRECT	DIRECT	INDIRECT
τίς; *who?, which?*	ὅστις	ποῦ; *(at) where?*	ὅπου
ποῖος; *of what kind?*	ὁποῖος	ποῖ; *(to) where?*	ὅποι
πόσος; *how big?, how much?* pl. *how many?*	ὁπόσος	πόθεν; *from where?*	ὁπόθεν
		πότε; *when?*	ὁπότε
πότερος; *which (of two)?*	ὁπότερος	πῶς; *how?*	ὅπως

The forms ending in -ος are declined as first and second declension adjectives (3.1/3); for the declension of ὅστις see note 1.

The difference between direct and indirect forms is one of use, not meaning. The indirect are used in indirect questions only, as ἐρωτᾷ ὅστις εἶ *he is asking who you are* (but see also note 2). The direct forms can be used in direct questions (τίς εἶ; *who are you?*) or in indirect ones (ἐρωτᾷ τίς εἶ *he is asking who you are*). When used in the latter context they give a touch of immediacy and vividness.

Where the original question begins with ἆρα (ἆρα εὐωχεῖ; *are you holding a party?*) or has no interrogative word at all (εὐωχεῖ;) the indirect version is introduced by εἰ *if/whether*: ἐρωτᾷ εἰ εὐωχεῖ *he is asking if* (or *whether*) *you are holding a party.*

As in indirect statements (8.1/3), the tense of the original direct question is retained in the indirect form.[2] As will be seen in the third example below, an indirect question is not always preceded by a verb of asking.

> τούτων ἕκαστον ἠρόμην εἴ τινές εἰσι μάρτυρες. *I asked each of them if there were any witnesses* (direct: ἆρα μάρτυρές τινές εἰσιν; *Are there any witnesses?*)
> ὁ κῆρυξ ἠρώτā τίς (or ὅστις) ἀγορεύειν βούλεται. *The herald used to ask who wanted to speak* (direct: τίς ἀγορεύειν βούλεται;).

---

[2] For the change of mood which may occur after an introductory historic verb, see 14.1/4*d*.

οὐ δεῖ σε εἰπεῖν πόσους (or ὁπόσους) πόνους ἔχεις. *You don't have to say how many troubles you have* (implying a direct question πόσους πόνους ἔχω; in the mind of the person addressed).

Notes

1 ὅστις is a combination of the relative pronoun ὅς (9.1/2) and the indefinite τις (10.1/1). There are some alternative forms:

		M.	F.	N.
SINGULAR	Nom.	ὅστις	ἥτις	ὅτι
	Acc.	ὅντινα	ἥντινα	ὅτι
	Gen.	οὗτινος, ὅτου	ἧστινος	οὗτινος, ὅτου
	Dat.	ᾧτινι, ὅτῳ	ᾗτινι	ᾧτινι, ὅτῳ
PLURAL	Nom.	οἵτινες	αἵτινες	ἅτινα, ἅττα
	Acc.	οὕστινας	ἅστινας	ἅτινα, ἅττα
	Gen.	ὧντινων, ὅτων	ὧντινων, ὅτων	ὧντινων, ὅτων
	Dat.	οἷστισι(ν), ὅτοις	αἷστισι(ν)	οἷστισι(ν), ὅτοις

The neuter singular ὅτι is sometimes printed ὅ τι in modern texts to avoid confusion with the conjunction ὅτι *that, because*. This distinction is not employed in this book; the context should show which is being used.

2 The indirect interrogative ὅστις is also used as an **indefinite relative** with the meaning *whoever*; ὅστις γαμεῖ πονηράν, μῶρός ἐστιν *whoever marries an evil woman is stupid*. The other indirect interrogatives are similarly used (ὅπου *wherever*, etc). For ὅπως, which has additional meanings, see the **Vocabulary**.

3 Just as the interrogative τίς becomes, with a change in accentuation, the indefinite τις (10.1/1), so the other direct interrogatives can be converted to indefinite pronouns and adverbs. Very common are που *somewhere*, ποτέ *at some time, once*, πως *somehow* (all enclitic).

10.1/3 First and third declension adjectives

The masculine and neuter of adjectives in this category belong to the third declension, but their feminine to the first. There are two types:

(a) Stems in υ

In this large class the nom. s. ends in -ύς, -εῖα, -ύ (all adjectives in υ are accented in the same way). ἡδύς *sweet* is declined:

	SINGULAR			PLURAL		
	M.	F.	N.	M.	F.	N.
Nom.	ἡδύς	ἡδεῖα	ἡδύ	ἡδεῖς	ἡδεῖαι	ἡδέα
Voc.	ἡδύ	ἡδεῖα	ἡδύ	ἡδεῖς	ἡδεῖαι	ἡδέα
Acc.	ἡδύν	ἡδεῖαν	ἡδύ	ἡδεῖς	ἡδείᾱς	ἡδέα
Gen.	ἡδέος	ἡδείᾱς	ἡδέος	ἡδέων	ἡδειῶν	ἡδέων
Dat.	ἡδεῖ	ἡδείᾳ	ἡδεῖ	ἡδέσι(ν)	ἡδείαις	ἡδέσι(ν)

(b) Stems in ντ

This class contains only a few adjectives but very many participles (12.1/1). The ντ of the stem is lost in all feminine forms and in the masculine and neuter dat. pl. (cf. γίγᾱς 5.1/1*b*). πᾶς *all* is declined:

	SINGULAR			PLURAL		
	M.	F.	N.	M.	F.	N.
N.V.	πᾶς	πᾶσα	πᾶν	πάντες	πᾶσαι	πάντα
Acc.	πάντα	πᾶσαν	πᾶν	πάντας	πάσᾱς	πάντα
Gen.	παντός	πάσης	παντός	πάντων	πᾱσῶν	πάντων
Dat.	παντί	πάσῃ	παντί	πᾶσι(ν)	πάσαις	πᾶσι(ν)

Like πᾶς are declined its emphatic forms ἅπᾱς and σύμπᾱς (which we must also translate by *all*). The only other adjectives in this group end in -εις (gen. -εντος), -εσσα, -εν, e.g. χαρίεις, χαρίεσσα, χαρίεν *graceful*, gen. s. χαρίεντος, χαριέσσης, χαρίεντος, dat. pl. χαρίεσι(ν), χαριέσσαις, χαρίεσι(ν).

Notes

1 In the predicative position πᾶς means *all*: περὶ πάντας τοὺς θεοὺς ἀσεβοῦσιν *they commit impiety with respect to all the gods*. In the attributive position it means *whole*: ἡ πᾶσα Σικελίᾱ *the whole of Sicily*. Without the article it means *every* in the singular, but *all* in the plural: πᾶσα πόλις *every city*; πάντες πολῖται *all citizens*.

2 μέλᾱς, μέλαινα, μέλαν *black* has a stem in ν (not ντ); gen. s. μέλανος, μελαίνης, μέλανος; dat. pl. μέλασι(ν), μελαίναις, μέλασι(ν). Exactly similar is τάλᾱς *miserable*.

10.1/4 Third declension adjectives

These adjectives are declined wholly within the third declension and fall into two groups. In both, the masculine and feminine have the same form.

(a) Stems in ον

These are declined like δαίμων (6.1/1*a*), except that the nom. voc. and acc. neuter ends in -ον in the singular and -ονα in the plural. An example is ἄφρων *senseless*:

	SINGULAR		PLURAL	
	M. & F.	N.	M. & F.	N.
Nom.	ἄφρων	ἄφρον	ἄφρον-ες	ἄφρον-α
Voc.	ἄφρον	ἄφρον	ἄφρον-ες	ἄφρον-α
Acc.	ἄφρον-α	ἄφρον	ἄφρον-ας	ἄφρον-α
Gen.	ἄφρον-ος	ἄφρον-ος	ἀφρόν-ων	ἀφρόν-ων
Dat.	ἄφρον-ι	ἄφρον-ι	ἄφρο-σι(ν)	ἄφρο-σι(ν)

Comparative adjectives in -ων (17.1/2*b*) are similarly declined.

(b) Stems in ες

These belong to the same type as neuter nouns in ες (6.1/1*c*). This is most obvious in the genitive and dative, where we find similar endings. ἀληθής *true* (stem ἀληθες-) is declined:

	SINGULAR		PLURAL	
	M. & F.	N.	M. & F.	N.
Nom.	ἀληθής	ἀληθές	ἀληθεῖς	ἀληθῆ
Voc.	ἀληθές	ἀληθές	ἀληθεῖς	ἀληθῆ
Acc.	ἀληθῆ	ἀληθές	ἀληθεῖς	ἀληθῆ
Gen.	ἀληθοῦς	ἀληθοῦς	ἀληθῶν	ἀληθῶν
Dat.	ἀληθεῖ	ἀληθεῖ	ἀληθέσι(ν)	ἀληθέσι(ν)

ἀληθῆ, ἀληθεῖς are contractions of ἀληθέ(σ)α, ἀληθέ(σ)ες. ἀληθεῖς as acc. pl. (m. and f.) is irregular; we would have expected ἀληθής

(< -ε(σ)ας). The n. pl. nom. voc. and acc. ἀληθῆ are only an apparent exception to the rule given at 3.1/1 (cf. γένος: pl. γένη < γένεσ-α, 6.1/1c).

The few adjectives with other stems are mostly compounds whose second element is a third declension noun, e.g. εὔχαρις (εὖ + χάρις) *charming*, stem εὐχαριτ-; εὔελπις (εὖ + ἐλπίς) *hopeful*, stem εὐελπιδ-.

Insight

Greek has a recorded history of over three thousand years and the modern language still has grammatical features and vocabulary that were part of its ancient form (cf. Unit 1). There are, however, many words that have been taken into the language as a result of immigration and invasion. These borrowings come from Latin, Italian, Albanian, Turkish and other sources. Among the more curious are σπίτι the modern Greek word for *house* that replaced the ancient οἰκία, and λουκάνικο, the normal word in modern Greek for *sausage*. Σπίτι comes from the Latin **hospitium**, whose original meaning *hospitality* developed into *a place in which to stay*; λουκάνικο is from the Latin **lūcānica,** a sausage from Lucania, a region in southern Italy where a popular form of sausage originated. Such Latin words were introduced as a result of migration from Italy to Greece early in the Christian era.

10.2 Greek reading

Starting with this unit no separate vocabularies will be given and you should look up all unfamiliar words in the vocabulary at the end of the book.

1# παχεῖα γαστὴρ λεπτὸν οὐ τίκτει νόον.

2# ὡς ἡδὺ τὴν θάλατταν ἀπὸ τῆς γῆς ὁρᾶν.

3# ὁ χρόνος ἅπαντα τοῖσιν ὕστερον φράσει.

4 ἡ εὐδαιμονία ἐστὶν ἐνέργειά τις τῆς ψυχῆς.

5 ὦ Μένανδρε καὶ βίε, πότερος ἄρ᾽ ὑμῶν πότερον ἀπεμιμήσατο;

6# τίς δ᾽ οἶδεν (*knows*) εἰ τὸ ζῆν μέν ἐστι κατθανεῖν,
τὸ κατθανεῖν δὲ ζῆν κάτω νομίζεται;

7 ὁ βίος βραχύς, ἡ δὲ τέχνη μακρή, ὁ δὲ καιρὸς ὀξύς, ἡ δὲ πεῖρα
σφαλερή, ἡ δὲ κρίσις χαλεπή.

8 σύντομος ἡ πονηρία, βραδεῖα ἡ ἀρετή.

9 ὅπου εὖ πράττει τις, ἐνταῦθα πατρίς.

10# ὅστις δὲ θνητῶν βούλεται δυσώνυμον
εἰς γῆρας ἐλθεῖν, οὐ λογίζεται καλῶς·
μακρὸς γὰρ αἰὼν μυρίους τίκτει πόνους·

11# ὡς ἡδὺ δούλοις δεσπότας χρηστοὺς λαβεῖν
καὶ δεσπόταισι δοῦλον εὐμενῆ δόμοις.

12# ἅπαντ᾽ ἐπαχθῆ πλὴν θεοῖσι κοιρανεῖν·
ἐλεύθερος γὰρ οὔτις ἐστὶ πλὴν Διός.

13 οἱ ἀμαθεῖς ὥσπερ ἐν πελάγει καὶ νυκτὶ φέρονται ἐν τῷ βίῳ.

14 ἡ γυνὴ ἔφη ὅτι αὐτάρκης κόσμος μοι ἡ τοῦ ἀνδρὸς ἀρετή.

15 ὅπου τις ἀλγεῖ, κεῖσε καὶ τὸν νοῦν ἔχει.

16 **Other proverbs**
(*i*) μισῶ μνήμονα συμπότην. (*ii*) δυσμενὴς ὁ τῶν γειτόνων
ὀφθαλμός. (*iii*) τὸν ἀτυχῆ καὶ πρόβατον δάκνει. (*iv*) ἀνὴρ ἄτεχνος
τοῖς πᾶσίν ἐστι δοῦλος. (*v*) γλυκὺς ἀπείρῳ πόλεμος. (*vi*) χρόνῳ τὰ
πάντα κρίνεται. (*vii*) ἐν νυκτὶ λαμπρός, ἐν φάει δ᾽ ἀνωφελής. (*viii*)
ἀλλήλας νίπτουσι χεῖρες. (*ix*) ὑπὸ παντὶ λίθῳ σκόρπιος καθεύδει.
(*x*) ῥᾴδια πάντα θεῷ. (*xi*) ἅπας ἐχῖνος τραχύς. (*xii*) ὃν ἡ τύχη
μέλανα γράψει τοῦτον ὁ πᾶς χρόνος οὐ δύναται λευκάναι.

17 **Stories about Diogenes**
The Greeks were fond of short, pithy anecdotes ending in a
bon mot. Diogenes, the philosopher of the fourth century BC

whose eccentric lifestyle made him a tourist attraction in the Athens of his day, is the subject of a large collection.

(*i*) ὁ Διογένης ᾔτει ποτὲ ἀνδρίαντα· ἐρωτηθεὶς (*having been asked*) δὲ διὰ τί τοῦτο ποιεῖ, μελετῶ, εἶπεν, ἀποτυγχάνειν.

(*ii*) ἐρωτηθεὶς ποῖον οἶνον ἡδέως πίνει, ἔφη, τὸν ἀλλότριον.

(*iii*) φιλάργυρον ᾔτει· ὅτε δὲ ἐβράδυνεν, ὁ Διογένης, ἄνθρωπε, εἶπεν, εἰς τροφήν σε αἰτῶ, οὐκ εἰς ταφήν.

(*iv*) ἐρωτηθεὶς πόθεν ἐστίν, κοσμοπολίτης, ἔφη.

(*v*) ὅτε εἶπέ τις κακὸν εἶναι τὸ ζῆν, οὐ τὸ ζῆν, ἔφη, ἀλλὰ τὸ κακῶς ζῆν.

Notes

1 The uncontracted νόον (= νοῦν, 6.1/2) shows that this is Ionic Greek (1.3).

3 τοῖσιν = τοῖς (3.1/1 note 3).

5 Menander was famous for his faithful representation of everyday life; πότερος ἄρ᾽ lit. *which of you two then ...?* (ἄρ᾽ = ἄρα an inferential particle which must be distinguished from ἆρα, 10.1/2*a*).

6 κατθανεῖν shortened form of καταθανεῖν (aor. inf. act. of καταθνήσκειν). *l.*2 δέ is postponed for metrical reasons (prose order would be τὸ δὲ κατθανεῖν); κάτω *below* i.e. in Hades.

7 The well-known aphorism of Hippocrates, the famous doctor of the 5th century BC. He wrote in Ionic Greek and the η of μακρή and σφαλερή would be ᾱ in Attic. By τέχνη Hippocrates meant the art of medicine.

9 ὅπου here (and in 15 below) is the relative adverb *where,* not the indirect interrogative.

10 Take δυσώνυμον with γῆρας *old age* (acc. s., 13.1/1*b*(iii)).

11 *l.*2 λαβεῖν is to be understood; δεσπόταισι has the longer form of the dat. pl. ending (3.1/1 note 3; cf. θεοῖσι in the next sentence); δόμοις dat. without preposition to express *place where* (23.1/2*n*) – translate by a singular.

12 κοιρανεῖν here takes the dative, not the genitive as is normal after verbs of ruling (13.1/2*a*); Διός gen. of Ζεύς (11.1/4)

14 For ὅτι introducing a **direct** statement see 8.1/3*b* note 2.

16 (*iv*) τοῖς πᾶσιν the article is added for emphasis (as also in (*vi*)). (*vi*) χρόνῳ *by time* dat. of instrument (11.1/2); τὰ πάντα cf. (*iv*) above. (*vii*) A phrase of abuse, not a sentence (cf. 6.2.7 (*iv*)). (*xii*) Although ὅν comes first, its antecedent is τοῦτον; δύναται *is able* from δύναμαι (on verbs with -αμαι instead of -ομαι see 19.1/3*b*).

17 (*i*) ᾔτει (< αἰτέω) *was begging [alms from]* + acc.; ποιεῖ on the tense see 10.1/2*b* (this also applies to πίνει (*ii*) and ἐστίν (*iv*)). (*ii*) with τὸν ἀλλότριον supply ἡδέως πίνω. (*iii*) ᾔτει see (*i*); εἰς *with regard to*, i.e. *for*.

Main points

• Both τίς (interrogative) and τις (indefinite) can be pronouns or adjectives

• Direct questions are normally introduced by a question word (as πόθεν *when?*) or by ἆρα, ἆρ᾽ οὐ, μῶν/μή as appropriate

• Interrogative pronouns, adjectives, etc. have a direct (τίς etc.) and an indirect (ὅστις etc.) form

• Indirect questions are introduced by the direct or indirect interrogative or by εἰ

• First and third declension adjectives decline their feminine form in the first declension but their masculine and neuter in the third

• Third declension adjectives have the same forms for the masculine and feminine but differ in the n. v. a. for the neuter; the three genders are declined wholly in the third declension

10.3 Extra reading

From this point extra reading will be included with certain units. Because it will consist of longer passages it will necessarily be somewhat harder than the other exercises. If you do not feel confident enough to tackle it when working your way through the book for the first time, it may conveniently be left until later.

The wisdom of Socrates

Socrates (469–399 BC) was to philosophy what Herodotus was to history. Previous thinkers had speculated on the physical nature of the world, but Socrates was the first to concern himself with moral and ethical problems. His uncompromising pursuit of truth made him so unpopular with his fellow citizens at Athens that, when he was brought to trial on a trumped-up charge of corrupting the young, he was convicted and executed. The following is from his defence in court, as reported by his pupil Plato; here Socrates explains the origin of his reputation (ὄνομα) for exceptional wisdom, which, he claims, is unjustified.

ἐγὼ γάρ, ὦ ἄνδρες Ἀθηναῖοι, δι᾽ οὐδὲν ἄλλ᾽ ἢ διὰ σοφίαν τινὰ τοῦτο τὸ ὄνομα ἔχω. ποίαν δὴ σοφίαν ταύτην; ἥπερ ἐστὶν ἴσως ἀνθρωπίνη σοφία· τῷ ὄντι γὰρ κινδυνεύω ταύτην εἶναι σοφός. οὗτοι δέ, οὓς ἄρτι ἔλεγον, δαιμονίαν τινὰ σοφίαν σοφοί εἰσιν, ἣν οὐκ ἔχω διηγεῖσθαι· οὐ γὰρ δὴ ἔγωγε αὐτὴν ἐπίσταμαι, ἀλλ᾽ ὅστις φησί, ψεύδεταί τε καὶ ἐπὶ διαβολῇ 5
τῇ ἐμῇ λέγει. καὶ ἐλπίζω ὑμᾶς, ὦ ἄνδρες Ἀθηναῖοι, μὴ θορυβήσειν μοι, μηδ᾽ εἰ δοκῶ τι ὑμῖν μέγα λέγειν· οὐ γὰρ ἐμὸν ἐρῶ τὸν λόγον ὃν λέγω, ἀλλ᾽ εἰς ἀξιόπιστόν τινα ἀνοίσω. τῆς γὰρ ἐμῆς, εἰ δή τίς ἐστι σοφία καὶ οἵα, μάρτυρα ὑμῖν παρέξομαι τὸν θεὸν τὸν ἐν Δελφοῖς. γνώριμος γάρ που ὑμῖν ἦν Χαιρεφῶν. οὗτος ἐμός τε ἑταῖρος ἦν ἐκ νέου καὶ ὑμῶν 10
τῷ πλήθει. καὶ εὔγνωστον ὑμῖν ἐστιν οἷος ἦν Χαιρεφῶν, ὡς παντάπασι σφοδρός. καὶ δή ποτε καὶ εἰς Δελφοὺς ἦλθε καὶ ἐτόλμησε μαντεύεσθαι, εἴ τίς ἐστι σοφώτερος ἢ (wiser than) ἐγώ. ἀνεῖλεν οὖν ἡ Πυθία οὐδένα σοφώτερον εἶναι.

Notes

l.1 ἀλλ᾽ = ἄλλο; ἤ *than*. *l*.2 ποίαν etc. supply λέγω; ἥπερ *[the one] which*, the suffix περ is added to the relative pronoun for emphasis. *l*.3 τῷ ὄντι *in reality, really* (12.1/1 note 1); ταύτην (*sc.* τὴν σοφίαν) accusative of respect (20.1/5) with σοφός, lit. *wise in respect of this [wisdom]*, i.e. *possessed of this wisdom* – the same construction occurs with σοφοί (*l*.4). *ll*.4f. οὐκ ἔχω *I am not able*; ἐπίσταμαι has -αμαι instead of -ομαι (19.1/3*b*); φησί *sc. that this is so*; ἐπί *with a view to* i.e *to arouse*; διαβολῇ τῇ ἐμῇ not *my prejudice* but *prejudice against me*; this use of the possessive adjective is the same as that of the objective genitive (23.1/1*c*). *l*.6 μή is used after ἐλπίζω (8.1/3*a* note 5) and consequently we also have μηδ᾽(έ) (7.1/6*c*), which here means *not even*, but, as we would not normally repeat the negative in such a construction in English, simply translate by *even*; θορυβήσειν μοι lit. *to be going to make a noise for me* i.e. *to be going to interrupt me*. *l*.7 ἐμόν predicative with τὸν λόγον, lit. *not [as] mine shall I tell the story which I am telling*. *ll*.8f. ἀνοίσω < ἀναφέρω; τῆς ... ἐμῆς (*sc.* σοφίας) with μάρτυρα *a witness of my [wisdom]*; εἰ ... οἵα two indirect questions to be taken with μάρτυρα *[as to] whether it is some sort of* (τις) *wisdom and what sort of [wisdom it is]* (the indefinite τις has an acute accent because of the following ἐστιν (see **Appendix** 8, *d*(ix)); it is **not** the interrogative τίς); τὸν θεόν i.e. Apollo. *ll*.10ff. που *I suppose, think*, the original meaning, which is also common, is *somewhere* (10.1/2*b* note 3); τε ... καί (*both ... and* but trans. simply by *and*) joins ἐμός and ὑμῶν; ἐκ νέου lit. *from [being] young*, i.e. *from youth*; ὑμῶν τῷ πλήθει lit. *to the people of you*, i.e. *to the [Athenian] democracy* (to be taken with ἑταῖρος, which may be here translated by one word and by another word with ἐμός); ὡς ... σφοδρός *how [he was] completely impetuous* Chaerephon had died before the trial (hence ἦν in the previous clause). *l*.12 καὶ δή *and indeed, and as a matter of fact*; ποτε καί ... *once even/actually* (he actually went to Delphi once). *l*.13 ἀνεῖλεν < ἀναιρέω.

Unit 11

11.1 Grammar

11.1/1 Root aorist, aorist passive and future passive

A few -ω verbs form their aorist active by adding endings directly to their basic stem or root without a suffix (such as σ in the weak aorist – 4.1/1) or a link vowel (such as ο/ε of the strong aorist endings – 7.1/1). The roots of all such verbs end in the long vowels ᾱ, η, ῡ or ω, and the endings applied to form the root aorist are -ν, -ς, -, -μεν, -τε, -σαν. As an example we may take the aorist of βαίνω go (root βη-).

	SINGULAR	PLURAL
1	ἔβην *I went*	ἔβημεν
2	ἔβης	ἔβητε
3	ἔβη	ἔβησαν
INFINITIVE	βῆναι	

Some other common verbs with root aorists are given below. Note that the form of the root cannot be predicted from the present stem.

	PRESENT STEM	ROOT	ROOT AORIST
(ἀπο) διδράσκω[1] *run away*	διδρασκ-	δρᾱ-	-έδρᾱν
φύω *cause to grow, produce*	φυ-	φῡ-	ἔφῡν
γιγνώσκω *get to know*	γιγνωσκ-	γνω-	ἔγνων
βιόω *live*	βιο-	βιω-	ἐβίων

φύω also has a regularly formed weak aorist active: ἔφῡσα. In such cases where a verb has two sets of aorist active forms, the root aorist is intransitive: ἔφῡν (*I grew* intr.); and the weak aorist transitive: ἔφῡσα (*I caused to grow, I produced*); cf. καταδύω

---

[1] This verb occurs only in compounds.

cause to sink; κατέδῡσα *I caused to sink*, κατέδῡν *I sank.*[2]
Examples are:

αἱ τρίχες ἔρρεον ἃς πρὶν ἔφῡσε τὸ φάρμακον. *the hairs fell out which the drug previously made grow.*
ἐλάᾱ ἐντὸς τῆς αὐλῆς ἔφῡ *an olive tree grew inside the courtyard.*

Another important verb with two aorists and a similar distinction between them is ἵστημι (19.1/1).

Only a few verbs, however, have a root aorist with an active meaning. Elsewhere the root aorist has developed a passive meaning and is normally classified as an aorist passive. An example is πνῑ́γω *strangle, choke* (tr.), which, like φύω, has a weak aorist ἔπνῑξα *I strangled, choked* (tr., e.g. ἐχθὲς ἔπνῑξα τὸν τοῦ γείτονος κύνα *yesterday I choked the neighbour's dog*) and what is really a root aorist ἐπνίγην *I choked* (intr., e.g. ὁ σὸς κύων, ἔφην, ἐπνίγη ἐν τῷ τοῦ πυρὸς καπνῷ 'Your dog', I said, 'choked in the smoke of the fire'). The original contrast between the transitive and intransitive aorists in verbs of this sort developed into one of active/passive, and forms such as ἐπνίγην were used in contexts where they must be interpreted as passive (ὁ ἐμὸς κύων, ἔφη, οὐκ ἐπνίγη καπνῷ 'My dog', he said, 'was not choked by smoke' – on this use of the dative see 11.1/2 below). Consequently most root aorists in -ην, (but not in -ᾱν, ῡν, or, with one exception, -ων) which could be interpreted as passive came to be so regarded and classified. This could not happen with intransitive verbs, such as βαίνω, whose meaning precludes any passive sense.

The total number of aorist passives in -ην is also small, but they formed the model for the vast majority of transitive verbs, where a special aorist passive stem was created by attaching the suffix θη to the root.[3] To this were added the same endings as for the root aorist. For this reason **all** aorist passive endings are of the **active** type; the aorist passive **never** has the passive endings of the other historic tenses (-μην, -σο, -το etc. 4.1/1 note 1).

---

[2] In these verbs the 3rd plural of the root aorist and of the weak aorist active are identical: ἔφῡσαν (from ἔφυ<σαν or ἔφυσ<αν).

[3] The η of the suffix undergoes change in some forms other than the indicative, e.g. the aor. pass. pple. λυθείς (12.1/1).

The aorist passive indicative (and corresponding infinitive) of λύω will be found in **Appendix 1**. This tense is included in the principal parts of verbs which show some irregularity (7.1/1 note 3) as the form it takes is not always predictable. We may, however, note:

(a) Most verbs whose present stem ends in a vowel or diphthong form their aorist passive stem regularly. In a few cases the suffix is enlarged to σθη on the analogy of dental stems (see below), e.g. ἠκούσθην *I was heard* (ἀκούω); ἐκελεύσθην *I was ordered* (κελεύω). In regular contracted verbs the final vowel of the present stem is lengthened in the same way as in the aorist active (5.1/2 note 2), e.g. ἐτῑμήθην (τῑμάω); ἐποιήθην (ποιέω); ἐδηλώθην (δηλόω).

(b) In palatal and labial stems (6.1/4) final κ and γ become χ, final π and β become φ (i.e. they are assimilated to the following θ by becoming aspirates), e.g. ἐφυλάχθην *I was guarded* (φυλάττω, stem φυλακ-); ἐπέμφθην *I was sent* (πέμπω, stem πεμπ-). In dental stems the final consonant becomes σ, e.g. ἐπείσθην *I was persuaded* (πείθω, stem πειθ-).

Occasionally (and unpredictably) a verb has a root aorist passive, e.g. ἐπνίγην (see above); ἐκόπην *I was cut* (κόπτω), sometimes both, e.g. ἐβλάβην, ἐβλάφθην *I was hurt* (βλάπτω; there is no difference in meaning).

The stem of the **future passive** is that of the aorist passive with an added σ (λυθησ-, τῑμηθησ-, κοπησ-). The endings are those of the present middle and passive: λυθήσομαι *I shall be loosened*; τῑμηθήσομαι *I shall be honoured*; κοπήσομαι *I shall be cut*. For the full future passive of λύω see **Appendix 1**.

Note

As mentioned in 8.1/2 some deponents are classified as **passive** because their aorist is passive, not middle, in form (most, however, have a **middle future**). Among the most common passive deponents are:

βούλομαι *wish*; fut. βουλήσομαι; aor. ἐβουλήθην
δύναμαι *be able*; fut. δυνήσομαι; aor. ἐδυνήθην
πορεύομαι *march*; fut. πορεύσομαι; aor. ἐπορεύθην

In the future and aorist of the first two η is inserted. δύναμαι has -αμαι, -ασαι, -αται etc., not -ομαι -ῃ, -εται etc. in the present (see 19.1/3*b*)

The difference between middle and passive deponents is simply one of **form**; both are active in **meaning**.

11.1/2 Agent and instrument

In English we can say *the policeman was hit by a demonstrator* and *the policeman was hit by a placard* but Greek makes a distinction between agent (*demonstrator*) and instrument (*placard*). An agent is a living being and agency is normally expressed by ὑπό with the genitive. An instrument is nearly always inanimate and the construction used for it is the dative without a preposition (examples have already occurred at 7.2.13 *l*.9, 9.2.13 *l*.2, 10.2.16(*vi*); in English we use either *by* or *with*: Ἀσπασίᾱ με τύπτει μήλοις *Aspasia is hitting me with apples* (instrument); ἡ Τροίᾱ ὑπὸ τῶν Ἑλλήνων ἐπορθήθη *Troy was sacked by the Greeks* (agent).

11.1/3 -ω verbs with stems in λ, μ, ν, ρ

Most verbs with these stems originally formed their present with a *y* suffix (6.1/4*b*). This combined with a preceding λ to give λλ, but disappeared after μ, ν, ρ, although, by way of compensation, a preceding ε, ι, υ was lengthened and a preceding α became αι. The future of these verbs is of the contracted type (-ῶ < -έω; 5.1/2 note 3); where a *y* suffix has been used in the present the future reverts to the original stem. In the weak aorist (which occurs in all common verbs of this group, except βάλλω *throw*) the sigma is dropped and the preceding vowel lengthened (note that here we have α > η except after vowels and ρ, where α becomes ᾱ; also, ε becomes ει). The following table shows the different possibilities:

PRESENT			FUTURE	AORIST
βάλλω	*throw*	(< βάλ-*y* ω)	βαλῶ	ἔβαλον
στέλλω	*send*	(< στέλ-*y* ω)	στελῶ	ἔστειλα
νέμω	*apportion*	(no *y* suffix)	νεμῶ	ἔνειμα
μένω	*wait*	(no *y* suffix)	μενῶ	ἔμεινα
σημαίνω	*indicate*	(< σημάν-*y* ω)	σημανῶ	ἐσήμηνα
μιαίνω	*stain*	(< μιάν-*y* ω)	μιανῶ	ἐμίᾱνα

PRESENT			FUTURE	AORIST
αἰσχύνω	*dishonour*	(< αἰσχύν-y ω)	αἰσχυνῶ	ἤσχῡνα
αἴρω	*lift*	(< ἄρ-y ω)	ἀρῶ	ἦρα
οἰκτίρω	*pity*	(< οἰκτίρ-y ω)	οἰκτιρῶ	ᾤκτῑρα

For the principal parts of ἐλαύνω *drive* and φέρω *carry*, which are irregular, see **Principal parts of verbs.**

The aorist passive of verbs in -αίνω and -ύνω ends in -άνθην and -ύνθην, e.g. ἐσημάνθην (σημαίνω); ᾐσχύνθην (αἰσχύνω). Likewise, we have ἤρθην from αἴρω, but the other verbs listed above which have an aorist passive are irregular.

11.1/4 Third declension nouns – stems in ευ, αυ, ου

A large number of masculine nouns end in -εύς (always so accented). Most common nouns of this type involve male occupations, e.g. ἱερεύς *priest*, ἱππεύς *horseman*. The names of some Homeric heroes are also of this type, as Ὀδυσσεύς, Ἀχιλλεύς. The genitive and dative singular endings are the same as for stems in ι (8.1/4).

The only examples of stems in αυ and ου are those given below:

	βασιλεύς (m) *king*	ναῦς (f) *ship*	γραῦς (f) *old woman*	βοῦς (m or f) *ox, cow*
SINGULAR				
Nom.	βασιλεύ-ς	ναῦ-ς	γραῦ-ς	βοῦ-ς
Voc.	βασιλεῦ	ναῦ	γραῦ	βοῦ
Acc.	βασιλέ-ᾱ	ναῦ-ν	γραῦ-ν	βοῦ-ν
Gen.	βασιλέ-ως	νε-ώς	γρᾱ-ός	βο-ός
Dat.	βασιλεῖ	νη-ΐ	γρᾱ-ΐ	βο-ΐ
PLURAL				
N.V.	βασιλῆς (or -εῖς)	νῆ-ες	γρᾶ-ες	βόες
Acc.	βασιλέ-ᾱς	ναῦς	γραῦς	βοῦς
Gen.	βασιλέ-ων	νε-ῶν	γρᾱ-ῶν	βο-ῶν
Dat.	βασιλεῦ-σι(ν)	ναυ-σί(ν)	γραυ-σί(ν)	βου-σί(ν)

Note also Ζεύς *Zeus*, which is irregular: voc. Ζεῦ, acc. Δία, gen. Διός, dat. Διΐ (in poetry there is an alternative stem, Ζην-, for the oblique cases, giving Ζῆνα, Ζηνός, Ζηνί).

11.1/5 Crasis

Crasis (κρᾶσις *mixing, blending*) is the contraction of a vowel or diphthong at the end of one word with a vowel or diphthong at the beginning of the following word. It is found chiefly in poetry but is not uncommon in the orators. Only a very small number of words occur as the first element of crasis, viz the relevant parts of the definite article, καί and a few others. Examples we have already met are κἄν (= καὶ ἐν 5.2.17) and αὑτός (= ὁ αὐτός), ταὐτοῦ etc. (9.1/3*b*). In all such cases elision (2.1/6*b*), even if theoretically possible, is never used in preference to crasis. The rules for crasis are:

(*a*) The first word loses its accent, if any.

(*b*) A vowel (always long) or diphthong resulting from crasis is marked with ᾽ (technically called **coronis** but identical in form with a smooth breathing), e.g. τοὔνομα (τὸ ὄνομα). When the second word begins with a rough breathing, a consonant preceding it in crasis (always κ or τ) is aspirated, e.g. θοἰμάτιον (τὸ ἱμάτιον). When, however, the first word is simply an aspirated vowel or diphthong (ὁ, οἱ etc.), the rough breathing is kept in crasis, e.g. οὑν (ὁ ἐν).

(*c*) The rules that apply for internal contraction in verbs (5.1/2) are generally followed, as in the above examples. There are, however, some combinations which do not occur in verbs, as well as some exceptions. We should note:

(i) When the definite article is combined with a word beginning with α, this α is always kept, e.g. ἅνθρωπος (ὁ ἄνθρωπος), αὑτός (ὁ αὐτός, 9.1/3*b*).

(ii) The αι of καί is dropped in certain combinations, e.g. κοὐ (καὶ οὐ), χἠ (καὶ ἡ).

....

Insight

When the police at Canberra, Australia's capital city, acquired a new launch to chase wrongdoers on the city's extensive lake they rang the local Greek professor for a suitable name. The quick-witted professor immediately suggested PLATYPUS. The police liked the suggestion as the name of this unique Australian animal, which lives in water, would give a certain local colour and be more user-friendly than NEMESIS (Νέμεσις *Retribution*), which had been used for police boats in the past. However, the professor was misleading them; πλατύπους is a compound of the two words πλατύς *wide, flat* and πούς *foot* and so means *flatfoot*, a rather offensive slang term for an officer of the law.

Πλατύς is declined like ἡδύς (10.1/4); for πούς see 5.1/1*a*.

11.2 Greek reading

1 ἡ τυραννὶς ἀδικίας μήτηρ ἔφυ.

2 ἀεὶ εὖ πίπτουσιν οἱ Διὸς κύβοι.

3# ἔστι τι κἂν κακοῖσιν ἡδονῆς μέτρον.

4# κοὐκ ἐμὸς ὁ μῦθος, ἀλλ᾽ ἐμῆς μητρὸς πάρα,
ὡς οὐρανός τε γαῖά τ᾽ ἦν μορφὴ μία·
ἐπεὶ δ᾽ ἐχωρίσθησαν ἀλλήλων δίχα
τίκτουσι πάντα κἀνέδωκαν (*sent up*) εἰς φάος
δένδρη, πετεινά, θῆρας, οὕς θ᾽ ἅλμη τρέφει
γένος τε θνητῶν.

5

5# κακὸν τὸ κεύθειν κοὐ πρὸς ἀνδρὸς εὐγενοῦς.

6 εἶπέ τις τῷ Σωκράτει, θάνατον σοῦ κατέγνωσαν οἱ Ἀθηναῖοι, ὁ δὲ εἶπεν, κἀκείνων ἡ φύσις (*sc.* θάνατον καταγιγνώσκει).

7 ἄμαξα τὸν βοῦν ἕλκει.

8 Advanced futility
(*i*) γραῦς χορεύει. (*ii*) τυφλῷ κάτοπτρον χαρίζῃ. (*iii*) ἄνεμον δικτύῳ θηρᾷς. (*iv*) λίθοις τὸν ἥλιον βάλλεις. (*v*) καλεῖ χελώνη τοὺς βοῦς βραδύποδας. (*vi*) σπόγγῳ πάτταλον κρούεις. (*vii*) πάτταλον ἐξέκρουσας παττάλῳ. (*viii*) τὴν ἀμίδα σανδάλῳ ἐπιφράττεις. (*ix*) οἴνῳ οἶνον ἐξελαύνεις.(*x*) αὐτὸς τὴν σαυτοῦ θύραν κρούεις λίθῳ.

9# πᾶσιν γὰρ ἀνθρώποισιν, οὐχ ἡμῖν μόνον,
ἢ καὶ παραυτίκ᾽ ἢ χρόνῳ δαίμων βίον
ἔσφηλε, κοὐδεὶς διὰ τέλους εὐδαιμονεῖ.

10# Odysseus explains to Neoptolemus that they must obtain the
bow of Philoctetes if Troy is to be captured.

τούτων γὰρ οὐδὲν ἀλγυνεῖ μ᾽ · εἰ δ᾽ ἐργάσῃ
μὴ ταῦτα, λύπην πᾶσιν Ἀργείοις βαλεῖς.
εἰ γὰρ τὰ τοῦδε τόξα μὴ ληφθήσεται,
οὐκ ἔστι (= ἔξεστι) πέρσαι σοι τὸ Δαρδάνου πέδον.

11 In 525 BC Egypt was conquered and permanently occupied
by the Persians, whose power in the eastern Mediterranean
continued to increase until their unsuccessful invasion of Greece
(480–479 BC). The subsequent rise of Athens encouraged the
Athenians to invade Egypt (c.461 BC), with disastrous results,
as Thucydides tells us in the introduction to his history.

οὕτω μὲν τὰ τῶν Ἑλλήνων πράγματα ἐφθάρη· καὶ ὀλίγοι ἀπὸ
πολλῶν διὰ τῆς Λιβύης ἐς Κυρήνην ἐπορεύθησαν καὶ ἐσώθησαν,
οἱ δὲ πλεῖστοι ἀπέθανον. Αἴγυπτος δὲ πάλιν ὑπὸ βασιλέα
ἐγένετο πλὴν Ἀμυρταίου τοῦ ἐν τοῖς ἕλεσι βασιλέως· τοῦτον
δὲ διὰ μέγεθός τε τοῦ ἕλους οὐκ ἐδύναντο ἑλεῖν καὶ ἅμα 5
σφόδρα μάχιμοί εἰσιν οἱ ἕλειοι. Ἰνάρως δὲ ὁ Λιβύων βασιλεύς,
ὃς τὰ πάντα ἔπραξε περὶ τῆς Αἰγύπτου, προδοσίᾳ ἐλήφθη καὶ
ἀνεσταυρώθη. ἐκ δὲ τῶν Ἀθηνῶν καὶ τῆς ἄλλης ξυμμαχίδος
πεντήκοντα τριήρεις διάδοχοι ἔπλευσαν ἐς Αἴγυπτον καὶ ἔσχον
κατὰ τὸ Μενδήσιον κέρας. ἀλλ᾽ αὐτοῖς ἔκ τε γῆς ἐπέπεσον πεζοὶ 10
καὶ ἐκ θαλάσσης Φοινίκων ναυτικὸν καὶ διέφθειραν τὰς πολλὰς
τῶν νεῶν. τὰ οὖν κατὰ τὴν μεγάλην στρατείαν Ἀθηναίων καὶ τῶν
ξυμμάχων ἐς Αἴγυπτον οὕτως ἐτελεύτησαν.

12 Euxitheos and Herodes were fellow passengers on a voyage to
Thrace. In the process of changing ships at Lesbos, Herodes
disappeared and Euxitheos was subsequently charged with his
murder. His speech of defence was written by Antiphon.

ἐπειδὴ δὲ μετεξέβημεν εἰς τὸ ἕτερον πλοῖον, ἐπίνομεν. καὶ
φανερὸν μέν ἐστιν ὅτι ὁ Ἡρώδης ἐξέβη ἐκ τοῦ πλοίου καὶ οὐκ

εἰσέβη πάλιν· ἐγὼ δὲ τὸ παράπαν οὐκ ἐξέβην ἐκ τοῦ πλοίου
τῆς νυκτὸς ἐκείνης. τῇ δὲ ὑστεραίᾳ, ἐπειδὴ ἀφανὴς ἦν ὁ ἀνήρ,
ἐζητεῖτο οὐδέν τι μᾶλλον ὑπὸ τῶν ἄλλων ἢ καὶ ὑπ' ἐμοῦ· καὶ εἴ 5
τῳ τῶν ἄλλων ἐδόκει δεινὸν εἶναι, καὶ ἐμοὶ ὁμοίως. καὶ εἷς τε
τὴν Μυτιλήνην ἐγὼ αἴτιος ἢ πεμφθῆναι ἄγγελον, καὶ ἐπεὶ ἄλλος
οὐδεὶς ἤθελε βαδίζειν, οὔτε τῶν ἀπὸ τοῦ πλοίου οὔτε τῶν αὐτοῦ
τοῦ Ἡρώδου ἑταίρων, ἐγὼ τὸν ἀκόλουθον τὸν ἐμαυτοῦ πέμπειν
ἕτοιμος ἦ. ἐπειδὴ δὲ ὁ ἀνὴρ οὔτε ἐν τῇ Μυτιλήνῃ ἐφαίνετο οὔτ' 10
ἄλλοθι οὐδαμοῦ, πλοῦς τε ἡμῖν ἐγίγνετο, καὶ τἄλλ' ἀνήγετο
πλοῖα ἅπαντα, ᾠχόμην κἀγώ.

Notes

1 ἔφῡ < φύω (11.1/1) the primary meaning of this root aorist is *was
born* but often, as here, it has the present sense *is*.

2 Διός gen. of Ζεύς (11.1/4).

3 τι with μέτρον; κακοῖσιν = κακοῖς (3.1/1 note 1).

4 *l*.1 κοὐκ = καὶ οὐκ (11.1/5); πάρα some disyllabic prepositions
can, in verse, be placed after the noun they govern, cf. δίχα in
l.3; when they are normally accented on the final syllable (as
with παρά, but not with δίχα), the accent is then thrown back
on to the first syllable. *l*.2 With a double subject (οὐρανός and
γαῖα) the verb sometimes agrees only with the nearer, hence ἦν;
τε ... τ(ε) lit. *both ... and* but simply trans. by *and*. *l*.4 τίκτουσι
vivid present, trans. *brought forth* (τίκτω can be used of either
parent); κἀνέδωκαν = καὶ ἀνέδωκαν (ἔδωκαν is the 3rd pl. aor.
ind. act. of δίδωμι *give*, 18.1/2 note 3). *l*.5 δένδρη acc. pl. of
δένδρον (13.1/1*c*); οὕς an antecedent meaning *creatures* is to be
understood; θ' i.e. τε; after the ε is elided, τ' becomes θ' because
of the rough breathing of ἅλμη.

6 καταγιγνώσκω *condemn* takes the gen. of the person condemned
and the accusative of what he is condemned to (23.1/1*k*(i));
κἀκείνων = καὶ ἐκείνων.

8 (*iv*) λίθοις instrumental dat. (11.1/2); βάλλεις here *pelt*.
(*vii*) ἐξέκρουσας < ἐκκρούω.

9 *l*.1 The datives should be translated by *for*. *l*.2 καί is here adverbial and emphasises the following word but need not be translated; βίον English idiom requires the plural. *l*.3 ἔσφηλε gnomic aorist (see note on 5.2.10); σφάλλω *trip up, cause to fall* (as in wrestling) is here (and often elsewhere) used metaphorically; κοὐδείς = καὶ οὐδείς.

10 The future tense in εἰ clauses (*l*.1 ἐργάσῃ and *l*.3 ληφθήσεται) is to be translated into English by a present; μή (as in *ll*.2 and 3) is the negative used in εἰ clauses (18.1/5) but in *l*.2 it is somewhat unusually placed after the verb it negates (cf. 2.1/6*a*(i)). *l*.3 Translate τὰ τόξα by a singular (the plural is often used for the singular in verse). *l*.4 On ἔστι = ἔξεστι see 21.1/4 note 1.

11 Thucydides uses the non-Attic spelling σσ for ττ (*l*.11 θαλάσσης), the old Attic form ξύν (ξυμ- etc. in compounds) for the normal σύν (*l*.8 ξυμμαχίδος, *l*.13 ξυμμάχων), and the old Attic ἐς for εἰς (*ll*.2, 9, 13). *l*.1 ἐφθάρη < φθείρω. *l*.3 ὑπό lit. *under*, i.e. *under the control of*; βασιλέᾱ at this period the Persian king was a figure of supreme importance and the Greeks referred to him simply as βασιλεύς. *l*.5. τε ... καί join the two reasons why Amyrtaeus could not be captured and in English we would supply *because* after ἅμα. *l*.7. τὰ πάντα see note on 10.2.16(*iv*); ἐλήφθη < λαμβάνω. *ll*.9f. διάδοχοι lit. *[as] relieving* i.e. *as a relieving force*; ἔσχον *put in*; τὸ Μενδήσιον κέρας the north-east arm of the Nile delta. *ll*.10ff. take αὐτοῖς with ἐπέπεσον (< ἐπιπίπτω), lit. *fell upon them*; τὰς πολλάς *the majority of, most of*; τὰ ... κατὰ τὴν ... cf. 5.1/3, lit. *the [things] with respect to the* ...

12 *l*.1 Translate μετεξέβημεν (< μετεκβαίνω) by a pluperfect *had transferred* (16.1/2); ἐπίνομεν *we began to drink* (inceptive imperfect 4.1/1). *l*.3 τὸ παράπαν οὐκ *not* ... *at all*; the adverb παράπαν is converted by τό to a noun equivalent (5.1/3), which functions here as an accusative of respect (20.1/5), lit. *[with respect to] the altogether*. *l*.5 οὐδέν τι μᾶλλον ὑπὸ ... ἢ ... ὑπό lit. *nothing more by* ... *than by* (οὐδέν τι *not at all* is also an accusative of respect). *ll*.6ff. τῳ = τινι (indefinite, 10.1/1); the καί of καὶ εἷς τε joins this sentence to the preceding one; τε is to be taken with the καί before ἐπεί (*l*.7) and the two link ἐγὼ αἴτιος ἦ ... with ἐγὼ ... ἕτοιμος ἦ; τε ... καί literally mean *both ... and* but translate here *not only ... but also* to give the necessary emphasis; πεμφθῆναι ἄγγελον accusative and infinitive (8.1/3*a*) after αἴτιος ἦ. *ll*.8f. οὔτε ... οὔτε continue the preceding negative οὐδείς, lit. *no-one ... neither from ... nor of*, but in English we would say *either ... or* (the rule given at 7.1/6 does not apply because οὔτε ... οὔτε do not negate the verb of this clause; cf. 10.3 *l*.6). *ll*.10ff. ἐπειδή is followed by three clauses with the second joined to the first by τε (*l*.11) and the third to the second by καί (*l*.11); πλοῦς *[the time for] sailing*; ἐγίγνετο lit. *was coming into being*, i.e *was starting*; τἆλλ᾽ = τὰ ἄλλα; κἀγώ = καὶ ἐγώ (11.1/5); ἀνήγετο impf. of ἀνάγομαι.

Main points

- Instead of a strong or weak aorist, a few verbs have a root aorist with the endings -ν, -ς, (no ending), -μεν, -τε, -σαν; these root aorists are active in meaning, e.g. ἔβην *I went* (< βαίνω)

- The aorist passive has active endings, which are the same as those of the root aorist

- The future passive is formed from the stem of the aorist passive

- An agent is expressed by ὑπό + gen., an instrument by the dative without a preposition

- Most verbs in λ, μ, ν, ρ have a suffix in the present tense that hides their true stem

- The declension of nouns in –εύς (as βασιλεύς) differs from that of other third declension nouns

- ναῦς, γραῦς, βοῦς are irregular

- Crasis can occur when καί, the definite article or a few other words are followed by a word beginning with a vowel or diphthong, e.g. καὶ ἐγώ > κἀγώ

Unit 12

12.1 Grammar

12.1/1 Participles

Participles are those parts of verbs which function as adjectives. They have tense (*killing* is present, *going to kill* future) and voice (*killing* is active, *being killed* passive). In Greek there are participles for all three voices in the present, future, and aorist (and also the perfect, 15.1/1) and they use the same stem as the corresponding indicatives (but the augment is dropped in the aorist). For the sake of completeness the following table includes perfect participles, which can be ignored until we treat these in 16.1/4.

ACTIVE
Present   m. λύ-ων (gen. λύ-οντος), f. λύ-ουσα, n. λῦ-ον *loosening*
Future   m. λύσ-ων (gen. λύσ-οντος), f. λύσ-ουσα, n. λῦς-ον *going to loosen, about to loosen*
Aorist   m. λύσ-ᾱς (gen. λύσ-αντος), f. λύσ-ᾱσα, n. λῦσ-αν *having loosened, after loosening*
Perfect   m. λελυκ-ώς (gen. λελυκ-ότος), f. λελυκ-υῖα, n. λελυκ-ός (*in a state of*) *having loosened*

MIDDLE
Present   λῡ-όμενος, -ομένη, -όμενον *ransoming*
Future   λῡσ-όμενος, -ομένη, -όμενον *going to ransom, about to ransom*
Aorist   λῡσ-άμενος, -αμένη, -άμενον *having ransomed, after ransoming*
Perfect   λελυ-μένος, -μένη, -μένον (*in a state of*) *having ransomed*

PASSIVE
Present   λῡ-όμενος, -ομένη, -όμενον *being loosened*
Future   λυθησ-όμενος, -ομένη, -όμενον *going to be loosened, about to be loosened*
Aorist   m. λυθ-είς (gen. λυθ-έντος), f. λυθεῖσα, n. λυθέν *having been loosened, after being loosened*

PASSIVE

Perfect   λελυ-μένος, -μένη, -μένον (*in a state of*) *having been loosened*

All active participles, together with that of the aorist passive, are declined like first and third declension adjectives (10.1/3). The declension of the aorist active participle is identical with that of πᾶς (10.1/3*b*). The present active and aorist passive are declined as follows:

SINGULAR

	M	F.	N.	M.	F.	N.
N.V.	λύων	λύουσα	λῦον	λυθείς	λυθεῖσα	λυθέν
Acc.	λύοντα	λύουσαν	λῦον	λυθέντα	λυθεῖσαν	λυθέν
Gen.	λύοντος	λυούσης	λύοντος	λυθέντος	λυθείσης	λυθέντος
Dat.	λύοντι	λυούσῃ	λύοντι	λυθέντι	λυθείσῃ	λυθέντι

PLURAL

N.V.	λύοντες	λύουσαι	λύοντα	λυθέντες	λυθεῖσαι	λυθέντα
Acc.	λύοντας	λυούσᾱς	λύοντα	λυθέντας	λυθείσᾱς	λυθέντα
Gen.	λυόντων	λυουσῶν	λυόντων	λυθέντων	λυθεισῶν	λυθέντων
Dat.	λύουσι(ν)	λυούσαις	λύουσι(ν)	λυθεῖσι(ν)	λυθείσαις	λυθεῖσι(ν)

The future active participle follows λύων. All middle participles and that of the future passive follow καλός (3.1/3). The present (and perfect) participle passive has the same form as the middle.

The meanings given above for the present and aorist participles simply reflect the temporal distinction between their corresponding indicatives: λύων *loosening*, λύσᾱς *having loosened*. This difference of time occurs in a sentence such as ἐργαζόμενοι μὲν ἠρίστων, ἐργασάμενοι δὲ ἐδείπνουν *they used to have breakfast while they were working* (lit. *working*), *but used to dine after they finished work* (lit. *having worked*), but the distinction is sometimes one of aspect (4.1/1), i.e. the present participle conveys the idea of continuation, the aorist of simple occurrence. An aorist participle so used can denote an action which happens **at the same time** as that of the finite verb of its clause (**coincidental** use), e.g. εὖ ἐποίησας ἀναμνήσᾱς με *you did well to remind me* (lit. *reminding*, not *having reminded*); ὑπολαβὼν ἔφη *he said in reply* (lit. *replying*, not *having replied*).

Notes

1 The present participle of εἰμί (*I am*) is ὤν, οὖσα, ὄν *being*; gen. s. ὄντος, οὔσης, ὄντος; dat. pl. οὖσι(ν), οὔσαις, οὖσι(ν). Its future participle is ἐσόμενος, -η, -ον (cf. 8.1/1 note 2); it has no others. The idiomatic expression τὸ ὄν (lit. *the [really] existing [thing]*) has the meaning *reality*; τῷ ὄντι is used in the sense *in reality, in truth* (on this use of the dative see 23.1/2*j*).

2 In tenses where they differ from λύω, contracted verbs, verbs with a contracted future, and verbs with stems in λ, μ, ν, ρ form their participles according to the rules already given for those tenses, e.g. the future active and aorist active participles of στέλλω are στελῶν (<έ + ων), στελοῦσα (< έ + ουσα), στελοῦν (< έ + ον) and στείλ-ᾱς, -ᾱσα, -αν.

3 Strong aorists take the participial endings of the present (cf. 7.1/1), e.g. active λαβών, -οῦσα, -όν;[1] middle λαβόμενος (< λαμβάνω).

4 The participles of root aorists are similar to those of the weak aorist active or the aorist passive, as the following examples show:
  (i) ἔγνων (γιγνώσκω): m. γνούς (gen. γνόντος), f. γνοῦσα, n. γνόν.
  (ii) ἔφῦν (φύω): m. φύς (gen. φύντος), f. φῦσα, n. φύν.
  (iii) -έδρᾱν (-διδράσκω, which occurs only in compounds): m. -δρᾱ́ς (gen. -δράντος), f. -δρᾶσα, n. -δράν.
  (iv) ἐπνίγην (πνίγω): m. πνιγείς (gen. πνιγέντος), f. πνιγεῖσα, n. πνιγέν.
  (v) ἔβην (βαίνω) follows -έδρᾱν: m. βᾱ́ς (gen. βάντος), f. βᾶσα, n. βάν (cf. ἔστην 19.1/1).

12.1/2 Uses of participles

(*a*) A participle in Greek can often be rendered by the same in English, but Greek regularly uses a participle and finite verb where

---

[1] Unlike the present active participle, the strong aorist active participle is always accented on the first syllable of its ending, hence λαμβάνων (pres.) but λαβών (aor.).

English would more naturally have two verbs joined by *and*: τοῦτο ποιήσας ἀπῆλθεν *he did this and went away* (lit. *having done this he went away*). In many other cases a subordinate clause should be used to translate a participle. The negative, when required, varies as indicated. When used within a clause participles can express:

(i) The **temporal relation** between two actions (negated by οὐ)

ἀφικόμενοι εἰς τὰς Ἀθήνας ἔλεξαν τάδε. *When they arrived* (lit. *having arrived*) *at Athens, they spoke as follows.*

Sometimes the temporal relation is made more precise by qualifying the participle with adverbs such as ἅμα *together with,* εὐθύς *immediately,* μεταξύ *in the middle of*:

μεταξὺ θύων ληκύθιον ἀπώλεσεν; *Did he lose his little oil-flask while* (lit. *in the middle of*) *sacrificing?* (on ἀπώλεσεν see 20.1/1 note 2).
ἅμα φεύγοντες τοὺς Ἕλληνας ἐτίτρωσκον. *While* (lit. *together with, at the same time as*) *fleeing they kept wounding the Greeks.*

ἄγων *leading,* ἔχων *having,* φέρων *carrying* are often to be translated simply by *with*: ἦλθεν ἔχων ξίφος *he came with a sword* (lit. *having a sword*).

(ii) **Cause** (negated by οὐ)
A participle used in this sense is often preceded by ἅτε *because* for a reason the writer or speaker sees as valid, or by ὡς *as* for a reason he does not vouch for. ὡς (which has many other uses – 22.1/1) here, and elsewhere, marks what follows as the subjective opinion of the person described and must often by translated by *thinking that, on the grounds that.* ἅτε is used only with phrases (with or without a participle):

ὁ Κῦρος, ἅτε τὸν χρῡσὸν ἔχων πάντα, ἐπικούρους ἐμισθώσατο. *Cyrus hired mercenaries because he had all the gold.*
ὁ βασιλεὺς τοὺς Πέρσᾱς εἶρξεν ὡς κατασκόπους ὄντας. *The king imprisoned the Persians on the ground that they were spies.*

οὐχ ἡγεμόνας ἔχων πλανᾷ ἀνὰ τὰ ὄρη. *Because you have no guides you are wandering over the mountains.*

(iii) **Concession** (negated by οὐ)
The participle is often preceded by καίπερ *although*, which, like ἅτε, is used only with phrases:

> ταῦτα φέρειν ἀνάγκη καίπερ ὄντα δύσφορα. *It is necessary* (lit. *[there is] necessity*) *to endure these things although they are* (lit. *although being*) *hard to bear.*
> δόξω γυναῖκα, καίπερ οὐκ ἔχων, ἔχειν. *I shall seem to have [my] wife, although I do not have [her]* (lit. *although not having*).

καί and καὶ ταῦτα (*and that [too]*) are used as equivalents of καίπερ:

> ἐν τῇ Ἰλιάδι οἱ ἥρωες ἰχθῦς οὐκ ἐσθίουσι καὶ ταῦτα ἐπὶ τῇ θαλάττῃ ὄντες. *In the Iliad the heroes do not eat fish although they are* (lit. *and that being*) *by the sea.*

(iv) **Condition** (negated by μή, as in conditional clauses, 18.1/5)
No introductory word is required: ἁμαρτήσῃ μὴ δράσας τάδε *you will make a mistake if you do not do this* (lit. *not having done these things*).

(v) **Purpose** (negated by οὐ)
With verbs of motion a future participle can be used by itself: ἥκομεν τοὺς σοὺς ἄθλους, Προμηθεῦ, ὀψόμενοι (< ὁράω) *we have come to see your ordeals, Prometheus*. Elsewhere the future participle is preceded by ὡς (cf. (ii) above; in both cases ὡς presents the attitude of the subject of the participle): συλλαμβάνει Κῦρον ὡς ἀποκτενῶν *he seizes Cyrus in order to kill [him]*. In these examples English uses an infinitive phrase to express purpose (for clauses expressing purpose see 14.1/4c(i)).

(vi) **Noun equivalent**
If preceded by the definite article, adjectives may function as nouns, as ὁ κακός *the evil man* (5.1/3). Since participles are adjectives, they can be treated in the same way. οἱ μανθάνοντες literally means *the learning [ones]* and, depending on the context, could be translated

those who are learning or (*the*) *learners* (in English the article is dropped if a general class is meant – 2.1/2 note 1):

ὡς ἡδὺ λεύσσειν τὸ φῶς τοῖς τε καλῶς πράττουσι καὶ τοῖς δυστυχοῦσιν. *How sweet [it is] both for those who are faring well and for those who are unfortunate to look upon the light* (i.e. *be alive*).

This use is negated by μή if a general class meant, but by οὐ if the reference is to a specific person or group:

οἱ μὴ εὐτυχοῦντες. lit. *the [class of] people who are not fortunate, i.e. the unfortunate.*
οἱ οὐκ εὐτυχοῦντες. *Those [particular] people who are not fortunate.*

(b) Genitive absolute

This construction (*absolute* here means *independent*), in its simplest form, involves a noun or pronoun and a participle which are both in the genitive case and which stand apart from (i.e. are **grammatically** independent of) the rest of the sentence; there is, of course, a connection in **sense** as otherwise there would be no point in putting the two together. We have an absolute construction (the nominative absolute) in English. Although it is a little clumsy, we can say *the Persians having sailed away, Miltiades returned to Athens.* In Greek this becomes τῶν Περσῶν ἀποπλευσάντων, ὁ Μιλτιάδης ἐπανῆλθεν εἰς τὰς Ἀθήνᾱς. The genitive absolute is employed in uses (i) – (iv) as detailed above and can be accompanied by ἅτε, ὡς, καίπερ when appropriate. It is negated by οὐ except when it expresses a condition (above (iv)).

τοῦτ᾽ ἐπράχθη Κόνωνος στρατηγοῦντος. *These things were done when Conon was general* (lit. *Conon being general*) (**temporal relation**).
ἅτε πυκνοῦ ὄντος τοῦ ἄλσους οὐκ εἶδον οἱ ἐντὸς τοὺς ἐκτός. *Because the grove was thick those inside did not see those outside* (lit. *inasmuch as the grove being thick*) (**cause**).
ἀποπλεῖ οἴκαδε καίπερ μέσου χειμῶνος ὄντος. *He sails home although it is midwinter* (lit. *although [it] being midwinter*) (**concession**).

ἀνέβη ἐπὶ τὰ ὄρη τῶν πολεμίων οὐ κωλυόντων. *He went up on to the mountains as the enemy did not prevent [him]* (lit. *the enemy not preventing*) (**cause**, hence οὐ).

ὡς ἡδὺ τὸ ζῆν μὴ φθονούσης τῆς τύχης. *How sweet [is] life if fortune is not jealous* (lit. *fortune not being jealous*) (**condition**, hence μή).

Insight

Julian, commonly called the Apostate, was the Roman emperor from AD 361 to 363 who attempted to suppress Christianity, the officially recognized religion for the previous thirty years. He was an accomplished scholar and on one occasion he was presented with a petition from Greek bishops anxious to preserve the rights of the Christian church. After glancing over it Julian replied ἔγνων, ἀνέγνων, κατέγνων *I recognized [it], I read [it], I condemned [it]*, thus rivalling Julius Caesar's famous **vēnī, vīdī, vīcī**. On the root aorist ἔγνων see 11.1/1.

12.2 Greek reading

1# ἀνὴρ ὁ φεύγων καὶ πάλιν μαχήσεται.

2 ἄρκτου παρούσης οὐ δεῖ ἴχνη ζητεῖν.

3# λίαν φιλῶν σεαυτὸν οὐχ ἕξεις φίλον.

4 ἑαυτὸν οὐ τρέφων κύνας τρέφει.

5# ὁ μὴ γαμῶν ἄνθρωπος οὐκ ἔχει κακά.

6 καπνὸν φεύγων εἰς τὸ πῦρ ἐνέπεσες.

7 ἀνὴρ φεύγων οὐ μένει λύρας κτύπον.

8 οἱ κύνες ἅπαξ δὴ καυθέντες λέγονται φοβεῖσθαι τὸ πῦρ.

9# θάψων γὰρ ἥκω Καίσαρ᾽, οὐκ ἐπαινέσων.

10 οὐδεὶς πεινῶν καλὰ ᾄδει.

11 ἄγροικός εἰμι τὴν σκάφην σκάφην λέγων;

12 ὁ δηχθεὶς ὑπὸ ὄφεως καὶ σχοινίον φοβεῖται.

13# ὁ γραμμάτων ἄπειρος οὐ βλέπει βλέπων.

14 χαλεπόν ἐστι πρὸς γαστέρα λέγειν ὦτα οὐκ ἔχουσαν.

15# ΠΡΟΜΗΘΕΥΣ
δέρκη θέαμα, τόνδε τὸν Διὸς φίλον,
οἴαις ὑπ᾽ αὐτοῦ πημοναῖσι κάμπτομαι.

ΩΚΕΑΝΟΣ
ὁρῶ, Προμηθεῦ, καὶ παραινέσαι γέ σοι
θέλω τὰ λῷστα καίπερ ὄντι ποικίλῳ.

16 ὁ Κῦρος ἐντεῦθεν ἐξελαύνει διὰ τῆς Λυκαονίας σταθμοὺς πέντε, παρασάγγας τριάκοντα, ταύτην δὲ τὴν χώραν ἐπέτρεψε διαρπάσαι τοῖς Ἕλλησιν ὡς πολεμίαν οὖσαν.

17# Ἡσιόδου ποτὲ βίβλον ἐμαῖς ὑπὸ χερσὶν ἑλίσσων
  Πύρρην ἐξαπίνης εἶδον ἐπερχομένην·
βίβλον δὲ ῥίψας ἐπὶ γῆν χερί, τοῦτ᾽ ἐβόησα·
  ἔργα τί μοι παρέχεις, ὦ γέρον Ἡσίοδε;

18# In this fragment from a lost play of Euripides the leader of a band of mystics greets Minos, the king of Cnossus in Crete, whose wife, Pasiphae, after an unfortunate experience with a bull, has given birth to the Minotaur.

Φοινικογενοῦς τέκνον Εὐρώπης
καὶ τοῦ μεγάλου Ζηνός, ἀνάσσων
Κρήτης ἑκατομπτολιέθρου,
ἥκω ζαθέους ναοὺς προλιπών...
ἁγνὸν δὲ βίον τείνομεν ἐξ οὗ
Διὸς Ἰδαίου μύστης γενόμην (= ἐγεν-),   5

καὶ νυκτιπόλου Ζαγρέως βούτης
τὰς ὠμοφάγους δαῖτας τελέσας
μητρί τ᾽ ὀρείᾳ δᾷδας ἀνασχὼν
μετὰ Κουρήτων,   10
βάκχος ἐκλήθην ὁσιωθείς.

Notes

2 ἄρκτου παρούσης gen. absolute (12.1/2b).

3 φιλῶν < φιλέων (pres. pple. m. nom. s. of φιλέω).

5 μή because a general class is meant (12.1/2a(vi)).

6 ἐνέπεσες < ἐμπίπτω.

8 δή emphasises ἅπαξ.

9 A translation of a line of Shakespeare, not a piece of original Greek; θάψων, ἐπαινέσων 12.1/2a(v).

10 καλά (n. pl.) trans. by an adverb.

13 βλέπων is used here concessively, *[though] seeing.*

14 ὦτα < οὖς

15 *l.*1 τόνδε τὸν Διὸς φίλον *this friend of Zeus* (i.e me, Prometheus) is in appositon to θέᾱμα (lit. *spectacle*). *l.*2 οἵαις (with πημοναῖς) lit. *with what sort of* dat. of instrument (11.1/2). *l.*3 παραινέω takes the dative (13.1/2b(i)); γε (lit. *at any rate* (13.1/3b)) need not be translated.

16 ἐξελαύνει vivid present (see note on 7.2.13 *l.*9); on the relation between σταθμούς and παρασάγγας see note on 7.2.9.

17 Hesiod, an early poet, wrote the Ἔργα καὶ Ἡμέραι (traditionally translated *Works and Days* but the real meaning is *Fields and Days [for ploughing them]*), which is the book referred to here. *l.*1 Books in antiquity were written on papyrus rolls and the reader kept his hands on top of a roll to manipulate it (hence ἐμαῖς ὑπὸ χερσίν *under my hands*). *l*.2 ἐπερχομένην *coming* (for this use of a participle see 15.1/2). *l*.4 ἔργα here *troubles,* but trans. by a singular – the author is punning on the title of the book he is reading (and wilfully misinterpreting the sense of ἔργα).

18 Europa, the daughter of Agenor, king of Tyre in Phoenicia (hence Φοινῑκογενής) was carried off by Zeus to Crete after the latter had taken the form of a bull (not related to the bull loved by Pasiphae); she subsequently gave birth to Minos. *ll*.1f. τέκνον vocative – with it we must take ἀνάσσων; the m. pple. (ἀνάσσων) is used because τέκνον, although neuter, refers to a male being, viz Minos – slight violations of strict grammatical agreement on this pattern are not rare (agreement according to the sense); Ζηνός see 11.1/4; ἀνάσσω *be king of, rule over* takes the genitive (13.1/2*a*(i)). *l*.4 προλιπών < προλείπω. *l*.5 τείνομεν lit. *we lead* but as ἐξ οὗ (*from what [time],* i.e. *since*) follows, English idiom requires *have led.* *l*.6 Διός see 11.1/4. *l*.7 νυκτιπόλου Ζαγρέως βούτης *[as] a herdsman of night-roaming Zagreus.* *l*.8 ὠμοφάγους δαῖτας *meals of raw flesh* were a regular feature of Dionysiac orgies (the beast was torn apart by the participants). *l*.9 μητρὶ ὀρείᾳ i.e. Cybele, another divinity worshipped with nightly orgies. *l*.11 ἐκλήθην < καλέω.

Main points

- Participles are the parts of verbs that function as adjectives

- Participles have tense (present, future, aorist, perfect) and voice

- Participles use the same stem as the indicative but drop the augment in the aorist

- Active participles and aorist passive participles are declined as first and third declension adjectives; other participles are declined as first and second declension adjectives

- Participles are used to show a temporal relationship, a cause, etc.

- When preceded by the definite article participles are used as nouns

- A genitive absolute consists of a noun or pronoun and a participle

---

12.3 Extra reading – Epigrams

For the Greeks an epigram was a short poem of two to twelve lines (we have already met examples at 9.2.3 and 12.2.17). The genre formed a sub-division of elegiac poetry because it was written in the elegiac metre (see **Appendix 9**; particular metres had, from an early stage in Greek literature, become the hallmarks of most poetical genres). Authors of epigrams used, although not very consistently, forms of words from Ionic and Homeric Greek (examples in 1, 3, 4, 8, 9). There was virtually no restriction on subject matter.

1# χρυσὸν ἀνὴρ εὑρὼν ἔλιπεν βρόχον· αὐτὰρ ὁ χρυσὸν
ὃν λίπεν οὐχ εὑρὼν ἧψεν ὃν εὗρε βρόχον.

2# ἡ Κύπρις τὴν Κύπριν ἐνὶ Κνίδῳ εἶπεν ἰδοῦσα,
φεῦ, φεῦ, ποῦ γυμνὴν εἶδέ με Πραξιτέλης;

3# πάντες μὲν Κίλικες κακοὶ ἀνέρες· ἐν δὲ Κίλιξιν
εἷς ἀγαθὸς Κινύρης, καὶ Κινύρης δὲ Κίλιξ.

4# εἴσιδεν Ἀντίοχος τὴν Λυσιμάχου ποτὲ τύλην
κοὐκέτι τὴν τύλην εἴσιδε Λυσίμαχος.

5# εἴκοσι γεννήσας ὁ ζωγράφος Εὔτυχος υἱοὺς
οὐδ᾿ ἀπὸ τῶν τέκνων οὐδὲν ὅμοιον ἔχει.

6# ἢ τὰ ῥόδα, ῥοδόεσσαν ἔχεις χάριν· ἀλλὰ τί πωλεῖς,
σαυτὴν, ἢ τὰ ῥόδα, ἠὲ συναμφότερα;

7# τὴν ψυχήν, Ἀγάθωνα φιλῶν, ἐπὶ χείλεσιν ἔσχον·
ἦλθε γὰρ ἡ τλήμων ὡς διαβησομένη.

8# ἣ σοβαρὸν γελάσασα καθ᾽ Ἑλλάδος, ἣ τὸν ἐραστῶν
    ἑσμὸν ἐπὶ προθύροις Λαῒς ἔχουσα νέων,
τῇ Παφίῃ τὸ κάτοπτρον· ἐπεὶ τοίη μὲν ὁρᾶσθαι
    οὐκ ἐθέλω, οἵη δ᾽ ἦν πάρος οὐ δύναμαι.

9# *They told me, Heraclitus, they told me you were dead* ...
εἶπέ τις, Ἡράκλειτε, τεὸν μόρον, ἐς δέ με δάκρυ
    ἤγαγεν, ἐμνήσθην δ᾽ ὁσσάκις ἀμφότεροι
ἤλιον ἐν λέσχῃ κατεδύσαμεν· ἀλλὰ σὺ μέν που,
    ξεῖν᾽ Ἁλικαρνησεῦ, τετράπαλαι σποδιή·
αἱ δὲ τεαὶ ζώουσιν ἀηδόνες, ᾗσιν ὁ πάντων   5
    ἁρπακτὴς Ἀΐδης οὐκ ἐπὶ χεῖρα βαλεῖ.

Notes

1 λίπεν = ἔλιπεν (aorist of λείπω) in Homer the augment is optional
in the imperfect and aorist, and unaugmented forms of these
tenses are often found in literary genres which use features of
Homeric language, cf. below 4.

2 Κύπρις another name for Aphrodite because of her association
with Cyprus (Κύπρος).

3 ἀνέρες (Homeric) = ἄνδρες.

4 εἴσιδεν = εἰσεῖδεν (< εἰσοράω) the augment is dropped as in λίπεν
(above 1); κοὐκέτι = καὶ οὐκέτι (11.1/5).

5 Eutychus apparently was a bad painter with an unfaithful wife;
οὐδ᾽(ἐ) *not even*, but trans. *even.*

6 ἡ τὰ ῥόδα (*sc.* ἔχουσα) *[you] the [woman having,* i.e. *with*
(12.1/2*a*(i))] *the roses* a concise form of address towards someone
whose name the speaker does not know.

7 *l.*1 φιλῶν *kissing* (despite some restrictions, male homosexuality
was common in Greek society, cf. 7.2.13). *l.*2 As the future
participle is used by itself to express purpose (12.1/2*a*(v)) ὡς

διαβησομένη means *thinking that it was going to cross over* (i.e. *with the idea of...* cf. 12.1/2a(ii)).

8 Lais (4th century BC), a beautiful courtesan now past her prime, dedicates her mirror to Aphrodite because she has no further use for it. The epigram consists of a single sentence and a main verb meaning *I dedicate* is to be supplied (the first two lines are in apposition to *I*, i.e. *I, the one who...*). *l*.1 σοβαρόν the n. acc. s. of the adjective is used adverbially, trans. *haughtily*; καθ᾽ i.e. κατά with elision and aspiration before the following initial aspirate; καθ᾽ Ἑλλάδος lit. *(laughing) against Greece*, i.e. *at Greece*. *l*.2 Trans. προθύροις as singular (the plural is often used for the singular in verse); take νέων (< νέος) with ἐραστῶν in the previous line. *l*.3 τῇ Παφίῃ i.e. to Aphrodite, whose temple at Paphos in Cyprus was famous; τοίη (= Attic τοιαύτη (21.1/3)) *of such a sort [as I am now]*, translate simply by *as I am now*; ὁρᾶσθαι middle voice *see myself* (8.1/1a). *l*.4 οἵη (= Attic οἵα) ... ἦν πάρος lit. *of what sort I was before*, trans. *as I was before*; with δύναμαι (on deponents in -αμαι see 19.1/3b) supply ὁρᾶσθαι from the previous line.

9 An epigram of Callimachus (3rd century BC), well known in its English translation (see **Appendix 9**). The person addressed is not the philosopher Heraclitus. *l*.1 τεός is the Homeric form of σός (cf. τεαί in *l*.5). *l*.2 ἐμνήσθην (aor. of μέμνημαι 19.1/3a) *I remembered*. *l*.3 *We sank the sun in conversation* i.e. we talked into the night. *l*.5 ζώουσιν Homeric for ζῶσιν (< ζάω); Heraclitus' nightingales were his poems, which, ironically, have not survived; ᾗσιν = αἷσιν (i.e. αἷς) – the dat. is governed by ἐπὶ ... βαλεῖ, *on to which*. *l*.6 ἐπὶ χεῖρα βαλεῖ = χεῖρα ἐπιβαλεῖ; in Homer when the first element of a compound verb (as ἐπιβάλλω) is a prepositional prefix (here ἐπί), it can be separated from the verbal element (here βάλλω) by one or more words (**tmesis** lit. *a cutting*).

Unit 13

....

13.1 Grammar

13.1/1 Oddities of declension

As we have now covered all regular nouns and adjectives, a few remaining oddities can be conveniently listed here. Only a very small number of nouns exist in each group.

(*a*) *Attic declension*
This subdivision oJf the second declension contains nouns which in Attic (and sometimes Ionic) end in -ως, but which in other dialects preserve the original -ος. Hence Homeric νᾱός (m) *temple* became first νηός (in Attic ᾱ >η except after a vowel or ρ) and then νεώς (cf. the gen. s. of πόλις, 8.1/4). νεώς is declined:

	SINGULAR	PLURAL
N.V.	νεώς	νεώ
Acc.	νεών	νεώς
Gen.	νεώ	νεών
Dat.	νεῴ	νεώς

Other nouns of this class are λεώς (m; Homeric λᾱός) *people*, Μενέλεως (Homeric Μενέλᾱος) *Menelaus*, λαγώς (m) *hare*, ἕως (f) *dawn* (singular only; the accusative is ἕω). The adjective ἵλεως *propitious* also belongs here (m.f. ἵλεως, n. ἵλεων; n. pl. ἵλεα). The masculine and neuter of πλέως *full* follow ἵλεως but its feminine, πλέᾱ, follows δικαίᾱ (3.1/3).

(*b*) *Third declension nouns in -ως, -ω, and -ας*
(i) ἥρως (m) *hero* is declined:

	SINGULAR	PLURAL
N.V.	ἥρως	ἥρω-ες
Acc.	ἥρω-α or ἥρω	ἥρω-ας
Gen.	ἥρω-ος	ἡρώ-ων
Dat.	ἥρω-ι or ἥρῳ	ἥρω-σι(ν)

Similarly declined are δμώς (m) *slave* and Τρῶες (m. pl.) *Trojans.*
αἰδώς (f) *shame* is irregular: *n.v.* αἰδώς; *acc.* αἰδῶ; *gen.* αἰδοῦς;
dat. αἰδοῖ (no plural).

(ii) πειθώ (f) *persuasion* has affinities with αἰδώς and is declined:
n. πειθώ; *v.* πειθοῖ; *acc.* πειθώ; *gen.* πειθοῦς; *dat.* πειθοῖ (no
plural). So also ἠχώ (f) *echo* and women's names such as Σαπφώ
and Καλυψώ.

(iii) In addition to neuter dental stems with a nominative in -ας (as
κέρας *horn, gen.* κέρατος, 5.1/1*a*), there are a few neuter nouns
in -ας whose declension is parallel to neuters in -ος (6.1/1*c*, i.e.
contraction has taken place after the loss of intervocalic sigma).
γέρας (n) *prize* is declined:

	SINGULAR		PLURAL	
N.V.	γέρας		γέρᾱ	(<α(σ)-α)
Acc.	γέρας		γέρᾱ	
Gen.	γέρως	(<α(σ)-ος)	γερῶν	(<ά(σ)-ων)
Dat.	γέραι	(<α(σ)-ι)	γέρασι(ν)	(<α(σ)-σι)

Similarly declined are γῆρας *old age,* κρέας *meat,* and also
κέρας when it means *wing of an army* (cf. 5.1/1*a*).

(c) Nouns declined in two ways
In English *brothers* and *brethren* are both plural forms of *brother,*
even though we attach a broader meaning to the second. In Greek,
anomalies of this sort sometimes reflect dialectal differences (as, e.g.,
between Homeric and Attic Greek), but some examples exist entirely
within Attic. These may involve alternative forms (as in υἱός), or an
apparent irregularity (as in δένδρον). The main examples are:

δάκρυον, -ου (n) *tear*; alternative n.v.a. in the singular: δάκρυ (as
in 12.3.9 *l.*1).

δένδρον, -ου (n) *tree* has an irregular dat. pl. δένδρεσι(ν). δένδρε(α)
in 13.2.22 *l.*2 is the Homeric and old Ionic form of the n.v.a.
plural, which can be contracted to δένδρη (11.2.4 *l.*5).

πῦρ, πυρός (n) *fire* (6.1/1*b*); the plural πυρά is second declension
(πυρῶν, πυροῖς) and means *watch-fires.*

σῖτος, -ου (m) *grain* (i.e. wheat or barley); the plural is neuter: σῖτα.

υἱός, -οῦ (m) *son* can be declined in the second declension throughout but also has the following third declension forms from an original nom. s. υἱύς (declined like ἡδύς – 10.1/3): gen. s. υἱέος; dat. s. υἱεῖ; nom. and acc. pl. υἱεῖς; gen. pl. υἱέων; dat. pl. υἱέσι(ν).

13.1/2 Verbs used with the genitive or dative

A transitive verb is defined as one that can be followed by the accusative case. Both the Greek πέμπω and the English *send* are transitive, and in the sentences Περικλῆς δῶρον ἔπεμψεν and *Pericles sent a gift* both δῶρον and *gift* are direct objects and therefore accusative. We might at first assume that if a verb is transitive in English its Greek equivalent will be the same. However, although this is true for the greater number of verbs, there are some which are transitive in one language but intransitive in the other.

The verb δειπνέω (*dine*) is transitive in Greek and so we can say ἄρτον δειπνῶ *I am dining [on] bread,* but we cannot say in English *I dine bread* because *dine* is an intransitive verb and must be followed by a preposition, not a direct object (in *I am dining on bread, bread* is accusative after the preposition *on*). Similarly, there are verbs which are transitive in English but not in Greek, but, whereas in English the logical object of an intransitive verb is preceded by a preposition (*dine on bread*), in Greek it is put into the genitive or dative. Greek verbs of this type can, to a large extent, be classified according to their meaning. The following are the main groups:

(*a*) *Verbs followed by the genitive* (see also 23.1/1*k*)
(i) Verbs of **ruling,** e.g. ἄρχω *rule;* κρατέω lit. *have power* (κράτος) *over;* βασιλεύω lit. *be king* (βασιλεύς) *of* (all three are normally translated by *rule*):

ἐν ἀμφιάλῳ Ἰθάκῃ βασιλεύσει Ἀχαιῶν. *He will rule the Achaeans in sea-girt Ithaca.*

(ii) Verbs of **desiring, needing, caring for,** e.g. ἐπιθῡμέω *desire;* ἐράω *love, desire* (sexually); δέομαι *need;* ἐπιμελέομαι *care for:*

οὐκ ἐρᾷ ἀδελφὸς ἀδελφῆς οὐδὲ πατὴρ θυγατρός. *A brother does not desire his sister, nor a father his daughter.*

(iii) Verbs of **perceiving, remembering, forgetting**, e.g. αἰσθάνομαι *perceive* (also + acc.); πυνθάνομαι *ascertain* (+ acc. of thing ascertained and gen. of informant; ἀκούω *hear, listen to* (+ acc. of thing heard, gen. of person heard); μέμνημαι (19.1/3a) *remember*; ἐπιλανθάνομαι *forget* (also + acc.):

> ταῦτα Κίρκης ἤκουσα. *I heard this from Circe* (but Κίρκης ἤκουσα *I heard* (or *listened to*) *Circe*).

(iv) Verbs of **reaching, obtaining, missing**, e.g. τυγχάνω *hit the mark, succeed, obtain*; ἁμαρτάνω *miss, fail to achieve*:

> τίνος πότμου ἔτυχεν; *What fate did he meet* (lit. *obtain*)?
> τῶν ἐλπίδων ἡμάρτομεν. *We did not realize* (lit. *missed*) *our hopes*.

(v) Verbs of **sharing**, e.g. μετέχω *share, have a share in*:

> πάντες οἱ πολῖται μετέχουσι τῆς ἑορτῆς. *All the citizens take part in* (lit. *share*) *the festival*.

(b) *Verbs followed by the dative*
(i) Verbs indicating that **the subject is asserting himself in some way over someone else**, e.g. παραινέω *advise*; βοηθέω (*run to*) *help, assist*; ὀργίζομαι *become angry with*; ἀπειλέω *threaten*; φθονέω *feel ill-will against, grudge*:

> φθονεῖν φασι μητρυιὰς τέκνοις. *They say that step-mothers feel ill-will against their children*.

(ii) Verbs indicating that **the subject is submitting himself in some way to somebody else**, e.g. πείθομαι (middle of πείθω) *obey*; πιστεύω *trust*; εἴκω *yield*:

> πατρὶ πείθεσθαι χρὴ τέκνα. *Children must obey their father*.

(iii) Verbs indicating **association of some sort**, e.g. ἕπομαι *follow*; ἐντυγχάνω *fall in with*; ἀπαντάω *meet*; πλησιάζω *approach, associate with*; μάχομαι *fight*; χράομαι *associate with* (people), *use* (things):

οὐδεὶς ἔτι ἡμῖν μάχεται. *No-one is fighting us any longer.*
τῷ δεσπότῃ ἑσπόμην (< ἕπομαι). *I followed my master.*

(iv) Verbs indicating **likeness,** e.g. ὁμοιόομαι, ἔοικα (19.1/3*a*) both
be like, resemble:

οὐ χρή σε ὁμοιοῦσθαι κακοῖς. *You should not be like bad men.*

Not all verbs which, by virtue of their meaning, we would expect
to belong to these groups do in fact take the genitive or dative, e.g.
φιλέω *love* and ὠφελέω *help* both take the accusative (we would
have expected the genitive and dative respectively). Some of the
verbs listed above (e.g. ἐπιλανθάνομαι) also take the accusative
with no difference in meaning. Full details will be found in the
vocabulary.

13.1/3 Further particles

The fundamental importance of particles (see 4.1/3) should now be
clear. Their use, especially as connectives, has been widely illustrated
in the reading exercises, and we have now met ἀλλά *but;* ἄρα* *then,
so;* γάρ* *for, as;* δέ* *and, but;* δήπου* *I presume, I should hope,
doubtless;* καί *and, even;* οὐδέ *and not, nor, not even;* οὖν* *therefore,
so, then;* τοι* *in truth, be assured, you know;* and που* *perhaps, I
suppose;* as well as the combinations μὲν*... δέ* *on the one hand ...
and/ but on the other hand,* τε*... καί and καί*... καί *both ... and,*
and καὶ δή* *and moreover.*

Some other particles of common occurrence are listed below:

(*a*) Particles with a **connective** function
δῆτα*: (i) in answers, particularly emphatic negative answers, οὐ
δῆτα *no indeed.*
(ii) in questions, πῶς δῆτα; *how then?,* τί δῆτα; *what (or
why) then?,* e.g. τί δῆτά με ζῆν δεῖ; *why then (or in that case)
should I live ?*

μήν* may be used (like δῆτα) to enliven a question, often in
combination with ἀλλά, e.g. ἀλλὰ τί μὴν δοκεῖς; *but (or well) what
then do you think?* By itself, τί μήν; has the meaning *of course:*

A. μισθωτῷ μᾶλλον ἐπιτρέπουσιν ἢ σοὶ τοὺς ἵππους; B. ἀλλὰ τί μήν;
  A. *Do they entrust the horses to a hireling rather than to you ?*
  B. *But of course* (lit. *But what then sc.if not that?*).

τοίνυν*: the temporal adverb νῦν (so accented) means *now, at present*. Unaccented νυν* is an inferential particle, *now* in the sense *then, therefore*, especially with imperatives (17.1/1): σπεῦδέ νυν *hurry up then*. τοίνυν, a strengthened form of νυν, likewise has a transitional or inferential force, *now then, furthermore, well now*, e.g. ἐπειδὴ τοίνυν ἐποιήσατο τὴν εἰρήνην ἡ πόλις ... *well now, since the city made peace* ...

(*b*) Particles which do not connect but convey **shades of tone, colour or emphasis**
γε* is an intensive and restrictive particle which affects the preceding word. Its literal meaning is *at least, at any rate, certainly, indeed*, e.g. ἔγωγε[1] *I for my part* (examples have already occurred at 9.2.12 *l.*9 and 10.3 *l.*5), but in English we would often simply use an emphatic tone of voice rather than an equivalent word, e.g. οἵδε κρινοῦσί γε εἰ χρή σε μίμνειν *they shall **judge** if you are to remain*; συγχωρεῖς τοῦτό γε καὶ σύ *even you admit **this***. It is also extremely common in replies to previous remarks, especially to questions, and is often to be rendered as *yes*:

  A. ἆρα στενάζει; B. κλαίει γε. A. *Is he groaning?* B. *Yes, he is weeping.*
  A. κενὸν τόδ᾽ ἄγγος ἢ στέγει τι; B. σά γ᾽ ἔνδυτα. A. *[Is] this vessel empty, or does it hold something?* B. *Yes, your garments.*

Sometimes it re-enforces a negative and must be translated by *no*:

  A. ἔστι τις λόγος; B. οὐδείς γε. A. *Is there some explanation?* B. *No, none.* (On ways of saying *yes* and *no* in Greek see 24.1/1).

δή* emphasizes the preceding word. *Indeed, certainly* are only approximate translations; the force of the particle would normally be conveyed to the hearer in English by the loudness of the voice or

---

[1] ἐγώ and γε are combined to form one word (with a different accent). Cf. below μέντοι (μέν + τοι), καίτοι (καί + τοι).

some accompanying emphatic gesture. δή is particularly common with adjectives or adverbs, e.g. ἅπαντες δή *absolutely everyone*; μόνος δή *quite alone*; πολλάκις δή *very often*. It may also convey irony or sarcasm, Σωκράτης ὁ σοφὸς δή *Socrates the wise* (the tone of voice in English will indicate whether *wise* is complimentary or ironical).

(*c*) Frequent **combinations** of particles

καὶ δή*: as well as being used as a lively connective, *and moreover* (e.g. καὶ δὴ τὸ μέγιστον *and moreover the principal point*) καὶ δή is common in replies to a command:

> A. οὔκουν ἐπείξει τῷδε δεσμὰ περιβαλεῖν; B. καὶ δὴ πρόχειρα ψάλια. A. *Hasten then to cast fetters round this fellow.* (lit. *won't you hasten ...?*) B. *There you are* (lit. *actually indeed*), *the chains [are] ready to hand.*

It is also used in making assumptions: καὶ δὴ πολέμιοί εἰσιν *and suppose they are hostile*. Note that καὶ δὴ καί means *and especially, and in particular*; in this combination the stress is laid on the word following the second καί:

> καὶ δὴ καὶ τότε ἅμ᾽ ἡμέρᾳ συνελέγημεν. *And on that particular occasion* (lit. *and then in particular*) *we gathered at dawn.*

Combinations with οὖν

(i) οὔκουν is merely a synonym for οὖν*, *therefore, accordingly, well then*:

> ἢ τοὺς ἀμύνεσθαι κελεύοντας πόλεμον ποιεῖν φήσομεν; οὔκουν ὑπόλοιπον δουλεύειν. *Or shall we say that those who urge [us] to defend ourselves are making war? Then (or in that case) it remains [for us] to be slaves.*

It is to be distinguished from οὔκουν (so accented), in which the negative retains its full force:

> οὔκουν, Προμηθεῦ, τοῦτο γιγνώσκεις, ὅτι ὀργῆς νοσούσης εἰσὶν ἰατροὶ λόγοι; *Do you not know this then, Prometheus, that when a temperament is sick* (lit. *a temperament being sick*

gen. absolute, 12.1/2*b*) *there are words [to act as] healers?* (see also the example given in (c) above).

(ii) δ᾽ οὖν has a resumptive force, *be that as it may,* used in dismissing a subject:

> εἰ δὴ δίκαια ποιήσω, οὐ γιγνώσκω. αἱρήσομαι δ᾽ οὖν ὑμᾶς. *If indeed I shall do what is right (lit. just things) I do not know; however that may be, I shall choose you.*

(iii) μὲν οὖν: this combination sometimes has no other force than the value of its two constituent parts (μέν looking forward to δέ, and οὖν *therefore*), but it can also be used to correct a previous statement, with the sense *no, on the contrary*:

> A. ἦ σὺ οὐδὲν ἡγῇ πράττειν τὸν γραμματιστήν; B. ἔγωγε ἡγοῦμαι μὲν οὖν. *A. Or do you think that the schoolmaster does nothing? B. On the contrary, I do think (sc. that he does something).*

Combinations with τοι*
(iv) καίτοι means *and yet, however*: καίτοι τί φημι; *and yet what am I saying?*

(v) μέντοι* is used either to emphasize, e.g. A. ἐγώ; B. σὺ μέντοι. *A. Me ? (lit. I) B. Yes, you;* or in an adversative sense, *however, yet,* often with an added γε:

> οὐ μέντοι οἵ γε Σκύθαι ταύτῃ εἰσέβαλον. *Yet the Scythians did not invade by this route.*

Other uses of particles will be explained as they occur in the reading.

··

Insight

In Greek legend Minos was a mighty king of a previous age who had ruled from Cnossus in Crete. A story told how the master craftsman Daedalus had, at the king's command, constructed a huge maze in which Minos could hide the monstrous offspring of his wife (cf.12.2.18). The traditional name for this was λαβύρινθος and its ruins were still visible in historical times. The site was excavated last century and discovered to be a vast palace belonging to an earlier stage of Greek culture, a symbol of which was a double-headed axe. When it was pointed out that λάβρυς was the word for such an axe in a pre-Greek language of the area and that -ινθος was a suffix indicating place (as in Κόρινθος *Corinth*) scholars realized that λαβύρινθος meant *the place of the double-headed axe* and was a name surviving from pre-Greek times.

13.2 Greek reading

1# καλόν γε γαστρὸς κἀπιθυμίας κρατεῖν.

2#   τῷ γήρᾳ φιλεῖ
χὠ νοῦς ὁμαρτεῖν καὶ τὸ βουλεύειν ἃ δεῖ.

3 τοῦτό τοι τἀνδρεῖον, ἡ προμηθία.

4# πανταχοῦ γε πατρὶς ἡ βόσκουσα γῆ.

5# σοφόν γέ τοί τι πρὸς τὸ βουλεύειν ἔχει
τὸ γῆρας, ὡς δὴ πόλλ᾽ ἰδόν τε καὶ παθόν.

6# ὦ τλῆμον ἀρετή, λόγος ἄρ᾽ ἦσθ᾽. ἐγὼ δέ σε
ὡς ἔργον ἤσκουν. σὺ δ᾽ ἄρ᾽ ἐδούλευες τύχῃ.

7# πατὴρ μὲν ἡμῖν Οἰδίπους ὁ Λαΐου,
ἔτικτε δ᾽ Ἰοκάστη με, παῖς Μενοικέως.
καλεῖ δὲ Πολυνείκη με Θηβαῖος λεώς.

8# οὐκ ἔστι Πειθοῦς ἱερὸν ἄλλο πλὴν λόγος,
καὶ βωμὸς αὐτῆς ἔστ᾽ ἐν ἀνθρώπου φύσει.

9 ὁ δύο λαγὼς διώκων οὐδέτερον καταλαμβάνει.

10 ὁ Κῦρος ἅτε παῖς ὢν καὶ φιλόκαλος καὶ φιλότιμος ἥδετο τῇ στολῇ.

11 ἀνάγκῃ οὐδὲ οἱ θεοὶ μάχονται.

12 κακὸν ἀναγκαῖον τὸ πείθεσθαι γαστρί.

13 τὴν Χάρυβδιν ἐκφυγὼν τῇ Σκύλλῃ περιέπεσες.

14 ὄνος πεινῶν οὐ φροντίζει ῥοπάλου.

15# τοῦ ζῆν γὰρ οὐδεὶς ὡς ὁ γηράσκων ἐρᾷ.

16# μόνος θεῶν θάνατος οὐ δώρων ἐρᾷ.

17 ὁ μηδὲν ἀδικῶν οὐδενὸς δεῖται νόμου.

18 τέτταρας δακτύλους θανάτου οἱ πλέοντες ἀπέχουσιν.

19 ἦρος χρῄζεις ἐπειδὴ παλαιὸν χιτῶνα ἔχεις.

20 Γοργὼ ἡ Λάκαινα, ἐρωτηθεῖσα ὑπό τινος Ἀττικῆς, διὰ τί ὑμεῖς ἄρχετε μόναι τῶν ἀνδρῶν αἱ Λάκαιναι; ὅτι, ἔφη, καὶ τίκτομεν μόναι ἄνδρας.

21 **A noteworthy pun**
Ἀντισθένης ὁ φιλόσοφος, πρὸς μειράκιόν τι μέλλον φοιτᾶν παρὰ αὐτὸν καὶ πυθόμενον τίνων αὐτῷ δεῖ, ἔφη, βιβλίου καινοῦ καὶ γραφείου καινοῦ καὶ πινακιδίου καινοῦ, τὸν νοῦν παρεμφαίνων.

22# ἡ γῆ μέλαινα πίνει,
πίνει δὲ δένδρε᾽ αὐτήν.
πίνει θάλασσα κρουνούς,
ὁ δ᾽ ἥλιος θάλασσαν,
τὸν δ᾽ ἥλιον σελήνη.
τί μοι μάχεσθ᾽, ἑταῖροι,
καὐτῷ θέλοντι πίνειν;

5

Notes

1 κἀπιθῡμίᾱς = καὶ ἐπιθῡμίᾱς (11.1/5).

2 φιλέω + infinitive *be accustomed to*; φιλεῖ is singular because it agrees with the closer of the two subjects; χὤ = καὶ ὁ (11.1/5); ἃ δεῖ is the object of βουλεύειν.

3 The subject τοῦτο (*sc.* ἐστί) anticipates ἡ προμηθίᾱ; τἀνδρεῖον = τὸ ἀνδρεῖον (11.1/5).

5 Take σοφόν ... τι together as the object of ἔχει (the subject is τὸ γῆρας); ὡς + participle to give a supposed reason (12.1/2*a*(ii)); πόλλ᾽ i.e. πολλά; ἰδόν < ὁράω; παθόν < πάσχω (both aorist participles are neuter nom. s. agreeing with γῆρας).

6 ἀρετή *virtue* was the philosophical ideal of the Stoics. These lines, whose exact source is unknown, were the last words of the Roman Brutus before committing suicide; ἄρ᾽ = ἄρα (distinguish from ἀρά); ἦσθ᾽= ἦσθα; ὡς *as* (22.1/1*a*(i)).

7 *l.*1 ἡμῖν trans. by a singular (royal plural – Polyneices in fact continues in the singular) *l.*2 ἔτικτε trans. as though aorist, *bore* (τίκτω is used idiomatically to mean *be parent of*).

9 λαγώς acc. pl. (13.1/1*a*).

12 τὸ πείθεσθαι is the subject; κακόν is used as a noun *an evil*.

15 ὡς *as* (cf. 6 above).

17 μηδέν, not οὐδέν, because a general class is meant (12.1/2*a*(vi)), lit. *the [person] doing wrong not at all* (adverbial acc., 20.1/5), i.e. *those who do no wrong.*

18 τέτταρας δακτύλους acc. of extent of space (7.1/7*d*); the width of four fingers was the normal thickness of the sides of an ancient ship.

19 ἦρος < ἔαρ (6.1/1*b*).

20 Spartan men prided themselves on manly virtues; they were not, however, male chauvinists, as the story shows; ὅτι *because*.

21 μέλλον acc. n. s. of the pres. act. pple. of μέλλω (here *intend*), to be taken with μειράκιον; δεῖ *there is need of* + gen. of thing needed and dat. of the person in need (cf. 21.1/4*b* and note 3); in Antisthenes' reply the genitives depend on an understood δεῖ (i.e. *you need ...*).

22 A poem in imitation of Anacreon (22.3). It is written in Ionic Greek as is shown by the forms θάλασσα and θέλοντι. *l*.1 The prose order would be ἡ μέλαινα γῆ. *l*.2 πίνει i.e. *draws nourishment from*; δένδρε' i.e. δένδρεα. *l*.6 μάχεσθ' i.e. μάχεσθε. *l*.7 καὐτῷ = καὶ αὐτῷ.

Main points

• A few nouns (as νεώς, γέρας) belong to small groups that are declined in different ways

• Some nouns (as δάκρυον) are declined in two ways

• Verbs that are transitive in English may have an intransitive Greek equivalent

• Verbs followed by the genitive can generally be classified by their meaning (ruling, desiring, etc.)

• The same applies to verbs followed by the dative (asserting, associating, etc.)

• Some particles connect (as δῆτα), some convey shades of meaning (as γε, δή)

• There are regular combinations of particles (καίτοι, μέντοι, etc.)

13.3 Extra reading – Plato (c. 429–347 BC)

All Plato's philosophical writings (except the *Apology*) are in the
form of discussions and arguments which are supposed to have taken
place on a particular occasion between various contemporaries. For
this reason they are called dialogues, but we have no way of telling
where factual reporting stops and Plato's imagination (or his desire
to expound his own ideas) begins. Some dialogues are in simple
dramatic form, whereas in others the conversation is reported by
one of the characters (the second extract is an example of the former,
the first of the latter). In all his dialogues (except the *Laws*) Plato
introduces his master, Socrates (10.3), as a protagonist, but nowhere
does he introduce himself.

(*i*) ΣΩΚΡΑΤΗΣ

ἐπορευόμην μὲν ἐξ Ἀκαδημείας εὐθὺ Λυκείου τὴν ἔξω τείχους ὑπ᾽
αὐτὸ τὸ τεῖχος. ἐπειδὴ δ᾽ ἐγενόμην κατὰ τὴν πυλίδα ᾗ ἡ Πάνοπος
κρήνη, ἐνταῦθα συνέτυχον Ἱπποθάλει τε τῷ Ἱερωνύμου καὶ
Κτησίππῳ τῷ Παιανιεῖ καὶ ἄλλοις μετὰ τούτων νεανίσκοις. καί με
προσιόντα (*approaching*) ὁ Ἱπποθάλης ἰδών, ὦ Σώκρατες, ἔφη, ποῖ 5
δὴ πορεύῃ καὶ πόθεν;
ἐξ Ἀκαδημείας, ἦν δ᾽ ἐγώ, πορεύομαι εὐθὺ Λυκείου.
δεῦρο δή, ᾗ δ᾽ ὅς, εὐθὺ ἡμῶν. οὐ παραβάλλεις; ἄξιον μέντοι.
ποῖ, ἔφην ἐγώ, λέγεις, καὶ παρὰ τίνας τοὺς ὑμᾶς;
δεῦρο, ἔφη, δείξας (*showing*) μοι ἐν τῷ καταντικρὺ τοῦ τείχους 10
περίβολόν τέ τινα καὶ θύραν. διατρίβομεν δέ, ᾗ δ᾽ ὅς, αὐτόθι ἡμεῖς τε
αὐτοὶ καὶ ἄλλοι πάνυ πολλοὶ καὶ καλοί.
ἔστιν δὲ δὴ τί τοῦτο, καὶ τίς ἡ διατριβή;
παλαίστρα, ἔφη, νέα· ἡ δὲ διατριβὴ τὰ πολλὰ ἐν λόγοις ὧν σε μετέχειν
ἐθέλομεν. 15
καλῶς γε, ἦν δ᾽ ἐγώ, ποιοῦντες· διδάσκει δὲ τίς αὐτόθι;
σὸς ἑταῖρός γε, ᾗ δ᾽ ὅς, καὶ ἐπαινέτης, Μίκκος.
μὰ Δία, ἦν δ᾽ ἐγώ, οὐ φαῦλός γε ἀνήρ, ἀλλ᾽ ἱκανὸς σοφιστής.
βούλει οὖν ἕπεσθαι, ἔφη, καὶ ὁρᾶν τοὺς ὄντας αὐτόθι;

(*ii*) ΕΥΚΛΕΙΔΗΣ – ΤΕΡΨΙΩΝ

ΕΥ. ἄρτι, ὦ Τερψίων, ἢ πάλαι ἐξ ἀγροῦ;
ΤΕΡ. ἐπιεικῶς πάλαι. καὶ σέ γε ἐζήτουν κατ᾽ ἀγορὰν καὶ ἐθαύμαζον
ὅτι οὐχ οἷός τ᾽ ἦ εὑρεῖν.

ΕΥ. οὐ γὰρ ἦ κατὰ πόλιν.

ΤΕΡ. ποῦ μήν;   5

ΕΥ. εἰς λιμένα καταβαίνων Θεαιτήτῳ ἐνέτυχον φερομένῳ ἐκ Κορίνθου
ἀπὸ τοῦ στρατοπέδου Ἀθήναζε.

ΤΕΡ. πότερον ζῶντι ἢ οὔ;

ΕΥ. ζῶντι καὶ μάλα μόλις· χαλεπῶς μὲν γὰρ ἔχει καὶ ὑπὸ τραυμάτων
τινῶν, μᾶλλον μὴν αὐτὸν αἱρεῖ τὸ νόσημα τὸ ἐν τῷ στρατεύματι.   10

ΤΕΡ. μῶν ἡ δυσεντερία;

ΕΥ. ναί.

ΤΕΡ. οἷον ἄνδρα λέγεις ἐν κινδύνῳ εἶναι.

ΕΥ. καλόν τε καὶ ἀγαθόν, ὦ Τερψίων, ἐπεί τοι καὶ νῦν ἤκουόν τινων
μάλα ἐγκωμιαζόντων αὐτὸν περὶ τὴν μάχην.   15

ΤΕΡ. καὶ οὐδέν γ᾽ ἄτοπον. ἀτὰρ πῶς οὐκ αὐτοῦ Μεγαροῖ κατέλυεν;

ΕΥ. ἠπείγετο οἴκαδε· ἐπεὶ ἔγωγ᾽ ἐδεόμην καὶ συνεβούλευον, ἀλλ᾽
οὐκ ἤθελεν. καὶ δῆτα προπέμψας αὐτόν, ἀνεμνήσθην καὶ ἐθαύμασα
Σωκράτους ὡς μαντικῶς ἄλλα τε δὴ εἶπε καὶ περὶ τούτου. δοκεῖ
γάρ μοι ὀλίγον πρὸ τοῦ θανάτου ἐντυχεῖν αὐτῷ μειρακίῳ ὄντι, καὶ   20
συγγενόμενός τε καὶ διαλεχθεὶς πάνυ ἀγασθῆναι αὐτοῦ τὴν φύσιν.

Notes

(*i*) The speaker is Socrates, who is going from the Academy, a park
with sporting facilities (i.e. a γυμνάσιον) lying north-west of ancient
Athens, to the Lyceum, a similar establishment to the east. The road
between the two skirted the north wall. *l*.1 τὴν ἔξω τείχους *sc*. ὁδόν
on/along the [road] outside the wall, this use of the accusative without
a preposition is classified as an acc. of spatial extent (7.1/7*d*). *l*.2 ἦ
where (*sc*. ἐστί). *l*.4 Παιανιεῖ (< Παιανεύς) an adjective meaning *of
the deme Paeania*; as the Athenians had only one personal name
(cf. 5.1/3 note 2) they were officially distinguished by the *deme*
(local administrative unit) to which they belonged. *l*.7 ἦν δ᾽ ἐγώ *said
I* a stereotyped formula, often used by Plato, which employs the
nearly defunct verb ἠμί *say* (18.1/1*a*) (δ᾽ is part of the formula and
should not be translated). *l*.8 δεῦρο often used as an order *[come]
over here*; ἦ δ᾽ ὅς *said he* the same formula as above but in its third
person singular version (the use of the relative ὅς as a demonstrative
pronoun is archaic). *l*.9 λέγεις *do you mean*; παρὰ τίνας τοὺς ὑμᾶς *sc*.
ὄντας *to whom the [group of] you being [am I to come]*? i.e. *who are
you to whom* etc. *l*.10 δείξας *showing* coincidental use of aor. pple.
(12.1/1). *l*.13 Supply ἐστί with ἡ διατριβή. *l*.14 τὰ πολλά lit. *for the*

many [times], i.e. *usually* (adverbial acc. 20.1/5); ὧν has λόγοις as its antecedent and is governed by μετέχειν, which takes the genitive of what is shared (13.1/2*a*(v)). *l*.16 καλῶς γε ... ποιοῦντες (*sc.* ἐθέλετε, to be supplied from ἐθέλομεν in the previous line) *doing well at any rate [you wish this]*, an expression of gratitude for their invitation.

(*ii*) The speakers are Eucleides and Terpsion. *l*.1 *sc.* ἦλθες the omission is typical of Plato's colloquial style. *l*.3 οἷός τ᾽ εἰμί an idiom meaning *I am able* (τ᾽ is not to be translated; on οἷος see 21.1/3). *l*.4 Terpsion has not been able to find Eucleides in the agora; in English the latter's reply would be *No, you couldn't, for I was not in the city*, but Greek omits the words *No, you couldn't* (which confirm the previous statement) and simply gives the reason *for I was not* etc. (24.1/1). *l*.8 πότερον introduces two alternative questions (10.1/2*a*) but is not to be translated; with ζῶντι supply ἐνέτυχες from ἐνέτυχον in *l*.6. *l*.9 ἔχω + adv. to express a state (cf. note on 8.2.9 *l*.1). *l*.10 μήν has an adversative sense (*but*) and balances the preceding μέν; the combination gives a stronger contrast than μὲν ... δέ. *l*.11 μῶν (10.1/2*a*) in his anxiety Terpsion is hoping for a negative answer. *l*.13 οἷον ... exclamatory *what a man ...!* (21.1/3) *l*.14 The Athenian male ideal was summed up in the phrase καλὸς κἀγαθός (here slightly varied), which can be translated *gentleman* (cf. 9.2.12 *l*.4). *l*.17 ἐπεί *since* introduces proof for the fact that Theaetetus was hurrying home, and governs the following three finite verbs; we would omit it in English; ἐδεόμην καὶ συνεβούλευον i.e. *him to stay*. *l*.18 καὶ δῆτα *in fact* (lit. *and indeed* but more emphatic than καὶ δή); translate προπέμψας by a finite verb and supply *and* before the next clause. *ll*.19f. Σωκράτους is genitive with ἀνεμνήσθην and ἐθαύμασα, lit. *remembered and admired Socrates, how prophetically he spoke* ... but English idiom requires *how prophetically Socrates spoke* ... (where appropriate, Greek often anticipates the subject of an indirect question in this way); ἄλλα τε ... καὶ περὶ τούτου lit. *both other [things] and about him*, i.e. *in particular about him*; ἄλλος τε καί is often used in the sense *particularly, especially*; δοκεῖ the subject is *he* (i.e. Socrates). *l*.21 διαλεχθείς < διαλέγομαι; ἀγασθῆναι < ἄγαμαι.

Unit 14

14.1 Grammar

14.1/1 Moods of the Greek verb

Mood is a characteristic of all finite forms[1] of the Greek verb (i.e. those that can stand alone in a clause). Up to now we have dealt only with the indicative, the mood used for facts. There are three other moods, the imperative, which expresses commands (17.1/1), and the subjunctive and optative. In a main clause the subjunctive can express the will of the subject, e.g. λύσωμεν (aor. subj. act.) τοὺς δούλους *let us free the slaves*, while the optative can express the wish of the speaker, e.g. μὴ γένοιτο (aor. opt. mid.) *may it not happen!* These uses illustrate, in part, an original distinction between what is **willed** or **expected** (subjunctive) and what is **desired** or considered **possible** (optative), but the functions of both moods have been expanded to such a degree that neither can be brought under a single definition.

In English we still possess some single-word subjunctive forms (*be that as it may*; *if I were you*) but the optative disappeared in the Germanic branch of Indo-European (1.3) before the evolution of English. Apart from the few relics of the subjunctive, we use auxiliary verbs (*let, may, would* etc.) for uses covered by these moods in Greek.

The subjunctive and optative exist in the present and aorist (and perfect, 16.1/4 note 1). There is also a future optative, but **no** future subjunctive. The distinction between the present and aorist forms of these moods is one of aspect (4.1/1) **not** time (for an exception see 14.1/4d). As with infinitives, the present subjunctive or optative is used for an action which is seen as going on, in the process of happening, or being repeated; the aorist subjunctive or optative is used for an action which is seen as a single event (cf. 4.1/1).

---

[1] The non-finite forms of verbs (i.e. participles and infinitives) are not considered as belonging to any mood.

14.1/2 Subjunctive mood

For complete table of λύω *see* **Appendix 1**.

The subjunctive has only one set of endings, which are applied to the present and aorist stems (the latter without the augment). The endings are formed by lengthening all the initial short vowels (even when the first element of a diphthong) of the present indicative endings:

Active: -ω, -ῃς, -ῃ, -ωμεν, -ητε, -ωσι(ν).
Middle and passive: -ωμαι, -ῃ, -ηται, -ωμεθα, -ησθε, -ωνται.

Note that ει becomes η but in ου > ω (3rd pl. act.) the second element of the diphthong disappears. As the aorist passive takes active endings (11.1/1), for the aorist passive subjunctive of λύω we have λυθῶ,[2] λυθῇς etc.

In the present subjunctive of contracted verbs the rules of contraction apply as for the indicative (5.1/2). Paradigms will be found in **Appendix 2**.

The endings for the subjunctive are classified as **primary** (4.1./1 note 1 and 8.1/1*f*.; we have -σι(ν) in the 3rd pl. act., -μαι in the 1st s. mid./ pass., etc.). This classification is relevant to the use of the subjunctive in certain subordinate clauses (14.1/4*c*).

Notes

1 The indicative and subjunctive coincide in a few forms, e.g. λύω, τιμῶ, τιμᾷς.

2 Strong aorists and root aorists have the normal subjunctive endings (i.e. -ω, -ῃς, -ῃ etc.), except for a few root aorists in -ων, which have -ω, -ῷς, -ῷ, -ωμεν, -ωτε, -ωσι(ν). An example is ἔγνων (γιγνώσκω), subj. γνῶ, γνῷς, γνῷ, γνῶμεν, γνῶτε, γνῶσι(ν); cf. the present and aorist subjunctive active of δίδωμι (18.1/2 note 1).

---

[2]The aorist passive subjunctive is always accented with a circumflex on the first syllable of the ending (the circumflex indicates contraction, λυθῶ < λυθέω etc.).

3 The subjunctive of εἰμί is identical with the endings of the present subjunctive of λύω, viz ὦ, ᾖς, ᾖ, ὦμεν, ἦτε, ὦσι(ν).

14.1/3 Optative mood

For complete table of λύω see **Appendix 1**.

The optative, like the subjunctive, uses the same stems as the indicative, but its endings show some variety between tenses. For λύω and other uncontracted -ω verbs we have:

(a) **Present and future active**: -οιμι, -οις, -οι, -οιμεν, -οιτε, -οιεν; e.g. λύοιμι, λύοις etc. (present); λύσοιμι, λύσοις, etc. (future).

(b) **Present and future, middle and passive**: -οιμην, -οιο, -οιτο, -οιμεθα, -οισθε, -οιντο; e.g. λῡοίμην (pres. mid./pass.), λῡσοίμην (fut. mid.), λυθησοίμην (fut. pass.).

(c) **Weak aorist active**: -αιμι, -ειας (or -αις), -ειε(ν) (or -αι), -αιμεν, -αιτε, -ειαν (or -αιεν); e.g. λύσαιμι, λύσειας, etc. The bracketed forms are less common.

(d) **Weak aorist middle**: -αιμην, -αιο, -αιτο, -αιμεθα, -αισθε, -αιντο; e.g. λῡσαίμην, λύσαιο, etc.

(e) In the **aorist passive** the final η of the stem is dropped (λυθη- > λυθ-) and to this are added: -ειην, -ειης, -ειη, -ειμεν, -ειτε, -ειεν; e.g. λυθείην, λυθείης, etc.

Contracted -ω verbs have different endings for the singular of the present optative active: -οιην, -οιης, -οιη. These, and the other present endings, contract according to the rules given at 5.1/2 (for paradigms see **Appendix 2**).

Present active	Present middle/passive
τῑμῴην (τῑμα-οίην), τῑμῴης, etc.	τῑμῴμην (τῑμα-οίμην), τῑμῷο, etc.
ποιοίην (ποιε-οίην), ποιοίης, etc.	ποιοίμην (ποιε-οίμην, ποιοῖο, etc.
δηλοίην (δηλο-οίην), δηλοίης, etc.	δηλοίμην (δηλο-οίμην), δηλοῖο, etc.

In the future, aorist, and perfect of contracted verbs the optative is formed by taking the appropriate stem and adding the normal endings.

The endings of the optative are classified as **historic** (4.1/1 note 1 and 8.1/1*f*; we have -ν in the 3rd pl. act., -μην in the 1st s. mid./ pass., etc.). This classification is relevant to the use of the optative in certain subordinate clauses (14.1/4*c*).

Notes

1 The optative of the strong aorist has the same endings as the present; e.g. the aorist optative active of μανθάνω is μάθοιμι, μάθοις, μάθοι, μάθοιμεν, μάθοιτε, μάθοιεν.

2 The root aorist ἔβην (βαίνω) has an optative βαίην, βαίης, βαίη, βαῖμεν, βαῖτε, βαῖεν (cf. the optative of -έδρᾱν which is -δραίην, -δραίης, etc.) but other root aorists in -ην have an optative in -ειην, -ειης, etc., just as that of the aorist passive. The optative of root aorists in -ων has the endings -οιην, -οιης, etc., and so from ἔγνων (γιγνώσκω) we have γνοίην, γνοίης, γνοίη, γνοῖμεν, γνοῖτε, γνοῖεν. The optative of root aorists in -υν is extremely rare.

3 The present optative of εἰμί is εἴην, εἴης, εἴη, εἶμεν, εἶτε, εἶεν. The future optative is ἐσοίμην, ἔσοιο, ἔσοιτο, etc.

14.1/4 *Uses of the subjunctive and optative*

The subjunctive and optative complement each other in several types of subordinate clauses, but in main clauses their uses are quite distinct.

(*a*) *Subjunctive in main clauses*
(i) The **jussive** subjunctive (negated by μή) is used for giving orders but, because we also have the imperative (17.1/1), its use is limited. In the first person plural (the singular is possible but not as common) it expresses self-exhortation or self-encouragement: μή, πρὸς θεῶν, μαινώμεθα *in the name of* (πρός) *the gods, let us not be mad!* The use of the second and third persons of the jussive subjunctive complements the imperative mood in the aorist. Both are treated at 17.1/1.

(ii) The **deliberative** subjunctive (negated by μή) is used exclusively in questions and indicates the uncertainty of the speaker about the future and what must be done (in English we use the verb *to be* followed by an infinitive):

εἴπωμεν ἢ σῑγῶμεν. *Are we to speak or keep silent?*
ποῖ φύγω μητρὸς χέρας; *Where am I to escape my mother's hands?*

(b) *Optative in main clauses*

The two uses of the optative in main clauses, to express a future wish and to express a future potential, are complemented by the indicative, which is used for both constructions in the present and past. For this reason we shall treat all forms of wishes at 21.1/1, of conditions at 18.1/5 and of potentials at 19.1/2.

(c) *Subordinate clauses where the subjunctive and optative complement each other*

In three types of subordinate clause the subjunctive is used after a main verb in a primary tense (4.1/1 note 1), the optative after a main verb in a historic tense. This reflects the fact that the subjunctive has primary endings (14.1/2) and the optative has historic endings (14.1/3).

In uses (i) and (ii) both subjunctive and optative can be literally translated by *may* or *might*. In (iii) both are to be translated by an indicative in English:

(i) Purpose clauses (negated by μή)

These can be introduced by ἵνα or ὅπως (both conjunctions meaning *in order that, so that*). The negative is μή, but a negated purpose clause can also be introduced by μή alone.

ἀποφεύγομεν ἵνα *(or* ὅπως*)* οἱ βάρβαροι μὴ ἔλωσιν ἡμᾶς. *We are fleeing so that the barbarians may not capture us.*
ἀπεφύγομεν ἵνα *(or* ὅπως*)* οἱ βάρβαροι μὴ ἔλοιεν ἡμᾶς. *We fled so that the barbarians might not capture us.*

In both cases ἵνα/ὅπως ... μή could be replaced by μή at the beginning of the purpose clause (μὴ οἱ βάρβαροι ἔλωσιν/ ἔλοιεν ἡμᾶς).

The subjunctive is often retained after a historic main verb, as this was regarded as producing a vivid effect (cf. vivid present, see note on 7.2.13 *l*.9). The second of the above examples would then become: ἀπεφύγομεν ἵνα (or ὅπως) οἱ βάρβαροι μὴ ἕλωσιν ἡμᾶς. As English has no way of bringing out the force of the subjunctive here, we must translate as previously.

(ii) **Noun clauses after verbs of fearing** (negated by οὐ)
The most common verb meaning *to fear* is φοβέομαι, which functions as a passive deponent with a middle future (11.1/1 note; it is not a true deponent as we also have an active φοβέω *terrify*). φοβέομαι and other verbs of fearing can be followed by a noun in the accusative: τὸν λέοντα φοβοῦμαι *I fear* (or *am afraid of*) *the lion*. They may also be followed by a clause which performs the same function as a noun (and hence is called a noun clause): *I am afraid that the lion may eat me.* Most (but not all) clauses of this sort have reference to a time subsequent to that of the main verb and in Greek are introduced by μή, which here, and elsewhere when used as a conjunction, can be literally translated by *lest*. The verb in the μή clause is put into the subjunctive after a main verb in a primary tense or into the optative after a main verb in a historic tense. As with purpose clauses, the subjunctive can be retained after a historic tense for a vivid effect.

> φοβοῦμαι μὴ ὁ λέων με φάγῃ. *I am afraid that* (lit. *lest*) *the lion may* (or *will*) *eat me.*
> ἐφοβήθην μὴ ὁ λέων με φάγοι (or φάγῃ). *I was afraid that the lion might* (or *would*) *eat me.*

If the μή clause is negated, the negative is οὐ:

> ὁ λέων φοβεῖται μὴ τροφὴν οὐχ εὕρῃ. *The lion is afraid that he may not find food.*

The noun clause can also have reference to the same time as, or a time anterior to, the verb of fearing. Here μή is followed by the indicative because what is feared either is happening or has happened:

> φοβοῦμαι μὴ ὁ λέων τὸν ἐμὸν φίλον νῦν ἐσθίει / τὴν ἐμὴν γυναῖκα ἐχθὲς ἔφαγεν. *I am afraid that the lion is now eating my friend / ate my wife yesterday.*

Where in English a verb of fearing is followed by an infinitive, Greek has the same construction:

αἱ ψύλλαι οὐ φοβοῦνται φαγεῖν τὸν λέοντα. *The fleas are not afraid to eat the lion* (or *of eating the lion*).

(iii) **Indefinite subordinate clauses** (negated by μή)
Certain temporal conjunctions (e.g. ἐπεί, ὅτε) may introduce a subordinate clause referring to the present or past and be followed by the indicative. Greek idiom here is very similar to that of English and we have already met examples (e.g. at 7.2.12). These clauses refer to single definite events. Another type of subordinate clause is that with an indefinite sense and is expressed in English by the addition of *ever*. In *I dislike what he is doing* the subordinate clause refers to a specific thing (viz the thing that he is doing), but in *I dislike whatever he does* the subordinate clause refers to a general class of thing (viz whatever thing he does), and so is called **indefinite**. Such clauses may be adjectival (as above), or adverbial, e.g. *I am going wherever my sister goes* (contrast *I am going to where my sister lives* where the adverbial clause refers to a definite place).

In Greek the construction used for these clauses in **primary sequence** (i.e. when the main verb is in a primary tense) is similar. The particle ἄν, which here[3] is the equivalent of *ever*, is added to the subordinate clause but in addition its verb is put into the subjunctive. ἄν coalesces with certain conjunctions, e.g. ὅταν *whenever* (= ὅτε + ἄν), ἐπειδάν (= ἐπειδή + ἄν) *whenever*. Examples of indefinite clauses in primary sequence are:

ὅταν τις κλέπτῃ, ζημιοῦται. *Whenever anyone steals he is punished.*
πράττουσιν ἃ ἂν βούλωνται. *They do whatever they want [to do].*

Compare the above with the definite relative clause in:

πράττουσιν ἃ βούλονται *they are doing [the things] which they want [to do].*

Because we can never be completely certain of what is going to happen in the future, the construction of ἄν + subjunctive is very

---

[3] ἄν has an entirely different force when used in a main clause (18.1/5).

common in subordinate temporal clauses with a future reference (cf.18.1/5). Often English idiom does not require us to translate ἄv:

ἡ Δίκη μάρψει τοὺς κακοὺς ὅταν τύχῃ *Justice will seize the wicked men when* (lit. *whenever*) *she finds [them].*

For indefinite subordinate clauses in **historic sequence** the optative **without** ἄv is used (we do **not** have the option of the primary construction as in (i) and (ii) above):

ὁ Κῦρος ἐθήρευεν ἀπὸ ἵππου ὁπότε γυμνάσαι βούλοιτο ἑαυτὸν καὶ τοὺς ἵππους *Cyrus used to hunt from horseback whenever* (or simply *when*) *he wanted to exercise himself and his horses.*

The negative for all indefinite clauses is μή:

ὁ μῶρος γελᾷ καὶ ὅταν τι μὴ γέλοιον ᾖ *fools laugh* (lit. *the fool laughs*) *even when something is not funny.*

(*d*) **Optative in indirect speech**
The optative has two further uses in subordinate clauses, one of which we shall deal with here (for the other see 18.1/5). In indirect speech which is introduced by a verb in a historic tense (*he said that ...; he asked if ...* etc.) all finite verbs **may** be put into the optative. There is no change in sense, and optatives of this sort are translated as indicatives:

ὁ Κλέανδρος εἶπεν ὅτι Δέξιππον οὐκ ἐπαινοίη (or ind. ἐπαινεῖ). *Cleander said that he did not commend Dexippus* (original: Δέξιππον οὐκ ἐπαινῶ *I do not commend Dexippus*).
εἶπεν ὅτι κατίδοι (or κατεῖδε, < καθοράω) στράτευμα. *He said that he had caught sight of an army* (original: κατεῖδον στράτευμα *I caught sight of an army;* on the use of the English pluperfect *had caught* see 16.1/2).
Ξενοφῶν οὐκ ἤρετο τί τὸ πάθος εἴη (or ἐστίν). *Xenophon did not ask what the misfortune was* (original: τί ἐστι τὸ πάθος; *what is the misfortune?*).

Finite verbs in indirect speech always retain the tense of the original direct speech (8.1/3*b*), and consequently the distinction between the present and aorist optative here involves time, **not** aspect, as the above examples show.

A verb in a future tense in direct speech can be put into the future optative when reported in historic sequence: εἶπον ὅτι τοῦτο ποιήσοιμι (or ποιήσω) *I said that I would do this* (original: τοῦτο ποιήσω *I shall do this*). The future optative has no other uses.

Notes

1 When an adverbial clause of reason (introduced by ὅτι *because*, ἐπεί *since*, etc.) occurs after a historic tense its verb is put into the optative if the speaker or writer wishes to ascribe a reason or motive to the subject of the main verb but does not vouch for it himself. This type of expression is called **virtual indirect speech** as no verb of saying, thinking, etc. is actually used. The subordinating conjunction is to be translated by *on the grounds that, thinking/saying that*:

οἱ Ἀθηναῖοι τὸν Περικλέα ἐκάκιζον ὅτι στρατηγὸς ὢν οὐκ ἐπεξάγοι. *The Athenians abused Pericles on the grounds that, [though] being general, he did not lead [them] out.*

2 When a deliberative question (τί ποιῶμεν; *what are we to do?*) is reported after a verb in a historic tense its verb may be put into the optative:

ἠποροῦμεν τί (or ὅτι) ποιοῖμεν *we were at a loss [as to]what we should do.*

The subjunctive may, however, be retained.

Insight

Ψῦχή *soul* is connected with the verb ψύχω *breathe* and originally meant *breath*. The combination of ψῦχή and σῶμα (*body*) made up a living being. At death the departure of the ψῦχή through the mouth was indicated by the noise made by the collapse of the lungs (the so-called death rattle) and it appeared in the outside world as a shadowy outline of the body it had left. The ψῦχή was then collected by the god Hermes

(Ἑρμῆς) who, in his function of ψῡχοπομπός (*soul-conductor*), brought it to the Underworld, and there it led a joyless existence as a gibbering ghost. It was unable to utter coherent speech because it lacked blood, the substance that gives life. If by some chance blood became available it could conduct a rational conversation. This happens in the eleventh book of the Odyssey when the living Odysseus visited the Underworld and revived the ψῡχαί of his mother and of others by letting them drink the blood of a sacrificed animal. Ψῡχοπομπός is a compound of ψῡχή and πέμπω, which can mean *conduct* as well as *send*.

14.2 Greek reading

In addition to translating, define each use of the subjunctive and optative.

1# ἔνεστι γάρ τις καὶ λόγοισιν ἡδονή,
λήθην ὅταν ποιῶσι τῶν ὄντων κακῶν.

2# πῶς οὖν μάχωμαι θνητὸς ὢν θείᾳ τύχῃ;

3# νοῦν χρὴ θεᾶσθαι, νοῦν· τί τῆς εὐμορφίας
ὄφελος, ὅταν τις μὴ καλὰς φρένας ἔχῃ;

4 ὃς ἂν δὶς ναυαγήσῃ, μάτην μέμφεται Ποσειδῶνα.

5 Σωκράτης ἔφη τοὺς μὲν πολλοὺς ἀνθρώπους ζῆν ἵνα ἐσθίωσιν,
αὐτὸς δὲ ἐσθίειν ἵνα ζῇ.

6 φάγωμεν καὶ πίωμεν· αὔριον γὰρ ἀποθνήσκομεν.

7# θεὸς αἰτίαν φύει βροτοῖς
ὅταν κακῶσαι δῶμα παμπήδην θέλῃ.

8# ὡς χαρίεν ἐσθ᾽ ἄνθρωπος ὅταν ἄνθρωπος ᾖ.

9# Α. τίς ἐστιν οὗτος; Β. ἰατρός. Α. ὡς κακῶς ἔχει
ἅπας ἰατρός, ἐὰν κακῶς μηδεὶς ἔχῃ.

10# σφόδρ᾽ ἐστὶν ἡμῶν ὁ βίος οἴνῳ προσφερής·
ὅταν ᾖ τὸ λοιπὸν μικρόν, ὄξος γίγνεται.

11 οἱ μὲν φοβούμενοι μὴ φύγωσι πατρίδα καὶ οἱ μέλλοντες
μάχεσθαι φοβούμενοι μὴ ἡττηθῶσιν οὔτε σίτου οὔτε ὕπνου
δύνανται λαγχάνειν διὰ τὸν φόβον· οἱ δὲ ἤδη φυγάδες, ἤδη δὲ
ἡττηθέντες δύνανται καὶ μᾶλλον τῶν εὐδαιμόνων ἐσθίειν καὶ
καθεύδειν.   5

12 πίθηκος ὁ πίθηκος κἂν (= καὶ ἐὰν) χρυσᾶ ἔχῃ σάνδαλα.

13 ἐφοβήθησαν οἱ Ἕλληνες μὴ προσάγοιεν οἱ Πέρσαι πρὸς τὸ κέρας
καὶ περιπτύξαντες ἀμφοτέρωθεν αὐτοὺς κατακόψειαν.

14 ὁ δὲ ἀνήρ, ὃν συνέλαβον, ἐρωτώμενος ποδαπὸς εἴη, Πέρσης μὲν
ἔφη εἶναι, πορεύεσθαι δ᾽ ἀπὸ τοῦ Τιριβάζου στρατεύματος ὅπως
ἐπιτήδεια λάβοι.

15 ὁ Διογένης, ἰδὼν τοξότην ἀφυῆ, παρὰ τὸν σκοπὸν ἐκάθισεν
εἰπών, ἵνα μὴ πληγῶ.

16#   τοῦ θανεῖν ἀπειρίᾳ
πᾶς τις φοβεῖται φῶς λιπεῖν τόδ᾽ ἡλίου.

17 ἔτρεχέ τις μὴ βρεχθείη καὶ εἰς βόθρον ἀπεπνίγη.

18 ἅμα δὲ τῇ ἡμέρᾳ συνελθόντες οἱ στρατηγοὶ ἐθαύμαζον ὅτι
Κῦρος οὔτε ἄλλον πέμποι σημανοῦντα ὅτι χρὴ ποιεῖν, οὔτε
αὐτὸς φαίνοιτο. ἔδοξεν οὖν αὐτοῖς συσκευασαμένοις ἃ εἶχον
καὶ ἐξοπλισαμένοις ἰέναι (to go) εἰς τὸ πρόσθεν. ἤδη δὲ ἐν ὁρμῇ
ὄντων, ἅμα ἡλίῳ ἀνέχοντι ἦλθε Προκλῆς ὁ Τευθρανίας ἄρχων   5
καὶ Γλοῦς ὁ Ταμῶ. οὗτοι δὲ εἶπον ὅτι Κῦρος μὲν ἀποθάνοι,
Ἀριαῖος δὲ ἐν τῷ σταθμῷ εἴη μετὰ τῶν ἄλλων βαρβάρων καὶ
λέγοι ὅτι ταύτην τὴν ἡμέραν περιμενοῖεν αὐτούς.

19 εἴ ποτε τοὺς στρατιώτας εὐτάκτως βαδίζοντας ἴδοι,
ἐπήνεσεν.

20# νόμον φοβηθεὶς οὐ ταραχθήσῃ νόμῳ.

Notes

1 *l*.1 ἔνεστι *is in* is followed by the dat. λόγοισιν. *l*.2 The first
two words would be in reverse order in prose; ὄντων (< ὤν) lit.
being, i.e. *existing*.

3 The pl. φρένες is very often used with the meaning of the
singular (here *mind*).

5 τοὺς πολλοὺς ἀνθρώπους *most people, the majority of people*
(cf. note on τοῖς πολλοῖς in 8.2.11 and on τὰ πολλά in 13.3(i)
l.14)

7 φύει here *plant*; βροτοῖς *in mortals* (dat. to express place where,
23.1/2*n*); take παμπήδην with κακῶσαι (*ruin completely*).

8 ὡς exclamatory *how* (also in 9, see 22.1/1*a*(ii)); χαρίεν (n.)
lit. *charming thing*; ἄνθρωπος (= ὁ ἄνθρωπος) expresses a
general class (3.1/2 note 1(ii) – translate simply *man* ; ἄνθρωπος
(penultimate word) i.e. *a [real] human being*.

9 A and B hold this conversation on seeing a destitute doctor; A's
second remark plays on two possible meanings of κακῶς ἔχω
(*a*) *I am destitute*, (*b*) *I am sick* (on ἔχω + adv. to express a state
see note on 8.2.9 *l*.1).

11 φεύγω + acc. here means *go/be in exile from* (17.1/5); λαγχάνειν
(+ gen., lit. *get*) should be translated *take* (the men spoken of
can obtain food and have time for sleep, but their fear prevents
them from taking either); δύνανται on deponents in -αμαι see
19.1/3*b*; μᾶλλον + gen. *more than* (genitive of comparison
17.1/4*a*).

13 προσάγω is here used intransitively, *advance*.

14 συνέλαβον (< συλλαμβάνω) take as 3rd pl., not as 1st s.

15 εἰπών coincidental use of the aorist pple. (12.1/1); πληγῶ 1st s.
aor. subj. pass. of πλήττω.

178

17 The pass. of βρέχω means *to get wet*; εἰς illustrates the pregnant use of prepositions (see on 9.2.13 *l*.13) – the person must have fallen **into** the hole before drowning **in** it. Consequently εἰς βόθρον is to be translated by *in a hole*.

18 *ll*.2f. πέμποι and φαίνοιτο opt. in indirect speech 14.1/4*d*; σημανοῦντα fut. pple. to express purpose, 12.1/2*a*(v); ὅτι here the indirect interrogative pronoun (10.1/2*b* note 1), trans. *what*; ἔδοξεν (< δοκέω) αὐτοῖς *it seemed good to them*, i.e. *they decided* (21.1/4). *ll*.4f. εἰς τὸ πρόσθεν *to the in front [place]*, i.e. *forward*; ὄντων is the pple. of a genitive absolute in which the subject (αὐτῶν) is omitted, lit. *[they] being already at the point of starting* (ὁρμῇ); ἦλθε is singular because it agrees with the nearer subject (Προκλῆς) only. *l*.6 ὁ Ταμῶ *the son of Tamos* (Ταμώς, which is declined like νεώς 13.1/1*a*), for this use of the definite article see 5.1/3 note 2. *l*.8 περιμενοῖεν the fut. opt. represents a fut. ind. in direct speech (14.1/4*d*).

19 As the optative in itself makes the εἰ clause indefinite (14.1/4*c*(iii)), ποτέ is really superfluous.

20 ταραχθήσῃ 2nd s. fut. ind. pass. of ταράττω.

Main points

- In addition to the indicative mood Greek has the subjunctive and optative moods

- The subjunctive mood in main clauses expresses an order or an uncertain question

- Certain subordinate clauses take the subjunctive for a primary tense but the optative for a historic tense

- The optative mood is used in indirect speech introduced by a historic tense

··

15.1 Grammar

15.1/1 Perfect indicative active

The perfect tense in both Greek and English expresses a present state resulting from an action in the past. κέκλεικα τὴν θύραν *I have closed the door* means that the door is now closed as a result of my past action of closing it. The aorist ἔκλεισα τὴν θύραν *I closed the door* describes a single past action, but tells us nothing about the present state of the door, not even whether it is still in existence. Because the perfect tense describes a present state it is classified as a **primary** tense (4.1/1 note 1). The perfect is by no means as common as the aorist and does not exist in every Greek verb.

There are two types of the perfect active, called **weak** and **strong**; only in the few verbs with both is there a difference in meaning (see note 2). There is a common set of endings (in the indicative -α, -ας, -εν, -αμεν, -ατε, -ᾱσι(ν)), but, whereas the strong perfect, like the strong aorist, has no suffix, the weak perfect has a suffixed κ which is attached in a way similar to that of the σ of the weak aorist (see below).

The stem of the perfect is normally modified by **reduplication**. Thus if a verb begins with a single consonant (except ρ) or with two consonants of which the second is λ, μ, ν, or ρ, the initial consonant is doubled with the insertion of ε; hence **weak** λέλυκα (λύω) *I have loosened*; πεπίστευκα (πιστεύω) *I have trusted*; κέκλεικα (κλείω) *I have closed*; **strong** γέγραφα (γράφω) *I have written*. When, however, the initial consonant is an aspirate (θ, φ, χ), it is reduplicated in its unaspirated form; τεθήρᾱκα (θηράω) *I have hunted*; πεφόνευκα (φονεύω) *I have murdered*; κεχόρευκα (χορεύω) *I have danced*.

In other cases the perfect stem is not reduplicated but simply augmented by the **temporal augment** (4.1/1 note 2(ii)) for verbs with an initial vowel or diphthong: ἦχα (ἄγω) *I have led*; ᾕρηκα (αἰρέω) *I have captured* (see also note 3); or by the **syllabic augment** (4.1/2 note 2(i)) for verbs beginning with ρ, a double consonant (ζ, ξ, ψ), or two consonants (the second not being λ, μ, ν, ρ): ἔρρῑφα (ῥίπτω) *I have thrown*; ἐζήτηκα (ζητέω) *I have sought*; ἔκτικα (κτίζω) *I have founded*.

The conjugation of λέλυκα (perf. ind. act. of λῡω) will be found in **Appendix 1**. An example of a strong perfect is ἔρρῑφα (ῥίπτω *throw*), which is conjugated: ἔρρῑφα, ἔρρῑφας, ἔρρῑφε(ν), ἐρρίφαμεν, ἐρρίφατε, ἐρρίφᾱσι(ν).

The weak perfect occurs mostly in:

(a) stems ending in vowels or diphthongs. Here the κ suffix is added to the present stem: κέκλεικα (κλείω). As in the aorist, the final vowel of most contracted verbs is lengthened: δεδήλωκα (δηλόω).

(b) stems ending in λ and ρ, where the κ suffix must be added to the original stem (i.e. the present stem stripped of any suffix, cf. 11.1./3): ἤγγελκα (ἀγγέλλω, i.e. ἀγγέλ-γω); ἦρκα (αἴρω, i.e. ἄρ-γω).

(c) dental stems (6.1/4), where the final dental is lost before the κ suffix: πέπεικα (πείθω); κεκόμικα (κομίζω, stem κομιδ-).

The strong perfect occurs in palatal and labial stems: πέφευγα (φεύγω); γέγραφα (γράφω). Often a final unaspirated consonant is aspirated (i.e. γ/κ > χ; β/π > φ): πέπρᾱχα (πρᾱττω stem πρᾱγ-); τέτριφα (τρίβω *rub* stem τριβ-). In many strong perfects an ε in the present stem is changed to ο: λέλοιπα (λείπω); πέπομφα (πέμπω). A few verbs with stems in other consonants have a strong perfect, e.g. γέγονα (γίγνομαι – note change in voice; the verb has another perfect γεγένημαι, which has the same meaning as γέγονα). For other examples of all types see **Principal parts of verbs**.

Notes

1 The strong perfect of some otherwise transitive verbs has an intransitive sense: ἐγείρω *I wake* (*somebody*) *up* (tr.), ἐγρήγορα (on this form see below note 3) *I have woken up* (intr.), i.e. *I am awake.*

2 πείθω and πράττω each have both a transitive and an intransitive perfect:
transitive: πέπεικα *I have persuaded*; πέπρᾱχα *I have done.*
intransitive: πέποιθα *I have confidence in* (+ dat.), i.e. *I trust*; πέπρᾱγα *I have fared.*
Note that πέποιθα can be translated by a present tense in English (*I trust*; cf. ἐγρήγορα above). A few other verbs (e.g. ὄλλῡμι, 20.1/1 note 2) follow πείθω and πράττω in having a transitive weak perfect and an intransitive strong perfect.

3 Some verbs which begin with α, ε, o reduplicate their entire initial syllable in addition to lengthening their original initial vowel:
ἀκήκοα (ἀκούω – the only common verb in a vowel stem which has a strong perfect).
ἐγρήγορα (ἐγείρω – the reduplicated syllable ἐγρ- also contains the ρ of the stem).

4 Many perfects are slightly irregular, e.g. βέβληκα (βάλλω); κέκληκα (καλέω); πέπτωκα (πίπτω).

15.1/2 Verbs used with participles

In the sentence Περικλέᾱ εἶδον ἐν τῇ ἀγορᾷ βαδίζοντα *I saw Pericles walking in the agora* the participle is not used in any of the ways mentioned in 12.1/2, where participles qualify either the finite verb of their clause or the clause itself. Here βαδίζοντα gives us further information (*I not only saw Pericles – I saw him walking*; cf. ex. in 12.2.17 *l*.2) and is called a **supplementary participle**. Participles can only be used in this way with verbs whose meaning permits it (as ὁράω in Greek and *see* in English). Most can be classified according to their meaning. With some the accompanying participle may occur in a case other than the accusative.

(*a*) Verbs of **knowing** and **perceiving**, e.g. ἐπίσταμαι (present tense as for δύναμαι, 19.1/3*b*) *know*; γιγνώσκω *recognize*; ὁράω *see*; αἰσθάνομαι *perceive*; πυνθάνομαι *ascertain*; ἀκούω *hear*; μανθάνω *learn*.

τῶν στρατιωτῶν τις εἶδε Κλέαρχον διελαύνοντα. *One of the soldiers saw Clearchus riding through.*

ἤκουσαν αὐτοῦ βοῶντος. *They heard him shouting* (genitive because ἀκούω is followed by the genitive of the person heard – 13.1/2a(iii)).

These verbs can also be followed by a noun clause introduced by ὅτι (8.1/3b):

ὁ Δωριεὺς εὖ ἠπίστατο ὅτι *(αὐτὸς)* σχήσει τὴν βασιλείαν. *Dorieus knew well that he (himself) would obtain the kingship.*

All such ὅτι clauses can, however, be converted to a participial phrase. When the subject of the participle is the same as the subject of the finite verb (as in the converted form of this example), the participle is put into the nominative; the subject itself will only be expressed if emphasis is required (normally some form of αὐτός; cf. nominative and infinitive, 8.1/3a): ὁ Δωριεὺς εὖ ἠπίστατο (αὐτὸς) σχήσων τὴν βασιλείαν (the meaning is the same as above).

When the subject of the participle is **not** the same as that of the finite verb both the participle and its subject are put into the accusative:

ἔμαθε τὴν Χερρόνησον πόλεις ἕνδεκα ἢ δώδεκα ἔχουσαν. *He learnt that the Chersonese had eleven or twelve cities* (= ὅτι ἡ Χερρόνησος ἔχει …).

Verbs of **knowing** and **learning** can also be followed by an **infinitive**, but in the sense of *know/learn how to* …: ἐπίσταμαι νεῖν *I know how to swim.*

(b) Verbs of **beginning, stopping, continuing**, e.g. ἄρχομαι (mid.) *begin* (doing something; the middle is more common than the active in this use); παύω *stop* (someone doing something); παύομαι (mid.) *stop* (doing something oneself); διατελέω *continue*. With such verbs in English we have sometimes a participle, sometimes an infinitive.

ὁ ἄνεμος ἐπαύσατο θύων. *The wind stopped raging.*
μόνοι Θρᾳκῶν διατελοῦσιν ὄντες ἐλεύθεροι. *Alone of the Thracians they continue to be free.*

γελῶντας ἐχθροὺς παύσομεν τῇ νῦν ὁδῷ. *With our present journey we will stop our enemies laughing.*

ἄρχομαι regularly takes a participle: ἄρξομαι διδάσκων *I shall begin teaching.* However, as with the English *begin*, an infinitive is also found: ἤρξαντο οἰκοδομεῖν *they began to build.*

(c) Verbs of **emotion**, e.g. ἥδομαι, χαίρω both *be pleased, take pleasure*; ἄχθομαι *be vexed*; αἰσχύνομαι *be ashamed.*

ἥδομαι ἀκούων σου φρονίμους λόγους. *I am pleased to hear wise words from you.*
οὐκ αἰσχύνῃ εἰς τοιαῦτα ἄγων τοὺς λόγους; *Aren't you ashamed at bringing the argument to such a point?* (lit. *to such things*).

αἰσχύνομαι may also be followed by an infinitive in the sense *be ashamed* to do something (and therefore not do it):

αἰσχύνομαί σε προσβλέπειν ἐναντίον. *I am ashamed to look at you straight in the face.*

Verbs of emotion may be followed by ὅτι and a finite verb with the same sense as their use with a participle. The first example above could be ἥδομαι ὅτι ἀκούω ... (lit. *I am pleased that I hear ...*). They are followed by the dative in clauses such as Πηνελοπείᾳ ἄχθομαι *I am annoyed with Penelope.*

(d) φαίνομαι *seem, be seen, be obvious.* Although φαίνομαι with an infinitive has the expected meaning *seem* (to be doing something), with a participle it means the same as δῆλός/φανερός εἰμι + participle, viz *I am obviously* (doing something).

φαίνονται οὐδὲν λέγειν. *They seem to be speaking nonsense* (lit. *saying nothing*).
φαίνονται οὐδὲν λέγοντες. *They are obviously speaking nonsense* (lit. *they, saying nothing, are obvious*).

(e) τυγχάνω *chance, happen* (to be doing something, i.e. *by chance I am [doing something]*; there is an etymological connection with τύχη *chance, fortune*). τυγχάνω is often used with a participle to express the idea that something has occurred fortuitously.[1]

> ἔτυχε τότε ἐλθών. *He happened to have come then* (lit. *he chanced having come then*).
> δηλώσω τὸ πᾶν ὃ παρὰ τοῦδε τυγχάνω μαθών. *I shall reveal the whole [matter] which I happen to have learnt from this man.*

(*f*) λανθάνω *escape the notice of* (+ acc.) and φθάνω *anticipate, be beforehand* can also be accompanied by a participle agreeing with their subject (in this construction they generally, but not always, have an object). As the main idea is contained in the participle, this will become the finite verb of the clause in an idiomatic translation.

> πάντας λανθάνει δάκρυα λείβων. *He sheds tears without anyone knowing* (lit. *he [in] shedding tears escapes the notice of all*).
> Μενέλεως ἡμᾶς ἔλαθε παρών. *Menelaus was present without us knowing* (lit. *Menelaus [in] being present escaped the notice of us*).
> ἔφθασαν τὸν χειμῶνα ἀνασπάσαντες τὰς ναῦς. *They hauled up their ships before winter* (lit. *they [in] hauling up their ships anticipated the winter*).
> ἔφθασαν οἱ Σκύθαι τοὺς Πέρσᾱς ἐπὶ τὴν γέφῡραν ἀφικόμενοι. *The Scythians arrived at the bridge before the Persians* (lit. *The Scythians [in] arriving at the bridge anticipated the Persians*).

The difference here between the present and aorist participle is one of **aspect**, not of time. A present participle indicates a **condition** or **process** (first and second examples), an aorist participle indicates an **event** (third and fourth examples). Cf. 12.1/1 and, for a similar distinction between the present and aorist infinitive, 4.1/1.

In sentences of this type it is, in fact, immaterial whether λανθάνω / φθάνω appear as the finite verb with an accompanying participle (as above), or as the participle (always aorist; the participle here has no temporal force) with an accompanying finite verb. Thus in the first and third examples we could have, with identical meanings: πάντας

---

[1] This verb must be distinguished from γίγνομαι, which means *happen* in the sense of *take place* (for its range of meanings see 8.1/2).

λαθὼν δάκρυα λείβει (lit. *escaping the notice of all, he sheds tears*);
φθάσαντες οἱ Σκύθαι τοὺς Πέρσας ἐπὶ τὴν γέφυραν ἀφίκοντο (lit. *the
Scythians, anticipating the Persians, arrived at the bridge*).

Insight

As mentioned in the Insight to Unit 14, the Underworld was
the abode of the shades of the dead (ψῦχαί). It was governed
by Πλούτων (Pluto) and his wife Περσεφόνη (Persephone),
whom he had abducted from the upper world. The shades
were not punished for any misdeeds of their earthly existence
except if they had been so foolish as to commit an offence
directly against the gods. Those who had done so were given
exemplary sentences. For attempting to seduce Ἥρα (Hera),
the queen of heaven, Ἰξίων (Ixion) was spread-eagled on an
ever-revolving wheel. Τάνταλος (Tantalus) had abused divine
hospitality and was subjected to eternal starvation through
being unable to reach the water and food in his immediate
vicinity. Τιτυός (Tityos) had tried to rape Λητώ (Leto), one
of Zeus' loves, and for punishment lay pegged to the ground
with two vultures forever gnawing at his liver. The fourth
offender was Σίσυφος (Sisyphus), who had also incurred the
displeasure of Zeus. He was condemned to push a large rock
to the top of a hill, only to see it roll back to the bottom; this
was to continue indefinitely.

15.2 Greek reading

1   σποδὸν φεύγων εἰς πῦρ ἐμπέπτωκα.

2   οὐδεὶς λανθάνει θεοὺς πονηρὰ ποιῶν.

3   καρκίνος ὀρθὰ βαδίζειν οὐ μεμάθηκεν.

4# ἅπαντές ἐσμεν εἰς τὸ νουθετεῖν σοφοί,
    αὐτοὶ δ᾽ ἁμαρτάνοντες οὐ γιγνώσκομεν.

5   εἴληφεν ἡ παγὶς τὸν μῦν.

6# ἀνὴρ γὰρ ὅστις ἥδεται λέγων ἀεί,
ἔλαθεν ἑαυτὸν τοῖς συνοῦσιν ὢν βαρύς.

7 σκορπίους βέβρωκεν.

8# ὅστις καθ᾽ ἑτέρου δόλια μηχανεύεται,
αὐτὸς καθ᾽ αὑτοῦ λανθάνει ποιῶν.

9 ἔτυχον ἐν τῇ ἀγορᾷ οἱ ὁπλῖται καθεύδοντες.

10 Μένων δῆλος ἦν ἐπιθυμῶν πλουτεῖν ἰσχυρῶς.

11 The crucifixion of Jesus
παρέλαβον οὖν τὸν Ἰησοῦν· καὶ βαστάζων ἑαυτῷ τὸν σταυρὸν
ἐξῆλθεν εἰς τὸν λεγόμενον Κρανίου Τόπον, ὃ λέγεται ἑβραϊστὶ
Γολγοθα, ὅπου αὐτὸν ἐσταύρωσαν, καὶ μετ᾽ αὐτοῦ ἄλλους δύο
ἐντεῦθεν καὶ ἐντεῦθεν, μέσον δὲ τὸν Ἰησοῦν. ἔγραψεν δὲ καὶ
τίτλον ὁ Πιλᾶτος καὶ ἔθηκεν (placed [it]) ἐπὶ τοῦ σταυροῦ, 5
ἸΗΣΟΥΣ Ὁ ΝΑΖΩΡΑΙΟΣ Ὁ ΒΑΣΙΛΕΥΣ ΤΩΝ ἸΟΥΔΑΙΩΝ.
τοῦτον οὖν τὸν τίτλον πολλοὶ ἀνέγνωσαν τῶν Ἰουδαίων, ὅτι
ἐγγὺς ὁ τόπος τῆς πόλεως ὅπου ἐσταυρώθη ὁ Ἰησοῦς. ἔλεγον οὖν
τῷ Πιλάτῳ οἱ ἀρχιερεῖς τῶν Ἰουδαίων, μὴ γράφε (do not write),
ὁ βασιλεὺς τῶν Ἰουδαίων, ἀλλ᾽ ὅτι ἐκεῖνος εἶπεν, βασιλεύς εἰμι 10
τῶν Ἰουδαίων. ἀπεκρίθη ὁ Πιλᾶτος, ὃ γέγραφα γέγραφα.

12 ἑπτὰ ἡμέρας, ἃς ἐπορεύοντο διὰ τῶν Καρδούχων, πάσας
μαχόμενοι διετέλεσαν.

13 Κλεάρετος, παρακαλέσας τοὺς στρατιώτας, ἦγεν ἐπὶ τὸ χωρίον·
πορευόμενον δ᾽ αὐτὸν ἔφθασεν ἡμέρα γενομένη.

14 According to Plutarch intellectual pleasures are much superior
to those of the body and therefore our reactions to the former
are much more enthusiastic.

ὁ Ἀρχιμήδης λουόμενος, ὥς φασιν, ἐκ τῆς ὑπερχύσεως ἐννοήσας
τὴν τοῦ στεφάνου μέτρησιν, οἷον ἔκ τινος κατοχῆς ἢ ἐπιπνοίας,
ἐξήλατο βοῶν, εὕρηκα, καὶ τοῦτο πολλάκις φθεγγόμενος
ἐβάδιζεν. οὐδενὸς δ᾽ ἀκηκόαμεν οὔτε γαστριμάργου οὕτως

περιπαθῶς βοῶντος, βέβρωκα, οὔτε ἐρωτικοῦ, πεφίληκα, μυρίων 5
ἀκολάστων γενομένων καὶ ὄντων.

15# Α. γεγάμηκε δήπου. Β. τί σὺ λέγεις; ἀληθινῶς
γεγάμηκεν, ὃν ἐγὼ ζῶντα περιπατοῦντά τε
κατέλιπον;

16 τὸ δὲ μέγα τεῖχος ἐπαύσαντο οἰκοδομοῦντες φοβούμενοι μὴ οὐχ
ἱκανὸν εἴη ἀντέχειν.

17# ὁρῶ δὲ τοῖς πολλοῖσιν ἀνθρώποις ἐγὼ
τίκτουσαν ὕβριν τὴν πάροιθ᾿ εὐπραξίαν.

Notes

3 ὀρθά acc. n. pl. used adverbially (= ὀρθῶς, cf. 20.1/5).

4 εἰς with respect to.

6 ἀνὴρ ... ὅστις lit. whatever man (ὅστις is here the indefinite
relative – 10.1/2b note 2) but translate the man who; ἔλαθεν
gnomic aor.; translate by present; συνοῦσι dat. pl. m. of the pres.
pple of σύνειμι.

9 As the subject is plural ἔτυχον must be 3rd pl.

10 δῆλος ἦν ἐπιθῦμῶν lit. was obvious desiring, i.e. it was obvious/
clear that M. desired.

11 l.3 Γολγοθα has no accent because it is not a Greek word. l.4
ἐντεῦθεν καὶ ἐντεῦθεν lit. from here and from there, i.e. on each
side. ll.7f. Take πολλοί with τῶν Ἰουδαίων and ἐγγύς with τῆς
πόλεως. l.8 ἔλεγον said the imperfect is used because the subject
is an unspecified number of individuals.

13 ἦγεν inceptive imperfect began to lead.

14 The famous story of Archimedes' discovery of the principle of
displacement (when two bodies of the same weight are submerged

they will displace the same amount of liquid only if they are of identical composition). Using this he was able to establish that his patron, Hiero of Syracuse, had been cheated by a jeweller who had been commissioned to make a crown of pure gold (the crown did not displace the same volume of water as an amount of gold of exactly equal weight). *ll*.4f. ἐβάδιζεν impf. to express repeated action *went about*; οὐδενὸς ... οὔτε ... οὔτε lit. *of no-one ... neither ... nor* but translate *neither of any ... nor of any* ...; ἀκηκόαμεν royal (or author's) plural. *l*.6 ἀκολάστων the adj. (*unrestrained, licentious*) is here used as a noun (*sensualist*).

16 φοβούμενοι μὴ οὐχ ... see 14.1/4*c*(ii).

17 τοῖς πολλοῖς *for the majority* (cf. 8.2.11); ὕβριν is governed by τίκτουσαν, which agrees with εὐπρᾱξίᾱν; πάροιθ᾽(ε) is an adv. but translate by an adj. *former*.

Main points

- The perfect tense expresses a present state

- Strong and weak perfects take the same endings

- Depending on its initial sound a verb has either reduplication or the temporal/syllabic augment in the prefect

- A wide range of Greek verbs is followed by a participle; their English equivalents are usually followed by either a participle or an infinitive; λανθάνω *escape the notice of* and φθάνω *anticipate* require special attention

15.3 Extra reading – Prometheus Bound (1)

This is the first of two passages from the *Prometheus Bound*, a play which has come down under the name of the first great Attic tragedian, Aeschylus (c.525–456 BC). Its plot, like that of nearly all tragedies, is taken from mythology.

Prometheus, who belonged to an older but minor order of divinities called Titans, had helped Zeus wrestle supreme control of heaven from his father Cronos. At this stage mankind lived in primitive squalor, but Prometheus took pity on them and gave them fire. This he was obliged to steal from heaven as it had been the exclusive possession of the gods. Zeus, incensed by the theft, ordered that Prometheus be fastened to a rock at the ends of the earth. In the following scene, with which the play opens, Zeus' henchman Κράτος (*Might*), who with his fellow lackey Βία (*Violence*) has escorted Prometheus to the rock, tells Hephaestus, the divine blacksmith, to execute Zeus' command.

ΚΡΑΤΟΣ

χθονὸς μὲν εἰς τηλουρὸν ἥκομεν πέδον,
Σκύθην ἐς οἶμον, ἄβροτον εἰς ἐρημίαν.
Ἥφαιστε, σοὶ δὲ χρὴ μέλειν ἐπιστολὰς
ἅς σοι πατὴρ ἐφεῖτο (*enjoined on*), τόνδε πρὸς πέτραις
ὑψηλοκρήμνοις τὸν λεωργὸν ὀχμάσαι   5
ἀδαμαντίνων δεσμῶν ἐν ἀρρήκτοις πέδαις.
τὸ σὸν γὰρ ἄνθος, παντέχνου πυρὸς σέλας,
θνητοῖσι κλέψας ὤπασεν. τοιᾶσδέ τοι
ἁμαρτίας σφε δεῖ θεοῖς δοῦναι (*to give* i.e. *to pay*) δίκην,
ὡς ἂν διδαχθῇ τὴν Διὸς τυραννίδα   10
στέργειν, φιλανθρώπου δὲ παύεσθαι τρόπου.

ΗΦΑΙΣΤΟΣ

Κράτος Βία τε, σφῷν μὲν ἐντολὴ Διὸς
ἔχει τέλος δὴ κοὐδὲν ἐμποδὼν ἔτι,
ἐγὼ δ᾽ ἄτολμός εἰμι συγγενῆ θεὸν
δῆσαι βίᾳ φάραγγι πρὸς δυσχειμέρῳ.   15
πάντως δ᾽ ἀνάγκη τῶνδέ μοι τόλμαν σχεθεῖν·
εὐωριάζειν γὰρ πατρὸς λόγους βαρύ.
τῆς ὀρθοβούλου Θέμιδος αἰπυμῆτα παῖ,
ἄκοντά σ᾽ ἄκων δυσλύτοις χαλκεύμασι
προσπασσαλεύσω τῷδ᾽ ἀπανθρώπῳ πάγῳ,   20
ἵν᾽ οὔτε φωνὴν οὔτε του μορφὴν βροτῶν
ὄψῃ, σταθευτὸς δ᾽ ἡλίου φοίβῃ φλογὶ
χροιᾶς ἀμείψεις ἄνθος· ἀσμένῳ δέ σοι
ἡ ποικιλείμων νὺξ ἀποκρύψει φάος
πάχνην θ᾽ ἑῴαν ἥλιος σκεδᾷ (*will scatter*) πάλιν·   25

ἀεὶ δὲ τοῦ παρόντος ἀχθηδὼν κακοῦ
τρύσει σ᾽, ὁ λωφήσων γὰρ οὐ πέφυκέ πω.

Notes

ll.1f. In poetry the demonstrative adjective, as well as the definite
article, can be omitted, and in English we would supply *this* with
πέδον, οἶμον and ἐρημίαν; take Σκύθην with οἶμον and ἄβροτον
with ἐρημίᾱν *l*.3 δέ is here used idiomatically in a clause following
a vocative and should not be translated; ἐπιστολάς is the subject of
μέλειν (which governs the dative σοί). *l*.4 πατήρ i.e. Zeus, whom
Homer calls *father of gods and men*. *l*.5 ὀχμάσαι aor. inf., to be
taken after ἐπιστολάς which it explains. *l*.7 ἄνθος *flower* but here
metaphorically *glory, pride*; παντέχνου lit. *[required] for all arts*
because fire was seen as necessary for any technological progress.
ll.8f. θνητοῖσι = θνητοῖς (3.1/1 note 3); κλέψᾱς ὤπασεν lit. *having
stolen ... he gave [it]*; τοιᾱσδέ ... ἁμαρτίᾱς gen. with δίκην (*penalty
for such a wrong*); σφε = αὐτόν, i.e. Prometheus. *l*.10 ὡς ἄν +
subj. expresses purpose (= ἵνα + subj. 14.1/4*c*(i)). *l*.11 παύεσθαι is
followed by a gen. (φιλανθρώπου ... τρόπου). *l*.12 σφῷν *for you two*
(24.1/4). *l*.13 κοὐδέν = καὶ οὐδέν (11.1/5). *l*.15 δῆσαι aor. inf. act. of
δέω *bind*. *ll*.16f. Supply ἐστί with both ἀνάγκη and βαρύ. *l*.19 σ᾽= σε
(also in *l*.27); δυσλύτοις χαλκεύμασι dat. of instrument (11.1/2). *l*.20
τῷδ᾽(ε) ἀπανθρώπῳ πάγῳ *to this ... the* dat. is governed by the προσ-
of προσπασσαλεύσω. *l*.21 ἵν᾽(α) (+ ind.) *where*; του = τινός (10.1/1).
l.22 ὄψῃ (< ὁράω) lit. *you will see* is appropriate to μορφήν but not
to φωνήν although it governs both – trans. *you will perceive*. *l*.23
χροιᾶς ἀμείψεις ἄνθος *you will alter* (i.e. *lose*) *the bloom* (lit. *flower*)
of [your] skin (through constant exposure to the sun Prometheus'
skin will become tanned and rough); ἀσμένῳ ... σοι *for you [being]
glad* dat. of reference (23.1/2*e*). *l*.25 θ᾽ i.e. τε. *l*.27 ὁ λωφήσων lit. *the
[one] going to relieve*; γάρ can be placed after the first phrase rather
than the first word; πέφῡκε (perf. of φύω is always intransitive) *has
been born*.

....

16.1 Grammar

16.1/1 Phrases and clauses of result

Result in English is usually expressed by a subordinate clause of the type (*he was so poor*) *that he couldn't buy food*, although we may omit *that* and say *he was so poor he couldn't buy food*. In Greek the corresponding conjunction, ὥστε *that, so that*, is always expressed. As in English, there is usually an anticipatory word in the main clause such as οὕτως *so, to such an extent*; τοιοῦτος *of this kind, of such a kind*; τοσοῦτος *so much*, pl. *so many* (on the declension of the last two see note 1 below).

ὥστε is usually followed by an **infinitive**, particularly where the result is to be marked as merely contemplated or in prospect and not stressed as a fact (here ὥστε is to be translated *as* – see first example). Where the subject of the infinitive is the same as the subject of the main verb, it is normally not expressed; where it is different, it is in the accusative (just as in the infinitive construction of indirect statement (8.1/3)). If the infinitive is negated, the negative is μή:

οὕτω σκαιὸς εἶ ὥστε μὴ δύνασθαι μανθάνειν. *You are so stupid as not to be able to understand.*
τοσαύτην κραυγὴν ἐποίησαν ὥστε τοὺς ταξιάρχους ἐλθεῖν. *They made such a din that the taxiarchs came* (i.e. *such a din as to cause the taxiarchs to come*).

ὥστε + infinitive may also express an **intended** result. The distinction between this and a purpose clause can be tenuous:

τοῦτο ποιοῦσιν ὥστε μὴ ἀποθανεῖν. *They are doing this so as not to die.*

ὥστε may also be followed by a finite verb in the **indicative** (negated by οὐ), but only where there is emphasis on the actual occurrence of the result; so οὕτω σκαιὸς εἶ ὥστε οὐ δύνασαι μανθάνειν would mean *you are so stupid that you [actually] cannot understand*:

ἐπέπεσε χιὼν ἄπλετος ὥστε ἀπέκρυψε καὶ τὰ ὅπλα καὶ τοὺς ἀνθρώπους. *An immense amount of* (lit. *boundless*) *snow fell so that it [actually] covered both the weapons and the men.*

Notes

1 τοιοῦτος and τοσοῦτος are compounds of οὗτος (9.1/1) and are inflected in the same way, except that the initial τ which οὗτος has in most forms is dropped: τοιοῦτος, τοιαύτη, τοιοῦτο(ν); τοσοῦτος, τοσαύτη, τοσοῦτο(ν) (unlike τοῦτο, the neuter s. nom. and acc. can end in ν).

2 ὥστε may be used to introduce an independent sentence, with much the same force as οὖν, i.e. *and so, therefore, consequently*:

οὐχ ἧκεν· ὥστε οἱ Ἕλληνες ἐφρόντιζον. *He had not come; consequently, the Greeks were worried.*

3 The English phrase *to such a pitch/point/degree of x* is expressed in Greek by εἰς τοῦτο or εἰς τοσοῦτο(ν) + genitive (cf. 23.1/1d):

εἰς τοσοῦτον ὕβρεως ἦλθον ὥστε ἔπεισαν ὑμᾶς ἐλαύνειν αὐτόν. *They reached such a pitch of insolence that they persuaded you to drive him out.*

4 ὥστε may also be used in the sense *on the condition that* to express a condition or proviso:

ὑπέσχοντο ὥστε ἐκπλεῖν. *They made a promise on condition that they should sail away.*

However, *on condition that* is more usually expressed by ἐφ᾽ ᾧ or ἐφ᾽ ᾧτε followed by an infinitive or, less frequently, by a future indicative:

ἐποιήσαντο εἰρήνην ἐφ᾽ ᾧ τὰ μακρὰ τείχη καθελόντες τοῖς Λακεδαιμονίοις ἔπεσθαι (or ἕψονται). *They made peace on condition that after taking down the long walls they would follow the Spartans.*

Both the infinitive and future indicative in conditions of this type are negated by μή.

5 For the use of a comparative + ἤ ὥστε, see 17.1/4c.

16.1/2 Pluperfect indicative active

The Greek pluperfect exists only in the indicative mood. It is normally to be translated by the same tense in English (*I had washed before you came*) but its use is much more restricted (see below).

The pluperfect is a **historic** tense (4.1/1 note 1) and its active stem is formed from that of the perfect active. Where the latter contains reduplication (15.1/1), the pluperfect active stem is formed by adding the augment, e.g.

PERFECT ACTIVE STEM	PLUPERFECT ACTIVE STEM
λελυκ- (λύω)	ἐλελυκ-
γεγραφ- (γράφω)	ἐγεγραφ-
πεπομφ- (πέμπω)	ἐπεπομφ-

Where, however, the perfect active stem is already augmented it is also used for the pluperfect without change, e.g. ἠχ- (ἄγω).

The pluperfect active endings are: -η, -ης, -ει(ν), -εμεν, -ετε, -εσαν. For the conjugation of ἐλελύκη *I had loosened* see **Appendix 1**.

The pluperfect is the past version of the perfect and thus expresses a state that existed in the past (cf. 15.1/1):

ἔθυον πρότερον οἱ Πελασγοὶ τοῖς θεοῖς, ὄνομα δὲ ἐποιοῦντο οὐδενὶ αὐτῶν· οὐ γὰρ ἀκηκόεσάν πω. *Formerly the Pelasgians used to sacrifice to the gods but gave a name to none of them; for they had not yet (πω) heard [their names] (i.e. they were in a state of ignorance about the names of the gods).*

The pluperfect is relatively uncommon in Greek. In English we often use the pluperfect in subordinate clauses to denote an action which happened two stages back in the past, e.g. *when the soldiers had assembled, Cyrus spoke as follows* (if we regard Cyrus' speaking as one stage back in the past, then the soldiers' assembling, which happened before Cyrus' speaking, is two stages back in the past). Greek, however, normally regards both actions as single past events and uses two aorists: ἐπεὶ οἱ στρατιῶται συνῆλθον, Κῦρος ἔλεξε τάδε (lit. *when the soldiers assembled ...*, which we can also say in English). It would be possible to regard the soldiers as being in a state of having assembled and so justify a Greek pluperfect, but in subordinate clauses of time and reason (and also relative clauses) this is rarely done.

16.1/3 Perfect and pluperfect indicative middle/passive

In both the perfect and pluperfect the middle and passive voices have the same forms.

PERFECT
The stem of the strong perfect active is retained in the middle/passive, but that of the weak perfect active loses its κ. Consequently the distinction between strong and weak perfects is not maintained. As, however, the stem of the perfect middle/passive is not always predictable, the first person perfect indicative middle/passive is included in the principal parts of irregular verbs (7.1/1 note 3 and **Principal parts of verbs**).

When a perfect middle/passive stem ends in a vowel or diphthong[1] (e.g. λελυ-, νένῑκη-) the endings -μαι, -σαι, -ται, -μεθα, -σθε, -νται are added (for the conjugation of λέλυμαι *I have ransomed* (mid.), *I have been loosened* (pass.) see **Appendix 1**).

When a perfect middle/passive stem ends in a consonant, a sound change is necessary in certain cases to assimilate the final

---

[1] This occurs only in verbs with a weak perfect active where the κ of the stem is preceded by a vowel or diphthong; the strong perfect ἀκήκοα (ἀκούω) has no passive in Classical Greek.

consonant of the stem to the initial consonant of the ending. With all consonant stems a succession of three consonants in the second and third plural is avoided; in the second plural the σ of the ending (-σθε) is dropped, but in the third plural Attic Greek sidesteps the difficulty by using a two-word periphrasis consisting of the perfect middle/passive participle (see 16.1/4) and the third plural present of εἰμί.

Consonant stems are classified in the same way as for the present tense (6.1/4 and 11.1/3):

(a) Palatal stems
The final palatal of the stem appears as γ before -μαι and -μεθα (and -μένοι of the participle), and as κ before -σαι (giving -ξαι) and -ται. In the second pl. κ + σθε > κθε > χθε (the κ is aspirated to assimilate it to θ). From φυλάττω *guard* (perf. mid./pass. stem πεφυλακ-) we have:

s.			PL.	
	1	πεφύλαγμαι		πεφυλάγμεθα
	2	πεφύλαξαι		πεφύλαχθε
	3	πεφύλακται		πεφυλαγμένοι εἰσί(ν)

When these forms are used as passives they mean *I have been guarded, you have been guarded,* etc. When they are used as middles their sense depends on the use of the middle involved in a particular context (8.1/1), i.e. *I have guarded myself* etc., or *I have guarded for myself* etc., or *I have had (something) guarded* etc. The participle used in the third plural varies in gender according to the subject. This applies to all forms of this type.

(b) Labial stems
The final labial of the stem appears as μ before -μαι and -μεθα (and -μένοι of the participle), and as π before -σαι (giving -ψαι) and -ται. In the second pl. π + σθε > πθε > φθε. From κρύπτω *hide* (perf. mid./ pass. stem κεκρυπ-) we have:

s.			PL.	
	1	κέκρυμμαι		κεκρύμμεθα
	2	κέκρυψαι		κέκρυφθε
	3	κέκρυπται		κεκρυμμένοι εἰσί(ν)

The passive meaning is *I have been hidden* etc.

(c) *Dental stems*

The final dental of the stem becomes σ before all endings. In the second person s. and pl. σσ > σ. From πείθω *persuade* (perf. mid./pass. stem πεπειθ-) we have:

s.		PL.	
1	πέπεισμαι		πεπείσμεθα
2	πέπεισαι		πέπεισθε
3	πέπεισται		πεπεισμένοι εἰσί(ν)

The passive meaning is *I have been persuaded* etc.

(d) *Stems in* λ, μ, ν, ρ

The final consonant of λ and ρ stems remains unchanged. ἀγγέλλω *announce,* σπείρω *sow* (perf. mid./pass. stems ἠγγελ-, ἐσπαρ-; the α of the latter is irregular) have ἤγγελμαι, ἤγγελσαι etc. and ἔσπαρμαι, ἔσπαρσαι etc. The final consonant of ν stems is dropped in some verbs, but in others becomes σ before -μαι, -μεθα, (and -μένοι). From κρίνω *judge,* φαίνω *show* (perf. mid./pass. stems κεκρι-, πεφαν-) we have:

s.		
1	κέκριμαι	πέφασμαι
2	κέκρισαι	πέφανσαι
3	κέκριται	πέφανται

PL.		
1	κεκρίμεθα	πεφάσμεθα
2	κέκρισθε	πέφανθε
3	κεκριμένοι εἰσί(ν)	πεφασμένοι εἰσί(ν)

The passive meaning is *I have been judged,* etc., *I have been shown,* etc.

-η is added to the few μ stems both in the perfect active and in the perfect middle/passive, e.g. νέμω *apportion,* νενέμηκα (act.), νενέμημαι (mid./pass.), 3 pl. νενέμηνται.

PLUPERFECT

The pluperfect indicative middle/passive uses the perfect middle/passive stem except that the syllabic augment is added when the latter is reduplicated, e.g. ἐλελυ- (λύω), ἐπεφυλακ- (φυλάττω); but ἐσπαρ- (σπείρω) is used for both perfect and pluperfect (cf. 16.1/2). The historic middle/passive endings are -μην, -σο, -το, -μεθα, -σθε, -ντο (cf. 8.1/1*f*). For the conjugation of ἐλελύμην *I had ransomed* (mid.), *I had been loosened* (pass.) see **Appendix 1**. With stems ending in a consonant the same sound changes are involved as with the perfect indicative middle/passive, and the perfect middle/passive participle with ἦσαν is used for the third plural, e.g.

s.			PL.	
	1	ἐπεφυλάγμην		ἐπεφυλάγμεθα
	2	ἐπεφύλαξο		ἐπεφύλαχθε
	3	ἐπεφύλακτο		πεφυλαγμένοι ἦσαν

The passive meaning is *I had been guarded* etc.

Note

Third **plural** endings in -αται (< νται) and -ατο (< ντο) occur in early Attic and other dialects, e.g. πεφυλάχαται (perf. – its passive meaning is *they have been guarded*), ἐπεφυλάχατο (pluperf. – its passive meaning is *they had been guarded*). These endings must be carefully distinguished from third **singular** endings in -ται and -το.

16.1/4 Other parts of the perfect tense

The perfect infinitives and participles are formed from the same stems as the corresponding indicatives (the reduplication or the temporal/syllabic augment of the perfect indicative stem is **not** dropped). The infinitive endings are -έναι (act.) and -σθαι (mid./pass.; with consonantal stems this ending undergoes the same changes as -σθε). The active participle is a first and third declension adjective (10.1/3) in -ώς, -υῖα, -ός (see below), and the middle/passive participle is a first and second declension adjective (3.1/3) in -μένος, -μένη, -μένον.[2] In the following table for λύω, φυλάττω, κρύπτω, πείθω, κρίνω only the masculine forms of the participles are given.

---

[2] The accent of all forms of the perfect middle/passive participle is on the second syllable from the end (paroxytone, see **Appendix 9**, b(*v*)).

Infinitives		Participles	
ACTIVE	MIDDLE/PASSIVE	ACTIVE	MIDDLE/PASSIVE
λελυκέναι	λελύσθαι	λελυκώς	λελυμένος
to *have loosened*	mid. *to have ransomed*	*having loosened*	mid. *having ransomed*
	pass. *to have been loosened*		pass. *having been loosened*
πεφυλαχέναι	πεφυλάχθαι	πεφυλαχώς	πεφυλαγμένος
κεκρυφέναι	κεκρύφθαι	κεκρυφώς	κεκρυμμένος
πεποιθέναι	} πεπεῖσθαι	πεποιθώς }	} πεπεισμένος[3]
πεπεικέναι		πεπεικώς	
κεκρικέναι	κεκρίσθαι	κεκρικώς	κεκριμένος

The corresponding forms of the aorist are sometimes to be translated in the same way as those of the perfect, but the meanings and uses of the two tenses are quite distinct. The perfect always expresses a state (on the meaning of the aorist see 4.1/1, 12.1/1).

λελυκώς is declined:

	SINGULAR			PLURAL		
	M.	F.	N.	M.	F.	N.
N.V.	λελυκώς	λελυκυῖα	λελυκός	λελυκότες	λελυκυῖαι	λελυκότα
Acc.	λελυκότα	λελυκυῖαν	λελυκός	λελυκότας	λελυκυίᾱς	λελυκότα
Gen.	λελυκότος	λελυκυίᾱς	λελυκότος	λελυκότων	λελυκυιῶν	λελυκότων
Dat.	λελυκότι	λελυκυίᾳ	λελυκότι	λελυκόσι(ν)	λελυκυίαις	λελυκόσι(ν)

Notes

1 A perfect subjunctive and perfect optative exist but are rare. The active is formed by adding to the active stem the endings -ω, -ῃς, -ῃ, -ωμεν, -ητε, -ωσι(ν) (subj., giving λελύκω etc.) and -οιμι, -οις, -οι, -οιμεν, -οιτε, -οιεν (opt., giving λελύκοιμι etc.). There are alternative active forms consisting of the perfect active participle and the appropriate part of εἰμί: λελυκὼς ὦ, etc. (subj.); λελυκὼς εἴην etc. (opt.). In the middle/passive the subjunctive and optative

---

[3] On the two perfect stems of πείθω see 15.1/1 note 2.

follow the latter pattern (subj. λελυμένος ὦ etc., opt. λελυμένος εἴην etc.) For tables see **Appendix 1**.

2 Greek has also a **future perfect** tense, which expresses a future state. For most verbs it exists only in the passive and is not common. Its stem is formed by adding σ to the perfect middle/passive stem (e.g. λελῦσ-), and to this are added the present middle/passive endings, viz λελύσομαι I *shall have been loosened*, λελύσῃ (-ει), λελύσεται, λελῦσόμεθα, λελύσεσθε, λελύσονται The future perfect occurs mostly with verbs whose perfect has a present meaning (19.1/3a) and for this reason is not included in Appendix 1.

Insight

Although the vast majority of the dead were condemned to spend a boring eternity in the Underworld the Greeks also developed the idea of a paradise for those who were particularly favored by the gods. This was Ἠλύσιον *Elysium*, which we first meet in Homer. In the Odyssey it is described as a place where *there is no snow or terrible storm or rain but with the gentle breath of the west wind Oceanus sends breezes to refresh mortals*, and one of the characters, Menelaus, is told that he will not die but be taken there while still living because he, by being married to Helen (another of Zeus' children), is the son-in-law of the lord of Olympus. Later poets relaxed the entry requirements and allowed admittance to noteworthy benefactors of humanity such as Harmodius and Aristogeiton, who killed an Athenian tyrant.

16.2 Greek reading

1 ἐπεὶ δὲ ἐπὶ τὰς σκηνὰς ἦλθον, οἱ μὲν ἄλλοι περὶ τὰ ἐπιτήδεια ἦσαν, στρατηγοὶ δὲ καὶ λοχαγοὶ συνῆλθον. καὶ ἐνταῦθα πολλὴ ἀπορία ἦν. ἔνθεν μὲν γὰρ ὄρη ἦν ὑπερύψηλα, ἔνθεν δὲ ὁ ποταμὸς τοσοῦτος ὥστε μηδὲ τὰ δόρατα ὑπερέχειν πειρωμένοις τοῦ βάθους.

2 ὁ Διογένης, ἐρωτηθεὶς διὰ τί οἱ ἀθληταὶ ἀναίσθητοί εἰσιν, ἔφη ὅτι κρέασιν ὑείοις καὶ βοείοις ἀνῳκοδόμηνται.

3 γαμεῖν κεκρικότα δεῖ.

4 πάντα τὸν βίον ἐν κινδύνοις διατελοῦμεν ὄντες, ὥστε οἱ περὶ ἀσφαλείας διαλεγόμενοι λελήθασιν αὑτοὺς τὸν πόλεμον εἰς ἅπαντα τὸν χρόνον κατασκευάζοντες.

5 κύνα δέρεις δεδαρμένην.

6 οἱ Ποτειδεᾶται προσδεχόμενοι τοὺς Ἀθηναίους ἐστρατοπεδεύοντο πρὸς Ὀλύνθου ἐν τῷ ἰσθμῷ, καὶ ἀγορὰν ἔξω τῆς πόλεως ἐπεποίηντο. καὶ στρατηγὸν μὲν τοῦ πεζοῦ παντὸς οἱ ξύμμαχοι ᾕρηντο Ἀριστέα, τῆς δὲ ἵππου Περδίκκαν.

7 ἐπεὶ οἱ βάρβαροι ἐκ τῆς χώρας ἀπῆλθον, οἱ Ἀθηναῖοι τὴν ἑαυτῶν πόλιν ἀνοικοδομεῖν παρεσκευάζοντο. τῶν γὰρ οἰκιῶν αἱ μὲν πολλαὶ ἐπεπτώκεσαν, ὀλίγαι δὲ περιῆσαν, ἐν αἷς αὐτοὶ ἐσκήνωσαν οἱ δυνατοὶ τῶν Περσῶν.

8 εἰς ἠκονημένας μαχαίρας ἡ αἲξ ἥκει.

9 καὶ τὴν μὲν νύκτα ἐνταῦθα διήγαγον· ἐπεὶ δ᾽ ἡμέρα ὑπέφαινεν, ἐπορεύοντο σιγῇ συντεταγμένοι ἐπὶ τοὺς πολεμίους· καὶ γὰρ ὀμίχλη ἐγένετο, ὥστε ἔλαθον ἐγγὺς προσελθόντες.

10 ἔπειτα δὲ καὶ πρὸς ἅπαντας τοὺς μετὰ Δημοσθένους ὁμολογία γίγνεται, ἐφ᾽ ᾧτε μὴ ἀποθανεῖν μηδένα, μήτε βιαίως, μήτε δεσμοῖς, μήτε σίτου ἐνδείᾳ.

11 Τιρίβαζος εἶπεν ὅτι σπείσασθαι βούλοιτο ἐφ᾽ ᾧ μήτε αὐτὸς τοὺς Ἕλληνας ἀδικεῖν, μήτ᾽ ἐκείνους καίειν τὰς οἰκίας, λαμβάνειν τε τὰ ἐπιτήδεια ὧν δέοιντο. ἔδοξε ταῦτα τοῖς στρατηγοῖς καὶ ἐσπείσαντο ἐπὶ τούτοις.

12 οὐδὲ βουλεύεσθαι ἔτι ὥρα, ὦ Σώκρατες, ἀλλὰ βεβουλεῦσθαι. μία δὲ βουλή· τῆσδε γὰρ τῆς νυκτὸς πάντα ταῦτα δεῖ πεπρᾶχθαι.

13 οὕτως οὖν οὐ ταὐτόν ἐστι θάρσος τε καὶ ἀνδρεία· ὥστε συμβαίνει τοὺς μὲν ἀνδρείους θαρραλέους εἶναι, μὴ μέντοι τούς γε θαρραλέους ἀνδρείους πάντας· θάρσος μὲν γὰρ καὶ ἀπὸ τέχνης γίγνεται ἀνθρώποις καὶ ἀπὸ θυμοῦ καὶ ἀπὸ μανίας, ὥσπερ ἡ δύναμις, ἀνδρεία δ' ἀπὸ φύσεως καὶ εὐτροφίας τῶν ψυχῶν γίγνεται.

14 οἱ Λακεδαιμόνιοι τὰς σπονδὰς προτέρους λελυκέναι τοὺς Ἀθηναίους ἡγοῦντο.

15 ἡ αἶξ οὔπω τέτοκεν.

16 Φίλιππος, ὁ πατὴρ τοῦ μεγάλου Ἀλεξάνδρου, φρούριόν τι βουλόμενος λαβεῖν ὀχυρόν, ὡς ἀπήγγειλαν οἱ κατάσκοποι χαλεπὸν εἶναι παντάπασι καὶ ἀνάλωτον, ἠρώτησεν εἰ χαλεπὸν οὕτως ἐστὶν ὥστε μηδὲ ὄνον προσελθεῖν χρυσίον κομίζοντα.

Notes

1 ἦλθον *had come* (16.1/2); περὶ ... ἦσαν *were busy with*; πειρωμένοις τοῦ βάθους lit. *for [them] testing the depth.*

2 ὅτι here *because*; ἀνῳκοδόμηνται < ἀνοικοδομέω.

3 κεκρικότα agrees with ἄνδρα understood, lit. *it is necessary for a man ...*

4 εἰς + acc. is used here instead of the plain acc. for emphasis (cf. 7.1/7*a*).

6 ᾕρηντο < αἱρέομαι *choose* (18.1/4); ἡ ἵππος *the cavalry.*

7 αἱ πολλαί *the majority, most* (cf. 8.2.11 and 15.2.17); ἐπεπτώκεσαν < πίπτω.

8 ἠκονημένᾱς < ἀκονάω.

9 ὑπέφαινεν, ἐπορεύοντο inceptive imperfects (*began to ...*).

11 βούλοιτο (and later δέοιντο) opt. in reported speech in historic sequence (14.1/4d); μήτε ... μήτ᾿ introduce the negated conditions (*that neither he ... nor they...*); the subject of λαμβάνειν is ἐκείνους from the previous phrase but note that it is **not** negated; ἔδοξε ταῦτα *these things seemed good.*

12 οὐδὲ ... ἔτι ὥρα supply ἐστί *nor [is it] still [the] time*; βεβουλεῦσθαι i.e. *to have finished deliberating.*

13 *l*.1 ταὐτόν *the same [thing]*; the subject of ἐστί is θάρσος and ἀνδρείᾱ (with double subjects the verb may agree with only the nearer one).

14 Take προτέρους with τοὺς Ἀθηναίους, which is the subject of λελυκέναι.

16 ὡς *when*; ἐστίν present tense because in indirect speech Greek always retains the tense of the original direct speech (7.1/3); Philip cynically implies that any fort can be captured if a sufficient bribe is offered to a potential traitor; προσελθεῖν the infinitive here denotes a **possible** result, *could approach.*

Main points

- Phrases and clauses of result are introduced by ὥστε

- The pluperfect expresses a state in the past; it exists only in the indicative

- For its stem the pluperfect adds an augment to reduplicated perfect stems; where a perfect stem itself has an augment this is retained in the pluperfect

- The perfect and pluperfect passive stem is the same as the active for verbs with a strong perfect but for verbs with a weak perfect the final κ of the active stem is dropped; a final consonant changes according to the ending

- A participle and an auxiliary verb (εἰσί, ἦσαν) are used for the third plural perfect and pluperfect passive

- Perfect infinitives and participles do not drop reduplication or the syllabic/temporal augment

16.3 Extra reading – Heracles

After an attack of madness, Heracles wakes up to find himself tied to a pillar and surrounded by destruction which he himself has unwittingly perpetrated. The passage is from the Ἡρακλῆς of Euripides (485–406 BC), the third of the great Attic tragedians.

> ἔμπνους μέν εἰμι καὶ δέδορχ᾽ ἅπερ με δεῖ,
> αἰθέρα τε καὶ γῆν τόξα θ᾽ ἡλίου τάδε.
> ὡς δ᾽ ἐν κλύδωνι καὶ φρενῶν ταράγματι
> πέπτωκα δεινῷ καὶ πνοὰς θερμὰς πνέω
> μετάρσι᾽, οὐ βέβαια πλευμόνων ἄπο.   5
> ἰδού, τί δεσμοῖς ναῦς ὅπως ὡρμισμένος
> νεανίαν θώρακα καὶ βραχίονα
> πρὸς ἡμιθραύστῳ λαΐνῳ τυκίσματι
> ἧμαι, νεκροῖσι γείτονας θάκους ἔχων;
> πτερωτὰ δ᾽ ἔγχη τόξα τ᾽ ἔσπαρται πέδῳ,   10
> ἃ πρὶν παρασπίζοντ᾽ ἐμοῖς βραχίοσιν
> ἔσῳζε πλευρὰς ἐξ ἐμοῦ τ᾽ ἐσῴζετο.
> οὔ που κατῆλθον αὖθις εἰς Ἅιδου πάλιν,
> Εὐρυσθέως δίαυλον ἐξ Ἅιδου μολών;
> ἀλλ᾽ οὔτε Σισύφειον εἰσορῶ πέτρον   15
> Πλούτωνά τ᾽ οὐδὲ σκῆπτρα Δήμητρος κόρης.
> ἔκ τοι πέπληγμαι· ποῦ ποτ᾽ ὢν ἀμηχανῶ;
> ὠή, τίς ἐγγὺς ἢ πρόσω φίλων ἐμῶν
> δύσγνοιαν ὅστις τὴν ἐμὴν ἰάσεται;

Notes

l.1 δέδορχ᾽ (= -κα) the perfect here is virtually an emphatic present *I really see*. *ll.3ff.* ὡς ... exclamatory, lit. *how I have fallen in a terrible wave* ... i.e. *into what a terrible wave* ...; μετάρσι᾽(α) ... βέβαια n.

acc. pl. used adverbially (20.1/5), lit. *how* (ὡς *l*.3) ... *I breathe warm breaths shallowly, not steadily from my lungs* (Heracles is panting but does not know why); ἄπο on the accent of disyllabic prepositions when they follow the word they govern see note on 11.2.4. *ll*.6f. Take ναῦς ὅπως together *like a ship*; ὡρμισμένος (< ὁρμίζω) *anchored*; νεανίαν here used adjectivally in the sense *sturdy* (not *youthful*, Heracles being no longer young); θώρακα καὶ βραχίονα lit. *with respect to chest and arm* this use of the accusative (called *accusative of respect*, 20.1/5) is used to clarify verbs and adjectives; here the accusatives tell where (i.e. with respect to what parts of his body) Heracles is anchored (ὡρμισμένος). *l*.9 ἧμαι (19.1/3*b*) *I sit*; θάκους trans. by a singular *seat* (the plural is often used for the singular in verse; cf. τόξα in *l*.10 and σκῆπτρα in *l*.16). *l*.10 The winged weapons (πτερωτὰ ἔγχη) are arrows; ἔσπαρται 3rd s. perf. ind. pass. of σπείρω. *l*.11 πρίν (here an adverb) *previously, formerly*; παρασπίζοντ᾽(α) governs the following dative, lit. *shielding my arms*. *l*.12 ἐξ = ὑπό *by*. *l*.14 Eurystheus was the king of Mycenae for whom Heracles had to complete his twelve labours (one of them, the descent to Hades to bring back Cerberus, is referred to here); Εὐρυσθέως δίαυλον lit. *the double course* (i.e. the descent and return) *of* (i.e. *prescribed by*) *Eurystheus*; μολών (aor. pple. of βλώσκω) to be taken with δίαυλον *going [on] the double course* (acc. of spatial extent, 7.1/7*d*). *ll*.15f. On Sisyphus see Insight to Unit 15; οὔτε ... τ᾽(ε) ... οὐδέ *neither ... or* (lit. *and*) ... *nor yet* (οὐδέ indicates a slight climax). *l*.16 The daughter of Demeter was Persephone, who was the wife of Pluto (= Hades; cf. Insight to Unit 15). *l*.17 ἐκ ... πέπληγμαι = ἐκπέπληγμαι (tmesis, see 12.3.9 *l*.6); ποῦ etc. lit. *wherever being am I helpless?* but the emphasis is on ὤν and we must translate *wherever am I in my helplessness?*

....

17.1 Grammar

17.1/1 Imperative mood: commands and prohibitions

The imperative mood is used for **commands**. In Greek it exists in the present and aorist tenses (and also the perfect – see note 4). The stem used is the same as that of the corresponding indicative. As well as second person imperatives (which we have in English), Greek also has imperatives in the **third** person with the meanings given below.

The imperative of λύω is

Present

		ACTIVE		MIDDLE/PASSIVE	
S.	2	λῦε	*loosen!*	λύου	mid. *ransom!* pass. *be loosened!*
	3	λυέτω	*let him loosen!*	λυέσθω	mid. *let him ransom!* pass. *let him be loosened!*
PL.	2	λύετε	*loosen!*	λύεσθε	mid. *ransom* pass. *be loosened!*
	3	λυόντων[1]	*let them loosen!*	λυέσθων	mid. *let them ransom!* pass. *let them be loosened!*

Aorist

		ACTIVE	MIDDLE	PASSIVE
S.	2	λῦσον	λῦσαι	λύθητι
	3	λυσάτω	λυσάσθω	λυθήτω
PL.	2	λύσατε	λύσασθε	λύθητε
	3	λυσάντων	λυσάσθων	λυθέντων

----

[1] Note that λυόντων, λυσάντων and λυθέντων can also be the gen. pl. of masculine and neuter of the corresponding participles.

The aorist is usually to be translated in the same way as the present but the two are not interchangeable. The difference, as elsewhere, is one of aspect. The present is used for an action which is seen as going on, in the process of happening or being repeated, the aorist for an action which is seen simply as an event. Sometimes this distinction can be brought out in English by using a verbal periphrasis:

κροῦσον (aor.) ἐκείνην τὴν μυῖαν. *Swat that fly!*
κροῦε (pres.) ἐκείνην τὴν μυῖαν. *Keep swatting that fly!*

Generally the present imperative is used with verbs which in themselves imply continual action, e.g. σπεῦδε βραδέως *hasten slowly*, while the aorist imperative is used with verbs which usually (but not necessarily) indicate a single act, e.g. καῦσον πῦρ ἐν τῇ ἑστίᾳ *light a fire in the hearth*.

Prohibitions (negative commands) are expressed with μή, e.g. μὴ πᾶσι πίστευε *do not trust everyone*; μηδεὶς τοῦτο ἀγνοείτω *let no-one be unaware of this,* but if the **aorist** aspect is appropriate the mood employed is always the **subjunctive**, not the imperative:

μὴ ἐπὶ δουλείαν ἑκὼν ἔλθῃς. *Do not go willingly to slavery.*
μηδεὶς θαυμάσῃ. *Let no-one be surprised.*

For the other use of this (jussive) subjunctive see 14.1/4*a*(i).

To express a very strong prohibition οὐ μή and the future indicative is used, e.g.

τί ποιεῖς; οὐ μὴ καταβήσει. *What are you doing? You shall (or must) not come down.*

Notes

1 The imperative of the strong aorist has the same endings as the present. From μανθάνω (aor. ἔμαθον) the aor. imp. act is μάθε, μαθέτω, μάθετε, μαθόντων. However, five strong aorist imperatives are irregularly accented on the last syllable in the second person singular: εἰπέ (λέγω), ἐλθέ (ἔρχομαι), εὑρέ (εὑρίσκω), ἰδέ (ὁράω), λαβέ (λαμβάνω).

2 The imperative of the root aorist (11.1/1) follows that of the aorist passive except that the ending for the 2nd s. is -θι, not -τι: from ἔγνων (γιγνώσκω) we have γνῶθι, γνώτω, γνῶτε, γνόντων.

3 The present imperative of contracted verbs is regular but, because of contraction, the 2nd s. forms are easily confused:

Active	τίμᾱ (τίμαε)	ποίει (ποίεε)	δήλου (δήλοε)
Mid./pass.	τῑμῶ (τῑμάου)	ποιοῦ (ποιέου)	δηλοῦ (δηλόου)

The position of the accent can be important for distinguishing between different forms, e.g. ποίει (imp.), ποιεῖ (ind.).

4 In addition to the present and aorist there is also a **perfect imperative**. The perfect imperative active consists of the perfect active participle and the imperative of εἰμί (see below note 6), e.g. λελυκὼς ἴσθι (lit. *be in a state of having loosened*); but the perfect imperative middle/passive has single-word forms, e.g. λέλυσο (lit. *be in a state of having been loosened*). This is rare except in verbs whose perfect has a present meaning (19.1/3*a*), e.g. μέμνησο *remember!* (< μέμνημαι). For these forms of λύω see **Appendix 1**.

5 The **infinitive** is sometimes used instead of the second person imperative, (cf. English *Not to worry*, i.e. *do not worry*):

πάντως, ὦ Κριτόβουλε, ἀπαληθεῦσαι πρὸς ἡμᾶς. *At any rate, Critobulus, tell the truth to us.*

6 The imperative of εἰμί is ἴσθι *be!*, ἔστω, ἔστε, ἔστων (or ὄντων). ἴσθι is also the 2nd s. imperative active of οἶδα (19.1/3*a*), with the meaning *know!*

7 Some imperatives have a fixed use:

χαῖρε, χαίρετε *hello* or *goodbye* (χαίρω *rejoice*)
ἔρρε, ἔρρετε *be damned! go to hell!* ἐρρέτω *let him/her/it be damned!* (ἔρρω *go to one's harm*)
ἄγε, ἄγετε; φέρε, φέρετε *come on! come now!* (by way of encouragement).

17.1/2 Comparison of adjectives and adverbs

Adjectives (and adverbs) have three degrees: **positive** *bad, sick, wonderful*; **comparative** *worse, sicker, more wonderful*; **superlative** *worst, sickest, most wonderful*. To give the three degrees of an adjective is to **compare** it. Some adjectives in English are compared regularly (*sick, wonderful*), some irregularly (*bad*). The same applies in Greek. By far the greater number of adjectives is compared by the addition of suffixes, and of these Greek has two sets:

(a) Comparative in -τερος, superlative in -τατος
In this type both the comparative in -τερος (f. -τερᾱ, n. -τερον) and the superlative in -τατος (f. -τατη, n. -τατον) are first and second declension adjectives (3.1/3). All regularly compared adjectives belong here. The way in which -τερος and -τατος are attached to the stem of an adjective depends on the class of its positive form:

(i) First and second declension adjectives (3.1/3) add -οτερος, -οτατος if the last syllable of their stem is long, but -ωτερος, -ωτατος if this is short (the stem is obtained by subtracting -ος from the nom. m. s., e.g. σοφός, stem σοφ-). A syllable is long if it contains either a long vowel, or a diphthong, or a short vowel followed by two consonants (the second not being λ, μ, ν, or ρ); a syllable is short if it contains a short vowel followed by a single consonant (for further details see **Appendix 9**). Examples are:

POSITIVE	STEM	COMPARATIVE	SUPERLATIVE
σοφός *wise*	σοφ-	σοφώτερος *wiser*	σοφώτατος *wisest*
δίκαιος *just*	δικαι-	δικαιότερος *more just*	δικαιότατος *most just*
ἔρημος *desolate*	ἐρημ-	ἐρημότερος *more desolate*	ἐρημότατος *most desolate*

Some 1st and 2nd declension adjectives belong to class (*b*) below. A few others belong to class (*a*) but are irregular, e.g. φίλος *dear*, compar. φιλαίτερος, supl. φιλαίτατος or φίλτατος.

(ii) Third declension adjectives (10.1/4) with a stem in ον add -εστερος, -εστατος, e.g. ἄφρων (stem ἀφρον-) *stupid*, ἀφρονέστερος *more stupid*, ἀφρονέστατος *most stupid*. Those with a stem in ες add -τερος, -τατος, e.g. ἀληθής (stem ἀληθεσ-) *true*, ἀληθέστερος, ἀληθέστατος.

(iii) First and third declension adjectives (10.1/3) in -εις follow χαρίεις, *charming*, χαριέστερος, χαριέστατος. Some in -υς follow γλυκύς, *sweet*, γλυκύτερος, γλυκύτατος but most are irregular (see below).

(b) *Comparative in* -(ῐ)ων, *superlative in* -ιστος
This group, which is much smaller, contains irregular adjectives from all classes. The stem of the positive form is sometimes changed for the other degrees of comparison. The following are the most common examples:

POSITIVE		COMPARATIVE	SUPERLATIVE
ἀγαθός	*good*	ἀμείνων	ἄριστος
		βελτίων	βέλτιστος
		κρείττων	κράτιστος
αἰσχρός	*ugly*	αἰσχίων	αἴσχιστος
ἀλγεινός	*painful*	ἀλγίων	ἄλγιστος
ἐχθρός	*hostile*	ἐχθίων	ἔχθιστος
ἡδύς	*sweet*	ἡδίων	ἥδιστος
κακός	*bad*	κακίων	κάκιστος
		χείρων	χείριστος
καλός	*beautiful*	καλλίων	κάλλιστος
μέγας	*great*	μείζων	μέγιστος
ὀλίγος	*small, few*	ἐλάττων	ἐλάχιστος
πολύς	*much*	πλείων	πλεῖστος
ῥᾴδιος	*easy*	ῥᾴων	ῥᾷστος
ταχύς	*swift*	θάττων	τάχιστος

Two adjectives (ἀγαθός and κακός) are compared in more than one way; κρείττων, κράτιστος (from ἀγαθός) can also mean *stronger, strongest* (cf. κράτος *power*).

Comparatives in this class are declined as third declension adjectives in ον (10.1/4a), but with some very important alternative forms (we can ignore the vocative, which is rare), e.g.

	SINGULAR		PLURAL	
	M. & F.	N.	M. & F.	N.
Nom.	μείζων	μεῖζον	μείζονες/μείζους	μείζονα/μείζω
Acc.	μείζονα/μείζω	μεῖζον	μείζονας/μείζους	μείζονα/μείζω
Gen.	μείζονος		μειζόνων	
Dat.	μείζονι		μείζοσι(ν)	

The alternatives are contracted versions of forms without ν (μείζω < μείζοα). The acc. pl. μείζους (< μείζοας) has an irregular contraction (ο + α normally produces ω, as in the singular). It is important to note that the forms in -ους may be **nom.** pl. as well as acc. pl.

πλείων *larger,* (pl.) *more* has a stem πλει- before ω/ου but πλει- or πλε- before ο (but always πλέον):

	SINGULAR		PLURAL	
	M. & F.	N.	M. & F.	N.
Nom.	πλείων	πλέον	πλείονες	πλείονα
			πλέονες	πλέονα
			πλείους	πλείω
Acc.	πλείονα	πλέον	πλείονας	πλείονα
	πλέονα		πλέονας	πλέονα
	πλείω		πλείους	πλείω
Gen.	πλείονος		πλειόνων	
	πλέονος		πλεόνων	
Dat.	πλείονι		πλείοσι(ν)	
	πλέονι		πλέοσι(ν)	

Adverbs formed from adjectives (e.g. σοφῶς *wisely*) have as their comparative the neuter **singular** nom./acc. of the comparative of the adjective (σοφώτερον *more wisely*), and as their superlative the neuter **plural** nom./acc. of the superlative (σοφώτατα *most wisely*). Of the few adverbs not formed from adjectives we may note μάλα *very,* μᾶλλον *more,* μάλιστα *most.*

Notes

1 The meaning of some adjectives (e.g. πᾶς *all*) precludes a comparative or superlative.

2 The adverbs μᾶλλον *more* and μάλιστα *most* are sometimes used to compare adjectives: μᾶλλον φίλος *more dear, dearer*; μάλιστα φίλος *most dear, dearest*.

3 ἥττων *lesser, weaker, inferior* has no positive. Its superlative (ἥκιστος) is only common as an adverb, ἥκιστα *least of all, not at all*.

17.1/3 Meaning of the comparative and superlative

Comparatives and superlatives in Greek are not always to be understood in the sense *more X* and *most X*. A comparative adjective is sometimes used where no comparison is expressed, and indicates a higher degree than the positive. English here uses *rather* or *too* (cf. also 17.1/4):

ὁ Κῦρος ἦν πολυλογώτερος. *Cyrus was rather talkative.*
αἱ ἐμαὶ διατριβαὶ ὑμῖν βαρύτεραι γεγόνασι καὶ ἐπιφθονώτεραι.
  My discourses have become too burdensome and odious for you.

Likewise, the superlative (without the definite article) is often used to express a very high degree:

καί ποτε ὄντος πάγου δεινοτάτου Σωκράτης ἐξῆλθεν ἱμάτιον ἔχων.
  And once when there was a very terrible frost Socrates went out wearing (lit. having) [only] a cloak.

As in English, a superlative adjective is preceded by the definite article when it means *the most X*: ὁ δεινότατος πάγος *the most terrible frost*. The article is omitted, however, when a superlative adjective is used as a predicate, e.g. ὁ Σωκράτης σόφωτατος πάντων ἐστίν *Socrates is wisest of all* (cf. 5.1/3).

17.1/4 Constructions involving the comparative and superlative

(*a*) In comparisons in English a comparative adjective or adverb is followed by *than*. In Greek ἤ *than* (which may elsewhere mean *or*) is used in the same way:

ἐν τοῖς ὄχλοις πιθανώτεροι οἱ ἀπαίδευτοι ἢ οἱ πεπαιδευμένοι. *Among crowds the uneducated [are] more persuasive than the educated (lit. the having been educated [people]).*
τὸ μὴ εἶναι κρεῖττον ἢ τὸ ζῆν κακῶς. *Not existing [is] better than living badly.*

ἤ is here a conjunction and what follows must be in the same case as what precedes. Whereas in English we can nowadays say *Socrates is wiser than me,* in Greek we must have Σωκράτης σοφώτερός ἐστιν ἢ ἐγώ; the first member of the comparison (Σωκράτης) is nominative and therefore the second member must also be nominative (hence ἐγώ).

There is, however, another construction, the **genitive of comparison**, in which the second member of the comparison is put into the genitive and ἤ is omitted:

ὁ χρῡσὸς κρείττων μῡρίων λόγων βροτοῖς. *For mortals gold [is] stronger than countless words.*
οὐδὲν σιωπῆς ἐστι χρησιμώτερον. *Nothing is more useful than silence.*

(*b*) A comparative may be accompanied by a dative of **measure of difference**: κεφαλῇ ἐλάττων *shorter by a head*; μείζων πολλῷ *greater by much,* i.e. *much greater.*

(*c*) In sentences of the type *he is too weak to help* ... Greek uses a comparative adjective followed by ἢ ὥστε and an infinitive (ὥστε here introduces a phrase of result – 16.1/1): μεῖζόν ἐστι τὸ κακὸν ἢ ὥστε φέρειν *the evil is too great to bear* (lit. *greater than so as to ...*).

(*d*) A superlative adjective or adverb is preceded by ὡς or ὅτι (both used here adverbially) for expressions such as ὡς (ὅτι) πλεῖστοι *as many as possible*; ὡς (ὅτι) τάχιστα *as quickly as possible.*

17.1/5 Active verbs used in a passive sense

The verb ἀποκτείνω does not occur in the passive. Instead, Greek uses the active forms of ἀποθνῇσκω (literally *die,* but in this context *be killed*): οἱ αἰχμάλωτοι ἀπέθανον ὑπὸ τῶν βαρβάρων *the captives were killed by the barbarians.* The passive sense of ἀπέθανον is here made clear by the agent construction ὑπό + gen. (11.1/2). Some indication of this sort is normally present.

Similarly, φεύγω (literally *flee*) and ἐκπίπτω (literally *fall out*) are used as the passive of ἐκβάλλω *banish, send into exile*:

> ἐκ Νάξου ἔφυγον πλούσιοί τινες ὑπὸ τοῦ δήμου. *Some wealthy men were exiled from Naxos by the people.*
>
> ἐκ γὰρ τῆς ἄλλης Ἑλλάδος οἱ πολέμῳ ἢ στάσει ἐκπίπτοντες παρ᾽ Ἀθηναίους οἱ δυνατώτατοι ἀνεχώρουν. *For when the most influential men were driven out of the rest of Greece by war or sedition, they used to withdraw to the Athenians* (lit. *those exiled by war ..., the most influential, ... used to ...*).

εὖ/κακῶς λέγω (+ acc.) *speak well/badly of* has the passive εὖ/κακῶς ἀκούω *be well/badly spoken of* (lit. *hear well/badly*):

> ἐμὲ κακῶς ἀκούσαντα ὑπὸ σοῦ μεγάλη ἔδακε λύπη. *I was deeply grieved when you spoke badly of me* (lit. *great grief bit me being badly spoken of by you*).

Likewise, εὖ/κακῶς ποιέω (+ acc.) *treat well/badly* has the passive εὖ/κακῶς πάσχω *be treated well/badly* (lit. *suffer well/badly*):

> οὐκ ἀεικὲς κακῶς πάσχειν ὑπὸ ἐχθρῶν. *[it is] not shameful to be badly treated by enemies.*

Insight

Legend tells us that when Constantine (AD 272–337; cf. Insight to Unit 9) was fighting a rival for supreme power at Rome, a fiery cross appeared in sky with the instruction τούτῳ νίκα *with this [sign]* (i.e. the symbol of Christianity) *conquer!* He went on to win and become emperor. Under his rule Christianity was officially recognized and became the favoured religion of the empire. Some versions of the story say that a Latin version also appeared, but as Constantine was fluent in both languages this would have been superfluous. On νίκα (2 s. imp. of νῑκάω) see 17.1/1 note 3.

17.2 Greek reading

1 A large number of pithy maxims current in antiquity were said to be inscribed on the columns of the temple of Apollo at Delphi. The following is a selection from surviving lists (the columns themselves no longer exist). The most famous are (*v*) and (*x*).

(*i*) ἀδικούμενος διαλλάττου. (*ii*) ἀλλοτρίων ἀπέχου. (*iii*) βραδέως ἐγχείρει. (*iv*) γαμεῖν μέλλε. (*v*) γνῶθι σεαυτόν. (*vi*) γονέας αἰδοῦ. (*vii*) φρόνει θνητά. (*viii*) ἐπὶ νεκρῷ μὴ γέλα. (*ix*) καιρὸν γνῶθι. (*x*) μηδὲν ἄγαν. (*xi*) πίνων μὴ πολλὰ λάλει. (*xii*) πλούτει δικαίως. (*xiii*) τύχην νόμιζε. (*xiv*) ὑβριζόμενος τιμωροῦ. (*xv*) υἱοῖς μὴ καταρῶ.

2# γύμναζε παῖδας· ἄνδρας οὐ γὰρ γυμνάσεις.

3 φοβερώτερόν ἐστι στρατόπεδον ἐλάφων ἡγουμένου λέοντος ἢ στρατόπεδον λεόντων ἡγουμένου ἐλάφου.

4# φοβοῦ τὸ γῆρας· οὐ γὰρ ἔρχεται μόνον.

5# καλῶς ἀκούειν μᾶλλον ἢ πλουτεῖν θέλε.

6# ῥόδον παρελθὼν μηκέτι ζήτει πάλιν.

7 δύο ὦτα ἔχομεν, στόμα δὲ ἕν, ἵνα πλείω μὲν ἀκούωμεν, ἥττω δὲ λέγωμεν.

8 Shorter proverbs
(*i*) ὀξύτερον οἱ γείτονες βλέπουσι τῶν ἀλωπέκων. (*ii*) πεζῇ βαδίζων μὴ φοβοῦ τὰ κύματα. (*iii*) φαγέτω με λέων καὶ μὴ ἀλώπηξ. (*iv*) ἴσθι καὶ λέων ὅπου χρὴ καὶ πίθηκος ἐν μέρει. (*v*) ἤν τις ἔμαξε μᾶζαν, ταύτην καὶ ἐσθιέτω. (*vi*) στρατηγοῦ παρόντος πᾶσα ἀρχὴ παυσάσθω. (*vii*) ὁ πλεόνων ἐρῶν καὶ τῶν παρόντων ἀποστερεῖται. (*viii*) σιτίον εἰς ἀμίδα μὴ ἐμβάλλειν. (*ix*) ξένος ὢν ἀκολούθει τοῖς ἐπιχωρίοις νόμοις. (*x*) τὸν φίλον κακῶς μὴ λέγε, μηδ᾽ εὖ τὸν ἐχθρόν. (*xi*) μὴ καταφρονήσῃς τοῦ πένητος εὐτυχῶν. (*xii*) μὴ κρίνετε ἵνα μὴ κριθῆτε. (*xiii*) αἱ δεύτεραί

πως φροντίδες σοφώτεραι. (*xiv*) οἱ πλεῖστοι κακοί. (*xv*) ἀεὶ τὰ
πέρυσι βελτίω.

9# ἀσπίδι μὲν Σαΐων τις ἀγάλλεται, ἣν παρὰ θάμνῳ,
   ἔντος ἀμώμητον, κάλλιπον (= κατέλιπον) οὐκ ἐθέλων·
   αὐτὸς δ᾽ ἐξέφυγον θανάτου τέλος· ἀσπὶς ἐκείνη
   ἐρρέτω· ἐξαῦτις κτήσομαι οὐ κακίω.

10 ὁ βασίλειος πῆχυς τοῦ μετρίου ἐστὶ πηχέως μείζων τρισὶ δακτύλοις.

11 The Spartans (οἱ Λάκωνες/Λακεδαιμόνιοι) were men of few
   words (hence our *laconic*) and had a reputation for a dry, blunt
   humour. Most of the following stories are about Spartan kings.
   (*i*) Εὐδαμίδας ἰδὼν ἐν Ἀκαδημείᾳ Ξενοκράτη ἤδη πρεσβύτερον
          μετὰ τῶν μαθητῶν φιλοσοφοῦντα καὶ πυθόμενος ὅτι τὴν
          ἀρετὴν ζητεῖ, πότε οὖν, εἶπεν, αὐτῇ χρήσεται;
   (*ii*) Ἀργείου δέ τινος λέγοντος, ὡς φαυλότεροι γίγνονται κατὰ
          τὰς ἀποδημίας οἱ Λάκωνες, ἀλλ᾽ οὐχ ὑμεῖς γε, ἔφη, εἰς τὴν
          Σπάρτην ἐλθόντες χείρονες ἀλλὰ βελτίονες γίγνεσθε.
   (*iii*) Ἆγις πρὸς ἄνθρωπον πονηρὸν ἐρωτῶντα τίς ἄριστος εἴη
          Σπαρτιάτης, εἶπεν, ὁ σοὶ ἀνομοιότατος.
   (*iv*) Ἀνταλκίδας, σοφιστοῦ μέλλοντος ἀναγιγνώσκειν ἐγκώμιον
          Ἡρακλέους, τίς γὰρ αὐτόν, ἔφη, ψέγει;
   (*v*) Θεαρίδας ξίφος ἀκονῶν ἠρωτήθη, εἰ ὀξύ ἐστιν, καὶ εἶπεν,
          ὀξύτερον διαβολῆς.
   (*vi*) Ἀρχέλαος, ἀδολέσχου κουρέως ἐρωτήσαντος αὐτόν, πῶς σε
          κείρω, ὦ βασιλεῦ; σιωπῶν, ἔφη.

12 ὁ Ἀριστοτέλης ἀκούσας ὑπό τινος λοιδορεῖσθαι, ἀπόντα με, ἔφη,
   καὶ μαστιγούτω.

13 οἱ σοφισταί, τἆλλα σοφοὶ ὄντες, τοῦτο ἄτοπον ἐργάζονται πρᾶγμα·
   φάσκοντες γὰρ ἀρετῆς διδάσκαλοι εἶναι πολλάκις κατηγοροῦσιν
   τῶν μαθητῶν ὡς ἀδικοῦσι σφᾶς, τοὺς μισθοὺς ἀποστεροῦντες
   καίπερ εὖ παθόντες ὑπ᾽ αὐτῶν.

14 πολλὴ ἔχθρα καὶ μῖσος ἀλλήλων τοῖς πολίταις ἐγγίγνεται, δι᾽ ἃ
   ἔγωγε μάλα φοβοῦμαι ἀεὶ μή τι μεῖζον ἢ ὥστε φέρειν κακὸν τῇ
   πόλει συμβῇ.

15 οἱ Λακεδαιμόνιοι ἐπρεσβεύοντο πρὸς τοὺς Ἀθηναίους ἐγκλήματα
ποιούμενοι, ὅπως σφίσιν ὅτι μέγιστη πρόφασις εἴη τοῦ πολεμεῖν,
ἢν (= ἐὰν) μή τι εἰσακούωσιν.

16 Κλέανδρος ἐτυράννευσε μὲν Γέλας ἑπτὰ ἔτη, ἀπέθανε δὲ ὑπὸ
Σαβύλλου ἀνδρὸς Γελῴου.

17# Ἐλπὶς καὶ σὺ Τύχη, μέγα χαίρετε· τὸν λιμέν' ηὗρον·
οὐδὲν ἐμοὶ χ' ὑμῖν· παίζετε τοὺς μετ' ἐμέ.

Notes

1 (ii) ἀπέχομαι is followed by the gen. (20.1/4). (x) Supply
an imperative such as ποίει. (xiii) νομίζω + acc. *believe in.*
(xiv) τῑμωροῦ < τῑμωρέου. (xv) καταρῶ < καταράου.

2 γάρ is here placed third word in its clause (cf. 15.3 *l.*27).

3 ἡγουμένου λέοντος and ἡγουμένου ἐλάφου are both genitive
absolutes (12.1/2*b*).

8 (iv) ἴσθι is here the 2nd s. imp. of εἰμί (17.1/1 note 6). (v) ἢν ...
μάζαν lit. *which bread* (ἢν is here the relative adjective, 9.1/2
note 3); ἔμαξε < μάττω. (vi) ἀρχή as an abstract noun can mean
magistracy but is used here concretely in the sense *officer.* (vii)
Both ἐράω *desire* (13.1/2*a*(ii)) and ἀποστερέομαι *be deprived of*
(20.1/4) are followed by the genitive, cf. ἀπέχου in 1(ii) above.
(viii) ἐμβάλλειν infinitive for imperative (17.1/1 note 5). (xv)
Supply ἦν.

9 A poem of Archilochus (7th cent. BC), the earliest figure in
Greek literature about whom we have any reliable information.
*l.*2 ἐντὸς ἀμώμητον is in apposition to ἢν in the previous line
*which, a blameless weapon, ... l.*3 θανάτου τέλος *[the] doom
of death* (a Homeric phrase). *l.*4 κακίω f. acc. s. to agree with
ἀσπίδα understood.

10 The *royal cubit* was that used by the Persians, the other was
standard in the Greek world.

11 (*i*) πυθόμενος *ascertaining*; Xenocrates was *looking for virtue* in the sense that he was investigating its nature from a philosophical point of view. (*ii*) This story is also about Eudamidas, who is the subject of ἔφη; γε emphasises ὑμεῖς. (*iii*) ἄριστος ... Σπαρτιάτης *[the] best Spartan* the article is not used with a predicate (5.1/3). (*iv*) For a down-to-earth Spartan, praising Heracles would have seemed as superfluous as praising motherhood; γάρ here introduces an ironical question 'Well, who ...?' (*vi*) κείρω aor. subj. in a deliberative question (14.1/4*a*(ii)) '*How am I to cut ...?*'

12 After ἀκούσας we have the infinitive construction for reported speech (8.1/3*a*), lit. *having heard [himself] to be abused* ...; ἀπόντα < ἄπειμι.

13 τἆλλα (= τὰ ἄλλα) adverbial accusative (20.1/5), *in other respects*; τοῦτο refers to what follows but the meaning is not *this extraordinary thing* (there is no definite article with ἄτοπον ... πρᾶγμα), but *an extraordinary thing [viz] this*; γάρ explains what precedes, but we would omit it in English; σφᾶς i.e. the sophists (9.1/4*a*); both ἀποστεροῦντες and παθόντες agree with the subject of ἀδικοῦσι (3 pl. pres. ind. act., **not** a pple.), i.e. the students; αὐτῶν also refers back to the sophists and is used instead of σφῶν for variety.

14 μῖσος ἀλλήλων *hatred of each other* (9.1/4*b*) i.e. *mutual hatred*.

15 ἐπρεσβεύοντο impf. to express repeated action (4.1/1); ποιούμενοι *making* the middle of ποιέω is used with nouns to indicate the involvement of the subject, cf. πόλεμον ποιεῖσθαι *to wage war*; εἰρήνην ποιεῖσθαι *to keep peace* but πόλεμον ποιεῖν *to cause a war* (but not necessarily be involved in it); εἰρήνην ποιεῖν *to impose peace* (on belligerents); ὅπως (= ἵνα) + opt. to express purpose after a historic tense (14.1/4*c*(i)).

16 Γέλᾱς Doric gen. s. of Γέλᾱ.

17 χαίρετε (17.1/1 note 7) is qualified by μέγα (here an adverb), lit. *farewell greatly* (the author is pleased to be rid of them); χ᾽ ὑμῖν elision for καὶ ὑμῖν (English idiom reverses the order, *you and me*) – the clause means *there is nothing for* (i.e. *between*) *you and me*; παίζετε (here imp.) + acc. *play with*.

Main points

- Positive commands are expressed by the imperative mood

- Negative commands are expressed by μή + present imperative or μή + aorist subjunctive as appropriate

- Regular adjectives have a comparative in -τερος and a superlative in -τατος

- Irregular adjectives have a comparative in -(ι)ων and a superlative in -ιστος

- Comparatives can also mean a higher degree (*rather, too*)

- Superlatives can also mean a very high degree (*very*)

- Comparatives can be followed by ἤ *than* or a genitive of comparison; they can also be followed by a dative of measure of difference

- ὡς/ὅτι with the superlative means *as* (*many/quickly*, etc.) *as possible*

- A few active verbs use other active verbs for their passive sense

17.3 Extra reading – Prometheus Bound (2)

Prometheus has revealed that he alone can save Zeus from an erotic liaison (euphemistically called γάμος *marriage*) which will rob him of his divine kingship. In the scene below, Hermes, the messenger of the gods, has come to force Prometheus to disclose his secret. Shortly after, the play ends with Prometheus persisting in his refusal.

ΕΡΜΗΣ

σὲ τὸν σοφιστήν, τὸν πικρῶς ὑπέρπικρον,
τὸν ἐξαμαρτόντ' εἰς θεοὺς ἐφημέροις
πορόντα τιμάς, τὸν πυρὸς κλέπτην λέγω·
πατὴρ ἄνωγέ σ' οὕστινας κομπεῖς γάμους
αὐδᾶν, πρὸς ὧν τ' ἐκεῖνος ἐκπίπτει κράτους·   5
καὶ ταῦτα μέντοι μηδὲν αἰνικτηρίως,
ἀλλ' αὔθ' ἕκαστα φράζε, μηδέ μοι διπλᾶς
ὁδούς, Προμηθεῦ, προσβάλης. ὁρᾷς δ' ὅτι
Ζεὺς τοῖς τοιούτοις οὐχὶ μαλθακίζεται.

ΠΡΟΜΗΘΕΥΣ

σεμνόστομός γε καὶ φρονήματος πλέως   1
ὁ μῦθός ἐστιν, ὡς θεῶν ὑπηρέτου.
νέον νέοι κρατεῖτε, καὶ δοκεῖτε δὴ
ναίειν ἀπενθῆ πέργαμ'· οὐκ ἐκ τῶνδ' ἐγὼ
δισσοὺς τυράννους ἐκπεσόντας ᾐσθόμην;
τρίτον δὲ τὸν νῦν κοιρανοῦντ' ἐπόψομαι   1
αἴσχιστα καὶ τάχιστα. μή τί σοι δοκῶ
ταρβεῖν ὑποπτήσσειν τε τοὺς νέους θεούς;
πολλοῦ γε καὶ τοῦ παντὸς ἐλλείπω. σὺ δὲ
κέλευθον ἥνπερ ἦλθες ἐγκόνει πάλιν·
πεύσῃ γὰρ οὐδὲν ὧν ἀνιστορεῖς ἐμέ.   2

Notes

*l.*1 Hermes' words are aggressive and rude. This shows itself in the
omission of the verb governing σέ (καλῶ *I am addressing*), trans.
you there, the clever one ... *ll.*2f. τὸν ἐξαμαρτόντ' (α) ... πορόντα lit.
the one who offended ... *[by] giving* (πορόντα aor. pple. of a defective
verb which only exists in the aor. and perf. and is listed under the
aor. ind. ἔπορον); take ἐφημέροις with πορόντα *giving* ... *to mortals*;
λέγω *I mean. l.*4 πατήρ i.e. Zeus; ἄνωγε *orders* from ἄνωγα a verb
perfect in form but present in meaning (cf. 19.1/3*a*); οὕστινας
(indirect interrogative, 10.1/2*b*) ... γάμους plural for singular. *l.*5
πρός (= ὑπό) ὧν *by which*; ἐκπίπτει for vividness the present is used
for the future in prophecies; κράτους (gen.) is governed by ἐκ-. *l.*6
Understand φράζε from the next line; καὶ ... μέντοι *and indeed, and
what is more*; μηδέν adverbial acc. (20.1/5) *in no way. ll.*7f. αὔθ'
(= αὐτά) ἕκαστα i.e. *each thing, every detail*; μηδέ ... προσβάλης

negative command (17.1/1). *l.*9 τοῖς τοιούτοις lit. *by such things* (i.e. *behaviour*). *l.*10 πλέως 13.1/1*a*. *l.*11 ὡς *for [the talk] of a lackey,* on this restrictive use of ὡς see 22.1/1*a*(vi). *l.*12 νέον is n. acc. s. used adverbially (20.1/5) and to be taken with κρατεῖτε, lit. *you rule newly,* i.e. *you have only just come to power;* δοκεῖτε *you think, expect;* δή adds a note of sarcasm *indeed.* *l.*14 δισσοὺς (= διττούς; the non-Attic form is used in Tragedy) τυράννους Uranus, the first king of the gods, had been dethroned by his son Cronus, who in turn was dethroned by Zeus (Prometheus sarcastically calls them τύραννοι). *l.*15 Supply ἐκπίπτοντα from ἐκπεσόντας in the previous line; ἐπόψομαι < ἐφοράω. *l.*16 μή ... σοι δοκῶ is a question expecting a negative answer (10.1/2*a*), lit. *surely I do not seem to you* (μή here = *surely not*); τί (the accent is from the enclitic σοι, see **Appendix 8**, *d*(ix)) acc. s. n. of the indefinite τις, here used as an adverbial acc. (20.1/5) *to some extent.* *l.*18 ἐλλείπω takes the gen. *I lack much* (πολλοῦ, i.e. of such behaviour), *in fact* (καί) *all* (lit. *the whole,* i.e. of such behaviour) – Prometheus is strongly emphasizing that he is not frightened of the new rulers of heaven. *l.*19 κέλευθον acc. of space traversed *along the road,* after ἐγκόνει (2nd s. pres. imp. of ἐγκονέω); ἥνπερ (< ὅσπερ, i.e. ὅς + περ) is an emphatic form of the relative. *l.*20 ὧν = τούτων ἅ *of those things which* the relative pronoun has been attracted into the case of the antecedent, and the latter then omitted (9.1/2 note 2).

Unit 18

....

18.1 Grammar

18.1/1 -μι verbs

-μι verbs fall into two groups:

(*a*) The suffixless class, where the endings of the present and imperfect are added directly to the stem without any suffix or link vowel, e.g. εἰ-μί (3.1/6) and φη-μί (7.1/2). There are nine other common verbs in this class:

> δίδωμι *give* and τίθημι *put, place* (18.1/2)
> εἶμι *I shall go* (18.1/3; distinguish from εἰμί *I am*)
> ἵστημι *make to stand* (19.1/1)
> ἵημι *let go, send forth* (20.1/2)
> δύναμαι *be able* and ἐπίσταμαι know (19.1/3b; the only common
>   deponents of this type)
> πίμπλημι *fill* and πίμπρημι *burn* (19.1/1 note 2)

From another such verb, ἠμί *say* (obsolescent in Attic) Plato often uses the forms ἦν *I said*, ἦ *he/she said* (13.3(i) *l*.7; both forms were originally imperfect).

(*b*) The -νῡμι class, where the stem of the present and imperfect has a νυ suffix (20.1/1).
Both classes differ from -ω verbs in the present and imperfect; of class (*a*) δίδωμι, τίθημι, ἵστημι, ἵημι also differ in the aorist active and middle (ἵστημι in the perfect and pluperfect as well). Elsewhere -μι verbs take the same suffixes and endings as -ω verbs.

18.1/2 δίδωμι *give*, τίθημι *put, place*

These two -μι verbs are closely parallel. In nearly all their forms an ο/ω in δίδωμι corresponds to an ε/η in τίθημι; and also οι to ει in optative forms, and ου to ει in forms other than those of the optative; the only exceptions are the 1st s. impf. act. (ἐδίδουν/ ἐτίθην), the present and aorist subjunctive (see note 1) and the perfect mid./pass. (δέδομαι etc. but τέθειμαι etc.). Both verbs form their present stem by reduplication with iota (cf. γιγνώσκω); as in the perfect tense (15.1/1), an aspirated consonant is reduplicated with the corresponding non-aspirate, hence τιθη- (not θιθη-). In both, the aorist active is weak in the singular, with κ (**not** σ) added to the long-vowel form of the root (δω-/θη-); in the plural the endings are added directly to the short-vowel form of the root (δο-/θε-; this is really a type of root aorist).

Their principal parts are:

PRESENT	FUTURE	AOR. ACT	PERF. ACT	PERF. MID./PASS	AOR. PASS
δίδωμι	δώσω	ἔδωκα	δέδωκα	δέδομαι	ἐδόθην
τίθημι	θήσω	ἔθηκα	τέθηκα	κεῖμαι (note 4) (τέθειμαι)	ἐτέθην

The future, perfect (act. and mid./pass.), and aorist passive are regular (see above 18.1/1). The present, imperfect, and aorist active forms, which require the greatest attention and should be mastered first, are set out here. The middle and passive forms are easily recognized from their endings (for full tables see **Appendix 5**)

		PRESENT		AORIST	
INDICATIVE					
s.	**1**	δίδωμι	τίθημι	ἔδωκα	ἔθηκα
	2	δίδως	τίθης	ἔδωκας	ἔθηκας
	3	δίδωσι(ν)	τίθησι(ν)	ἔδωκε(ν)	ἔθηκε(ν)
PL.	**1**	δίδομεν	τίθεμεν	ἔδομεν	ἔθεμεν
	2	δίδοτε	τίθετε	ἔδοτε	ἔθετε
	3	διδόᾱσι(ν)	τιθέᾱσι(ν)	ἔδοσαν	ἔθεσαν
INFINITIVE					
		διδόναι	τιθέναι	δοῦναι	θεῖναι
PARTICIPLE					
		διδούς, -όντος	τιθείς, -έντος	δούς, δόντος	θείς, θέντος
		διδοῦσα, -ούσης	τιθεῖσα, -είσης	δοῦσα, δούσης	θεῖσα, θείσης
		διδόν, -όντος	τιθέν, -έντος	δόν, δόντος	θέν, θέντος

	PRESENT		AORIST	

IMPERATIVE

s.	**2**	δίδου	τίθει	δός	θές
	3	διδότω	τιθέτω	δότω	θέτω
PL.	**2**	δίδοτε	τίθετε	δότε	θέτε
	3	διδόντων	τιθέντων	δόντων	θέντων

SUBJUNCTIVE (see note 1)

s.	**1**	διδῶ	τιθῶ	δῶ	θῶ
	2	διδῷς, etc.	τιθῇς, etc.	δῷς, etc.	θῇς, etc.

OPTATIVE

s.	**1**	διδοίην	τιθείην	δοίην	θείην
	2	διδοίης	τιθείης	δοίης	θείης
	3	διδοίη	τιθείη	δοίη	θείη
PL.	**1**	διδοῖμεν	τιθεῖμεν	δοῖμεν	θεῖμεν
	2	διδοῖτε	τιθεῖτε	δοῖτε	θεῖτε
	3	διδοῖεν	τιθεῖεν	δοῖεν	θεῖεν

IMPERFECT ACTIVE

ἐδίδουν, ἐδίδους, ἐδίδου, ἐδίδομεν, ἐδίδοτε, ἐδίδοσαν
ἐτίθην, ἐτίθεις, ἐτίθει, ἐτίθεμεν, ἐτίθετε, ἐτίθεσαν

Notes

1 The present and aorist subjunctive active of δίδωμι have the endings -ῶ, -ῷς, -ῷ, -ῶμεν, -ῶτε, -ῶσι(ν) (cf. 14.1/2 note 2). τίθημι has the regular endings (-ῶ, -ῇς, -ῇ etc.) but in both verbs the first syllable of the subjunctive endings has a circumflex as a result of contraction (διδῶ < διδόω, τιθῶ < τιθέω).

2 The present and imperfect active of δίδωμι can also mean *offer*.

3 The aorist active also has weak forms for the 3rd pl.: ἔδωκαν (= ἔδοσαν), ἔθηκαν (= ἔθεσαν); weak forms may also occur in the 1st and 2nd pl. (ἐδώκαμεν etc.) but are rare.

4 The **present** tense of the deponent κεῖμαι *lie* (19.1/3b) is generally used instead of the **perfect passive** of τίθημι in the sense *to have been put, placed, established*, e.g. οἱ νόμοι οἱ ὑπὸ τῶν βασιλέων κείμενοι (= τεθειμένοι) *the laws established by the kings*. Likewise ἐκείμην, the **imperfect** of κεῖμαι, is used for the **pluperfect passive** of τίθημι.

18.1/3 εἶμι *I shall come/go*

In Attic Greek prose the verb ἔρχομαι *come/go* occurs only in the present indicative. The remainder of its present tense (subjunctive, optative, imperative, infinitive, participle), and its future and imperfect are supplied by εἶμι which, though present in form, has in the indicative the future meaning *I shall come/go* (to be distinguished from εἰμί *I am*):

PRESENT	IND.	SUBJ.	OPT.	IMP.	INF.	PPLE.
	ἔρχομαι	ἴω	ἴοιμι	ἴθι	ἰέναι	ἰών
	I come/go					
FUTURE	εἶμι	——	ἴοιμι	——	ἰέναι	ἰών
	I shall come/go					
IMPERFECT	ᾖα					
	I was coming/going, used to come/go					

For a complete table of forms see **Appendix 3**. Note that ἴοιμι, ἰέναι and ἰών can be either present or future (the context will normally show which tense is meant). The aorist of ἔρχομαι is ἦλθον (7.1/1 note 2), and the perfect ἐλήλυθα.

18.1/4 Other verbs with principal parts from different roots

The English verb *to be* is a combination of separate and etymologically distinct words (*be, am, was* etc.). We have already seen the same in Greek with αἱρέω, λέγω, ὁράω, φέρω (7.1/1 note 2) as well as ἔρχομαι; other examples are ἐσθίω *eat*, πωλέω *sell*, ὠνέομαι *buy* (see **Principal parts of verbs**; the principal parts of all eight should now be learnt).

A particularly troublesome set is that associated with αἱρέω *take, capture*, whose passive is normally supplied by another verb, ἁλίσκομαι *be captured*, and whose middle αἱροῦμαι has the special sense *choose*. When used as a passive αἱροῦμαι normally means *be chosen*. These variations can be set out as follows:

PRESENT		FUTURE	AORIST	PERFECT
αἱρέω	I take, capture	αἱρήσω	εἷλον (stem ἑλ-)	ᾕρηκα
ἁλίσκομαι (pass.)	I am taken, am being captured	ἁλώσομαι	ἑάλων	ἑάλωκα
αἱροῦμαι (mid.)	I choose	αἱρήσομαι	εἱλόμην	ᾕρημαι
αἱροῦμαι (pass.)	I am being chosen	αἱρεθήσομαι	ᾑρέθην	ᾕρημαι

The moods, infinitives and participles of εἷλον *I took, captured* (stem ἑλ-, cf. 7.1/1 note 2) and of the root aorist ἑάλων *I was taken, was captured* are as follows:

IND.	SUBJ.	OPT.	IMP.	INF.	PPLE.
εἷλον	ἕλω	ἕλοιμι	ἕλε	ἑλεῖν	ἑλών
ἑάλων	ἁλῶ	ἁλοίην	ἅλωθι	ἁλῶναι	ἁλούς

ἑάλων is exactly parallel to ἔγνων (11.1/1), e.g. ind. ἑάλων, ἑάλως, ἑάλω, etc.

Notes

1 Most **compounds** of λέγω have the meaning *pick up, gather*, e.g. ἐκλέγω *pick out*, συλλέγω *collect*, καταλέγω *pick, choose* (and also *recount*). These compounds have principal parts from the stem λεγ- only, e.g. ἐκλέγω, ἐκλέξω, ἐξέλεξα, etc.

2 The alternative principal parts of λέγω (ἐρῶ, εἶπον etc.) are, however, used in the compounds of ἀγορεύω *speak in public*, e.g. ἀπαγορεύω *forbid* (fut. ἀπερῶ, aor. ἀπεῖπον), προαγορεύω *proclaim*.

18.1/5 Conditional sentences

Conditional sentences contain at least one main clause and one adverbial clause of condition; the latter is introduced by εἰ *if*. They fall into two clearly defined categories which, in both English and Greek, are distinguished by the form of the main clause:

Category 1

In the main clause English has the auxiliary verb *would* or *should* (or occasionally *could*), and Greek has the particle ἄν (see below). An English example is: *I would be sorry if you were not to persist with Greek*.

Category 2

In the main clause English does **not** have the auxiliary *would* or *should*, and Greek does **not** have the particle ἄν. An English example is: *I am sorry if you find Greek verbs difficult*.

There is a clear distinction between the two categories. The first is used in cases where something could have happened in the past, could be happening now, or could happen in the future. The cases covered by the second are also hypothetical (as all conditional sentences must be), but here, by not using *would* or *should* in English or ἄν in Greek, we express ourselves in a more positive and confident way.

Conditional clauses of both categories refer either to the future, present, or past. οὐ is used to negate main clauses[1] but the negative in the εἰ clause is μή. ἄν is postpositive and therefore never stands as first word in the main clause of conditional clauses of the first category.

The three time-frames of each category are given in Table 18.1.

We have already seen that the particle ἄν, when used with the subjunctive in subordinate clauses (14.1/4*c*(iii)), can be represented in English by *ever*. Here, however, it has no semantic equivalent. When in English we wish to express potentiality (as in the main clause of first category conditional sentences) we use an auxiliary verb (generally *would* or *should*), e.g. *I would have liked to see you*. ἄν, however, which expresses potentiality in Greek, is an adverbial particle and

---

[1]Unless these are in the form of a command (17.1/1) or wish (21.1/1).

Table 18.1

CATEGORY 1	CATEGORY 2
English *would/should* in the main clause	verb without *would/should* in the main clause
Greek ἄν in the main clause	no ἄν in the main clause

FUTURE

Conditional clause

εἰ + optative (pres. or aor.)	ἐάν (see note 2) + subjunctive (pres. or aor.)

Main clause

optative (pres. or aor.) + ἄν	future indicative
εἰ τοῦτο πράξειας, ἁμάρτοις ἄν.	ἐὰν τοῦτο πράξῃς, ἁμαρτήσει.
If you were to do this, you would be wrong.	*If you do this, you will be wrong.*

PRESENT

Conditional clause

εἰ + imperfect indicative	εἰ + present indicative

Main clause

imperfect indicative + ἄν	present indicative
εἰ τοῦτο ἔπραττες, ἡμάρτανες ἄν.	εἰ τοῦτο πράττεις, ἁμαρτάνεις.
If you were [now] doing this, you would be wrong.	*If you are doing this, you are wrong.*

PAST

Conditional clause

εἰ + aorist indicative	εἰ + imperfect or aorist indicative

Main clause

aorist indicative + ἄν	imperfect or aorist indicative
εἰ τοῦτο ἔπραξας, ἥμαρτες ἄν.	εἰ τοῦτο ἔπραττες, ἡμάρτανες.
If you had done this, you would have been wrong.	*If you used to do this, you were (used to be) wrong.*
	εἰ τοῦτο ἔπραξας, ἥμαρτες.
	If you did this, you were wrong.

modifies the verb to which it is attached: οὐκ ἐγένετο means *it did not happen*; οὐκ ἂν ἐγένετο means *it would not have happened*.

Notes

1 The meaning of εἰ ... ἔπρᾱττες/ἔπρᾱξας depends on what follows, i.e. on whether it is in a category 1 or category 2 sentence.

2 The conjunction ἐάν of the future time-frame of category 2 is a contraction of εἰ + ἄν (cf. ὅταν < ὅτε + ἄν, 14.1/4c(iii)). It may also be written as ἄν (to be distinguished from the particle ἄν – the latter has a short vowel) or ἤν in some dialects.

3 It is possible to combine certain time references within one sentence:

εἰ τοῦτο ἔπρᾱξας, ἐκινδύνευες ἄν. *If you had done that you would [now] be in danger.*
εἰ τοῦτο ἔπρᾱξας, κινδῡνεύεις. *If you did that you are in danger.*

4 In category 2 sentences with a future reference εἰ + fut. ind. is substituted for ἐάν + subj. where a **threat** or **warning** is implied:

ἀποκτενεῖς εἴ με γῆς ἔξω βαλεῖς. *You will kill [me] if you throw me out of the country.*

18.1/6 ἄκρος, μέσος, ἔσχατος

These three adjectives vary in meaning according to whether they are used in the attributive or predicative position (3.1/3b):

τὸ ἄκρον ὄρος *the high mountain*	ἄκρον τὸ ὄρος *the top of the mountain*
τὸ μέσον ὄρος *the middle mountain*	μέσον τὸ ὄρος *the middle of the mountain*
τὸ ἔσχατον ὄρος *the furthest mountain*	ἔσχατον τὸ ὄρος *the furthest part of the mountain*

For the predicative position we may also have τὸ ὄρος ἄκρον etc.

Arabic numerals (1, 2, 3, etc.) were not introduced into Europe until the Middle Ages. Earlier civilizations had their own individual systems of numeration. The Greeks used their own alphabet: α = 1, β = 2, γ = 3, δ = 4, ε = 5. Six was represented by a letter (the digamma) that had passed out of normal use but was retained as a numeral. The regular alphabet began again with 7, 8, 9, 10, which were represented by ζ, η, θ, ι. Quite fortuitously, these four letters make up a Greek word ζῆθι, which is the second singular imperative of ζάω *be alive, live.*

18.2 Greek reading

1 Κυμαῖός τις μέλι ἐπώλει. γευσαμένου δέ τινος καὶ εἰπόντος, πάνυ καλόν ἐστιν, εἰ μὴ γάρ, ἔφη, μῦς ἐνέπεσεν εἰς αὐτὸ οὐκ ἂν ἐπώλουν.

2 Λάκαινά τις πρὸς τὸν υἱὸν λέγοντα μικρὸν ἔχειν τὸ ξίφος εἶπε, καὶ βῆμα πρόσθες.

3 Proverbs
(*i*) ἐὰν ἡ λεοντῆ μὴ ἐξίκηται, τὴν ἀλωπεκῆν πρόσαψον. (*ii*) κυνὶ δίδως ἄχυρα, ὄνῳ δὲ ὀστᾶ. (*iii*) ἐπ᾽ ἄκρᾳ τῇ γλώττῃ τὸ φιλεῖν ἔχεις. (*iv*) ἂν (= ἐὰν) τοὺς φίλους μισῶμεν, τί ποιήσομεν τοὺς μισοῦντας; (*v*) εἰ τυρὸν εἶχον, οὐκ ἂν ἐδεόμην ὄψου. (*vi*) # φίλον δι᾽ ὀργὴν ἐν κακοῖσι μὴ προδῷς. (*vii*) # τὸ κέρδος ἡδύ, κἂν ἀπὸ ψευδῶν ἴῃ. (*viii*) δός τι καὶ λαβέ τι. (*ix*) # πλάνη βίον τίθησι σωφρονέστερον. (*x*) αἰσχρὸν εὐεργέτας προδοῦναι. (*xi*) ἐὰν ἔχωμεν χρήματα, ἕξομεν φίλους. (*xii*) ἴτω τὰ πράγματα ὅπη τῷ θεῷ φίλον.

4# εἰς Ῥόδον εἰ πλεῖν δεῖ, τις Ὀλυμπικὸν ἦλθεν ἐρωτῶν
τὸν μάντιν, καὶ πῶς πλεύσεται ἀσφαλέως·
χὠ μάντις, πρῶτον μὲν, ἔφη, καινὴν ἔχε τὴν ναῦν,
καὶ μὴ χειμῶνος, τοῦ δὲ θέρους ἀνάγου·
ταῦτα γὰρ ἢν ποιῇς, ἥξεις κἀκεῖσε καὶ ὧδε,   5
ἢν μὴ πειρατὴς ἐν πελάγει σε λάβῃ.

5 γέρων ποτὲ ξύλα κόψας καὶ ταῦτα φέρων πολλὴν ὁδὸν ἐβάδιζε. διὰ δὲ τὸν κόπον ἀποθέμενος τὸ φορτίον τὸν Θάνατον ἐπεκαλεῖτο. τοῦ δε Θανάτου φανέντος καὶ πυνθανομένου διὰ τίνα αἰτίαν ἐπεκαλεῖτο, ὁ γέρων ἔφη, ἵνα τὸ φορτίον τοῦτο ἄρας ἐπιθῇς μοι.

6# ἅπαν διδόμενον δῶρον, ἂν καὶ μικρὸν ᾖ, μέγιστόν ἐστιν, ἂν μετ᾽ εὐνοίας δοθῇ.

7 ὄφις, ἢν μὴ φάγῃ ὄφιν, δράκων οὐ γενήσεται.

8# γῆς ἐπέβην γυμνός, γυμνός θ᾽ ὑπὸ γαῖαν ἄπειμι·
καὶ τί μάτην μοχθῶ, γυμνὸν ὁρῶν τὸ τέλος;

9 **More stories about Diogenes**
(*i*) θαυμάζοντός τινος τὰ ἐν Σαμοθράκῃ ἀναθήματα ἔφη, πολλῷ ἂν ἦν πλείω εἰ καὶ οἱ μὴ σωθέντες ἀνετίθεσαν.
(*ii*) εἰς Μύνδον ἐλθὼν καὶ θεασάμενος μεγάλας τὰς πύλας, μικρὰν δὲ τὴν πόλιν, ἄνδρες Μύνδιοι, ἔφη, κλείσατε τὰς πύλας μὴ ἡ πόλις ὑμῶν ἐξέλθῃ.
(*iii*) δύσκολον ᾔτει· τοῦ δ᾽ εἰπόντος, ἐάν με πείσῃς, ἔφη, εἴ σε ἐδυνάμην πεῖσαι, ἔπεισα ἄν σε ἀπάγξασθαι.
(*iv*) λύχνον μεθ᾽ ἡμέραν ἅψας περιῄει λέγων, ἄνθρωπον ζητῶ.

10 In order to lure the Syracusan army away from Syracuse, the Athenians sent an agent who persuaded the Syracusans that they could surprise the Athenians at a neighbouring city, Catana. The ruse was totally successful. The passage is from Thucydides' account of the disastrous Athenian expedition to Sicily (415–413 B.C.).

οἱ δὲ στρατηγοὶ τῶν Συρακοσίων ἐπίστευσαν τῷ ἀνθρώπῳ πολλῷ ἀπερισκεπτότερον, καὶ εὐθὺς ἡμέραν ξυνθέμενοι ᾗ παρέσονται ἀπέστειλαν αὐτόν, καὶ αὐτοὶ προεῖπον πανδημεὶ πᾶσιν ἐξιέναι Συρακοσίοις. ἐπεὶ δὲ ἕτοιμα αὐτοῖς τὰ τῆς παρασκευῆς ἦν καὶ αἱ ἡμέραι ἐν αἷς ξυνέθεντο ἥξειν ἐγγὺς ἦσαν, πορευόμενοι ἐπὶ 5 Κατάνης ηὐλίσαντο ἐπὶ τῷ Συμαίθῳ ποταμῷ. οἱ δ᾽ Ἀθηναῖοι, ὡς ᾔσθοντο αὐτοὺς προσιόντας, ἀναλαβόντες τὸ στράτευμα ἅπαν τὸ ἑαυτῶν καὶ ἐπιβιβάσαντες ἐπὶ τὰς ναῦς καὶ τὰ πλοῖα ὑπὸ νύκτα ἔπλεον ἐπὶ τὰς Συρακούσας.

Notes

1 γάρ *yes*, *for* Greek has no word which corresponds exactly to the English *yes* and often the assent of a speaker is implied by particles (24.1/1).

2 μῑκρόν is in the predicative position (3.1/3*b*), i.e. *that he had his sword short*, i.e. *that the sword he had was short*; καί is adverbial (*as well*) but need not be translated; πρόθες < προστίθημι.

3 (*i*) πρόσαψον < προσάπτω. (*iv*) ποιέω + two accusatives *do [something] to/with* (22.1/2*f*(ii)). (*vii*) κἄν = καὶ ἐάν; ψευδῶν < ψεῦδος. (*ix*) τίθησι here *render* (xi) ἕξομεν < ἔχω. (*xii*) ἴτω 3rd s. imp. of ἔρχομαι (18.1/3 and **Appendix 3**); τῷ θεῷ φίλον (n. s.) *sc.* ἐστί *it is dear to God*.

4 *l*.1 εἰ *if* would be first word of its clause in prose. *l*.2 πλεύσεται lit. *he will sail*, but translate *he would sail*, because Greek retains the original tense in reported (indirect) speech (8.1/3 and 10.1/2*b*); ἀσφαλέως i.e. ἀσφαλῶς – the uncontracted form is Ionic (on Ionic forms in poetry see 1.3). *l*.3 χὠ = καὶ ὁ; καινήν predicative as in 2 above, lit. *have the ship [which you sail in] new*, i.e. *get a new ship*. *l*.4 χειμῶνος ... θέρους gen. of time within which (7.1/7*c*). *l*.5 ἤν = ἐάν (also in next line and in 7 below); κἀκεῖσε (=καὶ ἐκεῖσε) καὶ ὧδε lit. *both thither and hither*, i.e. *both there and back*.

5 ἀποθέμενος aor. mid. pple. of ἀποτίθημι; φανέντος gen. m. s. of the aor. pple. of φαίνομαι; πυνθανομένου *asking*; ἄρᾱς nom. m. s. of the aor. act. pple. of αἴρω; ἐπιθῇς 2nd s. aor. subj. act. of ἐπιτίθημι.

6 In both lines ἄν = ἐάν; ἐάν (or εἰ) καί normally *although* but here obviously *even if* (which is usually καὶ εἰ/ἐάν); δοθῇ 3rd s. aor. subj. pass. of δίδωμι.

7 φάγῃ 3rd s. aor. subj. act. of ἐσθίω.

8 θ᾽ i.e. τε.

9 (*i*) Samothrace, an island in the northern Aegean, was notorious for shipwrecks; the subject of ἔφη (and in (*ii*) and (*iii*)) is

Diogenes; πολλῷ dat. of measure of difference (17.1/4*b*); take καί *also* with what follows; οἱ μὴ σωθέντες (aor. pass. pple. of σῴζω) the negative μή is used because Diogenes is referring to a general class (12.1/2*a*(vi)); ἀνετίθεσαν *had dedicated* the imperfect, not the aorist, is used because the verb refers to **repeated** action in the past. (*ii*) μεγάλᾱς ... μῑκρᾱν both adjectives are predicative as in 2 above; μή introducing a negative purpose clause (14.1/4*c*(i)). (*iii*) τοῦ refers to the δύσκολος; ἀπάγξασθαι aor. inf. of ἀπάγχομαι (*iv*) περιῄει 3rd s. impf. of περιέρχομαι (18.1/3); μεθ᾽ ἡμέρᾱν *after day[break]* i.e. *by day*, cf. ἅμα τῇ ἡμέρᾳ.

10 *l.*1 πολλῷ (dat. of measure of difference, 17.1/4*b*) is to be taken with the following word. *l.*2 παρέσονται (< πάρειμι) on the future see note on πλεύσεται in 4 *l.*2 above (cf. ἥξεις in *l.*5). *ll.*3f. Take πᾶσιν ... Συρακοσίοις with προεῖπον (< προαγορεύω, 18.1/4 note 2); τὰ τῆς παρασκευῆς lit. *the [things] of their preparation* but trans. *their preparations*. *l.*6 ηὐλίσαντο < αὐλίζομαι. *l.*8 τὰ πλοῖα is acc. after ἐπί.

Main points

- δίδωμι, τίθημι belong to the group of -μι verbs without a suffix; the two are closely parallel

- Some verbs, such as ἔρχομαι, combine different words; the most difficult is αἱρέω

- Main clauses of category 1 conditionals have *would/should* in English and ἄν in Greek

- Main clauses of category 2 conditionals do **not** have *would/ should* in English and do **not** have ἄν in Greek

- Conditional sentences of both classes refer to the future, present or past; a different construction is used for each case

- The attributive and predicative positions of ἄκρος, μέσος, ἔσχατος determine their meaning

18.3 Extra reading – The sea, the sea !

The **Anabasis** of Xenophon (7.2.12) tells how an army of Greek mercenaries, after becoming embroiled in a dispute between rivals for the Persian throne, had to make their way back from Persia to Greece. The following passage describes their elation when, after many months of hardship, they finally reached the Black Sea.

καὶ ἀφικνοῦνται ἐπὶ τὸ ὄρος τῇ πέμπτῃ ἡμέρᾳ· ὄνομα δὲ τῷ ὄρει ἦν Θήχης. ἐπεὶ δὲ οἱ πρῶτοι ἐγένοντο ἐπὶ τοῦ ὄρους καὶ κατεῖδον τὴν θάλατταν, κραυγὴ πολλὴ ἐγένετο. ἀκούσας δὲ ὁ Ξενοφῶν καὶ οἱ ὀπισθοφύλακες ᾠήθησαν ἔμπροσθεν ἄλλους ἐπιτίθεσθαι πολεμίους· ἐπειδὴ δ᾽ ἡ βοὴ πλείων τε ἐγίγνετο καὶ ἐγγύτερον καὶ οἱ ἀεὶ ἐπιόντες 5 ἔθεον δρόμῳ ἐπὶ τοὺς ἀεὶ βοῶντας καὶ πολλῷ μείζων ἐγίγνετο ἡ βοὴ ὅσῳ δὴ πλείους ἐγίγνοντο, ἐδόκει δὴ μεῖζόν τι εἶναι τῷ Ξενοφῶντι, καὶ ἀναβὰς ἐφ᾽ ἵππον καὶ τοὺς ἱππέας ἀναλαβὼν παρεβοήθει· καὶ τάχα δὴ ἀκούουσι βοώντων τῶν στρατιωτῶν, θάλαττα θάλαττα, καὶ παρεγγυώντων. ἔνθα δὴ ἔθεον πάντες καὶ οἱ ὀπισθοφύλακες, καὶ τὰ 10 ὑποζύγια ἠλαύνετο καὶ οἱ ἵπποι. ἐπεὶ δὲ ἀφίκοντο πάντες ἐπὶ τὸ ἄκρον, ἐνταῦθα δὴ περιέβαλλον ἀλλήλους καὶ στρατηγοὺς καὶ λοχαγοὺς δακρύοντες.

Notes

l.1 ἀφικνοῦνται vivid present (see note on 7.2.13 *l*.8; cf. ἀκούουσι in *l*.10). *l*.4 ᾠήθησαν < οἴομαι. *ll*.5f. οἱ ἀεὶ ἐπιόντες (< ἐπέρχομαι) *those who kept coming up* refers to the different groups who went up the hill, but τοὺς ἀεὶ βοῶντας *those who kept shouting* refers to the ever-increasing group that could see the sea; δρόμῳ *at a run* is redundant after ἔθεον (inceptive imperfect *began to run* 4.1/1 footnote). *l*.7 ὅσῳ etc. lit. *by how much they became more [numerous]*; on ὅσος see 21.1/3; ἐδόκει ... τῷ Ξενοφῶντι lit. *it seemed to Xenophon*; μεῖζόν τι *something more serious*. *l*.8 παρεβοήθει and the imperfects in the following lines are inceptive (see above on ἔθεον). *l*.11 ἠλαύνετο has τὰ ὑποζύγια and οἱ ἵπποι as its subjects but it agrees with the nearer one, τὰ ὑποζύγια, which as a neuter plural takes a singular verb (3.1/1 note 2; for another example of a double subject see 16.2.13 *l*.1).

Unit 19

....

19.1 Grammar

19.1/1 ἵστημι *and its compounds*

ἵστημι *make to stand, set up* was originally σίστᾱμι with a present stem of the same formation as δίδωμι and τίθημι (i.e. reduplication with iota and no suffix). At an early stage in the history of Greek the initial sigma developed into a rough breathing; the resulting ἵστᾱμι (the form in most dialects) became ἵστημι in Attic with the regular change of ᾱ > η.[1] Consequently, where the alternation δω/δο occurs in δίδωμι and θη/θε in τίθημι we have στη/στα in ἵστημι; the alternation φη/φα in φημί (7.1/2) has the same explanation (the original form of the first person singular is φᾱμί).

The **present** and **imperfect** of ἵστημι are almost completely parallel to δίδωμι and τίθημι. In the active we have:

PRESENT

		IND.	IMP.	SUBJ.	OPT.
S.	**1**	ἵστημι		ἱστῶ	ἱσταίην
	2	ἵστης	ἵστη	ἱστῇς	ἱσταίης
	3	ἵστησι(ν)	ἱστάτω	ἱστῇ	ἱσταίη
PL.	**1**	ἵσταμεν		ἱστῶμεν	ἱσταῖμεν
	2	ἵστατε	ἵστατε	ἱστῆτε	ἱσταῖτε
	3	ἱστᾶσι(ν)	ἱστάντων	ἱστῶσι(ν)	ἱσταῖεν

INFINITIVE ἱστάναι
PARTICIPLE ἱστάς, ἱστᾶσα, ἱστάν; gen. ἱστάντος, ἱστάσης, ἱστάντος
IMPERFECT ἵστην, ἵστης, ἵστη, ἵσταμεν, ἵστατε, ἵστασαν

---

[1] This change, which occurs when ᾱ is not preceded by a vowel or ρ, is one of the more striking differences between Attic and most other dialects.

The **future** στήσω *I shall make to stand, shall set up* is also parallel, but we meet a divergence in the **aorist**. ἵστημι has two sets of forms (cf. the two aorists of φύω, 11.1/1):

(a) A weak aorist ἔστησα, which is transitive and means *I made to stand, set up*.

(b) A root aorist ἔστην (conjugated as ἔβην, 11.1/1), which is intransitive and means *I stood*.

Examples of these two aorists are:

ἔγχος ἔστησε πρὸς κίονα. *He stood his spear against a pillar* (transitive).
Ἀλκμήνης τόκος ἔστη σιωπῇ. *The son of Alcmene stood in silence* (intransitive).

The two aorists have identical forms in the 3rd pl. indicative active ἔστησαν (ἔστησ-αν from ἔστησα; ἔστη-σαν from ἔστην). Where this form occurs, only the context will show whether it is transitive or intransitive.

ἵστημι is also irregular in its **perfect** and **pluperfect**. Both tenses have a κ suffix in the singular of the indicative but elsewhere a stem without κ (ἐστα-) is normally used (see below). Because these tenses are intransitive (see below) they occur only in the active voice:

PERFECT

		IND.	IMP.	SUBJ.	OPT.
S.	1	ἔστηκα		ἑστῶ	ἑσταίην
	2	ἔστηκας	ἔσταθι	ἑστῇς	ἑσταίης
	3	ἔστηκε(ν)	ἑστάτω	ἑστῇ	ἑσταίη
PL.	1	ἔσταμεν		ἑστῶμεν	ἑσταῖμεν
	2	ἔστατε	ἔστατε	ἑστῆτε	ἑσταῖτε
	3	ἑστᾶσι(ν)	ἑστάντων	ἑστῶσι(ν)	ἑσταῖεν

INFINITIVE ἑστάναι
PARTICIPLES ἑστώς, ἑστῶσα, ἑστός gen. ἑστῶτος, ἑστώσης, ἑστῶτος
PLUPERFECT εἱστήκη, εἱστήκης, εἱστήκει(ν), ἔσταμεν, ἔστατε, ἔστασαν

Except for the imperative, forms with the stem ἑστα- have alternatives in ἑστηκ- (e.g. 3rd pl. ind. ἑστήκᾱσι(ν), inf. ἑστηκέναι) but these are less common.

The first syllable of the perfect stem was originally σεστ- with reduplication of σ, but, as in the present stem, the initial σ developed into a rough breathing, giving ἑστ-. Because ἑ is in fact the reduplication it is kept in **all** forms of the perfect (16.1/4). The initial εἱστ- of the singular of the pluperfect was originally ἐσεστ- with the syllabic augment and reduplication (quite irregularly the augment does not occur in the plural and hence the 1st and 2nd pl. forms are identical with those of the perfect).

Both perfect and pluperfect are intransitive and they are used as a **present** and **imperfect** tense respectively: ἕστηκα *I am standing* and εἱστήκη *I was standing*. The future perfect ἑστήξω *I shall stand* (cf 16.1/4 note 2) is also intransitive.

We may summarize these forms as follows:

	Transitive		**Intransitive**
PRESENT	ἵστημι *I am making to stand*	PERFECT	ἕστηκα *I am standing*
FUTURE	στήσω *I shall make to stand*	FUT. PERF.	ἑστήξω *I shall stand*
IMPERFECT	ἵστην *I was making to stand*	PLUPERFECT	εἱστήκη *I was standing*
WEAK AORIST	ἔστησα *I made to stand*	ROOT AORIST	ἔστην *I stood*

A comprehensive table of ἵστημι is given in **Appendix 5**. The present middle ἵσταμαι is intransitive and literally means *I am in the process of making myself stand* i.e. it represents a present **act** as opposed to the perfect, which represents a present **state** (*I am in a standing position*). The imperfect middle (ἱστάμην) and future middle (στήσομαι) are also intransitive but the weak aorist middle (ἐστησάμην) is transitive and means *I made (something) stand for myself.*

ἵστημι has many compounds and these retain the same distinctions between transitive and intransitive tenses. Among the most common are:

	Transitive tenses	Intransitive tenses
ἀνίστημι (ἀνά *up*)	*raise up; restore; cause to migrate, expel, uproot*	*rise up; be expelled; migrate*
ἀφίστημι (ἀπό *away*)	*remove; cause to revolt*	*go away from; revolt*
καθίστημι (κατά *down*)	*set down; put in a certain state; appoint; establish (laws etc.)*	*settle down; come into a certain state; be appointed; be established*

The middle voice of compounds of ἵστημι follows the pattern of the simple verb: οἱ βάρβαροι ἀφίστανται *the barbarians are in [the act of] revolt* (cf. οἱ βάρβαροι ἀφεστᾶσιν (perfect) *the barbarians are in [a state of] revolt*).

Examples of the above compounds are:

ἀνέστησαν καὶ Αἰγινήτᾱς τῷ αὐτῷ θέρει τούτῳ ἐξ Αἰγίνης Ἀθηναῖοι. *In this same summer the Athenians also expelled the Aeginetans from Aegina.*

Βοιωτοὶ οἱ νῦν ἑξηκοστῷ ἔτει μετὰ Ἰλίου ἅλωσιν ἐξ Ἄρνης ἀναστάντες ὑπὸ Θεσσαλῶν τὴν Βοιωτίᾱν ᾤκισαν. *In the sixtieth year after the capture of Troy the present Boeotians, after being expelled from Arne by the Thessalians, colonised Boeotia.*

εἰ τοὺς ξυμμάχους αὐτῶν ἀφιστάναι πειρᾱσόμεθα, δεήσει καὶ τούτοις ναυσὶ βοηθεῖν τὸ πλέον οὖσι νησιώταις. *If we try* (lit. shall try) *to make their allies revolt, we shall have to come to their assistance as well with a fleet because they are for the most part islanders* (lit. *it will be necessary to assist them also with ships, being [for] the greater [part] islanders.*)

πρῶτοι ἀπ᾽ αὐτῶν Μῆδοι ἤρξαντο ἀφίστασθαι. *The Medes were the first to start to revolt from them* (lit. *the Medes first started ...*).

κατέστησε τύραννον εἶναι παῖδα τὸν ἑαυτοῦ. *He appointed his own son to be tyrant.*

ἐς φόβον καταστάντων διαφθείρονται πολλοὶ Χαόνων. *When they were reduced to a state of panic many of the Chaonians were killed* (vivid present).

Notes

1 To distinguish the different forms of ἵστημι it is essential to remember that:
  (i)   ἱστ- occurs in all forms of the present and imperfect but nowhere else.
  (ii) ἐστ- occurs only in the aorist indicative.
  (iii) ἑστ- occurs in all forms of the perfect and in the pluperfect plural but nowhere else.
  (iv) εἱστ- occurs only in the pluperfect singular.

2 πίμπλημι *fill* and πίμπρημι *burn* (tr.) follow ἵστημι in the present and imperfect, e.g. the pres. ind. act. of the first is: πίμπλημι, πίμπλης, πίμπλησι(ν), πίμπλαμεν, πίμπλατε, πιμπλᾶσι(ν).

19.1/2 Potential clauses

Potential clauses express an action or state which has or had the potentiality of happening: *I wouldn't like to meet him on a dark night; Alcibiades would have been a disaster at our last party*. In Greek the construction is the same as for main clauses in category 1 conditional sentences (18.1/5; for the only complication see note 1 below); and the same is true in English, which uses *would* or *could* (although other auxiliaries such as *might* are also possible). As with conditional sentences (18.1/5) we have three time-frames:

Future   The optative (present or aorist as appropriate) with ἄν: τοῦτο οὐκ ἂν γένοιτο *that would not happen*.
Present The imperfect indicative with ἄν: τοῦτο οὐκ ἂν ἐγίγνετο *that would not be happening* or *happen* [*now* – to make a distinction between future and present English may need to add an adverb].
Past   The aorist indicative with ἄν: τοῦτο οὐκ ἂν ἐγένετο *that would not have happened*.

Notes

1 A future potential can be used as a form of politeness to make a statement or request less blunt, e.g. βουλοίμην ἄν *I should like* (cf. βούλομαι *I want*). ἐβουλόμην ἄν *I could wish* (*sc.* that something were now the case) is also frequently used with a past reference *I could have wished*; this is a relic of older use.

2 In a particular context it is sometimes possible to translate a present or future potential by *can*, instead of *could/would*; the above examples would then be translated *that can not happen/be happening*.

19.1/3 Oddities in verbs

(a) Perfects with a present meaning
As we have seen (15.1.1), the perfect expresses a state in the present resulting from an action in the past. The perfect of some Greek verbs is best expressed in English by the present tense of verbs which in themselves indicate a state. The most common examples are:

δέδοικα *I am afraid* (lit. *I have become alarmed*) from δείδω *be alarmed*. The aorist ἔδεισα is common and has the meaning *I was afraid*.

ἔγνωκα *I know* (lit. *I have recognized*) from γιγνώσκω *recognize*.

ἔοικα *I resemble, I seem* exists only in a few forms outside the perfect. Poetical forms in εἰκ- occur in the infinitive (εἰκέναι, otherwise ἐοικέναι) and participle (εἰκώς, εἰκυῖα, εἰκός, otherwise ἐοικώς etc.).

κέκτημαι,[2] lit. *I have acquired* or *I am in a state of having acquired* (< κτάομαι *acquire*), is normally to be translated by *I possess, own* (plpf. ἐκεκτήμην *I possessed, owned*; fut. perf. κεκτήσομαι *I shall possess, own*).

μέμνημαι *I remember* (lit. *I have reminded myself*) from μιμνήσκομαι *remind oneself*. The aorist passive ἐμνήσθην means *I remembered* (ex. at 12.3.9 *l*.2).

οἶδα *I know* exists only in the perfect, pluperfect, and future – see **Appendix 3**.

---

[2]This reduplication is an exception to the rule given at 15.1/1 (we would have expected ἐκτη-).

τέθνηκα I am dead (lit. I have died) from ἀποθνῆσκω die (the perfect is exceptional in never having the prefix ἀπο-, whereas the other tenses of the uncompounded verb are normally restricted to poetry). As with the perfect of ἵστημι (19.1/1) shorter forms occur, e.g. inf. τεθνάναι (for τεθνηκέναι), pple. τεθνεώς (for τεθνηκώς), opt. τεθναίην.

(b) Eccentric -μαι verbs

A few deponents end in -αμαι, not -ομαι, because they belong to the -μι class of verbs (18.1/1; cf. ἵσταμαι pres. mid./pass. of ἵστημι, 19.1/1). The only common examples are δύναμαι be able and ἐπίσταμαι know how to, understand (both passive deponents with a middle future – see **Principal parts of verbs**; we have already met some forms, e.g. 10.3 l.5). These differ from -ω verbs only in the present and imperfect. In these tenses δύναμαι is conjugated:

PRESENT
> INDICATIVE δύναμαι, δύνασαι, δύναται, δυνάμεθα, δύνασθε, δύνανται
> INFINITIVE δύνασθαι PARTICIPLE δυνάμενος, -η, -ον

IMPERFECT
> ἐδυνάμην, ἐδύνω (< -ασο), ἐδύνατο, ἐδυνάμεθα, ἐδύνασθε, ἐδύναντο.

For ἐδυν- we may also have ἠδυν-. The other moods of the present, where they occur, follow ἵστημι (19.1/1). The forms of ἐπίσταμαι are parallel.

Two similar verbs are κεῖμαι lie, be laid down and κάθημαι be seated, sit[3] which, because they both describe a continual action, exist only in the present, imperfect, and future. κεῖμαι is conjugated:

PRESENT
> INDICATIVE κεῖμαι, κεῖσαι, κεῖται, κείμεθα, κεῖσθε, κεῖνται
> INFINITIVE κεῖσθαι PARTICIPLE κείμενος, -η, -ον
> IMPERFECT ἐκείμην, ἔκεισο, ἔκειτο, ἐκείμεθα, ἔκεισθε, ἔκειντο
> FUTURE INDICATIVE κείσομαι, κείσῃ, etc.

---

[3] κάθημαι is used in prose but the uncompounded verb, ἧμαι, is found in verse (e.g. 16.3 l.9).

The forms of κάθημαι follow the same pattern. The other moods of the present of both verbs are rare. On the use of κεῖμαι for the perfect passive of τίθημι see 18.1/2 note 4.

19.2 Greek reading

1 λέγει που Ἡράκλειτος ὅτι πάντα χωρεῖ καὶ οὐδὲν μένει, καὶ ποταμοῦ ῥοῇ ἀπεικάζων τὰ ὄντα λέγει ὡς δὶς εἰς τὸν αὐτὸν ποταμὸν οὐκ ἂν ἐμβαίης.

2# νῆφε καὶ μέμνησ᾽ (= -σο) ἀπιστεῖν· ἄρθρα ταῦτα τῶν φρενῶν.

3 Πύρρων οὐδὲν ἔφη διαφέρειν ζῆν ἢ τεθνάναι. εἰπόντος δέ τινος, τί οὖν οὐκ ἀποθνήσκεις; ὅτι, ἔφη, οὐδὲν διαφέρει.

4# δοκεῖτε πηδᾶν τἀδικήματ᾽ εἰς θεοὺς
πτεροῖσι, κἄπειτ᾽ ἐν Διὸς δέλτου πτυχαῖς
γράφειν τιν᾽ αὐτά, Ζῆνα δ᾽ εἰσορῶντά νιν
θνητοῖς δικάζειν; οὐδ᾽ ὁ πᾶς ἂν οὐρανός,
Διὸς γράφοντος τὰς βροτῶν ἁμαρτίας,
ἐξαρκέσειεν οὐδ᾽ ἐκεῖνος ἂν σκοπῶν

5

πέμπειν ἑκάστῳ ζημίαν· ἀλλ᾽ ἡ Δίκη
ἐνταῦθά πουστιν ἐγγύς, εἰ βούλεσθ᾽ ὁρᾶν.

5 Proverbs and famous sayings

(*i*) ἐὰν δύνῃ ὁδεῦσαι, μὴ πλεύσῃς. (*ii*) τοῖς σεαυτοῦ πτεροῖς
ἑάλως. (*iii*) ἐκ παντὸς ξύλου Ἑρμῆς οὐκ ἂν γένοιτο. (*iv*) ὕδωρ
πίνων οὐδὲν ἂν τέκοις σοφόν. (*v*)# ὁ χρήσιμ᾽ εἰδώς, οὐχ ὁ
πόλλ᾽ εἰδώς, σοφός. (*vi*)# θεοῦ διδόντος οὐκ ἂν ἐκφύγοις κακά.
(*vii*) πάντες ἄνθρωποι τοῦ εἰδέναι ὀρέγονται φύσει. (*viii*) ὅταν
εὐπλοῇς, μάλιστα μέμνησο ζάλης. (*ix*) δός μοι ποῦ στῶ καὶ κινήσω
τὴν γῆν. (*x*) πολυμαθίη (= -ία) νόον ἔχειν οὐ διδάσκει· Ἡσίοδον
γὰρ ἂν ἐδίδαξε καὶ Πυθαγόρην (= -αν). (*xi*) τὸ φύσει πεφυκὸς οὐ
μεθίσταται. (*xii*) κούφως φέρειν δεῖ τὰς παρεστώσας τύχας. (*xiii*)
ἀθυμοῦντες ἄνδρες οὔπω τροπαῖον ἔστησαν. (*xiv*) ἄνθρωπος ὢν
μέμνησο. (*xv*) πάγην ἱστὰς ἐν πάγῃ ληφθήσῃ. (*xvi*) πόρρω ἐστὼς ὁ
θεὸς ἐγγύθεν βλέπει. (*xvii*) ἐπὶ ξυροῦ ἵσταται.

6# ὡς τοῖς κακῶς πράσσουσιν ἡδὺ καὶ βραχὺν
χρόνον λαθέσθαι τῶν παρεστώτων κακῶν.

7 One of the most famous Spartan kings was Leonidas, who
died with three hundred Spartan soldiers at Thermopylae in
an attempt to defend the pass against the invading Persians
(480 BC). The following are stories about him:

(*i*) Λεωνίδας πρός τινα εἰπόντα, πλὴν τοῦ βασιλεύειν ἡμῶν οὐδὲν
διαφέρεις, ἀλλ᾽ οὐκ ἄν, ἔφη, εἰ μὴ βελτίων ὑμῶν ἦν, ἐβασίλευον.
(*ii*) γενόμενος ἐν Θερμοπύλαις πρός τινα εἰπόντα, ἀπὸ τῶν
ὀϊστευμάτων τῶν βαρβάρων οὐδὲ τὸν ἥλιον ἰδεῖν ἔξεστιν, οὐκοῦν,
ἔφη, χαρίεν, εἰ ὑπὸ σκιᾷ αὐτοῖς μαχούμεθα.
(*iii*) Ξέρξου δὲ γράψαντος αὐτῷ, ἔξεστί σοι μὴ θεομαχοῦντι,
μετ᾽ ἐμοῦ δὲ ταττομένῳ, τῆς Ἑλλάδος μοναρχεῖν, ἀντέγραψεν,
εἰ τὰ καλὰ τοῦ βίου ἐγίγνωσκες, ἀπέστης ἂν τῆς τῶν ἀλλοτρίων
ἐπιθυμίας· ἐμοὶ δὲ κρείττων ὁ ὑπὲρ τῆς Ἑλλάδος θάνατος τοῦ
μοναρχεῖν τῶν ὁμοφύλων.
(*iv*) πάλιν δὲ τοῦ Ξέρξου γράψαντος, πέμψον τὰ ὅπλα, ἀντέγραψε,
μολὼν λαβέ.
The following epitaph for Leonidas and his men was written by
Simonides:
(*v*)# ὦ ξεῖν᾽, ἀγγέλλειν Λακεδαιμονίοις ὅτι τῇδε
κείμεθα, τοῖς κείνων ῥήμασι πειθόμενοι.

8 The normal way of publishing an official document in the Greek world was to cut the text on stone (usually marble) and display it in a prominent place. Many thousands of such inscriptions have survived. The following is an extract from the record of the Athenian settlement with the Euboean city of Chalcis after the Euboean revolt from the Athenian empire in 446 BC, and it gives the wording of the oath to be sworn by all adult males in Chalcis.

οὐκ ἀποστήσομαι ἀπὸ τοῦ δήμου τοῦ Ἀθηναίων οὔτε τέχνῃ
οὔτε μηχανῇ οὐδεμιᾷ οὐδ᾽ ἔπει οὐδὲ ἔργῳ, οὐδὲ τῷ ἀφισταμένῳ
πείσομαι, καὶ ἐὰν ἀφιστῇ τις, κατερῶ Ἀθηναίοις, καὶ τὸν φόρον
ὑποτελῶ Ἀθηναίοις ὃν ἂν πείθω Ἀθηναίους, καὶ ξύμμαχος
ἔσομαι οἷος ἂν δύνωμαι ἄριστος καὶ δικαιότατος, καὶ τῷ δήμῳ   5
τῷ Ἀθηναίων βοηθήσω καὶ ἀμυνῶ, ἐάν τις ἀδικῇ τὸν δῆμον τὸν
Ἀθηναίων, καὶ πείσομαι τῷ δήμῳ τῷ Ἀθηναίων.

Notes

1 τὰ ὄντα neuter pl., lit. *the being [things]*, i.e. *existing things*;
ὡς = ὅτι (8.1/3*b*)

2 ταῦτα is subject and ἄρθρα predicate.

3 οὐδὲν ἔφη cf. οὐ φημί (8.1/3*a* note 4); οὐδέν *in no respect, not
at all* (20.1/5); ζῆν and τεθνάναι (19.1/3*a*) are the subjects of
διαφέρειν; εἰπόντος ... τινος gen. absolute (12.1/2*b*).

4 *l*.1 δοκεῖτε *do you think*; τἀδικήματ᾽(α) (= τὰ ἀδ-) is the subject
of πηδᾶν. *l*.3 τιν᾽(α) *someone* is the subject of γράφειν and αὐτά
the object; νιν an obsolete pronoun used solely in verse; it exists
only in this form, which can function as the accusative of either
the singular or plural of any gender of the 3rd person unemphatic
pronoun (i.e. it can mean *him, her, it, them*); here it is the equivalent
of αὐτά (acc.), i.e. the ἀδικήματα. *l*.4 Take ἄν with ἐξαρκέσειεν.
l.6 ἐξαρκέσειεν < ἐξαρκέω (the ε is not lengthened, cf. 5.1/2 note
2) – the verb is to be taken before and after οὐδ᾽. *l*.8 ποῦστιν crasis
(11.1/5) for ποῦ ἐστιν; βούλεσθ᾽ i.e. βούλεσθε.

5 (*i*) δύνῃ 2nd s. pres. subj. of δύναμαι (the subjunctive is required
after ἐάν – 14.1/4*c*(iii)). (*ii*) ἑάλως < ἁλίσκομαι (18.1/4). (*iii*) Not

the god himself but a statue of him. (*iv*) ὕδωρ πίνων is the equivalent
of a conditional clause (*if you drink water* – 12.1/2*a*(iv)); τέκοις
2nd s. aor. opt. act. of τίκτω. (*v*) εἰδώς < οἶδα (19.1/3*a* and
Appendix 3). (*vii*) τοῦ εἰδέναι articular infinitive (5.1/3 – other
examples below in 7(*i*) and (*iii*)); ὀρέγομαι is followed by the
genitive (13.1/2*a*(ii)). (*viii*) μέμνησο cf.17.1/1 note 4. (*ix*) δός 2nd
s. aor. imp. act. of δίδωμι; στῶ (1st s. intr. aor. subj. of ἵστημι)
deliberative subjunctive in indirect speech (14.1/4*a*(ii)), *where
I am to stand*. (*x*) Written in Ionic (1.3); γάρ *for [otherwise]*.
(*xi*) πεφῡκός < φύω. (*xii*) παρεστώσας f. perf. pple. of παρίστημι.
(*xiii*) ἔστησαν gnomic aor. (see note on 5.2.10). (*xiv*) μέμνημαι is
followed, where appropriate, by a participle, not an infinitive (cf.
15.1/2*a*). (*xv*) ληφθήσῃ 2nd s. fut. ind. pass. of λαμβάνω.

6 παρεστώτων n. perf. pple. of παρίστημι.

7 (*i*) Take ἡμῶν with διαφέρεις, not with βασιλεύειν. (*ii*) οὐδέ *not
even*; ἔξεστιν (also in (*iii*)) an impersonal verb meaning *it is
possible* (21.1/4*a*); χαρίεν sc. ἔσται. (*iii*) Take ταττομένῳ (mid. of
τάττω, *drawing yourself up* (*with me*)) with σοι; τοῦ μοναρχεῖν
gen. of comparison (17.1/4*a*). (*iv*) μολών aor. pple. of βλώσκω.
(v) ξεῖν᾿(ε) = ξένε; ἀγγέλλειν infinitive used as imperative (17.1/1
note 5); κείνων = ἐκείνων.

8 *ll.*1f. The first negative, οὐκ, is reinforced by οὔτε ... οὔτε ...
οὐδεμιᾷ and οὐδ᾿ ... οὐδέ, lit. *I will not ... neither in no ... nor*,
etc. but trans. *I will not ... either in any ... or*, etc. (οὐδεμιᾷ
goes with both τέχνῃ and μηχανῇ); the fut. mid. ἀποστήσομαι
(< ἀφίστημι) is intransitive; τοῦ δήμου τοῦ Ἀθηναίων *the people*,
[*i.e.*] *the [people] of [the] Athenians* a regular formula in
inscriptions, trans. *the people of Athens*; ἔπει dat. s. of ἔπος.
*ll.*3ff. πείσομαι fut. of πείθομαι, not πάσχω; ἀφιστῇ 3rd s. pres.
subj. act., this is a transitive tense (19.1/1) but the verb here has
no object expressed – lit. *causes [others] to revolt*, i.e. *tries to
stir up revolt*; κατερῶ < καταγορεύω (18.1/4 note 2); ὑποτελῶ
fut. (5.1/2 note 2); τὸν φόρον ... ὃν ἂν πείθω Ἀθηναίους lit. *the
tribute whatever I persuade the Athenians*, i.e. *whatever tribute
I persuade the Athenians* (sc. *is appropriate*). *ll.*5ff. οἷος *of what
sort* (21.1/3) is given a general reference (*of whatever sort*)
because it is followed by ἄν and the subj. (14.1/4*c*(iii)), lit. *of

whatever sort best and most just I am able [to be]; the phrase ὁ δῆμος ὁ Ἀθηναίων is repeated to avoid any misunderstanding whatsoever.

Main points

- Some forms of ἵστημι are parallel to those of δίδωμι and τίθημι

- The weak aorist of ἵστημι is transitive but the root aorist is intransitive

- The compounds of ἵστημι have the same transitive/intransitive distinctions as ἵστημι itself

- Potential clauses are expressed in the same way as main clauses of a category 1 conditional sentences

- The perfect of some verbs has a present meaning

- Deponents ending in -αμαι belong to the -μι class of verbs

Unit 20

20.1 Grammar

20.1/1 Verbs in -νῡμι

The -νῡμι class (18.1/1) constitutes the more numerous subdivision of -μι verbs but presents no especial difficulty. All forms of the present and imperfect contain the suffix νῡ or νῠ; the present indicative, infinitive and participle, and the imperfect have endings without the o/e characteristic of -ω verbs (cf. 2.1/5 note 3), but the present subjunctive and optative have the same endings as λύω. The other tenses, which do not keep the νῡ/νῠ suffix, are formed in the same way as those of -ω verbs. An example is δείκνῡμι *show*, which has the principal parts δείκνῡμι, fut. δείξω, aor. act. ἔδειξα, perf. act. δέδειχα, perf. mid./pass. δέδειγμαι, aor. pass. ἐδείχθην. The present and imperfect of this verb are given in full in **Appendix 6**.

Notes

1 A number of verbs in this class end in -ννῡμι rather than -νῡμι, e.g. κεράννῡμι *mix*, σκεδάννῡμι *scatter*, κρεμάννῡμι *hang* (tr.; the intransitive meaning of this verb is supplied by the passive κρέμαμαι, which is conjugated like ἵσταμαι (19.1/1)).

2 ὄλλῡμι (originally ὄλ-νῡμι) *destroy*, *ruin*, *lose* (fut. ὀλῶ) has two aorists and two perfects. The weak forms of both are transitive and the strong intransitive (cf. 15.1/1 note 2):

AORIST	(weak)		*I destroyed/ruined/lost*
		ὤλεσα	
	(strong)	ὠλόμην	*I perished* (middle voice, not active!)
PERFECT	(weak)	ὀλώλεκα	*I have destroyed/ruined/lost*
	(strong)	ὄλωλα	*I have perished, am ruined or lost*

ὄλλῡμι in its uncompounded form occurs only in verse. In prose we find the compound ἀπόλλῡμι, which has the same meaning. Cf. the use of θνῄσκω in verse but ἀποθνῄσκω in prose (19.1/3*a*).

20.1/2 ἵημι and its compounds

ἵημι *let go, send forth* is another -μι verb of group (*a*) (18.1/1). Its present stem was originally σιση- (root ση/σε; cf. δίδωμι and τίθημι) but with the change of the initial sigma to a rough breathing (cf. ἵστημι 19.1/1) and the loss of intervocal sigma (cf. 6.1/1*c*) this was reduced to ἱη- (root ἡ/ἑ).

The principal parts of ἵημι are: pres. ἵημι, fut. ἥσω, aor. act ἧκα, perf. act. εἷκα, perf. pass. εἷμαι, aor. pass. εἵθην.

As will be seen from **Appendix 5** its present and imperfect tenses are exactly parallel to those of τίθημι except in the 3rd pl. pres. ind. act., where contraction has taken place (ἱᾶσι < ἱέᾱσι). The parallelism extends to nearly every other form, although it is obscured in some cases by contraction. Note that the sing. aor. act. ind. has a κ suffix as in τίθημι.

Almost all forms of ἵημι, except those of the present and imperfect, exist only in compounds. The following are the most common:

ἀφίημι	*send forth; discharge; let go*
ἐφίημι	*send; set on, send against;* (mid.) *aim at, desire*
μεθίημι	*let go, release; give up*
παρίημι	*pass over; let pass*

Examples of each of these compounds are:

πρέπει σοι τὴν ὀργὴν ἀφῑέναι εἰς τὸν βλάψαντά σε. *It is fitting for you to vent your anger on the man who harmed you.*
ἐὰν ἑλών τίς τινα ἀκουσίου φόνου καὶ σαφῶς ἐπιδείξᾱς μὴ καθαρόν, μετὰ ταῦτ᾽ αἰδέσηται καὶ ἀφῇ, οὐκέτ᾽ ἐκβαλεῖν κύριος τὸν αὐτόν ἐστιν. *If anyone convicts a man of involuntary homicide and clearly shows him to be polluted* (lit. *not pure*), *and then feels pity for him and releases him, he no longer has the power to cast the same person into exile.*

ἐφῆκε τὴν ἵππον ἐπὶ τοὺς Ἕλληνας. *He sent the cavalry against the Greeks.*

οὐ γὰρ τοῖς ἔθνεσιν ἔχθει ἐπίᾱσιν, ἀλλὰ τῶν ἐν τῇ Σικελίᾳ ἀγαθῶν ἐφῑέμενοι. *For they will not attack the races because of hatred but because they are aiming at the good things of Sicily.*

ἐλευθέρᾱν δέ με, ὡς ἐλευθέρᾱ θάνω, πρὸς θεῶν μεθέντες κτείνατε. *In the name of the gods, release me [to be] free, so that I may die free, and [then] kill me* (a woman is speaking).

εἰ μεθήσει τὴν ἀρχήν, ἄλλος τις ἀντ᾽ αὐτοῦ τύραννος καταστήσεται. *If he gives up his power, someone else will set himself up as tyrant in his stead.*

μὴ τοίνυν γιγνώσκοντές γε παρῶμεν αὐτὸ ἄρρητον. *Let us not then, since we know [it], pass it over unmentioned.*

χρὴ ἡμᾶς κατασκόπους μὴ πέμπειν μηδὲ διαμέλλειν καιρὸν παρῑέντας. *We ought not to send inspectors or to delay, letting an opportunity pass.*

20.1/3 Genitive of price or value

The genitive is used to express price or value with verbs and adjectives denoting buying, selling, valuing, and the like:

ὅταν δέῃ ἀργυρίου πρίασθαι ἢ ἀποδόσθαι ἵππον ... *Whenever it is necessary to buy or sell a horse for money ...*

τοῦτο δ᾽ ἐστὶν ὃ τῶν ἀνᾱλισκομένων χρημάτων πάντων Φίλιππος ὠνεῖται. *This is what Philip is buying with all the money which is being spent.*

Α. πόσου διδάσκει; Β. πέντε μνῶν. *A. What is his fee for teaching?* (lit. *for how much does he teach?*) *B. Five minae* (lit. *for five minae*).

ἡμᾶς οὐδενὸς λόγου ἀξιοῖ. *He thinks us of no account.*

σμῑκρὰ καὶ ὀλίγου ἄξια ἀνερωτᾷ. *He asks petty, insignificant questions* (lit. *things small and worth little*).

To *value highly/little/not at all* etc. is commonly expressed by ποιεῖσθαι and a genitive governed by περί: περὶ πολλοῦ (πλέονος, πλείστου) / ὀλίγου (ἐλάττονος, ἐλαχίστου)/ οὐδενὸς ποιεῖσθαι. Examples are:

τὰ πλείστου ἄξια περὶ ἐλαχίστου ποιεῖται, τὰ δὲ φαυλότερα περὶ πλέονος. *He values least what is worth most, and [values] more highly what is more trivial.*

ἀναγκαῖον ἐδόκει εἶναι τὸ τοῦ θεοῦ περὶ πλείστου ποιεῖσθαι. *It seemed essential to value most highly the god's [word].*

οὗτος ἅπαντας τοὺς πολίτας περὶ οὐδενὸς ἐποιήσατο. *He valued all the citizens at nothing.*

20.1/4 Genitive of separation

The genitive is used with verbs and adjectives denoting separation, cessation, prevention, hindrance, difference, etc. It is common with verbs compounded with ἀπό and ἐκ:

ἀπέχει τῶν Ἐπιπολῶν ἓξ ἢ ἑπτὰ σταδίους. *It is six or seven stades distant from Epipolae.*

ἔπαυσαν αὐτὸν τῆς στρατηγίᾱς. *They deposed him from his generalship.*

ἐκώλυον τῆς πορείᾱς αὐτόν. *They prevented him from passing* (lit. *from the passage*).

ἐψηφίσασθε ὑμεῖς αὐτὸν εἴργεσθαι τῆς ἀγορᾶς καὶ τῶν ἱερῶν. *You voted that he be excluded from the agora and the temples.*

οὐδὲν διοίσεις Χαιρεφῶντος. *You will be no different from Chaerephon.*

ἔργων πονηρῶν χεῖρ᾽ ἐλευθέρᾱν ἔχε. *Keep your hand free from wicked deeds.*

20.1/5 Accusative of respect or specification

The accusative may be used with a verb (usually intransitive) or an adjective to denote a thing with respect to which that verb or adjective is limited. A literal translation may be obtained by employing the words *with respect to* before the noun involved, but, to produce an idiomatic translation, it will often be necessary to recast the expression somewhat in English:

τὰς γνάθους ἀλγήσετε. *You will have a pain with respect to your jaws* i.e. *you'll have sore jaws.*

πόδας ὠκὺς Ἀχιλλεύς. *Swift-footed* (lit. *swift with respect to feet*) *Achilles.*

τυφλὸς τά τ᾽ ὦτα τόν τε νοῦν τά τ᾽ ὄμματ᾽ εἶ. *You are blind both in* (lit. *with respect to*) *ears and mind and eyes.*

τεῖχος πεντήκοντα μὲν πήχεων τὸ εὖρος, ὕψος δὲ διᾱκοσίων πήχεων. *A wall fifty cubits wide and two hundred cubits high* (lit. *of fifty cubits with respect to the width, and of two hundred with respect to height*).

λέξον ὅστις εἶ γένος. *Tell [me] who you are by race.*

Under this heading may also be included the so-called **adverbial accusatives**, e.g. οὐδέν *in no respect, not at all*; τι *to some extent*; τί *why* (lit. *with respect to what?*); πολύ *much, by far*; τὰ ἄλλα, τἆλλα *in other respects*; τοῦτον τὸν τρόπον *in this way*; τίνα τρόπον...; *in what way..? how...?* Examples of these have already occurred. We have also met the neuter accusative (both singular and plural) of adjectives employed in this way, e.g. ὀρθὰ βαδίζειν *to walk straight* (15.2.3, see also 16.3 *l.*5, 17.3 *l.*12). Adjectives so used are the equivalent of adverbs.

Insight

With us today Arabic numerals can indicate cardinal numbers (as *3 days*) or ordinals (as *10 January*, i.e. *the tenth of Jan.*). Similarly, the Greeks used α, β, γ, etc. to mean *first, second, third* as well as *1, 2, 3.* Consequently, α followed by ὥρα *hour* meant *the first hour [of the day].* An ingenious poet used the chance sequence of the letters ζ, η, θ, ι (see Insight, Unit 18) to show how a day should be properly spent:

Ἓξ ὧραι μόχθοις ἱκανώταται. αἵδε δὲ μετ’ αὐτὰς
γράμμασι δεικνύμεναι ΖΗΘΙ λέγουσι βροτοῖς.

Six hours are quite (lit. most) sufficient for labours; those [hours] after them say to mortals ‘Live!’ [by] indicating [this] with their letters.

The seventh hour begins the afternoon, which the poet recommends as a four-hour rest-break after the morning’s work.

On δεικνύμεναι (pres. pple. mid. of δείκνῡμι) see 20.1/1. The middle voice is used here in the same sense as the active.

20.2 Greek reading

1 νεανίας τίς ποτε νοσήσας εἶπε τῷ ἰατρῷ οὕτως ἀλγεῖν ὥστε
μὴ δύνασθαι μήτε καθῆσθαι μήτε κεῖσθαι μήτε ἑστάναι· ὁ δὲ
ἰατρός, ὦ φίλε, ἔφη, οὐδὲν ἄλλο σοι λοιπόν ἐστιν ἢ κρέμασθαι.

2# τίς δ᾽ οἶδεν εἰ ζῆν τοῦθ᾽ ὃ κέκληται θανεῖν,
τὸ ζῆν δὲ θνήσκειν ἐστί; πλὴν ὅμως βροτῶν
νοσοῦσιν οἱ βλέποντες, οἱ δ᾽ ὀλωλότες
οὐδὲν νοσοῦσιν οὐδὲ κέκτηνται κακά.

3 Proverbs and famous sayings
(*i*) δραχμῆς μὲν ἦλει, τεττάρων δὲ παύεται. (*ii*) ἡ κάμηλος
ἐπιθυμήσασα κεράτων καὶ τὰ ὦτα προσαπώλεσεν. (*iii*)# οὐκ
ἔστιν ὅστις πάντ᾽ ἀνὴρ εὐδαιμονεῖ. (*iv*) πολλοὶ στρατηγοὶ Καρίαν
ἀπώλεσαν. (*v*) ἀφεὶς τὰ φανερὰ μὴ δίωκε τὰ ἀφανῆ. (*vi*) χρόνος
δίκαιον ἄνδρα δείκνυσιν μόνος. (*vii*) ἐλέφαντος διαφέρεις οὐδέν.
(*viii*)# ἀπάτης δικαίας οὐκ ἀποστατεῖ θεός. (*ix*)# πολλῶν ἰατρῶν
εἴσοδός μ᾽ ἀπώλεσεν. (*x*) λέων εἶ τὴν τρίχα, ὄνος δὲ τὸν βίον.

4# An epic nose
τοῦ γρυποῦ Νίκωνος ὁρῶ τὴν ῥῖνα, Μένιππε,
   αὐτὸς δ᾽ οὖν μακρὰν φαίνεται εἶναι ἔτι·
ἀλλ᾽ ἥξει, μείνωμεν ὅμως· εἰ γὰρ πολύ, πέντε
   τῆς ῥινὸς σταδίους, οἴομαι, οὐκ ἀπέχει.
ἀλλ᾽ αὐτὴ μέν, ὁρᾷς, προπορεύεται· ἢν δ᾽ ἐπὶ βουνὸν   5
   ὑψηλὸν στῶμεν, καὐτὸν ἐσοψόμεθα.

5# τὴν κεφαλὴν βάπτων τις ἀπώλεσε τὰς τρίχας αὐτάς,
   καὶ δασὺς ὢν λίαν ᾠὸν ἅπαξ γέγονεν.

6 ἐπὶ τούτῳ Κλεάνωρ ἀνέστη καὶ ἔλεξεν ὧδε· ἀλλ᾽ ὁρᾶτε μέν,
ὦ ἄνδρες, τὴν βασιλέως ἐπιορκίαν καὶ ἀσέβειαν, ὁρᾶτε δὲ
τὴν Τισσαφέρνους ἀπιστίαν, ὅστις, λέγων ὡς γείτων τε εἴη τῆς
Ἑλλάδος καὶ περὶ πλείστου ἂν ποιήσαιτο σῶσαι ἡμᾶς, καὶ ἐπὶ
τούτοις αὐτὸς ὀμόσας ἡμῖν, αὐτὸς δεξιὰς δούς, αὐτὸς ἐξαπατήσας 5
συνέλαβε τοὺς στρατηγούς, καὶ οὐδὲ Δία ξένιον ᾐδέσθη, ἀλλὰ
Κλεάρχῳ καὶ ὁμοτράπεζος γενόμενος αὐτοῖς τούτοις ἐξαπατήσας
τοὺς ἄνδρας ἀπολώλεκεν.

7 ἀλλ', ὦ Σώκρατες, πειθόμενος τοῖς νόμοις μήτε παῖδας περὶ πλείονος ποιοῦ μήτε τὸ ζῆν μήτε ἄλλο μηδὲν πρὸ τοῦ δικαίου, ἵνα εἰς Ἅιδου ἐλθὼν ἔχῃς πάντα ταῦτα ἀπολογήσασθαι τοῖς ἐκεῖ ἄρχουσιν.

8 ὁ Σωκράτης φανερὸς ἦν οὐ τῶν τὰ σώματα πρὸς ὥραν, ἀλλὰ τῶν τὰς ψυχὰς πρὸς ἀρετὴν εὖ πεφυκότων ἐφιέμενος.

9# γραμματικοῦ θυγάτηρ ἔτεκεν φιλότητι μιγεῖσα
παιδίον ἀρσενικόν, θηλυκόν, οὐδέτερον.

10# Ζεὺς γὰρ τὰ μὲν μέγιστα φροντίζει βροτῶν,
τὰ μικρὰ δ' ἄλλοις δαίμοσιν παρεὶς ἐᾷ.

11 οἱ δ' ἐν τῇ Χίῳ μετὰ τοῦ Ἐτεονίκου στρατιῶται ὄντες, ἕως μὲν θέρος ἦν, ἀπό τε τῆς ὥρας ἐτρέφοντο καὶ ἐργαζόμενοι μισθοῦ κατὰ τὴν χώραν· ἐπεὶ δὲ χειμὼν ἐγένετο καὶ τροφὴν οὐκ εἶχον γυμνοί τε ἦσαν καὶ ἀνυπόδητοι, συνίσταντο ἀλλήλοις ὡς τῇ Χίῳ ἐπιθησόμενοι.   5

12# Polymnestor, who has been blinded by Hecuba, screams for vengeance but is restrained by Agamemnon.

ΠΟ. ὤμοι, τί λέξεις; ἦ γὰρ ἐγγύς ἐστί που;
σήμηνον, εἰπὲ ποῦ 'σθ', ἵν' ἁρπάσας χεροῖν
διασπάσωμαι καὶ καθαιμάξω χρόα.
ΑΓ. οὗτος, τί πάσχεις; ΠΟ. πρὸς θεῶν σε λίσσομαι,
μέθες μ' ἐφεῖναι τῇδε μαργῶσαν χέρα.   5
ΑΓ. ἴσχ'· ἐκβαλὼν δὲ καρδίας τὸ βάρβαρον
λέγ', ὡς ἀκούσας σοῦ τε τῆσδέ τ' ἐν μέρει
κρίνω δικαίως ἀνθ' ὅτου πάσχεις τάδε.

Notes

1 νοσήσας *having fallen sick* **not** *having been sick* as is shown by the context (technically called an **ingressive** aorist); μὴ δύνασθαι ... lit. *not to be able neither to ... nor to* i.e. *not to be able either to ... or to.*

2 *l.*1 τοῦθ' (τοῦτο) is the subject of the first clause after εἰ (supply ἐστί from the next line). *l.*2 πλὴν ὅμως *except however* (lit. *except nevertheless*). *l.*3 οἱ βλέποντες sc. *the light of day*, a regular expression for *the living*; οἱ ὀλωλότες (20.1/1 note 2) i.e. *the dead*.

3 (*i*) ηὔλει inceptive imperfect (4.1/1 footnote) *started to play the pipe*. (*ii*) καί adv. *also*. (*iii*) Lit. *there is not whatever man* ... i.e. *there is no man who* ... (on ὅστις, which is here used adjectivally, see 10.1/2*b* note 2). (*v*) μή negates the whole sentence, i.e. ἀφείς (aor. pple. of ἀφίημι) and δίωκε. (*x*) εἶ (< εἰμί) *you are*.

4 *l.*2 δ᾽ οὖν (13.1/3*c*(ii)) introduces a contrast *but/however* (οὖν does not have its normal meaning here). *ll.*3f. μείνωμεν jussive subj. (14.1/4*a*(i)); with εἰ γὰρ πολύ supply ἀπέχει from next line, lit. *for [even] if he is far away*; πέντε σταδίους acc. of spatial extent (7.1/7*d*); τῆς ῥινός *from his nose* gen. of separation (20.1/4). *l.*5 ἤν = ἐάν (18.1/5 note 2), which is followed by the subj. *l.*6 στῶμεν intr. aor. subj. of ἵστημι (19.1/1); καὐτόν (= καὶ αὐτόν) *him too*.

5 The participle ὤν has a concessive force *though being* (we might have expected an accompanying καίπερ (12.1/2*a*(iii)) but cf. λέγων, ὀμόσας, δούς in the next passage, which are used in the same way); take λίαν with δασύς (this unusual word order is dictated by metre).

6 *l.*1 ἀνέστη < ἀνίστημι. *l.*3 The indefinite relative ὅστις (10.1/2 note 2) is also used to introduce an adjectival clause which gives a reason, trans. *since he*; εἴη opt. in indirect speech in historic sequence (14.1/4*d*). *l.*5 ὀμόσας < ὄμνυμι. *ll.*6ff. οὐδέ *not even*; ἠδέσθη < αἰδέομαι; Κλεάρχῳ dat. with ὁμοτράπεζος (to share a meal automatically involved permanent ties of friendship and a violation of these was an offence against Ζεὺς ξένιος); καί *actually*; αὐτοῖς τούτοις (instrumental dat., 11.1/2) *by these very means*.

7 μήτε ἄλλο μηδέν *nor anything else* (7.1/6); πρό lit. *in preference to* but trans. *than*; εἰς is used with the gen. to mean *to the place/ house of* – the house of Hades is the Underworld, to which all souls (ψῡχαί) went after death; ἔχῃς *you may be able* (ἔχω + an infinitive means *be able*).

8 φανερὸς ἦν + pple. lit. *was clear(ly)* ... (cf.15.2.10); εὖ πεφῡκότων must be taken with both phrases beginning with τῶν; εὖ πεφῡκέναι (< φύω, the pple. is used here) means *to be well endowed by nature, to be naturally sound*; τὰ σώματα and τὰς ψῡχὰς are acc. of respect (20.1/5), but trans. *in body ... in soul* and trans. πρός (lit. *towards*) by *with respect to*.

9 μιγεῖσα f. aor. pass. pple. of μείγνῡμι; the lady gave birth to triplets, whose gender reflected her father's professional interests.

10 παρείς aor. act. pple. of παρῑημι.

11 ὥρᾱ *[produce of] the season*; γυμνοί lit. *naked* but here to be understood simply as *badly clothed*.

12 *l.*1 ἦ γάρ introduces a surprised question *is she really* ...? (ἦ = ἆρα). *l.*2 'σθ' i.e. ἐστί; χεροῖν is dat. dual (24.1/4), lit. *with two hands*. *l.*3 καθαιμάξω aor. subj. (as is διασπάσωμαι) after ἵνα (14.1/4c(i)); χρόα acc. s. of χρώς. *l.*4 The nom. οὖτος (which does not, in any case, have a voc.) expresses an impatient demand for the attention of the person addressed (here Polymnestor), trans. *you there!* or *what's this?*; τί πάσχεις lit. *what are you suffering?*, i.e. *what's wrong with you?*. *l.*5 μέθες 2nd s. aor. imp. act. of μεθῑημι; ἐφεῖναι aor. inf. of ἐφῑημι; *l.*6 τὸ βάρβαρον *the barbarous [element]* i.e. *savagery. ll.*7f. ὡς (here = ἵνα) introduces a purpose clause (22.1/1b(ii)), and consequently κρίνω is subjunctive.

Main points

- -νῡμι verbs only differ from -ω verbs in the present and imperfect

- ἵημι occurs mainly in compounds; its conjugation is very similar to that of τίθημι

- The genitive is used to express price, value and separation

- *With respect to [something]* is expressed by the accusative of respect or specification

Unit 21

21.1 Grammar

21.1/1 Wishes

Like potential clauses (19.1/2) and conditional sentences (18.1/5), wishes can have reference to the present, past or future. The negative used in wishes is always μή.

(*a*) Wishes for the **future** are expressed by the optative (present or aorist, according to the aspect involved – 14.1/1) and **may** be introduced by εἴθε or εἰ γάρ (*if only ... !*):

> ὑμῖν θεοὶ δοῖεν ἐκπέρσαι Πριάμου πόλιν. *May the gods grant that you sack* (lit. *give to you to sack*) *the city of Priam.*
> εἴθε γράψειεν ὡς χρή. *I wish that he would write as he should* (lit. *would that he would write as is necessary* or *if only he would ...*).

(*b*) Wishes for the **present** are expressed by the imperfect indicative and **must** be introduced by εἴθε or εἰ γάρ:

> εἰ γὰρ τοσαύτην δύναμιν εἶχον. *I wish I had so much power* (lit. *would that I had ...* or *if only I had ...*).
> εἴθ' εἶχες βελτίους φρένας. *I wish you had better thoughts.*

(*c*) Wishes for the **past** are expressed by the aorist indicative, also with an obligatory εἴθε/εἰ γάρ:

> εἴθ' εὕρομέν σε, ὦ Ἄδμητε, μὴ λῡπούμενον. *I wish we had not found you grieving, Admetus.*
> εἴθε σοι, ὦ Περίκλεις, τότε συνεγενόμην. *I wish I had been with you then, Pericles.*

In the nature of things only wishes for the future can be fulfilled (and then not always). Wishes for the present and past are futile protests against what is happening or has happened.

Note

A present or past wish may also be expressed by ὤφελον (the aorist of ὀφείλω *owe, be obliged to*), which has the meaning *ought*. It is followed by a present or aorist infinitive, depending on whether the wish is for the present or past. εἴθε/εἰ γάρ is optional:

ὤφελε Κῦρος ζῆν. *I wish Cyrus were alive* (lit. *Cyrus ought to be alive*).

μήποτ᾽ ὤφελον λιπεῖν τὴν Σκῦρον. *I wish I had never left Scyrus* (lit. *I ought never to have left ...*).

21.1/2 Further temporal conjunctions (ἕως, μέχρι, πρίν)

Each of these three words has more than one use, but all can be employed as subordinating conjunctions with the meaning *until*.

ἕως and μέχρι both take the same construction as certain other temporal conjunctions (ὅτε, ἐπειδή etc., see 14.1/4c(iii)). They are followed by the indicative when the clause they introduce refers to a definite event:

ταῦτα ἐποίουν μέχρι σκότος ἐγένετο. *They were doing these things until darkness fell* (lit. *happened*).

When the reference is to something anticipated (but we do not know if it eventuates or not), the indefinite construction is used (14.1/4c(iii)):

περιμένετε ἕως ἂν ἔλθω. *Wait until I come* (*or for me to come*).

ἔδοξεν αὐτοῖς προϊέναι ἕως Κύρῳ συμμείξειαν. *They decided* (lit. *it seemed good to them*, 21.1/4a) *to advance until they should meet Cyrus.*

With these conjunctions the indefinite construction can also refer to repeated action:

περιεμένομεν ἑκάστοτε ἕως ἀνοιχθείη τὸ δεσμωτήριον. *On each occasion we used to wait until the prison opened.*

πρίν has a wider range of constructions:

(*a*) When the main verb is **affirmative**, πρίν is followed by an infinitive (usually aorist) and has the meaning *before*:

ἐπὶ τὸ ἄκρον ἀνέβη Χειρίσοφος πρίν τινα αἰσθέσθαι τῶν πολεμίων. *Cheirisophus went up to the peak before any of the enemy noticed.*
λέγεται Ἀλκιβιάδης, πρὶν εἴκοσιν ἐτῶν εἶναι, Περικλεῖ διαλεχθῆναι περὶ νόμων. *Alcibiades is said to have conversed with Pericles about laws before he was twenty years old* (lit. *of twenty years*).

The rules governing the case of the subject of the infinitive are exactly the same as in the infinitive construction in indirect statement (8.1/3*a*); in the first example above, the subject (τινά) of the infinitive is not the same as the subject of the main verb and so is in the accusative.

(*b*) When the main verb is **negated** and πρίν can be translated by *until* or *before*, it has the same construction as ἕως and μέχρι:

οὐκ ἦν γένος ἀθανάτων πρὶν Ἔρως ξυνέμειξεν ἅπαντα. *There was not a race of immortals until* (or *before*) *Love mixed everything together.*
μὴ ἀπέλθετε πρὶν ἄν μου ἀκούσητε. *Do not go away until* (or *before*) *you hear me.*

(*c*) When the main verb is **negated** and πρίν must be translated by *before*, it has the same construction as in (*a*):

οὐδὲ πρὶν νῑκηθῆναι ἐθάρρει ὁ στρατηγός. *Not even before being defeated was the general confident* (πρίν cannot here be translated by *until*).

Notes

1 ἕως (and occasionally μέχρι) with the indicative can also mean *while, as long as*:

Κλέαρχος, ἕως πόλεμος ἦν τοῖς Λακεδαιμονίοις πρὸς τοὺς Ἀθηναίους, παρέμενεν. *As long as the Spartans were at war* (lit. *there was war for the Spartans*) *with the Athenians, Clearchus remained loyal.*

2 μέχρι may also function as a **preposition** (+ gen.) with the meaning *until, up to, as far as* (with reference to time or space): μέχρι τοῦ γόνατος *up to the knee*; μέχρι τούτου *up to this [time]*.

3 πρίν can also be used as an **adverb** meaning *before, formerly*: ἐν τῷ πρὶν χρόνῳ *in the previous time*.

4 οὐ is used to negate the indicative in the subordinate clauses described above, μή to negate the indefinite construction and also the infinitive after πρίν.

21.1/3 Further demonstrative and relative adjectives/pronouns

Greek possesses two series of adjectives, each containing a demonstrative, relative (and exclamatory), and interrogative form. One series, with the element -οσ-, refers to **quantity**, the other, with the element -οι-, refers to **quality**:

DEMONSTRATIVE	RELATIVE/EXCLAMATORY	INTERROGATIVE
τοσοῦτος, τοσόσδε *so much/many*	ὅσος *as much/many as; how much/many!*	πόσος *how big?; how much?* pl. *how many?*
τοιοῦτος, τοιόσδε *of this sort, such*	οἷος *of what sort; what a ...!*	ποῖος *of what sort?*

The relative/exclamatory and interrogative forms are first and second declension adjectives (3.1/3). On the declension of τοσοῦτος, τοιοῦτος see 16.1/1 note 1. τοσόσδε and τοιόσδε are compounds of τοσ/τοι + οσ (declined as καλός, 3.1/3) + δε. All can function as pronouns as well as adjectives.

We have already dealt with the interrogatives (10.1/2) and the use of τοσοῦτος and τοιοῦτος to anticipate an adverbial clause or phrase of result (16.1/1). We must also note that:

(*a*) τοιοῦτος is used with reference to what precedes in a narrative, τοιόσδε with reference to what follows. This is the principal use of the latter, e.g. οἱ μὲν τοιαῦτα εἶπον, οἱ δὲ Ἀθηναῖοι τοιάδε ἀπεκρίναντο *they said this* (lit. *such things as precede) and the Athenians replied as follows* (lit. *such things as follow*). οὗτος and ὅδε are used in the same way (9.1/1 note 1).

(*b*) τοσόσδε, like τοιόσδε, can refer to what follows but is generally the equivalent of τοσοῦτος.

(*c*) ὅσος and οἷος can introduce exclamations:

ὅσα πράγματα ἔχεις. *How much trouble* (lit. *how many things*) *you have!*
οἷα δράσας οἷα λαγχάνει κακά. *After what deeds what sufferings are his!* (lit. *what things having done what evil things he obtains!*).

(*d*) πάντες ὅσοι is used in the sense *all who* (lit. *all as many as*) instead of the expected πάντες οἵ:

πάντας ἐχθαίρω θεοὺς ὅσοι κακοῦσί μ᾽ ἐκδίκως. *I hate all the gods who unjustly wrong me.*

Very often ὅσος is used by itself in this sense:

οἱ Καδμεῖοι ὅσους κακοὺς εὗρον ... *All the Cadmeans whom I found wicked* ... (lit. *the Cadmeans as many as I found* ...).

(*e*) τοσοῦτος/ὅσος and τοιοῦτος/οἷος are used in sentences where ὅσος and οἷος introduce a comparison. As English does not have relatives of this sort some change is needed in translation:

οἷος ὁ πατήρ ἐστιν, τοιοῦτος καὶ ὁ υἱός. *Like father, like son* (lit. *of what sort the father is, of that sort [is] the son too*).
ἔχετε τοσούτους στρατιώτᾱς ὅσους οἱ Πέρσαι. *You have as many soldiers as the Persians* (*sc. have*; lit. *you have so many soldiers as many as the Persians*).

The relatives alone, without the corresponding demonstratives, may be used in this way:

οὐ μοι ἡ δύναμίς ἐστιν οἷᾱ πάρος ἦν. *I have not the same strength as I previously had* (lit. *there is not to me the strength of what sort* (= *of the sort which*) *there was previously*).

Notes

1 In verse τόσος and τοῖος often occur as the equivalents of τοσοῦτος and τοιοῦτος respectively.

2 οἷός τ᾽ εἰμί *I am able* is a stereotyped formula (example in 13.3(ii) *l.*3); τε here is purely idiomatic and is not to be translated, and οἷος has no relative force.

21.1/4 Further impersonal verbs

Impersonal verbs have no real subject. In English they are given a grammatical subject *it*, which is purely idiomatic and does not refer to anything. In Greek impersonal verbs are simply put in the 3rd singular. We have already met δεῖ and χρή *it is necessary,* which are followed by an infinitive whose subject, if expressed, is put into the accusative (examples at 3.2.12(*x*), 5.2.15 etc.). Other impersonals can be classified as follows:

(a) Impersonals followed by the dative and infinitive

δοκεῖ	*it seems good*	πρέπει	*it is fitting*
ἔξεστι	*it is allowed/possible*	προσήκει	*it concerns/is fitting*
λῡσιτελεῖ	*it is profitable*	συμφέρει	*it is expedient*
πάρεστι	*it is possible*		

Examples of ἔξεστι occur at 9.2.7 and 19.2.7(ii). Of the others we may cite:

> ταῦτα πρέπει μᾶλλον βαρβάροις ποιεῖν ἢ Ἕλλησιν. *It is more fitting for barbarians than Greeks to do these things.*
> οὔ σοι προσήκει φωνεῖν. *You have no business speaking* (lit. *it does not concern you to speak*).

δοκεῖ is usually to be translated by *think, intend, decide,* e.g. ὡς ἐμοὶ δοκεῖ *as I think* (lit. *as it seems good to me*); δοκεῖ αὐτῷ ἀπιέναι *he intends to leave*; ἔδοξε τοῖς Ἀθηναίοις μάχεσθαι *the Athenians decided to fight* (another example at 14. 2.18 *l.*3).

Some of the above verbs can be used personally, sometimes with a different meaning, e.g. πάρειμι *I am present.*

(b) **Impersonals followed by the dative of the person involved and the genitive of the thing**

μέτεστι μοι τούτου   *there is a share to me of this*, i.e. *I have a share in this*

μέλει μοι τούτου   *there is a concern to me of this*, i.e. *I am concerned about this*

μεταμέλει μοι τούτου   *there is repentance to me of this*, i.e. *I repent of this*

Examples are:

τοῖς θεοῖς δίκης μέλει. *The gods are concerned with justice.*
τί τοῦδέ σοι μέτεστι πρᾱγματος; *What concern* (lit. *share*) *have you in this business?*
ὑμῖν μεταμελησάτω τῶν πεπρᾱγμένων. *Repent of your deeds!* (lit. *let there be repentance* [3rd s. aor. imp. act.] *to you of the things done*).

(c) **Weather impersonals**
The various verbs for expressing weather conditions, as ὕει *it is raining*, νείφει *it is snowing*, are not strictly impersonals because Zeus, in his capacity as sky god, is their understood subject. We should, however, translate them by the impersonal English expression.

Notes

1 ἔστι (always so accented) is often used in the sense of ἔξεστι (examples at 9.2.13 *l.*5 and 11.2.10 *l.*4). For other cases of this accentuation see **Appendix 8,** *d*(x).

2 πάρα, μέτα (note accent!) are often used for πάρεστι, μέτεστι respectively.

3 When the impersonal δεῖ means *there is need of* it takes the same construction as class (b) (example in 13.2.21); in the sense *it is necessary* it is always followed by the infinitive.

21.1/5 Accusative absolute

The **participle** of an impersonal verb stands in the neuter singular **accusative** in a context where other verbs would be placed in the genitive absolute (cf. 12.1/2b); it has **no** subject. Such accusative absolutes are δέον *it being necessary*; ἐξόν, παρόν, παρέχον *it being possible*; μέλον *it being a care*; προσῆκον, πρέπον *it being fitting*; δόξαν *it having been decided*. Examples are:

ἐξὸν εἰρήνην ἔχειν, αἱρεῖται πολεμεῖν. *Although he can live in peace* (lit. *it being possible to have peace*), *he chooses to make war.*

δῆλον γὰρ ὅτι οἶσθα, μέλον γέ σοι. *For it [is] clear that you know, since you are interested [in the subject]* (lit. *it being a care to you*).

συνδόξαν τῷ πατρὶ καὶ τῇ μητρί, γαμεῖ τὴν Κυαξάρου θυγατέρα. *Since his father and mother approved* (lit. *it having seemed good also to ...*) *he married* (vivid present) *the daughter of Cyaxares.*

The accusative absolute is also found with expressions consisting of a neuter adjective and ὄν, such as ἀδύνατον ὄν *it being impossible*, αἰσχρὸν ὄν *it being disgraceful*, ἄδηλον ὄν *it being unclear*, e.g.

παρεκελεύοντο ἀλλήλοις κραυγῇ οὐκ ὀλίγῃ χρώμενοι, ἀδύνατον ὂν ἐν νυκτὶ ἄλλῳ τῳ σημῆναι. *They encouraged each other with* (lit. *using*) *no little shouting, since it was impossible* (lit. *it being impossible*) *by night to signal by any other [means].*

Insight

Croesus, the king of Lydia, wished to test the competence of the oracles in the eastern Mediterrean. Sending out messengers he gave instructions that on the hundredth day from leaving the royal capital each messenger should ask the oracle to which he had been dispatched what the king was doing at that time. What this would be Croesus told no one. The oracle of Delphi, after first stating that it knew everything, replied:

ὀδμή μ' ἐς φρένας ἦλθε κραταιρίνοιο χελώνης
ἑψομένης ἐν χαλκῷ ἅμ' ἀρνείοισι κρέεσσιν.

A smell has come (lit. *came*) *to [my] mind of a hard-shelled tortoise being boiled in bronze together with meat of a lamb* (lit. *lamb meat*).

At the appointed time Croesus was boiling the meat of a tortoise with mutton in a bronze pot as he supposed that such an eccentric action could hardly be detected by guesswork. As the reply of the Delphic oracle appeared to confirm its credentials as a reliable source of information Croesus went on to use it but in the end he was cruelly deceived (see 4.2.9). The answers of other oracles are not recorded; presumably they were all wrong. On φρήν cf. Insight to Unit 22.

21.2 Greek reading

1 Σπαρτιάτης τις εἰς Ἀθήνας ἐλθὼν καὶ ἰδὼν ἐν ἀποχωρήσει θακοῦντας ἐπὶ δίφρων ἀνθρώπους, μή μοι γένοιτο, εἶπεν, ἐνταῦθα καθίσαι ὅθεν οὐκ ἔστιν ἐξαναστῆναι πρεσβυτέρῳ.

2 Proverbs
(*i*) πρὶν τοὺς ἰχθῦς ἑλεῖν τὴν ἅλμην κυκᾷς. (*ii*) οὐ μέλει τῇ χελώνῃ μυιῶν. (*iii*) ἀεί με τοιοῦτοι πολέμιοι διώκοιεν. (*iv*) προσήκει τοῖς τέκνοις ἐντὸς θυρῶν λοιδορεῖσθαι. (*v*) οἷος ὁ τρόπος τοιοῦτος ὁ λόγος. (*vi*)# μηδένα νομίζετε εὐτυχεῖν πρὶν ἂν θάνῃ. (*vii*)# οἵαπερ ἡ δέσποινα τοία χἡ κύων. (*viii*)# νέῳ δὲ σιγᾶν μᾶλλον ἢ λαλεῖν πρέπει. (*ix*) ὦ οἵα κεφαλή, καὶ ἐγκέφαλον οὐκ ἔχει. (*x*)# μέτεστι τοῖς δούλοισιν δεσποτῶν νόσου. (*xi*)# μή μοι γένοιθ᾽ ἃ βούλομ᾽, ἀλλ᾽ ἃ συμφέρει. (*xii*) Ἅιδου πρωκτῷ περιπέσοις. (*xiii*)# εἴθ᾽ ἦν ἄφωνον σπέρμα δυστήνων βροτῶν.

3# ὅστις δὲ θνητῶν θάνατον ὀρρωδεῖ λίαν,
μῶρος πέφυκε· τῇ τύχῃ τῶνδε μέλει.
ὅταν δ᾽ ὁ καιρὸς τοῦ θανεῖν ἐλθὼν τύχῃ,
οὐδ᾽ ἂν πρὸς αὐλὰς Ζηνὸς ἐκφύγοι μολών.

4 ὅσοι γαμοῦσι γένει κρείττους γάμους οὐκ ἐπίστανται γαμεῖν.

5 οἵῳ τις ἂν τὸ πλεῖστον τῆς ἡμέρας συνῇ, τοιοῦτον ἀνάγκη
γενέσθαι καὶ αὐτὸν τοὺς τρόπους.

6 ἀναστὰς αὖθις Θώραξ ὁ Βοιώτιος, ὃς περὶ στρατηγίας Ξενοφῶντι
ἐμάχετο, ἔφη, εἰ ἐξέλθοιεν ἐκ τοῦ Πόντου, ἔσεσθαι αὐτοῖς
Χερρόνησον, χώραν καλὴν καὶ εὐδαίμονα, ὥστε ἐξεῖναι τῷ
βουλομένῳ ἐνοικεῖν, τῷ δὲ μὴ βουλομένῳ ἀπιέναι οἴκαδε.
γελοῖον δὲ εἶναι, ἐν τῇ Ἑλλάδι οὔσης χώρας πολλῆς καὶ ἀφθόνου,   5
ἐν τῇ βαρβάρων μαστεύειν. ἕως δ᾽ ἄν, ἔφη, ἐκεῖ γένησθε, κἀγὼ
ὑπισχνοῦμαι ὑμῖν τὸν μισθόν.

7 Διογένης ἰδών ποτε γυναῖκας ἀπ᾽ ἐλάας ἀπηγχονισμένας, εἴθε
γάρ, ἔφη, πάντα τὰ δένδρα τοιοῦτον καρπὸν ἤνεγκεν.

8# ὅστις δὲ πράσσει πολλά, μὴ πράσσειν παρόν,
μῶρος, παρὸν ζῆν ἡδέως ἀπράγμονα.

9 βουλευομένοις τοῖς στρατιώταις ἔδοξεν ἀποκρίνασθαι τάδε·
καὶ ἔλεξε Χειρίσοφος· ἡμῖν δοκεῖ, εἰ μέν τις ἐᾷ ἡμᾶς ἀπιέναι
οἴκαδε, διαπορεύεσθαι τὴν χώραν ὡς ἂν δυνώμεθα ἀσινέστατα·
ἢν δέ τις ἡμᾶς τῆς ὁδοῦ ἀποκωλύῃ, διαπολεμεῖν τούτῳ ὡς ἂν
δυνώμεθα κράτιστα.

10# Prometheus laments his lot
ἦ δυσπετῶς ἂν τοὺς ἐμοὺς ἄθλους φέροις,
ὅτῳ θανεῖν μέν ἐστιν οὐ πεπρωμένον·
αὕτη γὰρ ἦν ἂν πημάτων ἀπαλλαγή·
νῦν δ᾽ οὐδέν ἐστι τέρμα μοι προκείμενον
μόχθων πρὶν ἂν Ζεὺς ἐκπέσῃ τυραννίδος.   5

11 καὶ ὁ Κῦρος ἀκούσας τοῦ Γωβρύα τοιαῦτα τοιάδε πρὸς αὐτὸν
ἔλεξεν.

12# Medea resolves to murder her children
εἶεν· τί δράσεις, θυμέ; βούλευσαι καλῶς
πρὶν ἐξαμαρτεῖν καὶ τὰ προσφιλέστατα
ἔχθιστα θέσθαι. ποῖ ποτ᾽ ἐξῇξας τάλας;
κάτισχε λῆμα καὶ σθένος θεοστυγές.
καὶ πρὸς τί ταῦτα δύρομαι, ψυχὴν ἐμὴν   5

ὁρῶσ᾽ ἔρημον καὶ παρημελημένην
πρὸς ὧν ἐχρῆν ἥκιστα; μαλθακοὶ δὲ δὴ
τοιαῦτα γιγνόμεσθα πάσχοντες κακά;
οὐ μὴ προδώσεις, θυμέ, σαυτὸν ἐν κακοῖς.
οἴμοι δέδοκται· παῖδες, ἐκτὸς ὀμμάτων   10
ἀπέλθετ᾽· ἤδη γάρ με φοίνιον νέα
δέδυκε λύσσα θυμόν. ὦ χέρες χέρες,
πρὸς οἷον ἔργον ἐξοπλιζόμεσθα· φεῦ
τάλαινα τόλμης, ἢ πολὺν πόνον βραχεῖ
διαφθεροῦσα τὸν ἐμὸν ἔρχομαι χρόνῳ.   15

13 εἰς Λακεδαίμονα παραγενόμενός τις καὶ τὴν πρὸς τοὺς
πρεσβύτας τῶν νέων τιμὴν θεασάμενος, ἐν Σπάρτῃ μόνῃ, εἶπε,
λυσιτελεῖ γηράσκειν.

14# ἐχρῆν γὰρ ἡμᾶς σύλλογον ποιουμένους
τὸν φύντα θρηνεῖν εἰς ὅσ᾽ ἔρχεται κακά,
τὸν δ᾽ αὖ θανόντα καὶ πόνων πεπαυμένον
χαίροντας εὐφημοῦντας ἐκπέμπειν δόμων.

Notes

1 The Spartans, as well as living in a primitive simplicity where
a public toilet would have been unheard of, prided themselves
on old-fashioned virtues such as respect for people older than
oneself (cf. 13 below); ἔστιν = ἔξεστιν; ἐξαναστῆναι intr. aor. inf
of ἐξανίστημι.

2 (*i*) The brine is to boil the fish. (*iv*) Take τέκνοις with λοιδορεῖσθαι,
not with προσήκει. (*v*) Supply ἐστί with οἷος and with τοιοῦτος
(cf. (*vii*) below). (*vii*) χἠ = καὶ ἡ. (*ix*) οἶα exclamatory. (*x*) Take
δεσποτῶν with νόσου, and νόσου with μέτεστι. (*xi*) γένοιθ᾽ =
γένοιτο; βούλομ᾽ = βούλομαι (2.1/6*b* note); συμφέρει is not here
impersonal but has ἅ as its subject.

3 *l*.2 τῶνδε neuter *these things*. *l*.3 ἐλθὼν τύχῃ (3rd s. aor. subj. of
τυγχάνω) *chances to come* (15.1/2*e*).

4 γένει *in race* (dat. of respect, 23.1/2*m*).

5 συνῇ 3rd s. pres. subj. of σύνειμι, which takes a dative (here οἴῳ); ἀνάγκη *sc.* ἐστί; τοὺς τρόπους acc. of respect (20.1/5) with τοιοῦτον.

6 After ἔφη in *l.*2 we have a passage of indirect speech, but the last sentence of the passage is in direct speech with an extra ἔφη inserted (cf. 8.1/3*a* and 7.1/2 note 3). *l.*2 εἰ ἐξέλθοιεν represents in historic sequence ἐὰν ἐξέλθωσι of the original direct speech (14.1/4*c*(iii)); ἔσεσθαι αὐτοῖς lit: *there to be going to be for them,* i.e. *they would have. l.*4 τῷ ... μὴ βουλομένῳ the negative is μή because a general class is meant (12.1/2*a*(vi)), trans. *anyone who did not [so] wish. l.*6 ἐκεῖ γένησθε i.e. *you get there.*

7 ἀπηγχονισμένᾱς f. acc. pl. of the perf. pass. pple. of ἀπαγχονίζω; εἴθε + aor. expresses a wish for the past (21.1/1*c*).

8 The old Athenian aristocratic ideal was a life of leisure. In both lines παρόν is an acc. absolute (21.1/5). *l.*1 μή negates πράσσειν.

9 ἀπιέναι < ἀπέρχομαι (18.1/3); ὡς ... ἀσινέστατα lit. *in whatever way* (ὡς ἄν) *we can most harmlessly,* i.e. *doing the least possible harm.*

10 *l.*2 ὅτῳ the relative ὅστις can be used to introduce an adjectival clause which gives a **reason** (cf. note on 20.2.6 *l.*3). *l.*3 αὕτη *this* refers to what has just been mentioned (i.e. death), but is attracted into the gender of ἀπαλλαγή. *ll.*4f. νῦν δ᾽(έ) *but as it is;* take μόχθων with τέρμα; ἐκπίπτω is here acting as the pass. of ἐκβάλλω *throw out* (cf.17.1/5); τυραννίδος gen. of separation (20.1/4).

11 Take τοιαῦτα with ἀκούσᾱς, τοιάδε with ἔλεξεν; Γωβρύᾱς (1st declension) has the non-Attic gen. s. Γωβρύᾱ.

12 *l.*1 βούλευσαι 2nd s. aor. imp. mid. of βουλεύω. *l.*3 θέσθαι (< τίθημι) here *make;* ἐξῇξας 2nd s. aor. ind. act. of ἐξαΐσσω; τάλᾱς (10.1/3 note 2) is voc. (Medea is still addressing her θῡμός). *l.*5 πρὸς τί lit. *with a view to what,* i.e. *why. l.*6 ἔρημον is f. and agrees with ψῡχήν (ἔρημος is one of the few two termination adjectives (3.1/3) which are not compounds); παρημελημένην perf. pass. pple. of παραμελέω. *ll.*7f. πρὸς ὧν i.e. πρὸς (= ὑπὸ) τούτων οὕς (9.1/2 note 2); δὲ δή here introduces an emphatic question *And so ...? Then ... ?*; when a woman is using the royal plural, as with γιγνόμεσθα (= -μεθα, cf. 8.2.9 and ἐξοπλιζόμεσθα in *l.*13 below), she refers to herself with masculine pl. adjectives and participles, hence μαλθακοί and πάσχοντες; take τοιαῦτα ... κακά after πάσχοντες. *l.*9 οὐ μή + fut. ind. expresses a strong prohibition (17.1/1). *l.*10 δέδοκται *it is decided* (i.e. *by me*, lit. *it is in a state of seeming good [to me]*) - the impers. δοκεῖ (21.1/4*a*) is mid./pass. in the perfect; παῖδες voc. *ll.*11f. ἀπέλθετ᾿(ε) 2nd pl. aor. imp.; με ... δέδῦκε ... θῦμόν lit. *has entered me [with respect to] my heart*, i.e. *has entered my heart* (acc. of respect 20.1/5). *l.*14 τόλμης gen. of cause (23.1/1*k*(ii)) with τάλαινα *wretched [that I am] because of my daring*, Medea is talking about herself; πόνον i.e. the labour of bearing and raising her children. *l.*15 διαφθεροῦσα fut. pple. to express purpose (12.1/2*a*(v)).

14 *l.*1 ἐχρῆν = ἐχρῆν ἄν a common idiom which means *it should be necessary*, not *it was necessary*, because it expresses something which should be happening now (present potential, 19.1/2), trans. *we should ... l.*2 κακά is acc. of respect (20.1/5) after θρηνεῖν and the antecedent of εἰς ὅσ᾿(α) ἔρχεται, lit. *with respect to the troubles to how many he is coming*, i.e. *for all the toubles he is coming to* (21.1/3*d*). *ll.*3f. δ᾿(ὲ) αὖ *and in turn*; πόνων, δόμων gen. of separation (20.1/4); δόμων is also an example of the singular used for the plural, *from [his*, i.e. the dead man's] *house*.

Main points

- Wishes for the future are expressed by the optative, wishes for the present and past by the imperfect and aorist indicative respectively; with the latter two εἴθε or εἰ γάρ is obligatory but not with the optative

- ἕως and μέχρι (both *until*) are used with the indicative for a definite event, but with the subjunctive for an anticipated one

- πρίν with the meaning *before* (and not *until*) is followed by an infinitive

- πρίν after a negated verb with the meaning *before/until* has the same construction as ἕως and μέχρι

- The adjectives τοσοῦτος, ὅσος, πόσος refer to **quantity** but τοιοῦτος, οἷος, ποῖος refer to **quality**

- Some impersonal verbs are followed by the dative and infinitive, some by the dative and genitive

- Weather conditions are described by impersonals such as ὕει *it is raining*

- The accusative absolute is only used with impersonal verbs

21.3 Extra reading – love poetry

Love poetry had a long history in Greek. The first example below is from Mimnermus (7th century BC) but the others are much later (2 and 3 are attributed to Plato, whether correctly or not we have no means of telling; the authors of 4 and 5 are unknown). All are written in elegiacs (**Appendix 9**), the metre most associated with this genre.

1 τίς δὲ βίος, τί δὲ τερπνὸν ἄτερ χρυσῆς Ἀφροδίτης;
    τεθναίην, ὅτε μοι μηκέτι ταῦτα μέλοι,
κρυπταδίη φιλότης καὶ μείλιχα δῶρα καὶ εὐνή,
    οἷ᾽ ἥβης ἄνθεα γίγνεται ἁρπαλέα
ἀνδράσιν ἠδὲ γυναιξίν· ἐπεὶ δ᾽ ὀδυνηρὸν ἐπέλθῃ   5
    γῆρας, ὅ τ᾽ αἰσχρὸν ὁμῶς καὶ κακὸν ἄνδρα τιθεῖ,
αἰεί μιν φρένας ἀμφὶ κακαὶ τείρουσι μέριμναι
    οὐδ᾽ αὐγὰς προσορῶν τέρπεται ἠελίου,
ἀλλ᾽ ἐχθρὸς μὲν παισίν, ἀτίμαστος δὲ γυναιξίν·
    οὕτως ἀργαλέον γῆρας ἔθηκε θεός.   10
2 ἀστέρας εἰσαθρεῖς ἀστὴρ ἐμός· εἴθε γενοίμην
    οὐρανός, ὡς πολλοῖς ὄμμασιν εἰς σὲ βλέπω.
3 ἀστὴρ πρὶν μὲν ἔλαμπες ἐνὶ ζωοῖσιν Ἑῷος·
    νῦν δὲ θανὼν λάμπεις Ἕσπερος ἐν φθιμένοις.

4 πέμπω σοι μύρον ἡδύ, μύρῳ παρέχων χάριν, οὐ σοί·
  αὐτὴ γὰρ μυρίσαι καὶ τὸ μύρον δύνασαι.
5 Ἠοῦς ἄγγελε, χαῖρε, Φαεσφόρε, καὶ ταχὺς ἔλθοις
  Ἕσπερος, ἣν ἀπάγεις, λάθριος αὖθις ἄγων.

Notes

1 All deviations from Attic in this poem are Ionic (1.3). *l*.2 τεθναίην
  the shorter form of the perf. opt. of θνῄσκω (19.1/3*a*) – the opt.
  is used here to express a wish for the future (21.1/1*a*); ταῦτα
  (referring to the nouns in *l*.3) is the subject of μέλοι, which is
  not impersonal here and should be translated as though ind. (the
  verb has been assimilated to the mood of τεθναίην). *l*.3 κρυπταδίη
  = -ία. *l*.4 οἷ'(α) ... γίγνεται lit. *of what sort are*, i.e. *the sorts of
  things which*; ἄνθεα = ἄνθη (< ἄνθος). *l*.5 ἐπεὶ ... ἐπέλθῃ in this
  indefinite construction Attic would require ἄν (14.1/4*c*(iii)). *l*.6
  αἰσχρόν and κακόν (here *lowly, base*) are predicative after ἄνδρα
  τιθεῖ (= τίθησι), *makes a man both* (ὁμῶς) *ugly and base*—note
  here that we have ὁμῶς, **not** ὅμως *nevertheless*. *l*.7 φρένας ἀμφί =
  ἀμφὶ φρένας.

2 *l*.1 ἀστὴρ ἐμός is in apposition to *you*, the subject of εἰσαθρεῖς. *l*.2
  ὡς = ἵνα (βλέπω is subj., 14.1/4*c*(i)).

3 *l*.1 πρίν here an adverb *formerly*; ἀστὴρ ... Ἑῷος *the Morning
  Star*. *l*.2 Ἕσπερος *the Evening Star*; the Greeks knew that both
  were in fact the planet Venus (see 5 below), which makes the
  poet's fanciful identification of his lover with them all the more
  appropriate.

4 *l*.1 παρέχων χάριν *doing a favour*. *l*.2 καί *even* (μύρον has a very
  strong scent).

5 The poet, who supposes that the planet Venus in its guise as the
  Morning Star is taking away his girl friend, expresses the wish
  that it return quickly as the Evening Star and bring her back.
  l.1 Ἠοῦς gen. of Ἠώς. *l*.2 Ἕσπερος i.e. *[as] the Evening Star*; ἣν
  ἀπάγει ... ἄγων *bringing [the girl] whom you are [now] leading
  away*.

Unit 22

22.1 Grammar

22.1/1 Summary of the uses of ὡς

ὡς, originally an adverb of manner meaning *in which way, how,* came to have various uses as an adverb or as a conjunction. It may also occur as a preposition.

(a) ὡς *as an adverb*
(i) ὡς with participles and prepositional phrases

We have already seen how ὡς is used with participles of **cause** (12.1/2*a*(ii)) and **purpose** (12.1/2*a*(v)), reflecting the attitude (thought, opinion, intention, hope) of the subject of the participle without any implication of the belief or opinion of the writer or speaker. In this use, which also occurs with phrases introduced by a preposition, ὡς expresses an alleged reason or assumed motive, and may be translated *as if, in the opinion that, under the impression that, with the (avowed) intention of* etc.:

> συλλαμβάνει Κῦρον ὡς ἀποκτενῶν. *He seized* (vivid present) *Cyrus with the intention of putting him to death.*
> ἀγανακτοῦσιν ὡς μεγάλων τινῶν ἀπεστερημένοι. *They are annoyed in the belief that they have been deprived of some very great [benefits].*
> ἀνήγοντο ὡς ἐπὶ ναυμαχίᾱν. *They put out to sea with the intention of fighting* (lit. *as for a sea-battle*).
> ἀπέπλεον ὡς εἰς τὰς Ἀθήνᾱς. *They sailed away as if for Athens.*

(ii) ὡς exclamatory

ὡς *how ... !* is used in exclamations with adjectives, adverbs and verbs:

> ὡς ἀστεῖος ὁ ἄνθρωπος. *How charming the man is!*
> ὡς ἀδεῶς καὶ γενναίως ἐτελεύτᾱ. *How fearlessly and nobly he died!*
> ὥς μ᾽ ἀπώλεσας, γύναι. *How you have destroyed me, woman!*

(iii) ὡς with positive adverbs

ὡς may be used to emphasize positive adverbs: ὡς ἀληθῶς *in very truth*; ὡς ἑτέρως *quite otherwise*; ὡς αὕτως (often written ὡσαύτως) *in the same way, just so*.

Note too the common idiom where ὡς is added to the adverbs θαυμασίως and θαυμαστῶς (lit. *marvellously, wonderfully*) to express emphasis:

νῦν δὲ θαυμασίως ὡς ἄθλιος γέγονεν. *But now he has become prodigiously wretched.*
εὖ λέγει θαυμαστῶς ὡς σφόδρα. *He speaks marvellously well* (lit. *he speaks well marvellously very*).

(iv) ὡς with superlative adjectives and adverbs (see 17.1/4*d*)

(v) ὡς ἕκαστος/ἑκάτερος

ὡς is often combined with ἕκαστος (or ἑκάτερος) in the sense *each by himself, each severally* or *individually*:

ἄλλοι παριόντες ἐγκλήματα ἐποιοῦντο ὡς ἕκαστοι. *Others came forward and made their separate complaints* (lit. *each [group] by themselves*).
παυσάμενοι τῆς μάχης ὡς ἑκάτεροι ἡσυχάσαντες τὴν νύκτα ἐν φυλακῇ ἦσαν. *They ceased from fighting and on either side* (lit. *each side by themselves*) *remained quiet [but] on guard for the night.*

(vi) ὡς restrictive

ὡς may also be used to limit the validity of a statement, with the meaning *for*:

ἦν οὐδὲ ἀδύνατος, ὡς Λακεδαιμόνιος, εἰπεῖν. *He was not a bad speaker* (lit. *not unable to speak*) *either, for a Spartan* (or *considering that he was a Spartan*).
μακρὰ ὡς γέροντι ὁδός. *A long road, for an old man.*
φρονεῖ ὡς γυνὴ μέγα. *She has proud thoughts* (lit. *thinks big*), *for a woman.*

Restrictive ὡς is also found with the **infinitive** in certain idiomatic expressions which stand independent of the overall grammatical construction and which express some limitation or qualification of the sentence as a whole. This use is particularly common in the phrase ὡς ἔπος εἰπεῖν (or ὡς εἰπεῖν) *so to speak*, which usually modifies a sweeping statement with πᾶς or οὐδείς (or the like); occasionally it apologizes for a metaphor:

> ἀληθές γε ὡς ἔπος εἰπεῖν οὐδὲν εἰρήκασιν. *They have spoken virtually no word of truth* (lit. *nothing true so to speak*).
> Ἱππόλυτος οὐκέτ᾽ ἔστιν, ὡς εἰπεῖν ἔπος. *Hippolytus is as good as dead* (lit. *is no longer alive, so to speak*).
> ἰδιῶται ὡς εἰπεῖν χειροτέχναις ἀνταγωνισάμενοι. *Laymen, as it were, pitted against craftsmen* (the metaphorical use of ἀνταγωνισάμενοι is toned down).

(vii) **ὡς with numerals**

ὡς is used with numerals in the sense *about, nearly*:

> διέσχον ἀλλήλων βασιλεύς τε καὶ οἱ Ἕλληνες ὡς τριάκοντα στάδια. *The King and the Greeks were about thirty stades distant from each other*

ὡς is similarly used in the common phrase ὡς ἐπὶ τὸ πολύ *for the most part* (lit. *nearly so far as regards the much*).

(*b*) **ὡς** *as a conjunction*
(i) **In indirect speech,** *that* (see 8.1/3*b*)

(ii) **In purpose clauses,** *in order that* (see 14.1/4*c*(i))

Purpose clauses are generally introduced by ἵνα or ὅπως, but ὡς may also be used, especially in poetry and in Xenophon:

> διανοεῖται τὴν γέφυραν λῦσαι ὡς μὴ διαβῆτε. *He intends to break up the bridge in order that you may not cross.*

(iii) **In clauses of reason,** *as, since, because*

Causal clauses are regularly introduced by ὅτι, διότι *because, as,* ἐπεί, ἐπειδή *since,* but may also be introduced by ὡς. As in its use with the participle (see *a*(i) above), ὡς sometimes carries the implication that the reason given is the subjective opinion of the person described:

ἔπειτα δὲ ξύμβασιν ποιησάμενοι πρὸς τὸν Περδίκκᾶν, ὡς αὐτοὺς κατήπειγεν ἡ Ποτείδαια, ἀπανίστανται ἐκ τῆς Μακεδονίᾶς. *Then, when they had made an agreement with Perdiccas because (in their opinion) [the situation in] Potidaea was pressing them, they withdrew* (vivid present) *from Macedonia.*

(iv) **In temporal clauses,** *when, after*

ὡς may be used like ἐπεί (cf. 14.1/4*c*(iii)):

ὡς ᾔσθετο Κῦρον πεπτωκότα ἔφυγεν. *When he perceived that Cyrus had fallen, he fled.*

ὡς τάχιστα may be used for ἐπειδὴ τάχιστα in the sense *as soon as:*

ὡς τάχιστα ἥκομεν εἰς Μακεδονίᾶν, συνετάξαμεν τὸν πρεσβύτατον πρῶτον λέγειν. *As soon as we had come to Macedonia, we arranged for the eldest man to speak first.*

(v) **ὡς in clauses of manner**

ὡς may be used to introduce adverbial clauses of manner in the sense *as, according as, in which way,* often coupled with οὕτω(ς) *thus, so* in the principal clause. In such clauses the verb in the subordinate clause will be in the indicative mood if the action is marked as a fact:

ἐκέλευσε τοὺς Ἕλληνας, ὡς νόμος αὐτοῖς ἦν εἰς μάχην, οὕτω ταχθῆναι. *He ordered the Greeks to be drawn up as was their custom for battle* (lit. *as was their custom, so ... to be drawn up*).

But if the action has a future reference or is indefinite, the mood of the verb will follow the rules for indefinite clauses (cf. 14.1/4*c*(iii)), i.e. subjunctive with ἄν in primary sequence, optative without ἄν in historic sequence:

τὸ πέρας ὡς ἂν ὁ δαίμων βουληθῇ πάντων γίγνεται. *The end of all things comes about in whatever way the deity wishes.*
ξυνετίθεσαν ὡς ἕκαστόν τι ξυμβαίνοι. *They put [them] together as each [piece] fitted.*

The verb in the ὡς clause is often omitted, e.g. εἴθε πάντες σε φιλοῖεν ὡς ἐγώ *would that all loved you as I* (*sc. do*). Other examples occur at 13.2.6 and 15. ὡς is likewise frequently used to introduce clauses which are parenthetical: ὡς ἔοικε *as it seems*; ὡς ἔγῳμαι (= ἐγὼ οἶμαι) *as I think*; ὡς ἐμοὶ δοκεῖ *in my opinion* (lit. *as it seems to me*).

(c) **ὡς** *as a preposition*
ὡς as a preposition governs the accusative case and has the sense of *to, towards*. It is used only with **persons**:

ὡς Περδίκκαν ἔπεμψαν ἀμφότεροι πρέσβεις. *Both sides sent ambassadors to Perdiccas.*

22.1/2 Uses of cases (1) – accusative

Apart from its use as the case of the direct object of transitive verbs (2.1/3c) and after certain prepositions (2.1/3f; 3.1/5a), the accusative can function in a number of ways, some of which require rephrasing to be turned into normal English.

(*a*) *Accusative and infinitive* (see 8.1/3a, and cf. 16.1/1)

(*b*) *Accusative to express time how long* (see 7.1/7a)

(*c*) *Accusative to express spatial extent* (see 7.1/7d)

(*d*) *Accusative of respect or specification* (see 20.1/5)

(*e*) *Accusative absolute* (see 21.1/5)

(*f*) *Verbs taking two accusatives*

These occur in Greek as in English (*we chose him leader*; *they asked us our opinion*) and can be divided into two categories:

(i) Verbs of **making, considering, naming, choosing, appointing** etc. (factitive verbs), which take a direct object and an object complement (also called a predicate):

οἱ Θετταλοὶ καὶ οἱ Θηβαῖοι φίλον, εὐεργέτην, σωτῆρα τὸν Φίλιππον ἡγοῦντο. *The Thessalians and Thebans considered Philip* (direct object) *a friend, benefactor and saviour* (object complement).
τρεῖς τῶν ἐμῶν ἐχθρῶν νεκροὺς θήσω. *I shall make three of my enemies corpses.*

When such expressions are put into the passive, both accusatives become nominative:

Λασθένης φίλος ὠνομάζετο Φιλίππου *Lasthenes was called the friend of Philip.*

(ii) Verbs of **asking for** (αἰτέω), **teaching** (διδάσκω), **concealing** (κρύπτω), **depriving** (ἀποστερέω), **taking away** (ἀφαιρέομαι), and a few others, which may take two accusatives (one accusative of the person and the other of the thing involved). The construction of the corresponding verbs in English is not always the same:

ὁ πόλεμος ἀείμνηστον παιδείᾱν αὐτοὺς ἐπαίδευσεν. *The war taught them a lesson never to be forgotten.*
ἀποστερεῖ με τὴν τῑμήν. *He takes the honour from me.*
τὴν θυγατέρα ἔκρυπτε τὸν θάνατον τοῦ ἀνδρός. *He concealed her husband's death from his daughter.*

When such expressions are put into the passive, the thing involved remains in the accusative (**retained accusative**):

ἐκεῖνοι ἵππους ἀπεστέρηνται. *Those men have been deprived of their horses.*
οὐδὲν ἄλλο διδάσκεται ἄνθρωπος ἢ ἐπιστήμην. *A man is taught nothing else except knowledge.*

276

Under this heading also belong the phrases ἀγαθὰ (κακά, etc.) λέγειν τινά *to speak well (ill, etc.) of someone*, and ἀγαθὰ (κακά, etc.) ποιεῖν τινα *to do good (evil, etc.) to someone* and the like:

τοὺς Κορινθίους πολλά τε καὶ κακὰ ἔλεγεν. *He said many bad things about the Corinthians.*

Instead of the neuter pl. acc. of the adjective, however, we often find the adverbs εὖ/κακῶς, etc.:

τὸν μέντοι καὶ λόγῳ καὶ ἔργῳ πειρώμενον ἐμὲ ἀνιᾶν οὐκ ἂν δυναίμην οὔτ᾽ εὖ λέγειν οὔτ᾽ εὖ ποιεῖν. *However, I would be able neither to speak well of nor to do good to the man who tries to vex me both in word and in deed.*

For the passive of expressions using λέγω and ποιέω see 17.1/5.

(g) *Cognate accusative*

This describes an expression in which a noun and the verb (usually otherwise intransitive) by which it is governed are both derived from the same root (as in English *sing a song*):

νοσεῖ νόσον ἀγρίᾱν. *He is ill with a cruel disease.*
ἑωρᾶτε Σωκράτη πολλὴν φλυᾱρίᾱν φλυᾱροῦντα. *You used to see Socrates talking much nonsense.*

Except in poetry, the cognate accusative is usually accompanied by an adjective or other attribute.

Also included under this heading are accusatives used in exactly the same way with nouns not derived from the same root as the verb: ἠσθένησε ταύτην τὴν νόσον *he fell sick with this disease.*

Instead of a cognate noun in the accusative we may also find the neuter of an adjective used as an equivalent: Ὀλύμπια (acc. pl. n.) νῑκᾶν *to win an Olympic victory* (lit. *Olympic things*).

(h) *Accusative in oaths*

The accusative is regularly found in oaths, especially after the particles μά and νή. νή conveys strong affirmation; νὴ τὸν Δία *yes, by*

Zeus!, but μά may be either affirmative or negative, the choice being determined either simply by the context (as, e.g., in 23.2.5 *l*.4) or by adding ναί or οὐ: ναὶ μὰ τὸν Δία *yes, by Zeus!*; μὰ τὸν Ἀπόλλω, οὔκ *no, by Apollo!* (cf. 24.1/1*c*).

In these expressions we must understand the verb ὄμνῡμι *swear*, which can also be used with the accusative of the god's name in the sense *I swear by*:

ὄμνῡμι θεοὺς καὶ θεάς. *I swear by [all the] gods and goddesses.*

(*i*) **Accusative to express motion towards** (see 2.1/3*f*)
In poetry the accusative can be used with verbs of motion **without any preposition**:

Μήδεια πύργους γῆς ἔπλευσ᾽ Ἰωλκίᾱς. *Medea sailed to the towers of the Iolcian land.*

Insight

Φρήν is usually to be translated by *heart* or *mind*; the word is often used in the plural with the same meanings. However, it originally meant *midriff*, which was thought to be the seat of the emotions and of intelligence. We must often take care in translating the word in poetical contexts. A character in Aeschylus' *Prometheus Bound* (cf. 15.3) expresses her anxiety by saying κραδίᾱ φόβῳ φρένα λακτίζει. Is φρήν used here literally with the meaning *through fear [my] heart kicks [my] midriff* or does it have a transferred sense of *mind*? The first is more likely but we should translate the sentence as *my heart knocks at my breast for fear* as *kicks my midriff* might suggest the action of an over-enthusiastic footballer.

22.2 Greek reading

1# σὺ δ᾽ ὦ θεῶν τύραννε κἀνθρώπων Ἔρως,
ἢ μὴ δίδασκε τὰ καλὰ φαίνεσθαι καλά,
ἢ τοῖς ἐρῶσιν εὐτυχῶς συνεκπόνει
μοχθοῦσι μόχθους ὧν σὺ δημιουργὸς εἶ.

2   ἑσπέρα μὲν γὰρ ἦν, ἧκε δ᾽ ἀγγέλλων τις ὡς τοὺς πρυτάνεις ὡς
Ἐλάτεια κατείληπται. καὶ μετὰ ταῦτα οἱ μὲν εὐθὺς ἐξαναστάντες
μεταξὺ δειπνοῦντες τούς τ᾽ ἐκ τῶν σκηνῶν τῶν κατὰ τὴν ἀγορὰν
ἐξεῖργον καὶ τὰ γέρρα ἐνεπίμπρασαν, οἱ δὲ τοὺς στρατηγοὺς
μετεπέμποντο καὶ τὸν σαλπικτὴν ἐκάλουν· καὶ θορύβου πλήρης   5
ἦν ἡ πόλις. τῇ δ᾽ ὑστεραίᾳ ἅμα τῇ ἡμέρᾳ οἱ μὲν πρυτάνεις τὴν
βουλὴν ἐκάλουν εἰς τὸ βουλευτήριον, ὑμεῖς δ᾽ εἰς τὴν ἐκκλησίαν
ἐπορεύεσθε, καί, πρὶν ἐκείνην χρηματίσαι καὶ προβουλεῦσαι,
πᾶς ὁ δῆμος ἄνω καθῆτο. καὶ μετὰ ταῦτα ὡς ἦλθεν ἡ βουλὴ
καὶ ἀπήγγειλαν οἱ πρυτάνεις τὰ προσηγγελμέν᾽ ἑαυτοῖς καὶ   10
τὸν ἥκοντα παρήγαγον κἀκεῖνος εἶπεν, ἠρώτα μὲν ὁ κῆρυξ, τίς
ἀγορεύειν βούλεται; παρήει δ᾽ οὐδείς.

3   *In addition to translating, define each use of the accusative:*

(*i*) αἴτει καὶ τοὺς ἀνδριάντας ἄλφιτα. (*ii*) ἔστιν τις Σωκράτης σοφὸς
ἀνήρ, τά τε μετέωρα φροντιστὴς καὶ τὰ ὑπὸ γῆς πάντα ἀνεζητηκώς.
(*iii*) ἥκει καὶ τὰ τοῦ πάππου χρήματα ἡμᾶς ἀποστερήσων. (*iv*)#
ἦλθε πατρὸς ἀρχαῖον τάφον. (*v*)# πολλὰ διδάσκει μ᾽ ὁ πολὺς
βίοτος. (*vi*) Μέλητός με ἐγράψατο τὴν γραφὴν ταύτην. (*vii*) ὁ
Κῦρος ἦν εἶδος μὲν κάλλιστος, ψυχὴν δὲ φιλανθρωπότατος. (*viii*)
μὰ Δία, οὐκ εἶδον ἐμαυτοῦ ἀμείνω ὑλοτόμον. (*ix*) σπονδὰς καὶ
ξυμμαχίαν ἐποιήσαντο ἑκατὸν ἔτη. (*x*)# ὄμνυμι δ᾽ ἱερὸν αἰθέρ᾽,
οἴκησιν Διός.

4   *In addition to translating, define each use of* ὡς:

(*i*) ὡς ἡδὺ τῷ μισοῦντι τοὺς φαύλους ἐρημία. (*ii*)# κρύπτε μηδέν,
ὡς πάνθ᾽ ὁρῶν πάντ᾽ ἀναπτύσσει χρόνος. (*iii*)# τέκνα τοῦδ᾽ ἔκατι
τίκτομεν, ὡς θεῶν τε βωμοὺς πατρίδα τε ῥυώμεθα. (*iv*) κατέλαβε
τὴν ἀκρόπολιν ὡς ἐπὶ τυραννίδι. (*v*) πειρᾶσθαι δὲ χρὴ ὡς ῥᾷστα
τἀναγκαῖα (= τὰ ἀν-) τοῦ βίου φέρειν. (*vi*)# πόνος γάρ, ὡς λέγουσιν,
εὐκλείας πατήρ. (*vii*)# φεῦ, φεῦ, τὸ νικᾶν τἄνδιχ᾽ (= τὰ ἔνδικα)
ὡς καλὸν γέρας, τὰ μὴ δίκαια δ᾽ ὡς πανταχοῦ κακόν. (*viii*)# ὡς
ἡδὺς ὁ βίος, ἄν τις αὐτὸν μὴ μάθῃ. (*ix*)# δίδου πένησιν ὡς λάβῃς
θεὸν δότην. (*x*)# κρίνει φίλους ὁ καιρός, ὡς χρυσὸν τὸ πῦρ. (*xi*)#
μέμνησο νέος ὢν ὡς γέρων ἔσῃ ποτέ. (*xii*)# οὐ ζῶμεν ὡς ἥδιστα μὴ
λυπούμενοι; (*xiii*) ἀπέπλευσαν ἐξ Ἑλλησπόντου ὡς ἕκαστοι κατὰ
πόλεις. (*xiv*) ἄνδρες σοφοὶ ὡς ἀληθῶς.

5# ἦν Οἰδίπους τὸ πρῶτον εὐτυχὴς ἀνήρ,
εἶτ᾽ ἐγένετ᾽ αὖθις ἀθλιώτατος βροτῶν.

6# Deianeira laments the absence of her husband Heracles

πάθη μὲν οὖν δὴ πόλλ᾽ ἔγωγ᾽ ἐκλαυσάμην·
ἓν δ᾽, οἷον οὔπω πρόσθεν, αὐτίκ᾽ ἐξερῶ.
ὁδὸν γὰρ ἦμος τὴν τελευταίαν ἄναξ
ὡρμᾶτ᾽ ἀπ᾽ οἴκων Ἡρακλῆς, τότ᾽ ἐν δόμοις
λείπει παλαιὰν δέλτον ἐγγεγραμμένην   5
ξυνθήμαθ᾽, ἀμοὶ (= ἃ ἐμοὶ) πρόσθεν οὐκ ἔτλη ποτέ,
πολλοὺς ἀγῶνας ἐξιών, οὕτω φράσαι,
ἀλλ᾽ ὥς τι δράσων εἷρπε κοὐ θανούμενος.

7 καὶ πρῶτον πρὸς τοὺς Θρᾷκας ἐπολέμησα, ἐκ τῆς Χερρονήσου
αὐτοὺς ἐξελαύνων βουλομένους ἀφαιρεῖσθαι τοὺς Ἕλληνας
τὴν γῆν.

8# ὦ γῆρας, οἵαν ἐλπίδ᾽ ἡδονῆς ἔχεις,
καὶ πᾶς τις εἰς σὲ βούλετ᾽ ἀνθρώπων μολεῖν·
λαβὼν δὲ πεῖραν, μεταμέλειαν λαμβάνει,
ὡς οὐδέν ἐστι χεῖρον ἐν θνητῷ γένει.

9 ἐγὼ γάρ, ὦ Κέβης, νέος ὢν θαυμαστῶς ὡς ἐπεθύμησα ταύτης τῆς
σοφίας ἣν δὴ καλοῦσι περὶ φύσεως ἱστορίαν.

Notes

1 *l.*1 κἄν- = καὶ ἄν-. *ll.*3f. συνεκπόνει 2nd s. pres. imp. act., as the
accent indicates (the 3rd s. pres. ind. act would be συνεκπονεῖ);
ἐρῶσι and μοχθοῦσι (the latter agrees with the former) are m.
dat. pl. of the pres. act. pples. of ἐράω and μοχθέω respectively.

2 A famous passage of the orator Demosthenes in which he
describes how the Athenians in 339 BC received the news that
their enemy Philip of Macedon (father of Alexander the Great)
had captured a town only three days march from Athens. *ll.*1f.
ὡς τοὺς πρυτάνεις *to* (22.1/1*c*) *the prytaneis* (a committee of the

Council in charge of day-to-day administration); take ὡς (= ὅτι) Ἐλάτεια κατείληπται with ἀγγέλλων; κατείληπται 3rd s. perf. ind. pass. of καταλαμβάνω (the tense used in the original direct speech is kept, 8.1/3). *ll.*3f. μεταξὺ δειπνοῦντες 12.1/2*a*(i); τοὺς ἐκ τῶν σκηνῶν lit. *those from the stalls* but trans. *those in the stalls*; in this pregnant use of ἐκ (cf. note on 9.2.13 *l.*12, where the use is somewhat different) the choice of preposition has been influenced by ἐξεῖργον; the imperfect is often used for vivid effect in narrative, hence ἐξεῖργον, ἐνεπίμπρασαν (< ἐμπίμπρημι) etc. – trans. by the simple past (*cleared out, set fire to* etc.); the γέρρα (wicker-work of some kind) were set on fire to inform the Athenians of the emergency. *l.*7 ὑμεῖς i.e. the people (referred to as ὁ δῆμος in *ll.*9f.). *l.*9 ἄνω *above* i.e. on the Pnyx, a hill to the south-west of the Athenian agora which was used for meetings of the Assembly; καθῆτο impf. (19.1/3*b*); ὡς *when* (22.1/1*b*(iv)). *ll.*10f. τὰ προσηγγελμέν᾽(α) ἑαυτοῖς *the things reported* (perf.) *to them* (refl. because it refers back to the subject of the clause οἱ πρυτάνεις); τὸν ἥκοντα the person mentioned in the first line as having brought the message. *l.*12 παρῄει < παρέρχομαι (cf. 18.1/3).

3 (*i*) αἴτει 2nd s. pres. imp. act. (*ii*) ἔστιν here *there is*; ἀνεζητηκώς perf. act. pple. of ἀναζητέω. (*x*) Zeus dwelt in the heavens or upper air (αἰθήρ).

4 Supply ἐστί in (*i*), (*vi*), (*vii*), (*viii*). (*ii*) πάνθ᾽ i.e. πάντα. (*iii*) Take τοῦδ᾽ ἕκατι together – the phrase anticipates the ὡς clause. (*vii*) δ᾽(έ) is placed here after the first phrase, not the first word; with τὰ μὴ δίκαια supply τὸ νῑκᾶν. (*viii*) ἄν = ἐάν. (xi) ἔσῃ 2nd s. fut. ind. of εἰμί. (*xii*) μή with a pple. to express a condition (12.1/2*a*(iv)). (*xiv*) A phrase, not a sentence.

5 τὸ πρῶτον acc. of respect (20.1/5), *with respect to the first [period]*, i.e *at first*.

6 *ll.*1f. μέν and δέ contrast πάθη ... πόλλ᾽ (= πολλά) and ἕν (*sc.* πάθος); οὖν δή *so then, well as you know*; with οἷον οὔπω πρόσθεν supply ἐκλαυσάμην; ἐξερῶ fut. of ἐξαγορεύω (cf. 18.1/4 note 2). *ll*.3f. γάρ begins the explanation of the previous line and need not be translated; take ὁδὸν ... τὴν τελευταίαν as virtual cognate acc. (22.1/2*g*) with ὡρμᾶτ᾽(ο) *was setting out on* ...; οἴκων ... δόμοις plural for singular (a common use in poetry). *l*.6 ξυνθήμαθ᾽ (= -τα) a type of retained acc. (22.1/2*f*(ii)) with ἐγγεγραμμένην (*l*.5), *inscribed with signs* (ἐγγράφει ξυνθήματα δέλτῳ means *he inscribes signs on a tablet*; this can, somewhat illogically, be put into the passive δέλτος ἐγγράφεται ξυνθήματα with the original accusative retained, but we must translate *a tablet is inscribed with signs* – this differs from the examples in 22.1/2*f*(ii) in that ἐγγράφω takes an acc. and dat., not two accusatives); ἔτλη root aor. of τλάω. *l*.7 πολλοὺς ἀγῶνας ἐξιών *going out on many exploits* virtual cognate acc. (22.1/2*g*); οὕτω *thus, like this* as Deianeira goes on to explain later. *l*.8 ὡς ... *under the impression of going to do something, as [one] going to do something* (see note on 12.3.7).

8 *l*.2 πᾶς τις emphatic for πᾶς, lit. *every single one*; βούλετ᾽ i.e. βούλεται *l*.4 ὡς to introduce a clause of reason (22.1/1*b*(iii)).

9 θαυμαστῶς ὡς 22.1/1*a*(iii).

Main points

- ὡς is used to modify words and phrases; it can also function as a conjunction and as a preposition

- Both the direct and the complementary object are put in the accusative after certain verbs (*making, considering, naming, etc.*), e.g. *they made him general*

- Verbs meaning *ask for, teach, conceal, deprive*, etc. also take two accusatives

- The cognate accusative occurs in such phrases as *sing a song*

- The accusative is also used in oaths and to express motion towards (the latter is poetical)

22.3 Extra reading – Anacreontea

Anacreon was an Ionic poet of the sixth century BC. His personal poetry was famous but very little has survived. It attracted many imitators in antiquity and some of their poems (as 1 below) have come down under his name. The second poem is certainly genuine.

1 μακαρίζομέν σε, τέττιξ,
  ὅτε δενδρέων ἐπ᾽ ἄκρων
  ὀλίγην δρόσον πεπωκὼς
  βασιλεὺς ὅπως ἀείδεις·
  σὰ γάρ ἐστι κεῖνα πάντα,   5
  ὁπόσα βλέπεις ἐν ἀγροῖς,
  ὁπόσα τρέφουσιν ὗλαι.
  σὺ δὲ τίμιος βροτοῖσιν,

  θέρεος γλυκὺς προφήτης.
  φιλέουσι μέν σε Μοῦσαι,   10
  φιλέει δὲ Φοῖβος αὐτός,
  λιγυρὴν δ᾽ ἔδωκεν οἴμην.
  τὸ δὲ γῆρας οὔ σε τείρει,
  σοφέ, γηγενές, φίλυμνε,
  ἀπαθὴς δ᾽, ἀναιμόσαρκε,   15
  σχεδὸν εἶ θεοῖς ὅμοιος.

2 πολιοὶ μὲν ἡμὶν ἤδη
  κρόταφοι, κάρη τε λευκόν,
  χαρίεσσα δ᾽ οὐκέτι ἤβη
  πάρα, γηράλεοι δ᾽ ὀδόντες.
  γλυκεροῦ δ᾽ οὐκέτι πολλὸς   5
  βιότου χρόνος λέλειπται·

  διὰ ταῦτ᾽ ἀνασταλύζω
  θαμὰ Τάρταρον δεδοικώς.
  Ἀΐδεω γάρ ἐστι δεινὸς
  μυχός, ἀργαλέη δ᾽ ἐς αὐτὸν   10
  κάθοδος· καὶ γὰρ ἕτοιμον
  καταβάντι μὴ ἀναβῆναι.

Notes

1 *l.*2 δενδρέων (Ionic for δένδρων, cf. 13.1/1*c*) ἐπ᾽ ἄκρων *on the tops of trees* (18.1/6). *l.*4 βασιλεὺς ὅπως = ὅπως (*like*) βασιλεύς. *ll.*5f. πάντα, ὁπόσα (= ὅσα, as also in *l.*7) 21.1/3*d.* *l.*8 Supply εἶ (< εἰμί); βροτοῖσιν *among mortals* (dat. of reference, 23.1/2*e*). *ll.*9ff. Three examples of the use of uncontracted forms in Ionic, θέρεος (= θέρους, cf. 6.1/1*c*), φιλέουσι (= φιλοῦσι), φιλέει (= φιλεῖ). *l.*12 λιγυρήν = -ήν.

2 *l.*1 Supply εἰσί; ἡμίν (= ἡμῖν) plural for singular (the dative is one of possession, 23.1/2*c*). *l.*2 κάρη, an irregular noun, is neuter, hence λευκόν. *l.*4 πάρα = πάρεστι (cf. 21.1/4 note 2 but here it is not used impersonally). *ll.*7f. Take θάμα with ἀνασταλύζω; δεδοικώς 19.1/3*a.* *l.*9 Ἀΐδεω = Attic Ἄιδου (gen. of Ἄιδης), on the ending cf. 25.1/2*b*(i). *l.*10 ἀργαλέη = -έᾱ. *l.*11 ἕτοιμον *[it is] fixed* the neuter singular adj. is used in impersonal expressions.

Unit 23

23.1 Grammar

23.1/1 Uses of cases (2) – genitive

Apart from its use as the case of possession (2.1/3d) and after certain prepositions (2.1/3g, 3.1/5b), the genitive can function in a number of ways with another noun, verb, adjective or even adverb. Although the genitive is often to be translated by *of*, in some of its uses a different rendering in English is required.

(*a*) *Possessive genitive* (see 2.1/3d)
In this use the genitive denotes ownership, possession or some looser association: ἡ τοῦ Δημοσθένους οἰκίᾱ *the house of Demosthenes* (or *Demosthenes' house*); οἱ Σόλωνος νόμοι *the laws of* (*made by*) *Solon*; τὰ τῆς πόλεως *the [affairs] of the city*. In certain very restricted contexts a possessive genitive qualifies a missing noun, which can easily be supplied; the most common are *wife, son/daughter* (cf. 5.1/3 note 2), *place of abode*:

> Ἀλέξανδρος ὁ Φιλίππου. *Alexander, [son] of Philip.*
> Ἄρτεμις ἡ Διός. *Artemis, [daughter] of Zeus.*
> ἐν Ἀρίφρονος. *At Ariphron's (in [the house] of Ariphron).*
> ἐν Διονύσου. *At [the shrine] of Dionysus* (cf. *at St. Paul's*).

(*b*) *Genitive of characteristic*
In English we may say *it is the part/duty/nature/characteristic*, etc. *of someone to do something*. In Greek this is expressed simply by the use of the third singular of εἰμί plus the genitive. In translation from Greek the appropriate English word to be supplied must be determined from the context:

> οὔτοι γυναικός ἐστιν ἱμείρειν μάχης. *It is indeed not a woman's part to long for battle.*
> δοκεῖ δικαίου τοῦτ᾽ εἶναι πολίτου. *This seems to be the duty of a just citizen.*

(c) Subjective and objective genitive

An **objective** genitive stands in the same relation to a noun or adjective as an object does to a transitive verb. In *Socrates' love of the truth dominated his life*, the genitive *of the truth* is objective because the sense connection between *truth* and *love* is the same as between an object and a verb (we could say, with the same meaning, *Socrates loved the truth; this dominated his life*). Examples in Greek are: φόβος τοῦ γήρως *fear of old age,* τὸ κράτος τῆς θαλάττης *the command of the sea,* ἔρως τῆς ἀρετῆς *love of virtue.* Because this use is more extensive in Greek than in English we must sometimes translate it by a different preposition: ὁ τοῦ κυνὸς λόγος *the story about the dog,* νίκη τῶν ἡδονῶν *victory over pleasures.* A **subjective** genitive, on the other hand, stands in the same relation to a noun as a subject does to a verb: νίκη τῶν βαρβάρων *victory of the barbarians* (i.e. οἱ βάρβαροι νικῶσιν *the barbarians are victorious*). This use is only a variety of the possessive genitive.

Sometimes, however, we must decide from the context whether a genitive is subjective or objective. ὁ τῶν Ἑλλήνων φόβος can mean *the Greeks' fear* (i.e. *the fear felt by the Greeks*) (subjective), as well as *the fear of the Greeks* (i.e. *the fear inspired by the Greeks*) (objective). A possessive adjective (9.1/5b) usually represents a subjective genitive, but may on occasion be the equivalent of an objective genitive: φιλίᾳ τῇ ἐμῇ can mean *through friendship for me* as well as *through my friendship.* Cf. ἐπὶ διαβολῇ τῇ ἐμῇ in 10.3 *l.*6.

(d) Partitive genitive

In this construction the genitive denotes the whole and the noun or pronoun on which it depends denotes a part of that whole

> μέρος τι τῶν βαρβάρων. *A part of the barbarians.*
> οἱ ἄδικοι τῶν ἀνθρώπων. *The unjust among men.*
> ὀλίγοι αὐτῶν. *Few of them.*
> οἱ πρεσβύτατοι τῶν στρατηγῶν. *The oldest of the generals.*

The partitive genitive may also occur by itself as the object of a verb: τῆς γῆς ἔτεμον *they ravaged [part] of the land* (τὴν γῆν ἔτεμον would mean *they ravaged the [whole] land*). It can also be used predicatively:

Σόλων τῶν ἑπτὰ σοφιστῶν ἐκλήθη. *Solon was called [one] of the Seven Sages.*

This use of the genitive also occurs with abstract nouns after the phrase εἰς τοῦτο (τοσοῦτο) ἀφικνεῖσθαι (ἥκειν etc.) *to reach this (such a) pitch/point/stage of* (cf. 16.1/1 note 3):

εἰς τοῦτο θράσους καὶ ἀναιδείᾱς ἀφίκετο. *He reached such a pitch of boldness and shamelessness.*
εἰς τοῦθ᾽ ὕβρεως ἥκει. *He has come to such a pitch of insolence.*

Under this heading also belongs the **chorographic** genitive, or genitive of **geographic definition**:

ἔπλευσαν τῆς Ἰταλίᾱς εἰς Τάραντα. *They sailed to Tarentum in Italy* (lit. *[a part] of Italy*).
τῆς Σικελίᾱς οἱ Συρᾱκόσιοι. *The Syracusans in Sicily.*

Compare the use of the genitive with adverbs of place, e.g. εἰδέναι ὅπου γῆς ἐστιν *to know where in the world he is* (cf. 2.2.11).

(e) Genitive of explanation
The genitive may be used as the equivalent of a noun in apposition which gives an explanation or definition of the preceding noun. The construction in English is generally the same:

ὦ πόλι Θηβῶν. *O city of Thebes* (i.e. *O city, viz Thebes*).
τέλος θανάτου. *The end of death* (i.e. *the end that is death*).
ὕπνου δῶρον. *The gift of sleep.*

(f) Genitive of price or value (see 20.1/3)

(g) Genitive of time within which (see 7.1/7c)

(h) Genitive absolute (see 12.1/2b)

(i) Genitive of comparison (see 17.1/4a)

286

(*j*) **Genitive of separation** (see 20.1/4)

(*k*) **Genitive with verbs** (see 13.1/2*a*)
At 13.1/2*a* we considered certain intransitive verbs which take the genitive. Two other groups are followed by an accusative and a genitive:

(i) Verbs of **accusing, acquitting, condemning, prosecuting** and the like are generally followed by an accusative of the person involved and a genitive of the crime or charge. Such verbs are αἰτιάομαι *accuse*, γράφομαι *indict*, διώκω *prosecute*:

> ὁ Μέλητος ἀσεβείᾱς ἐμὲ ἐγράψατο. *Meletus indicted me for impiety.*
> διώξομαί σε δειλίᾱς. *I shall prosecute you for cowardice.*

However, verbs of accusing and condemning which are compounded with κατά (such as κατηγορέω *accuse*, καταγιγνώσκω *give judgement against, condemn*, κατακρίνω *give sentence against*, καταψηφίζομαι *vote against*) reverse the normal construction, and so take a genitive of the person and an accusative of the crime or penalty:

> ἐγὼ δ᾽ ῡ̔μῶν δέομαι μὴ καταγνῶναι δωροδοκίᾱν ἐμοῦ. *I ask you not to condemn me for bribery.*
> ἐμοῦ Φιλιππισμὸν κατηγορεῖ. *He accuses me of siding with Philip.*

(ii) A genitive of **cause** can follow verbs of **emotion**. Such verbs are θαυμάζω *wonder at*, ζηλόω *admire*, οἰκτῑ́ρω *pity*, etc.:

> τούτους τῆς τόλμης θαυμάζω. *I wonder at these men for* (or *because of*) *their boldness.*
> τοῦ πάθους ᾤκτῑρεν αὐτόν. *He pitied him for his suffering.*

A genitive of cause can also occur with adjectives: εὐδαίμων τοῦ τρόπου *happy in his way of life*.

(*l*) **Genitive of exclamation**
This genitive, which is often coupled with an interjection (φεῦ *alas* (of grief), *ah, oh* (of astonishment); οἴμοι *alas*), is akin to the genitive

of cause as it gives the reason for the speaker's astonishment or grief:

οἴμοι ταλαίνης τῆσδε συμφορᾶς. *Alas for this wretched plight!*
φεῦ φεῦ τῆς ὥρᾱς, τοῦ κάλλους. *Ah, what youthful bloom, what beauty!*
εἶπε πρὸς αὑτόν, τῆς τύχης. *He said to himself, 'What luck!'*

23.1/2 Uses of cases (3) – dative

The Greek dative is an amalgam of three cases:

- the **dative proper**, generally to be translated *to* or *for*, indicating the person (or thing) involved in an action (the recipient, the person advantaged or disadvantaged, etc.);

- the old **instrumental** case, denoting that *by* which or *with* which an action is done or accompanied;

- the original **locative** case, which expressed *place where* and *time when*.

Some of these uses were distinguished and made more precise by the use of prepositions (cf. 2.1/3*h*, 3.1/5).

Dative proper

(*a*) *Verbs governing the dative*

(i) Verbs followed by a direct object (accusative) and an indirect object (dative – 2.1/3*e*), such as verbs of **giving, saying, promising**:

Κῦρος δίδωσιν αὐτῷ μῡρίους δᾱρεικούς. *Cyrus gives him 10,000 darics.*
ὑπισχνοῦμαί σοι δέκα τάλαντα. *I promise you ten talents.*

However, many verbs of **reproaching, blaming** and the like, which in English take a direct object of the person involved, in Greek take a **dative** of the person and an accusative of the thing (when expressed):

> μὴ πάθωμεν ὃ ἄλλοις ἐπιτῑμῶμεν. *Let us not get into a situation for which we censure others* (lit. *let us not experience [the thing] which we censure in others*).
> αἰσχύνομαί σοι τοῦτ᾽ ὀνειδίσαι. *I am ashamed to reproach you with this.*
> τί ἂν μοι μέμφοιο; *What would you blame me for?*

The English construction which allows the indirect object of a verb in the active voice to be made the subject of the same verb in the passive *(I was given this land)* is generally impossible in Greek. ταύτην τὴν χώρᾱν μοι ἔδωκε *he gave me this land* becomes αὕτη ἡ χώρᾱ μοι ὑπ᾽ αὐτοῦ ἐδόθη *this land was given to me by him.* ἐδόθην would mean *I was given* in the sense *I was handed over.* For an exception see note on 22.2.6 *l.5*.

(ii) **Intransitive verbs** followed by the dative (see 13.1/2*b*)

(iii) **Impersonal verbs** followed by the dative (see 21.1/4)

(b) Dative with adjectives, adverbs and nouns
The dative is used with certain **adjectives** whose English equivalent is usually followed by *to* or *for.* These include φίλος *dear, friendly*; ἐχθρός *hateful, hostile*; ἴσος *equal*; ὅμοιος *like, resembling*; ἀνόμοιος *unlike, dissimilar*:

> τύραννος ἅπᾱς ἐχθρὸς ἐλευθερίᾳ καὶ νόμοις ἐναντίος. *Every tyrant [is] hostile to freedom and opposed to laws.*
> ποιεῖτε ὅμοια τοῖς λόγοις. *You are acting in accordance with* (lit. *doing things like*) *your words.*

Compare ὁ αὐτός with the dative *the same as* (9.1/3*b*).

A similar use of the dative is found after some **adverbs**:

> ἀκολούθως τοῖς νόμοις. *In accordance with the laws.*
> ὁμολογουμένως τῇ φύσει ζῆν. *To live in agreement with nature.*

The same is true of some **nouns**, especially those related to verbs of similar meaning which take the dative:

ἐπιβουλὴ ἐμοί. *A plot against me.*
κοινωνίᾱ τοῖς ἀνδράσιν. *Association with men.*

(c) *Dative of possession*
The dative is used with εἶναι (and verbs of similar meaning such as ὑπάρχειν and γίγνεσθαι) to denote the owner or possessor:

οἰκεῖοί μοί εἰσι καὶ υἱεῖς. *I have relatives and sons* (lit. *relatives and sons are to me*).
τῷ δικαίῳ παρὰ θεῶν δῶρα γίγνεται. *The just man has gifts* (lit. *gifts come into being for the just man*) *from the gods.*

(d) *Dative of advantage and disadvantage*
The dative is used to indicate the person or thing for whose advantage or disadvantage something is done:

πᾶς ἀνὴρ αὑτῷ πονεῖ. *Every man works for himself* (advantage).
ἄλλο στράτευμα αὐτῷ συνελέγετο. *Another army was being gathered for him* (advantage).
ἥδε ἡ ἡμέρᾱ τοῖς Ἕλλησι μεγάλων κακῶν ἄρξει. *This day will be the beginning of great troubles for the Greeks* (disadvantage).

Sometimes this use cannot be translated by *for*:

σῖτον αὐτοῖς ἀφεῖλεν. *He took food away from them.* (lit. *he took food away to their disadvantage*).

For the other construction used with verbs meaning *take away* see 22.1/2*f*(ii).

(e) *Dative of reference or relation*
Similarly, the dative may be used to denote a person or thing to whose case a statement is limited:

τριήρει ἐστὶν εἰς Ἡράκλειαν ἡμέρᾱς μακρᾶς πλοῦς. *For a trireme it is a long day's voyage to Heraclea.*

This dative is often used to denote *in the eyes of* or *in the judgement of*:

ἡμῖν Ἀχιλλεὺς ἄξιος τῖμῆς. *In our eyes* (lit. *for us*) *Achilles [is] worthy of honour.*
ἀνάξιοι πᾶσίν ἐστε δυστυχεῖν. *In the eyes of all* (lit. *for all*) *you are unworthy to suffer misfortune.*

A participle in the dative singular is used in this way with an indefinite reference:

Ἐπίδαμνος ἐν δεξιᾷ ἐστιν εἰσπλέοντι ἐς τὸν Ἰόνιον κόλπον. *Epidamnus is on the right as one sails into* (lit. *in relation to one sailing into*) *the Ionian Gulf.*
ἔλεγον ὅτι ἡ ὁδὸς διαβάντι τὸν ποταμὸν ἐπὶ Λῦδίᾶν φέροι. *They said that, when one had crossed the river, the road led to Lydia.*

Compare also the phrase ὡς συνελόντι εἰπεῖν *to speak concisely, in a word* (lit. *so to speak for one having brought [the matter] together*).

(*f*) *Ethic dative* (a purely conventional term, with no connection with ethics)
The dative of the first or second person pronouns can be used simply to attract the attention of the person addressed. There is no grammatical connection with the surrounding words. This so-called ethic dative is usually to be represented in English by *I beg you, please, let me tell you, you know*, and the like.

καί μοι μὴ θορυβήσητε. *And, I beg you, don't make a clamour.*
Ἀρταφέρνης ὑμῖν Ὑστάσπου ἐστὶ παῖς. *Artaphernes, you know, is Hystaspes' son.*

(*g*) *Dative of the agent*
This use, replaced in most contexts by ὑπό + gen., is found with the perfect and pluperfect passive (very rarely with other tenses):

πάνθ᾽ ἡμῖν πεποίηται. *Everything has been done by us.*
ἐπειδὴ αὐτοῖς παρεσκεύαστο. *When they had made their preparations* (lit. *it had been prepared by them*).

For the dative of the agent with verbal adjectives, see 24.1/5*b*.

Instrumental dative

(h) *Dative of instrument* (see 11.1/2)

(i) *Dative of cause*

The dative may denote cause: ῥίγει ἀπωλλύμεθα *we were perishing from* (or *because of*) *cold*. Often the noun in the dative denotes an emotional or mental condition:

> ὕβρει καὶ οὐκ οἴνῳ τοῦτο ποιεῖ. *He does this through insolence and not because he is drunk* (lit. *because of wine*).
> ἠπείγοντο πρὸς τὸν ποταμὸν τοῦ πιεῖν ἐπιθυμίᾳ. *They were hurrying towards the river because of their desire to drink* (lit. *because of a desire for drinking*).

Occasionally cause may also be expressed by ὑπό with the genitive:

> οὐκ ἐδύνατο καθεύδειν ὑπὸ λύπης. *He could not sleep because of* (or *for*) *grief*.

(j) *Dative of manner and attendant circumstances*
The dative may be used to denote the manner in which something is done or the circumstances accompanying an action:

> οἱ Ἀθηναῖοι παντὶ σθένει ἐπεκούρησαν. *The Athens helped with all their strength* (manner).
> ἀτελεῖ τῇ νίκῃ ἀπῆλθον. *They went away with their victory incomplete* (attendant circumstance).

Normally a noun used in this way is qualified by an adjective (as above). Some nouns, however, are regularly employed by themselves as datives of manner and are virtually the equivalent of adverbs: βίᾳ *by force, forcibly*; δρόμῳ *at a run*; ἔργῳ *in fact, in deed*; λόγῳ *in word, in theory*; σιγῇ *in silence*; σπουδῇ *hastily*; φύσει … νόμῳ *by nature … by convention*; compare also τῷ ὄντι *in reality* (see 12.1/1 note 1); τούτῳ τῷ τρόπῳ *in this way*.

Under this category are also included the datives of feminine adjectives with a noun understood: ταύτῃ *in this way*; ἰδίᾳ *privately*; δημοσίᾳ *publicly*; πεζῇ *on foot*.

(k) *Dative of accompaniment*

We have already met this use of the dative with αὐτός (see 9.1/3a(ii)). The dative by itself is particularly common in military contexts (the **military dative**) to denote the forces with which a journey or expedition is made:

Ἀθηναῖοι ἐφ᾽ ἡμᾶς πολλῇ στρατιᾷ ὥρμηνται. *The Athenians have made an expedition against us with a large force.*

(l) *Dative of measure of difference* (see 17.1/4b)

(m) *Dative of respect*

As well as an accusative of respect (20.1/5) we may also find the dative used in a similar way: ἀνὴρ ἡλικίᾳ ἔτι νέος *a man still young in age*; ὀνόματι σπονδαί *a truce in name [alone]*.

Locative dative

(n) *Dative of place where*

In poetry **place where** may be expressed by the dative **without a preposition**: Κρονίδης αἰθέρι ναίων *the son of Cronos living in the sky*. In Attic prose, however, a preposition is generally required (2.1/3h), except with some place names, e.g. Μαραθῶνι *at Marathon*. Traces of the old locative endings remain in such forms such as: Ἀθήνησι (= ἐν Ἀθήναις) *at Athens*; Φαληροῖ (= ἐν Φαλήρῳ) *at Phalerum*; cf. οἴκοι *at home*; these words are usually classified as adverbs.

(o) *Dative of time when* (see 7.1/7b)

Insight

Several eminent philosophers established schools in particular places of Athens to disseminate their teachings. These continued to function after the deaths of their founders. The Ἀκαδήμεια was an open-air gymnasium where Plato taught from early in the fourth century BC; the name became synonymous with his philosophy and gives us the term *Academy*. Aristotle began in the Lyceum (Λύκειον), another open-air gymnasium where his pupils cogitated on his teachings while *walking around* (περιπατοῦντες) and so were called Peripatetics. Zeno taught in the Στοὰ ποικίλη *the Painted Stoa*, a roofed colonnade in the centre of Athens that gave its name to his philosophy, Stoicism. Epicurus lectured in his own private garden, which had no special designation. Later, when Athens became the university city of the Roman Empire, young Romans came there to study, principally at its philosophical schools. These continued until AD 529 when they were closed by the emperor Justinian in his desire to purge Athens of non-Christian institutions.

23.2 Greek reading

1 *In addition to translating, define each use of the genitive and dative:*

(*i*)# ὦ φίλον ὕπνου θέλγητρον, ἐπίκουρον νόσου. (*ii*) ἤθελε τῶν μενόντων εἶναι. (*iii*) ὦ Πόσειδον, τῆς τέχνης. (*iv*)# πενίαν φέρειν οὐ παντός, ἀλλ᾽ ἀνδρὸς σοφοῦ. (*v*) τούτῳ πάνυ μοι προσέχετε τὸν νοῦν. (*vi*) πολλαὶ θεραπεῖαι τοῖς ἰατροῖς εὕρηνται. (*vii*) ὕπνος πέφυκε σωμάτων σωτηρία. (*viii*) τὸν αὐτὸν αἰνεῖν καὶ ψέγειν ἀνδρὸς κακοῦ. (*ix*) τοιοῦτο ὑμῖν ἐστιν ἡ τυραννίς, ὦ Λακεδαιμόνιοι. (*x*)# ταῦτα Ζεὺς οἶδεν Ὀλύμπιος, αἰθέρι ναίων. (*xi*) αἰτιῶνται αὐτὸν κλοπῆς. (*xii*) οἱ ἄνθρωποι διὰ τὸ αὐτῶν δέος τοῦ θανάτου ψεύδονται. (*xiii*) ἐφοβοῦντο μὴ οἱ Ἀθηναῖοι μείζονι παρασκευῇ ἐπέλθωσιν. (*xiv*) κραυγῇ πολλῇ ἐπίασιν. (*xv*) ὄνομα τῷ μειρακίῳ ἦν Πλάτων. (*xvi*)# τέχνη ἀνάγκης ἀσθενεστέρα μακρῷ. (*xvii*)# ζηλῶ σε τοῦ νοῦ, τῆς δὲ δειλίας στυγῶ. (*xviii*) ἐγὼ τῶν κρεῶν ἔκλεπτον. (*xix*)# ἆρ᾽ ὑμῖν οὗτος ταῦτ᾽ ἔδρασεν ἔνδικα; (*xx*) θεοῖς ταῦτα ἐποίησαν. (*xxi*) στυγνὸς ἦν καὶ τῇ φωνῇ τραχύς. (*xxii*) ὁ στρατὸς ἀφίκετο τῆς Ἀττικῆς ἐς Οἰνόην. (*xxiii*) ὁρᾶτε τὴν βασιλέως ἐπιορκίαν. (*xxiv*) οὐκ εἰμὶ τοῖς πεπραγμένοις δύσθυμος.

2 ὁ Διογένης, Ἀναξιμένει τῷ ῥήτορι παχεῖ ὄντι προσελθών, ἐπίδος καὶ ἡμῖν, ἔφη, τοῖς πτωχοῖς τῆς γαστρός· καὶ γὰρ αὐτὸς κουφισθήσει καὶ ἡμᾶς ὠφελήσεις.

3# ἦν γάρ τις αἶνος ὡς γυναιξὶ μὲν τέχναι
μέλουσι, λόγχῃ δ᾽ ἄνδρες εὐστοχώτεροι.
εἰ γὰρ δόλοισιν ἦν τὸ νικητήριον,
ἡμεῖς ἂν ἀνδρῶν εἴχομεν τυραννίδα.

4# καὶ νῦν παραινῶ πᾶσι τοῖς νεωτέροις
μὴ πρὸς τὸ γῆρας ἀναβολὰς ποιουμένους
σχολῇ τεκνοῦσθαι παῖδας· οὐ γὰρ ἡδονή,
γυναικί τ᾽ ἐχθρὸν χρῆμα πρεσβύτης ἀνήρ·
ἀλλ᾽ ὡς τάχιστα. καὶ γὰρ ἐκτροφαὶ καλαὶ   5
καὶ συννεάζων ἡδὺ παῖς νέῳ πατρί.

5   One of the accusations brought against Socrates (10.3) was that
he did not believe in the traditional gods. In the *Apology* of Plato
(see 13.3), which is an account of his trial, he is represented as
interrogating one of his accusers on this charge.

ΜΕΛΗΤΟΣ – ΣΩΚΡΑΤΗΣ

ΜΕ. ταῦτα λέγω, ὡς τὸ παράπαν οὐ νομίζεις θεούς.
ΣΩ. ὦ θαυμάσιε Μέλητε, τί ταῦτα λέγεις; οὐδὲ ἥλιον οὐδὲ
σελήνην ἄρα νομίζω θεοὺς εἶναι, ὥσπερ οἱ ἄλλοι ἄνθρωποι;
ΜΕ. μὰ Δί᾽, ὦ ἄνδρες δικασταί, ἐπεὶ τὸν μὲν ἥλιον λίθον φησὶν
εἶναι, τὴν δὲ σελήνην γῆν.   5
ΣΩ. Ἀναξαγόρου οἴει κατηγορεῖν, ὦ φίλε Μέλητε; καὶ οὕτω
καταφρονεῖς τῶνδε καὶ οἴει αὐτοὺς ἀπείρους γραμμάτων εἶναι
ὥστε οὐκ εἰδέναι ὅτι τὰ Ἀναξαγόρου βιβλία τοῦ Κλαζομενίου
γέμει τούτων τῶν λόγων; καὶ δὴ καὶ οἱ νέοι ταῦτα παρ᾽ ἐμοῦ
μανθάνουσιν, ἃ ἔξεστιν δραχμῆς ἐκ τῆς ὀρχήστρας πριαμένοις 10
Σωκράτους καταγελᾶν, ἐὰν προσποιῆται ἑαυτοῦ εἶναι, ἄλλως
τε καὶ οὕτως ἄτοπα ὄντα; ἀλλ᾽, ὦ πρὸς Διός, οὑτωσί σοι δοκῶ;
οὐδένα νομίζω θεὸν εἶναι;
ΜΕ. οὐ μέντοι μὰ Δία οὐδ᾽ ὁπωστιοῦν.
ΣΩ. ἄπιστός γ᾽ εἶ, ὦ Μέλητε, καὶ ταῦτα μέντοι, ὡς ἐμοὶ δοκεῖς, 15
σαυτῷ. ἐμοὶ γὰρ δοκεῖ οὑτοσί, ὦ ἄνδρες Ἀθηναῖοι, πάνυ εἶναι
ὑβριστὴς καὶ ἀκόλαστος, καὶ ἀτεχνῶς τὴν γραφὴν ὕβρει τινὶ καὶ
ἀκολασίᾳ καὶ νεότητι γράψασθαι. ἔοικεν γὰρ ὥσπερ αἴνιγμα
συντιθέντι διαπειρωμένῳ, ἆρα γνώσεται Σωκράτης ὁ σοφὸς δὴ
ἐμοῦ χαριεντιζομένου καὶ ἐναντί᾽ ἐμαυτῷ λέγοντος, ἢ ἐξαπατήσω 20

αὐτὸν καὶ τοὺς ἄλλους τοὺς ἀκούοντας; οὗτος γὰρ ἐμοὶ φαίνεται
τὰ ἐναντία λέγειν αὐτὸς ἑαυτῷ ἐν τῇ γραφῇ ὥσπερ ἂν εἰ εἴποι·
ἀδικεῖ Σωκράτης θεοὺς οὐ νομίζων, ἀλλὰ θεοὺς νομίζων. καίτοι
τοῦτό ἐστι παίζοντος.

Notes

1 (*i*) ὕπνου θέλγητρον 23.1/1*e*. (*iv*) Supply ἐστί (cf. (*viii*) and (*xvi*)).

2 ἐπίδος 2nd. s. aor. imp. act. of ἐπιδίδωμι; τῆς γαστρός 23.1/1*d*;
κουφισθήσει 2nd s. fut. ind. pass.

3 *l*.2 Supply εἰσί with ἄνδρες. *l*.3 Lit. *for if the prize of victory were
through guiles* (dat. of instrument), i.e. *were [won] by guiles.*

4 *ll*.2f. ἀναβολὰς ποιοῦμαι (mid.) *I make delays* i.e. for myself – the
active would mean *I make delays (for others)*, cf. 8.1/1*b*; the middle
is used in the same way with τεκνοῦσθαι; οὐ ... ἡδονή (ἐστι) i.e. in
producing children in old age. *l*.5 ὡς τάχιστα is contrasted with
σχολῇ (*l*.3), i.e. have children as quickly as possible; ἐκτροφαί
(plural for singular) *the rearing [of children]*, i.e. *rearing children.*
l.6 The neuter adj. ἡδύ is predicate *[is] a pleasant [thing]* (ἐστί is
understood), cf. 5.2.5(*i*).

5 *l*.1 ταῦτα trans. *this* (the neuter plural is often used where we
would have the singular in English); τὸ παράπαν οὐ *not at all*,
cf. note on 11.2.12 *l*.3; νομίζεις *believe in*. *l*.2 οὐδὲ ... οὐδέ *not
even ... nor* (**not** *neither ... nor* which is οὔτε ... οὔτε) – note that
this question is **not** marked by any introductory word (the same
applies to all the questions in what Socrates says next). *l*.4 μὰ
Δί᾽ (α) here *no, by Zeus* (22.1/2*h*). *l*.6 Anaxagoras of Clazomenae
was a philosopher of the generation before Socrates who taught
that the sun and moon were material bodies suspended in the sky
(the sun was a burning rock about the size of the Peloponnese);
the traditional belief was that they were divinities. *ll*.7f. τῶνδε
i.e. the jurymen; αὐτοὺς ... ὥστε lit. *them to be inexperienced in
letters with the result ...,* i.e. *that they are [so] illiterate that ...;*
οὐκ εἰδέναι an exception to the rule given at 24.1/2*e* – ὥστε +
inf. is often negated by οὐ when it follows the inf. construction

of indirect speech (here αὐτοὺς ... εἶναι); *ll.*10ff. ἄ is the object of πριαμένοις, lit. *which having bought ... it is allowed* (ἔξεστιν) *[to them] to mock* (καταγελᾶν)... i.e *which they can buy ... and [then] laugh at ...*; δραχμῆς gen. of price (20.1/3); ἐκ τῆς ὀρχήστρᾱς lit. *from the orchestra* (a part of the Athenian agora where books were sold) but English idiom requires *in the orchestra*; ἑαυτοῦ εἶναι *[them* i.e. the doctrines of Anaxagoras*] to be his* (lit. *of himself* possessive gen., 23.1/1*a*); ἄλλως τε καί *especially*; ἄτοπα ὄντα agrees with the understood subject of εἶναι. *l.*15 καὶ ταῦτα μέντοι *and that* (cf. note on *l.*1) *too* (ταῦτα refers to the clause ἄπιστός γ᾽ εἶ *you are not to be believed*). *ll.*17ff. ὕβρει τινί, ἀκολασίᾳ datives of cause (23.1/2*i*); ὥσπερ (lit. *as if*) tones down the metaphor (cf. 22.1/1*a*(vi) for ὡς used in the same way) and need not be translated; αἴνιγμα object of συντιθέντι which agrees with διαπειρωμένῳ, *[a man] composing a riddle making trial [of me]*, i.e. *[a man] making trial [of me] [by] composing ...* (the actual riddle is ἆρα ... ἀκούοντας). *ll.*19f. δή adds a note of sarcasm to ὁ σοφός; ἐμοῦ ... ἐναντί᾽(α) ἐμαυτῷ λέγοντος (*saying [things] opposite to myself*, i.e. *contradicting myself*) gen. absol. with two participles (*will S. realize when I ... ?*). *l.*22 ὥσπερ ἂν εἰ (= ὥσπερ εἰ) εἴποι *as if he were to say. l.*24 παίζοντος gen. of characteristic (23.1/1*b*). In the next section of the Apology Socrates goes on to prove his assertion that Meletus is contradicting himself.

Main points

• Uses of genitive – subjective, objective, partitive, explanatory, etc.

• Uses of dative – advantage, disadvantage, reference, agent, cause, manner and attendant circumstance, accompaniment, respect, place where, etc.

23.3 Extra reading – further elegiac poetry

Of the following, 1-5 are epitaphs, which were nearly always written in elegiac couplets (**Appendix 9**). Other examples of epitaphs occur at 9.2.3 and 19.2.7(*v*).

1 ναυηγοῦ τάφος εἰμί· ὁ δ᾽ ἀντίον ἐστὶ γεωργοῦ·
  ὡς ἁλὶ καὶ γαίῃ ξυνὸς ὕπεστ᾽ Ἀΐδης.

2 τῇδε Σάων ὁ Δίκωνος Ἀκάνθιος ἱερὸν ὕπνον
  κοιμᾶται· θνῄσκειν μὴ λέγε τοὺς ἀγαθούς.

3 δωδεκετῆ τὸν παῖδα πατὴρ ἀπέθηκε Φίλιππος
  ἐνθάδε, τὴν πολλὴν ἐλπίδα, Νικοτέλην.

4 On the Spartans who died fighting the Persians at Plataea
  ἄσβεστον κλέος οἵδε φίλῃ περὶ πατρίδι θέντες
  κυάνεον θανάτου ἀμφιβάλοντο νέφος·
  οὐδὲ τεθνᾶσι θανόντες, ἐπεί σφ᾽ ἀρετὴ καθύπερθεν
  κυδαίνουσ᾽ ἀνάγει δώματος ἐξ Ἀΐδεω.

5 Αἰσχύλον Εὐφορίωνος Ἀθηναῖον τόδε κεύθει
  μνῆμα καταφθίμενον πυροφόροιο Γέλας·
  ἀλκὴν δ᾽ εὐδόκιμον Μαραθώνιον ἄλσος ἂν εἴποι
  καὶ βαθυχαιτήεις Μῆδος ἐπιστάμενος.

6 δάκρυα σοὶ καὶ νέρθε διὰ χθονός, Ἡλιοδώρα,
  δωροῦμαι στοργᾶς λείψανον εἰς Ἀΐδαν,
  δάκρυα δυσδάκρυτα· πολυκλαύτῳ δ᾽ ἐπὶ τύμβῳ
  σπένδω νᾶμα πόθων, μνᾶμα φιλοφροσύνας·
  οἰκτρὰ γὰρ οἰκτρὰ φίλαν σε καὶ ἐν φθιμένοις Μελέαγρος   5
  αἰάζω, κενεὰν εἰς Ἀχέροντα χάριν.
  αἰαῖ, ποῦ τὸ ποθεινὸν ἐμοὶ θάλος; ἅρπασεν Ἅιδας,
  ἅρπασεν, ἀκμαῖον δ᾽ ἄνθος ἔφυρε κόνις.
  ἀλλά σε γουνοῦμαι, γᾶ παντρόφε, τὰν πανόδυρτον
  ἠρέμα σοῖς κόλποις, μᾶτερ, ἐναγκάλισαι.   10

Notes

1 *l.*1 ὁ *sc.* τάφος. *l.*2 ὡς exclamatory (22.1/1*a*(ii)); ὕπεστ᾽ (ι) < ὕπειμι.

2 ὁ Δίκωνος (23.1/1*a*); ἱερὸν ὕπνον cognate acc. (22.1/2*g*) with
κοιμᾶται.

3 *l.*1 ἀπέθηκε < ἀποτίθημι. *l.*2 τὴν πολλὴν ἐλπίδα is in apposition to
παῖδα.

4 *l*.1 περὶ ... θέντες tmesis (12.3.9 *l*.6 note) for περιθέντες (the image is from putting a wreath on a person's head). *l*.2 ἀμφιβάλοντο (= ἀμφεβάλοντο) a Homeric form without the augment (25.1/2*d*(i)) – the image here is of putting on a mantle. *l*.3 τεθνᾶσι shorter form of τεθνήκᾱσι (19.1/3*a*); σφ᾽(ε) here *them*. *l*.4 κυδαίνουσ᾽(α) f. nom. pple.; in prose the order of the last three words would be ἐκ δώματος Ἀΐδεω (= Ἅιδου, cf. 22.3.2 *l*.9 and 25.1/2*b*(i)).

5 *l*.1 Εὐφορίωνος *[son] of E.*, 23.1/1*a* (the article can be omitted). *l*.2 καταφθίμενον (Homeric aorist mid. pple.) *dead* (trans. *who died*); πυροφόροιο (= -ου, 25.1/2*b*(ii)) Γέλᾱς Homeric use of gen. to denote place where. *ll*.3f. Μαραθώνιον ἄλσος the grove at Marathon (a village to the north of Athens) which celebrated the Athenian victory over an invading Persian force in 490 BC. Aeschylus had distinguished himself in the battle and set more value on this than on any literary achievements, if the tradition assigning the epitaph to him is correct. The subject of εἴποι is both ἄλσος and Μῆδος (with double subjects of this sort the verb may agree with the closer noun). *l*.4 ἐπιστάμενος *sc. it*, i.e. Aeschylus' ἄλκη.

6 The poem has a smattering of Doric forms, which are sometimes used in elegiac poetry; these involve ᾱ for Attic η: στοργᾶς, Ἀΐδᾶν (= Ἀΐδην) (*l*.2); μνᾶμα, φιλοφροσύνᾱς (*l*.4); Ἀΐδᾱς (*l*.7); γᾶ, τᾱ́ν (*l*.9); μᾶτερ (*l*.10). *ll*.2f. Take στοργᾶς with λείψανον, which is in apposition to δάκρυα. *l*.4 μνᾶμα is in apposition to νᾶμα. *l*.5 οἰκτρὰ ... οἰκτρά n. pl. acc. used adverbially (20.1/5), *piteously*. *l*.6 κενεᾶν ... χάριν is in apposition to the whole of the preceding clause; Acheron, one of the rivers of the Underworld, is used here to mean the Underworld itself. *l*.7 ἐμοί indicates possession (23.1/2*c*); ἅρπασεν = ἥρπασεν (cf. ἀμφιβάλοντο in 4 *l*.2 above). *l*.10 ἐναγκάλισαι 2nd s. aor. imp. mid. of ἐναγκαλίζομαι.

Unit 24

24.1 Grammar

24.1/1 Yes and no

Greek has four ways of answering questions where in English we would use *yes* or *no*. In answer to the question ἆρα τοῦτο εἶπας; *Did you say this?* we may have:

(*a*) the key word of the question repeated either affirmatively or negatively:

εἶπον	*yes* (lit. *I said [it]*)
οὐκ εἶπον	*no* (lit. *I did not say [it]*)

(*b*) the personal pronoun with γε:

ἔγωγε	*yes* (lit. *I at any rate [said it]*)
οὐκ ἔγωγε	*no*

(*c*) by ναί *yes* and οὔ *no*; or by a phrase such as πάνυ μὲν οὖν *certainly*; οὐδαμῶς *certainly not*. This can take the form of an abbreviated question, e.g. πῶς γὰρ οὔ; *of course* (lit. *for how not?*); or of an oath (22.1/2*h*).

(*d*) a short clause such as ἀληθῆ λέγεις *you speak [the] truth* (lit. *true things*).

Sometimes one speaker in a conversation makes a comment on what the other speaker has said (which may or may not have been a question), and we must infer from his words whether he is agreeing or not:

A. σὺ γ᾽ οὔπω σωφρονεῖν ἐπίστασαι. B. σὲ γὰρ προσηύδων οὐκ ἄν.
A. *You do not yet know prudence* (lit. *how to be prudent*). B. *[No], for I would not be speaking to you (sc. if I did).*

Other examples have already occurred at 13.3(ii) *l*.4 and 18.2.1.

24.1/2 Summary of uses of οὐ and μή

Both οὐ and μή are to be translated by *not*. Their uses, which involve distinctions which we do not make in English, can be classified as follows:

(*a*) In **main clauses**
οὐ is used as the negative in:

(i)   Statements of fact
(ii) Suppositions (i.e. in the main clause of a category 1 conditional sentence (18.1/5) and potential clauses (19.1/2))
(iii) Direct questions expecting the answer *yes*

μή is used as the negative in:

(i) Constructions expressing an order or desire, i.e. prohibitions (17.1/1), exhortations (14.1/4*a*(i)), and wishes (21.1/1)
(ii) Direct questions expecting the answer *no* (10.1/2*a*) and in deliberative questions (14.1/4*a*(ii))

(*b*) When the verb of an **adverbial clause** is negated, μή is used in clauses of purpose (14.1/4*c*(i)), condition (18.1/5), and for indefinite adverbial clauses (14.1/4*c*(iii) and 21.1/2 note 4); elsewhere the negative is οὐ.

(*c*) When the verb of an **adjectival clause** is negated, μή is used if the clause has an indefinite or general sense whether the indefinite construction (14.1/4*c*(iii)) is used or not, e.g.

οὐ γὰρ ἃ πράττουσιν οἱ δίκαιοι, ἀλλ᾽ ἃ μὴ πράττουσι, ταῦτα λέγεις.
You are speaking not of those things which the just do, but [of those things] which they do not do.

(*d*) οὐ is used to negate the verb of a **noun clause**, i.e. in indirect statements when expressed by a ὅτι/ὡς clause (8.1/3*b*), indirect questions (10.1/2*b*), and clauses following verbs of fearing (14.1/4*c*(ii)).

(*e*) **Infinitives** are always negated by μή, except in the infinitive construction for indirect statement after verbs of saying and thinking (8.1/3*a*).

(*f*) **Participles** are negated by οὐ except:
    (i) when used with the article to denote a general class (12.1/2*a*(vi)); this also applies to adjectives, e.g. οἱ μὴ ἀγαθοί *the [general class of] people who are not good*, but οἱ οὐκ ἀγαθοί *the [particular] people who are not good*.
    (ii) when used conditionally (12.1/2*a*(iv)).

(*g*) οὐ μή with the fut. ind. expresses a strong prohibition (17.1/1).

(*h*) οὐ μή with the aor. subj. expresses a strong denial:

οὐ μὴ παύσωμαι φιλοσοφῶν. *I shall certainly not stop studying philosophy.*

(*i*) *Or not* as an alternative question in indirect speech is either ἢ οὔ or ἢ μή:

ὑμῶν δέομαι σκοπεῖν εἰ δίκαια λέγω ἢ μή (or ἢ οὔ). *I ask you to examine whether I am speaking justly or not.*

24.1/3 Diminutives

Nouns can be modified by the addition of a suffix to indicate something smaller, e.g. *booklet* (< *book*), *islet* (< *isle*). The modified form is called a **diminutive**. Greek has a number of diminutive suffixes but the most common is -ιον, e.g. παιδίον *little child* (παῖς, stem παιδ-). All diminutives in -ιον (including those from proper names) are 2nd declension neuters, even when they denote living beings.

Very often diminutives are used to indicate affection and familiarity without any real connotation of smallness, e.g. πατρ-ίδιον *daddy* (< πατήρ with the suffix -ίδιον), Σωκρατίδιον *dear little/old Socrates*. Occasionally a diminutive has lost any special meaning and replaced the original noun, e.g. θηρίον *wild beast* (< θήρ, which has the same meaning but is used mainly in verse).

Diminutives were a feature of the colloquial language, and consequently are not found in literary genres written in an elevated style, such as tragedy. They are, however, very common in comedy, and in the dialogues of Plato, who aimed at reproducing the everyday speech of educated Athenians. An amusing example occurs in Aristophanes' *Clouds* where Strepsiades wakes his adult son by coaxing him with the diminutive of his name:

πῶς δῆτ᾽ ἂν ἥδιστ᾽ αὐτὸν ἐπεγείραιμι; πῶς; Φειδιππίδη, Φειδιππίδιον.
How could I wake him most gently? How? Pheidippides, dear little Pheidippides.

24.1/4 Dual number

In addition to the singular and plural, Indo-European (1.3) also had a dual number, which was used for two persons or objects. In Homer it is still frequent, but in Attic Greek of the fifth and fourth centuries BC its use is generally confined to two persons or things closely associated or normally considered to form a pair, e.g. two brothers, sisters, hands, eyes, but even here it is optional. Its endings do not show anything like the same variety as either the singular or plural.

In **verbs** the same stems are used as elsewhere. There is **no** first person dual. In the second person the dual endings are identical for the primary and historic tenses but in the third person endings there is a distinction between primary and historic forms (cf. 4.1/1 note 1 and 8.1/1*f*):

	ACTIVE		MIDDLE/PASSIVE	
	Primary	*Historic*	*Primary*	*Historic*
2	-τον	-τον	-σθον	-σθον
3	-τον	-την	-σθον	-σθην

In -ω verbs the link vowel (cf. 8.1/1*d*) is the same as in the singular and plural except that we have ε (not ο/ε) in the present, imperfect and future.

For λύω in the **indicative** we have:

		ACTIVE		MIDDLE/PASSIVE		
PRESENT	2	λύ-ετον *you two loosen*		λύ-εσθον		
	3	λύ-ετον *two (people) loosen*		λύ-εσθον		
FUTURE	2	λύσ-ετον	mid.	λύσ-εσθον	pass.	λυθήσ-εσθον
	3	λύσ-ετον		λύσ-εσθον		λυθήσ-εσθον
IMPERFECT	2	ἐλύ-ετον		ἐλύ-εσθον		
	3	ἐλū-έτην		ἐλū-έσθην		
AORIST	2	ἐλύσ-ατον	mid.	ἐλύσ-ασθον	pass.	ἐλύθη-τον
	3	ἐλūσ-άτην		ἐλūσ-άσθην		ἐλυθή-την
PERFECT	2	λελύκ-ατον		λέλυ-σθον		
	3	λελύκ-ατον		λέλυ-σθον		
PLUPERFECT	2	ἐλελύκ-ετον		ἐλέλυ-σθον		
	3	ἐλελυκ-έτην		ἐλελύ-σθην		

The **subjunctive** mood takes the primary endings (cf.14.1/2), giving for both second and third persons λύ-ητον (pres. act.) and λύ-ησθον (pres. mid./pass.), etc. (the η represents the lengthening of ε in λύ-ε-τον, λύ-ε-σθον of the indicative).

The **optative** takes the historic endings (cf.14.1/3) with the same preceding diphthong as occurs in the singular and plural of the tenses which have an optative (i.e. οι/αι/ει), e.g. pres. act. 2 λύ-οιτον, 3 λū-οίτην; aor. act. 2 λύσ-αιτον, 3 λūσ-αίτην; aor. pass. 2 λυθ-εῖτον, 3 λυθ-είτην.

The 2nd person dual of the **imperative** is the same as in the indicative. The 3rd person dual of the imperative is rare.

The dual endings for **nouns** and the dual forms of the **article** and **personal pronouns** are:

	NOUNS (Declension)			ARTICLE M.F.N.	PERSONAL PRONOUNS	
	1st	2nd	3rd			
N.V.A.	-ᾱ	-ω	-ε	τώ	νώ *we two*	σφώ *you two*
Gen. Dat.	-αιν	-οιν	-οιν	τοῖν	νῷν	σφῷν

The article has the same forms for all genders, and the demonstrative pronouns follow the same pattern (τούτω/τούτοιν from οὗτος; τώδε/τοῖνδε from ὅδε). In each declension **adjectives** (and αὐτός and participles) take the same endings as nouns.

Because the dual is not obligatory we often find dual and plural forms used indiscriminately:

> δύο ἄνδρες προσελθόντε Ἄγιδι διελεγέσθην. *Two men came forward and* (lit. *having come forward*) *were talking with Agis* (we might have expected ἄνδρε instead of δύο ἄνδρες).

24.1/5 Verbal adjectives in -τος/-τός and -τέος

(*a*) We have already met many verbal adjectives in -τος/-τός. Most have a prefix, in many cases the negative ἀ-/ἀν-, e.g. ἔμφυτος (ἐν + φυτος), ἄβατος (ἀ + βατος), but some have none, e.g. χυτός. They can be either:

(i)   the equivalent of a perfect passive participle, e.g. εὔγνωστος *well-known*, ἔμφυτος *inborn*, χυτός *melted*

(ii) the equivalent of a present participle active, e.g. ἀνόητος *stupid* (lit. *not perceiving*)

(iii) an adjective denoting possibility, e.g. ἄβατος *impassable*, βιωτός *livable*.

Some can be either (i) or (iii), e.g. ἀόρᾱτος *unseen/invisible*.

(*b*) The verbal adjective in -τέος differs from the above in being considered a normal part of a verb, although, in its neuter singular form, it is given a separate listing in dictionaries. It is formed by replacing θη of the aorist passive stem with -τέος, e.g. φιλητέος (<φιλέω, aor. pass ἐφιλήθην), κελευστέος (<κελεύω, aor. pass. ἐκελεύσθην); and has the meaning of a present passive participle but with the added idea of necessity. The literal translation of φιλητέος εἰμί is *I am needing-to-be-loved*, i.e. *I must be loved*. The agent is expressed by the dative (23.1/2g), not by ὑπό + gen.:

> ὁ ποταμὸς ἡμῖν ἐστι διαβατέος. *The river is needing-to-be-crossed-over by us*, i.e. *we must cross over the river.*
> ἐκείνη σοι οὐ φιλητέα. *That woman [is] not needing-to-be-loved by you*, i.e. *you must not love that woman.*

The neuter singular (and occasionally the neuter plural) of the verbal adjective can be used **impersonally**: διαβατέον ἡμῖν ἐστιν *it is needing-to-be-crossed-over (there must be a crossing over) by us*, i.e. *we must cross over*. The verbal adjective of a transitive verb can, when used impersonally, take an object: τὸν ποταμὸν ἡμῖν ἐστι διαβατέον *it is needing-to-be-crossed-over the river (there must be a crossing over the river) by us*, i.e. *we must cross over the river*. There is no difference in meaning between ὁ ποταμός ἐστι διαβατέος and τὸν ποταμόν ἐστι διαβατέον.

Sometimes a literal translation of an impersonal verbal adjective is impossible:

> τῷ ἀδικοῦντι δοτέον ἐστὶ δίκην. *The [person] doing wrong must pay the penalty* (the closest translation is *there must-be-a-paying of the penalty* ...).

The neuter plural of the verbal adjective has exactly the same meaning. We may equally well have τὸν ποταμόν ἐστι διαβατέα or τὸν ποταμόν ἐστι διαβατέον.

24.1/6 Verbs of precaution and striving

When these verbs, which include ἐπιμελέομαι, εὐλαβέομαι both *take care*, σπουδάζω *be eager/busy*, σκοπέω *consider, take heed*, are followed by a clause (*take care that ..., be eager that ...* etc.), this is expressed by ὅπως with the future indicative. The future indicative is retained even after main verbs in a historic tense. The ὅπως clause is negated by μή:

> ὅπως ἀμυνούμεθα, οὐδεὶς παρασκευάζεται οὐδὲ ἐπιμελεῖται. *No-one is making preparations or taking care that we should defend ourselves.*

δεῖ σκοπεῖν ὅπως τὰ παρόντ᾽ ἐπανορθωθήσεται. We must take heed
that the present state of affairs be remedied.
ἐσκόπουν ὅπως αὐτὸς ἀπολυθήσομαι τῆς ἐγγύης. I was taking heed
that I myself be freed from the pledge

Less often ὅπως is followed by the subjunctive or optative, as in
purpose clauses (14.1/4c(i)):

οὐ φυλάξεσθε ὅπως μὴ δεσπότην εὕρητε; Will you not be on your
guard that you do not find a master?
ἐπεμελεῖτο ὁ Κῦρος ὅπως μήποτε οἱ στρατιῶται ἀνίδρωτοι γενόμενοι
ἐπὶ τὸ ἄριστον εἰσίοιεν. Cyrus took care that the soldiers should
never come to breakfast without working up a sweat (lit. being
without a sweat).

Note

Sometimes a main verb in the imperative such as σκόπει/σκοπεῖτε see
to it is omitted and we are left with nothing but ὅπως and the future
indicative:

ὅπως ἔσεσθε ἄνδρες ἄξιοι τῆς ἐλευθερίας. [See to it] that you show
yourselves (lit. will be) men worthy of freedom!

24.1/7 Verbs of hindering, preventing, forbidding, denying

In English, verbs with these and similar meanings take various
constructions (I prevented him from entering, we forbid you to
do this). In Greek they are always followed by an infinitive which
is accompanied by the negative μή; the latter is redundant from
an English point of view: εἴργω ὑμᾶς μὴ μάχεσθαι I hinder you
from fighting; ἀπαγορεύομεν αὐτὸν μὴ οἰκοδομεῖν we forbid him
to build. When the main verb is itself negated, the infinitive is
accompanied by a double redundant negative μὴ οὐ: οὐκ εἴργω ὑμᾶς
μὴ οὐ μάχεσθαι I do not hinder you from fighting. However, κωλύω
prevent is usually followed by a simple infinitive without μή or
μὴ οὐ:

κωλύω αὐτὸν ἱππεύειν. I prevent him from riding.
οὐ κωλύω αὐτὸν βαδίζειν. I do not prevent him from walking.

Insight

Perhaps the most controversial philosopher of antiquity was Epicurus (d. 270 BC), who postulated that pleasure is the beginning and end of living happily; pleasures are to be graded according to the pain they might involve, and the most desirable pleasures are those that involve the least pain. This has always been understood by some as an excuse for unrestrained indulgence in the pleasures of the flesh, and Epicurus has been held up as justifying debauchery, as exemplified in the expression *the fattest hog in Epicurus' sty*. However, this was not what he intended and he himself led a very simple life. On one occasion he wrote to a friend, πέμψον μοι τῡροῦ κυθριδίον ἵν' ὅταν βούλωμαι πολυτελεύσασθαι δύνωμαι *send me a little pot of cheese so that I shall be able to have a feast whenever I wish*.

24.2 Greek reading

1 *In addition to translating, explain each use of a negative:*

(*i*)# ὁ μηδὲν εἰδὼς οὐδὲν ἐξαμαρτάνει. (*ii*) μηδένα φίλον ποιοῦ πρὶν ἂν ἐξετάσῃς πῶς κέχρηται τοῖς πρότερον φίλοις. (*iii*) πᾶν ποιοῦσιν ὥστε μὴ δοῦναι δίκην. (*iv*) οὐδὲν ἐπράχθη διὰ τὸ μὴ τὸν ἄρχοντα παρεῖναι. (*v*) οὐκ οἶδα πότερον πορευθῶ ἢ μή. (*vi*) δέδοικα μὴ οὐχ ἱκανοὺς ἔχω οἷς τὸν χρυσὸν δῶ. (*vii*) θάρρει, ὦ Κῦρε, οὐ μή σε κρύψω πρὸς ὅντινα βούλομαι ἀφικέσθαι. (*viii*) οἱ δ' ἔφασαν ἀποδώσειν τοὺς νεκροὺς ἐφ' ᾧ μὴ καίειν τὰς κώμας. (*ix*)# τὸ μὴ δίκαιον ἔργον οὐ λήθει θεούς. (*x*) τί ἐμποδὼν μὴ οὐκ ἀποθανεῖν αὐτούς; (*xi*) φίλος ἐβούλετο εἶναι τοῖς μέγιστα δυναμένοις ἵνα ἀδικῶν μὴ διδοίη δίκην. (*xii*)# εἰ μὴ καθέξεις γλῶτταν, ἔσται σοι κακά. (*xiii*)# οὐκ ἂν δύναιο μὴ καμὼν εὐδαιμονεῖν. (*xiv*)# οὐ μὴ δυσμενὴς ἔσει φίλοις. (*xv*) εἰπὼν ἃ θέλεις, ἀντάκου' ἃ μὴ θέλεις. (*xvi*) ἢ δεῖ χελώνης κρέα φαγεῖν ἢ μὴ φαγεῖν. (*xvii*) δύνασαί μοι λέγειν εἰ διδακτὸν ἡ ἀρετὴ ἢ οὔ; (*xviii*) οὐδεὶς ἀπαρνήσεται μὴ οὐχὶ ἐπίστασθαι τὰ δίκαια. (*xix*) ἐφοβεῖτο μὴ οὐ δύναιτο ἐκ τῆς χώρας ἐξελθεῖν. (*xx*) μὴ ἀπέλθητε πρὶν ἂν ἀκούσητε.

2 θεραπευτέον τοὺς θεούς, τοὺς φίλους εὐεργετητέον, τὴν πόλιν ὠφελητέον, τὴν Ἑλλάδα πειρατέον εὖ ποιεῖν, τὴν γῆν

θεραπευτέον, τῶν βοσκημάτων ἐπιμελητέον, τὰς πολεμικὰς
τέχνας μαθητέον.

3# ὁ φόβος, ὅταν τις αἵματος μέλλῃ πέρι
λέγειν καταστὰς εἰς ἀγῶν᾽ ἐναντίον,
τό τε στόμ᾽ εἰς ἔκπληξιν ἀνθρώπων ἄγει
τὸν νοῦν τ᾽ ἀπείργει μὴ λέγειν ἃ βούλεται.

4 ὑμᾶς εὐλαβεῖσθαι δεῖ ὅπως μηδὲν ὧν ἰδίᾳ φυλάξαισθ᾽ ἄν, τοῦτο
δημοσίᾳ ποιοῦντες φανήσεσθε.

5 οὗτοι πάντες οἱ νόμοι κεῖνται πολὺν ἤδη χρόνον, ὦ ἄνδρες
δικασταί, καὶ οὐδεὶς πώποτ᾽ ἀντεῖπεν μὴ οὐ καλῶς ἔξειν αὐτούς.

6 εὐλαβοῦ μὴ φανῇς κακὸς γεγώς.

7 Socrates tells of an encounter with two sophists whom he has
previously met (sophists were teachers who travelled about
from one Greek city to another).

ἠσπαζόμην οὖν αὐτὼ ἅτε διὰ χρόνου ἑωρακώς· μετὰ δὲ τοῦτο
εἶπον πρὸς τὸν Κλεινίαν· ὦ Κλεινία, τώδε μέντοι τὼ ἄνδρε σοφώ,
Εὐθύδημός τε καὶ Διονυσόδωρος, οὐ τὰ σμικρὰ ἀλλὰ τὰ μεγάλα·
τὰ γὰρ περὶ τὸν πόλεμον ἐπίστασθον.
εἰπὼν οὖν ταῦτα κατεφρονήθην ὑπ᾽ αὐτοῖν· ἐγελασάτην οὖν ἄμφω   5
βλέψαντε εἰς ἀλλήλω, καὶ ὁ Εὐθύδημος εἶπεν· οὗτοι ἔτι ταῦτα, ὦ
Σώκρατες, σπουδάζομεν, ἀλλὰ παρέργοις αὐτοῖς χρώμεθα.
κἀγὼ θαυμάσας εἶπον· καλὸν ἄν που τὸ ἔργον ὑμῶν εἴη, εἰ
τηλικαῦτα πράγματα πάρεργα ὑμῖν τυγχάνει ὄντα, καὶ πρὸς θεῶν
εἴπετόν μοι τί ἐστι τοῦτο τὸ καλόν;   10
ἀρετήν, ἔφη, ὦ Σώκρατες, οἰόμεθα οἵω τ᾽ εἶναι παραδοῦναι
κάλλιστ᾽ ἀνθρώπων καὶ τάχιστα.
ὦ Ζεῦ, οἷον, ἦν δ᾽ ἐγώ, λέγετον πρᾶγμα· πόθεν τοῦτο τὸ ἕρμαιον
ηὕρετον; ἐγὼ δὲ περὶ ὑμῶν διενοούμην ἔτι, ὥσπερ νυνδὴ ἔλεγον,
ὡς τὸ πολὺ τοῦτο δεινοῖν ὄντοιν, ἐν ὅπλοις μάχεσθαι, καὶ ταῦτα   15
ἔλεγον περὶ σφῷν· ὅτε γὰρ τὸ πρότερον ἐπεδημήσατον, τοῦτο
μέμνημαι σφὼ ἐπαγγελλομένω.

8 μετὰ τοῦτον Ξενοφῶν εἶπεν· ἐγὼ δ᾽ οὕτω γιγνώσκω. εἰ μὲν
ἀνάγκη μάχεσθαι, τοῦτο δεῖ παρασκευάσασθαι ὅπως ὡς κράτιστα

μαχούμεθα. εἰ δὲ βουλόμεθα ὡς ῥᾷστα ὑπερβάλλειν, τοῦτό μοι δοκεῖ σκεπτέον εἶναι ὅπως ὡς ἐλάχιστα μὲν τραύματα λάβωμεν, ὡς ἐλάχιστα δὲ σώματα ἀποβάλωμεν.   5

9 σκεπτέον πότερον δίκαιον ἐμὲ ἐνθένδε πειρᾶσθαι ἐξιέναι μὴ ἀφιέντων Ἀθηναίων ἢ οὐ δίκαιον.

10 Α. εἰπέ μοι, ἔστι σοι ἀγρός; Β. οὐκ ἔμοιγε.

11 καὶ μὴν εἰ ὑφησόμεθα καὶ ἐπὶ βασιλεῖ γενησόμεθα, τί οἰόμεθα πείσεσθαι; ὃς καὶ τοῦ ὁμομητρίου ἀδελφοῦ καὶ τεθνηκότος ἤδη ἀποτεμὼν τὴν κεφαλὴν καὶ τὴν χεῖρα ἀνεσταύρωσεν· ἡμᾶς δὲ, οἷς κηδεμὼν μὲν οὐδεὶς πάρεστιν, ἐστρατεύσαμεν δὲ ἐπ᾽ αὐτὸν ὡς δοῦλον ἀντὶ βασιλέως ποιήσοντες καὶ ἀποκτενοῦντες εἰ   5 δυναίμεθα, τί ἂν οἰόμεθα παθεῖν; ἆρ᾽ οὐκ ἂν ἐπὶ πᾶν ἔλθοι ὡς ἡμᾶς τὰ ἔσχατα αἰκισάμενος πᾶσιν ἀνθρώποις φόβον παράσχῃ τοῦ στρατεῦσαί ποτε ἐπ᾽ αὐτόν; ἀλλ᾽ ὅπως τοι μὴ ἐπ᾽ ἐκείνῳ γενησόμεθα πάντα ποιητέον.

Notes

1 (*i*) οὐδέν adverbial acc. (20.1/5). (*ii*) ποιοῦ 2nd s. pres. imp. mid.; κέχρηται < χράομαι; πρότερον here an adverb (cf. οἱ νῦν, 5.1/3) but trans. by an adjective. (*v*) πορευθῶ (aor. subj. of πορεύομαι) deliberative subj. (14.1/4*a*(ii)) in indirect speech (cf. δῶ in (*vi*)). (*vii*) θάρρει (< θάρρε-ε) pres. imp.; κρύψω is here aor. subj. (24.1/2*h*). (*viii*) ἐφ᾽ ᾧ 16.1/1 note 4. (*x*) ἐμποδών *sc.* ἐστί; because the construction appropriate after a negated verb of hindering, preventing etc. (μὴ οὐ) is used here, we know that the question expects the answer *nothing* and so counts as a virtual negation. (*xi*) μέγιστα adverb (17.1/2). (*xii*) καθέξεις < κατέχω. (*xiv*) οὐ μή + fut. ind., 17.1/1. (*xv*) ἀντάκου᾽(ε) imp. (*xvi*) κρέᾱ acc. pl. of κρέας (13.1/1*b*(iii)).

2 ἐστί is very often omitted with verbal adjectives and must be supplied with each example here.

3 A murder trial is being described. *l*.1 ὁ φόβος is the subject of ἄγει (*l*.3); take πέρι with αἵματος (see note on 11.2.4 *l*.1). *l*.2

καταστάς intr. aor. pple. of καθίστημι. *ll.*3f. Take ἀνθρώπων with στόμ᾽(α) and νοῦν.

4 ὅπως ... φανήσεσθε (2nd pl. fut. pass. of φαίνω) see 24.1/6; φυλάξαισθ᾽(ε) ἄν potential optative (19.1/2).

5 κεῖνται is used here as the perf. pass of τίθημι (18.1/2 note 4); ἕξειν fut. act. inf. of ἔχω.

6 μή = ὅπως μή.

7 The passage has many dual forms (24.1/4). *l.*1 ἑωρᾱκώς perf. act. pple. of ὁράω. *l.*2 μέντοι emphatic, not adversative (13.1/3*c*(v)). *l.*3. τὰ σμῑκρὰ ... τὰ μεγάλα acc. of respect with σοφώ in *l.*2 (20.1/5). *ll.*7f. παρέργοις here predicative with αὐτοῖς, *them* (αὐτοῖς)*[as] subordinate issues*. *l.*8 θαυμάσᾱς coincidental use of the aor. pple. (12.1/1), *marvelling*; ἄν ... εἴη potential opt. (19.1/2), lit. *would be*, but trans. *must be*. *l.*10 εἴπετον 2nd dual aor. imp. act. *l.*12 κάλλιστ᾽(α) ἀνθρώπων καὶ τάχιστα lit. *most excellently and speedily of men*, i.e. *as excellently and speedily as is humanly possible*. *l.*13 οἷον exclamatory (21.1/3); ἦν δ᾽ ἐγώ *said I* (18.1.1*a*). *l.*15 ὡς τὸ πολύ (= ὡς ἐπὶ τὸ πολύ) *for the most part*, 22.1/1*a*(vii); τοῦτο (acc. of respect with δεινοῖν (20.1/5)) anticipates ἐν ... μάχεσθαι; δεινοῖν ὄντοιν agrees with ὑμῶν in *l.*14, although the latter is plural, not dual (note that Socrates somewhat illogically goes on to use the dual pronoun σφῷν).

8 οὕτω anticipates the following sentence, lit. *I think* (γιγνώσκω) *thus*; each τοῦτο anticipates the ὅπως clause which follows it and need not be translated; ὡς + supl. 17.1/4*d*.

9 Supply ἐστί with both σκεπτέον (see note on 2 above) and δίκαιον; ἀφιέντων gen. pl. of the pres. act. pple. of ἀφίημι.

10 ἔμοιγε 24.1/1*b*.

11 *ll.*1ff. καὶ μήν *and further*; ὑφησόμεθα fut. mid. of ὑφίημι; τί etc. *what do we think we shall suffer* (cf. 8.1/3*a*); ὅς lit. *who* (the antecedent is βασιλεῖ) but trans. *he* (the relative pronoun is often used to join a sentence with what precedes); καί (before τοῦ and before τεθνηκότος) *even*, but trans. the second by *and that too* for variety; take ἤδη with τεθνηκότος. *ll.*3ff. ἡμᾶς is the subject of παθεῖν in *l.*6; οἷς ... πάρεστιν lit. *for whom there is no protector at hand*; before ἐστρατεύσαμεν we must supply the relative οἵ from the preceding οἷς, and the two adjectival clauses can be translated *who have no protector at hand but* (δέ) *who campaigned against him* (ἐπ᾽ αὐτόν); ὡς + fut. pple. (12.1/2*a*(v)); εἰ δυναίμεθα indefinite construction in historic sequence (14.1/4*c*(iii)), lit. *if ever we could*; ἄν ... παθεῖν represents ἄν πάθοιμεν in direct speech (potential opt., 19.1/2), and the subject of the infinitive (ἡμᾶς in *l.*3) is, quite irregularly, inserted in the acc. although it is the same as the subject of οἰόμεθα – trans. *what do we think we would suffer.* *ll.*6ff. ἆρ᾽ οὐκ (10.1/2*a*); ἐπὶ πᾶν lit. *to everything* i.e. *to any lengths*; ὡς introduces a purpose clause (22.1/1*b*(ii)); τὰ ἔσχατα acc. of respect (20.1/5), lit. *in respect of the worst things*, i.e. *in the worst [possible] ways*; take τοῦ στρατεῦσαι ... as objective gen. (23.1/1*c*) with φόβον, *fear of campaigning*; the clause ὅπως ... γενησόμεθα is governed by ποιητέον (ἐστίν) (ὅπως + fut. after a verb of striving 24.1/6).

Main points

- There are four ways of giving a positive or negative answer corresponding to *yes/no*

- The uses of οὐ and μή differ in main and subordinate clauses, and with infinitives and participles

- Diminutives are used to show affection or familiarity as well as size

- The dual number has separate endings; its use is restricted in Attic Greek

- Verbal adjectives end in -τος , -τός and -τέος; those in -τέος indicate necessity

- Verbs of precaution and striving are normally followed by ὅπως + future

- Verbs of hindering, preventing, forbidding, denying, if not negated themselves, are followed by μή + infinitive, but if negated, are followed by μὴ οὐ + infinitive

24.3 Extra reading – The Think Tank

Old Comedy is the term given to the form of comic drama which flourished in Athens during the fifth century BC. Two of its main characteristics, comic situations and unbridled criticism of contemporaries, can be seen in the following passage from Aristophanes' *Clouds*, which was a stinging attack on Socrates and what were popularly supposed to be his intellectual interests. In this scene Strepsiades, a stupid and uneducated Athenian of the older generation, has just gained admittance to Socrates' Φροντιστήριον (*Think Tank*) in order to improve himself.

ΣΤΡΕΨΙΑΔΗΣ–ΜΑΘΗΤΗΣ

ΣΤ.   πρὸς τῶν θεῶν, τί γὰρ τάδ᾽ ἐστί; εἰπέ μοι.
ΜΑ.   ἀστρονομία μὲν αὑτηί. ΣΤ. τουτὶ δὲ τί;
ΜΑ.   γεωμετρία. ΣΤ. τοῦτ᾽ οὖν τί ἐστι χρήσιμον;
ΜΑ.   γῆν ἀναμετρεῖσθαι. ΣΤ. πότερα τὴν κληρουχικήν;
ΜΑ.   οὔκ, ἀλλὰ τὴν σύμπασαν. ΣΤ. ἀστεῖον λέγεις.   5
    τὸ γὰρ σόφισμα δημοτικὸν καὶ χρήσιμον.
ΜΑ.   αὕτη δέ σοι γῆς περίοδος πάσης. ὁρᾷς;
    αἵδε μὲν Ἀθῆναι. ΣΤ. τί σὺ λέγεις; οὐ πείθομαι,
    ἐπεὶ δικαστὰς οὐχ ὁρῶ καθημένους.
ΜΑ.   ὡς τοῦτ᾽ ἀληθῶς Ἀττικὸν τὸ χωρίον.   10
ΣΤ.   φέρε τίς γὰρ οὗτος οὑπὶ τῆς κρεμάθρας ἀνήρ;
ΜΑ.   αὐτός. ΣΤ. τίς αὐτός; ΜΑ. Σωκράτης. ΣΤ. ὦ Σωκράτης.
    ἴθ᾽ οὗτος, ἀναβόησον αὐτόν μοι μέγα.
ΜΑ.   αὐτὸς μὲν οὖν σὺ κάλεσον· οὐ γάρ μοι σχολή.
ΣΤ.   ὦ Σώκρατες,
    ὦ Σωκρατίδιον.

ΣΩΚΡΑΤΗΣ

       τί με καλεῖς, ὦ 'φήμερε;   15

ΣΤ. πρῶτον μὲν ὅτι δρᾷς, ἀντιβολῶ, κάτειπέ μοι.

ΣΩ. ἀεροβατῶ καὶ περιφρονῶ τὸν ἥλιον.

ΣΤ. ἔπειτ' ἀπὸ ταρροῦ τοὺς θεοὺς ὑπερφρονεῖς,

      ἀλλ᾽ οὐκ ἀπὸ τῆς γῆς, εἴπερ; ΣΩ. οὐ γὰρ ἄν ποτε

      ἐξηῦρον ὀρθῶς τὰ μετέωρα πράγματα,   20

      εἰ μὴ κρεμάσας τὸ νόημα καὶ τὴν φροντίδα.

Notes

The Φροντιστήριον of Aristophanes' play (he seems to have coined the word himself) was a school where various sciences were both investigated and taught. In the opening lines a pupil shows Strepsiades pieces of equipment, which, for humorous effect, are given the names of the sciences (astronomy and geometry) in which they are used. *l*.1 γάρ explains why Strepsiades has used the exclamation πρὸς τῶν θεῶν (*in the name of the gods*) but should not be translated. *l*.2 αὐτηί, τουτί emphatic forms of αὕτη, τοῦτο with the suffix ί, before which a final short vowel is dropped. *l*.3 οὖν *well, so*; τί lit. *in what respect*. *l*.4 When the pupil replies that the purpose of geometry is to measure land, Strepsiades, who is unable to rise above self-interested parochialism, asks if the land involved is for κλῆροι, which were allotments of foreign land confiscated by the state and given to poorer Athenian citizens. The term for this allocation was κληρουχίᾱ *cleruchy*. πότερα introduces alternative questions (10.1/2*a*) but the second, ἢ οὔ *or not*, is omitted; κληρουχικήν *sc.* γῆν *land for cleruchies*. *ll*.5f. Strepsiades finds the idea of measuring the whole earth attractive because he supposes that this would mean distributing it to needy Athenians. *l*.7 σοι ethic dat. (23.1/2*f*). *l*.9 Large juries were a prominent feature of the Athenian legal system, which was often the butt of Aristophanes' humour. *l*.10 A main clause meaning *I assure you* must be supplied. *l*.11 At this point Socrates appears overhead suspended from the end of a crane (see note on *l*.18); φέρε 17.1/1 note 7; οὑπί = ὁ ἐπί. *l*.12 αὐτός was used to mean *the master* (cf. Irish use of *himself*); ὦ Σωκράτης (nom. **not** voc.) an exclamation *Ah, [it's] Socrates*. *l*.13 ἴθ᾽(ι) 2nd s. pres. imp. of ἔρχομαι (18.1/3); οὗτος *you there!* (see note on 20.2.12 *l*.4). *l*.15 Σωκρατίδιον 24.1/3; ὦ 'φήμερε i.e. ὦ ἐφ- (initial elision of this type (prodelision) is poetical). *l*.16 ὅτι indirect form of τί, 10.1/2*b* note 1. *ll*.17f. Socrates, who is comically represented as some sort of divine being, says he is thinking about (περιφρονῶ) the sun but Strepsiades perversely takes περιφρονῶ in its other meaning *despise* and replies with the unequivocal ὑπερφρονεῖς; ἀπὸ ταρροῦ *from your mat* although Strepsiades speaks of a basket in *l*.11 – Socrates is apparently sitting on a mat which is suspended at each corner from the gib of the crane and so resembles a basket. *l*.19 ἀλλ᾽ (ά) trans. *and* as there is no strong contrast; εἴπερ *if indeed [that's what you're really doing]* Strepsiades expresses himself cautiously because he cannot understand what Socrates is up to; οὐ γὰρ ἄν ... lit. *for I would not ...* i.e. *yes, for I would not ...* (24.1/1). *l*.21 εἰ μὴ κρεμάσας *except by* (lit. *if not*) *suspending* (εἰ is here followed by a phrase, not a clause).

....

25.1 Grammar

25.1/1 Homeric Greek

The language of the *Iliad* and *Odyssey* is an older version of Ionic (1.3) with elements from other dialects. It differs to some extent from Attic in **phonology** (the individual sounds of words), **morphology** (the different forms which some words can take), and **syntax** (grammatical constructions and uses). Listed below are the main differences which occur in the passages in 25.2, together with examples from them.

A good introduction to Homer is G.S. Kirk *Homer and the Epic* (Cambridge U.P.).

25.1/2 Differences in phonology and morphology

(*a*) *Vowels and diphthongs*
(i)   Contraction is not always observed, e.g. αἰδέομαι (1 *l*.3 in 25.2).
(ii) ᾱ becomes η after ε, ι and ρ, e.g. κρατερή (1 *l*.19).
(iii) Diphthongs are sometimes broken up into two vowels, e.g. ἐϋμμελίω (1 *l*.10, = εὐ-); χήτεϊ (1 *l*.24, = χήτει).
(iv) Homeric Greek sometimes has σσ where the Attic has σ, e.g. ὅσσον (1 *l*.15)

(*b*) *Case endings*
(i)   -εω, -ω (= Attic -ου) for the gen. s. of first declension masculines, e.g. ἐϋμμελίω (1 *l*.10).
(ii) -οιο (= Attic -ου) for the gen. s. of the second declension, e.g. πολέμοιο (1 *l*.4).
(iii) -άων (= Attic -ῶν) for the gen. pl. of the first declension, e.g. ῥοάων (2 *l*.8).
(iv) -εσσι (= Attic -σι) for the dat. pl. of some third declension nouns, e.g. Τρώεσσι (1 *l*.6).

(v) -ῃσι (= Attic -αις) for the dat. pl. of the first declension, e.g. κονίῃσι (1 *l*.14)

(vi) πολύς has an irregular nom. pl. m. πολέες (1 *l*.13).

(vii) The gen. s. of σύ is σεῦ (1 *l*.15).

(*c*) *Verbal endings*

(i) -ῃσι(ν) (= Attic -ῃ) for the 3rd s. subj. act., e.g. εἴπῃσιν (1 *l*.20).

(ii) -ατο (= Attic -ντο) for the 3rd pl. mid. and pass. of certain tenses (cf. 16.1/3 note), e.g. ἥατο (2 *l*.2).

(iii) -εν (= Attic -ησαν) for the 3rd pl. of the aor. ind. pass. and root aorists in -ην, e.g. ἔφανεν (2 *l*.5).

(iv) -έμεν (= Attic -ειν) for the pres. (and strong aor.) inf. act., e.g. μενέμεν (4 *l*.16).

(v) The pres. inf. of εἰμί is ἔμμεναι (1 *l*. 5), not εἶναι.

(*d*) *Verbal stems*

(i) The augment is frequently omitted, e.g. μάθον (1 *l*.5, = ἔμαθον).

(ii) The aor. ind. stem of εἶπον (< λέγω) is given a syllabic augment, προσέειπε (1 *l*.1, = προσεῖπε).

(iii) The pres. pple. of εἰμί is ἐών, ἐοῦσα, ἐόν (see 1 *l*.17)

(*e*) A few words have a different form, e.g. αἰ (1 *l*.4, = εἰ *if*); ἦμαρ (1 *l*.9, = ἡμέρᾱ).

25.1/3 Differences in syntax

(*a*) What became the definite article in Attic is a third person pronoun in Homer, e.g. τήν (1 *l*.1) *her* (= αὐτήν). A relic of this use survives in Attic in the idiom οἱ μὲν ... οἱ δέ (5.1/3).

(*b*) The future tense exists in Homer (e.g. ἔσσεται 1 *l*.9), but the future can also be expressed by the subjunctive with or without ἄν or κε (an equivalent of ἄν which Homer often uses), e.g. κεν ... ἄγηται (1 *ll*.15f.) *will lead*; ἄν ὀλώλῃ (1 *l*.9) *will be destroyed* (the perfect expresses a future state, lit. *will be in a state of having perished*); εἴπῃσιν (1 *l*.20) *will say*. Further, the optative with ἄν (or κε) does not always have a strong future potential sense as in Attic, and is sometimes to be translated by a simple future, e.g. κεν ... ὑφαίνοις *you will weave* (1 *l*.17).

25.2 Readings from Homer

The Attic equivalent of certain Homeric words and endings is given in the right-hand margin. The Homeric forms so explained (e.g. ἱρή,1 *l.*9) are not listed separately in the vocabulary.

The Homeric poems are written in hexameters (**Appendix 9**).

1 Hector talks with his wife Andromache

τὴν δ᾽ αὖτε προσέειπε μέγας κορυθαίολος Ἕκτωρ·		-εἶπε
ἦ καὶ ἐμοὶ τάδε πάντα μέλει, γύναι· ἀλλὰ μάλ᾽ αἰνῶς		
αἰδέομαι Τρῶας καὶ Τρωάδας ἑλκεσιπέπλους,		
αἴ κε κακὸς ὣς νόσφιν ἀλυσκάζω πολέμοιο·		-ου
οὐδέ με θυμὸς ἄνωγεν, ἐπεὶ μάθον ἔμμεναι ἐσθλὸς	5	ἔμαθον, εἶναι
αἰεὶ καὶ πρώτοισι μετὰ Τρώεσσι μάχεσθαι,		Τρωσί
ἀρνύμενος πατρός τε μέγα κλέος ἠδ᾽ ἐμὸν αὐτοῦ.		
εὖ γὰρ ἐγὼ τόδε οἶδα κατὰ φρένα καὶ κατὰ θυμόν·		
ἔσσεται ἦμαρ ὅτ᾽ ἄν ποτ᾽ ὀλώλῃ Ἴλιος ἱρὴ		ἔσται, ἱερή (= -ά)
καὶ Πρίαμος καὶ λαὸς ἐϋμμελίω Πριάμοιο.	10	-ίου, -ου
ἀλλ᾽ οὔ μοι Τρώων τόσσον μέλει ἄλγος ὀπίσσω,		τόσον, ὀπίσω
οὔτ᾽ αὐτῆς Ἑκάβης οὔτε Πριάμοιο ἄνακτος		-ου
οὔτε κασιγνήτων, οἵ κεν πολέες τε καὶ ἐσθλοὶ		πολλοί
ἐν κονίῃσι πέσοιεν ὑπ᾽ ἀνδράσι δυσμενέεσσιν,		-ίαις, δυσμενέσιν
ὅσσον σεῦ, ὅτε κέν τις Ἀχαιῶν χαλκοχιτώνων	15	ὅσον, σοῦ
δακρυόεσσαν ἄγηται, ἐλεύθερον ἦμαρ ἀπούρας·		
καί κεν ἐν Ἄργει ἐοῦσα πρὸς ἄλλης ἱστὸν ὑφαίνοις,		οὖσα
καί κεν ὕδωρ φορέοις Μεσσηΐδος ἢ Ὑπερείης		φοροίης (= φέροις)
πόλλ᾽ ἀεκαζομένη, κρατερὴ δ᾽ ἐπικείσετ᾽ ἀνάγκη.		
καί ποτέ τις εἴπησιν ἰδὼν κατὰ δάκρυ χέουσαν·	20	εἴπῃ
Ἕκτορος ἥδε γυνή, ὃς ἀριστεύεσκε μάχεσθαι		
Τρώων ἱπποδάμων, ὅτε Ἴλιον ἀμφιμάχοντο.		ἀμφεμάχοντο
ὣς ποτέ τις ἐρέει· σοὶ δ᾽ αὖ νέον ἔσσεται ἄλγος		ἐρεῖ, ἔσται
χήτεϊ τοιοῦδ᾽ ἀνδρὸς ἀμύνειν δούλιον ἦμαρ.		
ἀλλά με τεθνηῶτα χυτὴ κατὰ γαῖα καλύπτοι,	25	τεθνεῶτα
πρίν γέ τι σῆς τε βοῆς σοῦ θ᾽ ἑλκηθμοῖο πυθέσθαι.		-ου

2 The Trojans camp on the the plain outside Troy

οἱ δὲ μέγα φρονέοντες ἐπὶ πτολέμοιο γεφύρας		-οῦντες, πολέμου
ἥατο παννύχιοι, πυρὰ δέ σφισι καίετο πολλά.		ἧντο, ἐκαίετο
ὣς δ᾽ ὅτ᾽ ἐν οὐρανῷ ἄστρα φαεινὴν ἀμφὶ σελήνην		

φαίνετ᾽ ἀριπρεπέα, ὅτε τ᾽ ἔπλετο νήνεμος αἰθήρ· -ἦ
ἔκ τ᾽ ἔφανεν πᾶσαι σκοπιαὶ καὶ πρώονες ἄκροι   5 ἐφάνησαν
καὶ νάπαι· οὐρανόθεν δ᾽ ἄρ᾽ ὑπερράγη ἄσπετος αἰθήρ,
πάντα δὲ εἴδεται ἄστρα, γέγηθε δέ τε φρένα ποιμήν·
τόσσα μεσηγὺ νεῶν ἠδὲ Ξάνθοιο ῥοάων   τόσα, -ου, ῥοῶν
Τρώων καιόντων πυρὰ φαίνετο Ἰλιόθι πρό.   ἐφαίνετο, Ἰλίου
χίλι᾽ ἄρ᾽ ἐν πεδίῳ πυρὰ καίετο, πὰρ δὲ ἑκάστῳ   10 ἐκαίετο, παρά
ἧατο πεντήκοντα σέλα πυρὸς αἰθομένοιο.   ἧντο, -ου
ἵπποι δὲ κρῖ λευκὸν ἐρεπτόμενοι καὶ ὀλύρας
ἑσταότες παρ᾽ ὄχεσφιν ἐΰθρονον Ἠῶ μίμνον.   ἑστῶτες, ὄχεσιν,
                                                  ἔμιμνον

3 The beginning of the Odyssey

ἄνδρα μοι ἔννεπε, Μοῦσα, πολύτροπον, ὃς μάλα πολλὰ
πλάγχθη, ἐπεὶ Τροίης ἱερὸν πτολίεθρον ἔπερσε·   ἐπλάγχθη, -ᾶς
πολλῶν δ᾽ ἀνθρώπων ἴδεν ἄστεα καὶ νόον ἔγνω,   εἶδεν, ἄστη, νοῦν
πολλὰ δ᾽ ὅ γ᾽ ἐν πόντῳ πάθεν ἄλγεα ὃν κατὰ θυμόν, ἔπαθεν, ἄλγη
ἀρνύμενος ἥν τε ψυχὴν καὶ νόστον ἑταίρων.   5
ἀλλ᾽ οὐδ᾽ ὣς ἑτάρους ἐρρύσατο, ἱέμενός περ·   καίπερ
αὐτῶν γὰρ σφετέρῃσιν ἀτασθαλίῃσιν ὄλοντο,   -αις, -αις, ὤλοντο
νήπιοι, οἳ κατὰ βοῦς Ὑπερίονος Ἠελίοιο   Ἡλίου
ἤσθιον· αὐτὰρ ὁ τοῖσιν ἀφείλετο νόστιμον ἦμαρ.

4 The Lotus-eaters

ἔνθεν δ᾽ ἐννῆμαρ φερόμην ὀλοοῖς ἀνέμοισι   ἐφερόμην
πόντον ἐπ᾽ ἰχθυόεντα· ἀτὰρ δεκάτῃ ἐπέβημεν
γαίης Λωτοφάγων, οἵ τ᾽ ἄνθινον εἶδαρ ἔδουσιν.   γῆς
ἔνθα δ᾽ ἐπ᾽ ἠπείρου βῆμεν καὶ ἀφυσσάμεθ᾽ ὕδωρ,   ἔβημεν, ἠφυσάμεθα
αἶψα δὲ δεῖπνον ἕλοντο θοῆς παρὰ νηυσὶν ἑταῖροι. 5 εἵλοντο, -αις,
                                                  ναυσίν
αὐτὰρ ἐπεὶ σίτοιό τ᾽ ἐπασσάμεθ᾽ ἠδὲ ποτῆτος,   -ου, ἐπασάμεθα
δὴ τότ᾽ ἐγὼν ἑτάρους προΐειν πεύθεσθαι ἰόντας
οἵτινες ἀνέρες εἶεν ἐπὶ χθονὶ σῖτον ἔδοντες,   ἄνδρες
ἄνδρε δύω κρίνας, τρίτατον κήρυχ᾽ ἅμ᾽ ὀπάσσας.   ὀπάσας
οἱ δ᾽ αἶψ᾽ οἰχόμενοι μίγεν ἀνδράσι Λωτοφάγοισιν· 10 ἐμίγησαν
οὐδ᾽ ἄρα Λωτοφάγοι μήδονθ᾽ ἑτάροισιν ὄλεθρον   ἐμήδοντο
ἡμετέροις, ἀλλά σφι δόσαν λωτοῖο πάσασθαι.   ἔδοσαν, -οῦ
τῶν δ᾽ ὅστις λωτοῖο φάγοι μελιηδέα καρπόν,   -οῦ, μελιηδῆ
οὐκέτ᾽ ἀπαγγεῖλαι πάλιν ἤθελεν οὐδὲ νέεσθαι,   νεῖσθαι
ἀλλ᾽ αὐτοῦ βούλοντο μετ᾽ ἀνδράσι Λωτοφάγοισι   15 ἐβούλοντο
λωτὸν ἐρεπτόμενοι μενέμεν νόστου τε λαθέσθαι.   μένειν

τοὺς μὲν ἐγὼν ἐπὶ νῆας <u>ἄγον</u> κλαίοντας ἀνάγκῃ,   ἦγον
<u>νηυσὶ</u> δ' ἐνὶ γλαφυρῇσιν ὑπὸ ζυγὰ <u>δῆσα</u> <u>ἐρύσσας</u>.   ναυσί, -αῖς,
                                         ἔδησα, ἐρύσας
αὐτὰρ τοὺς ἄλλους <u>κελόμην</u> ἐρίηρας ἑταίρους   ἐκελόμην
σπερχομένους <u>νηῶν</u> <u>ἐπιβαινέμεν</u> ὠκειάων,   20   νεῶν, -βαίνειν, -ῶν
μή πώς τις λωτοῖο φαγὼν <u>νόστοιο</u> λάθηται.   -οῦ, -ου
οἱ δ' αἶψ' <u>εἴσβαινον</u> καὶ ἐπὶ κληῖσι καθῖζον,   εἰσέβαινον
ἑξῆς δ' ἑζόμενοι <u>πολιὴν</u> ἅλα <u>τύπτον</u> ἐρετμοῖς.   πολιάν, ἔτυπτον

Notes

1 *l*.1 τήν = αὐτήν (25.1/3*a*). *l*.2 ἦ *indeed*; τάδε is the subject of μέλει.
l.4 αἴ κε = ἐάν (ἀλυσκάζω is subj.); κακὸς ὥς *like a coward* (ὡς
is accented when it follows the word it qualifies); take νόσφιν
with πολέμοιο. *l*.5 με ... ἄνωγεν *orders me [to do this]*. *l*.7 The
genitives are to be translated *for*; ἐμὸν αὐτοῦ = ἐμοῦ αὐτοῦ, lit.
of me myself. *l*.9 ὅτ'(ε) *when*; translate ἄν ... ὀλώλῃ (strong perf.
subj. of ὄλλῡμι) as a future (25.1/3*b*). *l*.11 τόσσον (= normal Attic
τοσοῦτο) agrees with ἄλγος (which is the subject of μέλει) and
is balanced by ὅσσον in *l*.15 (21.1/3*e*). *l*.12. Ἑκάβης, Πριάμοιο
(together with κασιγνήτων (*l*.13) and σεῦ (*l*.15)) are objective
genitives (23.1/1*c*) with ἄλγος (*l*.11), *grief for* ... *ll*.13f. κεν ...
πέσοιεν fut. potential (19.1/2) but trans. *may fall*; ὑπ'(ό) + dat.
(= gen. in Attic) *by, at the hands of*. *ll*.15f. κεν ... ἄγηται lit. *will
lead for himself* (25.1/3*b*; ἐλεύθερον ἦμαρ lit. *free day* a regular
Homeric expression for *freedom*, trans. *day of liberty* (similiar
expressions occur in *l*.24 below and in 3 *l*.9). *ll*.17f. The two
examples of κε + opt. are potential (Hector is stating something
that may possibly happen), but are better translated *will weave ...
and carry* (25.1/3*b*); πρός *at the command of*; Μεσσηΐδος ἤ
Ὑπερείης gen. of separation (20.1/4) *from M. or H*. *l*.19 πόλλ'
(i.e. πολλά) adverbial acc. (20.1/5) *much*; ἐπικείσετ'(αι). *l*.20
εἴπῃσι (subj., 25.1/2*c*(i)) *will say* (25.1/3*b*); κατὰ δάκρυ χέουσαν
= καταχέουσαν δάκρυ (tmesis, 12.3.9 *l*.6 note). *l*.22f. Take Τρώων
ἱπποδάμων with ἀριστεύεσκε (= ἠρίστευε) *was best of the* etc. *l*.23
ὥς (= οὕτως) *thus*. *l*.24 χήτεϊ (= χήτει) + gen. *because of the lack*
(dat. of cause 23.1/2*i*); δούλιον ἦμαρ cf. ἐλεύθερον ἦμαρ (*l*.16).
l.25 κατὰ ... καλύπτοι tmesis as in *l*.20—the opt. expresses a wish
for the future (21.1/1).

2 *l.*1 *The embankments of war* apparently means the places where battles were normally fought. *l.*2 παννύχιοι is an adj. (*staying all night*) but trans. *all night long*; σφισι (= αὐτοῖς) is not here reflexive. *l.*3 ὡς ... ὅτ'(ε) *as when* introduces a simile. *ll.*4f. φαίνετ'(αι); aorists such as ἔπλετο and ἔφανεν are often interspersed among presents in Homeric similes and should be translated by the present; ἔκ ... ἔφανεν tmesis (see on 1 *l.*20 above). *l.*6 ὑπερράγη root aor. of ὑπορρήγνῡμι. *l.*7 τε is often used to mark similes and has no connective force; φρένα acc. of respect (20.1/5). *l.*8 τόσσα agrees with πυρά (*l.*9) and brings out the point of the simile. *l.*9 Τρώων καιόντων gen. abs. (12.1/2*b*); Ἰλιόθι πρό = πρὸ Ἰλίου (the suffix -θι, which denotes *place from which*, is used as the equivalent of the genitive ending). *l.*11 σέλα = σέλαι dat. s. of σέλας (cf. 13.1/1*b*(iii)). *l.*14 The ending of ὄχεσφιν (< ὄχος) is peculiar to Homer and is generally the equivalent of the dat. pl., as here.

3 *l.*1 πολλά *much* (20.1/5). *l.*2 πλάγχθη 3rd s. aor. ind. (without augment) of πλάζομαι. *l.*4 ὅ γ'(ε) *he* (25.1/3*a*; γε is often added to ὁ in this use and is not to be translated); ὅν **not** the relative but a 3rd person reflexive possessive adjective, ὅς, ἥ, ὅν (*his, her, its*), which did not survive in Attic—take with θῡμόν. *his own heart* but trans. simply by *his heart* (but ἥν ... ψῡχήν (*l.*5) *his own life* because of the contrast with νόστον ἑταίρων). *l.*5 ἀρνύμενος *trying to win.* *l.*6 ὥς *so, thus* (cf. 1 *l.*23 above); ἱέμενός (< ἵημι) περ lit. *although striving.* *l.*7 αὐτῶν ... σφετέρῃσιν *their own* (αὐτῶν lit. *of them* is added for particular emphasis); ἀτασθαλίῃσιν plural for singular. *ll.*8f. νήπιοι *fools* in apposition to the subject of ὄλοντο (*l.*7); κατὰ ... ἤσθιον tmesis; ὁ *he*, i.e. Helios; τοῖσιν (= αὐτοῖς) *from them*, dat. of disadvantage (23.1/2*d*).

4 *l.*2 δεκάτῃ sc. ἡμέρᾳ. *l.*3 οἵ τ'(ε) *who*, **not** *and who*—in Homer τε is added to the relative when the antecedent is a class (here the Lotus-eaters). *l.*5 ἕλοντο lit. *took for themselves* (the mid. of αἱρέω does not here have the meaning *choose*). *l.*6 ἐπασσάμεθ'(α) < πατέομαι. *l.*7 δή here not postpositive as in Attic; προΐειν 1st s. impf. ind. act. of προΐημι; ἰόντας (<εἶμι) here fut. pple. (18.1/3) to express purpose (12.1/2*a*(v)). *l.*8 οἵτινες indirect interrogative (10.1/2*b* note 1); εἶεν opt. in historic sequence (14.1/4*d*). *l.*9 ἄνδρε acc. dual, 24.1/4; τρίτατον κήρυχ' ἄμ' (= κήρυκα ἄμα) lit. *a third together* (i.e. *with them*) [as] *herald*. *l*.12 σφι = αὐτοῖς; λωτοῖο partitive gen. (23.1/1*d*) with δόσαν, lit. *gave of lotus*, i.e. *gave some lotus* (cf. λωτοῖο φαγών *eating some lotus l*.21 below). *l*.13 τῶν = αὐτῶν; ὅστις ... φάγοι indefinite adj. clause (14.1/4*c*(iii)), *whoever ate*. *l*.15 αὐτοῦ (adv.) *there*. *l*.17 ἄγον ... ἀνάγκῃ *I brought by force* (the impf. here and in the following lines is used for vividness and should be translated by a simple past). *l*.21 μή πώς τις ... *lest somehow* (πως) *anyone* ...

Insight

Homer was always regarded as the greatest of poets but no reliable information about him survived from the period in which he lived. For Greeks of the fifth century BC and later he was a figure from the dim past. One of the Homeric hymns speaks of him as τυφλὸς ἀνήρ, οἰκεῖ δὲ Χίῳ ἔνι παιπαλοέσσῃ *a blind man and he dwells on rugged Chios*. His blindness was the only personal detail preserved by tradition, if, in fact, that was true. Many cities claimed him as a native. An epigram tells us:

Ἑπτὰ πόλεις διερίζουσιν περὶ ῥίζαν Ὁμήρου
Σμύρνα, Ῥόδος, Κολοφών, Σαλαμίς, Ἴος, Ἄργος, Ἀθῆναι.

Seven cities dispute over the origin of Homer: Smyrna, Rhodes, Colophon, Salamis, Ios, Argos, Athens.

There are other lists with different, and sometimes more, names.

Since the nineteenth century many scholars have thought that the Iliad and Odyssey were not written by a single person but were the result of a long tradition of oral poetry handed down from one generation of poets to another. Other scholars have questioned whether such a process could have produced works of such excellence.

For suggestions for further study see the Internet website http://ancientgreek.org

Appendices

Appendix 1: Conjugation of λύω loosen

ACTIVE

		Present	Imperfect	Future	Aorist	Perfect	Pluperfect
		Indicative					
s.	1	λύ-ω	ἔλῡ-ον	λύσ-ω	ἔλῡσ-α	λέλυκ-α	ἐλελύκ-η
		I loosen, etc.	I was loosening, etc.	I will loosen	I loosened	I have loosened	I had loosened
	2	λύ-εις	ἔλῡ-ες	λύσ-εις	ἔλῡσ-ας	λέλυκ-ας	ἐλελύκ-ης
	3	λύ-ει	ἔλῡ-ε(ν)	λύσ-ει	ἔλῡσ-ε(ν)	λέλυκ-ε(ν)	ἐλελύκ-ει(ν)
pl.	1	λύ-ομεν	ἐλύ-ομεν	λύσ-ομεν	ἐλύσ-αμεν	λελύκ-αμεν	ἐλελύκ-εμεν
	2	λύ-ετε	ἐλύ-ετε	λύσ-ετε	ἐλύσ-ατε	λελύκ-ατε	ἐλελύκ-ετε
	3	λύ-ουσι(ν)	ἔλῡ-ον	λύσ-ουσι(ν)	ἔλῡσ-αν	λελύκ-ᾱσι(ν)	ἐλελύκ-εσαν
		Subjunctive					
s.	1	λύ-ω			λύσ-ω	λελύκ-ω[1]	
	2	λύ-ῃς			λύσ-ῃς	λελύκ-ῃς	
	3	λύ-ῃ			λύσ-ῃ	λελύκ-ῃ	
pl.	1	λύ-ωμεν			λύσ-ωμεν	λελύκ-ωμεν	
	2	λύ-ητε			λύσ-ητε	λελύκ-ητε	
	3	λύ-ωσι(ν)			λύσ-ωσι(ν)	λελύκ-ωσι(ν)	
		Optative					
s.	1	λύ-οιμι		λύσ-οιμι	λύσ-αιμι	λελύκ-οιμι[1]	
	2	λύ-οις		λύσ-οις	λύσ-ειας (λύσ-αις)	λελύκ-οις	
	3	λύ-οι		λύσ-οι	λύσ-ειε(ν) (λύσ-αι)	λελύκ-οι	
pl.	1	λύ-οιμεν		λύσ-οιμεν	λύσ-αιμεν	λελύκ-οιμεν	
	2	λύ-οιτε		λύσ-οιτε	λύσ-αιτε	λελύκ-οιτε	
	3	λύ-οιεν		λύσ-οιεν	λύσ-ειαν (λύσ-αιεν)	λελύκ-οιεν	
		Imperative					
s.	2	λῦ-ε			λῦσ-ον	λελυκὼς ἴσθι	
	3	λῡ-έτω			λῡσ-άτω	λελυκὼς ἔστω	
pl.	2	λύ-ετε			λύσ-ατε	λελυκότες ἔστε	
	3	λῡ-όντων			λῡσ-άντων	λελυκότες ὄντων	
		Infinitive					
		λύ-ειν		λύσ-ειν	λῦσ-αι	λελυκ-έναι	
		Participle					
		λύ-ων		λύσ-ων	λύσ-ᾱς	λελυκ-ώς	
		λύ-ουσα		λύσ-ουσα	λύσ-ᾱσα	λελυκ-υῖα	
		λῦ-ον		λῦσ-ον	λῦσ-αν	λελυκ-ός	

---

[1]See also 16.1/4 note 1.

		Present	Imperfect	Future	Aorist	Perfect	Pluperfect
		Indicative					
s.	1	λύ-ομαι	ἐλῡ-όμην	λύσ-ομαι	ἐλῡσ-άμην	λέλυ-μαι	ἐλελύ-μην
	2	λύ-η (-ει)	ἐλύ-ου	λύσ-η (-ει)	ἐλύσ-ω	λέλυ-σαι	ἐλέλυ-σο
	3	λύ-εται	ἐλύ-ετο	λύσ-εται	ἐλύσ-ατο	λέλυ-ται	ἐλέλυ-το
pl.	1	λῡ-όμεθα	ἐλῡ-όμεθα	λῡσ-όμεθα	ἐλῡσ-άμεθα	λελύ-μεθα	ἐλελύ-μεθα
	2	λύ-εσθε	ἐλύ-εσθε	λύσ-εσθε	ἐλύσ-ασθε	λέλυ-σθε	ἐλέλυ-σθε
	3	λύ-ονται	ἐλύ-οντο	λύσ-ονται	ἐλύσ-αντο	λέλυ-νται	ἐλέλυ-ντο
		Subjunctive					
s.	1	λύ-ωμαι			λύσ-ωμαι	λελυμένος ὦ	
	2	λύ-η			λύσ-η	λελυμένος ἦς	
	3	λύ-ηται			λύσ-ηται	λελυμένος ἦ	
pl.	1	λῡ-ώμεθα			λῡσ-ώμεθα	λελυμένοι ὦμεν	
	2	λύ-ησθε			λύσ-ησθε	λελυμένοι ἦτε	
	3	λύ-ωνται			λύσ-ωνται	λελυμένοι ὦσι(ν)	
		Optative					
s.	1	λῡ-οίμην		λῡσ-οίμην	λῡσ-αίμην	λελυμένος εἴην	
	2	λύ-οιο		λύσ-οιο	λύσ-αιο	λελυμένος εἴης	
	3	λύ-οιτο		λύσ-οιτο	λύσ-αιτο	λελυμένος εἴη	
pl.	1	λῡ-οίμεθα		λῡσ-οίμεθα	λῡσ-αίμεθα	λελυμένοι εἶμεν	
	2	λύ-οισθε		λύσ-οισθε	λύσ-αισθε	λελυμένοι εἶτε	
	3	λύ-οιντο		λύσ-οιντο	λύσ-αιντο	λελυμένοι εἶεν	
		Imperative					
s.	2	λύ-ου			λῦσ-αι	λέλυ-σο	
	3	λῡ-έσθω			λῡσ-άσθω	λελύ-σθω	
pl.	2	λύ-εσθε			λύσ-ασθε	λέλυ-σθε	
	3	λῡ-έσθων			λῡσ-άσθων	λελύ-σθων	
		Infinitive					
		λύ-εσθαι		λύσ-εσθαι	λύσ-ασθαι	λελύ-σθαι	
		Participle					
		λῡ-όμενος,		λῡσ-όμενος,	λῡσ-άμενος,	λελυ-μένος,	
		-ομένη,		-ομένη,	-αμένη,	-μένη,	
		-όμενον		-όμενον	-άμενον	-μένον	

Note

In all forms of the perfect which are made up of a perfect participle and εἰμί the participle must agree with the subject of the verb in number and gender.

PASSIVE

The forms for the present, imperfect, perfect and pluperfect are the same as for the middle; for the future perfect passive see 16.1/4 note 2.

Future

		Indicative	Optative		
s.	1	λυθήσ-ομαι	λυθησ-οίμην		
	2	λυθήσ-ῃ (-ει)	λυθήσ-οιο	**Infinitive**	λυθήσ-εσθαι
	3	λυθήσ-εται	λυθήσ-οιτο	**Participle**	λυθησ-όμενος,
pl.	1	λυθησ-όμεθα	λυθησ-οίμεθα		-ομένη,
	2	λυθήσ-εσθε	λυθήσ-οισθε		-όμενον
	3	λυθήσ-ονται	λυθήσ-οιντο		

Aorist

		Indicative	Subjunctive	Optative	Imperative
s.	1	ἐλύθη-ν	λυθ-ῶ	λυθ-είην	
	2	ἐλύθη-ς	λυθ-ῇς	λυθ-είης	λύθη-τι
	3	ἐλύθη	λυθ-ῇ	λυθ-είη	λυθή-τω
pl.	1	ἐλύθη-μεν	λυθ-ῶμεν	λυθ-εῖμεν	
	2	ἐλύθη-τε	λυθ-ῆτε	λυθ-εῖτε	λύθη-τε
	3	ἐλύθη-σαν	λυθ-ῶσι(ν)	λυθ-εῖεν	λυθέ-ντων

Infinitive λυθῆ-ναι   **Participle** λυθ-είς, λυθ-εῖσα, λυθ-έν

Appendix 2: Conjugation of contracted verbs (present and imperfect)

τῑμάω *honour*

		ACTIVE		MIDDLE/PASSIVE	
		Present	Imperfect	Present	Imperfect
Indicative					
s.	1	τῑμῶ	ἐτίμων	τῑμῶμαι	ἐτῑμώμην
	2	τῑμᾷς	ἐτίμᾱς	τῑμᾷ	ἐτῑμῶ
	3	τῑμᾷ	ἐτίμᾱ	τῑμᾶται	ἐτῑμᾶτο
pl.	1	τῑμῶμεν	ἐτῑμῶμεν	τῑμώμεθα	ἐτῑμώμεθα
	2	τῑμᾶτε	ἐτῑμᾶτε	τῑμᾶσθε	ἐτῑμᾶσθε
	3	τῑμῶσι(ν)	ἐτίμων	τῑμῶνται	ἐτῑμῶντο
Subjunctive					
s.	1	τῑμῶ		τῑμῶμαι	
	2	τῑμᾷς		τῑμᾷ	
	3	τῑμᾷ		τῑμᾶται	
pl.	1	τῑμῶμεν		τῑμώμεθα	
	2	τῑμᾶτε		τῑμᾶσθε	
	3	τῑμῶσι(ν)		τῑμῶνται	
Optative					
s.	1	τῑμῴην		τῑμῴμην	
	2	τῑμῴης		τῑμῷο	
	3	τῑμῴη		τῑμῷτο	
pl.	1	τῑμῷμεν		τῑμῴμεθα	
	2	τῑμῷτε		τῑμῷσθε	
	3	τῑμῷεν		τῑμῷντο	
Imperative					
s.	2	τίμᾱ		τῑμῶ	
	3	τῑμάτω		τῑμάσθω	
pl.	2	τῑμᾶτε		τῑμᾶσθε	
	3	τῑμώντων		τῑμάσθων	
Infinitive					
		τῑμᾶν		τῑμᾶσθαι	
Participle					
		τῑμῶν, τῑμῶσα, τῑμῶν		τῑμώμεν-ος, -η, -ον	

ποιέω *make, do*

		ACTIVE		MIDDLE/PASSIVE	
		Present	Imperfect	Present	Imperfect
Indicative					
s.	1	ποιῶ	ἐποίουν	ποιοῦμαι	ἐποιούμην
	2	ποιεῖς	ἐποίεις	ποιῇ (-εῖ)	ἐποιοῦ
	3	ποιεῖ	ἐποίει	ποιεῖται	ἐποιεῖτο
pl.	1	ποιοῦμεν	ἐποιοῦμεν	ποιούμεθα	ἐποιούμεθα
	2	ποιεῖτε	ἐποιεῖτε	ποιεῖσθε	ἐποιεῖσθε
	3	ποιοῦσι(ν)	ἐποίουν	ποιοῦνται	ἐποιοῦντο
Subjunctive					
s.	1	ποιῶ		ποιῶμαι	
	2	ποιῇς		ποιῇ	
	3	ποιῇ		ποιῆται	
pl.	1	ποιῶμεν		ποιώμεθα	
	2	ποιῆτε		ποιῆσθε	
	3	ποιῶσι(ν)		ποιῶνται	
Optative					
s.	1	ποιοίην		ποιοίμην	
	2	ποιοίης		ποιοῖο	
	3	ποιοίη		ποιοῖτο	
pl.	1	ποιοῖμεν		ποιοίμεθα	
	2	ποιοῖτε		ποιοῖσθε	
	3	ποιοῖεν		ποιοῖντο	
Imperative					
s.	2	ποίει		ποιοῦ	
	3	ποιείτω		ποιείσθω	
pl.	2	ποιεῖτε		ποιεῖσθε	
	3	ποιούντων		ποιείσθων	
Infinitive					
		ποιεῖν		ποιεῖσθαι	
Participle					
		ποιῶν, ποιοῦσα, ποιοῦν		ποιούμεν-ος, -η, -ον	

δηλόω *make clear, show*

		ACTIVE		MIDDLE/PASSIVE	
		Present	Imperfect	Present	Imperfect
		Indicative			
s.	1	δηλῶ	ἐδήλουν	δηλοῦμαι	ἐδηλούμην
	2	δηλοῖς	ἐδήλους	δηλοῖ	ἐδηλοῦ
	3	δηλοῖ	ἐδήλου	δηλοῦται	ἐδηλοῦτο
pl.	1	δηλοῦμεν	ἐδηλοῦμεν	δηλούμεθα	ἐδηλούμεθα
	2	δηλοῦτε	ἐδηλοῦτε	δηλοῦσθε	ἐδηλοῦσθε
	3	δηλοῦσι(ν)	ἐδήλουν	δηλοῦνται	ἐδηλοῦντο
		Subjunctive			
s.	1	δηλῶ		δηλῶμαι	
	2	δηλοῖς		δηλοῖ	
	3	δηλοῖ		δηλῶται	
pl.	1	δηλῶμεν		δηλώμεθα	
	2	δηλῶτε		δηλῶσθε	
	3	δηλῶσι(ν)		δηλῶνται	
		Optative			
s.	1	δηλοίην		δηλοίμην	
	2	δηλοίης		δηλοῖο	
	3	δηλοίη		δηλοῖτο	
pl.	1	δηλοῖμεν		δηλοίμεθα	
	2	δηλοῖτε		δηλοῖσθε	
	3	δηλοῖεν		δηλοῖντο	
		Imperative			
s.	2	δήλου		δηλοῦ	
	3	δηλούτω		δηλούσθω	
pl.	2	δηλοῦτε		δηλοῦσθε	
	3	δηλούντων		δηλούσθων	
		Infinitive			
		δηλοῦν		δηλοῦσθαι	
		Participle			
		δηλῶν, δηλοῦσα, δηλοῦν		δηλούμεν-ος, -η, -ον	

Appendix 3: Conjugation of εἰμί be, ἔρχομαι (and εἶμι) come/go, φημί say, οἶδα know

(The last is perfect in form but present in meaning; it has been classified below according to its meaning.)

		εἰμί be	ἔρχομαι come/go (18.1/3)	φημί say	οἶδα know (19.1/3a)
Present indicative					
s.	1	εἰμί	ἔρχομαι	φημί	οἶδα
	2	εἶ	ἔρχῃ (-ει)	φῄς	οἶσθα
	3	ἐστί(ν)	ἔρχεται	φησί(ν)	οἶδε(ν)
pl.	1	ἐσμέν	ἐρχόμεθα	φαμέν	ἴσμεν
	2	ἐστέ	ἔρχεσθε	φατέ	ἴστε
	3	εἰσί(ν)	ἔρχονται	φασί(ν)	ἴσᾱσι(ν)
Present subjunctive					
s.	1	ὦ	ἴω	φῶ	εἰδῶ
	2	ᾖς	ἴῃς	φῇς	εἰδῇς
	3	ᾖ	ἴῃ	φῇ	εἰδῇ
pl.	1	ὦμεν	ἴωμεν	φῶμεν	εἰδῶμεν
	2	ἦτε	ἴητε	φῆτε	εἰδῆτε
	3	ὦσι(ν)	ἴωσι(ν)	φῶσι(ν)	εἰδῶσι(ν)
Present optative					
s.	1	εἴην	ἴοιμι	φαίην	εἰδείην
	2	εἴης	ἴοις	φαίης	εἰδείης
	3	εἴη	ἴοι	φαίη	εἰδείη
pl.	1	εἶμεν	ἴοιμεν	φαῖμεν	εἰδεῖμεν
	2	εἶτε	ἴοιτε	φαῖτε	εἰδεῖτε
	3	εἶεν	ἴοιεν	φαῖεν	εἰδεῖεν
Present imperative					
s.	2	ἴσθι	ἴθι	φαθί	ἴσθι
	3	ἔστω	ἴτω	φάτω	ἴστω
pl.	2	ἔστε	ἴτε	φάτε	ἴστε
	3	ἔστων or ὄντων	ἰόντων	φάντων	ἴστων
Present infinitive					
		εἶναι	ἰέναι	φάναι	εἰδέναι
Present participle					
		ὤν, οὖσα, ὄν	ἰών, ἰοῦσα, ἰόν	# φάς, φᾶσα, φάν	εἰδώς, εἰδυῖα, εἰδός

Imperfect indicative

s.					
	1	ἦ *or* ἦν	ἦα	ἔφην	ᾔδη
	2	ἦσθα	ᾔεισθα	ἔφησθα *or* ἔφης	ᾔδησθα
	3	ἦν	ᾔει(ν)	ἔφη	ᾔδει(ν)
pl.	1	ἦμεν	ᾖμεν	ἔφαμεν	ᾖσμεν
	2	ἦτε	ᾖτε	ἔφατε	ᾖστε
	3	ἦσαν	ᾖσαν *or* ᾖσαν	ἔφασαν	ᾔδεσαν *or* ᾖσαν

Future indicative

s.					
	1	ἔσομαι	εἶμι	φήσω	εἴσομαι
	2	ἔσῃ (-ει)	εἶ	φήσεις	εἴσῃ (-ει)
	3	ἔσται	εἶσι(ν)	φήσει	εἴσεται
pl.	1	ἐσόμεθα	ἴμεν	φήσομεν	εἰσόμεθα
	2	ἔσεσθε	ἴτε	φήσετε	εἴσεσθε
	3	ἔσονται	ἴᾱσι(ν)	φήσουσι(ν)	εἴσονται

The other parts of the future are regular. εἰμί, φημί and οἶδα do not exist in other tenses. For the other parts of ἔρχομαι see **Principal part of verbs.** The optative, infinitive and participle of εἶμι may also have a future meaning (18.1/3).

Appendix 4: Root aorists (11.1/1)

ἔβην (βαίνω) and ἔγνων (γιγνώσκω) are conjugated:

		Ind.	Subj.	Opt.	Imp.	
s.	1	ἔβην	βῶ	βαίην		
	2	ἔβης	βῇς	βαίης	βῆθι	Infinitive βῆναι
	3	ἔβη	βῇ	βαίη	βήτω	
pl.	1	ἔβημεν	βῶμεν	βαῖμεν		
	2	ἔβητε	βῆτε	βαῖτε	βῆτε	Participle βάς, βᾶσα, βάν
	3	ἔβησαν	βῶσι(ν)	βαῖεν	βάντων	

s.	1	ἔγνων	γνῶ	γνοίην		
	2	ἔγνως	γνῷς	γνοίης	γνῶθι	Infinitive γνῶναι
	3	ἔγνω	γνῷ	γνοίη	γνώτω	
pl.	1	ἔγνωμεν	γνῶμεν	γνοῖμεν		
	2	ἔγνωτε	γνῶτε	γνοῖτε	γνῶτε	Participle γνούς,
	3	ἔγνωσαν	γνῶσι(ν)	γνοῖεν	γνόντων	γνοῦσα, γνόν

Appendix 5: Conjugation of δίδωμι give, τίθημι put, place, ἵημι let go, send forth, ἵστημι make stand

(For full details of which tenses of ἵστημι are transitive and which are intransitive see 19.1/1.) Many of the forms of ἵημι occur only in compounds.

		δίδωμι	τίθημι	ἵημι	ἵστημι
			ACTIVE		

Present indicative

s.	1	δίδωμι	τίθημι	ἵημι	ἵστημι
	2	δίδως	τίθης	ἵης	ἵστης
	3	δίδωσι(ν)	τίθησι(ν)	ἵησι(ν)	ἵστησι(ν)
pl.	1	δίδομεν	τίθεμεν	ἵεμεν	ἵσταμεν
	2	δίδοτε	τίθετε	ἵετε	ἵστατε
	3	διδόᾱσι(ν)	τιθέᾱσι(ν)	ἱᾶσι(ν)	ἱστᾶσι(ν)

Present subjunctive

s.	1	διδῶ	τιθῶ	ἱῶ	ἱστῶ
	2	διδῷς	τιθῇς	ἱῇς	ἱστῇς
	3	διδῷ	τιθῇ	ἱῇ	ἱστῇ
pl.	1	διδῶμεν	τιθῶμεν	ἱῶμεν	ἱστῶμεν
	2	διδῶτε	τιθῆτε	ἱῆτε	ἱστῆτε
	3	διδῶσι(ν)	τιθῶσι(ν)	ἱῶσι(ν)	ἱστῶσι(ν)

Present optative

s.	1	διδοίην	τιθείην	ἱείην	ἱσταίην
	2	διδοίης	τιθείης	ἱείης	ἱσταίης
	3	διδοίη	τιθείη	ἱείη	ἱσταίη
pl.	1	διδοῖμεν	τιθεῖμεν	ἱεῖμεν	ἱσταῖμεν
	2	διδοῖτε	τιθεῖτε	ἱεῖτε	ἱσταῖτε
	3	διδοῖεν	τιθεῖεν	ἱεῖεν	ἱσταῖεν

Present imperative

s.	2	δίδου	τίθει	ἵει	ἵστη
	3	διδότω	τιθέτω	ἱέτω	ἱστάτω
pl.	2	δίδοτε	τίθετε	ἵετε	ἵστατε
	3	διδόντων	τιθέντων	ἱέντων	ἱστάντων

Present infinitive

		διδόναι	τιθέναι	ἱέναι	ἱστάναι

Present participle

		διδούς	τιθείς	ἱείς	ἱστάς
		διδοῦσα	τιθεῖσα	ἱεῖσα	ἱστᾶσα
		διδόν	τιθέν	ἱέν	ἱστάν

Imperfect indicative

s.	1	ἐδίδουν	ἐτίθην	ἵην	ἵστην
	2	ἐδίδους	ἐτίθεις	ἵεις	ἵστης
	3	ἐδίδου	ἐτίθει	ἵει	ἵστη
pl.	1	ἐδίδομεν	ἐτίθεμεν	ἵεμεν	ἵσταμεν
	2	ἐδίδοτε	ἐτίθετε	ἵετε	ἵστατε
	3	ἐδίδοσαν	ἐτίθεσαν	ἵεσαν	ἵστασαν

Future indicative

s.	1	δώσω etc.	θήσω etc.	ἥσω etc.	στήσω etc.

The other parts of the future active are formed regularly with the same stems (δωσ-, θησ-, ἡσ-, στησ-).

Aorist indicative

					Transitive	*Intransitive*
s.	1	ἔδωκα	ἔθηκα	ἧκα	ἔστησα	ἔστην
	2	ἔδωκας	ἔθηκας	ἧκας	ἔστησας	ἔστης
	3	ἔδωκε(ν)	ἔθηκε(ν)	ἧκε(ν)	ἔστησε(ν)	ἔστη
pl.	1	ἔδομεν	ἔθεμεν	εἷμεν	ἐστήσαμεν	ἔστημεν
	2	ἔδοτε	ἔθετε	εἷτε	ἐστήσατε	ἔστητε
	3	ἔδοσαν	ἔθεσαν	εἷσαν	ἔστησαν	ἔστησαν

On the alternative forms for the plural of ἔδωκα and ἔθηκα see 18.1/2 note 3.

Aorist subjunctive

s.	1	δῶ	θῶ	ὧ	στήσω	στῶ
	2	δῷς	θῇς	ἧς	στήσῃς	στῇς
	3	δῷ	θῇ	ᾗ	στήσῃ	στῇ
pl.	1	δῶμεν	θῶμεν	ὧμεν	στήσωμεν	στῶμεν
	2	δῶτε	θῆτε	ἧτε	στήσητε	στῆτε
	3	δῶσι(ν)	θῶσι(ν)	ὧσι(ν)	στήσωσι(ν)	στῶσι(ν)

Aorist optative

s.	1	δοίην	θείην	εἵην	στήσαιμι	σταίην
	2	δοίης	θείης	εἵης	στήσειας (-αις)	σταίης
	3	δοίη	θείη	εἵη	στήσειε(ν) (-αι)	σταίη
pl.	1	δοῖμεν	θεῖμεν	εἷμεν	στήσαιμεν	σταῖμεν
	2	δοῖτε	θεῖτε	εἷτε	στήσαιτε	σταῖτε
	3	δοῖεν	θεῖεν	εἷεν	στήσειαν (-αιεν)	σταῖεν

Aorist imperative

s.	2	δός	θές	ἕς	στῆσον	στῆθι
	3	δότω	θέτω	ἕτω	στησάτω	στήτω
pl.	2	δότε	θέτε	ἕτε	στήσατε	στῆτε
	3	δόντων	θέντων	ἕντων	στησάντων	στάντων

Aorist infinitive

	δοῦναι	θεῖναι	εἷναι	στῆσαι	στῆναι

Aorist participle

	δούς	θείς	εἵς	στήσᾶς	στάς
	δοῦσα	θεῖσα	εἷσα	στήσᾶσα	στᾶσα
	δόν	θέν	ἕν	στῆσαν	στάν

Perfect and pluperfect

The perfect and pluperfect active of δίδωμι, τίθημι, ἵημι are formed regularly from the stems δεδωκ-, τεθηκ-, εἱκ-.

The perfect and pluperfect active of ἵστημι (which are intransitive – see 19.1/1) are conjugated as follows:

Perfect

		Indicative	Subjunctive	Optative	Imperative
s.	1	ἕστηκα	ἑστῶ	ἑσταίην	
	2	ἕστηκας	ἑστῇς	ἑσταίης	ἕσταθι
	3	ἕστηκε(ν)	ἑστῇ	ἑσταίη	ἑστάτω
pl.	1	ἕσταμεν	ἑστῶμεν	ἑσταῖμεν	
	2	ἕστατε	ἑστῆτε	ἑσταῖτε	ἕστατε
	3	ἑστᾶσι(ν)	ἑστῶσι(ν)	ἑσταῖεν	ἑστάντων

Infinitive ἑστάναι Participle ἑστώς, ἑστῶσα, ἑστός
On alternative forms in ἑστηκ- see 19.1/1

Pluperfect s. εἱστήκη (I stood), εἱστήκης, εἱστήκει, pl. ἕσταμεν, ἕστατε, ἕστασαν.

MIDDLE

Present indicative

s.	1	δίδομαι	τίθεμαι	ἵεμαι	ἵσταμαι
	2	δίδοσαι	τίθεσαι	ἵεσαι	ἵστασαι
	3	δίδοται	τίθεται	ἵεται	ἵσταται
pl.	1	διδόμεθα	τιθέμεθα	ἱέμεθα	ἱστάμεθα
	2	δίδοσθε	τίθεσθε	ἵεσθε	ἵστασθε
	3	δίδονται	τίθενται	ἵενται	ἵστανται

Present subjunctive

s.	1	διδῶμαι	τιθῶμαι	ἱῶμαι	ἱστῶμαι
	2	διδῷ	τιθῇ	ἱῇ	ἱστῇ
	3	διδῶται	τιθῆται	ἱῆται	ἱστῆται
pl.	1	διδώμεθα	τιθώμεθα	ἱώμεθα	ἱστώμεθα
	2	διδῶσθε	τιθῆσθε	ἱῆσθε	ἱστῆσθε
	3	διδῶνται	τιθῶνται	ἱῶνται	ἱστῶνται

Present optative

s.	1	διδοίμην	τιθείμην	ἱείμην	ἱσταίμην
	2	διδοῖο	τιθεῖο	ἱεῖο	ἱσταῖο
	3	διδοῖτο	τιθεῖτο	ἱεῖτο	ἱσταῖτο
pl.	1	διδοίμεθα	τιθείμεθα	ἱείμεθα	ἱσταίμεθα
	2	διδοῖσθε	τιθεῖσθε	ἱεῖσθε	ἱσταῖσθε
	3	διδοῖντο	τιθεῖντο	ἱεῖντο	ἱσταῖντο

Present imperative

s.	2	δίδοσο	τίθεσο	ἵεσο	ἵστασο
	3	διδόσθω	τιθέσθω	ἱέσθω	ἱστάσθω
pl.	2	δίδοσθε	τίθεσθε	ἵεσθε	ἵστασθε
	3	διδόσθων	τιθέσθων	ἱέσθων	ἱστάσθων

Present infinitive

δίδοσθαι   τίθεσθαι   ἵεσθαι   ἵστασθαι

Present participle

διδόμεν-ος, -η, -ον   τιθέμεν-ος, -η, -ον   ἱέμεν-ος, -η, -ον   ἱστάμεν-ος, -η, -ον

Imperfect indicative

s.	1	ἐδιδόμην	ἐτιθέμην	ἱέμην	ἱστάμην
	2	ἐδίδοσο	ἐτίθεσο	ἵεσο	ἵστασο
	3	ἐδίδοτο	ἐτίθετο	ἵετο	ἵστατο
pl.	1	ἐδιδόμεθα	ἐτιθέμεθα	ἱέμεθα	ἱστάμεθα
	2	ἐδίδοσθε	ἐτίθεσθε	ἵεσθε	ἵστασθε
	3	ἐδίδοντο	ἐτίθεντο	ἵεντο	ἵσταντο

Future indicative

s.	1	δώσομαι etc.	θήσομαι etc.	ἥσομαι etc.	στήσομαι etc.

The other parts of the future middle are formed regularly with the same stems (δωσ-, θησ-, ἡσ-, στησ-).

Aorist

The only aorist middle of ἵστημι is weak (and transitive), ἐστησάμην, conjugated in exactly the same way as ἐλυσάμην (see **Appendix 1**). The aorist middle of the other verbs are conjugated as follows:

Aorist indicative

s.	1	ἐδόμην	ἐθέμην	εἵμην
	2	ἔδου	ἔθου	εἷσο
	3	ἔδοτο	ἔθετο	εἷτο
pl.	1	ἐδόμεθα	ἐθέμεθα	εἵμεθα
	2	ἔδοσθε	ἔθεσθε	εἷσθε
	3	ἔδοντο	ἔθεντο	εἷντο

Aorist subjunctive

s.	1	δῶμαι	θῶμαι	ὧμαι
	2	δῷ	θῇ	ἧ
	3	δῶται	θῆται	ἧται
pl.	1	δώμεθα	θώμεθα	ὥμεθα
	2	δῶσθε	θῆσθε	ἧσθε
	3	δῶνται	θῶνται	ὧνται

Aorist optative

s.	1	δοίμην	θείμην	εἵμην
	2	δοῖο	θεῖο	εἷο
	3	δοῖτο	θεῖτο	εἷτο
pl.	1	δοίμεθα	θείμεθα	εἵμεθα
	2	δοῖσθε	θεῖσθε	εἷσθε
	3	δοῖντο	θεῖντο	εἷντο

Aorist imperative

s.	2	δοῦ	θοῦ	οὗ
	3	δόσθω	θέσθω	ἔσθω
pl.	2	δόσθε	θέσθε	ἔσθε
	3	δόσθων	θέσθων	ἔσθων

Aorist infinitive

δόσθαι θέσθαι ἕσθαι

Aorist participle

δόμεν-ος, -η, -ον θέμεν-ος, -η, -ον ἕμεν-ος, -η, -ον

Perfect and pluperfect

The perfect and pluperfect middle/passive of δίδωμι and ἵημι are formed regularly from the stems δεδο- and εἱ- (e.g. perfect middle/passive indicative δέδομαι, δέδοσαι etc., εἷμαι, εἷσαι etc). Similar forms exist for τίθημι (τέθειμαι, τέθεισαι etc.) but on the perfect passive of this verb see 18.1/2 note 4. The perfect middle/passive forms of ἵστημι are rare.

PASSIVE

As with other verbs, the forms for the present, imperfect, perfect and pluperfect are the same as for the middle. The future and aorist passive follow λύω (see **Appendix 1**):

Future indicative

δοθήσομαι τεθήσομαι ἑθήσομαι σταθήσομαι

Aorist indicative

ἐδόθην ἐτέθην εἵθην ἐστάθην

Appendix 6: Conjugation of δείκνῡμι (present and imperfect)

For the other tenses of δείκνῡμι see 20.1/1.

		ACTIVE		MIDDLE/PASSIVE	
		Present	Imperfect	Present	Imperfect
Indicative					
s.	1	δείκνῡμι	ἐδείκνῡν	δείκνυμαι	ἐδεικνύμην
	2	δείκνῡς	ἐδείκνῡς	δείκνυσαι	ἐδείκνυσο
	3	δείκνῡσι(ν)	ἐδείκνῡ	δείκνυται	ἐδείκνυτο
pl.	1	δείκνυμεν	ἐδείκνυμεν	δεικνύμεθα	ἐδεικνύμεθα
	2	δείκνυτε	ἐδείκνυτε	δείκνυσθε	ἐδείκνυσθε
	3	δεικνύᾱσι(ν)	ἐδείκνυσαν	δείκνυνται	ἐδείκνυντο
Subjunctive					
s.	1	δεικνύω		δεικνύωμαι	
	2	δεικνύῃς		δεικνύῃ	
	3	δεικνύῃ		δεικνύηται	
pl.	1	δεικνύωμεν		δεικνυώμεθα	
	2	δεικνύητε		δεικνύησθε	
	3	δεικνύωσι(ν)		δεικνύωνται	
Optative					
s.	1	δεικνύοιμι		δεικνυοίμην	
	2	δεικνύοις		δεικνύοιο	
	3	δεικνύοι		δεικνύοιτο	
pl.	1	δεικνύοιμεν		δεικνυοίμεθα	
	2	δεικνύοιτε		δεικνύοισθε	
	3	δεικνύοιεν		δεικνύοιντο	
Imperative					
s.	2	δείκνῡ		δείκνυσο	
	3	δεικνύτω		δεικνύσθω	
pl.	2	δείκνυτε		δείκνυσθε	
	3	δεικνύντων		δεικνύσθων	
Infinitive					
		δεικνύναι		δείκνυσθαι	
Participle					
		δεικνύς, δεικνῦσα, δεικνύν		δεικνύμεν-ος, -η, -ον	

Appendix 7: Numerals

Cardinals

For the declension of εἷς, δύο, τρεῖς, τέτταρες see 7.1/5a. διᾱκόσιοι, τριᾱκόσιοι etc. follow the plural of καλός (3.1/3).

1	εἷς	20	εἴκοσι(ν)
2	δύο	30	τριάκοντα
3	τρεῖς	40	τετταράκοντα
4	τέτταρες	50	πεντήκοντα
5	πέντε	60	ἑξήκοντα
6	ἕξ	70	ἑβδομήκοντα
7	ἑπτά	80	ὀγδοήκοντα
8	ὀκτώ	90	ἐνενήκοντα
9	ἐννέα	100	ἑκατόν
10	δέκα	200	διᾱκόσιοι
11	ἕνδεκα	300	τριᾱκόσιοι
12	δώδεκα	400	τετρακόσιοι
13	τρεῖς καὶ δέκα	500	πεντακόσιοι
14	τέτταρες καὶ δέκα	600	ἑξακόσιοι
15	πεντεκαίδεκα	700	ἑπτακόσιοι
16	ἑκκαίδεκα	800	ὀκτακόσιοι
17	ἑπτακαίδεκα	900	ἐνακόσιοι
18	ὀκτωκαίδεκα	1,000	χίλιοι
19	ἐννεακαίδεκα	10,000	μύριοι

The cardinals *two thousand, three thousand* etc. are compounds of the appropriate numeral adverbs and χίλιοι, e.g. δισχίλιοι, τρισχίλιοι etc.; likewise we have δισμύριοι *twenty thousand*, τρισμύριοι *thirty thousand* etc.

	Ordinals	Adverbs
1	πρῶτος	ἅπαξ
2	δεύτερος	δίς
3	τρίτος	τρίς
4	τέταρτος	τετράκις
5	πέμπτος	πεντάκις
6	ἕκτος	ἑξάκις
7	ἕβδομος	ἑπτάκις
8	ὄγδοος	ὀκτάκις
9	ἔνατος	ἐνάκις
10	δέκατος	δεκάκις

The ordinals are normal first and second declension adjectives (3.1/3), except that the feminine of ὄγδοος is ὀγδόη (not -ᾱ).

Appendix 8: Accentuation

The basic features of Greek accentuation are described at 1.1/2, and information given there is not repeated below.

The following terms are used to describe words according to their accent:

Oxytone – a word with an acute on its final syllable, e.g. ποταμός.

Paroxytone – a word with an acute on its penultimate (i.e. last syllable but one), e.g. λόγος.

Proparoxytone – a word with an acute on its last syllable but two, e.g. ἄνθρωπος.

Perispomenon – a word with a circumflex on its final syllable, e.g. ποταμοῦ.

Properispomenon – a word with a circumflex on its penultimate, e.g. δῶρον.

Barytone – a word with a grave on its final syllable, e.g. ποταμὸν εἶδον *I saw a* river.

These are the only places in which each accent can occur (we cannot, for example, have an acute on the last syllable but three, or a circumflex on the last syllable but two).

For purposes of accentuation a syllable is long if it contains a long vowel or diphthong, and short if it contains a short vowel, except that **all endings in -αι and -οι, apart from those of the optative, are counted as short.**[1]

The length of the final syllable of a word and, to a lesser extent, of its penultimate is important for accentuation because:

- a word can only be proparoxytone if its final syllable is short, e.g. ἄνθρωπος.
- a word can only be properispomenon if its final syllable is short; as a circumflex must in any case stand on a long vowel or diphthong, a word so accented must end in - �‿ , or be a disyllable consisting of - �‿ , e.g. πολῖται, γλῶττα. Conversely, if such a word is accented on

---
[1] The rules in verse are different; see **Appendix 9**

its penultimate, the accent must be a circumflex, and this is why we get the change of accent from πολίτης to πολῖται (the reverse in γλῶττα/γλώττης).

For purposes of accentuation words are divided into five categories:

(a) Nouns, adjectives and pronouns

There are no overall rules about the position of the accent in the nominative singular of nouns or in the nominative masculine singular of adjectives and pronouns, and we must simply learn that ποταμός is oxytone but λόγος is paroxytone. There are some rules for certain small groups which can be learnt by observation, e.g. nouns in -ευς are always oxytone (as βασιλεύς); the accent of comparative and superlative adjectives is always as far from the end of the word as possible (σοφός but σοφώτερος, σοφώτατος).

Once, however, we know where a noun, adjective or pronoun is accented in the nominative (masculine) singular, it is easy to deduce how its other forms will be accented because the accent stays on the same syllable as far as this is allowed by the rules given above for proparoxytones and perispomenons. In λόγος, for example, the accent remains unchanged (λόγε, λόγον, λόγου, λόγῳ, λόγοι, λόγους, λόγων, λόγοις), but in ἄνθρωπος the accent must become paroxytone when the ending is long: ἄνθρωπε, ἄνθρωπον, ἀνθρώπου, ἀνθρώπῳ, ἄνθρωποι, ἀνθρώπους, ἀνθρώπων, ἀνθρώποις (ἄνθρωποι because -οι does **not** count as long – see above).

In many third declension nouns the genitive singular is a syllable longer than the nominative singular, e.g. σῶμα (properispomenon, not paroxytone, because it is a disyllable of the form - ˘ ; see above): σώματος, σώματι, σώματα (the accent must change to an acute because the added short syllable makes all three forms proparoxytone), σωμάτων (the added syllable is long and therefore the accent must become paroxytone), σώμασι.

We must, however, note:

(i) Where a first or second declension word has an acute on its final syllable in the nominative singular, this becomes a circumflex in the genitive and dative (in both singular and plural, cf. 2.1/2 note 3), e.g. from ποταμός we have ποταμέ, ποταμόν, ποταμοῦ, ποταμῷ, ποταμοί, ποταμούς, ποταμῶν, ποταμοῖς.² For an example of an adjective so accented see καλός (3.1/3).

(ii) All first declension nouns are perispomenon in the genitive plural (2.1/2 note 4), e.g. χωρῶν (< χώρα), νεανιῶν (< νεανίας). This does **not** apply to the gen. f. pl. of adjectives when this form would not otherwise differ from the masculine, e.g. μεγάλων is both gen. m. pl. and gen. f. pl. of μέγας. Where, however, the masculine and feminine forms differ, the rule holds, e.g. χαρίεις, gen. m. pl. χαριέντων, gen. f. pl. χαριεσσῶν.

(iii) In the third declension, monosyllabic nouns are accented on the final syllable of the genitive and dative, in both singular and plural, e.g. αἴξ, αἶγα, αἰγός, αἰγί, αἶγες, αἶγας, αἰγῶν, αἰξί. An exception is the gen. pl. of παῖς (παίδων). Of polysyllabic nouns γυνή also follows this pattern (γυνή, γύναι (5.1/1 note 1), γυναῖκα, γυναικός, γυναικί, γυναῖκες, γυναῖκας, γυναικῶν, γυναιξί), and ἀνήρ, μήτηρ and πατήρ follow it in the gen. and dat. s. (6.1/1b). For the accentuation of πᾶς see 10.1/3b.

(iv) The accent in the genitive (s. and pl.) of third declension nouns with stems in ι and of some with stems in υ (8.1/4) is quite irregular: πόλεως, πόλεων (< πόλις); πήχεως, πήχεων (<πῆχυς).

(v) Contracted nouns and adjectives (6.1/2) follow the same rules as for contracted verbs (below b(i)).

(b) Verbs

With verbs the accent falls as far from the end of a word as possible (here too final -αι and -οι count as short, **except in optative endings**). In forms such as ἀκουετε, ἀκουουσι, κελευεσθαι, ἐκελευσαν the final short syllable shows that they must be proparoxytone: ἀκούετε, ἀκούουσι, κελεύεσθαι, ἐκέλευσαν (in disyllabic forms such as ἑλε and λῦε the accent goes back to the penultimate but becomes properispomenon in λῦε because of its long ῦ: ἕλε but λῦε). In κελευω, προφερει, ἐλυθην, where the final syllable is long, the accent is paroxytone: κελεύω, προφέρει, ἐλύθην.

---

² The Attic declension (13.1/1a) is an exception.

We must, however, note:

(i) In the forms of contracted verbs where contraction occurs, the accent follows that of the original uncontracted form according to the following rules:

- If the accent is on neither of the syllables to be contracted it remains unchanged, e.g. ἐποίει (< ἐποίε-ε).
- If the accent is on the first of the two syllables to be contracted it becomes a circumflex on the contracted syllable, e.g. ποιεῖ (< ποιέ-ει); νῑκῶμεν (< νῑκά-ομεν).
- If the accent is on the second of the two syllables to be contracted it stays as an acute on the contracted syllable, e.g. ἐτῑμώμεθα (< ἐτῑμα-όμεθα); τῑμῴην (< τῑμα-οίην).

(ii) Certain forms of uncontracted -ω verbs and of -μι verbs are in origin contracted and for this reason the first syllable of their endings is always accented. These are:

- the aorist subjunctive passive of all verbs, e.g. λυθῶ, λυθῇς, λυθῇ, λυθῶμεν, λυθῆτε, λυθῶσι.
- the subjunctive and optative of both present (act., mid./pass.) and aorist (act., mid.) of δίδωμι, τίθημι, ἵημι and their compounds, e.g. διδῶ, διδοῖμεν, ἀποδῶ, ἀποδοῖμεν.

(iii) In all strong aorists the first syllable of the ending always carries the accent in the active participle (e.g. λαβών, λαβοῦσα, λαβόν), the active and middle infinitives (λαβεῖν, λαβέσθαι), and the 2nd s. imperative middle (λαβοῦ).

(iv) The first syllable of the ending also carries the accent in participles in -εις, -ους and -ως, e.g. λυθείς, λυθεῖσα, λυθέν; τιθείς, τιθεῖσα, τιθέν; διδούς, διδοῦσα, διδόν; λελυκώς, λελυκυῖα, λελυκός.

(v) In certain participles and infinitives the accent is always either paroxytone or properispomenon, depending on whether it stands on a short or long syllable. These are:

- infinitives in -σαι (weak aorist active), e.g. λῦσαι, νῑκῆσαι, αἰνέσαι.
- infinitives in -ναι (perf. act., aor. pass., root aor. act., and certain active infinitives of -μι verbs), e.g. λελυκέναι, λυθῆναι, γνῶναι, διδόναι.

- the infinitive and participle of the perf. mid./pass., e.g. νενῑκῆσθαι, λελυμένος.

(vi) In compound verbs the accent cannot fall further back than the augment, e.g. ἀπῆγον (< ἀπάγω), παρέσχον (< παρέχω), or the last vowel of a prepositional prefix, e.g. παράδος (< παραδίδωμι).

(c) *Adverbs, conjunctions, interjections, particles, prepositions*
These have only one form and therefore their accent does not vary, e.g. σοφῶς *wisely,* ὅταν *whenever,* εὖ *well,* except for oxytones becoming barytones (1.1/2). A few words which would otherwise be included here are enclitic or atonic and so come under categories (*d*) or (*e*).

(d) *Enclitics*
An enclitic combines with the preceding word for pronunciation, and can affect its accentuation. When quoted by themselves (in paradigms, dictionaries, etc.) monosyllabic enclitics are written with no accent (e.g. γε), disyllabics as oxytone (e.g. ποτέ), except for τινῶν.

The total number of enclitics is small and consists of:

(i) The present indicative of εἰμί *I am* and φημί *say*, with the exception in both cases of the 2nd singular.
(ii) The unemphatic forms of the personal pronouns, viz με, μου, μοι; σε, σου, σοι; ἑ, οὑ, οἱ.
(iii) All forms of the indefinite τις (10.1/1).
(iv) The indefinite adverbs ποτέ, που, πω, πως.
(v) The particles γε, νυν, περ, τε.

The rules for enclitics are:

(vi) An enclitic has no accent when it follows a word accented on its final syllable, e.g. ποταμῶν τινων. If this word has a final acute (i.e. is oxytone), this accent is kept, e.g. ποταμός τις.
(vii) If the preceding word is paroxytone a monosyllabic enclitic has no accent but a disyllabic enclitic keeps the accent on its final syllable, e.g. ἵππος τις, ἵπποι τινές.

(viii) If the preceding word is proparoxytone or properispomenon, an enclitic, whether monosyllabic or disyllabic, has the effect of adding an acute to the final syllable, e.g. ἄνθρωπός τις, ἄνθρωποί τινες, δῶρόν τι, δῶρά τινα.

(ix) In groups of two or more enclitics all are accented except the last, e.g. ἡμεῖς γέ ποτέ πού τι εἴδομεν *we at any rate once saw something somewhere.*

(x) ἐστί is accented on its first syllable (ἔστι) when:

- it denotes existence, e.g. Ἱππόλυτος οὐκέτ᾽ ἔστιν *Hippolytus is no longer alive.*
- it stands for ἔξεστι (21.1/4 note 1).
- it follows ἀλλά, εἰ, καί, οὐκ, μή, τοῦτο, ὡς.
- it begins a clause.

(*e*) *Atonics*

Atonics are monosyllables which have no accent unless followed by an enclitic. These are:

- the nom. m. and f. (s. and pl.) of the article (ὁ, ἡ, οἱ, αἱ), εἰ, οὐ, ὡς.
- the prepositions εἰς, ἐκ, ἐν.

Of these, however, οὐ is accented if it occurs as the last word of a clause (ex. at 5.2.21 *l.*2), and ὡς if it occurs after the word it qualifies or is used in the sense of *thus* (exx. at 25.2.1 *ll.*4, 23).

Notes

1 A few words which we would expect to be properispomenon are in fact paroxytone: οὔτε, μήτε, εἴθε, ὥστε and compound demonstratives and relatives whose second element is -δε, -περ and -τις (οἵδε, αἵπερ, ἥτις etc.).

2 τίς and τί never become barytone (10.1/1).

3 Certain disyllabic prepositions throw their accent back on to their first syllable when they follow the noun they govern (example at 11.2.4 *l.* 1).

Appendix 9: Greek verse

(a) The nature of Greek verse, long and short syllables

Greek poetry was composed on an entirely different principle from that employed in English. It was not constructed by arranging stressed syllables in patterns, nor with a system of rhymes. Greek poets employed a number of different metres, all of which consist of certain fixed arrangements of **long and short syllables**. In English verse, whether rhymed or not, the length and rhythm of a line is determined by the number and arrangement of its stressed syllables:

> They tóld me, Heraclítus, they tóld me yoú were déad;
> They broúght me bitter néws to heár and bitter teárs to shéd.
> I wépt, as I remémbered how óften yoú and Í
> Had tíred the sún with tálking and sént him down the ský.
> And nów that thou art lýing, my deár old Cárian guést,
> A hándful of gréy áshes, long lóng ago at rést,
> Stíll are thy pleásant voíces, thy níghtingales, awáke,
> For deáth he taketh áll away, but thém he cánnot táke.

In this translation of a poem of Callimachus (12.3.9) the poet, William Johnston Cary, has changed the position of stressed syllables in some lines for purposes of rhythm and emphasis. No comparable variation is possible in Greek poetry because its structure is much more formal. Every line of verse consists of a succession of long and short syllables whose number and order are prescribed by the metre used; word accent, which in any case is different from that of English (1.1/2), plays no part. To scan a line (i.e. indicate its metre) syllables are marked with a macron (—) when long and a micron (◡) when short (to avoid a confusion, accents and breathings are omitted and capitals are not used for vowels when marking long and short syllables):

εῑπε̆ τῐ̆ς η̄ρᾱκλεῑτε̆ τε̄ο̄ν μο̆ρο̆ν ε̄ς δε̆ με̆ δᾱκρῠ (first line of 12.3.9)

The rules for determining the length of syllables are:

(i) Vowels are classified as short (α, ε, ι, ο, υ) or long (ᾱ, η, ῑ, ῡ, ω). For metrical purposes all diphthongs are long (this is not true for accentuation – see **Appendix 8**).
(ii) A short syllable must contain a short vowel followed by either a single consonant or no consonant at all.
(iii) A syllable is long if it contains:

either a long vowel or diphthong. When, however, either occurs at the end of a word and the following word does not begin with a consonant, the long vowel or diphthong is shortened, μοῦ ἔννἔπἔ.[1]

or a short vowel followed by two consonants (ζ, ξ, ψ count as double consonants but θ, φ, χ do not; breathings have no metrical value). When a short vowel occurs before certain combinations of two consonants where the second is λ, μ, ν, ρ, the syllable may be long or short.

(iv) In counting consonants after a final short vowel of a word no account is taken of word division, hence τεὸν μορον, τὸ σχημα.

(*b*) *Metrical feet, the hexameter, pentameter and iambic trimeter*
A metrical foot is made up of certain combinations of long and short syllables. Of the numerous possibilities only the following need concern us:

Dactyl	— �‿ ˿	Iamb	˿ —
Spondee	— —	Trochee	— ˿

The metre used for epic and pastoral was the hexameter; the combination of one hexameter and one pentameter forms an elegiac couplet (see below).

---

[1] Epic correption (i.e. shortening). It occurs in hexameters and pentameters but is completely avoided in iambic trimeters (on these terms see below).

The **hexameter** (< ἕξ + μέτρον) consists of six feet. The first four can be either dactyls or spondees, the fifth is almost always a dactyl and the sixth can be either a spondee or trochee. This can be represented as follows:

— ⏑⏑ | — ⏑⏑ | — ⏑⏑ | — ⏑⏑ | — ⏑⏑ | — ⏑

The upright lines show the syllable division between one foot and the next. They do **not** necessarily coincide with word division. The first two lines of the Odyssey (25.2.3) are scanned:

ᾱν-δρᾰ μοῐ | ε̄ν-νε̆-πε̆ | Μοῡ-σᾰ ‖ πŏ- | λῡτ-ρŏ-πŏν | ŏς μᾰ-λᾰ | πŏ̄λ-λᾰ
πλᾱγ-χθη̄ ε̆- | πεῑ Τροῑ- | η̄ς ‖ ῐ-ε̆- | ρο̄ν πτŏ-λῐ̆- | ε̄θ-ρŏν ε̆- | πε̄ρ-σε̆.

It was felt that the rhythm of a hexameter would be impaired if there were a break between words at the end of the third foot as a line so composed would fall into two equal halves. To avoid this, there is always a break between words (**caesura** *cut* or *break*) either (*a*) after the first syllable of the third foot (as in the second line above), or (*b*) after the second syllable of the third foot when a dactyl (as in the first line above), or (*c*) after the first syllable of the fourth foot. The caesura is marked by two vertical lines, as in the above examples.

A pentameter following a hexameter makes up an **elegiac couplet**, and is by convention indented (e.g. 12.3). It does not occur by itself. The elegiac couplet was the metre of elegiac poetry, a broad literary genre which included epigram and certain narrative, didactic, and occasional poetry. The pentameter consists of two halves of two and a half feet each; the division between the two is marked by a break between words (here called **diaeresis**, not **caesura** because it occurs at the end, not in the middle of a metrical unit; it also is marked by two vertical lines). The metrical pattern of the **pentameter** is:

— ⏑⏑ | — ⏑⏑ | — ‖ — ⏑⏑ | — ⏑⏑ | ⏑

Examples (from 12.3.1 and 3) are:

ὂν λῐ-πὲν | οὐχ εὖ- | ρῶν ‖ ἤ-ψὲν ὂν | εὖ-ρὲ βρὸ- | χὸν
εῖς ἄ-γᾰ- | θὸς Κῐ-νῠ- | ρῆς ‖ καῖ Κῐ-νῠ- | ρῆς δὲ Κῐ- | λῑξ

The **iambic trimeter** is the chief metre used for dialogue and speeches
in drama because it was considered the metre which came closest to
the rhythm of normal speech. It consists of three pairs of iambs but
more variation was allowed than in the hexameter or pentameter. Its
basic form is:

$$\smile\!\!\!- \; — \; \smile \; — \; | \; \smile\!\!\!- \; — \; \smile \; — \; | \; \smile\!\!\!- \; — \; \smile \; \smile\!\!\!-$$

A caesura occurs after either the fifth or seventh syllables. Examples
of iambic trimeters (from 15.2.4) are:

ἄ-πᾱν-τὲς ἒς- | μὲν ‖ εῖς τὸ νοῦ- | θὲ-τεῖν σὸ-φοῖ
αῦ-τοῖ δ ἄ-μᾱρ-| τᾰ-νῶν- τὲς‖ οῦ| γῑγ-νῶς- κὸ-μὲν

Included in the reading are poems in some of the many other metres
used by Greek poets (an example occurs at 12.2.18, which is written
in anapaests).

Key to exercises in Greek reading and extra reading sections

Explanations and more literal interpretations are given in round brackets. Some words which have no specific equivalent in the Greek original but which must be supplied in English are enclosed in square brackets. Translations from Greek authors are generally as literal as possible and should not be taken as reflecting the style of the original.

When *God* is written with an initial capital letter, the Judeo-Christian deity should only be understood in passages from the Bible. Elsewhere the Greek original (θεός) does not indicate what particular divinity is meant.

References are given for longer prose passages, for whole poems and for extracts from verse of more than two lines. In these references Roman numerals refer to books (e.g. of Thucydides), Arabic to chapters in prose works but in poetry to lines. Fragments of the Greek tragedians are given the number assigned to them in Nauck's edition (*Fragmenta Tragicorum Graecorum*). *A.P.* is the abbreviation of *Anthologia Palatina,* an enormous collection of shorter Greek poems whose present form dates from Byzantine times; it has a supplement entitled *App(endix) Plan(udea).* In both the latter works the reference is first to book (Roman), then to poem number (Arabic).

1.2

1 Aristotelēs (Aristotle), Aristophanēs, Dēmosthenēs, Hērodotos (Herodotus), Theokritos (Theocritus), Kallimachos (Callimachus), Pindaros (Pindar), Platōn (Plato).

2 akmē, anathema, analūsis, antithesis, asbestos, automaton, aphasiā, bathos, genesis, diagnōsis, dogma, drāma, zōnē, ēthos, ēchō, ideā, kīnēma, klīmax, kosmos, krisis, kōlon, metron, miasma, nektar, nemesis, orchēstrā, pathos, skēnē, stigma, hubris, hupothesis, chaos, charaktēr, psūchē.

3 (*a*) Agamemnōn, Achilleus (Achilles), Hektōr (Hector), Helenē (Helen), Odusseus (Odysseus), Patroklos (Patroclus), Pēnelopeia (Penelope) *(all are characters in Homer).*

(*b*) Athēnai (Athens), Argos, Thēbai (Thebes), Korinthos (Corinth), Spartē (Sparta), Krētē (Crete), Rhodos (Rhodes), Samos *(all are places in Greece).*

2.2

(1) Odysseus has come from Troy, but Poseidon destroys his ship on (*or* at) Scheria. (2) Odysseus flees out of (*or* from) the sea and hides himself beneath [an] olive-tree near the shore. (3) In a dream Athena says to (*or* tells) the princess Nausicaa that she must (it is necessary [for her] to) wash the clothes on the shore. (4) At daybreak (*or* dawn) Nausicaa brings the clothes in [a] wagon from her house to the sea. (5) In the wagon there is also food for Nausicaa and her companions. (6) The girls quickly wash the clothes near the olive-tree where Odysseus is sleeping. (7) Then (*or* next) the girls throw the clothes on to the shore. (8) They wash themselves and eat the food which they have in the wagon. (9) While they are playing on the shore, Nausicaa

throws [a] ball but the ball falls into [a] whirlpool. (10) The girls' shouts (the shouts of the girls) awaken Odysseus and frighten him. (11) Odysseus wonders where in the world he has come to, and suddenly creeps from the olive-tree. (12) He frightens Nausicaa and her companions. (13) But Nausicaa stays on the shore because Athena puts courage into her heart. (14) Odysseus says to (or tells) Nausicaa that he has come from Ogygia. (15) Nausicaa says to (or tells) her companions that they must (it is necessary [for them] to) provide Odysseus with food and clothes (provide food and clothes to Odysseus). (16) She wishes (or is willing) to bring Odysseus to her father's house (the house of her father) but she fears (or is afraid of) the citizens' blame (the blame of the citizens) if they see her with Odysseus. (17) So Nausicaa and the girls bring the clothes back to the house in the wagon, but Odysseus waits outside.

In 2, 4 and 9 the indefinite article, which does not exist in Greek, has to be supplied in the English.

Analysis of sentence 13 (according to the steps given in 2.2)

ἀλλ᾽ ἡ Ναυσικάα ἐν τῇ ἀκτῇ ἀναμένει διότι ἡ Ἀθηνᾶ τὴν ἀνδρείᾱν εἰς τὴν καρδίᾱν εἰσβάλλει.

(*a*) ἀλλ᾽ (= ἀλλά) conjunction *but*; ἡ feminine nominative singular of the definite article (2.1/2); Ναυσικάα can be either nominative or vocative singular but, as ἡ precedes, it must be the former (the voc. would normally be preceded by ὦ (2.1/3), **never** by the article) – note that the article **must** agree in number, gender and case with the noun it qualifies (2.1/2 note 1; cf. τῇ ἀκτῇ, ἡ Ἀθηνᾶ, τὴν ἀνδρείᾱν, τὴν καρδίᾱν); ἐν preposition governing the dative *in, on, among,* and we would expect the following words to be in this case, which they are: τῇ ἀκτῇ dative singular of ἡ ἀκτή *the shore*; ἀναμένει 3rd person singular present indicative active of ἀναμένω *wait, stay* (the corresponding form of λύω would be λύει); διότι conjunction *because*; ἡ Ἀθηνᾶ nominative singular (the same reasoning applies as for ἡ Ναυσικάα); τὴν ἀνδρείᾱν accusative singular of ἡ ἀνδρείᾱ lit. *the courage*; εἰς preposition governing the accusative *to, into,* and we would expect the following words to be in this case, which they are: τὴν καρδίᾱν accusative singular of ἡ καρδίᾱ *the heart*; εἰσβάλλει 3rd person present indicative active of εἰσβάλλω *throw into, invade.*

(*b*) There are two finite verbs, ἀναμένει and εἰσβάλλει; therefore we have two clauses.

(*c*) Because ἀλλ᾽(ά) stands as first word it must link this sentence with the previous one. As we have two clauses and διότι comes after the first finite verb, this conjunction must introduce the second clause.

(*d*) In the first clause ἡ Ναυσικάα is nominative and therefore must be the subject of ἀναμένει (we note that the verb agrees with ἡ Ναυσικάα in the way prescribed at the beginning of 2.1/4). ἐν τῇ ἀκτῇ *on the shore* (*on* seems more appropriate with *shore* than *in* or *among*) must be an adverbial phrase qualifying the verb. The clause therefore means *but Nausicaa* (the definite article can be used with proper names in Greek (2.1/2 note 1(iii)), but is never so employed in English) *stays* (or *waits*) *on the shore.* In the second clause ἡ Ἀθηνᾶ, which is nominative, must be the subject of εἰσβάλλει (note the agreement as in the previous clause). τὴν ἀνδρείᾱν is accusative and is **not** preceded by a preposition; therefore it must be the object of the verb as it can have no other grammatical function in the clause. We may translate *because Athena throws courage* (the definite article is not to be translated – 2.1/2 note 1(i)) *into*; the other meaning of εἰσβάλλω, *invade,* makes no sense in this context. εἰς τὴν καρδίᾱν *into the heart* must be an adverbial phrase qualifying the verb but we have one too many *in/into* – the problem is solved by reference to the note on (7) and we can translate *because Athena throws courage into the heart* (*to,* the other meaning of εἰς, does not seem appropriate here).

(*e*) The conjunction διότι shows that the second clause gives the reason for the first and we can put both together as *but Nausicaa stays on the shore because Athena throws courage into the heart.* English idiom requires that we specify whose heart is involved (obviously Nausicaa's, as otherwise the reason introduced by διότι would have no point – on this use of the Greek definite article see note on (1)). Also *put* seems more in accordance with English idiom than *throw* (all possible translations of some words cannot be given in either vocabularies or dictionaries). We now have: *But Nausicaa stays on the shore because Athena puts courage into her heart.*

3.2

(1) Millionaires (the very rich) are not good. (2) A large city is [a] large desert (*or* wilderness). (3) Poverty stimulates skills (*i.e.* necessity is the mother of invention). (4) [A] corpse does not bite (*i.e.* dead men tell no tales). (5) (*i*) Many [are] friends of [the] table, not of truth. (*ii*) Good fortune has many friends ([is] many-friended). (*iii*) Man [is] [a] political animal. (*iv*) Death [is] immortal (*or* deathless). (*v*) Slaves have no leisure ([there is] not leisure to/for slaves). (*vi*) Without health life [is] no life (*or* unlivable). (*vii*) Flattery [is a] disease of friendship. (*viii*) [A] wicked man [is] long-lived. (6) Fortune's great gifts involve (have) fear. (7) Wicked friends bear wicked fruit. (8) The sowing (procreation) of children is a self-inflicted (self-chosen) grief. (9) Gifts persuade [the] gods. (10) Neither [a] drinking-party without company nor wealth without virtue is pleasurable (*lit.* has pleasure). (11) For [a] human being the unexamined life [is] not worth living. (12) (*i*) A large number of (*lit.* many) frogs send messengers to the son of Cronos (*i.e.* Zeus) because they desire [a] monarch. (*ii*) The messengers say to the son of Cronos on behalf of the frogs, 'Just son of Cronos, you are master of the gods. Are you willing to provide the frogs with [a] master?' (*lit.* provide [a] master to the frogs). (*iii*) The son of Cronos is very surprised and hurls [a] large log into the frogs' marsh. (*iv*) The log frightens the frogs and they quickly run away, but they begin to be suspicious, since the log does not move (*lit.* is motionless). (*v*) Later they step on to the log without fear and say 'Stranger, are you [a] god or [a] human being or [an] animal?' (*vi*) Since it says nothing at all, they consider that it is despicable that they have such a master and they send messengers again to the son of Cronos about [a] new monarch. (*vii*) The messengers say to the son of Cronos, 'Master, you must (it is necessary [for you] to) send the frogs (to the frogs) another monarch since the first is motionless and idle.' (*viii*) The master of the gods is angry with the frogs and sends [a] great hydra. (*ix*) The hydra is pitiless and eats the frogs. (*x*) The fable makes [it] clear that one (*or* we) must (it is necessary [for one/us] to) bear (i.e. put up with) idle masters since active masters often bear (i.e. bring) hardships.

Analysis of sentence 10 (according to the steps given in 2.2)

οὔτε συμπόσιον χωρὶς ὁμιλίας οὔτε πλοῦτος χωρὶς ἀρετῆς ἡδονὴν ἔχει.

(*a*) οὔτε ... οὔτε conjunctions *neither ... nor*; συμπόσιον, which is neuter, could be either nominative or accusative singular (the vocative is virtually ruled out by the meaning of the word, *drinking-party*); χωρίς preposition governing the genitive *without*; ὁμιλίας could be either genitive singular or accusative plural of ὁμιλίᾱ *company, companionship*, but as it is preceded by a preposition governing the genitive it must be the former; πλοῦτος nominative singular *wealth*; χωρίς as before; ἀρετῆς genitive singular of ἀρετή *courage, excellence, virtue*; ἡδονήν accusative singular of ἡδονή *pleasure*; ἔχει 3rd person singular present indicative active of ἔχω *have*.

(*b*) and (*c*) The one finite verb, ἔχει, indicates that we have only one clause.

(*d*) and (*e*) οὔτε ... οὔτε (like *neither ... nor* in English) join elements of equal grammatical weight. Therefore, since πλοῦτος is nominative, συμπόσιον is also nominative, and both are the subject of ἔχει (the verb is singular just as it would be in a similar construction in English, e.g. *neither my wife nor my dog was waiting for me*). As the accusative ἡδονήν is not preceded by a preposition it must be the object of ἔχει. We may now translate: *neither drinking-party without company nor wealth without virtue has pleasure* (of the possible meanings of ἀρετή *courage* and *excellence* are not appropriate as a combination of either with wealth would hardly seem to produce pleasure). English, however, would normally put the indefinite article (which does not exist in Greek) before *drinking-party*. Also, *is pleasurable* or *is enjoyable* would be more idiomatic than *has pleasure*. Our final version then could be: *neither a drinking-party without company nor wealth without virtue is pleasurable*.

4.2

(1) Pleasures [are] mortal, virtues immortal. (2) The beggar did not have bread, and was buying cheese. (3) Praise [is the] reward of virtue, and (*or* but) censure of wickedness. (4) [The] Egyptians [are] clever at contriving ways and means. (5) Necessity [is] law for slaves, but law [is] necessity for free men. (6) Once long ago [the] Milesians were brave. (7) [An] eagle does not hunt flies. (8) (*i*) You are spitting into [the] sky. (*ii*) You are plaiting [a] rope out of sand. (*iii*) You are sowing [the] sea. (*iv*) You are teaching [a] horse to run on to [a] plain. (*v*) You have come after [the] feast. (*vi*) You are whipping [a] corpse. (*vii*) You are shearing [an] ass. (*viii*) You are singing the victory-song before the victory. (*ix*) You are kicking against [the] pricks (*i.e.* of a goad). (*x*) You are bringing the war-engines after the war. (9) Croesus, the Lydian king (king of the Lydians), wanted to destroy the Persian empire (empire of the Persians). For, according to the Delphic oracle (*lit.* oracle at Delphi), he was destined to put an end to a mighty empire. But finally he put an end to his own empire, but not that (*lit.* the [empire]) of the Persians. After the Persians' victory Cyrus, the Persian king (*lit.* king of the Persians), made Croesus go up on to [a] great pyre, and Croesus began to consider the words of Solon the Athenian: no-one of men [is, *i.e.* can be considered] happy before his death. So he quietly awaited his death. But because Croesus was both pious and good, Cyrus ordered his soldiers to bring him down from the pyre and spoke as follows, 'Croesus, who among (*lit.* of) men persuaded you to make an expedition [as an] enemy instead of [as a] friend against my land?' But Croesus said, 'Cyrus, I (*lit.* I on the one hand) made an expedition against you, but the god (*lit.* but on the other hand the god) at Delphi persuaded me to make the expedition. For I am not foolish nor do I wish to have war instead of peace. For in peace-time the young men bury the old, but in war-time the old [bury] the young. But this was the god's pleasure (*lit.* this thing was dear to the gods).' So Cyrus set him free and made [him] sit nearby. And Croesus spoke once more, 'Cyrus, what are your soldiers doing?' 'They are plundering your city,' said Cyrus, 'and carrying off your wealth.' 'They are not plundering my city', said Croesus, 'nor my wealth. For I have nothing (*lit.* nothing is to me). [It is] **you** [whom] they are plundering.' After this he (i.e. Croesus) was dear to him; for Cyrus respected his wisdom. (Based on Herodotus i. 86-88)

Analysis of sentence 5 (according to the steps given in 2.2)

τοῖς μὲν δούλοις ἡ ἀνάγκη νόμος, τοῖς δὲ ἐλευθέροις ἀνθρώποις ὁ νόμος ἀνάγκη.

(*a*) μὲν ... δέ *on the one hand ... and/but on the other hand* indicate that we have two balanced grammatical elements (4.1/3); τοῖς ... δούλοις dative plural *to/for the slaves* (on the meaning of the dative with living things see 2.1/3e); ἡ ἀνάγκη nominative singular *the necessity* but to be translated *necessity* in view of 2.1/2 note 1(i); νόμος nominative singular *law*; τοῖς ... ἐλευθέροις ἀνθρώποις dative plural *to/for the free men*; ὁ νόμος nominative singular *the law*; ἀνάγκη nominative singular *necessity*.

(*b*) There are no finite verbs! However, even without the hint given in the note on (1), we learn from 3.1/3*b* and 3.1/6 that εἰμί is often omitted in clauses where something is predicated of something else. The fact that in each half of the sentence we have two nominatives suggests that this is what we have here. Since we have **two** balanced elements the appropriate part of εἰμί (viz ἐστί) is to be supplied in each. Therefore we have two clauses.

(c) The comma after νόμος shows the division between clauses.

(d) In τοῖς ... νόμος the definite article with ἀνάγκη shows that this is the subject; the absence of the definite article with νόμος shows that it is the predicate. The basic meaning (leaving aside μέν) is therefore *for the slaves* (the other meaning of the dative, *to*, is not appropriate) *necessity is law*. In τοῖς ... ἀνάγκη we realize that ὁ νόμος must be translated by *law* and not *the law* because it is parallel with ἀνάγκη and must mean the abstract concept of law, not a particular law. We then have *for the free men law is necessity*.

(e) We can translate μὲν ... δέ by *but* with the second clause. However, when we put both halves together we realize that we are dealing with a proverb and that the general class of slaves and the general class of free men are meant. We must, therefore, omit the definite article with each in English (2.1/2 note 1(ii)), and we have: *Necessity is law for slaves, but law is necessity for free men.*

5.2

(1) Time educates the wise. (2) Silence has many fine [points] (*i.e.* silence is golden). (3) Human beings have many troubles, strangers (*lit.* there are many troubles to human beings). (4) [One] must not (it is not necessary to) keep former evils in mind (*lit.* bear ... in memory). (5) (*i*) Quietness (*or* peace and quiet) [is] a fine [thing]. (*ii*) Fine [things] [are] difficult. (*iii*) Moderation [is] best. (*iv*) [A] big book [is] [a] big evil. (*v*) The property (*lit.* the [things]) of friends [is] shared. (*vi*) Hermes [is] shared. (*vii*) [A] small evil [is] [a] big blessing. (*viii*) Different [things] [are] beautiful to different [people] (*i.e.* some people like one thing, others another). (*ix*) The tongue [is] [the] cause of (*or* responsible for) many troubles. (*x*) Doing [is] difficult, giving the order (*sc.* to do it) [is] easy. (*xi*) Getting drunk (*or* drunkenness) [is] [a] bad remedy for (*i.e.* way to get rid of) woe. (*xii*) One learns by experience (lit. sufferings [are] lessons). (*xiii*) [A] bad egg comes from (*lit.* [is] of) [a] bad crow. (*xiv*) Trust the land, mistrust the sea (*lit.* [the] land [is] [a] trustworthy [thing], [the] sea [an] untrustworthy [thing]). (*xv*) Even an ant can get angry (*lit.* [there is] bile (anger) even in [an] ant). 6 (*i*) One must find a wife amongst one's own class (*lit.* it is necessary [*sc.* for a person] to marry from among those who are similar. (*ii*) [A] fool speaks foolish [things]. (*iii*) You have your feet out of trouble (*lit.* foot outside mud). (*iv*) [The] pot boils, friendship lives. (*v*) You are shaving (*or* bearding) [a] lion. (*vi*) You are weeping on [your] step-mother's tomb (*i.e.* being hypocritical). (7) Alas, alas, greatness (*lit.* great things) also suffers great evils. (8) [The] roughness of [the] road tests [the] serviceability of [the] ass. (9) Man is only (*or* nothing but) breath and shadow. (10) Fortune guides art, not art fortune. (11) Money [is] responsible for many evils for men. (12) Woman, silence is becoming (*lit.* brings decoration) for women. (13) Even for [an] old man, [it is] [a] fine [thing] to learn wisdom (*lit.* wise things). (14) The Athenians sent Thucydides the [son] of Olorus to the general of those in Thrace. (15) One should seek neither companionship (*or* company) from [a] corpse nor [a] favour from [a] miser. (16) Victory is sufficient for the free. (17) Even among rustics there is love of culture. (18) The wolf changes his coat (*lit.* hair), not his mind. (19) Money finds friends for men. (20) [A] mob [is] [a] poor judge of [a] fine matter. (21) To some of the Egyptians, therefore, crocodiles are sacred, to others [they are] not, but they treat [them] as enemies. Those around Thebes and [those around] the swamp of Moeris strongly believe that they are (*lit.* them to be) sacred. Both groups keep (*or* rear) one crocodile and train [it], and put rings made of glass in its ears and anklets round its front feet, and provide special food and offerings. So while the crocodiles are alive, they are treated very well, and after their death the Egyptians embalm them and bury them in sacred tombs. But those around the city [of] Elephantine actually eat them; for they do not consider [them] to be sacred. (Adapted from Herodotus ii.69)

6.2

From this point on the definite and indefinite articles which must be supplied for translation are no longer bracketed.

(1) (*i*) The guards guarded the Persians (φυλάττω). (*ii*) Did you hide the golden horse? (κρύπτω). (*iii*) The Athenians and the Spartans joined in an expedition (συστρατεύω). (*iv*) He wrote many things on the rock (ἐγγράφω). (*v*) The gods will do many great things (πράττω). (*vi*) Socrates taught us (διδάσκω). (*vii*) They damaged the house of Pericles (βλάπτω). (*viii*) We fought a sea-battle in the harbour (ναυμαχέω). (2) Bronze is the mirror of form (i.e. of the body), wine of the mind. (3) Hand washes hand, fingers [wash] fingers. (4) Speech is silver, silence is golden. (5) O God, how mortals have no escape from evils [which are] innate or (*or* and) sent by the gods! (*lit.* how there is not to mortals [an] escape...). (6) (*i*) You are writing on (*lit.* into) water. (*ii*) You are building on (*lit.* into) sand. (*iii*) [You are bringing] an owl to Athens (*cf.* coals to Newcastle). (*iv*) You are measuring the waves. (*v*) You are looking for bird's milk. (*vi*) You are teaching iron to float (*lit.* sail). (*vii*) You are lending light to the sun. (*viii*) You are pouring wine for frogs. (*ix*) You are beating the air. (*x*) He is making an elephant out of a fly (*i.e.* a mountain out of a molehill). (7) (*i*) The mind is a great check (*lit.* bit) of the soul. (*ii*) The Greeks [are] always children, an old Greek does not exist. (*iii*) For a mother (*or* for mothers) children are the anchors of [her] life. (*iv*) Lions at home, but foxes (*i.e.* cowards) in battle. (*v*) The mind sees and the mind hears. (*vi*) The arms (*lit.* hands) of tyrants [are] long. (*vii*) Ares (War) [is] a friend of falsehood (*lit.* friendly to false things). (*viii*) Athens [is] the Greece of Greece. (*ix*) You are comparing a bee with a cicada. (*x*) A daughter [is] a difficult possession. (8) The wind [kindles] fire, intimacy kindles love. (9) According to Socrates no-one errs willingly. (10) The wise man should not think after (*i.e.* repent) but before (*lit.* it is necessary for the wise man not to...). (11) The Athenian ambassadors withdrew to the army, but the generals built a wall around the Melians. Later, a small garrison of the allies remained there and continued to besiege (*lit.* was besieging) the place, while the rest of the soldiers withdrew by land and by sea. Afterwards the Melians pulled down the Athenians' blockading wall, since not many of the guards were present. But later the Athenians sent out another army from Athens, and they now vigorously prosecuted the siege. There was treachery (*or* treachery broke out) among the Melians, and they capitulated to the Athenians. And they (*i.e.* the Athenians) killed the men among (*lit.* of) the Melians, and enslaved the women and children. And later they sent out many settlers and colonised the place. (Adapted from Thucydides v.114–116)

7.2

(1) The proverb bids us not to move the immovable (*lit.* unmovable [things]). (2) [It is] altogether not easy to find what is right (*or* justice). (3) Ischomachus said, 'Socrates, in winter a house should be well exposed to the sun, but in summer well-shaded.' (4) We do not have either weapons or horses (*or* we have neither weapons nor horses). (5) No falsehood spreads for long (a length of time). (6) So for one day the Athenians encamped there. But on the following day Alcibiades called an assembly and ordered them to fight both at sea, on land and against the fortifications. 'For', he said, 'we have no money, whereas the enemy have plenty.' (7) All human beings die (*lit.* no one of human beings does not die). (8) (*i*) One swallow does not make a spring. (*ii*) Old men [are] children for a second time. (*iii*) You see three things in two. (*iv*) One man [is] no man. (*v*) One day does not make (a man) wise. (*vi*) The tongue leads many [people] to destruction. (*vii*) In war it is not possible to make a mistake twice. (*viii*) It is possible to recognize a lion from his claw-marks (i.e. to judge a person from a characteristic mark). (9) Cyrus marched forth three stages (*or* days' marches) through Lydia, [a distance of] twenty-two parasangs, to the river Maeander. Its

breadth was two plethra. (10) The world [is] a stage, life an entrance: you come, you see, you depart. (11) Someone said to Socrates, 'Megacles speaks ill of you'. And he replied, 'Yes, for he does not know how (*lit*. has not learnt) to speak well.' (12) Callicratidas held the right wing of the Peloponnesians. His steersman, Hermon, said, 'It is a good [idea] to retreat (*lit*. sail away); for the Athenian triremes are very strong.' But Callicratidas said, 'It is shameful to flee.' The triremes fought [for] a long time, at first in close order, and then scattered. When Callicratidas fell overboard into the sea and was killed and Protomachus the Athenian and his men (*lit*. those with him) defeated the left wing with [their] right wing, thereupon the Peloponnesians fled (*lit*. there was a flight of...) to Chios and Phocaea, while the Athenians sailed back to Arginousae. And so of the Athenians the Spartans sank 25 triremes, whereas of the Peloponnesians the Athenians [sank] nine Laconian [triremes], and of their allies as well about 60. (Adapted from Xenophon *Hellenica* i. 6. 32) (13) For, when Simon came to my house at night, he forced (*lit*. knocked out) the doors and entered the women's apartments, where my sister and nieces were. At first the men in the house ordered him to go away, but he refused. Then they forcibly pushed him out. But he discovered where we were dining and did a thing most extraordinary and incredible. He called me out from inside, and as soon as I had come out, he immediately attempted to strike me; and when I pushed him away, he began to pelt me with stones (*or* throw stones at me). Although he missed me, he hit Aristocritus with a stone and gashed his forehead. (Adapted from Lysias *Against Simon* 6-8)

8.2

(1) God and Nature do nothing without reason. (2) [It is] not easy to change a wicked nature. (3) Wicked slander wipes out whole cities. (4) Jesus Christ, son of God, Saviour (*the symbol is the fish*, ἰχθύς *being an acronym of the phrase*). (5) Gold does not tarnish (*lit*. is not stained). (6) Do you think that others will save Greece, but you will run away? (7) As a result of looking at [someone] people fall in love. (8) The possession of virtue alone is secure. (9) Alas, alas, how true the old saying is: we old men are nothing but (no other thing except) noise and [outward] appearance; we creep along [as] copies of dreams; there is no sense in [us] but we think we are sane. (Euripides, fragment 25) (10) An elephant does not bite a mouse. (11) For most people the search for truth [is pursued] without taking pains, and they turn rather to what is ready to hand. (12) The Lacedaemonians sent a herald and carried across the corpses (*or* had the corpses carried across). (13) It was wonder which made men begin to pursue philosophy both now and originally (*lit*. because of the fact of wondering men both now and at first began...). (14) The mountain laboured, and then gave birth to a mouse. (15) Hunger is (*lit*. becomes) the teacher of many [things.] (16) The Scythians do not wash with (*or* in) water. (17) (*i*) In the beginning God made the heaven and the earth. And the earth was invisible and unformed, and darkness [was] upon the abyss, and the spirit of God moved upon the water. And God said, 'Let there be (*lit*. be born) light.' And there was light (*lit*. light came into being). And God saw that the light was beautiful. And God made a division between the light and the darkness. And God called the light day and the darkness he called night. (*Genesis* 1.1-5). (*ii*) I turned about and I saw beneath the sun that the race [is] not to the nimble, nor war to the strong, nor bread to the wise, nor wealth to the intelligent. (*Ecclesiastes* 9.11) (18) Zenothemis contrived a wicked crime in collaboration with Hegestratus. They went around borrowing (*lit*. were borrowing) money in Syracuse. When they got the money, they used to send it home to Marseilles, and they loaded (*lit*. brought into) nothing on board (*lit*. into) the ship. Since the contract stipulated repayment of (*lit*. was to repay) the money after the arrival in port of the ship, they plotted to sink the ship; for they wished to defraud their creditors. Accordingly, when they were two or three days out from

land (*lit.* had sailed away a voyage of ... days), Hegestratus began to cut through the bottom of the ship during the night, while Zenothemis passed the time on deck (*lit.* above) with the other passengers. But when a noise was heard (*lit.* happened), those on the ship perceived that some mischief was taking place down below, and went to the rescue. As Hegestratus was being caught and assumed that he would be badly treated, he took to his heels (*lit.* fled) and jumped into the sea. In this way then, as he deserved, a bad man, he came to a bad end (*lit.* he died badly). ([? Demosthenes] *Against Zenothemis* 4-6, slightly adapted)

9.2

(1) Death [is] beautiful [for those] to whom life brings humiliation. (2) The wise man carries round his substance within (*lit.* in) himself. (3) Mighty in war [was] Timocritus, whose tomb this [is]; Ares spares not the brave, but the cowardly. (*A.P.* vii. 269). (4) Cleon said that not he himself but that man was general. (5) The same [people] [say] the same [remarks] about the same [subjects] to the same [people]. (6) You are telling me my [own] dream (*i.e.* nothing I don't already know). (7) Then that man said, 'Well, if there is need of anything else (*lit.* another thing) in addition to what (*lit.* these things which) Xenophon says, it will be possible to do it immediately.' After this Xenophon spoke as follows: '[It is] clear that we must march where we will have supplies; and I hear that there are fine villages which are twenty stades away.' (Xenophon *Anabasis* iii. 2. 33-34.) (8) A friend is another self (*or* alter ego). (9) Pythagoras was the first to name philosophy and himself a philosopher. (10) [We] must compare them with each other; for thus we will consider if they will differ from each other. (11) The Greeks mistrust each other (*lit.* are mistrustful towards themselves). (12) After dinner Cyrus asked, 'Tigranes, where then is that man who used to hunt with us? You seemed to me to admire him very much.' 'My father here put him to death', he said. 'For he said that he was corrupting me. And yet, Cyrus, he was a fine man, for even when he was about to die, he summoned me and said, "Tigranes, you must not be angry because your father is putting me to death; for he does this not because of malice, but because of ignorance. And what (*lit.* which things) men do wrong through ignorance, I believe [they do] this against their will".' (Xenophon *Cyropaedia*, iii.1.38, adapted) (13) Demosthenes, who saw that the Lacedaemonians intended to attack by land and by sea (*lit.* both with ships and with infantry), began to make his own preparations (*lit.* make preparations himself also), and hauled up under the fortification the triremes which remained to him, and armed the sailors from them with shields of poor quality and mostly made of osier; for it was impossible to procure arms in [this] deserted place, and even these (*sc.* which they had) they got from a thirty-oared pirate-ship and a pinnace belonging to (*lit.* of) [some] Messenians, who were there. Of these Messenians there were about forty hoplites. Accordingly, he posted the majority of his own men at the strong points of the place facing the mainland, while (*lit.* and) he himself picked out sixty hoplites and a few archers and began to go outside the wall (*sc.* of the fortification) towards the sea, [to the point] where he particularly expected the enemy (*lit.* those men) would attempt to land. So he posted his hoplites at this point right beside the sea (*lit.* towards the sea itself). (Thucydides iv. 9, adapted)

10.2

(1) A fat belly does not generate a fine mind. (2) How sweet [it is] to look at the sea from the land. (3) Time will explain everything to posterity (*lit.* those [who come] later). (4) Happiness is an activity of the soul. (5) O Menander and life, which one of you then imitated which? (6) Who knows if life is death, and [if] down below death is considered life? (7) Life [is] short, art long (*i.e.* the art of medicine is extensive and requires a long time to master), opportunity fleeting (*lit.* swift), experiment

perilous, and judgement difficult. (8) Wickedness [is] quick (*lit.* brief), virtue slow. (9) Where a man fares well, there [is his] native-land. (10) Whoever of mortals wishes to arrive at (*lit.* go/come into) hateful old age, does not reckon well; for a long life begets countless woes. (11) How sweet [it is] for slaves to get decent masters and for masters [to get] a well-disposed slave in [their] house. (12) Everything [is] burdensome except to rule over the gods. For no one is free except Zeus. (13) Ignorant [people] are carried along in life as if on the high sea and in darkness. (14) The woman said, 'My husband's virtue is sufficient adornment for me.' (15) Where a man has a pain, there he applies (*lit.* has) his mind too. (16) (*i*) I hate a drinking-companion who remembers (*lit.* a mindful drinking-companion). (*ii*) Hostile [is] the eye of neighbours. (*iii*) Even a sheep bites an unlucky man. (*iv*) An unskilled man is a slave of (*lit.* to) everyone. (*v*) War [is] sweet to the inexperienced. (*vi*) Time decides everything (*lit.* everything is decided by time). (*vii*) Bright in darkness, but useless in daylight. (*viii*) Hands wash each other. (*ix*) Under every stone sleeps a scorpion. (*x*) Everything [is] easy for God (or a god). (*xi*) Every hedgehog [is] prickly. (*xii*) The whole of time cannot whiten the man (*lit.* this [man]) whom Fate paints (*lit.* will paint) black. (17) (*i*) Diogenes was once begging [alms] from a statue. [When he was] asked why he was doing this, he said, 'I am practising failure (*lit.* to fail to obtain).' (*ii*) [When he was] asked what kind of wine he liked to drink (*lit.* drank gladly), he said, 'Someone else's.' (*iii*) He was begging [alms] from a miser. When he hesitated (*lit.* was slow), Diogenes said, 'Fellow, I'm begging [alms] from you for food, not for burial.' (*iv*) [When he was] asked where he was from, he said, '[I am] a citizen of the world.' (*v*) When someone said that life was bad, he said, 'Not life, but a bad life.'

10.3

For, gentlemen of Athens, I have this reputation for no other reason (*lit.* on account of nothing else) than a certain wisdom. What sort of wisdom [do I say] this [is]? [Just that] which is perhaps human wisdom. For in reality I am likely to be (or I am probably) wise in this wisdom. But these men, whom I was just now mentioning, are wise in a sort of superhuman wisdom, which I am unable to describe. For I, at any rate, do not understand it, and (*lit.* but) whoever says [that I do], is lying and speaking to arouse prejudice against me. I hope, men of Athens, that you will not interrupt me, even if I seem to you to be saying something extravagant (*lit.* big). For the story which I will tell is not mine, but I will refer [you] to someone who is worthy of credit. For I shall furnish you with the god of (*lit.* at) Delphi [as] witness of my [wisdom], [as to] whether it is actually some sort of wisdom and of what sort it is. Chaerephon was familiar to you, I think. He was a comrade of mine from youth and a partisan of the democracy. And it is well known to you what sort [of a person] Chaerephon was, how impetuous in all respects. As a matter of fact, he actually went to Delphi once and dared to ask the oracle if anyone was wiser than I. The Pythian [priestess] answered that no one was wiser. (Plato *Apology* 20d-21a, slightly adapted)

11.2

From this point on the relevant part of the verb to be *which must be supplied for translation is not normally bracketed.*

(1) Tyranny is the mother of injustice. (2) The dice of Zeus always fall luckily (*lit.* well). (3) There is some degree (*lit.* measure) of pleasure even in troubles. (4) And the story is not mine, but [comes] from my mother, that heaven and earth were one shape; but when they were separated apart from each other, they brought forth everything and sent up to the light trees, winged creatures, wild beasts and [the creatures] which the sea nourishes and the race of men. (Euripides, fragment 484)

(5) Concealment (*lit.* the act of hiding) is wicked and not the mark of a well-born man. (6) Someone said to Socrates, 'The Athenians condemned you to the death', and he said, "And Nature [is condemning] them [to death]". (7) The wagon pulls the ox. (8) (*i*) An old woman is dancing. (*ii*) You are graciously giving a mirror to a blind man. (*iii*) You are hunting the wind with a net. (*iv*) You are throwing stones at the sun (*lit.* pelting the sun with stones). (*v*) The/a tortoise is calling the oxen slow-footed. (*vi*) You are striking a peg with a sponge. (*vii*) You knocked out a peg with a peg (*i.e.* in solving one problem you created another). (*viii*) You are blocking up (*i.e.* repairing) the chamber-pot with a sandal. (*ix*) You are driving out wine with wine. (*x*) You yourself are striking your own door with a stone. (9) For, for all mankind, not only for us, either straightaway or in [the course of] time, God trips up [one's] life, and no one is happy throughout (*or* forever). (Euripides, fragment 273) (10) For none of these things will distress me. But if you do not do this (*lit.* these things), you will inflict (*lit.* throw) grief upon all the Argives (*i.e.* Greeks). For if we do not get this man's bow (*lit.* this man's bow will not be taken), it is not possible for you to ravage the land of Dardanus. (Sophocles *Philoctetes* 66–69) (11) Thus the venture (*lit.* things) of the Greeks came to naught (*lit.* was destroyed). And out of many a few made their way through Libya to Cyrene and were saved, but most were killed. Egypt again came (*lit.* became) under the control of the King [of Persia], except Amyrtaeus, the king in the marshes. They (*i.e.* the Persians) were unable to capture him both because of the extent of the marsh and at the same time [because] the marsh-people are particularly warlike. Inaros the Libyan king (*lit.* king of the Libyans), who had conducted (*lit.* done) the whole Egyptian venture (*lit.* everything with respect to Egypt), was captured by treachery and impaled. Fifty triremes from Athens and the rest of the confederacy sailed [as a] relieving [force] to Egypt and put in at the Mendesian arm [of the Nile]. But foot-soldiers attacked them from the land and a fleet of Phoenicians from the sea and destroyed most of the ships. So ended the great expedition (*lit.* the [things] with respect to the great expedition) of the Athenians and their allies against (*lit.* into) Egypt. (Thucydides i.110, adapted) (12) When we had transferred to the other ship, we began to drink. It is clear that Herodes disembarked from the ship and did not re-embark (*lit.* go on board again). I did not disembark at all from the ship that night. On the following day, when the man was not to be seen, he was looked for in no way more [vigorously] by the others than by me (*i.e.* I looked for him as vigorously as anyone); and if it (his disappearance) seemed serious to any of the others, [it did so] equally to me (i.e. if anyone considered it a serious matter, I did). Not only (*lit.* both) was I responsible for a messenger being sent to Mytilene, but (*lit.* and), since no one else was willing to go, either of those on (*lit.* from) the ship or of the companions of Herodes himself, I was prepared to send my own servant. But when the man did not appear either in Mytilene or anywhere else, and the wind was fair (*lit.* sailing [time] was coming into being) for us and all the other ships were putting out to sea, I too departed. (Antiphon *Murder of Herodes* 23–24, slightly adapted)

12.2

Where participial phrases have been expanded into subordinate clauses (e.g. in 1-5 below; see 12.1/2a) the words added in English have not been enclosed in square brackets.

(1) The man who runs away will also fight again (*or* lives to fight another day). (2) When a bear is present (*or* around) one need not look for tracks. (3) If you love yourself too much you will not have a friend. (4) Although he does not feed himself, he feeds [his] dogs. (5) The person who does not marry has no troubles. (6) In trying to flee (*lit.* fleeing) the smoke you fell into the fire. (7) A man who is running away does not wait for the sound of the lyre. (8) It is said that dogs burnt just once are

afraid of fire (*lit.* dogs ... are said to fear ...). (9) For I have come to bury Caesar, not to praise [him]. (10) No one who is hungry sings sweet songs (*lit.* beautiful things). (11) Am I a bumpkin (*lit.* boorish) if I call a trough a trough? (12) The man who has been bitten by a serpent fears even a little rope. (13) The man who is illiterate (*lit.* inexperienced in letters) sees nothing although he has sight (*lit.* does not see [although] seeing). (14) It is difficult to speak to [one's] belly, since it does not have ears. (15) Prometheus: 'You behold [this] spectacle, [me] this friend of Zeus, with what woes I am bent by him.' Ocean: 'I see, Prometheus, and I wish to give you the best advice (*lit.* advise the best things to you), subtle (*or* ingenious) as you are (*lit.* though being).' (Aeschylus *Prometheus Bound* 304ff.) (16) From there Cyrus marched out though Lycaonia five stages, [a distance of] thirty parasangs, and he allowed the Greeks to plunder this country on the grounds that it was hostile. (17) Once when turning a book of Hesiod beneath my hands I suddenly saw Pyrrha approaching; and throwing the book to the ground with my hand I shouted this, 'Why do you give me trouble, old Hesiod?' (*A.P.* ix.161) (18) Child of Phoenician-born Europa and great Zeus, ruling over Crete of a hundred cities, I have come leaving sacred (*lit.* very holy) temples ... And we have led a chaste life since I became a mystic of Idaean Zeus, and, having conducted feasts of raw flesh as a herdsman of night-roaming Zagreus and held up torches for the mountain-wandering mother with the Curetes, I was sanctified and called an initiate of Bacchus. (Euripides, fragment 472)

12.3

(1) A man, finding [some] gold, left a noose; but the man who did not find the gold which he had left, fastened the noose (*i.e.* to hang himself) which he had found. (*A.P.* ix.44) (2) The Cyprian, seeing [the statue of] the Cyprian (*i.e.* of herself) in Cnidos, said, 'Alas, alas, where did Praxiteles see me naked?' (*App. Plan.* 162) (3) All Cilicians are bad men; but among the Cilicians [there is] one good man, [viz] Cinyres, but even Cinyres is Cilician. (*A.P.* xi. 236) (4) Once Antiochus laid eyes on (*lit.* looked at) Lysimachus' cushion, and Lysimachus never again (*lit.* no longer) laid eyes on his cushion. (*A.P.* xi. 315) (5) Although he produced twenty sons, Eutychus the painter has no likeness even among (*lit.* from) his children (*i.e.* he has as little success in producing lifelike paintings as in fathering children from a faithless wife). (*A.P.* xi. 215) (6) You [with] the roses, you have a rosy charm. But what are you selling, yourself, or the roses, or both together? (*A.P.* v. 81) (7) As I was kissing Agathon, I checked my soul at [my] lips; for it had come, poor wretch, with the idea of crossing over. (*A.P.* v. 78) (8) I who laughed haughtily at Greece, I, Laïs, who kept the swarm of young lovers in [my] porch, [dedicate] [my] mirror to the Paphian; since such [as I am now] I do not wish to see myself, and such as I was formerly I am unable [to see myself]. (*A.P.* vi. 1) (9) Someone told [me], Heraclitus, of your death, and brought tears (*lit.* a tear) to me, and I remembered how often both of us laid the sun to rest in conversation. But you, I suppose, my friend from Halicarnassus, are ashes long, long ago. But your nightingales (*i.e.* poems) live on, upon which Hades, the ravisher of all things, shall not lay his hand. (Callimachus epigram 2).

13.2

(1) [It] is a fine [thing] indeed to be master of one's belly and one's desire[s]. (2) Both common-sense and proper deliberation (*lit.* deliberating on what it is necessary [to do]) are accustomed to accompany old age. (3) This is bravery (*lit.* the brave thing), [that is to say] forethought. (4) Everywhere the land which feeds [you is your] native-land. (5) Old age, you know, has a certain wisdom (*lit.* something wise) indeed with respect to deliberation (*or* planning), since indeed it has seen and experienced much (*lit.* as having seen and experienced many things). (6) O unfortunate virtue, you

were [a mere] word then; yet I practised you as something real (*lit.* a fact, *i.e.* as though you really existed). But you were a slave to chance after all. (7) Oedipus, the son of Laius, is my father (*lit.* father for us), and Iocaste, the daughter of Menoeceus, bore me; and the Theban people call me Polyneices (Euripides *Phoenissae* 288–290). (8) There is no temple of Persuasion other than speech, and her altar is in the nature of man. (9) He who chases two hares catches neither. (10) Cyrus, inasmuch as he was a child and liked elegance and distinction, was pleased with his clothes. (11) Not even the gods fight against necessity. (12) Obedience to one's stomach is a necessary evil. (13) In escaping Charybdis you have fallen into (*lit.* in with) Scylla. (14) A hungry ass pays no heed to the cudgel. (15) No-one desires life as much as the man who is growing old. (16) Death alone of the gods does not desire gifts. (17) The man who does no wrong needs no law (*sc.* to protect him). (18) Sailors (*or* those who sail) are [only] four fingers away from death. (19) You have a need of spring since you have an old cloak (*i.e.* spring [and not winter] is the right season for the threadbare cloak you are wearing). (20) The Spartan [woman] Gorgo, asked by an Attic (*i.e.* Athenian) [woman], 'Why do you Spartan [women] alone rule your men (*or* husbands)?' said, 'Because we alone also give birth to [real] men.' (21) In reply to a certain lad who was intending to attend his classes and enquired what he needed (*lit.* of what things there is a need to him), Antisthenes the philosopher said, "A new book and a new pencil and a new writing-tablet", stressing the nous. (*The pun on* καινοῦ *and* καὶ-νοῦ *is virtually untranslatable, although in American pronunciation it comes across in 'new' and 'nous'.*) (22) The black earth drinks, and the trees drink it (*i.e.* from it); the sea drinks the streams, the sun the sea, and the moon the sun. Why do you fight with me [my] friends (*or* comrades), when I myself also wish to drink? (Anacreontea 19)

13.3

(*i*) I was making my way from the Academy straight to the Lyceum along the [road] outside the wall, close under the wall (*lit.* beneath the wall) itself. When I came to (*lit.* was in the region of) the postern gate where the spring of Panops is, there I fell in with Hippothales, the [son] of Hieronymus, and Ctesippus of Paiania, and [some] other young men [who were] with them. Seeing me approach, Hippothales said, 'Socrates, where are you going and where [have you come] from?' 'From the Academy', I said, 'on my way (*lit.* I'm making my way) straight to the Lyceum.' '[Come] over **here**', he said, 'straight to us. Aren't you going to come over (*lit.* do you not come near)? Yet it's worthwhile.' 'Where do you mean', I said, 'and who are you to whom [I am to come]?' 'Over here', he said, showing me right opposite (*lit.* in the [spot] right opposite) the wall a sort of enclosure and door. 'We spend our time here,' he said, 'both we ourselves and a lot of other fine [fellows].' 'And what is this [place] then, and how do you spend your time (*lit.* what is [your] manner of spending time)?' 'A new wrestling-school', he said. 'And we usually spend our time in discussions, in which we wish you to share.' 'That's very kind of you (*lit.* doing well indeed)', I said. 'And who teaches here?' 'Your own friend', he said, 'and admirer, Miccus.' 'My goodness (*lit.* by Zeus)', I said, 'he's not unimportant (*lit.* the man [is] not insignificant), he's a competent teacher.' 'Well then, do you want to follow [me]', he said, 'and to see those who are here?' (Plato *Lysis* 203a–204a)

(*ii*) *Eucleides.* Just [in] from the country, Terpsion, or [did you arrive] some time ago? *Terpsion.* Quite some time ago. I was looking for you in (*lit.* throughout) the agora and was surprised that I could not find [you]. *E.* [No, you couldn't], for I was not in the city. *T.* Where [were you] then? *E.* As I was going down to [the] harbour I met Theaetetus being carried to Athens from the camp at (*lit.* from) Corinth. *T.* Alive or dead? *E.* Alive, but only just (*lit.* and very hardly). For he's in a bad way actually because of some wounds, but more [than that] the disease which [has broken out] in the army is afflicting him. *T.* You don't mean dysentery, do you? *E.* Yes, I do. *T.* What a man [this is who] you say is in danger. *E.* A real gentleman (*lit.* fine and good), Terpsion, and (*lit.* since), you know, just now I was listening to some [people] singing his praises (*lit.* praising him very much) in connection with the battle. *T.* And [that's] not at all strange. But how [is it that] he did not stay (*or* lodge) here in Megara? *E.* He was hurrying [to get] home. I asked him and advised him [*sc.* to stay], but he refused. In fact, as I escorted [him home] I recalled with admiration how prophetically Socrates had spoken in particular about him (*lit.* I recalled and marvelled at Socrates how prophetically he had spoken both other things indeed and about this man). For I think that (*lit.* he seems to me to...), a little before his death, he (Socrates) met him when he was a lad, and after being with [him] and conversing [with him], greatly admired his character. (Plato *Theaetetus* 142a-c)

14.2

The abbreviations P.S. (Primary sequence) and H.S. (Historic sequence) are used in defining the uses of the subjunctive/optative here.

(1) For there is a certain pleasure even in words, if (*lit.* whenever) they create a forgetfulness of [one's] existing troubles (*indefinite, P.S.*). (2) How then am I, a [mere] mortal (*lit.* being mortal), to fight against divine fortune (*or* fortune sent by the gods)? (*deliberative subjunctive*). (3) [It is] the mind [that one] must look at, the mind; what advantage [is there] in (*lit.* of) bodily beauty, if (*lit.* whenever) a person does not have a beautiful (i.e. noble) mind? (*indefinite, P.S.*). (4) Whoever is shipwrecked twice, blames Poseidon without reason (*i.e.* he should have taken Poseidon's hint the first time) (*indefinite, P. S.*). (5) Socrates said that most men live in order that they may eat, whereas he himself ate in order that he might live (*purpose, subjunctive retained in H.S.*). (6) Let us eat and drink; for tomorrow we die (*jussive subjunctive.*). (7) God plants (*lit.* produces) a fault (*lit.* blame) in mortals whenever he wishes to ruin a family completely (*indefinite, P. S.*). (8) What a charming creature (*lit.* how charming) is man when (*lit.* whenever) he is a [real] man (*indefinite, P.S.*). (9) *A.* Who is this man? *B.* A doctor. *A.* What a bad state every doctor is in if (*lit.* if ever) no one [else] is in a bad state! (*indefinite, P.S.*). (10) Our life is very like wine: whenever what remains (*or* the remains) is small, it becomes vinegar (*indefinite, P.S.*). (11) Those who are afraid that they may go into exile from their native land and those who, being about to fight, are afraid that they may be defeated are not able to take (*lit.* get) either food or sleep because of their fear; but those who are already in exile or (*lit.* and) already defeated can eat and sleep even more (*or* better) than those blessed with good fortune (*fear for the future, P.S.*). (12) A monkey is a monkey even if it has golden sandals (*indefinite, P.S.*). (13) The Greeks were afraid that the Persians might advance against the wing and, outflanking them on both sides, might cut them to pieces (*fear for the future, H.S.*). (14) When the man whom they had seized was asked from what country he came (*lit.* was; *indirect question, H.S.*), he said that he was a Persian, and that he was proceeding from Tiribazos' army in order that he might get provisions (*purpose clause, H.S.*). (15) When Diogenes saw an archer with no natural skill, he sat down beside the target saying, 'In order that I may not be hit' (*purpose clause in direct quotation, hence not H.S.*). (16) Through inexperience of death every man is afraid to leave the light of this sun (*lit.* this light of the sun). (17) A man was running so as not to get wet, and was drowned in a hole (*purpose clause, H.S.*). (18) When the generals assembled at daybreak, they were surprised that Cyrus neither sent someone else to tell [them] what to do (*lit.* it is necessary to do) nor appeared himself (*indirect statement, H.S.*). So they decided to pack up what they had and put on their full (ἐξ-) armour and move forwards. When they were already on the point of starting, at sunrise there came Procles, the ruler of Teuthrania, and Glus, the [son] of Tamos. They reported that Cyrus had been killed,

but that Ariaeus was at the halting place with the rest of the barbarians and was saying that they would wait for them throughout this day (*indirect statement, H.S.*). (Xenophon *Anabasis* ii. 1. 2-3, slightly adapted) (19) If ever he saw the soldiers going in good order, he praised [them] (*indefinite, H.S.*). (20) If you fear the law (*lit.* fearing the law) you will not be troubled by the law.

15.2

(1) [While] avoiding [the] ashes I have fallen into [the] fire (*i.e.* out of the frying-pan into the fire). (2) No-one does wicked [deeds] without the gods' knowing (*lit.* no-one escapes the notice of the gods doing wicked things). (3) A crab has not learned (*i.e.* does not know how) to walk straight. (4) We are all wise in giving warnings (*lit.* with respect to warning), but we do not realise when we ourselves make mistakes. (5) The trap has caught the mouse. (6) For the man who takes pleasure in constantly speaking does not realise (*lit.* escaped his own notice) that he is wearisome to his companions (*lit.* those who are with [him]). (7) He has eaten scorpions. (8) Whoever devises treachery (*lit.* crafty things) against another is doing this against himself unawares (*lit.* escapes [his own] notice doing this himself against himself). (9) The hoplites happened to be sleeping in the agora. (10) It was clear that Menon desired (*lit.* Menon was obvious desiring) to be exceedingly rich. (11) So they took Jesus; and carrying his own cross (*lit.* the cross for himself) he went forth to the so-called Place of a Skull, which in Hebrew is called Golgotha, where they crucified him, and with him two others one on each side (*lit.* from this side and from this side), and Jesus in the middle. Pilate also wrote a title (*or* inscription) and placed [it] on the cross, JESUS OF NAZARETH THE KING OF THE JEWS. Many of the Jews read this title, because the place where Jesus was crucified was near the city. Accordingly, the chief priests of the Jews said to Pilate, 'Do not write "The King of the Jews", but "He claimed to be the King of the Jews"' (*lit.* but that, 'he said, "I am the King ..."'). Pilate replied, 'What I have written, I have written.' (John 19.16–22) (12) For all seven days during which they were marching through [the territory of] the Kurds they continued to fight. (13) When Clearetus had encouraged his soldiers, he began to lead them against the place, but day broke while he was still marching (*lit.* day happening anticipated him marching). (14) When Archimedes was washing himself, so the story goes (*lit.* as they say), he discovered from the overflow (*sc.* of the water-level in his bath) how to measure (*lit.* the measuring of) the crown, and as if possessed or inspired (*lit.* just as from some possession or inspiration), he jumped out shouting, 'I've found [it]', and went about saying this over and over again (*lit.* often). But we have heard neither of any glutton shouting so passionately, 'I have eaten', nor of any lover [shouting] 'I have kissed', though countless sensualists existed in the past and [still] exist [now]. (Plutarch *Moralia* 1094C) (15) *A.* He is married, I believe. *B.* What are you saying? Is he really married, [the man] whom I left alive and on his feet (*lit.* living and walking about)? (16) They stopped building the large wall because they feared (*lit.* fearing) that it would not be sufficient to hold out. (17) I see that for the majority of people former prosperity gives birth to insolence.

15.3

Might. We have come to [this] distant region of the earth, to [this] Scythian tract, to [this] wilderness where no men live. Hephaestus, you must concern yourself with the commands (*lit.* it is necessary that the commands be of concern to you) which the Father (*i.e.* Zeus) enjoined on you, to bind fast this wrong-doer on [these] rocks with lofty cliffs in unbreakable fetters of adamantine bonds. For [it was] your glory, the flame of fire on which all arts depend, [which] he stole and bestowed on mortals.

[It is] for such a wrong, you know, [that] he must pay the penalty to the gods, in order that he may be taught (*or* learn) to accept the sovereignty of Zeus, and cease from his man-loving ways. *Hephaestus.* Might and Violence, for you two the command of Zeus has indeed fulfilment (*or* has been fulfilled) and nothing is still in [your] way, but I lack the heart to bind by force to [this] stormy ravine a god [who is my] kinsman. Yet for all that, I must (*lit.* there is necessity for me to) take the heart for this; for [it is] a grievous [matter] to disregard the words of the Father. O lofty-minded son of straight-counselling Themis, against your will and mine (*lit.* you being unwilling I being unwilling) will I fasten you in (*or* with) inextricable brazen bonds to this rock far from men, where you will perceive (*lit.* see) neither the voice nor the shape of anyone of mortals, but grilled by the sun's radiant flame you will alter the bloom of your skin; and you will be glad when (*lit.* to you being glad) night with her embroidered cloak will hide the light and [when] the sun will scatter the morning frost again; the burden of your present suffering (*lit.* the present trouble) will continually distress you; for the one who will relieve [it *or* you] is not yet born. (Aeschylus *Prometheus Bound* 1–27)

16.2

(1) When they had come to their tents, the rest (*sc.* of the soldiers) were busy about the provisions, while generals and captains met together. And at this point there was much despondency. For on one side there lay (*lit.* were) very high mountains, and on the other side the river was so deep (*lit.* of such a size) that not even their spears were above [the water] when they tested the depth. (2) When Diogenes was asked why athletes were stupid, he said, 'Because they have been built up with pork and beef.' (3) One must marry [only] after making a [proper] choice. (4) We are involved in constant (*lit.* we continue being in) dangers throughout all our life, so that those who talk about security do not realise (*lit.* have escaped their own notice) that they are preparing for war for the whole of time. (5) You are flaying a flayed bitch (*i.e.* you are flogging a dead horse). (6) The Potideans, waiting for the Athenians, were camped on the isthmus on the side towards Olynthus, and they had established a market outside the city. And the allies had chosen Aristeus [as] general of the whole infantry and Perdiccas of the cavalry. (7) When the barbarians had left their land, the Athenians began to make preparations to rebuild their city. For of the houses most had collapsed, although a few survived, in which the chief men of the Persians had themselves lodged. (8) The goat has come to knives [already] sharpened (*i.e.* one is asking for trouble). (9) They passed the night there. But when day began to break, they proceeded to march in silence against the enemy, drawn up in battle-order; for a mist had also appeared, so that they came up close without being seen (*lit.* escaped notice approaching near). (10) Then an agreement was made (*lit.* comes into being (*vivid pres.*)) with respect to all those with Demosthenes as well, on condition that no-one would die either through violence (*lit.* violently) or imprisonment (*lit.* bonds) or lack of food. (11) Tiribazus said that he wished to make a treaty on condition that neither he himself would harm the Greeks nor would they burn the houses but (*lit.* and) would take the provisions that they needed. These [terms] were accepted by (*lit.* seemed good to) the generals and they made a treaty on these terms. (12) Nor is it still the time, Socrates, to be deliberating but to have finished deliberating. There is [only] one plan: all this must be completed (*or* over and done with) within this night. (13) So boldness and courage are not the same thing. Consequently the result is (*lit.* it results) that the courageous are bold but not that the bold are courageous, for boldness, like strength, comes to men from art and from anger and from madness but courage from nature and proper nurture of the soul (*lit.* souls). (14) The Spartans considered that the Athenians were first in violation of (*lit.* to be in a state of having broken) the treaty. (15) The goat has not yet given birth (*i.e.* don't

count your chickens before they're hatched.) (16) Philip, the father of Alexander the Great, wanted (*lit.* wanting) to capture a strong fort. When his scouts reported that it was difficult in all respects and impregnable, he asked if it was so difficult that not even an ass carrying gold could approach [it].

16.3

I am alive and I behold what I ought to, the sky, the earth and these shafts of sun[light]. But what a terrible turmoil (*lit.* wave, surf) and confusion of mind I have fallen into (*lit.* in) and what warm breath I breathe, shallow, not steady from my lungs. Look, why am I sitting anchored like a ship with bonds on (*lit.* with respect to) my sturdy chest and arms to this stone-carved pillar (*lit.* chiselled work made of stone) broken in half, sitting next to corpses (*lit.* having a seat neighbouring corpses)? My winged weapons and bow lie scattered on the ground, which formerly shielded my arms and protected my flanks and were protected by me. Surely I have not descended back to [the house] of Hades again, having [just] completed (*lit.* having gone) the double course from Hades set by Eurystheus? But neither do I see the stone of Sisyphus or Pluto nor yet the sceptre of Demeter's daughter. I am indeed bewildered. Wherever am I in my helplessness? Help, who is there of my friends near or far who will cure my bewilderment? (Euripides *Heracles* 1089–1107)

17.2

(1) (*i*) If (*or* when) you are wronged (*lit.* being wronged), settle your differences. (*ii*) Keep away from other people's property. (*iii*) Don't hurry when you undertake something (*lit.* undertake slowly). (*iv*) Don't rush into marriage (*lit.* delay getting married). (*v*) Know yourself (*i.e.* your human limitations). (*vi*) Respect your parents. (*vii*) Think [only] mortal thoughts (*lit.* mortal things). (*viii*) Don't laugh over a corpse. (*ix*) Know the right moment. (*x*) Nothing in excess. (*xi*) When you drink, don't talk too much (*lit.* prattle many things). (*xii*) Use your wealth fairly (*lit.* be wealthy justly). (*xiii*) Believe in fortune. (*xiv*) If (*or* when) you are insulted, avenge yourself. (*xv*) Don't curse your sons. (2) Train your children; for you will not train [them when they are] men. (3) An army of deer led by a lion is more frightening than an army of lions led by a deer. (4) Fear old age; for it does not come alone. (5) Choose a good reputation rather than wealth (*lit.* wish to be well spoken of rather than to be rich). (6) When you have passed a rose do not seek it any longer again. (7) We have two ears but one mouth, in order that we may hear more but speak less. (8) (*i*) Neighbours have sharper eyes (*lit.* see more sharply) than foxes. (*ii*) When you are walking on foot do not fear the waves. (*iii*) Let a lion eat me, not a fox (*i.e.* if I come to grief may it be at the hands of a worthy opponent). (*iv*) Be both a lion where it is required (*lit.* necessary) and a monkey in turn (*i.e.* be prepared to assume a role suited to a particular situation). (*v*) What[ever] bread a man has kneaded, let him eat it as well. (*vi*) When the general is present, let all the officers stop (*sc.* giving orders). (*vii*) The man who desires more is also deprived of what he has (*lit.* the things which are present). (*viii*) Don't throw food into a chamberpot. (*ix*) When you are a foreigner follow the local customs. (*x*) Don't speak ill of your friend or well of your enemy. (xi) If (*or* when) you are prosperous, don't despise the poor. (xii) Judge not, that you be not judged. (xiii) Second thoughts are somehow wiser. (xiv) Most people are rogues. (xv) Things last year were always better. (9) One of the Saii exults in a shield, which I left unwillingly, a blameless weapon, by a thicket. But I myself escaped the doom of death; to hell with that shield; I'll get another just as good (*lit.* once more I shall obtain [one] not worse). (Archilochus 6) (10) The royal cubit is three fingers greater (*or* longer) than the standard cubit. (11) (*i*) When Eudamidas saw Xenocrates, who was now rather old, studying philosophy in the Academy with his students and

ascertained that he was searching for virtue, he said, 'So when will he [be able to] use it?' (*ii*) When a certain Argive was saying that the Spartans became worse when they were abroad (*lit.* during their absences from home), he (*i.e.* Eudamidas) said, 'But you, when you come to Sparta, do not become worse but better.' (*iii*) To a wretch who was asking [him] who the best Spartan was Agis said, 'The one who is most unlike you.' (*iv*) When a teacher was about to read out an encomium of Heracles, Antalcidas said, 'Well, who's criticizing him?' (*v*) When Thearidas was sharpening a sword he was asked if it was sharp, and he said, 'Sharper than slander.' (*vi*) When a garrulous barber asked Archelaus, 'How would you like it, your Majesty (*lit.* how am I to cut your hair, O King)?' Archelaus said, 'In silence (*lit.* keeping quiet).' (12) When Aristotle heard that he was being abused by someone, he said, 'Let him also whip me when I'm not there (*lit.* being absent).' (13) Although they are wise in other respects, the sophists do something extraordinary *viz* (*lit.* do an extraordinary thing [viz] this) they claim to be teachers of virtue, yet they often accuse their students of wronging them (*lit.* that they wrong them), by withholding their fees, although they have been well treated by them (*i.e.* if the sophists had really been able to teach their students virtue, the latter would not have failed to pay their fees). (14) Much enmity and mutual hatred is innate in our citizens, on account of which I am always fearful that some disaster too great to bear may fall upon the city. (15) The Lacedaemonians kept sending embassies to the Athenians to make complaints, in order that they might have (*lit.* there might be to them) as great a pretext as possible for going to war, in case they (the Athenians) did not pay any attention. (16) Cleander was tyrant of Gela for seven years, but he was killed by Sabyllus, a man from Gela. (17) Hope and you, Luck, a long farewell; I have found the harbour. There's nothing [more] between you and me. Have your fun with those [who come] after me.

17.3

Hermes. You there, the clever one, bitterly bitter to the extreme, you who offended against the gods by giving honours to mortals, you the thief of fire I mean; the Father orders you to tell [him] of the marriage of which you boast and by which he is [to be] cast out of his power. And what is more, do not [tell] it (*lit.* these things) in riddling fashion, but explain each detail as it is, and do not inflict a double journey on me, Prometheus. You see that Zeus is not softened by such behaviour. *Prometheus.* Haughty and full of arrogance is your talk, for a lackey of the gods. New you are and new your power (*lit.* you [being] new wield new power), and you think indeed that you dwell in citadels free from woe. [Yet] have I not seen two rulers cast out from them? And as the third I shall behold the present lord (*sc.* cast out) most shamefully and most speedily. You don't imagine, do you, (*lit.* surely I do not seem to you in some respect) that I am terrified and cower before these new gods? I'm far removed, indeed completely removed, from that. Hasten back along the road you came; for you will find out none of the things which you question me about. (Aeschylus *Prometheus Bound* 944–963)

18.2

(1) A man from Cyme was selling honey. When someone tasted it and said, 'It's very good', he said, '[Yes,] for if a mouse had not fallen into it, I would not be selling it.' (2) A Spartan woman, in answer to her son who was saying that the sword which he had was short, said, 'Add a step' (*i.e.* take a step closer to your enemy to make up for the shortness of your sword). (3) (*i*) If the lion-skin does not suffice, put on the fox-skin (*i.e.* if behaving like a lion doesn't help, behave like a fox). (*ii*) You are giving a dog bran, and an ass bones (*i.e.* you are doing things the wrong way). (*iii*) You

keep your love on the tip of your tongue. (*iv*) If we hate our friends, what shall we do to those who hate [us]? (*v*) If I had cheese, I would not want a cooked meal (*i.e.* the small luxury of cheese would be enough – spoken of those who did not indulge themselves overmuch). (*vi*) [When] a friend [is] in trouble do not betray [him] because of anger. (*vii*) Gain is sweet, even if it comes from lies. (*viii*) Give something and take something. (*ix*) Wandering makes life more reasonable (*i.e.* travel broadens the mind). (*x*) [It is] disgraceful to betray one's benefactors. (*xi*) If we have money, we will have friends. (*xii*) Let matters proceed as God wills (*lit.* as is dear to the god). (4) A man came asking the seer Olympicus whether he should sail to Rhodes and how he would sail in safety; and the seer replied, 'First, have a new ship, and put out to sea not in winter but in summer; for if you do this, you will go both there and [back] here, unless a pirate captures you at sea.' (*A.P.* xi. 162) (5) Once an old man had cut some wood and was walking a long road carrying it. Because of fatigue he laid aside the load and called upon Death. When Death appeared and asked for what reason he was calling upon him, the old man said, 'So that you may lift up this load and put it on me.' (6) Every gift which is given, even if it is small, is very great, if it is given with goodwill. (7) If a snake does not eat a snake, it will not become a dragon (*i.e.* to rise in the world one must be ruthless). (8) Naked I set foot upon the earth, and naked I shall go away below the earth; and why do I vainly toil when I see the end naked? (9) (*i*) When someone was surprised at [the number of] the dedications in Samothrace, he said, 'There would be far more if those who were not saved had also made dedications.' (*ii*) When he came to Myndus and observed that the gates were big whereas the city was small, 'Men of Myndus', he said, 'Shut the gates lest your city gets out (*or* escapes).' (*iii*) He was asking a bad-tempered man [for alms]. When [the latter] said, '[Yes,] if you persuade me', [Diogenes] replied, 'If I were able to persuade you, I would have persuaded you to hang yourself.' (*iv*) Lighting (*lit.* having lit) a lamp in broad daylight, he used to go about saying, 'I'm looking for a [genuine] human being.' (10) The Syracusan generals trusted the fellow much too incautiously and immediately agreed upon a day on which they would be present and sent him back, while (*lit.* and) they themselves gave warning to the Syracusans beforehand that they would all go out in full force. When their preparations were complete and the days were at hand on which they had agreed to come, proceeding in the direction of Catana they encamped at the river Symaethus. When the Athenians perceived that they were approaching, they took all their own army and, putting it on board the ships and boats, sailed under cover of night against Syracuse. (Thucydides vi. 65, slightly adapted)

18.3

They arrived at the mountain on the fifth day; the name of (*lit.* to) the mountain was Theches. When the vanguard got on to [the summit of] the mountain and looked down at the sea, much shouting arose. Hearing [this], Xenophon and the rearguard thought that other enemy forces were attacking up in front. But when (*or* since) the shouting was becoming greater and closer and those who kept coming up in succession were running quickly towards those who were continually shouting and the shouting became much louder in proportion as the numbers increased (*lit.* they were becoming more), it seemed to Xenophon to be something more serious. He mounted his horse and taking the cavalry set off to the rescue. And very soon they heard the soldiers shouting, "The sea, the sea!" and passing the word along. Thereupon all the rearguard also began to run, and the draught animals and the horses were driven along. When they had all arrived at the summit, they then began to embrace each other in tears, including generals and captains. (Xenophon *Anabasis* iv. 7. 21–25, slightly adapted)

19.2

(1) Heraclitus says somewhere that everything is in motion (*or* flux) and nothing stays still, and likening existing things (*lit.* the being [things]) to the stream of a river he says that you could not (*or* cannot) step twice into the same river. (2) Keep sober and remember to distrust; these (*i.e.* sobriety and distrust) are the limbs of the mind. (3) Pyrrho said that there was no difference between life and death (*lit.* being alive or being dead differed in no way). And when someone said, 'Why then do you not die?', he said, 'Because it makes no difference.' (4) Do you think that crimes (*or* sins) leap up with wings to the gods, and then someone writes them on the leaves of Zeus' tablet, and Zeus looks at them and gives judgements for mortals? The whole of heaven would not suffice if Zeus were writing [down] the sins of mortals nor would he (*i.e.* Zeus) examining [them] [suffice] to send a penalty to each man. No (*lit.* but), Justice is here somewhere near, if you wish to see. (Euripides, fragment 506) (5) (*i*) If you are able to travel (*sc.* by land), do not go by sea (*lit.* sail). (*ii*) You were caught by your own feathers (*i.e.* hoist with your own petard). (*iii*) A [statue of] Hermes cannot (*lit.* could not) be made out of every (*or* any) log. (*i.e.* you can't make a silk purse out of a sow's ear). (*iv*) If you drink water you will (*lit.* would) produce nothing wise. (*v*) The man who knows what is useful (*lit.* useful things), not the man who knows much (*lit.* many things), is wise. (*vi*) If God gives [it], you cannot (*lit.* could not) escape evil (*lit.* evil things). (*vii*) All men naturally (*or* by nature) strive after knowledge (Aristotle). (*viii*) Whenever you are having a fine voyage, be especially mindful of squalls (*lit.* a squall). (*ix*) Give me somewhere to stand (*lit.* where I am to stand) and I shall move the earth (Archimedes). (*x*) Much learning does not teach [one] to have wisdom; for (*sc.* otherwise) it would have taught Hesiod and Pythagoras (Heraclitus). (*xi*) That which exists naturally does not change. (*xii*) [One] must bear lightly [one's] present (*lit.* standing beside) fortunes. (*xiii*) Despondent men never yet (*lit.* not yet) set up a trophy. (*cf.* faint heart never won fair lady.) (*xiv*) Remember that you are a human being. (*xv*) If you set a trap, you will be caught in a trap. (*xvi*) Although he stands far off God sees from near at hand. (*xvii*) He stands on the razor['s edge] (*i.e.* he is in a difficult situation). (6) How sweet [it is] for those in distress to forget their present troubles even for a short time. (7) (*i*) To a man who said, 'Except for the fact that you are King you are in no way different from us', Leonidas said, 'But I wouldn't be King if I were not better than you.' (*ii*) When he arrived at Thermopylae, to a man who said, 'Because of the barbarians' arrows it is not even possible to see the sun,' he said, 'So [it will be] nice, if we fight (*lit.* will fight) them beneath the shade.' (*iii*) When Xerxes wrote to him, 'It is possible for you by not fighting against God but by ranging yourself with me, to be sole ruler of Greece', he wrote in reply, 'If you knew (*i.e.* understood) the fine things of life, you would have refrained from the desire for other people's possessions; for me death on behalf of Greece is better than being sole ruler over my own race (*lit.* those of the same stock).' (*iv*) When Xerxes wrote again, 'Send (*i.e.* surrender) your arms', he wrote in reply, 'Come and get them!' (*v*) Stranger, tell the Spartans that we lie here, in obedience to (*lit.* obeying) their commands (*lit.* words). (8) I shall not revolt from the people of Athens (*lit.* of the Athenians) either in any way or means or in word or deed, nor shall I obey anyone who revolts (*lit.* the revolting man), and if anyone tries to stir up revolt, I shall denounce [him] to the Athenians; and I shall pay to the Athenians whatever tribute I persuade the Athenians [is appropriate]; and I shall be as excellent and just an ally as I am able (*lit.* I shall be an ally of whatever sort I may be able best and most just), and I shall come to the help of the people of Athens and I shall ward off anyone who (*lit.* if anyone) does wrong to the people of Athens, and I will obey the people of Athens. (*Inscriptiones Graecae* i³ 40.21–32)

20.2

(1) Once a young man fell sick and said to his doctor that he was in such pain that he was unable either to sit or lie [down] or stand; the doctor said, 'My friend, you have no

alternative but (*lit.* there is no other thing left to you than) to hang.' (2) Who knows if what is called death [is] life, and life is death? Except, however, [that] those of mortals who are alive (*lit.* see [*sc.* the light of day]) fall sick, whereas those who are dead never (*lit.* not at all) fall sick nor suffer ill (*lit.* possess troubles). (Euripides, fragment 833) (3) (*i*) He started to play the flute for a drachma, and stops (*sc.* playing it) for four. (*ii*) The camel who conceived a desire for horns lost his ears too. (*iii*) There is no man who is fortunate in all respects. (*iv*) Many generals lost Caria (*cf.* too many cooks spoil the broth). (*v*) Do not let go what is visible and choose what is invisible. (*vi*) Time alone shows a just man. (*vii*) You are in no way different from an elephant. (*viii*) God does not stand aloof from a just deceit. (*ix*) A visit from (*lit.* entrance of) many doctors destroyed me. (*x*) Your appearance is like a lion's but your life is like an ass's (*lit.* you are a lion as regards your hair, but an ass as regards your life). (4) I see the nose of hook-nosed Nico, Menippus; however, he himself seems to be still far off; but he'll come, let's wait after all. For if [he is] far [away], he is not, I suppose, five stades from (i.e. behind) his nose. But, as you see, it precedes [him] itself. If we stand on (*lit.* on to) a high mound, we'll see him too. (*A.P.* xi. 406) (5) When he was dyeing his head (*i.e.* his hair) a man lost his hair itself, and although he was very hairy he has completely become an egg. (6) Thereupon, Cleanor stood up and spoke as follows: 'Come, gentlemen, you see the perjury and impiety of the King, and you see the faithlessness of Tissaphernes, since, although he used to say that he was a neighbour of Greece and that he would consider it most important to save us, and although he himself swore an oath to us to confirm this (*lit.* upon these things) and himself gave pledges, he himself deceived and seized our generals, and he did not even respect Zeus God of Hospitality, but after actually sitting at the same table as Clearchus deceived him by these very means and has [now] destroyed the men.' (Xenophon *Anabasis* iii. 2.4.) (7) Well, Socrates, obey the laws and regard (*lit.* obeying the laws, regard) neither children nor life nor anything else more highly than justice, in order that, when you go [down] to [the house] of Hades you may be able to plead all this in your defence to those who rule there. (8) Socrates manifestly longed not for those who were naturally sound in body with respect to beauty but for those who were naturally sound in soul with respect to virtue. (9) The daughter of a grammarian, after making love (*lit.* having mingled in sexual intercourse), produced a masculine child, a feminine [child], [and] a neuter [child]. (10) For Zeus gives thought to the greatest [affairs] of mortals, but leaves unimportant [matters] to other gods and lets them be. (11) While it was summer, the soldiers who were in Chios with Eteonicus supported themselves both from [the produce of] the season and by working for hire around the countryside. But when winter came on, and they had no sustenance and they were badly clothed and without shoes, they began to conspire amongst themselves (*lit.* with each other) to attack Chios. (12) *Polymnestor.* Alas, what will you say? Is she really somewhere nearby? Show [me], tell [me] where she is, in order that I may seize [her] with my hands and tear [her] apart and bloody [her] flesh. *Agamemnon.* What's this, what's wrong with you? *Po.* In the name of the gods I beseech you, let me lay my raging hand[s] on her. *Ag.* Stop; cast [this] savagery from [your] heart and speak, so that, when I have heard both you and her in turn, I may fairly decide for what reason (*lit.* in return for what thing) you are treated thus (*lit.* suffer these things). (Euripides *Hecuba* 1124–1131)

21.2

(1) When a certain Spartan came to Athens and saw men sitting on stools in a [public] toilet, he said, 'May it not happen to me to sit in a place from which (*lit.* there from where) it is not possible to rise up for (*i.e.* to give my seat to) an older man.' (2) (*i*) You are stirring the brine before you catch the fish (*cf.* first catch your hare, then cook it). (*ii*) A tortoise is not concerned about flies. (*iii*) May such enemies always pursue me. (*iv*) One should (*lit.* it is fitting to) scold children indoors.

(*v*) One's speech reflects one's way of life (*lit.* of what sort [is one's] way of life, of such a sort [is one's] speech). (*vi*) Count no man fortunate (*lit.* consider no-one to be fortunate) until he dies. (*vii*) Dogs resemble their mistresses (*lit.* of what sort the mistress, of such a sort also the bitch). (*viii*) It is fitting for a child to be silent rather than to chatter. (*ix*) Oh, what a head, and it does not have a brain! (*x*) Slaves share their masters' sickness. (*xi*) May I not have (*lit.* may there not be to me) what I want but what it is advantageous (*sc.* for me to have). (*xii*) May you fall into (*lit.* in with) Hades' anus! (*i.e* may you die!) (*xiii*) Would that (*or* I wish that) the offspring of wretched men were dumb. (3) Whoever of mortals fears death too much, is by nature stupid; [for] this (*lit.* these things) is the concern of Chance. But whenever the moment of death chances to come, he could not escape [it] even if he went to the halls of Zeus. (Sophocles, fragment 865) (4) All who marry above themselves (*lit.* as many as marry marriages better in race) do not know [how] to marry. (5) A man's character is of necessity affected by the sort of people with whom he spends most of his time. (*lit.* with what sort of [a person] a man associates for the greatest part of the day, of such a sort as regards to character it is necessary for him too to become). (6) Next stood up Thorax the Boeotian, who was struggling with Xenophon about the generalship, and said that, if they got out of the Black Sea, they would have (*lit.* there would be to them) the Chersonnese, a beautiful and blessed country, so that it was possible for anyone who [so] wished to dwell there, and anyone who did not to go off home. It was ridiculous, when there was much bountiful land in Greece, to be searching for [it] in the [country] of the barbarians. 'And until you get (*lit.* become) there, I too promise you pay.' (Xenophon *Anabasis* v.6.25–26) (7) Once when Diogenes saw [some] women hanging by nooses from an olive-tree, he said, 'I wish that all trees had borne such a fruit.' (8) Whoever does (*or* tries to do) many things if it is possible not to do [them], [is] foolish, if it is possible to live a quiet (*lit.* free from business) life pleasantly. (9) In deliberation (*lit.* deliberating) the soldiers decided to reply as follows (*lit.* the following things) and Cheirisophus was their spokesman (*lit.* spoke): 'We are resolved, if we are allowed (*lit.* someone allows us) to go off home, to proceed through the country doing the least possible harm; but if anyone [tries to] hinder us from the journey, to fight it out with him as vigorously as possible.' (10) Indeed [it is] with difficulty [that] you would bear **my** ordeals, to whom it is not fated to die (*or* since it is not fated for me to die); for this (*i.e.* death) would be a deliverance from [my] woes; but as it is, there is no end of toils appointed for me until Zeus is cast out from [his] sovereignty. (Aeschylus *Prometheus Bound* 752–756) (11) When Cyrus had listened to such words from Gobryas he spoke to him as follows. (12) Well, what will you do, [my] heart? Consider well before you err and make most hateful what is [now] most dear (*lit.* the dearest things). Wherever did you rush forth, you wretch? Check [your] arrogance and strength hated of the gods. And why (*lit.* with a view to what) do I lament like this (*lit.* these things), seeing my life desolate and abandoned by those who should least (*sc.* have abandoned me)? Do we then become cowards when we suffer such evils? Do not betray yourself, [my] heart, in [the midst of] troubles. Alas, it is decided; children, go away from [my] sight (*lit.* eyes); for already a new frenzy has entered my bloody heart; O [my] hands, [my] hands, for what a [terrible] task we are preparing ourselves; alas, wretched [that I am] because of [my] daring, [I] who go to destroy in a brief moment the [product of] my great labour. (Neophron, fragment 2) (13) When a man came to Lacedaemon and beheld the respect shown by (*lit.* of) the young towards the old, he said, 'In Sparta alone it is profitable to grow old.' (14) We should meet together and (*lit.* making a meeting) lament over a new-born baby (*lit.* the one [just] born) for all the troubles it is coming to, and in turn farewell with sounds of triumph the man who has died and is freed from troubles as we send him forth from his house (*lit.* farewelling [and] shouting in triumph send forth). (Euripides, fragment 449)

21.3

(1) What life [can there be], what joy without golden Aphrodite? May I die, when these things are no longer my concern (*lit.* a care to me), [viz] secret love and gentle gifts and bed (*or* sex), the sorts of things which are the attractive flowers of youth for men and women. But when distressing old age comes on, [old age] which makes a man both ugly and base, evil cares always distress him in his heart (*or* mind), nor is he glad when he looks upon the rays of the sun, but [he is] hateful to boys and dishonoured by women. So painful did God make old age. (Mimnermus 1) (2) You, [who are] my star, gaze at the stars. Would I might become the sky, in order that I might see you with many eyes. (3) Formerly you shone among the living [like] the Morning Star; but now you have died you shine [like] the Evening Star among the dead. (4) I am sending you sweet perfume, [thus] doing a favour to the perfume, not to you; for you yourself are able to give fragrance even to perfume. (5) Hail, Messenger of Dawn, Bringer of Light, and may you come [back] quickly [as the] Evening Star, bringing secretly back again [the girl] whom you are [now] leading away.

22.2

(1) You, Love, ruler of gods and men, either do not teach beauty to appear beautiful or assist lovers (*lit.* those who are in love) with good fortune, as they suffer the pains of which you are the author. (Euripides, fragment 136) (2) For it was evening, and someone had come to the prytaneis with the report (*lit.* announcing) that Elatea had been captured. After this some of them got up immediately in the middle of dinner, cleared out the people in the stalls throughout the market-place, and set fire to the wicker-work, while others sent for the generals and summoned the trumpeter. The city was filled with commotion. On the following day at dawn the prytaneis called the councillors (*lit.* the council) into the Council-chamber, while you proceeded to the Assembly, and before they dealt with the matter and framed a draft resolution the whole people was seated on the hill (*i.e.* the Pnyx; *lit.* above). After this, when the Council had arrived and the prytaneis had announced what had been reported to them and had introduced the messenger (*lit.* the one who had come) and he had spoken, the herald put the question, 'Who wishes to speak?' And no one came forward. (Demosthenes *On the Crown* 169–170) (3) (*i*) Ask even statues for [your] daily bread (*double acc.*) (*i.e.* you're not getting anything from me!). (*ii*) There is a certain Socrates, a wise man, who speculates on (*lit.* a deep thinker about) the heavens above (*lit.* things high in the air; *accusative of respect*) and has investigated everything beneath the earth (*direct object*). (*iii*) He has come to take from us even the property of [our] grandfather (*double acc.*). (*iv*) He came to the ancient tomb of [his] father (*acc. of motion towards*). (*v*) [My] long life teaches me many things (*double acc.*). (*vi*) Meletus brought this indictment against me (*direct object*; *cognate acc.*). (*vii*) Cyrus was very handsome in appearance and very humane in spirit (*acc. of respect*). (*viii*) [No], by Zeus (*acc. in oath*), I did not see a woodcutter (*direct obj.*) better than myself. (*ix*) They made a treaty and alliance for a hundred years (*acc. to express time how long*). (*x*) I swear by the holy sky, the dwelling of Zeus (*acc. in oath*). (4) (*i*) How sweet [a thing] [is] solitude to the man who hates common people (*exclamatory adv.*). (*ii*) Hide nothing, for all-seeing (*lit.* seeing everything) time unfolds everything (*causal conjunction*). (*iii*) We bear children for this reason [viz] that we may protect the altars of the gods and [our] native land (*conjunction introducing purpose clause*). (*iv*) He seized the acropolis to gain sole power (*lit.* as for tyranny; *adv. introducing prepositional phrase*). (*v*) [We/one] must try to bear the constraints (*lit.* the necessary things) of life as lightly (*lit.* easily) as possible (ὡς + *supl.*). (*vi*) Effort, as/so they say, is the father of fame (*conjunction introducing a parenthetical clause*, 22.1/1*b*(v)). (*vii*) Alas, alas, how fine a prize is a just victory (*lit.* to win just things), but how absolutely evil is an unjust victory (*lit.*

[to win] unjust things) (*exclamatory adv.*). (*viii*) How sweet is life, if a man does not understand it (*exclamatory adv.*). (*ix*) Give to the poor, in order that you find god a giver (*conjunction introducing purpose clause*). (*x*) Time judges friends as fire [judges] gold (*conjunction introducing a clause of manner*). (*xi*) When you are young remember that one day you will be old (ὡς = ὅτι, *indirect statement*). (*xii*) Do we not live as pleasantly as possible if we do not grieve? (ὡς + *supl.*). (*xiii*) They sailed away from the Hellespont separately to their cities (22.1/1*a*(v)). (*xiv*) Really wise men (ὡς *with positive adv.*). (5) At first Oedipus was a fortunate man, [but] then he became the most wretched of mortals. (6) Well, as you know, I have wept for many sufferings, but now I shall speak of one [suffering] such as [I have] not yet [wept for] before. When [my] lord Heracles was setting out on his last journey from home, at that time he left in the house an ancient tablet inscribed with signs, which he had never brought himself to explain to me like this before, when he went forth on [his] many exploits, but he used to go as one who was about to do something [notable] and not as one about to die. (Sophocles *Trachiniae* 153–160) (7) I made war first against the Thracians, driving them from the Hellespont as they wanted to take the country from the Greeks. (8) O old age, what hope of pleasure you have, and every single man wishes to live through (*lit.* come) to you. But when he has made trial [of you], he regrets (*sc.* that he has; *lit.* takes regret) because there is no worse evil among the mortal race. (Euripides, fragment 1080) (9) For I, Cebes, when young, had an enormous desire (*lit.* desired enormously) for this wisdom which they call the investigation into (*lit.* of) nature.

22.3

(1) We congratulate you, grasshopper, when on the tops of the trees you sing like a king, after drinking a little dew; for yours are all those things which you see in the fields, [all those things] which the woods nourish. You [are] held in honour among mortals, sweet harbinger of summer. The Muses love you, and Phoebus himself loves [you], and gave [you] a shrill power of song. Old age does not distress you, o skilful, earth-born lover of song, and since you know not suffering (*lit.* [being] unsuffering), o [creature of] bloodless flesh, you are nearly equal to the gods. (Anacreontea 34) (2) My (*lit.* to us) temples [are] now grey, and my head white, and no longer is graceful youth at hand, and my teeth are aged. No longer is there left much time of sweet life; for this reason (*lit.* on account of these things) I weep often in fear of Tartarus. For terrible is the inner chamber of Hades, and painful the path down to him; and further [it is] fixed for the man who has gone down not to come up [again]. (Anacreon 50)

23.2

(1) (*i*) O sweet charm of sleep (*gen. of explanation*), ally against sickness (*objective gen.*). (*ii*) He wanted to be [one] of those who remained (*partitive gen.*). (*iii*) O Poseidon, what skill! (*gen. of exclamation*). (*iv*) To bear poverty is not [the nature] of everyone, but of a wise man (*gen. of characteristic*). (*v*) Pay close attention (*lit.* apply the mind very much) to this man (*dat. of indirect object*), I beg you (*ethic dat.*). (*vi*) Many treatments have been found by doctors (*dat. of agent*). (*vii*) Sleep is naturally a safeguard of the body (*lit.* of bodies; *objective gen.*). (*viii*) [It is the mark] of a wicked man to praise and blame the same person (*gen. of characteristic*). (*ix*) Such is tyranny for you, Lacedaemonians (*dat. of reference* or *ethic dat.*). (*x*) Olympian Zeus, dwelling in the sky (*dat. of place where*), knows this. (*xi*) They accuse him of theft (*verb of accusing, gen. of charge*). (*xii*) Men lie because of their own (*subjective/possessive gen.*) fear of death (*objective gen.*). (*xiii*) They were afraid that the Athenians might attack with a greater force (*military dat.*). (*xiv*) They will approach with much shouting (*dat. of manner*). (*xv*) The boy's name (*lit.* the name to the boy;

dat. of possession) was Plato. (*xvi*) Art is weaker by far (*dat. of measure of difference*) than necessity (*gen. of comparison*). (*xvii*) I admire you for [your] intelligence, but I loathe [you] for [your] cowardice (*both gen. of cause*). (*xviii*) I tried to steal [some] of the meat (*partitive gen.*). (*xix*) In your eyes (*dat. of reference*) did this man do these things justly? *or* Did this man do these things justly for you? (*dat. of advantage*) (*xx*) They did these things for the gods (*dat. of advantage*). (*xxi*) He was loathsome and rough in his voice (*dat. of respect*). (*xxii*) The army arrived at Oenoe in Attica (*chorographic gen.*). (*xxiii*) You see the king's perjury (*subjective/possessive gen.*). (*xxiv*) I am not disheartened by what has happened (*gen. of cause*). (2) Diogenes went up to Anaximenes the orator who was fat and said, 'Give [some] of your belly to us the poor too; for you both will be lightened yourself and will help us.' (3) There was a saying that wiles are the concern of women, whereas men are of surer aim with the spear. For if the prize of victory were [won] by guiles, we would have sovereignty over men. (Euripides, fragment 321) (4) And now I advise all younger [men] not to produce children tardily, making delays up to old age (*or* until they are old). For [this] (*i.e.* producing children in old age) is no pleasure, and an old man is a hateful thing to (*or* for) a woman. But [do it] as quickly as possible. For rearing [children] is beautiful and a boy sharing his youth with a youthful father is a pleasant [thing]. (Euripides, fragment 317) (5) *Meletus.* This [is what] I say, that not at all do you believe in the gods. *Socrates.* You really amaze me in speaking like this, Meletus (*lit.* o amazing Meletus, why do you say this?). Do I not even believe then that the sun or the moon are gods, as the rest of mankind [do]? *Me.* [No], by Zeus, gentlemen of the jury, since he says that the sun is a stone and the moon earth. *So.* Do you think that you are accusing Anaxagoras, my dear Meletus? And do you so despise these men and think that they are [so] illiterate (*lit.* inexperienced in letters) that they do not know that the books of Anaxagoras of Clazomenae are full of such statements? And moreover the youth learn these [doctrines], do they, from me, which they can buy for a drachma in (*lit.* from) the orchestra and [then] laugh at Socrates if he claims they are his own, especially since they are so absurd? Well, for heaven's sake (*lit.* O by Zeus), is this what you think of me (*lit.* do I seem thus to you)? Do I not believe in any god? *Me.* No indeed, by Zeus, not in the very least. *So.* You are not to be believed, Meletus, and that too, as it seems (*lit.* you seem) to me, [even] by yourself. For this man appears to me, men of Athens, to be very violent and unrestrained, and simply to have brought this indictment through (*or* because of) violence and lack of restraint and youthful folly. For he seems like a man making trial [of me] [by] composing a riddle: 'Will Socrates the wise recognize that I am joking and contradicting myself, or shall I deceive him and the rest of those who are listening [to me]?' For he appears to me to contradict himself in the indictment, as if he were to say, 'Socrates is a wrong-doer [by] not believing in the gods, but by believing in the gods.' And yet this is the [mark *or* conduct] of a joker (*lit.* of [someone] joking). (Plato *Apology* 26c–27a)

23.3

(1) I am the tomb of a ship-wrecked [sailor]; and the one opposite [is the tomb] of a farmer; for Hades lies beneath, common to [both] sea and land. (2) Here Saon, the [son] of Dico, of Acanthus, slumbers in holy sleep (*lit.* sleeps a holy sleep); do not say that the good die. (3) Philip, his father, laid (*or* buried) here his twelve-year-old son, his great hope, Nicoteles. (4) These men, having invested (*lit.* placed round) their dear native-land with imperishable glory, put on the dark cloud of death; but they are not dead in death (*lit.* having died), since from above their valour glorifies them and raises them from the house of Hades. (Simonides 121 D) (5) This monument hides Aeschylus, son of Euphorion, the Athenian, who died in wheat-bearing Gela; but of his famous valour the grove of Marathon could tell, and the long-haired Mede who knew it. (6) Tears I give to you, Heliodora, even below through the

earth, a remnant of love [sent] to Hades, tears sorely wept; and on [your] much-lamented tomb I pour the stream of [my] longing, the memorial of [my] affection. Piteously, piteously I Meleager lament you, my dear (*lit.* dear you), even among the dead, an empty favour to (*or* for) Acheron. Alas, where is my flower (*lit.* shoot *or* sprout) [sorely] missed? Hades snatched [her], snatched [her], and the dust marred the flower of her youth (*lit.* the blooming flower). But I implore you, all-nurturing Earth, gently clasp her, all-lamented (*lit.* the all-lamented [girl]), to your bosom, O Mother. (Meleager *A.P.* vii.476)

24.2

(1) *Where a negative is involved, the relevant subsection of 24.1/2 is given after the appropriate explanatory term.* (*i*) The man who knows nothing (*generic* (*f*)) makes no mistakes (*statement* (*a*)). (*ii*) Consider no one a friend (*prohibition/negative command* (*a*)) until you examine how he has treated his previous friends. (*iii*) They do everything so as not to be punished (*infinitive* (*e*)). (*iv*) Nothing (*statement* (*a*)) was done because of the fact that the archon was not present (*infinitive* (*e*)). (*v*) I do not know (*statement* (*a*)) whether to travel (*lit.* I am to travel) or not (*deliberative question* (*a*)). (*vi*) I am afraid that I do not have (*noun clause* (*d*)) sufficient [people] to whom I am to give the gold. (*vii*) Take courage, Cyrus, I shall not hide (*strong denial* (*h*)) from you [the person] to whom I wish to go (*lit.* arrive). (*viii*) And they said that they would give back the corpses on condition that [they] did not burn (*infinitive* (*e*)) the villages. (*ix*) The deed which is not just (*generic* (*f*)) does not escape (*statement* (*a*)) the notice of the gods. (*x*) What is to prevent them from dying? (*verb of preventing is virtually negative because the answer* nothing *is expected* (24.1/7)). (*xi*) He wanted to be a friend of (*lit.* friendly to) those who were most powerful in order that, when he did wrong, he might not be punished (*purpose clause* (*b*)). (*xii*) If you don't check (*conditional clause* (*b*)) your tongue, you will have troubles (*lit.* troubles will be to you). (*xiii*) You cannot (*lit.* could not) be prosperous if you do not toil (*participle used conditionally* (*f*)). (*xiv*) You **shall** not be hostile to your friends (*strong prohibition* (*g*)). (*xv*) If you say what you want (*sc.* to say), [then] hear in turn what you don't want (*sc.* to hear) (*general adjectival clause* (*c*)). (*xvi*) [We/one] must either eat tortoise meat or not eat [at all] (*infinitive* (*e*)). (*xvii*) Can you tell me whether virtue can be taught (*lit.* is a teachable [thing]) or not? (*alternative question* (*i*) – μή *is also possible*). (*xviii*) No-one will deny that he knows what is just (*lit.* just things) (*negated verb of denying* (24.1/7). (*xix*) He was afraid that he would not be able to go out of the country (*noun clause* (*d*)). (*xx*) Do not go away until you hear (*prohibition/negative command* (*a*)). (2) We must worship the gods, benefit our friends, help the city, try to do good to Greece, cultivate the land, look after the cattle, [and] learn the arts of war. (3) When anyone is brought to (*lit.* into) a hostile (*lit.* opposing) trial and is about to speak about bloodshed, fear brings the mouth of men to consternation and hinders the mind from saying what it wishes. (Euripides, fragment 67) (4) You must beware not to be obviously doing publicly any of things which you would privately guard against. (5) All these laws have been in existence (*lit.* made) for a long time now, gentlemen of the jury, and no-one ever yet denied that they would be good. (6) Take care not to reveal your low birth (*lit.* lest you may appear being born lowly). (7) So I greeted the two of them, since I had not seen them for some time (*lit.* as having seen [them] after a time); and after this I said to Cleinias, 'Cleinias, these two men, you know, Euthydemus and Dionysodorus, are skilled not in trivialities (*lit.* little things) but in important matters. For they know all about (*lit.* the things about) war.' They despised me for saying this (*lit.* when I said this I was despised by them); so they both laughed, looking at each other, and Euthydemus said, 'We do **not**, Socrates, concern ourselves with these things any longer, but deal with them [as] subordinate issues.' And I said admiringly, 'Your business must be a

fine one, if such important matters happen to be subordinate for you; in the name of the gods, tell me what this [fine] business is.' 'Virtue,' he said, 'Socrates, [is what] we think we are able to deliver as excellently and speedily as is humanly possible.' 'Zeus,' I said, 'what a [splendid] thing. Where (*lit.* from where) did you find this treasure? I was still thinking about you, as I said just now, as for the most part being clever at this, [i.e.] fighting under arms, and this [is what] I was saying about you; for when you visited [us] before, I remember that this [is what] the pair of you professed.' (Plato *Euthydemus* 273c–e) (8) After him (*lit.* this man) Xenophon said, 'And I am of the following opinion (*lit.* think thus). If it is necessary [for us] to fight, we must make preparations to fight as vigorously as possible; but if we wish to cross as easily as possible, I think we should consider how we may receive as few wounds as possible and lose as few lives as possible.' (9) We must consider whether it is right or not (*lit.* just ... or not just) for me to try to leave from here without the permission of the Athenians (*lit.* the Athenians not letting [me] go). (10) *A.* Tell me, do you have a field? *B.* No, I don't. (11) And further if we submit and come into the power of the king, what do you think we shall suffer? He cut off the head and hand of even his brother by the same mother and [that too] when already dead, and impaled them. As for us, who have no protector and [who] made an expedition against him with the intention of making him a slave instead of a king and of killing him if we could, what do you think we would suffer? Surely he would go to any lengths so that, by inflicting the worst outrages on us, he might instill in all men fear of ever campaigning against him? But everything must be done so that we do not come into his power. (Xenophon *Anabasis* iii. 1.17f.)

24.3

Strepsiades. In the name of the gods, what is this (*lit.* these things)? Tell me. *Student.* This is astronomy. *Str.* And what's this? *St.* Geometry. *Str.* So what's it (*lit.* this thing) useful for? *St.* To measure out land. *Str.* [Do you mean land] for cleruchies? *St.* No, [land] as a whole. *Str.* What you say is attractive (*lit.* you say an attractive [thing]). For the device is democratic (*or* popular) and useful. *St.* And this, notice, is a map of the whole world. Do you see? Here is Athens. *Str.* What do you mean? I don't believe [you], for I cannot (*lit.* do not) see [any] jurymen sitting [there]. *St.* [I assure you] that this area is truly Attic (*or* Attica). *Str.* Come now, who's this man in the basket? *St.* The master. *Str.* Who's the master? *St.* Socrates. *Str.* Ah, [it's] Socrates. You there, go [and] call him loudly for me. *St.* No, **you** call [him] yourself. I don't have the time. *Str.* Socrates! dear little Socrates! *Socrates* Why do you call me, creature of a day? *Str.* In the first place, tell me, I pray, what are you doing. *So.* I tread the air and my thoughts centre round the sun (*lit.* I think about the sun). *Str.* Then you're looking down on the gods from [your] mat, and (*lit.* but) not from the earth, if [indeed that's what you're doing]. *So.* [Yes] for I would never have correctly discovered heavenly phenomena, except by suspending [my] perception and thought. (Aristophanes *Clouds* 200–209, 218–229)

25.2

(1) Again mighty Hector of the gleaming helmet addressed her: 'Indeed all this is **my** concern, [my] wife; but I am terribly afraid of the Trojans and the Trojan women with their trailing robes, if, like a coward, I shrink away far from the fighting. Nor does my spirit [so] order me, since I have learned always to be brave and to fight among the foremost [ranks of the] Trojans, winning great glory both for my father and for myself. For I know this well in my heart and in my soul: there will come (*lit.* be) a day when holy Ilium will be destroyed, and Priam and the people of Priam of the fine ash-spear. But [it is] not so much grief for the Trojans hereafter [which]

troubles me, neither for Hecuba herself nor for lord Priam nor for [my] brothers, who, many and brave, may fall in the dust at the hands of the enemy (lit. hostile men), as [grief] for you, when one of the bronze-clad Achaeans will lead you away in tears, taking away [your] day of liberty; and living (lit. being) in Argos you will weave a web at the command of another [woman] (i.e. a mistress), and carry water from [the spring] Messeis or Hypereia, much unwilling, but strong necessity will be upon [you]. And one day a man seeing you shedding tears will say: "This is the wife of Hector, who was the best of the horse-taming Trojans at fighting [at the time] when they (i.e. the Greeks) besieged Ilium." Thus one day will someone speak; and for you it will be a fresh grief because of the lack of such a husband to ward off the day of slavery. But may earth heaped up cover me in death before I hear your scream when you are taken away by force (lit. both your scream and your being carried off).' (Iliad vi. 440–465) (2) All night long they sat with high thoughts (lit. thinking big) along the embankments of war, and their fires blazed in great numbers (lit. many). Just as when in the sky the stars are seen conspicuous[ly] around the bright moon, when the air becomes windless; and there appear all the lookout-places and the tops of the headlands and the glens; and from heaven the boundless air is rent beneath, and all the stars are seen, and the shepherd rejoices in his heart. So many shone the fires as the Trojans lit [them] in front of Ilium, between the ships and the streams of Xanthus. A thousand fires then were blazing in the plain, and beside each one sat fifty [men] in the gleam of the blazing fire. And the horses, feeding on white barley and wheat, stood beside the chariots and waited for fair-throned Dawn. (Iliad viii. 553–565) (3) Tell me, Muse, of the man of many wiles, who wandered far and wide (lit. very much), after he had sacked the holy citadel of Troy. He saw the cities of many men and came to know [their] minds, and on the sea he suffered many griefs in his heart, striving to win his own life and the home-coming of [his] companions. But not even so did he save [his] companions, strive as he might, for they perished by their own presumptuousness, fools, who devoured the cattle of Hyperion the Sun [God]; and he took from them the day of [their] home-coming. (Odyssey i.1–9) (4) From there I was carried along for nine days by baneful winds over the sea full of fish; but on the tenth [day] we stepped on to the land of the Lotus-Eaters, who feed on [that] flowery food. There we set foot on the mainland and drew water, and [my] companions quickly took their meal beside the swift ships. But when we had partaken of food and drink, then I sent ahead [some of my] companions to go and find out what sort of men were living (lit. eating food) in [this] land, choosing two men and sending a third with [them] as herald. They went off and quickly fell in with the Lotus-Eaters (lit. the Lotus-eating men]. Nor did the Lotus-Eaters plot destruction for our companions, but gave them [some] lotus to taste. Whoever of them ate the honey-sweet fruit of the lotus was no longer willing to report back [to us] or return, but wished to remain there with the Lotus-Eaters, feeding on lotus, and to forget [his] home-coming. Forcibly I brought them [back] in tears to the ships, and I dragged [them] and bound [them] under the benches in the hollowed ships. Then I ordered the rest of my trusty companions to embark with haste (lit. hurrying) on the swift ships, lest any of them might somehow eat of the lotus and forget their home-coming. They went quickly on board and sat down at the benches, and sitting in order they smote the grey sea with the oars. (Odyssey ix. 82–104)

Principal parts of verbs

Present	Future	Aorist	Perfect	Perfect mid. pass.	Aorist passive
ἀγγέλλω *announce*	ἀγγελῶ	ἤγγειλα	ἤγγελκα	ἤγγελμαι	ἠγγέλθην
ἄγω *lead*	ἄξω	ἤγαγον	ἦχα	ἦγμαι	ἤχθην
(ἐπ-) αἰνέω *praise*	αἰνέσομαι (αἰνέσω)	ᾔνεσα	ᾔνεκα	ᾔνημαι	ᾐνέθην
αἱρέω *take*; mid. *choose*	αἱρήσω	εἷλον	ᾕρηκα	ᾕρημαι	ᾑρέθην
αἴρω *raise*	ἀρῶ	ἦρα	ἦρκα	ἦρμαι	ἤρθην
αἰσθάνομαι *perceive*	αἰσθήσομαι	ᾐσθόμην		ᾔσθημαι	
αἰσχύνω *dishonour*	αἰσχυνῶ	ᾔσχῡνα			ᾐσχύνθην
ἀκούω *hear*	ἀκούσομαι	ἤκουσα	ἀκήκοα		ἠκούσθην
ἁλίσκομαι *be captured*	ἁλώσομαι	ἑάλων	ἑάλωκα		
ἁμαρτάνω *err*	ἁμαρτήσομαι	ἥμαρτον	ἡμάρτηκα	ἡμάρτημαι	ἡμαρτήθην
ἀμύνω *ward off*	ἀμυνῶ	ἤμῡνα			
ἀνᾱλίσκω *spend*	ἀνᾱλώσω	ἀνήλωσα	ἀνήλωκα	ἀνήλωμαι	ἀνηλώθην
ἀνοίγνῡμι *open*	ἀνοίξω	ἀνέῳξα	ἀνέῳχα	ἀνέῳγμαι	ἀνεῴχθην
ἀποκρίνομαι *answer*	ἀποκρινοῦμαι	ἀπεκρῑνάμην		ἀποκέκριμαι	
ἄρχω *begin, rule*	ἄρξω	ἦρξα		ἦργμαι	ἤρχθην
ἀφικνέομαι *arrive*	ἀφίξομαι	ἀφῑκόμην		ἀφῖγμαι	
βαίνω *go*	βήσομαι	ἔβην	βέβηκα		
βάλλω *throw*	βαλῶ	ἔβαλον	βέβληκα	βέβλημαι	ἐβλήθην
βλάπτω *hurt, injure*	βλάψω	ἔβλαψα	βέβλαφα	βέβλαμμαι	ἐβλάφθην ἐβλάβην

Present	Future	Aorist	Perfect	Perfect mid. pass.	Aorist passive
βοάω *shout*	βοήσομαι	ἐβόησα			
βούλομαι *wish*	βουλήσομαι			βεβούλημαι	ἐβουλήθην
γαμέω *marry* (with man as subject)	γαμῶ	ἔγημα	γεγάμηκα		
γαμέομαι *marry* (with woman as subject)	γαμοῦμαι	ἐγημάμην		γέγαμημαι	
γελάω *laugh*	γελάσομαι	ἐγέλασα			ἐγελάσθην
γίγνομαι *become*	γενήσομαι	ἐγενόμην	γέγονα	γεγένημαι	
γιγνώσκω *know*	γνώσομαι	ἔγνων	ἔγνωκα	ἔγνωσμαι	ἐγνώσθην
γράφω *write*	γράψω	ἔγραψα	γέγραφα	γέγραμμαι	ἐγράφην
δάκνω *bite*	δήξομαι	ἔδακον		δέδηγμαι	ἐδήχθην
δεῖ impers. *it is necessary*	δεήσει	ἐδέησε			
δείκνῡμι *show*	δείξω	ἔδειξα	δέδειχα	δέδειγμαι	ἐδείχθην
δέομαι *need, ask*	δεήσομαι			δεδέημαι	ἐδεήθην
δέχομαι *receive, await*	δέξομαι	ἐδεξάμην		δέδεγμαι	ἐδέχθην
δέω (A) *want, lack*	δεήσω	ἐδέησα			
δέω (B) *bind*	δήσω	ἔδησα	δέδεκα	δέδεμαι	ἐδέθην
διαλέγομαι *converse*	διαλέξομαι			διείλεγμαι	διελέχθην
διδάσκω *teach*	διδάξω	ἐδίδαξα	δεδίδαχα	δεδίδαγμαι	ἐδιδάχθην
δίδωμι *give*	δώσω	ἔδωκα	δέδωκα	δέδομαι	ἐδόθην
διώκω *pursue*	διώξομαι	ἐδίωξα	δεδίωχα		ἐδιώχθην
δοκέω *seem, think*	δόξω	ἔδοξα		δέδογμαι	
δύναμαι *be able, can*	δυνήσομαι			δεδύνημαι	ἐδυνήθην

Present	Future	Aorist	Perfect	Perfect mid. pass.	Aorist passive
ἐάω *allow, let alone*	ἐάσω	εἴᾱσα	εἴᾱκα	εἴᾱμαι	εἰάθην
ἐγείρω *arouse*	ἐγερῶ	ἤγειρα	ἐγρήγορα (intr.) *I am awake*		
ἐθέλω *wish, be willing*	ἐθελήσω	ἠθέλησα	ἠθέληκα		
εἴργω *imprison, prevent*	εἴρξω	εἶρξα		εἶργμαι	εἴρχθην
ἐλαύνω *drive*	ἐλῶ (= άω)	ἤλασα	ἐλήλακα	ἐλήλαμαι	ἠλάθην
ἐλέγχω *examine, confute*	ἐλέγξω	ἤλεγξα		ἐλήλεγμαι	ἠλέγχθην
ἕλκω *drag, draw*	ἕλξω	εἵλκυσα	εἵλκυκα	εἵλκυσμαι	εἱλκύσθην
ἐπίσταμαι *understand*	ἐπιστήσομαι				ἠπιστήθην
ἕπομαι *follow*	ἕψομαι	ἑσπόμην			
ἐργάζομαι *work*	ἐργάσομαι	ἠργασάμην		εἴργασμαι	ἠργάσθην
ἔρχομαι *come, go*	εἶμι	ἦλθον	ἐλήλυθα		
ἐρωτάω *ask a question*	ἐρωτήσω ἐρήσομαι	(ἠρώτησα) ἠρόμην	ἠρώτηκα	ἠρώτημαι	ἠρωτήθην
ἐσθίω *eat*	ἔδομαι	ἔφαγον	ἐδήδοκα	ἐδήδεσμαι	
εὑρίσκω *find*	εὑρήσω	ηὗρον	ηὕρηκα	ηὕρημαι	ηὑρέθην
ἔχω *have*	ἕξω σχήσω	ἔσχον	ἔσχηκα	ἔσχημαι	
ζάω *live*	ζήσω/ζήσομαι βιώσομαι	ἐβίων	βεβίωκα		
ἥδομαι *be pleased*	ἡσθήσομαι				ἥσθην
θάπτω *bury*	θάψω	ἔθαψα		τέθαμμαι	ἐτάφην
θαυμάζω *wonder*	θαυμάσομαι	ἐθαύμασα	τεθαύμακα	τεθαύμασμαι	ἐθαυμάσθην
(ἀπο-)θνήσκω *die*	θανοῦμαι	ἔθανον	τέθνηκα		
θύω *sacrifice*	θύσω	ἔθῡσα	τέθυκα	τέθυμαι	ἐτύθην

Present	Future	Aorist	Perfect	Perfect mid. pass.	Aorist passive
ἵημι send	ἥσω	ἧκα	εἷκα	εἷμαι	εἵθην
ἵστημι place, make stand	στήσω	ἔστησα (tr.) ἔστην (intr.)	ἔστηκα (intr.)	ἔσταμαι	ἐστάθην
καίω burn	καύσω	ἔκαυσα	κέκαυκα	κέκαυμαι	ἐκαύθην
καλέω call	καλῶ	ἐκάλεσα	κέκληκα	κέκλημαι	ἐκλήθην
κελεύω order, bid	κελεύσω	ἐκέλευσα	κεκέλευκα	κεκέλευσμαι	ἐκελεύσθην
κλαίω weep	κλαύσομαι	ἔκλαυσα		κέκλαυμαι	
κλέπτω steal	κλέψω	ἔκλεψα	κέκλοφα	κέκλεμμαι	ἐκλάπην
κομίζω convey, bring	κομιῶ	ἐκόμισα	κεκόμικα	κεκόμισμαι	ἐκομίσθην
κρίνω judge	κρινῶ	ἔκρῑνα	κέκρικα	κέκριμαι	ἐκρίθην
κτάομαι acquire	κτήσομαι	ἐκτησάμην		κέκτημαι possess	ἐκτήθην
(ἀπο-)κτείνω kill	κτενῶ	ἔκτεινα	ἔκτονα		
λαγχάνω obtain by lot	λήξομαι	ἔλαχον	εἴληχα	εἴληγμαι	ἐλήχθην
λαμβάνω take	λήψομαι	ἔλαβον	εἴληφα	εἴλημμαι	ἐλήφθην
λανθάνω escape the notice of, lie hidden (ἐπι-)	λήσω	ἔλαθον	λέληθα		
λανθάνομαι forget	λήσομαι	ἐλαθόμην		λέλησμαι	
λέγω (A) say	λέξω ἐρῶ	ἔλεξα εἶπον	εἴρηκα	λέλεγμαι εἴρημαι	ἐλέχθην ἐρρήθην
λέγω (B) pick up, gather	λέξω	ἔλεξα	εἴλοχα	εἴλεγμαι (λέλεγμαι)	ἐλέγην
λείπω leave	λείψω	ἔλιπον	λέλοιπα	λέλειμμαι	ἐλείφθην
μανθάνω learn	μαθήσομαι	ἔμαθον	μεμάθηκα		
μάχομαι fight	μαχοῦμαι μαχήσομαι	ἐμαχεσάμην		μεμάχημαι	

378

Present	Future	Aorist	Perfect	Perfect mid. pass.	Aorist passive
μέλει impers. *it is a care* (ἐπι-)	μελήσει	ἐμέλησε	μεμέληκε		
μελέομαι *care for*	μελήσομαι			μεμέλημαι	ἐμελήθην
μέλλω *intend*	μελλήσω	ἐμέλλησα			
μένω *remain* (ἀνα-)	μενῶ	ἔμεινα	μεμένηκα		
μιμνήσκω *remind*	μνήσω	ἔμνησα		μέμνημαι *remember*	ἐμνήσθην *remembered*
νέω *swim*	νεύσομαι	ἔνευσα	νένευκα		
νομίζω *think*	νομιῶ	ἐνόμισα	νενόμικα	νενόμισμαι	ἐνομίσθην
οἶδα *know*	εἴσομαι	ᾔδη (19.1/3)			
οἴομαι (also οἶμαι) *think*	οἰήσομαι				ᾠήθην
(ἀπ-) ὄλλυμι *destroy, lose*	ὀλῶ	ὤλεσα	ὀλώλεκα (tr.) ὄλωλα (intr. *I am ruined*)		
(ἀπ-) ὄλλυμαι *be lost, perish*	ὀλοῦμαι	ὠλόμην			
ὄμνυμι *swear*	ὀμοῦμαι	ὤμοσα	ὀμώμοκα	ὀμώμο(σ)μαι	ὠμό(σ)θην
ὁράω *see*	ὄψομαι	εἶδον	ἑόρᾱκα ἑώρᾱκα	ἑώρᾱμαι ὦμμαι	ὤφθην
ὀργίζομαι *become angry*	ὀργιοῦμαι			ὤργισμαι	ὠργίσθην
ὀφείλω *owe*	ὀφειλήσω	ὠφείλησα ὤφελον (21.1/1)	ὠφείληκα		
πάσχω *suffer*	πείσομαι	ἔπαθον	πέπονθα		
πείθω *persuade*	πείσω	ἔπεισα	πέπεικα (tr.) πέποιθα (intr. *trust*)	πέπεισμαι	ἐπείσθην
πέμπω *send*	πέμψω	ἔπεμψα	πέπομφα	πέπεμμαι	ἐπέμφθην
πίμπλημι *fill*	πλήσω	ἔπλησα	πέπληκα	πέπλησμαι	ἐπλήσθην
πίνω *drink*	πίομαι	ἔπιον	πέπωκα	πέπομαι	ἐπόθην

Present	Future	Aorist	Perfect	Perfect mid. pass.	Aorist passive
πίπτω *fall*	πεσοῦμαι	ἔπεσον	πέπτωκα		
πλέω *sail*	πλεύσομαι	ἔπλευσα	πέπλευκα	πέπλευσμαι	
πράττω *do*	πράξω	ἔπραξα	πέπρᾱχα (tr.) πέπρᾱγα (intr. *have fared*)	πέπρᾱγμαι	ἐπράχθην
πυνθάνομαι *ascertain*	πεύσομαι	ἐπυθόμην		πέπυσμαι	
πωλέω *sell*	ἀποδώσομαι	ἀπεδόμην	πέπρᾱκα	πέπρᾱμαι	ἐπράθην
ῥήγνῡμι *break*	ῥήξω	ἔρρηξα	ἔρρωγα (intr. *am broken*)		ἐρράγην
ῥίπτω *throw*	ῥίψω	ἔρρῑψα	ἔρρῑφα	ἔρρῑμμαι	ἐρρίφθην
σκεδάννῡμι *scatter*	σκεδῶ (= άω)	ἐσκέδασα		ἐσκέδασμαι	ἐσκεδάσθην
σπείρω *sow*	σπερῶ	ἔσπειρα	ἔσπαρκα	ἔσπαρμαι	ἐσπάρην
στέλλω *send, equip*	στελῶ	ἔστειλα	ἔσταλκα	ἔσταλμαι	ἐστάλην
σφάλλω *trip up*	σφαλῶ	ἔσφηλα		ἔσφαλμαι	ἐσφάλην
σῴζω *save*	σώσω	ἔσωσα	σέσωκα	σέσῳσμαι	ἐσώθην
τελέω *finish*	τελῶ	ἐτέλεσα	τετέλεκα	τετέλεσμαι	ἐτελέσθην
τέμνω *cut*	τεμῶ	ἔτεμον	τέτμηκα	τέτμημαι	ἐτμήθην
τίθημι *place, put*	θήσω	ἔθηκα	τέθηκα	τέθειμαι	ἐτέθην
τίκτω *beget*	τέξομαι	ἔτεκον	τέτοκα		
τιτρώσκω *wound*	τρώσω	ἔτρωσα		τέτρωμαι	ἐτρώθην
τρέπω *turn*	τρέψω	ἔτρεψα	τέτροφα	τέτραμμαι	ἐτράπην ἐτρέφθην
τρέφω *nourish*	θρέψω	ἔθρεψα	τέτροφα	τέθραμμαι	ἐτράφην ἐθρέφθην
τρέχω *run*	δραμοῦμαι	ἔδραμον	δεδράμηκα		
τυγχάνω *hit, happen*	τεύξομαι	ἔτυχον	τετύχηκα		

Present	Future	Aorist	Perfect	Perfect mid. pass.	Aorist passive
τύπτω strike	τυπτήσω	ἐτύπτησα			
ὑπισχνέομαι promise	ὑποσχήσομαι	ὑπεσχόμην	ὑπέσχημαι		
φαίνω show	φανῶ	ἔφηνα	πέφαγκα (tr. *I have shown*) πέφηνα (intr. *I have appeared*)	πέφασμαι	ἐφάνθην (*I was shown [to be]*) ἐφάνην (intr. *I appeared*)
φέρω bring, carry	οἴσω	ἤνεγκον	ἐνήνοχα	ἐνήνεγμαι	ἠνέχθην
φεύγω flee	φεύξομαι	ἔφυγον	πέφευγα		
φημί say	φήσω	ἔφησα (ἔφην impf.)			
φθάνω anticipate	φθήσομαι	ἔφθασα ἔφθην (like ἔστην)			
(δια-)φθείρω destroy, corrupt	φθερῶ	ἔφθειρα	ἔφθαρκα	ἔφθαρμαι	ἐφθάρην
φοβέομαι fear	φοβήσομαι			πεφόβημαι	ἐφοβήθην
φύω produce	φύσω	ἔφῦσα (tr.) ἔφῦν (intr. *grew, was*)	πέφῡκα (intr. *am by nature, am*)		
χαίρω rejoice	χαιρήσω		κεχάρηκα		ἐχάρην
χράομαι use	χρήσομαι	ἐχρησάμην		κέχρημαι	ἐχρήσθην
χρή impers. *it is necessary*	χρῆσται	χρῆν, ἐχρῆν (both impf.)			
ὠνέομαι buy	ὠνήσομαι	(ἐπριάμην)		ἐώνημαι	ἐωνήθην

Vocabulary

In using the vocabulary the following should be noted:

(a) In addition to the abbreviations given at the end of the **Introduction** the sign † is used:

(i) **before** a simple verb whose principal parts are given in the previous section.

(ii) **after** a compound verb whose simple form is included in the same list.

(b) The feminine and neuter forms of adjectives and the genitive of nouns are nearly always abbreviated and will **not** necessarily have the same accent as the form given in full, e.g. the genitive of ἄβυσσος is ἀβύσσου, but these are listed below as ἄβυσσος, -ου; in these cases the accent of the abbreviated form must be deduced from the rules for accentuation given in **Appendix 8**.

(c) The form of the article which accompanies each noun indicates its gender.

ἄβατος, -ον *impassable*
ἄβιος, -ον *unlivable, unsupportable*
ἄβροτος, -ον *without men, deserted by men*
ἄβυσσος, -ου, ἡ *abyss*
ἀγαγ- aor. stem of ἄγω
ἀγαθός, -ή, -όν *good, noble, brave*
   ἀγαθὰ λέγω *speak well of* (+acc., 22.1/2*f*(ii))
   ἀγαθὰ ποιέω *do good to* (+acc., 22.1/2*f*(ii))
Ἀγάθων, -ωνος, ὁ Agathon (tragic poet)
ἀγάλλομαι *glory, exult in* (+dat.)
ἄγαμαι (aor. ἠγάσθην) *admire*
Ἀγαμέμνων, -ονος, ὁ Agamemnon (Greek commander at Troy)
ἄγαν (adv.) *too much, excessively*
ἀγανακτέω *be annoyed*

ἀγαπάω *love*
†ἀγγέλλω *report, announce*
ἄγγελος, -ου, ὁ *messenger*
ἄγγος, -ους, τό *vessel, urn*
Ἆγις, -ιδος, ὁ Agis (King of Sparta)
ἄγκυρα, -ας, ἡ *anchor*
ἀγνοέω *not to know, fail to understand*
ἄγνοια, -ας, ἡ *ignorance*
ἁγνός, -ή, -όν *chaste*
ἀγορά, -ᾶς, ἡ *place of assembly, market-place; agora*
ἀγοράζω *buy in the market*
ἀγορεύω *speak* (in assembly); *proclaim*
ἄγριος, -ᾱ, -ον *fierce, cruel*
ἄγροικος, -ον *from the country, rustic, boorish*
ἀγρός, -οῦ, ὁ *field, country, farm*

ἀγρυπνέω *lie awake, pass sleepless nights*

†ἄγω *lead, bring*

ἄγω καὶ φέρω *plunder*

ἀγών, -ῶνος ὁ *contest, trial, competition, exploit*

ἀδαμάντινος, -ον *adamantine, of steel*

ἀδελφή, -ῆς, ἡ *sister*

ἀδελφιδῆ, -ῆς, ἡ *niece*

ἀδελφός, -οῦ, ὁ *brother*

ἀδεῶς (adv.) *fearlessly*

ἄδηλος, -ον *unclear*

ἀδικέω *be unjust, commit a crime; wrong, injure* (+acc.)

ἀδίκημα, -ατος, τό *crime, wrong*

ἀδικίᾱ, -ᾱς, ἡ *injustice, wrong-doing*

ἄδικος, -ον *unjust, dishonest*

ἀδίκως (adv.) *unjustly*

Ἄδμητος, -ου, ὁ *Admetus* (King of Pherae, husband of Alcestis)

ἀδολέσχης, -ου, ὁ *idle talker, babbler*; (as. adj.) *garrulous*

ἀδύνατος -ον *impossible; incapable*

ᾄδω *sing*

ἀεί (adv.) *always, continually; in succession*

ἀείδω = ᾄδω

ἀεικής, -ές *shameful*

ἀείμνηστος, -ον *not to be forgotten*

#ἀεκαζόμενος, -η, -ον *unwilling(ly)*

#ἀεροβατέω *tread the air*

ἀετός, -οῦ, ὁ *eagle*

ἀηδών, -όνος, ἡ *nightingale*

ἀήρ, -έρος, ὁ *air*

ἀθάνατος, -ον *immortal*

Ἀθηνᾶ, -ᾶς, ἡ *Athena*

Ἀθήναζε (adv.) *to Athens*

Ἀθῆναι, -ῶν, αἱ *Athens*

Ἀθηναῖος, -ᾱ, -ον *Athenian*

Ἀθήνηθεν (adv.) *from Athens*

Ἀθήνησι(ν) (adv.) *at Athens*

ἀθλητής, -οῦ, ὁ *athlete*

ἄθλιος, -ᾱ, -ον *wretched, miserable*

ἆθλον, -ου, τό *prize*

ἆθλος, -ου, ὁ *contest; ordeal*

ἀθροίζω *gather together* (tr.)

ἀθρόος, -ᾱ, -ον *all together, all at once, in a body*

ἀθῡμέω *be despondent*

#αἰ = εἰ

#αἰάζω *bewail, lament*

#αἰαῖ (exclamation) *alas!*

Αἴγῑνα, -ης, ἡ *Aegina* (island in the Saronic Gulf near Athens)

Αἰγῑνήτης, -ου, ὁ *man of Aegina*

Αἰγύπτιος, -ᾱ, -ον *Egyptian*

Αἴγυπτος, -ου, ἡ *Egypt*

αἰδέομαι *respect; feel pity for; stand in awe of, fear*

Ἅιδης, -ου (also # Ἀΐδης), ὁ *Hades* (god of the underworld)

εἰς Ἅιδου *to the house of Hades, to the underworld* (23.1/1a)

αἰδώς, -ους, ἡ *sense of shame, modesty, respect* (13.1/1b(i))

#αἰεί = ἀεί

#αἰέν = ἀεί

αἰθήρ, -έρος, ὁ *upper air, sky*

αἴθομαι *burn, blaze*

αἰκίᾱ, -ᾱς, ἡ *suffering, misery*

αἰκίζομαι *maltreat*

αἷμα, -ατος, τό *blood; bloodshed, murder*

Αἵμων, -ωμος, ὁ *Haemon* (son of Creon)

†αἰνέω *praise*

αἴνιγμα, -ατος, τό *riddle*

αἰνικτηρίως (adv.) *riddlingly, in riddling fashion*

αἰνίττομαι *speak in riddles*

#αἶνος, -ου, ὁ *tale, story*

αἰνῶς (adv.) *terribly*

αἴξ, αἰγός, ὁ/ἡ goat
#αἰπυμήτης, -ου (adj.) with high
        thoughts, lofty-minded
αἱρέομαι choose, elect
†αἱρέω take, capture; convict
        (18.1/4)
†αἴρω lift, raise up; set sail; exalt
†αἰσθάνομαι perceive, notice,
        realise (+gen. or acc.,
        13.1/2a(iii))
Αἰσχίνης, -ου, ὁ Aeschines
        (Athenian orator)
αἰσχρός, -ά, -όν ugly (of people);
        base, shameful, disgraceful
        (compar. αἰσχίων, supl.
        αἴσχιστος)
Αἰσχύλος, -ου, ὁ Aeschylus (tragic
        poet)
αἰσχύνη, -ης, ἡ shame, disgrace
αἰσχύνομαι be ashamed (15.1/2c);
        feel shame before
†αἰσχύνω dishonour, disgrace
αἰτέω ask (for) (+double acc.,
        22.1/2f(ii)); ask alms of (+acc.)
αἰτίᾱ, -ᾱς, ἡ reason, cause;
        responsibility, blame; charge,
        accusation; fault
αἰτιάομαι accuse
αἴτιος, -ᾱ, -ον responsible (for),
        guilty (of) (+gen.)
#αἶψα (adv.) quickly, forthwith
αἰών, -ῶνος, ὁ life, lifetime; age
Ἀκαδήμεια, -ᾱς, ἡ the Academy
        (park and gymnasium in
        Athens)
Ἀκάνθιος, -ᾱ, -ον of Acanthus
        (city in Macedonia)
ἀκατασκεύαστος, -ον unformed
ἀκήκοα perf. ind. of ἀκούω
ἀκίνητος, -ον motionless,
        immovable
#ἀκμαῖος, -ᾱ, -ον in full bloom, at
        the prime
ἀκμή, -ῆς, ἡ prime, zenith

ἀκολασίᾱ, -ᾱς, ἡ lack of restraint
ἀκόλαστος, -ον undisciplined,
        unrestrained, licentious
ἀκολουθέω follow, accompany
        (+dat.)
ἀκόλουθος, -ου, ὁ servant, slave
ἀκολούθως (adv.) in accordance
        with (+dat.)
ἀκονάω sharpen
ἀκούσιος, -ον against one's will,
        involuntary
†ἀκούω hear, listen (to) (+gen. of
        person, gen. or acc. of thing,
        13.1/2a(iii)); be spoken of
        (17.1/5)
ἀκρῑβῶς (adv.) accurately, exactly,
        carefully
ἄκρον, -ου, τό peak, summit
ἀκρόπολις, -εως, ἡ acropolis,
        citadel
ἄκρος, -ᾱ, -ον high; top of (18.1/6)
Ἀκταίων, -ωνος, ὁ Actaeon
        (mythological character)
ἀκτή, -ῆς, ἡ shore, coast
ἄκων, ἄκουσα, ἆκον unwilling(ly)
ἀλγέω feel pain, be in pain;
        grieve; suffer
ἄλγος, -ους, τό grief, pain,
        suffering
ἀλγῡνω grieve, distress (+acc.)
Ἀλέξανδρος, -ου, ὁ Alexander (the
        Great, of Macedon)
ἀλήθεια, -ᾱς, ἡ truth
ἀληθεύω tell the truth
ἀληθής, -ές true
        τὰ ἀληθῆ (τἀληθῆ) the truth
ἀληθινῶς (adv.) truly, really
ἀληθῶς (adv.) truly, really
        ὡς ἀληθῶς in very truth
Ἁλικαρνᾱσσεύς, -έως, ὁ man from
        Halicarnassus
†ἁλίσκομαι be caught; be convicted
        (18.1/4)
ἀλκή, -ῆς, ἡ valour, bravery

Ἄλκηστις, -ιδος, ἡ   *Alcestis* (wife
    of Admetus)
Ἀλκιβιάδης, -ου, ὁ   *Alcibiades*
    (Athenian general and
    statesman)
ἄλκιμος, -ον   *brave*
ἀλλά (conj.)   *but; well, now*
ἀλλάττω   *change*
ἀλλήλους, -ᾱς, -α (reciprocal
    pron.)   *each other, one
    another* (9.1/4*b*)
ἄλλοθι (adv.)   *elsewhere*
ἄλλομαι (aor. ἡλάμην)   *leap*
ἄλλος, -η, -ο (9.1/3)   *other, the rest
    of; as well, besides* (7.2.12 *l.*
    13)
    ἄλλος ... ἄλλον   *one ...
        another* (cf. note on
        5.2.5(viii))
ἄλλοτε (adv.)   *at other times*
ἀλλότριος, -ᾱ, -ον   *someone else's;
    alien*
ἄλλως (adv.)   *otherwise; in vain*
    ἄλλως τε καί   *especially*
ἄλμη, -ης, ἡ   *sea-water, brine; sea*
ἄλογος, -ον   *speechless; irrational*
ἅλς, ἁλός, ἡ   *sea*
ἄλσος, -ους, τό   *grove*
ἀλυσκάζω   *shun, shrink away*
ἄλφιτα, -ων, τά   *barley-groats;
    daily-bread*
ἀλωπεκῆ, -ῆς, ἡ   *fox-skin*
ἀλώπηξ, -εκος, ἡ   *fox*
ἅλωσις, -εως, ἡ   *capture*
ἅμα (adv.)   *at the same time;*
    (prep.+dat.) *at the same time
    as, together with*
    ἅμα μέν ... ἅμα δέ   *partly ...
        partly*
    ἅμα ἡλίῳ ἀνέχοντι   *at sunrise*
    ἅμα (τῇ) ἡμέρᾳ   *at dawn*
ἀμαθής, -ές   *ignorant*
ἀμαθίᾱ, -ᾱς, ἡ   *ignorance, stupidity*
ἅμαξα, -ης, ἡ   *wagon*

ἁμαρτ- aor. stem of ἁμαρτάνω
ἁμαρτάνω   *err; do wrong; make a
    mistake;* (+gen., 13.1/2*a*(iv))
    miss, fail to achieve
ἁμαρτίᾱ, -ᾱς, ἡ   *fault, wrong, sin*
ἀμείβω   *change, alter*
ἀμείνων, -ον   *better* (compar. of
    ἀγαθός)
ἀμηχανέω   *be at a loss/helpless*
ἀμίς, -ίδος, ἡ   *chamber-pot*
ἄμμος, -ου, ἡ   *sand*
†ἀμύνω   *keep/ward off,* (acc. of
    person kept off and dat. of
    person defended); in mid.,
    defend oneself against (+acc.)
Ἀμυρταῖος, -ου, ὁ   *Amyrtaeus*
ἀμφί (prep.+acc.)   *about, around*
#ἀμφίαλος, -ον   *sea-girt*
ἀμφιβάλλομαι†   *throw around,
    put on*
ἀμφιδέᾱ, -ᾱς, ἡ   *bracelet, anklet*
#ἀμφιμάχομαι†   *besiege*
ἀμφότερος, -ᾱ, -ον   *both*
ἀμφοτέρωθεν (adv.)   *from/on both
    sides*
ἄμφω, -οιν, τώ (dual)   *both*
ἀμώμητος, -ον   *blameless*
ἄν untranslatable particle: in a
    main clause (+ind. or opt.)
    with a potential/conditional
    sense (19.1/2, 18.1/5);
    in a subordinate clause
    (+subj.) with an indef. sense
    (14.1/4*c*(iii))
ἄν = ἐάν
ἀνά (prep.+acc.)   *up, up along;
    throughout, over*
ἀναβαίνω†   *go up; come up;
    mount*
ἀναβιβάζω   *make go up*
ἀναβοάω†   *call upon*
ἀναβολή, -ῆς, ἡ   *putting off,
    delaying*
ἀναγιγνώσκω†   *read, read aloud*

ἀναγκάζω force, compel
ἀναγκαῖος, -ᾱ, -ον necessary,
    constraining
ἀνάγκη, -ης, ἡ necessity,
    compulsion, force
    ἀνάγκη ἐστί it is necessary
    (+dat. and inf.)
ἀνάγω† bring up, raise; (mid.) set
    sail, put out to sea
ἀναδίδωμι† give forth, send up
ἀναζητέω investigate
ἀνάθεμα, -ατος, τό anything
    dedicated (especially to evil);
    an accursed thing
ἀνάθημα, -ατος, τό dedication
ἀναίδεια, -ᾱς, ἡ shamelessness
#ἀναιμόσαρκος, -ον with bloodless
    flesh
ἀναιρέω† pick up; give a response
    (of an oracle)
ἀναίσθητος, -ον without feeling,
    stupid
ἀναίτιος, -ον innocent
ἀναλαμβάνω† take up, take with
    one
†ἀνᾱλίσκω spend
ἀνάλῡσις, -εως, ἡ loosening,
    releasing; resolution (of a
    problem)
ἀνάλωτος, -ον not able to be
    captured, impregnable
ἀναμένω† wait, stay, wait for
    (+acc.)
ἀναμετρέομαι measure carefully
ἀναμιμνήσκω† remind; (pass.)
    recall to mind, remember
#ἄναξ, -ακτος, ὁ lord, king
Ἀναξαγόρᾱς, -ου, ὁ Anaxagoras
    (philosopher of Clazomenae
    in Asia Minor)
Ἀναξιμένης, -ους, ὁ Anaximenes
    (early philospher)
ἀνάξιος, -ον unworthy
ἀναπτύσσω unfold, disclose

ἀνασπάω (aor. -έσπασα) haul up;
    tear up, pull down
ἀνάσσω rule over (+gen.,
    13.1/2a(i))
#ἀνασταλύζω weep, sob
ἀνασταυρόω impale
ἀνατίθημι† dedicate, make a
    dedication
ἀναφέρω† bring back, refer
ἀναχωρέω withdraw, retreat,
    retire
ἀνδρ- stem of ἀνήρ
ἀνδραποδίζω enslave
ἀνδράποδον, -ου, τό captive; slave
ἀνδρείᾱ, -ᾱς, ἡ manliness, courage
ἀνδρεῖος, -ᾱ, -ον manly, brave
ἀνδριάς, -άντος, ὁ statue
ἄνεμος, -ου, ὁ wind
ἀνεξέταστος, -ον without enquiry
    or investigation
ἀνερ - = ἀνδρ -
ἀνερωτάω† ask questions
ἄνευ (prep.+gen.) without
ἀνέχω† hold up, lift up; intr. rise
    up
    ἅμα ἡλίῳ ἀνέχοντι at sunrise
ἀνήρ, ἀνδρός, ὁ man, husband
ἄνθινος, -η, -ον flowery
ἀνθίστημι† (mid. and intr. tenses
    of act.) withstand, resist,
    oppose (+dat.)
ἄνθος, -ους, τό flower, bloom; glory
ἀνθρώπινος, -η, -ον human
ἄνθρωπος, -ου, ὁ/ἡ human being,
    person; man; fellow
ἄνθρωπος crasis for ὁ ἄνθρωπος
ἀνιάω distress, vex
ἀνίδρωτος, -ον without raising a
    sweat
ἀνίστημι† raise up; restore; cause
    to migrate, expel, uproot;
    (mid. and intr. tenses of act.)
    rise up, stand up; migrate, go
    away (19.1/1)

ἀνιστορέω   make enquiry about, ask about, (+double acc.)
ἀνόητος -ον   foolish
†ἀνοίγνῡμι   open
ἀνοικοδομέω   build up; rebuild
ἀνόμημα, -ατος, τό   transgression, sin
ἀνόμοιος, -ον (also -ᾱ, -ον)   unlike, dissimilar (+dat.)
ἀνταγορεύω (aor. ἀντεῖπον, 18.1/4 note 2)   speak against, deny
ἀνταγωνίζομαι   struggle against, vie with (+dat.)
ἀντακούω   hear in turn
Ἀνταλκίδᾱς, -ου, ὁ   Antalcidas (Spartan general)
ἀντεῖπον aor. of ἀνταγορεύω
ἀντέχω†   hold out, withstand
ἀντί (prep.+gen.)   instead of, in return for
ἀντιβολέω   entreat, beseech
ἀντιγράφω   write in reply
ἀντιδίδωμι†   give in return
ἀντίθεσις, -εως, ἡ   opposition, antithesis
ἀντιλέγω†   argue against, oppose
ἀντίον (adv.)   opposite
Ἀντίοχος, -ου, ὁ   Antiochus
Ἀντισθένης, -ους, ὁ   Antisthenes (philosopher)
ἀνυποδησίᾱ, -ᾱς, ἡ   going barefoot
ἀνυπόδητος, -ον   without shoes
ἄνω (adv.)   above, up above
#ἄνωγα (perf. with pres. sense, 19.1/3a)   command, order
ἀνωφελής, -ές   useless
ἄξενος, -ον   inhospitable
ἀξιόπιστος, -ον   worthy of credit, trustworthy
ἄξιος, -ᾱ, -ον   worthy (of), deserving (+gen.), worthwhile
ἀξιόω   think worthy of
ἀόρᾱτος, -ον   unseen, invisible
ἀπαγγέλλω†   announce, report

ἀπαγορεύω   forbid (18.1/4 note 2)
ἀπάγχομαι   hang oneself
ἀπαγχονίζω   hang by a noose
ἀπάγω†   lead/take away
ἀπαθής, -ές   not suffering
ἀπαίρω†   sail away, depart
ἀπαλλαγή, -ῆς, ἡ   deliverance
ἀπαλῡνω   make tender/delicate
ἀπάνθρωπος, -ον   far from men, desolate
ἀπανίστημι†   withdraw
ἀπαντάω   go to meet, meet (+dat., 13.1/2b(iii))
ἅπαξ (adv.)   once only, once
ἀπαραίτητος -ον   unmoved by prayer, inexorable
ἀπαρνέομαι   deny
ἅπᾱς, ἅπᾱσα, ἅπαν   all, the whole of
ἀπατάω   deceive
ἀπάτη, -ης, ἡ   deceit
ἀπέθανον aor. of ἀποθνῄσκω
ἀπεικάζω   liken, compare
ἀπειλέω   threaten (+dat., 13.1/2b(i))
ἄπειμι   be absent
ἀπείργω†   hinder, prevent
ἀπειρίᾱ, -ᾱς, ἡ   inexperience
ἄπειρος, -ον   ignorant of, inexperienced in (+gen.)
ἀπείρως ἔχω   be without experience
ἀπενθής, -ές   free from grief/woe
ἀπερισκέπτως (adv.)   incautiously
ἀπέρχομαι†   go away, depart
ἀπέχω†   be distant from (+gen.); (mid.) keep one's hands off, keep away from (+gen.)
ἀπιστέω   distrust
ἀπιστίᾱ, -ᾱς, ἡ   faithlessness
ἄπιστος, -ον   incredible; untrustworthy, not to be believed; mistrustful
ἀπίστως ἔχω   be mistrustful

ἄπλετος, -ον *boundless, immense*
ἄπλους, -ῆ, -οῦν *simple* (6.1/2)
ἀπό (prep.+gen.) *from, away from*
ἀποβαίνω† *land*
ἀποβάλλω† *throw away, lose*
ἀποδημίᾱ, -ᾱς, ἡ *being abroad or away from one's country*
ἀποδιδράσκω (fut. -δράσομαι aor. -έδρᾱν) *run away, escape, flee*
ἀποδίδωμι† *give back, return, repay*; (mid.) *sell*
ἀποθαν- aor. stem of ἀποθνῄσκω
ἀποθνῄσκω† *die, be killed* (17.1/5; for the perfect see 19.1/3a)
ἄποικος, -ου, ὁ *settler, colonist*
†ἀποκρίνομαι *answer*
ἀπόκρισις, -εως, ἡ *answer, reply*
ἀποκρύπτω *hide from sight*; (mid.) *conceal for one's own purposes*
ἀποκτείνω† *kill*
ἀποκωλύω *hinder from*
ἀπολέγομαι *pick out*
ἀπολεσ- aor.stem of ἀπόλλῡμι
ἀπόλλῡμι† *kill, ruin, destroy, lose* (20.1/1 note 2)
  ἀπωλόμην *I was killed*
  ἀπόλωλα *I am lost/dead/ruined*
Ἀπόλλων, -ωνος, ὁ *Apollo* (acc. either -ωνα or -ω)
ἀπολογέομαι *defend oneself, speak in one's defence; plead in one's defence* (+acc.)
ἀπολογίᾱ, -ᾱς, ἡ *speech in one's defence*
ἀπολύω *free, release*
ἀπομῑμέομαι *imitate, copy*
ἀποπίπτω† *fall overboard*
ἀποπλέω† *sail away*
ἀποπνίγομαι *choke, suffocate, be drowned*
ἀπορέω *be at a loss, be in difficulty*
ἀπορίᾱ, -ᾱς, ἡ *lack of provisions, want; perplexity, difficulty*

ἀποστατέω *stand aloof from* (+gen.)
ἀποστέλλω† *send, send away*
ἀποστερέω *deprive of, rob, defraud, refuse payment of*
ἀποστροφή, -ῆς, ἡ *turning away from, escape*
ἀπότακτος, -ον *set apart for special use*
ἀποτειχίζω *wall off*
ἀποτέμνω† *cut off*
ἀποτίθημι† *put away, bury*; (mid.) *lay aside*
ἀποτρέχω† *run away, run off*
ἀποτυγχάνω† *fail to obtain*
#ἀπούρᾱς (epic aor. pple. of ἀπαυράω) *having taken away*
ἀποφαίνω† *reveal, show*
ἀποφέρω† *carry away*
ἀποφεύγω† *flee, run off; be acquitted*
ἀποχωρέω *go away, depart*
ἀποχώρησις, -εως, ἡ *privy, public toilet*
ἀπραγμόνως (adv.) *without trouble*
ἀπράγμων, -ονος *free from business, not meddling in public affairs*
ἅπτω *fasten, fix; light* (a lamp); (mid.) *touch* (+gen.)
ἀπωθέω (aor. ἀπέωσα) *push away*
ἀπώλεσα aor. of ἀπόλλῡμι
ἄρα* (inferential particle) *then, consequently, after all*
ἆρα interrog. particle (10.1/2a)
ἀργαλέος, -ᾱ, -ον *painful, troublesome*
Ἀργεῖοι, -ων, οἱ *Argives*; (poet.) *Greeks*
Ἀργεῖος, -ᾱ, -ον *Argive*; (poet.) *Greek*

Ἀργινοῦσαι, -ῶν, αἱ   Arginousae
(islands) (scene of Athenian
naval victory)
Ἄργος, -ους, τό   Argos
ἀργός, -όν   idle, lazy
ἀργύριον, -ου, τό   silver, money
ἀργυροῦς, -ᾶ, -οῦν   made of silver,
silver
ἀρετή, -ῆς, ἡ   courage; excellence,
virtue
Ἄρης, -ου ὁ,   Ares (god of war)
ἄρθρον, -ου, τό   joint, limb
Ἀριαῖος, -ου, ὁ   Ariaeus
ἀριθμός, -οῦ, ὁ   number, amount,
total
#ἀριπρεπής, -ές   very bright,
conspicuous
ἀριστάω   have breakfast
ἀριστερός, -ά, -όν   left
Ἀριστεύς, -έως, ὁ   Aristeus
ἀριστεύω   be best, be best at
(+inf.)
Ἀριστόκριτος, -ου, ὁ   Aristocritus
ἄριστον, -ου, τό   breakfast
ἄριστος, -η, -ον   best; bravest (supl.
of ἀγαθός)
Ἀριστοτέλης, -ους, ὁ   Aristotle
(philosopher)
Ἀριστοφάνης, -ους, ὁ   Aristophanes
(comic poet)
Ἀρίφρων, -ονος, ὁ   Ariphron
ἄρκτος, -ου, ἡ   bear
ἁρμόζει (impers.)   it is fitting, it
suits
ἄρνειος, -α, -ον adj. of ἀρήν   lamb
Ἄρνη, -ης, ἡ   Arne (place in
Thessaly)
ἄρνυμαι   win
ἁρπάζω   seize, plunder, snatch
ἁρπακτής, -οῦ, ὁ   robber, ravisher
#ἁρπαλέος, -ᾱ, -ον   attractive,
alluring
ἄρρηκτος, -ον   unbroken,
unbreakable

ἄρρητος, -ον   unspoken,
unmentioned
ἀρσενικός, -ή, -όν   male, masculine
Ἀρταφέρνης, -ους, ὁ   Artaphernes
Ἄρτεμις, -ιδος, ἡ   Artemis
(goddess)
ἄρτημα, -ατος, τό   ear-ring
ἄρτι (ἀρτίως) (adv.)   newly,
recently, just now
ἄρτος, -ου, ὁ   bread
ἀρχαῖος, -ᾱ, -ον   ancient, old;
former
Ἀρχέλᾱος, -ου, ὁ   Archelaus (King
of Sparta)
ἀρχή, -ῆς, ἡ   beginning; rule,
power; empire; office,
magistracy, board of
magistrates, magistrate, officer
ἀρχιερεύς, -έως, ὁ   high priest
Ἀρχιμήδης, -ους, ὁ   Archimedes
(Syracusan mathematician and
inventor)
†ἄρχω   rule, rule over, command
(+gen., 13.1/2a(i))
(+pple.)   begin (of something
continued by others); (mid.)
begin (of something continued
by oneself)
ἄρχων, -οντος, ὁ   archon
(magistrate)
ἀσαφής, -ές   obscure, unclear
ἄσβεστος, -ον (also -η,
-ον)   unquenchable,
inextinguishable, imperishable
ἀσέβεια, -ᾱς, ἡ   impiety,
irreverence (to gods)
ἀσεβέω   commit impiety
ἀσθένεια, -ᾱς, ἡ   weakness, illness
ἀσθενέω   be weak/ill
ἀσθενής, -ές   weak, ill
ἀσινέστατα (supl. adv.)   most/very
harmlessly
ἀσῑτέω   be without food
ἀσκέω   practise, exercise, train

ἄσμενος, -η, -ον   glad, pleased
ἀσπάζομαι   greet
Ἀσπασίᾱ, -ᾱς, ἡ   Aspasia (mistress
  of Pericles)
ἄσπετος, -ον   enormously great,
  boundless
ἀσπίς, -ίδος, ἡ   shield
ἀστεῖος, -ᾱ, -ον   charming,
  attractive
ἀστήρ, -έρος, ὁ   star
ἀστρονομίᾱ, -ᾱς, ἡ   astronomy
ἄστυ, -εως, τό   city, town
ἀσφάλεια, -ᾱς, ἡ   safety, security
ἀσφαλής, -ές   safe, secure
ἀσφαλῶς (adv.)   safely
ἀταλαίπωρος, -ον   without taking
  pains, not painstaking
ἀτάρ (conj.)   but
ἀτασθαλίᾱ, -ᾱς, ἡ   presumptuous
  sin, wickedness
ἄτε (particle)   as if, as; (causal) in
  as much as, since, seeing that,
  because, as (+pple. 12.1/2a(ii))
ἀτελής, -ές   incomplete
#ἄτερ (prep.+gen.)   without
ἄτεχνος, -ον   unskilled
ἀτεχνῶς (adv.)   simply, just
ἄτη, -ης, ἡ   ruin
ἀτῑμάζω   dishonour
ἀτίμαστος, -ον   dishonoured
ἀτῑμίᾱ -ᾱς, ἡ   dishonour; loss of
  citizen rights
ἄτῑμος, -ον   dishonoured; deprived
  of citizen rights
ἄτολμος, -ον   not daring, lacking
  the heart to
ἄτοπος, -ον   out of place,
  extraordinary, strange, absurd
Ἀττικός, -ή, -όν   Attic, Athenian
Ἀττική (sc. γῆ), -ῆς   Attica
ἀτυχής, -ές   unlucky, unfortunate
αὖ (adv.)   again, moreover
αὐγή, -ῆς, ἡ   ray, beam
#αὐδάω   speak, say, utter, tell

αὐθαίρετος, -ον   self-chosen, self-
  inflicted
αὖθις (adv.)   again; in turn, next,
  on the other hand
αὐλέω   play the flute
αὐλή, -ῆς, ἡ   courtyard, hall
αὐλίζομαι   encamp
αὔριον (adv.)   tomorrow
#αὐτάρ (conj.)   but, then
αὐτάρκης, -ες   sufficient
#αὖτε (adv.)   again, in turn
αὐτίκα (adv.)   at once, immediately
αὐτόθι (adv.)   on the spot, here
αὐτόματον, -ου, τό   accident
αὐτόν, -ήν, -ό (pron.)   him, her, it
  (4.1/2; 9.1/3c)
αὐτός, -ή, -ό   self (9.1/3a)
  ὁ αὐτός   the same (9.1/3b)
αὑτός crasis for ὁ αὐτός
αὐτοῦ (adv.)   here, there, on the
  spot
ἀφαιρέω†   take away (from),
  remove; (mid.) deprive (of) (+
  double acc., 22.1/2f(ii))
ἀφανής, -ές   unseen, vanished, not
  to be seen
ἀφανίζω   make unseen, wipe out,
  destroy
ἀφασίᾱ, -ᾱς, ἡ   speechlessness
ἀφεῖναι aor. inf. of ἀφίημι
ἄφθονος, -ον   abundant, plentiful;
  bountiful
ἀφίημι†   send forth; discharge; let
  go
†ἀφικνέομαι arrive,   come
ἀφῑκόμην aor. of ἀφικνέομαι
ἀφίστημι†   remove; make to revolt;
  (mid. and intr. tenses of act.)
  withdraw; revolt (19.1/1)
Ἀφροδίτη, -ης, ἡ   Aphrodite
  (goddess of love)
ἄφρων, -ον   senseless, foolish
ἀφυής, -ές   without natural talent/
  skill

#ἀφύσσομαι draw (a liquid) for
    oneself
ἄφωνος, -ον dumb, speechless
Ἀχαῖοι, -ων, οἱ Achaeans, Greeks
Ἀχέρων, -οντος, ὁ Acheron (river
    in the underworld)
ἀχθηδών, -όνος, ἡ burden
ἄχθομαι be annoyed/displeased at
    (+dat.)
Ἀχιλλεύς, -έως, ὁ Achilles (hero
    in Iliad)
ἄχυρα, -ων, τά chaff, bran

βαδίζω (fut. βαδιοῦμαι) walk, go
βάθος, -ους, τό depth
βαθύς, -εῖα, -ύ deep
#βαθυχαιτήεις, -εσσα, -εν long-
    haired
†βαίνω go, come; walk
Βάκχος, -ου, ὁ Bacchus (another
    name for Dionysus)
#βάκχος, -ου, ὁ person initiated
    into the rites of Bacchus
†βάλλω throw, hit, pelt; inflict
βάπτω dip; dye
βάρβαρος, -ον barbarian, foreign
βαρύνομαι be weighed down
βαρύς, -εῖα, -ύ heavy; wearisome
βασίλεια, -ᾱς, ἡ princess, queen
βασιλείᾱ, -ᾱς, ἡ kingship
βασίλειος, -ᾱ, -ον royal
βασιλεύς, -έως, ὁ king
βασιλεύω be king, rule (+gen.,
    13.1/2a(i))
#βαστάζω lift up, carry
βάτραχος, -ου, ὁ frog
βέβαιος, -ον (also -ᾱ, -ον) secure,
    steady
βέβρωκα perf. of βιβρώσκω
βέλος, -ους, τό missile
βέλτιστος, -η, -ον best (supl. of
    ἀγαθός)
βελτίων, -ον better (compar. of
    ἀγαθός)

βῆμα, -ατος, τό step
βίᾱ, -ᾱς, ἡ force, violence
    πρὸς βίᾱν by force
βιάζομαι use force, force one's
    way
βιαίως (adv.) violently
βιβλίον, -ου, τό book
βίβλος, -ου, ἡ book
βιβρώσκω (perf. βέβρωκα) eat
βίος, -ου, ὁ life; means of life;
    livelihood
#βίοτος, -ου, ὁ life
βιόω live
βιωτός, -όν to be lived, worth
    living
βλάβη, -ης, ἡ damage
†βλάπτω hurt, injure; damage
βλέπω see, look (at); see the light
    of day, be alive
βληθείς, -εῖσα, -έν aor. pple. pass.
    of βάλλω
#βλώσκω (fut. μολοῦμαι, aor. ἔμολον,
    perf. μέμβλωκα) go
†βοάω shout
βόειος, -ᾱ, -ον of beef
βοή, -ῆς, ἡ shout, shouting
βοήθεια, -ᾱς, ἡ help, aid
βοηθέω (run to) help (+dat.,
    13.1/2b(i))
βόθρος, -ου, ὁ hole, pit
Βοιωτίᾱ, -ᾱς, ἡ Boeotia (state in
    north central Greece)
Βοιωτός, -οῦ, ὁ a Boeotian
βοσκήματα, -ων, τά cattle
βόσκω feed, nourish
βουλευτήριον, -ου, τό council-
    chamber
βουλεύω plan, resolve, determine,
    deliberate; (mid.) discuss,
    deliberate, consider; plot
βουλή, -ῆς, ἡ plan, counsel, advice;
    council
†βούλομαι wish, want
#βουνός, -οῦ, ὁ hill, mound

βοῦς, βοός, ὁ/ἡ ox, bull, cow
#βούτης, -ου, ὁ herdsman
βραδέως (adv.) slowly
βραδύνω be slow, hesitate
#βραδύπους, -πουν (gen. -ποδος)
    slow-footed
βραδύς, -εῖα, -ύ (compar. βραδίων,
    supl. βράδιστος) slow
βραχίων, -ονος, ὁ arm
βραχύς, -εῖα, -ύ short, brief; small,
    little
βρέχω wet (tr.)
#βροτός, -οῦ, ὁ mortal man
βρόχος, -ου, ὁ noose
βρῶμα, -ατος, τό food
Βυζάντιον, -ου, τό Byzantium
    (city on the west side of the
    Bosporus)
βωμός, -οῦ, ὁ altar

#γαῖα, -ᾱς, ἡ = γῆ
γάλα, -ακτος, τό milk
†γαμέω (+acc.) marry (with the
    man as subject); (mid., +dat.)
    marry (with the woman as
    subject)
γάμος, -ου, ὁ marriage
γάρ* (connecting particle) for, as
γαστήρ, -τρός, ἡ stomach, belly
    (6.1/1b)
γαστρίμαργος, -ον gluttonous
γε* (particle) at least; at any rate,
    certainly, indeed (13.1/3b)
γεγένημαι perf. of γίγνομαι
γεγενημένα, -ων, τά events,
    occurrences, the past
#γέγηθα (perf. with pres. sense, from
    γηθέω) rejoice
γέγονα perf. of γίγνομαι
#γεγώς = γεγονώς (perf. pple. of
    γίγνομαι)
γείτων, -ονος, ὁ neighbour;
    (as adj.+dat.) neighbouring
Γέλᾱ, -ᾱς, ἡ Gela (city in Sicily)

†γελάω laugh
γέλοιος (also γελοῖος), -ᾱ, -ον
    funny, ridiculous
Γελῷος, -ᾱ, -ον of Gela
γέλως, -ωτος, ὁ laughter
γέμω be full of (+gen.)
γεν- aor. stem of γίγνομαι
γένεσις, -εως, ἡ birth, coming into
    being
γενναῖος, -ᾱ, -ον noble, well-born,
    noble-minded
γενναίως (adv.) nobly
γεννάω beget, produce
γένος, -ους, τό race; kind
γεραιός, -ά, -όν old
γέρας, -ως, τό prize, privilege
    (13.1/1 b(iii))
γέρρα, -ων, τά wicker-work
γέρων, -οντος, ὁ old man
γεύομαι taste
γέφῡρα, -ᾱς, ἡ bridge,
    embankment
γεωμετρίᾱ, -ᾱς, ἡ geometry
γεωργός, -οῦ, ὁ farmer
γῆ, γῆς, ἡ land, earth, ground
    κατὰ γῆν by land
    ποῦ (τῆς) γῆς; where on earth?
γηγενής, -ές earth-born
γημ- aor. stem of γαμέω
#γηράλεος, -ᾱ, -ον aged, old
γῆρας, -ως, τό old age (13.1/1
    b(iii))
γηράσκω grow old
γίγᾱς, -αντος, ὁ giant
†γίγνομαι become, be, be born;
    happen, take place
†γιγνώσκω get to know, recognise,
    realize; think, resolve, decide
γίνομαι = γίγνομαι
Γλαῦκος, -ου, ὁ Glaucus
γλαῦξ, -αυκός, ἡ owl
#γλαφυρός, -ά, -όν hollow,
    hollowed
Γλοῦς, -οῦ, ὁ Glus

γλυκερός, -ά, -όν sweet
γλυκύς, -εῖα, -ύ sweet
γλῶττα, -ης, ἡ tongue
γνάθος, -ου, ἡ jaw
γνούς, γνοῦσα, γνόν aor. pple. of
    γιγνώσκω
γνῶθι 2nd s. imp. of ἔγνων
γνώμη, -ης, ἡ judgment, opinion,
    mind, purpose
γνώριμος, (-η), -ον well-known,
    familiar
γονεύς, -έως, ὁ parent
γόνυ, -ατος, τό knee (5.1/1 note 1)
Γοργώ, -οῦς, ἡ Gorgo
#γουνόομαι implore, entreat
γράμμα, -ατος, τό written
    character, letter
γραμματικός, -οῦ, ὁ grammarian
γραμματιστής, -οῦ, ὁ schoolmaster
γραῦς, γρᾱός, ἡ old woman
    (11.1/4)
γραφεῖον, -ου, τό pencil
γραφή, -ῆς, ἡ writing, drawing;
    indictment, charge, case
†γράφω write; draw, paint; (mid.)
    indict, charge
γρῡπός, -ή, -όν hook-nosed,
    aquiline
Γύλιππος, -ου, ὁ Gylippus
    (Spartan general)
γυμνάζω exercise, train
γυμνός, -ή, -όν naked; lightly/
    poorly clad
γυναικωνῖτις, -ιδος, ἡ women's
    apartments
γυνή, -αικός, ἡ woman, wife
    (5.1/1 note1)
γύψ, γῡπός, ὁ vulture
Γωβρύᾱς, -ᾱ, ὁ Gobryas (Persian
    general)

δαιμόνιος, -ᾱ -ον miraculous,
    supernatural
δαίμων, -ονος, ὁ god, deity

δαίς, δαιτός, ἡ feast
δακ- aor. stem of δάκνω
δάκνω bite; worry
δάκρυ see δάκρυον
δακρυόεις, -εσσα, -εν weeping, in
    tears
δάκρυον, -ου, τό tear (alternative
    nom. δάκρυ 13.1/1c)
δακρύω weep
δακτύλιος, -ου, ὁ ring
δάκτυλος, -ου, ὁ finger
δανείζω lend; (mid.) borrow
δανειστής, -οῦ, ὁ creditor
Δάρδανος, -ου, ὁ Dardanus
    (founder of Troy)
δᾱρεικός, -οῦ, ὁ daric (Persian
    gold coin)
δᾴς, δᾳδός, ἡ torch
δασύς, -εῖα, -ύ hairy, shaggy
δέ* (connecting particle) and, but
    δ᾽ οὖν* be that as it may
    (13.1/3c)
δέδαρμαι perf. mid./pass. of δέρω
δέδοικα I fear, am afraid (19.1/3a)
#δέδορκα see, look upon (perf. of
    δέρκομαι)
†δεῖ (impers.) it is necessary (+acc.
    and infin.); there is a need of
    (+gen., 21.1/4 note 3)
#δείδω be alarmed
†δείκνῡμι show (20.1/1 and
    Appendix 6)
δειλίᾱ, -ᾱς, ἡ cowardice
δειλός, -ή, -όν miserable,
    wretched, cowardly
δειμαίνω (+acc.) be afraid of, fear
δεινός, -ή, -όν terrible, serious,
    strange; clever at (+inf.)
δειπνέω dine, have dinner, dine on
    (+acc.)
δεῖπνον, -ου, τό dinner
δέκα (indecl. adj.) ten
δεκατός, -ή, -όν tenth
δέλτος, -ου, ἡ writing-tablet

δελφίς, -ῖνος, ὁ *dolphin*
Δελφοί, -ῶν, οἱ *Delphi*
δένδρον, -ου, τό *tree* (13.1/1c)
δένδρεον, -ου, τό *tree*
δεξιά, -ᾶς, ἡ *right hand*
 δεξιὰν δίδωμι *give a pledge*
δεξιός, -ά, -όν *on the right hand;*
 clever
Δέξιππος, -ου, ὁ *Dexippus*
†δέομαι *need, implore, ask* (+gen.,
 13.1/2a(ii))
δέον (acc. absol.) *it being*
 necessary (21.1/5)
δέος, -ους, τό *fear*
#δέρκομαι *see, behold*
δέρω (perf. mid./pass. δέδαρμαι)
 flay
δεσμός, οῦ, ὁ (alternative pl. δεσμά,
 τά) *bond*
δεσμωτήριον, -ου, τό *prison*
δέσποινα, -ης, ἡ *mistress*
δεσπότης, -ου, ὁ *master*
δεῦρο (adv.) *here, over here*
δεύτερος, -α, -ον *second*
†δέχομαι *receive*
δέω (Α) *need, want, lack* (+gen.)
 πολλοῦ δέω *I am far from*
 πολλοῦ δεῖ *far from it!*
†δέω (B) *bind, tie*
δή* (particle) *indeed, certainly*
 (13.1/3b)
δῆλος, -η, -ον *visible, clear,*
 obvious
δηλόω *make clear, show, reveal*
Δημέας, -ου, ὁ *Demeas*
δημηγορέω *make a public*
 speech
Δημήτηρ, -τρος, ἡ *Demeter*
 (corn-goddess, mother of
 Persephone)
δημιουργός, -οῦ, ὁ *craftsman;*
 maker, author
δῆμος, -ου, ὁ *the people;*
 democracy; deme

Δημοσθένης, -ους, ὁ *Demosthenes*
 (fifth-century Athenian
 general; fourth-century orator)
δημόσιος, -ᾱ, -ον *public, of the*
 state
δημοσίᾳ *publicly*
δημοτικός, -ή, -όν *democratic,*
 popular
δήξομαι fut. of δάκνω
δήπου* (particle) *I presume, I*
 should hope, doubtless
δῆτα* (particle) *indeed; then*
 (13.1/3a)
δηχθ- aor. pass. stem of δάκνω
Δία acc. of Ζεύς (11.1/4)
διά (prep.+acc.) *because of, on*
 account of; (+gen.) *through,*
 across
 διὰ τί; *why?*
διαβαίνω† *cross, cross over*
διαβάλλω† *slander*
διαβατέον *one must cross* (24.1/5)
διαβολή, -ῆς, ἡ *slander*
διάγνωσις, -εως, ἡ *[act of]*
 distinguishing, deciding
διάγω† *carry over; pass, spend* (of
 time); *live, pass one's life*
διάδοχος, -ον *succeeding, relieving*
διαθρύπτω *enervate, pamper*
διάκειμαι (+adv.) *be in certain*
 state/mood
διακλέπτω† *steal and secrete,*
 appropriate
διακομίζομαι† *carry across*
διακόπτω *cut through*
διᾱκόσιοι, -αι, -α 200
†διαλέγομαι *converse with* (+dat.)
διαλλάττομαι *reconcile one's*
 differences
διαμέλλω† *delay*
διανοέομαι *intend, plan; think,*
 suppose
διάνοια, -ᾱς, ἡ *intention, plan*
διαπειράομαι *make trial of*

διαπίμπλημι† *fill with* (+gen.)

διαπολεμέω *fight it out* (*with someone*, dat.)

διαπορεύομαι *march/proceed through* (+acc.)

διαρπάζω *plunder*

διασπάομαι (aor. -εσπασάμην) *tear apart*

διατελέω† *accomplish; continue*

διατίθημι† *dispose; put in a certain state of body or mind*

διατριβή, -ῆς, ἡ *way/manner of spending time*

διατρίβω *pass/waste* (time)

δίαυλος, -ου, ὁ *double course* (i.e. the race up the stadium and back)

διαφέρω† *differ from* (+gen.); *make a difference; be superior to* (+gen.)

διαφθείρω† *destroy; corrupt*

διαχωρίζω *separate, divide*

διδακτός, -ή, -όν *able to be taught*

διδάσκαλος, -ου, ὁ *teacher*

†διδάσκω *teach, train*

-διδράσκω see ἀποδιδράσκω

δίδωμι *give, offer, grant* (18.1/2)

διελαύνω† *ride through*

διεξέρχομαι† *go through, relate*

διερίζω *contend, dispute*

διέχω† *be separated/distant from* (+gen.)

διηγέομαι *explain, relate, describe*

δικάζω *be a juror; judge, give judgement*

δίκαιος, -ᾱ, -ον *just, honest, upright*

δικαιοσύνη, -ης, ἡ *justice, honesty*

δικαίως (adv.) *justly*

δικαστήριον, -ου, τό *law-court*

δικαστής, -οῦ, ὁ *juror, dicast, judge*

δίκη, -ης, ἡ *lawsuit;* (legal) *satisfaction; justice; penalty;* (personified, with cap.) *Justice*

δίκην δίδωμι *be punished, pay the penalty*

δίκην λαμβάνω *punish, exact one's due from* (παρά+gen.)

δίκτυον, -ου, τό *net, hunting-net*

Δίκων, -ωνος, ὁ *Dico*

δίνη, -ης, ἡ *whirlpool*

Διογένης, -ους, ὁ *Diogenes* (philosopher)

διόλλῡμι† *destroy utterly*

Διονῡσόδωρος, -ου, ὁ *Dionysodorus*

Διόνῡσος, -ου, ὁ *Dionysus* (god of wine)

διότι (conj.) *because*

διπλοῦς, -ῆ, -οῦν *double*

δίς (adv.) *twice*

διττός (δισσός), -ή, -όν *two-fold, two*

δίφρος, -ου, ὁ *stool*

δίχα (adv., or prep.+gen.) *apart, apart from*

διψάω *be thirsty* (5.1/2 note 4)

†διώκω *pursue, chase, prosecute*

#δμώς, δμωός, ὁ *slave taken in war* (13.1/1*b*(i))

δόγμα, -ατος, τό *opinion, belief; decision, judgement*

†δοκέω *seem, seem good; be thought; consider* (self) *to be; think;*

δοκεῖ (impers., +dat. and inf.) *it seems a good idea;* δοκεῖ μοι *I decide* (21.1/4a)

#δόλιος, -ᾱ, -ον *crafty, deceitful*

#δόλος, -ου, ὁ *trick, guile*

#δόμος, -ου, ὁ *house, home*

δόξα, -ης, ἡ *reputation, fame; opinion*

δόξαν (acc. abs.) *it having been decided* (21.1/5)

δόρυ, -ατος, τό   spear
δοτέον   one must give (24.1/5)
δότης, -ου, ὁ   giver
δουλείᾱ, -ᾱς, ἡ   slavery
δουλεύω   be a slave
#δούλιος, -ᾱ, -ον   of slavery
δοῦλος, -ου, ὁ   slave
δουλόω   enslave
δούς, δοῦσα, δόν, aor. pple. of
   δίδωμι
δράκων, -οντος, ὁ   dragon, serpent
δρᾶμα, -ατος, τό   play, drama
δραμεῖν aor. inf. of τρέχω
δραστήριος, -ον   active
δραχμή, -ῆς, ἡ   drachma (coin)
δράω   do, act
δρόμος, -ου, ὁ   race; δρόμῳ at a
   run, at full speed
δρόσος, -ου, ἡ   dew
†δύναμαι   be able (19.1/3b); be
   powerful
   μέγα δύναμαι   be very powerful
δύναμις, -εως, ἡ   power, ability,
   force, strength
δυνατός, -ή, -όν   able, possible;
   strong, powerful; οἱ δυνατοί
   the chief men
δύο   two (7.1/5a)
#δύρομαι (= ὀδύρομαι)   lament
δύσγνοια, -ᾱς, ἡ   ignorance,
   bewilderment
#δυσδάκρῡτος, -ον   sorely wept
δυσεντερίᾱ, -ᾱς, ἡ   dysentery
δύσθῡμος, -ον   disheartened,
   despondent
δύσκολος, -ον   bad-tempered
#δύσλυτος, -ον   indissoluble,
   inextricable
δυσμενής, -ές   hostile
δυσπετῶς (adv.)   with difficulty
δυσσεβής, -ές   impious, ungodly,
   profane
#δύστηνος, -ον   wretched
δυστυχέω   be unlucky/unfortunate

δυστυχής, -ές   unlucky, unfortunate
δυστυχίᾱ, -ᾱς, ἡ   misfortune
δύσφορος, -ον   hard to bear
δυσχείμερος, -ον   wintry, stormy
#δυσώνυμος, -ον   having an ill
   name, hateful
δύω (A)   enter, get into
δύω (B) = δύο   two
δώδεκα (indecl. adj.)   twelve
#δωδεκέτης, -ου   twelve years old
#δῶμα, -ατος, τό   house; family
δωρέομαι   present, give
Δωριεύς, -έως, ὁ   Dorieus (half-
   brother of Spartan king
   Cleomenes)
δωροδοκίᾱ, -ᾱς, ἡ   bribery
δῶρον, -ου, τό   gift, bribe

ἑ (indir. refl. pron.)   him, her, it
   (9.1/4a)
ἑάλων aor. of ἁλίσκομαι
ἐάν (conj., +subj.)   if, if ever
ἔαρ, ἦρος, τό (the season of)
   spring
ἑαυτόν, -ήν, -ό (refl. pron.)
   himself, herself, itself (9.1/4a)
†ἐάω   allow, permit; let alone, let be
ἔβην aor. of βαίνω
ἑβραϊστί (adv.)   in Hebrew
ἐγγελάω†   laugh at (+dat.)
ἐγγίγνομαι†   be born in, appear
   among
ἐγγράφω†   write in/on, inscribe;
   enrol, enlist
ἐγγύη, -ης, ἡ   pledge, surety
ἔγγυθεν (adv.)   from nearby
ἐγγύς (adv., or prep.+gen.)   near,
   nearby
†ἐγείρω   arouse, awaken (perf.
   ἐγρήγορα I am awake)
ἐγενόμην aor. of γίγνομαι
ἐγκέφαλος, -ου, ὁ   brain
ἔγκλημα, -ατος, το   accusation,
   complaint

ἔγκλημα ποιέομαι *make a complaint*

#ἐγκονέω *be quick, hasten*

ἐγκωμιάζω *praise*

ἐγκώμιον, -ου, τό *encomium, eulogy; victory-song*

ἔγνων aor. of γιγνώσκω

ἐγρήγορα perf. of ἐγείρω

ἐγχειρέω *attempt, try; attack* (+dat.)

ἔγχος, -ους, τό *weapon, spear*

ἐγώ (pron.) *I* (4.1/2)

ἔγωγε *I at least; I for my part*

ἐγῷμαι = ἐγὼ οἶμαι

#ἐγών = ἐγώ

ἔδαφος, -ους, τό *bottom*

ἐδόθην aor. pass. of δίδωμι

ἔδομαι fut. of ἐσθίω

#ἔδω *eat*

ἐδωδή, -ῆς, ἡ *food*

ἔδωκα aor. of δίδωμι

ἕζομαι *seat oneself, sit*

†ἐθέλω *am willing, wish*

ἔθηκα aor. of τίθημι

ἔθνος, -ους, τό *nation, tribe, race*

ἔθρεψα aor. of τρέφω

εἰ (conj.) *if*

  εἰ γάρ or εἴθε *would that, I wish that* (to introduce wishes, 21.1/1)

  εἰ δὲ μή *but if not, otherwise*

εἶ 2nd s. of εἰμί *be* or εἶμι *shall come/go*

εἴασα aor. of ἐάω

#εἶδαρ, -ατος, τό *food*

εἰδείην opt. of οἶδα

εἰδέναι inf. of οἶδα

#εἴδομαι *be seen, appear*

εἶδον aor. of ὁράω

εἶδος, -ους, τό *form, shape, appearance; beauty*

εἰδώς, εἰδυῖα, εἰδός *knowing* (pple. of οἶδα)

εἶεν (particle) *well, well then*

εἴθε see εἰ

εἴκοσι(ν) (indecl. adj.) *twenty*

εἴκω *give way, yield* (+dat.,13.1/2b(ii))

εἰκώς, -υῖα, -ός *like, resembling* (+dat.,19.1/3a)

εἴληφα perf. of λαμβάνω

εἰλόμην aor. of αἱρέομαι

εἷλον aor. of αἱρέω

εἰμί *be* (3.1/6 and **Appendix 3**)

εἶμι *shall come/go* (inf. ἰέναι; impf. ᾖα, 18.1/3 and **Appendix 3**)

#εἰν = ἐν

εἶναι *to be* (inf. of εἰμί)

εἰπ- aor. act./mid. stem of λέγω or of ἀγορεύω in compounds

εἴπερ (strengthened form of εἰ) *if indeed*

εἶπον aor. of λέγω and of ἀγορεύω in compounds (18.1/4 note 2)

†εἴργω *shut up, imprison; prevent, hinder, exclude*

εἴρηκα perf. act. of λέγω

εἴρημαι perf. mid./pass. of λέγω

εἰρήνη, -ης, ἡ *peace*

  εἰρήνην ἄγω *live in/be at peace*

  εἰρήνην ποιέομαι *make peace*

εἰς (prep.+acc.) *to, into, on to; with regard to, in relation to*

  εἰς τοσοῦτο/τοῦτο (+gen., 23.1/1d) *to such a pitch/point/degree of*

εἷς, μία, ἕν *one* (7.1/5a)

#εἷς 2nd s. of εἰμί or εἶμι

εἰσάγω† *introduce*

#εἰσαθρέω *look/gaze at*

εἰσακούω† *give ear, pay attention*

εἰσβαίνω† *go into, go on board*

εἰσβάλλω† *throw into; invade*

εἰσβολή, -ῆς, ἡ *invasion*

εἰσέρχομαι† *enter, go inside*

εἴσοδος, -ου, ἡ *entrance; visit*

εἴσομαι fut. of οἶδα

εἰσοράω† *behold, look at*
εἰσπλέω† *sail in*
εἰσφέρω† *bring/carry into*
εἶτα (adv.) *then, next*
εἴτε ... εἴτε *whether ... or*
εἶχον impf. of ἔχω
εἴωθα *I am accustomed*
εἰωθώς, -υῖα, -ός *customary, usual*
ἐκ (prep.+gen.; before vowel ἐξ)
    out of, from
Ἑκάβη, -ης, ἡ *Hecuba* (wife of
    Priam)
ἕκαστος, -η, -ον *each, every*
    ὡς ἕκαστος *each individually*
    (22.1/1a(v))
ἑκάστοτε (adv.) *on each occasion*
ἑκάτερος, -ᾱ -ον *each* (of two)
    ὡς ἑκάτερος *each (of two)*
    individually (22.1/1a(v))
#ἕκατι (prep.+gen.) *on account of,*
    for the sake of (usually comes
    after word it governs)
#ἑκατομπτολίεθρος, -ον *with a*
    hundred cities
ἑκατόν (indecl. adj.) *100*
ἐκβαίνω† *step out, go forth;*
    disembark
ἐκβάλλω† *throw out, expel* (into
    exile)
#ἐκδίκως (adv.) *unjustly*
ἐκεῖ (adv.) *there*
ἐκεῖθεν (adv.) *from there*
ἐκεῖνος, -η, -ο (pron. and adj.
    9.1/1) *that*
ἐκεῖσε (adv.) *(to) there*
ἐκκαίω† *kindle*
ἐκκαλέω† *call* (someone) *out*
ἐκκλησίᾱ, -ᾱς, ἡ *assembly*
ἐκκόπτω *knock out*
ἐκκρούω *knock out*
ἐκλέγω *pick out* (18.1/4 note 1)
ἐκμανθάνω† *learn thoroughly*
ἑκουσίως (adv.) *willingly*
ἐκπέμπω† *send out*

#ἐκπέρθω *destroy utterly*
ἐκπῑ́πτω† *fall out; be thrown out;*
    be banished, be sent into exile
    (17.1/5)
ἐκπλέω† *sail out/off*
ἔκπληξις, -εως, ἡ *panic,*
    consternation
ἐκπλήττω *strike with panic,*
    frighten; amaze
ἐκπρᾱ́ττω† *bring to pass,*
    accomplish
ἐκτός (adv., and prep.+gen.)
    outside
ἐκτροφή, -ῆς, ἡ *bringing up,*
    rearing
Ἕκτωρ, -ορος, ὁ *Hector* (Trojan
    hero in *Iliad*)
ἐκφαίνομαι† *appear, shine out/*
    forth
ἐκφέρω† *carry out*
ἐκφεύγω† *escape*
ἑκών, -οῦσα, -όν *willing(ly),*
    wittingly
ἑλ- aor. act./mid. stem of αἱρέω
ἐλάᾱ, -ᾱς, ἡ *olive-tree*
ἔλαβον aor. of λαμβάνω
ἔλαθον aor. of λανθάνω
Ἐλάτεια, -ᾱς, ἡ *Elatea* (town in
    Phocis)
ἐλᾱ́ττων, -ον *smaller; fewer; less*
†ἐλαύνω *drive* (tr. and intr.); *drive*
    out; march
ἔλαφος, -ου, ὁ/ἡ *deer*
ἐλάχιστος, -η, -ον *smallest, least;*
    fewest
ἔλαχον aor. of λαγχάνω
ἐλέγχω *test, examine*
ἑλεῖν aor. inf. act. of αἱρέω
ἕλειος, -ον *living in the*
    marshes
Ἑλένη, -ης, ἡ *Helen*
ἐλευθερίᾱ, -ᾱς, ἡ *freedom*
ἐλεύθερος, -ᾱ, -ον *free*
ἐλευθερόω *set free*

Ἐλεφαντίνη, -ης, ἡ   Elephantine
(city in Egypt)
ἐλέφᾱς, -αντος, ὁ   elephant
ἐλήλυθα perf. of ἔρχομαι
ἐλήφθην aor. pass. of λαμβάνω
ἐλθ- aor. stem of ἔρχομαι
ἔλιπον aor. of λείπω
ἑλίσσω   turn
#ἑλκεσίπεπλος, -ον   with trailing
robes
#ἑλκηθμός, -οῦ, ὁ   [act of] being
carried off, seizure
†ἕλκω   pull, drag
Ἑλλάς, -άδος, ἡ   Greece
ἐλλείπω†   be lacking in, fall short
of (+gen.)
Ἕλλην, -ηνος, ὁ   a   Greek
Ἑλληνικός, -ή, -όν   Greek
Ἑλλήσποντος, -ου, ὁ   the
Hellespont
ἕλος, -ους, τό   marsh
ἐλπίζω   hope, expect
ἐλπίς, -ίδος, ἡ   hope
ἔμαθον aor. of μανθάνω
ἐμαυτόν, -ήν (refl. pron.)   myself
(9.1/4a)
ἐμβαίνω†   step on/into, embark,
board
ἐμβάλλω†   throw in, put in
ἔμολον aor. of βλώσκω
ἐμός, -ή, -όν (poss. adj.)   my, mine
ἔμπειρος, -ον   experienced,
skilled
ἐμπίμπλημι†   fill
ἐμπίμπρημι   burn, set on fire
ἐμπίπτω†   fall into/on/upon
ἔμπνους, -ουν   alive
ἐμποδών (adv.)   in the way (+dat.)
ἔμπροσθεν (adv.)   in front, ahead
ἐμπρόσθιος, -ον   in front, fore
ἐμφανής, -ές   open, obvious
ἔμφυτος, -ον   inborn, innate
ἐν (prep.+dat.)   in, on, among
ἐν τούτῳ meanwhile

ἐναγκαλίζομαι   take in one's arms,
clasp
ἐναντίον (+gen.)   opposite, facing;
(as adv.) face to a face
ἐναντιόομαι   oppose, withstand
(+dat.)
ἐναντίος, -ᾱ, -ον   opposite, facing,
opposed to
ἐνδεεστέρως (compar. adv.)   in
a more/rather deficient/
inadequate way
ἔνδεια, -ᾱς, ἡ   lack
ἐνδίδωμι†   give in, surrender
ἔνδικος, -ον   just, legitimate
ἔνδοθεν (adv.)   from inside
ἔνδον (adv.)   inside
#ἔνδυτα, -ων, τά   clothes
ἐνεγκ- aor. act./mid. stem of φέρω
ἐνεδρεύω   lie in ambush
ἔνειμι   be in (+dat.)
ἔνεστι (impers.)   it is possible
(+dat.)
ἕνεκα (prep.+gen.)   because of, for
the sake of (usually follows its
noun)
ἐνέργεια, -ᾱς, ἡ   activity, operation
ἔνθα (adv.)   thereupon
ἐνθάδε (adv.)   here
ἔνθεν (adv.)   from there;
thereafter;
ἔνθεν μὲν . . . ἔνθεν δέ   on one
side . . on the other
#ἐνί = ἐν
ἐννέα (indecl. adj.)   nine
#ἐννέπω (and ἐνέπω)   tell, tell of
#ἐννῆμαρ (adv.)   for nine days
ἐννοέω   consider, understand;
discover
ἐνοικέω   dwell in, inhabit
ἐνταῦθα (adv.)   here, there, at this
point
ἐντεῦθεν (adv.)   from then; from
here/there, thereupon
ἐντολή, -ῆς, ἡ   order, command

ἐντός (prep.+gen.)   *within, inside*
#ἔντος, -ους, τό   *weapon*
ἐντυγχάνω†   *fall in with,
    meet with, come upon*
    (+dat.,13.1/2b(iii))
ἐξ = ἐκ
ἕξ (indecl. adj.)   *six*
ἐξαγορεύω (fut. ἐξερῶ, 18.1/4
    note 2)   *make known, speak
    of; speak out, utter aloud*
ἐξάγω†   *lead, bring out*
ἐξαιρέω†   *take out, remove*
ἐξαΐσσω   *rush forth*
ἐξαίφνης (adv.)   *suddenly*
ἐξακόσιοι, -αι, -α *600*
ἐξάλλομαι (aor. ἐξηλάμην)   *jump
    out*
ἐξαμαρτάνω†   *make a mistake; do
    wrong against* (εἰς + acc.)
ἐξανίστημι† (mid. and intr. tenses
    of act.)   *stand up from, get
    up from* (a table)
ἐξαπατάω   *deceive, trick*
ἐξαπίνης (adv.)   *suddenly*
ἐξαρκέω   *be quite enough, suffice*
#ἐξαῦτις (adv.)   *once more, anew*
ἐξείργω†   *shut out from, drive out*
ἐξελαύνω†   *drive out, expel, exile;
    (intr.) march out*
ἐξέρχομαι†   *go out, come out*
#ἐξερῶ fut. of ἐξαγορεύω
ἔξεστι (impers.)   *it is allowed/
    possible* (+dat. and inf.,
    21.1/4a)
ἐξετάζω   *examine*
ἐξευρίσκω†   *find out, discover*
ἐξήκοντα (indecl. adj.)   *sixty*
ἐξηκοστός, -ή, -όν   *sixtieth*
ἐξηλάμην aor. of ἐξάλλομαι
ἑξῆς (adv.)   *in order, in a row*
ἐξικνέομαι (principal parts as for
    ἀφικνέομαι)   *suffice*
ἐξόν (acc. absol.)   *it being
    permitted/possible* (21.1/5)

ἐξοπλίζομαι   *arm oneself
    completely*
ἔξω (+gen.)   *outside*
ἔξω fut. of ἔχω
ἐξωθέω   *push out*
ἔοικα   *resemble, seem*
    (+dat.,13.1/2b(iv)) (19.1/3a)
    ἔοικε (impers.)   *it seems*
ἑορτή, -ῆς, ἡ   *feast, festival*
ἐπαγγέλλομαι†   *profess, make
    profession of*
ἔπαθον aor. of πάσχω
ἐπαινέτης, -ου, ὁ   *admirer*
ἐπαινέω†   *praise, commend*
ἔπαινος, -ου, ὁ   *praise*
ἐπανέρχομαι†   *return*
ἐπανορθόω   *remedy* (a situation)
ἐπάνω (prep.+gen.)   *upon*
ἐπαχθής, -ές   *burdensome*
ἐπεγείρω†   *awaken, rouse up*
ἐπεί (conj.)   *since, when*
ἐπείγομαι   *hurry, hasten; be eager*
ἐπειδάν (conj.+subj.)   *when (ever)*
ἐπειδή (conj.)   *when, since,
    because*
    ἐπειδὴ τάχιστα   *as soon as*
ἔπειμι†   *be upon*
ἔπειτα (adv.)   *then, next*
ἐπεξάγω†   *lead out against*
ἐπέρχομαι†   *go against, attack*
    (+dat.); *come on, approach*
ἐπερωτάω†   *ask* (a question)
ἐπέχω†   *hold back, check*
ἐπί (prep.) (+acc.)   *on to, to,
    against;* (+gen.) *on; in the
    direction of; in the time of;*
    (+dat.) *at, on, upon; with a
    view to; in the power of*
ἐπιβαίνω†   *step on to* (+gen. or
    dat.)
ἐπιβάλλω†   *throw upon, impose
    upon*
ἐπιβάτης, -ου, ὁ   *passenger*
ἐπιβιβάζω   *put on board*

ἐπιβουλεύω *plot against*
ἐπιβουλή, -ῆς, ἡ *plot*
ἐπιγίγνομαι† *come after*
Ἐπίδαμνος, -ου, ἡ *Epidamnus*
  (town on the east coast of
  Adriatic)
Ἐπίδαυρος, -ου, ἡ *Epidaurus*
  (town in southern Greece)
ἐπιδείκνῡμι† *prove, show,*
  demonstrate; exhibit,
  display
ἐπιδημέω *come to stay in a place,*
  visit
ἐπιδίδωμι† *give in addition*
ἐπιεικής, -ές *reasonable,*
  moderate, fair
ἐπιεικῶς (adv.) *fairly, quite*
ἐπιθόμην aor. of πείθομαι
ἐπιθῡμέω *desire, yearn for*
  (+gen.,13.1/2a(ii))
ἐπιθῡμίᾱ, -ᾱς, ἡ *desire, passion*
ἐπικαλέομαι† *call upon, summon*
ἐπίκειμαι *lie upon, be upon*
ἐπικουρέω *help, remedy* (+dat.)
ἐπίκουρος, -ου, ὁ *helper, ally;* (pl.)
  mercenaries
ἐπιλανθάνομαι† *forget* (+acc. or
  gen.,13.1/2a(iii))
ἐπιμέλεια, -ᾱς, ἡ *concern, care*
†ἐπιμελέομαι *care for*
  (+gen.,13.1/2a(ii)), *take care*
ἐπιμελητέον *one must take care of*
  (+gen.) (24.1/5)
ἐπιορκίᾱ, -ᾱς, ἡ *perjury*
ἐπιπίπτω† *fall upon, attack* (+dat.)
ἐπίπνοια, -ᾱς, ἡ *inspiration*
Ἐπιπολαί, -ῶν, αἱ *Epipolae*
  (plateau above Syracuse)
ἐπιπονέω *labour on*
ἐπισκοπέω *inspect, examine,*
  observe
†ἐπίσταμαι *know how to;*
  understand (19.1/3b)
ἐπιστέλλω† *send to*

ἐπιστήμη, -ης, ἡ *understanding,*
  knowledge
ἐπιστολή, -ῆς, ἡ *order, command;*
  (pl.) *letter, epistle*
ἐπιστρέφω† *turn about*
ἐπιτήδεια, -ων, τά *necessities of*
  life, provisions
ἐπιτήδειος, -ᾱ, -ον *suitable, useful*
  for; friendly
ἐπιτίθημι† *put/place upon* (+dat.);
  (mid.) *attack* (+dat.)
ἐπιτῑμάω *censure* (+dat.)
ἐπιτρέπω† *entrust; allow* (+dat.)
ἐπιτρέχω† *overrun*
ἐπιφέρομαι† *move* (intr.)
ἐπίφθονος, -ον *burdensome*
ἐπιφράττω *block up*
ἐπιχαίρω† *rejoice at* (+dat.)
ἐπιχειρέω *attempt, take in hand*
  (+dat.,13.1/2b(iii))
ἐπιχώριος, -ον (also -ᾱ, -ον) *of the*
  country, local
#ἔπλετο 3rd s. aor. of πέλομαι
ἕπομαι *follow* (+dat.,
  13.1/2b(iii))
#ἔπορον (aor., no pres. exists) *give,*
  furnish
ἔπος, -ους, τό *word*
  ὡς ἔπος εἰπεῖν *so to speak*
  (22.1/1a(vi))
ἐπριάμην aor. of ὠνέομαι
ἑπτά (indecl. adj.) *seven*
ἐραστής, -οῦ, ὁ *lover*
ἐράω *love, desire passionately*
  (+gen.,13.1/2a(ii))
†ἐργάζομαι *work, perform, do*
ἔργον, -ου, τό *task, labour,*
  job, deed, action; fact,
  achievement; field
  ἔργῳ *in fact, indeed*
  ἔργα παρέχω *give trouble*
#ἐρέπτομαι *feed on* (+acc.)
#ἐρετμόν, οῦ, τό *oar*
ἐρέω fut. of λέγω

ἐρημίᾱ, -ᾱς, ἡ solitude, desert,
    wilderness
ἔρημος (also ἐρῆμος), -ον empty,
    deserted, desolate, devoid
#ἐρίηρος, -ον (m. pl. nom. ἐρίηρες,
    acc. ἐρίηρας) trusty,
    faithful
Ἐρῑνύες, -ων, αἱ the Erinyes (divine
    avengers of crime)
ἔρις, -ιδος, ἡ strife (acc. ἔριν)
ἔρμαιον, -ου, τό godsend, windfall,
    treasure
ἑρμηνεύς, -έως, ὁ interpreter
Ἑρμῆς, -οῦ, ὁ Hermes
Ἕρμων, -ωνος, ὁ Hermon
ἕρπω creep, crawl; move about,
    spread; go
ἔρρω go to one's harm, go to hell
#ἐρύω drag
†ἔρχομαι come, go (18.1/3 and
    Appendix 3)
ἔρως, -ωτος, ὁ love, desire;
    (personified, with cap.) Love
†ἐρωτάω ask (aor. ἠρόμην)
ἐρωτικός, -ή, -όν amorous, in love
ἐς = εἰς
ἐσθίω eat
#ἐσθλός, -ή, -όν brave
ἑσμός, -οῦ, ὁ swarm
ἔσομαι fut. of εἰμί (be) (3rd s.
    ἔσται)
ἐσοράω see εἰσοράω
ἔσπαρμαι perf. mid./pass. of σπείρω
ἑσπέρᾱ, -ᾱς, ἡ evening
ἕσπερος, -ον of/at evening; (as m.
    noun with cap.) the Evening
    Star
ἑσπόμην aor. of ἕπομαι
ἔσται 3rd s. fut. of εἰμί (be)
ἑστηκώς, -υῖα, -ός standing (perf.
    pple. of ἵσταμαι) (or ἑστώς,
    -ῶσα, -ός) (19.1/1)
ἔστι it is possible (21.1/4 note1);
    there is

ἔσχατος, -η, -ον furthest, last;
    worst (18.1/6)
ἔσχον aor. of ἔχω
ἑταίρᾱ, -ᾱς, ἡ female companion;
    prostitute, courtesan
ἑταῖρος (epic also ἕταρος), -ου, ὁ
    companion, comrade
Ἐτεόνῑκος, -ου, ὁ Eteonicus
    (Spartan commander)
ἕτερος, -ᾱ -ον (pron. and adj.) one
    or the other of two
ἑτέρως (adv.) in the other way
    ὡς ἑτέρως quite otherwise
ἔτι (adv.) still, yet; further
    ἔτι καὶ νῦν even now
ἑτοιμάζω get ready, prepare
ἕτοῖμος, -η, -ον ready, ready to
    hand, prepared; fixed, certain
ἔτος, -ους, τό year
ἐτραπόμην aor. of τρέπομαι
ἔτυχον aor. of τυγχάνω
εὖ (adv.) well
    εὖ λέγω speak well of (+acc.,
    22.1/2f(ii))
    εὖ ποιέω treat well, do good to
    (+acc., 22.1/2f(ii))
    εὖ πράττω fare well, be
    prosperous
εὐγενής, -ές noble, well-born;
    generous
εὔγνωστος, -ον well-known
εὐδαιμονέω prosper, thrive; be
    happy
εὐδαιμονίᾱ, -ᾱς, ἡ prosperity,
    happiness
εὐδαίμων, -ον blessed with good
    fortune; happy; rich
Εὐδᾱμίδᾱς, -ου, ὁ Eudamidas
εὐδόκιμος, -ον famous, glorious
εὕδω sleep
εὔελπις, -ι hopeful (stem εὐελπιδ-)
εὐεργεσίᾱ, -ᾱς, ἡ kindness, service
εὐεργετέω do good to, benefit
εὐεργέτης, -ου, ὁ benefactor

εὐεργετητέον   one must benefit (24.1/5)

εὐήλιος, -ον   sunny, with a sunny aspect

#εὔθρονος (epic ἐΰ-), -ον   fair-throned

εὐθύ (+gen.)   straight towards

Εὐθύδημος, -ου, ὁ   Euthydemus

εὐθύς (adv.)   at once, straightaway

εὔκλεια, -ᾱς, ἡ   fame, glory

Εὐκλείδης, -ου, ὁ   Eucleides

εὐλαβέομαι   be cautious, beware, take care

εὔλογος, -ον reasonable, sensible

εὐμενής, -ές   well-disposed, kindly, favourable

Εὐμενίδες, -ων, αἱ   the Kindly Ones (euphemism for the Erinyes)

#εὐμμελίης (epic ἐΰ-), -ου   armed with a good ash spear

εὐμορφίᾱ, -ᾱς, ἡ   beauty of form or body

εὐνή, -ῆς, ἡ   bed; marriage; sex

εὔνοια, -ᾱς, ἡ   good will

εὔνους, -ουν   well-disposed

#εὐπλοέω   have a fine voyage

εὐπορίᾱ, -ᾱς, ἡ   abundance, means

εὐπρᾱξίᾱ, -ᾱς, ἡ   prosperity

εὑρ- aor. act./mid. stem of εὑρίσκω

εὕρηκα perf. of εὑρίσκω

Εὐρῑπίδης, -ου, ὁ   Euripides (tragic poet)

†εὑρίσκω   find; get; invent

εὖρος, -ους, τό   breadth

εὐρύς, -εῖα, -ύ   broad, wide

Εὐρυσθεύς, -έως, ὁ   Eurystheus (King of Mycenae)

Εὐρώπη, -ης, ἡ   Europa (character in mythology)

εὔσκιος, -ον   well-shaded

εὔστοχος, -ον   aiming well

εὐτάκτως (adv.)   in good order

εὐτροφίᾱ, -ᾱς, ἡ   proper nurture

εὐτυχέω   be fortunate/lucky

εὐτυχής, -ές   fortunate, lucky

εὐτυχίᾱ, -ᾱς, ἡ   good fortune

Εὔτυχος, -ου, ὁ   Eutychus

εὐτυχῶς (adv.)   with good fortune

εὐφημέω   shout in triumph

Εὐφορίων, -ωνος, ὁ   Euphorion (father of Aeschylus)

εὔχαρις, -ι   charming (stem εὐχαριτ-)

εὐχή, -ῆς, ἡ   prayer

εὔχομαι   pray

εὐώνυμος, -ον   of good name or omen; euphemistically for left, on the left hand (the side of a bad omen)

#εὐωριάζω   disregard, neglect

εὐωχέομαι   have a feast/party

ἐφ᾽ = ἐπί
    ἐφ᾽ ᾧτε   on condition that (+inf. or fut. ind., 16.1/1 note 4)

ἐφάνην aor. of φαίνομαι

ἐφήμερος, -ον   living but a day; mortal

ἔφην impf. of φημί (7.1/2)

ἐφίημι†   send; set on, send against; allow; (mid.) aim at, long for, desire (+gen.)

ἐφίστημι†   set over, appoint

ἐφοράω†   oversee, observe, watch

ἔφυγον aor. of φεύγω

ἔφῡν   be naturally, was naturally (see φύω)

#ἐχθαίρω   hate

ἐχθές (adv.)   yesterday

ἔχθιστος supl. of ἐχθρός

ἔχθος, -ους, τό   hatred

ἔχθρᾱ, -ᾱς, ἡ   enmity, hostility

ἐχθρός, -ά -όν hostile (supl. ἔχθιστος)

ἐχθρός, -οῦ, ὁ   (personal) enemy

ἐχῖνος, -ου, ὁ   hedgehog

ἐχρῆν impf. of χρή

ἐχυρός, -ά, -όν   strong, secure

†ἔχω   *have, hold, check*; (intr.) *land, put in*; (+adv.) *be in a certain condition*; (+inf.) *be able*

ἕψω   *boil*

ἑῷος, -ᾱ, -ον   *of the morning*

ἑώρᾱκα perf. of ὁράω

ἑώρων impf. of ὁράω

ἕως (conj.) (+ἄν + subj.)   *until*; (+ opt.) *until*; (+ind.) *while, until* (21.1/2)

ἕως, ἕω (acc. ἕω), ἡ   *dawn* (13.1/1*a*)

Ζαγρεύς, -έως, ὁ   *Zagreus* (another name of Dionysus)

#ζάθεος, -ᾱ, -ον   *very holy, sacred*

ζάλη, -ης, ἡ   *squall, storm*

†ζάω   *be alive, live, pass one's life*

ζεύγνῡμι   *yoke, bind, join*

Ζεύς, Διός, ὁ   *Zeus* (poetical also Ζῆνα, Ζηνός, Ζηνί)

ζέω   *boil*

ζηλόω   *admire, envy, emulate*

ζημίᾱ, -ᾱς, ἡ   *fine, penalty, loss*

ζημιόω   *fine, punish*

Ζηνόθεμις, -ιδος, ὁ   *Zenothemis*

ζητέω   *look for, seek* (+acc.)

ζήτησις, -εως, ἡ   *search, inquiry, investigation*

ζυγόν, -οῦ, τό   *yoke*; *bench* (of ship)

ζωγράφος, -ου, ὁ   *painter*

ζωγρέω   *take prisoners* (alive)

ζώνη, -ης, ἡ   *belt, girdle*

ζῷον, -ου, τό   *animal, creature*

ζωός, -ή, -όν   *alive, living*

ζώω = ζάω   *live, pass one's life*

ἤ   *or; than*

ἦ (particle)   *indeed, really*

ἦ 1st s. impf. of εἰμί   (*be*)

ἦ δ' ὅς   *said he* (see note on 13.3(i) *l*.7)

ᾗ (adv.)   *where*

ᾖα impf. of ἔρχομαι/εἶμι

ἡβάω   *be a young man*

ἥβη, -ης, ἡ   *youth*

ἤγαγον aor. of ἄγω

ἡγεμών, -όνος, ὁ   *leader, guide*

ἡγέομαι   *lead* (+dat.); *think, consider*

Ἡγέστρατος, -ου, ὁ   *Hegestratus*

#ἠδέ (conj.)   *and*

ᾔδει 3rd s. past of οἶδα (19.1/3 and **Appendix 3**)

ᾔδεσαν 3rd pl. past of οἶδα (19.1/3 and **Appendix 3**)

ἡδέως (adv.)   *with pleasure, gladly, sweetly, pleasantly*

ἤδη (adv.)   *(by) now, already, from now on*

ᾔδη 1st s. past of οἶδα (19.1/3 and **Appendix 3**)

†ἥδομαι   *enjoy, be pleased with* (+dat.)

ἡδονή, -ῆς, ἡ   *pleasure*

ἡδύς, -εῖα, -ύ   *sweet, pleasant, enjoyable* (supl. ἥδιστος) (10.1/3*a*)

ἠέ (= ἤ)   *or*

#ἠέλιος = ἥλιος

ἦθος, -ους, τό   *custom, usage, character*; (in pl.) *manners, customs*

ἥκιστα (adv.)   *least of all, no, not at all*

ἠκονημένος, -η, -ον perf. mid./pass. pple. of ἀκονάω

ἥκω   *have come* (fut. ἥξω *will come*)

ἦλθον aor. of ἔρχομαι/εἶμι

ἡλικίᾱ, -ᾱς, ἡ   *time of life, age*

Ἡλιοδώρᾱ, -ᾱς, ἡ   *Heliodora*

ἥλιος, -ου, ὁ   *sun*; (personified, with cap.) *Sun-god*

Ἠλύσιον, -ου, τό   *Elysium*

ἧμαι   *be seated, sit*

#ἦμαρ, -ατος, τό   *day*

ἡμεῖς (pron.)   we (4.1/2)
ἡμέρᾱ, -ᾱς, ἡ   day
  ἅμα (τῇ) ἡμέρᾳ   at dawn
  καθ᾽ ἡμέρᾱν   daily, by day
ἡμέτερος, -ᾱ, -ον (poss. adj.)   our
#ἡμίθραυστος, -ον   half-broken,
  broken in half
ἥμισυς, -εια, -υ   half
#ἦμος (conj.)   when
ἤν = ἐάν
ἦν 1st or 3rd s. impf. of εἰμί   be
ἦν δ᾽ ἐγώ   said I (see note on
  13.3(i) l.7)
ἤνεγκον aor. of φέρω
ἧπαρ, -ατος, τό   liver
ἤπειρος, -ου, ἡ   mainland; continent
ἠπιστάμην impf. of ἐπίσταμαι
Ἥρᾱ, -ᾱς, ἡ   Hera (consort of
  Zeus)
Ἡράκλεια, -ᾱς, ἡ   Heraclea (town
  on Black Sea)
Ἡράκλειτος, -ου, ὁ   Heraclitus
Ἡρακλῆς, -κλέους, ὁ   Heracles
  (= Hercules)
ἠρέμα (adv.)   gently, softly
Ἡρόδοτος, -ου, ὁ   Herodotus
  (historian)
ἠρόμην aor. of ἐρωτάω
Ἡρώδης, -ου, ὁ   Herodes
ἥρως, -ωος, ὁ   hero (13.1/1b(i))
ἦσαν 3rd pl. impf. of εἰμί   be
ἦσθα 2nd s. impf. of εἰμί   be
ἥσθην aor. of ἥδομαι
ᾐσθόμην aor. of αἰσθάνομαι
Ἡσίοδος, -ου, ὁ   Hesiod (early
  Greek poet)
ἡσυχάζω   be quiet, keep quiet
ἡσυχῇ   quietly, gently
ἡσυχίᾱ, -ᾱς, ἡ   peace, quiet
ἥσυχος, -η, -ον   quiet, peaceful
ἡττάομαι   be defeated
ἥττων, ἧττον (compar. adj.)   lesser,
  weaker, inferior (17.1/2
  note 3)

ηὗρον aor. of εὑρίσκω
Ἥφαιστος, -ου, ὁ   Hephaestus (god
  of fire)
ἠχώ, -οῦς, ἡ   echo (13.1/1b(ii))
#ἠώς, ἠοῦς, ἡ   dawn; (personified,
  with cap.) Dawn

θᾱκέω   sit
θᾶκος, -ου, ὁ   seat
θάλαττα, -ης, ἡ (Ionic θάλασσα) sea
Θαλῆς, -οῦ, ὁ   Thales (philosopher
  from Miletus)
#θάλος, -ους, τό   shoot, sprout
θαμά (adv.)   often
θάμνος, -ου, ὁ   bush, thicket
θαν- aor. stem of θνῄσκω
θάνατος, -ου, ὁ   death
†θάπτω   bury, honour with funeral
  rites
θαρράλεος, -ᾱ, -ον   bold
θαρρέω   be of good courage, take
  courage, be confident
θάρσος (Attic θάρρος), -ους, τό
  boldness
θᾱ́ττων, θᾶττον   quicker (compar.
  of ταχύς,17.1/2b)
θαῦμα, -ατος, τό   wonder, marvel;
  astonishment
†θαυμάζω   wonder,marvel at
  (+gen.); be surprised; admire
  (+acc.)
θαυμάσιος, -ᾱ -ον   wonderful,
  strange; extraordinary
θαυμασίως (adv.)   marvellously,
  wonderfully
  θαυμασίως ὡς   exceedingly,
  prodigiously (22.1/1a(iii))
θαυμαστῶς (adv.)   marvellously,
  wonderfully
  θαυμαστῶς ὡς   marvellously
  (22.1/1a(iii))
θε- aor. act./mid. stem of τίθημι
θέᾱ, -ᾱς, ἡ   sight
θεά, -ᾶς, ἡ   goddess

Θεαίτητος, -ου, ὁ   Theaetetus
θέᾱμα, -ατος, τό   sight, spectacle
θεάομαι   watch, gaze at, look at,
    observe
Θεαρίδᾱς, -ου, ὁ   Thearidas
θεᾱτής, -οῦ, ὁ   spectator
θεήλατος, -ον   sent by the gods
θεῖος, -ᾱ, -ον   divine, of the gods
θέλγητρον, -ου, τό   charm, spell
θέλω   wish, be willing (Ionic for
    ἐθέλω)
θέμενος, -η, -ον aor. pple. of τίθεμαι
θέμις, -ιδος, ἡ   that which is meet
    and right; justice; right
    θέμις ἐστί   it is right
Θέμις, -ιδος, ἡ   Themis (mother of
    Prometheus)
Θεμιστοκλῆς, -κλέους, ὁ
    Themistocles (Athenian
    statesman)
Θεόκριτος, -ου, ὁ   Theocritus
    (pastoral poet)
θεομαχέω   fight against (a) god
θεός, -οῦ, ὁ/ἡ   god(dess)
    πρὸς θεῶν   in the name of the
    gods
#θεοστυγής, -ές   hated by the gods
θεραπείᾱ, -ᾱς, ἡ   service, treatment
θεραπευτέον   one must look after/
    worship (24.1/5)
θεραπεύω   look after, tend; look
    after the interests of, protect
#θεράπων, -οντος, ὁ   servant
Θερμοπύλαι, -ῶν, αἱ   Thermopylae
θερμός, -ή, -όν   hot
θέρος, -ους, τό   summer
θές   place! put! (2nd s. aor. imp.
    act. of τίθημι)
θέσθαι aor. inf. of τίθεμαι
Θετταλός, -οῦ, ὁ   a Thessalian
θέω   run
Θῆβαι, -ῶν, αἱ   Thebes
Θηβαῖοι, -ων, οἱ   Thebans
Θηβαῖος, -ᾱ, -ον   of Thebes, Theban

θήκη, -ης, ἡ   tomb
θηλυκός, -ή, -όν   female, feminine
θῆλυς, -εια, -υ   female
θήρ, θηρός, ὁ   wild beast
θηράω   hunt
θηρεύω   hunt
θηρίον, -ου, τό   wild beast
Θήχης, -ου, ὁ   (Mt.) Theches
†θνήσκω   die
θνητός, -ή, -όν   mortal
θοἰμάτιον crasis for τὸ ἱμάτιον
#θοός, -ή, -όν   quick, swift
θορυβέω   make a disturbance/din
θόρυβος, -ου, ὁ   noise, din,
    clamour, commotion
Θουκῡδίδης, -ου, ὁ   Thucydides
    (historian)
Θρᾴκη, -ης, ἡ   Thrace
Θρᾷξ, Θρᾳκός, ὁ   Thracian
θράσος, -ους, τό   boldness
θρασύς, -εῖα, -ύ   bold, brave
θρεψ- aor. act./mid. stem of τρέφω
θρηνέω   bewail, lament over
θρίξ, τριχός, ἡ   hair (5.1/1 note 1)
θυγάτηρ, -τρός, ἡ   daughter (6.1/1b)
θῡμός, -οῦ, ὁ   spirit, heart; anger
θύρᾱ, -ᾱς, ἡ   door
θυσίᾱ, -ᾱς, ἡ   sacrifice
†θύω (A)   sacrifice
θύω (B)   rage
θώραξ, -ᾱκος, ὁ   trunk, chest
    (of body)
Θώραξ, -ᾱκος, ὁ   Thorax
    (a Boeotian)

ἰάομαι   heal, cure
ἰᾱτρός, -οῦ, ὁ   doctor, healer
ἰδ- aor. act./mid. stem of ὁράω
Ἰδαῖος, -ᾱ, -ον   of Mt. Ida (in
    Crete), Idaean
ἰδέᾱ, -ᾱς, ἡ   form, shape, type
ἰδίᾳ (adv.)   privately
ἴδιος, -ᾱ, -ον   private, personal,
    one's own

ἰδιώτης, -ου, ὁ   *private individual;*
    layman
ἰδού (adv.) *look! here! hey!*
ἰέναι inf. of ἔρχομαι/εἶμι (18.1/3
    and **Appendix 3**)
ἰερά, -ῶν, τά   *rites, sacrifices*
ἰερεῖα, -ων, τά   *offerings*
ἰερεύς, -έως, ὁ   *priest*
ἰερόν, -οῦ, τό   *temple, sanctuary*
ἰερός, -ά, -όν   *sacred, holy*
Ἱερώνυμος, -ου, ὁ   *Hieronymus*
†ἵημι   *let go, launch, send forth*
    (20.1/2); (mid., poet.) *be*
    eager, strive
Ἰησοῦς, -οῦ, ὁ   *Jesus*
Ἰθάκη, -ης, ἡ   *Ithaca* (island home
    of Odysseus)
ἴθι 2nd s. imp. of ἔρχομαι/εἶμι
    (18.1/3 and **Appendix 3**)
ἱκανός, -ή, -όν   *sufficient;*
    competent, capable (+inf.)
ἱκετεύω   *beg, supplicate*
ἱκέτης, -ου, ὁ   *suppliant*
ἵλεως, -ων   *propitious* (13.1/1*a*)
Ἰλιάς, -άδος, ἡ   *Iliad* (epic poem
    by Homer)
#ʼΙλιόθι epic equivalent of gen. of
    Ἴλιος/Ἴλιον
Ἴλιον, -ου, τό   *Ilium, Troy*
Ἴλιος, -ου, ἡ   *Ilium, Troy*
ἱμάτιον, -ου, τό   *cloak;* (pl.) *clothes*
#ἱμείρω   *long for, desire* (+gen.)
ἵνα (conj.) (+subj. or opt.)   *in*
    order that, to (14.1/4*c*(i));
    (+ind.) *where*
Ἰνάρως, -ω, ὁ   *Inaros* (King of
    Libya)
Ἰξίων, -ονος, ὁ   *Ixion*
Ἰοκάστη, -ης, ἡ   *Iocasta* (mother
    and wife of Oedipus)
Ἰόνιος, -ᾱ, -ον   *Ionic, Ionian*
Ἴος, -ου, ἡ   *Ios* (island in the
    Aegean)
Ἰουδαῖος, -ου, ὁ   *Jew*

ἱππεύς, -έως, ὁ   *horseman, cavalry;*
    rider
ἱππεύω   *ride*
#ἱππόδαμος, -ον   *horse-taming*
Ἱπποθάλης, -ους, ὁ   *Hippothales*
Ἱπποκράτης, -ους, ὁ   *Hippocrates*
Ἱππόλυτος, -ου, ὁ   *Hippolytus*
Ἱππόνῑκος, -ου, ὁ   *Hipponicus*
ἱπποπόταμος, -ου, ὁ   *hippopotamus*
ἵππος, -ου, ὁ   *horse;* ἡ *cavalry*
    ἀπὸ (ἀφʼ) ἵππου   *from horseback*
ἴσᾱσι 3rd pl. of οἶδα (**Appendix 3**)
ἴσθι 2nd s. imp. of εἰμί and οἶδα
    (**Appendix 3**)
ἰσθμός, -οῦ, ὁ   *isthmus*
ἴσμεν 1st pl. of οἶδα (**Appendix 3**)
ἴσος, -η, -ον   *equal to* (+dat.)
†ἵστημι   *make to stand;* (mid. and
    intr. tenses of act.) *stand*
    (19.1/1)
ἱστορίᾱ, -ᾱς, ἡ   *enquiry,*
    investigation
ἱστός, -οῦ, ὁ   *loom; web*
Ἴστρος, -ου, ὁ   *Danube*
#ἴσχε (2nd s. imp. of ἴσχω, a form of
    ἔχω)   *stop!*
Ἰσχόμαχος, -ου, ὁ   *Ischomachus*
ἰσχῡρός, -ά, -όν   *powerful, strong*
ἰσχῡρῶς (ad.)   *very much,*
    exceedingly
ἴσως (adv.)   *perhaps*
Ἰταλίᾱ, -ᾱς, ἡ   *Italy*
#ἰχθυόεις, -εσσα, -εν   *full of fish*
ἰχθῡς, -ύος, ὁ   *fish*
ἴχνος, -ους, τό   *track, footstep*
ἴω subj. of ἔρχομαι/εἶμι (**Appendix 3**)
Ἰώλκιος, -ᾱ, -ον   *of Iolcus* (city in
    Thessaly)
ἰών, ἰοῦσα, ἰόν pple. of ἔρχομαι/εἶμι
    (**Appendix 3**)

κἀγώ crasis for καὶ ἐγώ
Καδμεῖος, -ᾱ, -ον *Cadmean* (i.e.
    Theban)

καθαιμάττω *make bloody, stain with blood*
καθαιρέω† *take down, destroy*
καθαίρω† *cleanse, purify*
καθαρός, -ά, -όν *free from guilt/ defilement, pure*
καθεύδω *sleep*
κάθημαι *be seated* (19.1/3*b*)
καθίζω *sit down* (tr.and intr.); (mid.) *sit down* (intr.)
καθίστημι† *set down; put in a certain state; appoint; establish*; (mid. and intr.tenses of act.) *settle down; come into a certain state; be appointed; be established*
κάθοδος, -ου, ἡ *way down*
καθοράω† *see, catch sight of, look down on*
καθύπερθεν (adv.) *from above*
καί (conj.) *and*; (adv.) *also; even; actually, in fact*
  καὶ . . . καί *both . . . and*
  τε* . . . καί *both . . . and*
  καὶ γάρ *in fact; yes, certainly*
  καὶ δή *and really, moreover; as a matter of fact; look!; let us suppose* (13.1/3*c*)
  καὶ δὴ καί *and especially, and in particular*
  καὶ μήν *what's more; look!*
καινός, -ή, -όν *fresh, new, novel*
καίπερ *although* (+pple. 12.1/2*a*(iii))
καιρός, -οῦ, ὁ *right time; opportunity; time; crisis*
Καῖσαρ, -αρος, ὁ *Caesar*
καίτοι (particle) *and yet, however* (13.1/3*c*(iv))
†καίω *burn, kindle, set fire to*
κακηγορίᾱ, -ᾱς, ἡ *slander*
κακίᾱ, -ᾱς, ἡ *wickedness*
κακίζω *abuse*

κακίων, -ον *worse* (compar. of κακός)
κακοδαίμων, -ον *unlucky, unfortunate*
κακόνοια, -ᾱς, ἡ *malice*
κακός, -ή, -όν *bad, evil, wicked; cowardly; mean, lowly*; (neuter used as noun) *trouble*
  κακὰ (κακῶς) λέγω *speak ill of* (+acc., 22.1/2*f*(ii))
  κακὰ (κακῶς) ποιέω *treat badly; do harm to* (+acc., 22.1/2*f*(ii))
κακόω *ruin; wrong, maltreat*
κακῶς (adv.) *badly, wickedly*
  κακῶς ἔχω *be in a bad state/ condition*
καλεσ- aor. act./mid. stem of καλέω
καλέω *call, summon; name*
Καλλικρατίδᾱς, -ου, ὁ *Callicratidas*
Καλλίμαχος, -ου, ὁ *Callimachus* (Alexandrian poet)
κάλλιστος, -η, -ον *most beautiful* (supl. of καλός)
καλλίων, -ον *more beautiful* (compar. of καλός)
κάλλος, -ους, τό *beauty*
καλός, -ή, -όν *beautiful, good, fine; honourable*
Καλυψώ, -οῦς, ἡ *Calypso* (nymph who detained Odysseus on the island Ogygia) (13.1/1*b*(ii))
καλῶς (adv.) *well, rightly*
  καλῶς ἔχω *be in a good state/ condition*
κάμηλος, -ου, ὁ/ἡ *camel*
κάμνω (aor. ἔκαμον) *toil, labour*
κάμπτω *bend*
κἄν crasis for καὶ ἄν and καὶ ἐάν
κἀν crasis for καὶ ἐν
καπνός, -οῦ, ὁ *smoke*
καρδίᾱ, -ᾱς, ἡ *heart*
Καρδοῦχοι, -ων, οἱ *Kurds*

#κάρη, -ητος, τό head
Κᾱρίᾱ, -ᾱς, ἡ Caria (region in
    S.W. Asia Minor)
καρκίνος, -ου, ὁ crab
καρπός, -οῦ, ὁ fruits, harvest
καρτερός, -ά, -όν strong, mighty
#κασίγνητος, -ου, ὁ brother
κατά (prep.) (+acc.) in, on, at; in
    the region of; by, according to;
    down, throughout, during; in
    relation to, with respect to
    κατὰ γῆν καὶ κατὰ θάλατταν by
      land and by sea
    (+gen.) below, down from;
      against
καταβαίνω† go down, come down
καταβιβάζω make go down, bring
    down
καταγελάω† laugh at, mock
    (+gen.)
καταγιγνώσκω† condemn (acc.of
    the charge, gen.of the person,
    23.1/1k(i))
καταγορεύω (fut. κατερῶ, 18.1/4
    note 2) denounce
κατάγω† take/lead down; bring
    back/restore (from exile)
καταδουλόω enslave
καταδύω make to sink, lay to rest
#καταθνῄσκω† die
κατακαλύπτω cover over
κατάκειμαι lie down
κατακόπτω cut to pieces
κατακρίνω† give sentence against
    (acc. of penalty, gen. of
    person, 23.1/1k(i))
καταλαμβάνω† overtake, come
    across; seize, catch, capture
καταλέγω pick, choose; recount
    (18.1/4 note 1)
καταλείπω† leave behind,
    bequeath
κατάλυσις, -εως, ἡ overthrow,
    destruction

καταλύω bring to an end, destroy;
    finish; (intr.) stay, lodge
καταμείγνῡμι† mix in, combine
Κατάνη, -ης, ἡ Catana (city in
    Sicily)
καταντικρύ (prep.+gen.) right
    opposite
καταπαύω put an end to (+acc.)
καταπῑπτω† fall down
καταπλέω† sail down/back
κατάπλους, -ου, ὁ arrival in port
καταράομαι call down curses on
    (+dat.)
κατασκευάζω prepare, arrange
κατάσκοπος, -ου, ὁ scout, spy;
    inspector
καταστρέφομαι subdue, subject to
    oneself
καταστροφή, -ῆς, ἡ overthrowing;
    conclusion
#καταφθίμενος, -η, -ον dead
καταφρονέω despise, look down
    on (+gen.)
καταχέω pour down, shed
καταψηφίζομαι vote against (acc.
    of penalty, gen. of person,
    23.1/1k(i))
κατέλιπον aor. of καταλείπω
κατεπείγω press hard
κατέρχομαι† go down/back;
    return from exile
κατεσθίω† eat up, devour
κατέχω† hold back, check
κατηγορέω accuse (acc. of charge,
    gen. of person, 23.1/1k(i))
κατίσχω hold back, check
κατόπιν (adv., and prep.+gen.)
    after
κάτοπτρον, -ου, τό mirror
κατοχή, -ῆς, ἡ possession (by a
    spirit)
κάτω (adv.) below, down
καυσ- fut. and aor. act./mid. stem
    of καίω

#κε(ν) = ἄν
Κέβης, -ητος, ὁ   Cebes
κεῖμαι   lie; be placed (19.1/3b)
κεῖνος, -η, -ο = ἐκεῖνος
κείρω   cut (the hair), shear
κεῖσε = ἐκεῖσε
κέκρικα perf. of κρίνω
κέκτημαι   own, possess (perf. of
   κτάομαι 19.1/3a)
#κέλευθος, -ου, ἡ   road, path
κελευστέον   one must order
   (24.1/5)
†κελεύω   order, urge, tell . . . to, bid
κέλης, -ητος, ὁ   fast-sailing ship,
   pinnacle
#κέλομαι   urge, order, command
#κενεός, -ά, -όν = κενός
κενός, -ή, -όν   empty
κέντρον, -ου, τό   goad
κεράννῡμι   mix
κέρας, -ᾱτος, τό   horn; branch (of
   a river); with gen. κέρως, wing
   of an army/fleet (13.1/1b(iii))
κέρδος, -ους, τό   gain; profit
#κεύθω   hide, conceal
κεφαλή, -ῆς, ἡ   head
κηδεμών, -όνος, ὁ   protector
κῆρυξ, -υκος, ὁ   herald
Κίλιξ, -ικος, ὁ   a Cilician
κινδῡνεύω   be in danger, run a
   risk; be likely to (+inf.)
κίνδῡνος, -ου, ὁ   danger
κῑνέω   move
κῑνημα, -ατος, τό   movement
Κινύρης, -ου, ὁ   Cinyres
Κίρκη, -ης, ἡ   Circe (enchantress
   in Odyssey on the island of
   Aeaea)
κίων, -ονος, ἡ   pillar
Κλαζομένιος, -ᾱ, -ον   of/from
   Clazomenae
†κλαίω weep;   weep for, lament;
   (mid.) bewail to oneself
κλαυσ- aor. act./mid. stem of κλαίω

Κλέανδρος, -ου, ὁ   Cleander
Κλεάνωρ, -ορος, ὁ   Cleanor
Κλεάρετος, -ου, ὁ   Clearetus
Κλέαρχος, -ου, ὁ   Clearchus
Κλεινίᾱς, -ου, ὁ   Cleinias
κλείω   close, shut
κλέος, -ους, τό   glory
κλέπτης -ου, ὁ   thief
†κλέπτω steal
Κλέων, -ωνος, ὁ   Cleon (Athenian
   politician)
κληθείς, -εῖσα, -έν aor. pass. pple.
   of καλέω
#κληΐς, -ῖδος, ἡ   rowing-bench
κληρουχικός, -ή, -όν   belonging to
   a cleruchy
κλῖμαξ, -ακος, ἡ   ladder, stairway
κλοπή, -ῆς, ἡ   theft
κλύδων, -ωνος, ὁ   wave, surf;
   turmoil
κλωπεύω steal
Κνίδος, -ου, ἡ   Cnidos (city in Asia
   Minor)
κοιμάομαι   sleep, slumber
κοινῇ (adv.)   in common
κοινός, -ή, -όν   common, shared,
   public
κοινωνίᾱ, -ᾱς, ἡ   association,
   intercourse
κοινωνός, -οῦ, ὁ   partner
#κοιρανέω   be lord/master of, rule
   over (+gen.)
κολάζω punish
κολακείᾱ, -ᾱς, ἡ   flattery
Κολοφών, -ῶνος, ἡ   Colophon (city
   in Asia Minor)
κόλπος, -ου, ὁ   bosom; gulf
†κομίζω   carry, convey, bring;
   (mid.) acquire, recover
κομπέω   boast of
#κονίᾱ, -ᾱς, ἡ   dust
#κόνις, -εως, ἡ   dust
Κόνων, -ωνος, ὁ   Conon (Athenian
   admiral)

κόπος, -ου, ὁ *exertion, fatigue*
κόπτω *cut; knock on*
κόραξ, -ακος, ὁ *crow*
κόρη, -ης, ἡ *maiden, girl*
Κορίνθιοι, -ων, οἱ *Corinthians*
Κορίνθιος, -ᾱ, -ον *from Corinth*
Κόρινθος, -ου, ἡ *Corinth*
#κορυθαίολος, -ον *with gleaming helmet*
κοσμοπολίτης, -ου, ὁ *citizen of the world*
κόσμος, -ου, ὁ *decoration, ornament; order; universe; world*
κοὐ(κ) crasis for καὶ οὐ(κ)
κουρεύς, -έως, ὁ *barber*
Κουρῆτες, -ων, οἱ *Curetes* (minor divinities associated with orgiastic rites)
κουφίζω *lighten, make light*
κοῦφος, -η, -ον *light, nimble*
κούφως (adv.) *lightly*
κραδία, -ᾱς, ἡ *heart*
κρᾱνίον, -ου, τό *skull*
κραταίρῑνος, -ον *hard-shelled*
#κρατερός, -ᾱ́, -όν *hard, strong*
κρατέω *hold sway/power over, rule, control; defeat* (+gen., 13.1/2a(i))
κρᾱτήρ, -ῆρος, ὁ *mixing-bowl*
κράτιστος, -η, -ον *best, strongest* (supl. of ἀγαθός, κρείττων)
κράτος -ους, τό *strength, power; supremacy; (personified) Might*
   κατὰ κράτος *vigorously*
κρατύ́νω *strengthen*
κραυγή, -ῆς, ἡ *shouting, din*
κρέας, -ως, τό *meat* (13.1/1b(iii))
κρείττων, -ον *stronger, greater; better* (compar. of ἀγαθός)
κρεμάθρᾱ, -ᾱς, ἡ *hanging basket*

κρεμάννῡμι *hang* (tr.); (mid. κρέμαμαι) *hang* (intr.)
κρήνη, -ης, ἡ *spring*
Κρήτη, -ης, ἡ *Crete*
#κρῑ̂ (nom. and acc. s. only), τό *barley*
†κρῑ́νω *judge, decide; select, choose*
κρίσις, -εως, ἡ *judgment; decision; dispute; trial*
κριτής, -οῦ, ὁ *judge*
Κροῖσος, -ου, ὁ *Croesus* (King of Lydia)
κροκόδῑλος, -ου, ὁ *crocodile*
Κρονίδης, -ου, ὁ *son of Cronos* (i.e. Zeus)
κρόταφοι, -ων, οἱ *temples* (of forehead)
#κρουνός, -οῦ, ὁ *spring, stream*
κρούω *strike, knock*
#κρυπτάδιος, -ᾱ, -ον *secret, clandestine*
κρύπτω *keep secret, hide; bury; cover*
†κτάομαι *acquire, get; (perf.) own, possess* (19.1/3a)
†κτείνω *kill*
κτῆμα, -ατος, τό *(a) possession*
Κτήσιππος, -ου, ὁ *Ctesippus*
κτῆσις, -εως, ἡ *possession*
κτίζω *found, build*
κτύπος, -ου, ὁ *din, noise*
κυάνεος, -ᾱ, -ον *dark, black*
Κυαξάρης, -ου, ὁ *Cyaxares* (uncle of Cyrus)
κυβερνήτης, -ου, ὁ *helmsman, captain*
κύβος, -ου, ὁ *(a) die; (mostly in pl.) dice*
#κῡδαίνω *glorify*
κυθρίδιον, -ου, τό *little jar*
κυκάω *stir*
κῦμα, -ατος, τό *wave*
Κυμαῖος, -ᾱ, -ον *of or from Cyme* (city in Asia Minor)

Κύπρις, -ιδος, ἡ the Cyprian
(goddess), Cypris (a name of
Aphrodite, from the island of
Cyprus)
Κῡρήνη, -ης, ἡ Cyrene (city in N.
Africa)
κῡριος, -ᾱ, -ον having power/
authority
Κῦρος, -ου, ὁ Cyrus (1. founder of
the Persian empire; 2. younger
son of Darius II)
κύων, κυνός, ὁ/ἡ dog
κῶλον, -ου, τό limb
κωλύω prevent, stop (+acc. and
inf., 24.1/7)
κώμη, -ης, ἡ village
Κωνσταντινουπόλις, -εως,
ἡ Constantinople

λαβ- aor. act./mid. stem of
λαμβάνω
λαβύρινθος, -ου, ὁ Labyrinth
λαγχάνω obtain by lot; win as a
portion, get (+gen.)
λαγώς, -ώ, ὁ hare (13.1/1a)
λαθ- aor. act./mid. stem of λανθάνω
λάθρᾳ (adv.) secretly
#λάθριος, -ον secret, secretly
#λάϊνος, -η, -ον of stone
Λάϊος, -ου, ὁ Laius (father of
Oedipus)
Λᾱῖς, -ῖδος, ἡ Lais
Λάκαινα, -ης, ἡ Laconian
(Spartan) woman
Λακεδαιμόνιος, -ου, ὁ
Lacedaemonian, Spartan
Λακεδαίμων, -ονος, ἡ
Lacedaemon, Sparta
λακτίζω kick
Λάκων, -ωνος, ὁ Laconian,
Spartan
Λακωνικός, -ή, -όν Laconian,
Spartan
λαλέω talk, prattle, chatter

†λαμβάνω take, get, capture
δίκην λαμβάνω punish, exact
one's due from (παρά+gen.)
λαμπρός, -ά, -όν bright, brilliant,
famous
λάμπω shine
†λανθάνω escape notice of
(15.1/2f); (mid.) forget
#λᾱός, -οῦ, ὁ people
Λασθένης, -ους, ὁ Lasthenes
λαχ- aor. act./mid. stem of λαγχάνω
λέγω speak, say, tell, mean
οὐδὲν λέγω speak/talk nonsense
λείβω pour; let flow, shed
†λείπω leave, abandon
λείψανον, -ου, τό remnant
λέληθα perf. of λανθάνω
λεοντῆ, -ῆς, ἡ lion-skin
λεπτός, -ή, -όν subtle, fine;
delicate, thin
λέσχη, -ης, ἡ conversation
λευκαίνω (aor. ἐλεύκανα) make
white, whiten
λευκός, -ή, -όν white
#λεύσσω look upon, behold
λέων, -οντος, ὁ lion
Λεωνίδᾱς, -ου, ὁ Leonidas
(Spartan king)
λεωργός, -όν villainous; (as noun)
wrong-doer
#λεώς, -ώ, ὁ people (13.1/1a)
λήθη, -ης, ἡ forgetfulness
λήθω = λανθάνω
ληκύθιον, -ου, τό little oil-flask
#λῆμα, -ατος, τό arrogance,
audacity
ληστρικός, -ή, -όν belonging to
pirates
Λητώ, -οῦς, ἡ Leto
ληφθ- aor. pass. stem of λαμβάνω
λήψομαι fut. of λαμβάνω
λῑᾱν (adv.) very, exceedingly; too
much
Λιβύη, -ης, ἡ Libya

Λίβυς, -υος, ὁ *a Libyan*
λιγυρός, -ά, -όν *clear, shrill*
λίθινος, -η, -ον *made of stone* (see also χυτός)
λίθος, -ου, ὁ *stone*
λιμήν, -ένος, ὁ *harbour*
λίμνη, -ης, ἡ *lake* (especially marshy)
λῑμός, -οῦ, ὁ *hunger, famine*
#λίσσομαι *beg, beseech*
λογίζομαι *calculate, reckon, consider*
λόγος, -ου, ὁ *speech, tale, word, account; argument; reason, explanation*
λόγχη, -ης, ἡ *spear, javelin*
λοιδορέω *abuse, revile;* (mid., +dat.) *abuse, scold*
λοιπός, -ή, -όν *left, remaining*
λούω *wash (the body);* (mid.) *wash oneself*
λόφος, -ου, ὁ *hill*
λοχᾱγός, -οῦ, ὁ *company commander, captain*
Λῡδίᾱ, -ᾱς, ἡ *Lydia* (territory in west of Asia Minor)
Λῡδός, -οῦ, ὁ *Lydian*
Λυκαονίᾱ, -ᾱς, ἡ *Lycaonia* (country in Asia Minor)
Λύκειον, -ου, τό *the Lyceum* (park and gymnasium in Athens)
Λύκιος, -ου, ὁ *Lycius*
λύκος, -ου, ὁ *wolf*
Λυκοῦργος, -ου, ὁ *Lycurgus* (traditional Spartan legislator)
λῡπέω *cause distress to, annoy, grieve;* (mid.) *be distressed, grieve*
λύπη, -ης, ἡ *pain, grief*
λύρᾱ, -ᾱς, ἡ *lyre*
Λῡσίμαχος, -ου, ὁ *Lysimachus*
λῡσιτελεῖ (impers.) *it is profitable* (+dat. and inf., 21.1/4a)

#λύσσα, -ης, ἡ *frenzy, raging madness*
λυτήριον, -ου, τό *remedy, deliverance*
λύχνος, -ου, ὁ *lamp*
λύω *loosen, release; break up;* (mid.) *ransom*
λῷστος, -η, -ον (supl. adj.) *best*
λωτός, -οῦ, ὁ *lotus*
Λωτοφάγοι, -ων, οἱ *Lotus-Eaters*
λωφάω *lighten, relieve*

μά (particle of asseveration, affirmative or negative) *yes by ..., no by ... !* (+acc., 22.1/2h))
μᾶζα, -ης, ἡ *barley bread*
μαθ- aor. act./mid. stem of μανθάνω
μάθημα, -ατος, τό *lesson*
μαθήσομαι fut. of μανθάνω
μαθητέον *one must learn* (24.1/5)
μαθητής, -οῦ, ὁ *student*
Μαίανδρος, -ου, ὁ *Maeander* (river in Phrygia)
μαίνομαι *rage, be furious, be mad*
μακαρίζω *congratulate*
μακάριος, -ᾱ, -ον *blessed, happy*
Μακεδονίᾱ, -ᾱς, ἡ *Macedonia*
μακρόβιος, -ον *long-lived*
μακρός, -ά, -όν *long, large, big*
  μακρᾱ́ν (adv. acc.) *far off*
  μακρῷ *by far*
μάλα (adv.) *very; quite*
μαλθακίζομαι *be softened*
μαλθακός, -ή, -όν *faint-hearted, cowardly*
μάλιστα (supl. of μάλα) *especially, particularly; yes*
μᾶλλον (compar. of μάλα) *more; rather*
†μανθάνω *learn, understand;* (+inf.) *learn how to*
μανίᾱ, -ᾱς, ἡ *madness*
μαντεύομαι *consult an oracle*

μαντικῶς (adv.) *prophetically*
μάντις, -εως, ὁ *seer, prophet*
Μαραθών, -ῶνος, ὁ *Marathon* (in Attica)
    Μαραθῶνι *at Marathon*
Μαραθώνιος, -ᾱ, -ον *of Marathon*
#μαργῶν, -ῶσα, -ῶν (pple. of μαργάω) *raging*
#μάρπτω *take hold of, seize*
μαρτυρέω *give evidence, bear witness*
μαρτυρίᾱ, -ᾱς, ἡ *evidence, testimony*
μάρτυς, -υρος, ὁ/ἡ *witness*
Μασσαλίᾱ, -ᾱς, ἡ *Marseilles*
μαστεύω *seek, search after*
μαστῑγοφόρος, -ου, ὁ *whip-bearer*
μαστῑγόω *whip, flog*
μαστίζω *whip, flog*
μάτην (adv.) *in vain; without reason*
μάτηρ = μήτηρ
μάττω *knead*
μάχαιρα, -ᾱς, ἡ *knife*
μάχη, -ης, ἡ *battle, fight*
μάχιμος, -η, -ον *warlike*
†μάχομαι *fight* (+dat., 13.1/2b(iii))
Μεγακλῆς, -έους, ὁ *Megacles*
Μεγαροῖ (adv.) *in/at Megara*
μέγας, μεγάλη, μέγα (stem μεγαλ-; 3.1/3) *great, big; tall; important; loud*
μέγεθος, -ους, τό *size*
μέγιστος, -η, -ον *greatest* (supl. of μέγας)
μεθίημι† *let go, release; give up; allow*
μεθίστημι† (mid. and intr. tenses of act.) *change, alter* (intr.)
μεθύω *be drunk*
μείγνῡμι (also μῑγ-, aor. pass. ἐμίγην) *mix, join;* (pass.) *be joined, mix with, have sexual intercourse with* (+dat.)

Μειδίᾱς, -ου, ὁ *Meidias*
μείζων, -ον *greater* (compar. of μέγας)
#μείλιχος, -ον *gentle, kind*
μειράκιον, -ου, τό *lad, boy*
μέλας, -αινα, -αν *black* (10.1/3 note 2)
Μελέαγρος, -ου, ὁ *Meleager* (poet and philosopher)
†μέλει (impers.) *there is a care/concern* (+dat. of pers. and gen. of thing, 21.1/4b)
μελετάω *practise*
Μέλητος, -ου, ὁ *Meletus* (accuser of Socrates)
μέλι, -ιτος, τό *honey*
#μελιηδής, -ές *honey-sweet*
μέλιττα, -ης, ἡ *bee*
†μέλλω *be destined to; be about to, be going to; intend; hesitate*
μέλον (acc. absol.) *it being a care* (21.1/5)
#μέλω (for principal parts see under μέλει) *be of concern*
μέμνημαι (perf.) *remember* (+gen., 13.1/2a(iii)) (19.1/3a)
μέμφομαι *blame, criticize, find fault with* (+dat. or acc.)
μὲν* . . . δέ* *on the one hand . . . and/but on the other* (4.1/3)
μὲν οὖν *no, on the contrary* (13.1/3c(iii))
Μένανδρος, -ου, ὁ *Menander* (writer of New Comedy)
Μενδήσιος, -ᾱ, -ον *of Mendes* (a town in the Nile Delta), *Mendesian*
Μενέλᾱος, -ου, ὁ *Menelaus* (brother of Agamemnon, husband of Helen)
Μενέλεως, -ω, ὁ *Menelaus* (13.1/1a)
Μένιππος, -ου, ὁ *Menippus*
Μενοικεύς, -έως, ὁ *Menoeceus*

μέντοι* (particle) *really,*
    you know; however, yet
    (13.1/3*c*(v))
†μένω *remain, stay, wait (for); be*
    at rest, be still
Μένων, -ωνος, ὁ *Meno*
μέριμνα, -ης, ἡ *care*
μέρος, -ους, τό *share, part*
    ἐν μέρει *in turn*
#μεσηγύ (adv., and
    prep.+gen.) *between*
μέσος, -η, -ον *middle (of), in the*
    middle (18.1/6)
Μεσσηῖς, -ῖδος, ἡ *Messeis*
    (a spring)
Μεσσήνιος, -ᾱ, -ον *Messenian*
μέτα = μέτεστι (21.1/4 note 2)
μετά (prep.) (+acc.) *after;* (+gen.)
    with; (+dat., poetic) *among*
μεταβάλλω† *change, alter* (tr. and
    intr.)
μεταβολή, -ῆς, ἡ *change*
μεταγιγνώσκω† *change one's*
    mind; repent (of)
μεταδίδωμι† *give a share of* (+dat.
    of pers. and gen. of thing)
μεταμέλει† (impers.) *there is*
    repentance (+dat. of pers. and
    gen. of thing, 21.1/4*b*)
μεταμέλεια, -ᾱς, ἡ *regret*
μετανοέω *think afterwards,*
    change one's mind, repent
μεταξύ (adv.) *in the middle;*
    (+pple.) *in the middle of doing*
    something (12.1/2*a*(i))
μεταπέμπομαι† *summon, send for*
μετάρσιος, -ον *superficial, shallow*
μετεκβαίνω† *go from one place*
    into another, transfer
μέτεστι (impers.) *there is a share*
    (+dat. of pers. and gen. of
    thing, 21.1/4*b*)
μετέχω† *share in* (+gen.,
    13.1/2*a*(v))

μετέωρος, -ον *high in the air*
    τὰ μετέωρα *things in the*
    heaven above, astronomical
    phenomena
μετρέω *measure*
μέτρησις, -εως, ἡ *measurement*
μέτριος, -ᾱ, -ον *moderate,*
    reasonable, fair, average;
    standard
μετρίως (adv.) *in moderation*
μέτρον, -ου, τό *measure, due*
    measure, moderation
μέτωπον, -ου, τό *forehead*
μέχρι (prep.+gen.) *until, up to, as*
    far as; μέχρι οὗ *until;* (conj.)
    until (21.1/2)
μή *no(t);* (+imp. or aor.
    subj.) *don't* (17.1/1); (+subj.)
    lest; inviting a neg. answer
    (10.1/2*a*); (on other uses see
    24.1/2)
μηδαμῶς (adv.) *not at all, in no*
    way
μηδέ (conj.and adv.) *nor, not even*
Μήδεια, -ᾱς, ἡ *Medea* (wife of
    Jason)
μηδείς, μηδεμίᾱ, μηδέν *no, no one,*
    nothing
Μηδικός, -ή, -όν *of the Medes*
    τὰ Μηδικά (*sc.* πράγματα) *the*
    Persian Wars
#μήδομαι *plot, plan, devise*
Μῆδος, -ου, ὁ *a Mede; a Persian*
μηκέτι (adv.) *no longer*
μῆκος, -ους, τό *length*
Μήλιοι, -ων, οἱ *Melians*
μῆλον, -ου, τό *apple*
μήν* (particle) *then, indeed;*
    further (13.1/3*a*)
    τί μήν; *of course*
μήν, -ός, ὁ *month*
μηνῡτής, -οῦ, ὁ *informer*
μηνῡ́ω *give information*
μήποτε (adv.) *never*

μήπω (adv.)   not yet
μήτε . . . μήτε   neither . . . nor
μήτηρ, -τρός, ἡ   mother (6.1/1b)
μητρυιά, -ᾶς, ἡ   step-mother
μηχανάομαι   devise, contrive;
    procure for oneself
μηχανεύομαι = μηχανάομαι
μηχανή, -ῆς, ἡ   device, plan; means;
    engine of war
μιαίνω   stain, pollute
μίασμα, -ατος, τό   stain, pollution
Μίκκος, -ου, ὁ   Miccus
μῑκρός, -ά, -όν   small, short, little,
    petty
Μῑλήσιος, -ᾱ, -ον   of Miletus,
    Milesian
Μιλτιάδης, -ου, ὁ   Miltiades
    (Athenian general)
μίμημα, -ατος, τό   imitation
μιμνήσκομαι   remind oneself
μίμνω = μένω
#μιν (acc. s. pron. of 3rd
    pers.)   him, her, it
μῑσέω   hate
μισθόομαι   hire
μισθός, -οῦ, ὁ   hire, pay, reward
μισθωτός, -οῦ, ὁ   hireling, hired
    servant
μῖσος, -ους, τό   hatred
μνᾶ, μνᾶς, ἡ   mina (100 drachmas)
μνᾶμα = μνῆμα
μνῆμα, -ατος, τό   monument, tomb;
    memorial
μνήμη, -ης, ἡ   remembrance,
    memory
μνήμων, -ονος   mindful,
    unforgetting
μοῖρα, -ᾱς, ἡ   fate, lot, destiny; death
Μοῖρις, -εως, ἡ   Moeris (lake in
    Egypt)
μόλις (adv.)   hardly, scarcely, with
    difficulty
#μολών, -οῦσα, -όν   having come/
    gone (aor. pple. of βλώσκω)

μοναρχέω   be sole ruler over
    (+gen.)
μοναρχίᾱ, -ᾱς, ἡ   monarchy
μόναρχος, -ου, ὁ   monarch
μόνον (adv.)   only, merely
    οὐ μόνον ... ἀλλὰ καί   not only
    ... but also
μόνος, -η, -ον   alone, only
#μόρος, -ου, ὁ   fate, destiny, doom;
    death
μορφή, -ῆς, ἡ   shape, form
Μοῦσα, -ης, ἡ   Muse
μουσική, -ῆς, ἡ   music (including
    poetry)
μοχθέω   labour, toil
μόχθος, -ου, ὁ   toil, hardship
μῦθος, -ου, ὁ   story, fable
μυῖα, -ᾱς, ἡ   fly
Μυκῆναι, -ῶν, αἱ   Mycenae (city in
    S. Greece)
Μύνδιος, -ᾱ, -ον   Myndian
Μύνδος, -ου, ὁ   Myndus (city in
    Caria)
μυρίζω   make fragrant
μύριοι, -αι, -α   10,000
μῡρίος, -ᾱ, -ον   numberless,
    countless
μύρμηξ, -ηκος, ὁ   ant
μύρον, -ου, τό   perfume
μῦς, μυός, ὁ   mouse
μύστης, -ου, ὁ   initiate
Μυτιλήνη, -ης, ἡ   Mytilene (chief
    city of Lesbos)
μυχός, -οῦ, ὁ   inner chamber
μῶν; (adv.)   surely not? (10.1/2a)
μῶρος, -ᾱ, -ον   stupid, foolish

Ναζωραῖος, -ᾱ, -ον   of Nazareth
ναί (particle)   yes (22.1/2h, 24.1/1)
ναίω   dwell, abide
νᾶμα, -ατος, τό   stream
νᾱός, -οῦ, ὁ   temple
νάπη, -ης, ἡ   glen
ναυᾱγέω   suffer shipwreck

ναυηγός, -όν ship-wrecked
ναυμαχέω fight a sea battle
ναυμαχίᾱ, -ᾱς, ἡ naval battle
ναῦς, νεώς, ἡ ship (11.1/4)
Ναυσικάᾱ, -ᾱς, ἡ Nausicaa
    (daughter of Alcinous, King of
    Phaeacians)
ναύτης, -ου, ὁ sailor
ναυτικόν, -οῦ, τό fleet
ναυτικός, -ή, -όν naval
νεᾱνίᾱς, -ου, ὁ young man
νεᾱνίσκος, -ου, ὁ young man
νείφει (impers.) it is snowing
    (21.1/4c)
νεκρός, -οῦ, ὁ corpse
νέκταρ, -αρος, τό nectar
νέμεσις, -εως, ἡ retribution
νέμω distribute, apportion, allot,
    assign
#νέομαι go back, return
νέος, -ᾱ, -ον young; new; strange,
    unexpected
    ἐκ νέου from childhood
νεότης, -ητος, ἡ youthfulness,
    youthful folly
#νέρθε (adv.) beneath, below
νέφος, -ους, τό cloud
†νέω swim
νεώς, -ώ, ὁ temple (13.1/1a)
νή (particle of asseveration) yes by
    ... ! (+acc.; 22.1/2h)
νήνεμος, -ον windless, calm
νήπιος, -ᾱ, -ον childish, foolish
νησιώτης, -ου, ὁ islander
νῆσος, -ου, ἡ island
νήφω be sober (literally or
    metaphorically)
Νικαία, -ᾱς, ἡ Nicaea (city in Asia
    Minor)
νῑκάω win, defeat
νίκη, -ης, ἡ victory, conquest
νῑκητήριον, -ου, τό prize of victory
Νῑκίᾱς, -ου, ὁ Nicias
Νῑκοτέλης, -ους, ὁ Nicoteles

Νίκων, -ωνος, ὁ Nico
#νιν* (acc.) him, her, it, them
νίπτω wash
νοέω perceive
νόημα, -ατος, τό thought,
    perception
†νομίζω acknowledge, think, believe
    (in); treat as customary; (of a
    legislator) enact
νόμος, -ου, ὁ law, convention,
    observance
νόος = νοῦς
νοσέω be sick/ill
νόσημα, -ατος, τό a disease, illness,
    plague
νόσος, -ου, ἡ disease, illness
νοστέω return
#νόστιμος, -ον belonging to one's
    return/homecoming
#νόστος, -ου, ὁ homecoming
#νόσφι(ν) (adv., and prep.+gen.)
    afar off, away from
νουθετέω warn, rebuke
νοῦς (νόος), νοῦ, ὁ mind, sense,
    intelligence (6.1/2)
    ἐν νῷ ἔχω have in mind, intend
#νυκτιπόλος, -ον night-roaming
νῦν (adv.) now, at present
νυν* well then; now then
νυνδή (adv.; strengthened form of
    νῦν) just now
νύξ, νυκτός, ἡ night, darkness
    ὑπὸ νύκτα under cover of night

Ξανθίππη, -ης, ἡ Xanthippe
Ξάνθος, -ου, ὁ Xanthus (another
    name for river Scamander at
    Troy)
ξεῖνος = ξένος
ξένιος, -ᾱ, -ον belonging to
    friendship and hospitality
    (used as a title of Zeus, as god
    of hospitality)
Ξενοκράτης, -ους, ὁ Xenocrates

ξένος, -ου, ὁ   foreigner, alien,
    stranger; guest; host
Ξενοφῶν, -ῶντος, ὁ   Xenophon
    (Athenian historian and
    general)
Ξέρξης, -ου, ὁ   Xerxes (Persian
    king)
ξίφος, -ους, τό   sword
ξυγ- = συγ-
ξύλον, -ου, τό   (piece of) wood, log
ξυμ- = συμ-
ξύν = σύν
ξυν- = συν-
ξῡνός, -ή, -όν   common
ξυρέω   shave
ξυρόν, -οῦ, τό   razor

ὁ, ἡ, τό   the (2.1/2, 3.1/1)
    ὁ μὲν ... ὁ δέ   the one ... the
        other, one man ... another
        (5.1/3)
    οἱ μὲν ... οἱ δέ   some ... others
        (5.1/3)
    ὁ δέ   and/but he (5.1/3)
ὅδε, ἥδε, τόδε   this (pron. and adj.,
    9.1/1)
ὁδεύω   travel (by land)
ὀδμή, -ῆς, ἡ   smell
ὁδός, -οῦ, ἡ   road, way, journey
ὀδούς, -όντος, ὁ   tooth
ὀδυνηρός, -ά, -όν   painful
ὀδύρομαι   lament
Ὀδυσσεύς, -έως, ὁ   Odysseus (hero
    of the Odyssey)
ὅθεν (rel. adv.)   from where
οἷ (rel. adv.)   (to) where
οἱ see ἑ (9.1/4a)
†οἶδα   know (19.1/3 and
    Appendix 3)
    χάριν οἶδα   be grateful to
        (+dat.)
Οἰδίπους, -ποδος, ὁ   Oedipus (son
    of Laius, king of Thebes)
οἴκαδε (adv.)   homewards

οἰκεῖος, -ᾱ, -ον   related, domestic;
    private; one's own
οἰκεῖος, -ου, ὁ   relative
οἰκέτης, -ου, ὁ   house-slave
οἰκέω   dwell (in), live, inhabit
οἴκημα, -ατος, τό   room
οἴκησις, -εως, ἡ   dwelling
οἰκίᾱ, -ᾱς, ἡ   house
οἰκίζω   colonise
οἰκοδομέω   build a house
οἰκοδόμημα, -ατος, τό   building,
    structure
οἰκοδομίᾱ, -ᾱς, ἡ   building,
    structure
οἴκοθεν (adv.)   from home
οἴκοι (adv.)   at home
οἶκος, -ου, ὁ   house, home
οἰκτίρω   pity
οἰκτρός, -ά, -όν   piteous
†οἶμαι, οἴομαι   think
#οἴμη, -ης, ἡ   way/power of song
οἴμοι (interjection)   alas! oh dear!
#οἶμος, -ου, ὁ   tract, strip of land
Οἰνόη, -ης, ἡ   Oenoë (town in
    Attica)
οἶνος, -ου, ὁ   wine
οἰνοχοέω   pour wine
οἴομαι see οἶμαι
οἷον   as, just as
#οἷος, -ᾱ, -ον (note smooth
    breathing)   alone
οἷος, -ᾱ, -ον   what a ...!
    (exclamation); of what sort, of
    the kind which (21.1/3)
    οἷός τ᾽ εἰμί   be able to (+inf.,
        21.1/3 note 2)
οἷοσπερ strengthened form of οἷος
οἰσ- fut. stem of φέρω
ὀΐστευμα, -ατος, τό   arrow
οἰσύϊνος, -η, -ον   made of osier/
    wickerwork
οἴχομαι   be off, depart, be gone
ὀκτώ (indecl. adj.)   eight
ὀλ- aor. stem of ὄλλυμαι

ὄλβιος, -ᾱ, -ον *happy, blessed*
ὄλεθρος, -ου, ὁ *destruction*
ὀλεσ- aor. stem of ὄλλῡμι
ὀλιγαρχίᾱ, -ᾱς, ἡ *oligarchy*
ὀλίγος, -η, -ον *small, few, little*
†ὄλλῡμι *destroy, kill, lose* (20.1/1 note 2)
#ὀλοός, -ή, -όν *destructive, baneful*
Ὄλορος, -ου, ὁ *Olorus* (father of Thucydides)
ὅλος, -η, -ον *whole, complete*
Ὀλυμπικός, -οῦ, ὁ *Olympicus* (name of a seer)
Ὀλύμπιος, -ᾱ, -ον *Olympian*
  Ὀλύμπια νῑκάω *win an Olympic victory* (22.1/2g)
Ὄλυνθος, -ου, ἡ *Olynthus*
ὄλυραι, -ῶν, αἱ *a one-seeded wheat* (used as fodder for horses)
#ὁμαρτέω *accompany* (+dat.)
Ὅμηρος, -ου, ὁ *Homer* (author of *Iliad* and *Odyssey*)
ὁμῑλέω *be in company with, associate with* (+dat.)
ὁμῑλίᾱ, -ᾱς, ἡ *company, companionship*
ὁμίχλη, -ης, ἡ *mist, fog*
#ὄμμα, -ατος, τό *eye*
†ὄμνῡμι *swear, swear by* (+acc., 22.1/2h)
ὁμοιόομαι *be like, resemble* (+dat., 13.1/2b(iv))
ὅμοιος, -ᾱ, -ον *like, similar to* (+dat.)
ὁμοίως (adv.) *in the same way, likewise*
ὁμολογέω *agree*
ὁμολογίᾱ, -ᾱς, ἡ *agreement*
ὁμολογουμένως (adv.) *in agreement/conformity with* (+dat.)
ὁμομήτριος, -ᾱ, -ον *born of the same mother*

ὁμόνοια, -ᾱς, ἡ *agreement, harmony*
ὁμοτράπεζος, -ον *eating at the same table with* (+dat.)
ὁμοῦ (adv.) *together (with)* (+dat.)
ὁμόφῡλος, -ον *of the same race or stock*
ὅμως (adv.) *nevertheless, however*
#ὁμῶς (adv., accompanying two words joined by καί) *both*
ὄν see ὤν
ὄναρ (nom. and acc. only), τό *dream*; (as adv.) *in a dream*
ὀνειδίζω *reproach, chide, insult* (+dat.)
ὄνειδος, -ους, τό *insult, rebuke*
ὄνειρος, -ου, ὁ (also ὄνειρον, -ου, τό) *dream*
ὄνομα, -ατος, τό *name, reputation*
  ὀνόματι *in/by name*
ὀνομάζω *call, name*
ὄνος, -ου, ὁ/ἡ *ass*
ὄνυξ, -υχος, ὁ *claw, nail*
ὄξος, -ους, τό *vinegar*
ὀξύς, -εῖα, -ύ *sharp, keen; quick, swift*
#ὀπάζω *give, bestow; make to follow*
ὅπη (adv.) *in what way, how, as*
ὄπισθε (adv.) *behind*
ὀπισθοφύλαξ, -ακος, ὁ *member of rear-guard*
#ὀπίσω (adv.) *hereafter*
ὅπλα, -ων, τά *weapons, arms*
  ἐν ὅπλοις *under arms*
ὁπλίζω *equip, arm*
ὁπλίτης, -ου, ὁ *hoplite*
ὁπόθεν (rel. adv.) *from where*
ὅποι (rel. adv.) *to where*
ὁποῖος, -ᾱ, -ον *of what kind* (10.1/2b)
ὁπόσος, -η, -ον *how big, how much*; (pl.) *how many* (10.1/2b)

ὁπόταν (conj.+subj.) *whenever* (14.1/4*c*(iii))

ὁπότε (conj.) *when*; (+opt.) *whenever* (14.1/4*c*(iii))

ὅπου (rel. adv.) *where, wherever*; (indir. interrog.) *where*

ὅπως (adv.) *how* (in answer to πῶς;); *how*; (poet.) *like, as*; (conj.+subj. or opt.) *in order that, to* (14.1/4*c*(i))

ὁπωστιοῦν (adv.) *in any way whatever*

†ὁράω *see, look at*

ὀργή, -ῆς, ἡ *temperament; anger* ἐν ὀργῇ ἔχω *be angry with* (+acc.)

†ὀργίζομαι (aor. ὠργίσθην) *become angry with* (+dat., 13.1/2*b*(i))

ὀρέγομαι *strive after* (+gen.)

ὄρειος, -ᾱ, -ον *of the mountains, mountain-wandering*

Ὀρέστης, -ου, ὁ *Orestes* (son of Agamemnon)

#ὀρθόβουλος, -ον *straight-counselling, wise*

ὀρθός, -ή, -όν *straight; correct; right*

ὀρθόω *set upright; guide aright*

ὀρθῶς (adv.) *correctly*

ὅρκος, -ου, ὁ *oath*

ὁρμάομαι *set off, start out; make an expedition*

ὁρμή, -ῆς, ἡ *setting oneself in motion* ἐν ὁρμῇ εἰμι *be on the point of starting*

ὁρμίζω *moor, anchor*

ὄρνῑς, -ῑθος (acc. ὄρνιν, 5.1/1 note 2), ὁ/ἡ *bird*

ὄρος, -ους, τό *mountain*

ὅρος, -ου, ὁ *boundary*

ὀρρωδέω *fear, dread*

ὀρχήστρᾱ, -ᾱς, ἡ *orchestra* (the dancing-space in the theatre and also a section of the agora where books were sold)

ὅς, ἥ, ὅ (rel. pron., 9.1/2) *who, which*

#ὅς, ἥ, ὅν (refl. poss. adj.) *his, her, its*

ὅσιος, -ᾱ, -ον *holy, sacred; pious, devout*

ὁσιόω *sanctify*

ὅσος, -η, -ον *how much/many/ great!* (exclamation); *as much/ many as* (21.1/3)

ὅσοσπερ, ὅσηπερ, ὅσονπερ *as great as, as many as*

ὅσπερ, ἥπερ, ὅπερ (rel. pron.) *the very one who/which*

#ὁσσάκις (interrog. adv.) *how often*

ὅστις, ἥτις, ὅτι (indef. rel. pron. and indir. interrog., 10.1/2*b*) *who(ever), which(ever), what(ever)*

ὀστοῦν, -οῦ, τό *bone*

ὅσῳ (+compar.) *the more* (lit. *by how much*)

ὅταν (conj.+subj.) *whenever* (14.1/4*c*(iii))

ὅτε (conj.) *when*

ὅτι (A) (conj.) *that; because* (+supl.) *as ... as possible* (17.1/4*d*)

ὅτι (B) neuter nom./acc. s. of ὅστις

ὅτου = οὗτινος

ὅτῳ = ᾧτινι

οὐ (οὐκ, οὐχ) *no(t)* οὐ μόνον ... ἀλλὰ καί *not only ... but also*

οὐ see ἑ (9.1/4*a*)

οὗ (rel. adv.) *where*

οὐδαμοῦ (adv.) *nowhere*

οὐδαμῶς (adv.) *in no way; not at all*

οὐδέ (conj.) *and not, nor*; (adv.) *not even*

οὐδείς, οὐδεμίᾱ, οὐδέν no, no one,
    nothing
οὐδέν (adverbial acc.) in no
    respect, not at all
οὐδέποτε (adv.) never
οὐδέπω (adv.) not yet
οὐδέτερος, -ᾱ, -ον neither of two;
    neuter (of gender)
οὐκ = οὐ
οὐκέτι (adv.) no longer
οὔκουν (particle) not ... therefore
    (13.1/3c(i))
οὐκοῦν (particle) therefore,
    accordingly (13.1/3c(i))
οὖν* (particle) therefore, so, then
    οὖν δή well, as you know
οὑν crasis for ὁ ἐν
οὕνεκα = ἕνεκα
οὔποτε (adv.) never
οὔπω (adv.) not yet
#οὐρανόθεν (adv.) from heaven
οὐρανός, -οῦ, ὁ sky, heaven;
    (personified, with cap.)
    Uranus
οὖς, ὠτός, τό ear
οὐσίᾱ, -ᾱς, ἡ property, wealth,
    substance, means
οὔτε ... οὔτε neither ... nor
οὔτις, οὔτινος no one
οὔτοι (adv.) indeed not
οὗτος, αὕτη, τοῦτο (pron. and adj.,
    9.1/1) this; οὗτος can express
    you there!
    οὑτοσί (strengthened form) this
    man here
οὕτω(ς) (adv.) thus, so, in this way;
    to such an extent, so much
οὑτωσί strengthened form of οὕτως
οὐχ = οὐ
οὐχί emphatic form of οὐ
ὀφείλω owe; be bound, ought (see
    21.1/1 note)
ὄφελος, -ους, τό help, use,
    advantage

ὀφθαλμός, -οῦ, ὁ eye
ὄφις, -εως, ὁ serpent
ὄχλος, -ου, ὁ crowd, mob
#ὀχμάζω bind fast
#ὄχος, -ους, τό chariot
ὀχυρός, -ᾱ, -όν strong, secure
ὀψέ (adv.) late
ὄψις, -εως, ἡ vision, sight; face
ὄψομαι fut. of ὁράω
ὄψον, -ου, τό cooked food, a made
    dish; delicacies

πάγη, -ης, ἡ trap, snare
#παγίς, -ίδος, ἡ trap, snare
πάγος, -ου, ὁ crag, rock; frost
παθ- aor. stem of πάσχω
πάθημα, -ατος, τό suffering,
    misfortune
πάθος, -ους, τό suffering,
    experience
Παιανιεύς, -έως, ὁ of the deme
    Paeania
παιδαγωγός, -οῦ, ὁ tutor
παιδείᾱ, -ᾱς, ἡ education,
    teaching, lesson; culture;
    childhood
παιδεύω train, teach, educate
παιδίον, -ου, τό child; slave
παίζω play, make sport of (+acc.),
    joke at (πρός+acc.)
παιπαλόεις -εσσα, -εν rugged
παῖς, παιδός, ὁ/ἡ child, boy, girl;
    slave
πάλαι (adv.) long ago
παλαιός, -ά, -όν ancient, (of) old
παλαίστρᾱ, -ᾱς, ἡ wrestling-
    school, palaestra
παλαίτατος, -η, -ον supl. of παλαιός
πάλιν (adv.) back again, again
παμπήδην (adv.) entirely,
    completely
παμπλούσιος, -ον very rich
πανδημεί (adv.) in a body, in full
    force

παννύχιος, -ον *all night long*
#πανόδυρτος, -ον *all-lamented*
Πάνοψ, -οπος, ὁ *Panops*
παντάπᾱσι(ν) (adv.) *in every
    respect*
πανταχόθεν (adv.) *from all
    directions*
πανταχοῦ (adv.) *everywhere;
    absolutely, altogether*
πανταχῶς (adv.) *in all ways,
    altogether*
παντελῶς (adv.) *completely,
    outright*
#πάντεχνος, -ον *assisting all the
    arts*
πάντοθεν (adv.) *from every side*
#παντρόφος, -ον *all-nurturing*
πάντως (adv.) *in all ways,
    especially*
πάνυ (adv.) *very (much)*
    πάνυ γε, πάνυ μὲν οὖν *certainly,
    of course* (13.1/3c(iii))
πάππος, -ου, ὁ *grandfather*
#πάρ = παρά
πάρα = πάρεστι (21.1/4 note 2)
παρά (prep.) (+acc.) *along, beside;
    against, contrary to; compared
    with;* (+gen.) *from;* (+dat.)
    with, beside, in the presence of
παραβαίνω† *transgress*
παραβάλλω† *compare* (+παρά
    and acc.); (intr.) *come near,
    approach*
παραβοηθέω *come to help* (+dat.);
    assist
παραγγέλλω† *give an order*
παραγίγνομαι† *be present; come
    to, arrive at*
παράγω† *bring forward, introduce*
παραδίδωμι† *hand over, deliver*
παραδωσ- fut. act./mid. stem of
    παραδίδωμι
παραινέω† *advise* (+dat.,
    13.1/2b(i))

παρακαλέω† *summon; invite;
    encourage*
παράκειμαι *lie/be placed beside*
    (+dat.)
παρακελεύομαι† *exhort,
    encourage* (+dat.)
παραλαμβάνω† *take/receive from*
παραμελέω (< παρά + ἀμελέω)
    disregard, pay no heed to
παραμένω† *remain; remain loyal*
παράπαν (adv.) *altogether,
    absolutely* (also τὸ παράπαν)
παραπλέω† *sail by, sail close to*
παραπλήσιος, (-ᾱ), -ον *very similar
    to* (+dat. or καί)
παρασάγγης, -ου, ὁ *parasang* (a
    Persian measure of distance of
    c. 6 kilometres)
παρασκευάζω *prepare, equip;*
    (mid.) *make one's preparations*
παρασκευή, -ῆς, ἡ *preparation,
    equipping; force*
παρασπίζω *bear a shield beside,
    shield* (+dat.)
παραυτίκα (adv.) *immediately,
    straight away*
παρεγγυάω *pass (the word) along*
πάρειμι *be at hand; be present; be
    near* (+dat.)
    πάρεστι (impers.) *it is possible
    for* (+dat. and inf., 21.1/4a)
παρελαύνω† *drive past*
παρεμφαίνω† *emphasise*
πάρεργον, -ου, τό *subordinate
    issue*
παρέρχομαι† *pass, go by; come
    forward*
παρέχον (acc. abs.) *it being
    possible/allowed* (21.1/5)
παρέχω† *give to, provide; offer,
    furnish, cause*
    πράγματα παρέχω *cause trouble*
    παρέχει (impers.) *it is possible/
    allowed* (+dat. and inf.)

παρθένος, -ου, ἡ girl, maiden
παρίημι† pass over; let pass;
    leave,allow, admit
παρίστημι† (mid. and intr. tenses of
    act.) stand beside, be near/
    at hand
παριών, -οῦσα, -όν pple. of
    παρέρχομαι
πάροδος, -ου, ἡ passage, entrance
πάροιθε (adv.) formerly
παροιμίᾱ, -ᾱς, ἡ proverb
παρόν (acc. absol.) it being
    possible (21.1/5)
πάρος (adv.) previously; before
    (= πρίν)
παρών, -οῦσα, -όν pple. of
    πάρειμι, be present
πᾶς, πᾶσα, πᾶν (10.1/3b) all, every
    ὁ πᾶς the whole
†πάσχω undergo; experience; suffer
    εὖ/κακῶς πάσχω be well/badly
    treated (17.1/5)
#πατέομαι (aor. ἐπασάμην) eat of,
    partake of (+gen.)
πατήρ, -τρός, ὁ father (6.1/1b)
πατρίδιον, -ου, τό daddy
πατρίς, -ίδος, ἡ fatherland, native
    land
Πάτροκλος, -ου, ὁ Patroclus
    (friend of Achilles)
πάτταλος, -ου, ὁ peg
παύω (tr.) stop; depose; (mid., intr.)
    stop, cease from (+gen. or pple.)
Πάφιος, -ᾱ, -ον from Paphos,
    Paphian; (as fem. noun) the
    Paphian (sc. goddess, a name
    of Aphrodite derived from
    Paphos in Cyprus)
πάχνη, -ης, ἡ hoar-frost
παχύς, -εῖα, -ύ thick, stout, fat
πέδη, -ης, ἡ fetter
πεδίον, -ου, τό plain
πέδον, -ου, τό ground, land,
    region

πεζομαχέω fight on foot/land
πεζός, -ή, -όν on foot
    πεζοί foot soldiers, infantry
    πεζῇ on foot
†πείθω persuade; (mid.) believe,
    trust, obey (+dat., 13.1/2b(ii))
πειθώ, -οῦς, ἡ persuasion;
    obedience (13.1/1b(ii))
πεινάω be hungry (5.1/2 note 4)
πεῖρα, -ᾱς, ἡ attempt, experiment,
    trial
Πειραιεύς (acc. -αιᾶ, gen. -αιῶς,
    dat. -αιεῖ), ὁ Piraeus (port of
    Athens)
πειράομαι try; test (+gen.)
πειρᾱτέον one must try (24.1/5)
πειρᾱτής, -οῦ, ὁ pirate
πείσομαι fut. of πάσχω or πείθομαι
πέλαγος, -ους, τό sea, high sea
πέλας (adv.+gen.) near; nearby
Πελασγοί, -ῶν, οἱ Pelasgians
#πέλομαι (ἔπλετο 3rd s. strong
    aor.) be
Πελοποννήσιοι, -ων,
    οἱ Peloponnesians
Πελοπόννησος, -ου, ἡ Peloponnese
πέμπτος, -η, -ον fifth
†πέμπω send; conduct
πένης, -ητος poor (man)
πένθος, -ους, τό grief, sorrow,
    mourning
πενίᾱ, -ᾱς, ἡ poverty
πέντε (indecl. adj.) five
πεντήκοντα (indecl. adj.) fifty
πέποιθα (strong perf. of
    πείθω) trust, rely on (+dat.)
πέπονθα perf. of πάσχω
πεπρωμένος, -η, -ον destined, fated
πέπτωκα perf. of πίπτω
πέπυσμαι perf. of πυνθάνομαι
πέπωκα perf. of πίνω
περ* = καίπερ; -περ at the end of a
    word (e.g. ὅσπερ) is emphatic
πέρας, -ατος, τό end

#πέργαμα, -ων, τά citadel, acropolis
Περδίκκᾱς, -ου, ὁ Perdiccas
#πέρθω ravage, destroy, sack
περί (prep.) (+acc.) about,
  around; (+gen.) about,
  concerning; (+dat.) in, on,
  about
  περὶ (+acc.) εἰμί be busy with
  περὶ πολλοῦ ποιέομαι value
  highly (+acc.) (20.1/3)
περιάγω† lead round
περιβάλλω† throw round;
  embrace
περίβολος, -ου, ὁ enclosure
περιγίγνομαι† remain over; excel
περίειμι survive, remain
περιέπω† treat
περιεργάζομαι† waste one's
  labour
περιέρχομαι† go round, walk
  round
Περικλῆς, -κλέους, ὁ Pericles
  (Athenian statesman)
περιμένω† wait, wait for (+acc.)
περίοδος, -ου, ἡ chart, map
περιοράω† overlook, allow
περιπαθῶς (adv.) passionately
περιπατέω walk around
περιπίπτω† fall in with, encounter
  (+dat.)
περίπλους, -ου,
  ὁ circumnavigation
περιπτύσσω outflank
περιτειχίζω build a wall round
περιτείχισμα, -ατος, τό wall of
  circumvallation, blockading
  wall
περιτίθημι† put around, bestow
  on
περιφέρω† carry round
περιφρονέω think about/around;
  despise
Περσεφόνη, -ης, ἡ Persephone
Πέρσης, -ου, ὁ Persian

πέρυσι (adv.) last year
πεσ- aor. stem of πίπτω
#πετεινός, -ή, -όν winged
πέτομαι fly
πέτρᾱ, -ᾱς, ἡ rock, cliff
πέτρος, -ου, ὁ stone, boulder
πεύθομαι = πυνθάνομαι
πεύσομαι fut. of πυνθάνομαι
πέφῡκα be by nature, be naturally
  (see φύω)
πῆ (interrog. particle) where?
  how?
πηδάω leap, jump
πηλός, -οῦ, ὁ mud
#πῆμα, -ατος, τό woe, misery,
  calamity
#πημονή, -ῆς, ἡ woe, misery
Πηνελόπεια, -ᾱς, ἡ Penelope (wife
  of Odysseus)
πῆχυς, -εως, ὁ forearm; cubit
πιέζομαι be oppressed/distressed
πιθ- aor. act./mid. stem of πείθομαι
πιθανός, -ή, -όν persuasive
πίθηκος, -ου, ὁ monkey
πικρός, -ά, -όν bitter, harsh, severe
πικρῶς (adv.) bitterly
Πῑλᾶτος, -ου, ὁ (Pontius) Pilate
†πίμπλημι fill with (+gen. or dat.)
  (19.1/1 note 2)
πίμπρημι burn (tr.) (19.1/1 note 2)
πινακίδιον, -ου, τό writing-tablet
Πίνδαρος, -ου, ὁ Pindar (lyric
  poet)
†πίνω drink
†πίπτω fall
πιστεύω trust (+dat., 13.1/2b(ii))
πίστις, -εως, ἡ pledge, assurance;
  good faith; trust
πιστός, -ή, -όν reliable,
  trustworthy, faithful
#πλάζομαι (aor. ἐπλάγχθην) wander
πλανάομαι wander
πλάνη, -ης, ἡ wandering
πλατύπους, -οδος flat-footed

πλατύς, -εῖα, -ύ   broad, flat
Πλάτων, -ωνος, ὁ   Plato
   (philosopher)
πλέθρον, -ου, τό   plethron
   (c. 30 metres)
πλεῖστος, -η, -ον   most (supl. of
   πολύς)
πλείων, πλέον   more (compar. of
   πολύς,17.1/2b)
πλέκω   plait; devise, contrive
πλέον (adv.)   more
πλεύμων, -ονος, ὁ   lung
πλευρά, -ᾶς, ἡ   rib, flank
πλεύσομαι fut. of πλέω
πλέω   sail
πλέως, -ᾱ, -ων   full of (+gen.)
   (13.1/1a)
πληγή, -ῆς, ἡ   blow, stroke, lash
πλῆθος, -ους, τό   number, crowd;
   the people
πλήν (adv.)   but, except; (also
   prep.+gen.) except, except for
πλήρης, -ες   full
πλησιάζω   approach (+dat.,
   13.1/2b(iii))
πλησίος, -ᾱ, -ον   near, close to
   (+gen.)
πλησμονή, -ῆς, ἡ   repletion
πλήττω   strike, hit
πλοῖον, -ου, τό   vessel, ship, boat
πλοῦς (πλόος), -οῦ, ὁ   sailing,
   voyage; time for sailing
   (6.1/2)
πλούσιος, -ᾱ, -ον   rich, wealthy
πλουτέω   be rich
πλοῦτος, -ου, ὁ   wealth
Πλούτων, -ωνος, ὁ   Pluto (god of the
   underworld)
πλύνω   wash (clothes)
πνεῦμα, -ατος, τό   breath
πνέω (aor. ἔπνευσα)   breathe
πνίγω   choke, strangle; ἐπνίγην
   (root aor.) choked (intr.)
πνοή, -ῆς, ὁ   breath

ποδαπός, -ή, -όν   from what
   country?
ποθεινός, -ή, -όν   longed for,
   desired
πόθεν (interrog. adv.)   from where?
πόθος, -ου, ὁ   longing, desire
ποῖ (interrog. adv.)   to where?
ποῖ τῆς γῆς   to where in the
   world?
ποιέω   make, do; (mid.) make,
   think, consider
ἀγαθὰ (εὖ) ποιέω   treat well, do
   good to (+acc., 22.1/2f(ii))
κακὰ (κακῶς) ποιέω   treat badly,
   harm (+acc., 22.1/2f(ii))
ποιητέον   one must make/do
   (24.1/5)
ποιητής, -οῦ, ὁ   poet
#ποικιλείμων, -ον   with embroidered
   coat
ποικίλος, -η, -ον   many-coloured;
   subtle, ingenious
ποιμήν, -ένος, ὁ   shepherd
ποῖος, -ᾱ, -ον;   of what sort?
πολεμέω   make war
πολεμικός, -ή, -όν   military, martial
πολέμιοι, -ων, οἱ   the enemy
πολέμιος, -ᾱ, -ον   hostile, enemy
πόλεμος, -ου, ὁ   war
πολιορκέω   besiege
#πολιός, -ά, -όν   grey
πόλις, -εως, ἡ   city, city-state
πολῑτείᾱ, -ᾱς, ἡ   citizenship;
   constitution
πολῑτεύομαι   be a citizen
πολίτης, -ου, ὁ   citizen
πολῑτικός, -ή, -όν   political
πολλάκις (adv.)   often
πολλός Ionic for πολύς
#πολύκλαυτος, -ον   much lamented
πολύλογος, -ον   talkative
πολυμαθίᾱ, -ᾱς, ἡ   much learning
Πολυνείκης, -ους, ὁ   Polynices (son
   of Oedipus)

πολύς, πολλή, πολύ (stem πολλ-;
    3.1/3)   *much* (pl. *many*); *long*
πολλοῦ δεῖ   *far from it!*
πολλοῦ δέω   *I am far from*
πολλῷ   *by far*
πολύ (adv. acc.)   *very, much*
οἱ πολλοί *the majority; the mob*
ὡς ἐπὶ τὸ πολύ   *for the most part*
    (22.1/1*a*(vii))
πολυτελεύομαι   *feast luxuriously*
#πολύτροπος, -ον   *of many wiles* (or
    much travelled)
πολύφιλος, -ον   *having many
    friends*
πονέω   *toil, labour*
πονηρίᾱ, -ᾱς, ἡ   *wickedness*
πονηρός, -ᾱ́, -όν   *wicked, bad; of
    poor quality; wretched*
πόνος, -ου, ὁ   *toil, labour; distress,
    trouble, stress, suffering*
πόντος, -ου, ὁ   *sea;* (with cap.) *the
    Black Sea*
πορείᾱ, -ᾱς, ἡ   *course, passage*
πορεύομαι *march, journey, travel*
πορθέω   *destroy, plunder, sack*
πορίζομαι   *procure*
πόρρω (adv.)   *far away*
πορών pple. of ἔπορον
Ποσειδῶν, -ῶνος, ὁ   *Poseidon* (god
    of the sea) (acc. Ποσειδῶ)
πόσος, -η, -ον;   *how big?, how
    much?;* pl. *how many?*
ποταμός, -οῦ, ὁ   *river*
ποτέ*   *once, ever*
πότε; (interrog. adv.)   *when?*
Ποτείδαια, -ᾱς, ἡ   *Potidea* (city in
    northern Greece)
Ποτειδεᾶται, -ῶν, οἱ   *Potideans*
πότερα = πότερον (introducing
    alternative questions, 10.1/2*a*)
πότερον ... ἤ ...   *whether ... or ..?*
πότερος, -ᾱ, -ον;   *which (of two)?*
#ποτής, -ῆτος, ἡ   *drink*
#πότμος, -ου, ὁ   *fate*

που*   *somewhere, anywhere; I
    suppose*
ποῦ; (adv.)   *where?*
πούς, ποδός, ὁ   *foot*
πρᾶγμα, -ατος, τό   *thing; business,
    negotiation; affair;* (in pl.)
    trouble
πράγματα παρέχω   *cause
    trouble*
Πραξιτέλης, -ους, ὁ   *Praxiteles*
    (sculptor)
πράσσω = πράττω
πράττω   *do, carry out, get on, fare*
    εὖ (or καλῶς) πράττω   *fare well,
    be prosperous*
    κακῶς πράττω   *fare badly, be in
    distress*
πρέπει (impers.)   *it befits, it is
    proper for* (+dat., 21.1/4*a*)
πρέπον (acc. absol.)   *it being fitting*
    (21.1/5)
πρέσβεις, -εων, οἱ   *ambassadors*
    (8.1/4 note)
πρεσβεύομαι   *send an embassy*
πρεσβευτής, -οῦ, ὁ   *ambassador*
πρεσβύτερος, -ᾱ, -ον   *older, rather
    old*
Πρίαμος, -ου, ὁ   *Priam* (King of
    Troy)
πρίασθαι aor. inf. of ὠνέομαι
πρίν (adv.)   *before, formerly;*
    (conj.) *before, until* (21.1/2)
πρό (prep.+gen.)   *before, in front
    of*
    πρὸ τοῦ   *previously*
προαγορεύω (aor. προεῖπον, 18.1/4
    note 2)   *proclaim*
προάγω†   *lead on/forward*
προαιρέομαι†   *choose in
    preference*
προαισθάνομαι†   *perceive
    beforehand*
προβάλλω†   *put forward; expose*
πρόβατον, -ου, τό   *sheep*

προβουλεύω   make a preliminary resolution (of the Council, for referral to the Assembly)
πρόγονος, -ου, ὁ   forebear, ancestor
προδίδωμι†   betray
προδοσίᾱ, -ᾱς, ἡ   treachery
προεῖπον aor. of προαγορεύω
προέρχομαι†   go forward, advance
προθῡμέομαι   be ready, eager
προθῡμίᾱ, -ᾱς, ἡ   desire, eagerness, goodwill
πρόθῡμος, -ον   ready, eager, willing
πρόθυρον, -ου, τό   porch, front door
προΐημι†   send forth
προκείμενος, -η, -ον   proposed, appointed
Προκλῆς, -έους, ὁ   Procles
προλείπω†   leave, abandon
προμάχομαι†   fight in defence of
Προμηθεύς, -έως, ὁ   Prometheus (giver of fire to mortals)
προμηθίᾱ, -ᾱς, ἡ   forethought
προνοέω   think beforehand
πρόνοια, -ᾱς, ἡ   foresight, providence
προπέμπω†   escort
προπορεύομαι   go in front, precede
πρός (prep.) (+acc.) to, towards; (+gen.) in name of, by; under protection of, at the command of; suiting, befitting, the mark of; (poet.) by (= ὑπό), on the side of, towards; (+dat.) near, in addition to
προσαγγέλλω†   report to
προσαγορεύω (aor. προσεῖπον, 18.1/4 note 2)   address
προσάγω†   bring towards/forward; (intr.) advance
προσαπόλλῡμι†   lose in addition
προσάπτω   fasten on, put on
προσαυδάω   speak to, address
προσβάλλω†   attack, assault (+dat.)

προσβλέπω   look at
προσδέομαι†   be in want/need of besides
προσδέχομαι†   await, wait for, expect
προσδίδωμι†   give in addition
προσεθίζομαι   accustom oneself
πρόσειμι   be present/at hand
προσεῖπον aor. of προσαγορεύω
προσέρχομαι†   go/come towards, advance, approach
προσέχω†   bring near, apply to
   προσέχω τὸν νοῦν   pay attention to (+dat.)
προσήκει (impers.)   it concerns, it is fitting (+dat. and inf., 21.1/4a)
προσῆκον (acc. absol.)   it being fitting (21.1/5)
πρόσθε(ν) (adv.)   previously; before; (+gen.) in front of
προσκαλέω†   summon
προσοράω†   look at
προσπασσαλεύω   nail fast to, fasten
προσπίπτω†   fall upon; meet; attack (+dat.)
προσποιέομαι   claim, pretend
προστάττω   assign to
προστίθημι†   put to, add
προστρέχω†   run towards
προσφερής, -ές   similar, like (+dat.)
προσφιλής, -ές   dear, beloved
πρόσω (adv.)   far off
πρότερον (adv.)   formerly, previously
πρότερος, -ᾱ, -ον   first (of two); previous
προτίθημι†   set before
προτρέπω†   urge on, impel
πρόφασις, -εως, ἡ   pretext, excuse
προφέρω†   bring forward
προφήτης, -ου, ὁ   harbinger
πρόχειρος, -ον   ready to hand

πρυτάνεις, -εων, οἱ *prytaneis*
(the 50 members of the tribe
presiding in the Council or
Assembly)
πρωκτός, -οῦ, ὁ *anus*
#πρών, -ῶνος (epic nom. pl.
πρώονες), ὁ *headland*
Πρωτόμαχος, -ου, ὁ *Protomachus*
πρῶτον (adv., also τὸ πρῶτον) *first,
at first*
πρῶτος, -η, -ον *first*
πτερόν, -οῦ, τό *wing*
πτερωτός, -ή, -όν *winged*
#πτολίερθρον, -ου, τό *citadel*
πτυχή, -ῆς, ἡ *leaf* (of book)
πτύω *spit*
πτωχός, -οῦ, ὁ *beggar*
πυθ- aor. stem of πυνθάνομαι
Πῡθαγόρᾱς, -ου, ὁ *Pythagoras*
(philosopher)
Πῡθίᾱ, -ᾱς, ἡ *the Pythia* (the
priestess of Pythian Apollo at
Delphi)
πυκνός, -ή, -όν *thick, dense*
πύλη, -ης, ἡ *gate*
πυλίς, -ίδος, ἡ *postern gate*
†πυνθάνομαι *inquire, ascertain, learn*
(+acc. and gen., 13.1/2*a*(iii))
πῦρ, πυρός, τό *fire*; (pl. πυρά,
13.1/1*c*) *watch-fires,
beacons, fire-signals*
πυρά, -ᾶς, ἡ *funeral pyre*
πύργος, -ου, ὁ *tower*
#πῡροφόρος, -ον *wheat-bearing*
Πύρρη, -ης, ἡ *Pyrrha* (woman's
name)
Πύρρων, -ωνος, ὁ *Pyrrho*
(philosopher of Elis)
πω* *yet*
πωλέω *sell*
πώποτε* *ever yet*
πως* *somehow*
πῶς; *how?*
πῶς γὰρ οὔ; *of course*

ῥᾴδιος, -ᾱ, -ον *easy*
ῥᾳδίως (adv.) *easily, lightly*
ῥᾷστος, -η, -ον *easiest, very easy*
(supl. of ῥᾴδιος)
ῥᾴων, -ον *easier* (compar. of
ῥᾴδιος)
ῥέω *flow; fall/drop off*
†ῥήγνῡμι *break, shatter, burst*
ῥῆμα, -ατος, τό *word*
ῥήτωρ, -ορος, ὁ *orator, politician*
ῥῖγος, -ους, τό *frost, cold*
ῥίζα, -ης, ἡ *root; origin*
†ῥίπτω *throw*
ῥίς, ῥῑνός, ἡ *nose*
#ῥοδόεις, -εσσα, -εν *rosy*
ῥόδον, -ου, τό *rose*
Ῥόδος, -ου, ἡ *Rhodes*
ῥοή, -ῆς, ἡ *stream*
ῥόπαλον, -ου, τό *club, cudgel*
ῥοῦς (ῥόος), -οῦ, ὁ *stream* (6.1/2)
ῥυθμός, -οῦ, ὁ *rhythm*
#ῥύομαι (aor. ἐρρυσάμην) *save,
rescue*
Ῥωμαῖος, -ου, ὁ *Roman*
Ῥώμη, -ης, ἡ *Rome*
ῥώμη, -ης, ἡ *strength, force*

Σάβυλλος, -ου, ὁ *Sabyllus*
Σάϊοι, -ων, οἱ *Saii* (Thracian
tribe)
Σαλαμίς, -ῖνος, ἡ *Salamis* (island in
the Saronic gulf)
σαλπικτής (and σαλπιγκτής), -οῦ,
ὁ *trumpeter*
Σαμοθρᾴκη, -ης, ἡ *Samothrace*
(island in Aegean)
Σάμος, -ου, ἡ *Samos* (island in
Aegean)
σάνδαλον, -ου, τό *sandal*
Σαπφώ, -οῦς, ἡ *Sappho* (poetess of
Lesbos) (13.1/1*b*(ii))
σατράπης, -ου, ὁ *satrap* (Persian
governor)
σαφηνίζω *make clear, explain*

σαφής, -ές clear, plain, true
  τὸ σαφές the truth
σαφῶς (adv.) clearly
Σάων, -ωνος, ὁ Saon
σεαυτόν, -ήν (also σαυτ-; reflex.
  pron.) yourself (9.1/4a)
σέβομαι revere, worship
σεισμός, -οῦ, ὁ earthquake
σέλας, -ως, τό flame, gleam
σελήνη, -ης, ἡ moon
σεμνός, -ή, -όν revered, holy;
  august, majestic
#σεμνόστομος, -ον haughty
σῆμα, -ατος, τό mound, tomb
σημαίνω signal, indicate, show
σημεῖον, -ου, τό signal, sign
σθένος, -ους, τό strength, might
σῑγάω be quiet, keep silent
σῑγή, -ῆς, ἡ silence
σίδηρος, -ου, ὁ iron
Σικελίᾱ, -ᾱς, ἡ Sicily
Σίκελοι, -ων, οἱ Sicels (indigenous
  Sicilians)
Σίμων, -ωνος, ὁ Simon
#Σῑσύφειος, -ᾱ, -ον of Sisyphus
Σίσυφος, -ου, ὁ Sisyphus
σῑτία, -ων, τά provisions, food
σῖτος, -ου, ὁ food (pl. τὰ σῖτα
  (13.1/1c))
σιωπάω be silent
σιωπή, -ῆς, ἡ silence
σκαιός, -ά, -όν clumsy, stupid
σκάφη, -ης, ἡ trough, tub, bowl
†σκεδάννῡμι (fut. σκεδῶ[-άω])
  scatter
σκεπτέον one must consider
  (24.1/5)
σκέπτομαι examine, look carefully
  at, consider
σκεύη, -ῶν, τά gear, furniture
σκηνή, -ῆς, ἡ tent; stage (in
  theatre); stall, booth
σκηνόω lodge, take up one's
  abode

σκῆπτρον, -ου, τό sceptre, staff
σκιά, -ᾶς, ἡ shadow, shade
σκοπέω consider, examine, take
  heed
σκοπιά, -ᾶς, ἡ lookout-place
σκοπός, -οῦ, ὁ mark (at which one
  aims), target
σκορπίος, -ου, ὁ scorpion
σκότος, -ου, ὁ (also -ους,
  τό) darkness
Σκύθης, -ου, ὁ a Scythian (also as
  adj. in poetry)
Σκύλλα, -ης, ἡ Scylla (a sea-
  monster)
Σκῦρος, -ου, ἡ Scyrus (island in
  Aegean)
σμῑκρός, -ά, -όν small, short, little
Σμύρνα, -ης, ἡ Smyrna (city in Asia
  Minor)
σοβαρός, -ά, -όν pompous,
  haughty
Σόλων, -ωνος, ὁ Solon (Athenian
  statesman and poet)
σός, σή, σόν (poss. adj.) your (s.)
σοφίᾱ, -ᾱς, ἡ wisdom
σόφισμα, -ατος, τό clever device
σοφιστής, -οῦ, ὁ sophist, thinker,
  teacher, sage
σοφός, -ή, -όν wise, clever,
  brilliant, accomplished
Σπάρτη, -ης, ἡ the city of Sparta
Σπαρτιάτης, -ου, ὁ Spartiate (a full
  citizen of Sparta)
Σπάρτωλος, -ου, ἡ Spartolus (city)
†σπείρω sow (with seed), engender;
  scatter
σπείσασθαι aor. inf. of σπένδομαι
σπένδω pour (a drink offering);
  (mid.) pour libations; make a
  treaty
σπέρμα, -ατος, τό seed; offspring
#σπέρχομαι hurry, hasten
σπόγγος, -ου, ὁ sponge
σποδιά, -ᾶς, ἡ heap of ashes, ashes

σποδός, -οῦ, ἡ *ashes, embers*
σπονδή, -ῆς, ἡ *libation;* (pl.) *treaty, truce*
σπορά, -ᾶς, ἡ *sowing; begetting*
σποράς, -άδος (adj.) *scattered*
σπουδάζω *be busy about, concern oneself about* (+acc.)
σπουδή, -ῆς, ἡ *zeal, haste, seriousness*
στάδιον, -ου, τό (plur. -α and -οι) *stade* (c. 200 metres)
#σταθευτός, -ή, -όν *scorched, grilled*
σταθμός, -οῦ, ὁ *station, halting-place; stage, day's march*
στάς, στᾶσα, στάν (root aor. pple. of ἵστημι)
στάσις, -εως, ἡ *faction, sedition, discord*
σταυρός, -οῦ, ὁ *stake; cross* (for crucifixion)
σταυρόω *crucify*
στέγω *contain, hold*
†στέλλω *send; equip*
στενάζω *groan*
στένω *groan*
στέργω *love; be content with, accept*
στέφανος, -ου, ὁ *crown, wreath, garland*
στίγμα, -ατος, τό *tattoo-mark*
στοά, -ᾶς, ἡ *roofed colonnade*
στολή, -ῆς, ἡ *clothing, clothes*
στόμα, -ατος, τό *mouth*
#στοργή, -ῆς, ἡ *love*
στρατεία, -ᾶς, ἡ *expedition, campaign*
στράτευμα, -ατος, τό *army; expedition, campaign*
στρατεύομαι *advance with an army or fleet; wage war*
στρατεύω *serve in war; send a force, make an expedition*
στρατηγέω *be general*

στρατηγία, -ᾶς, ἡ *generalship*
στρατηγός, -οῦ, ὁ *general, commander*
στρατιά, -ᾶς, ἡ *army*
στρατιώτης, -ου, ὁ *soldier*
στρατοπεδεύω *make camp, encamp* (also mid.)
στρατόπεδον, -ου, τό *camp, army*
στρατός, -οῦ, ὁ *army*
στρεπτός, -οῦ, ὁ *collar*
Στρεψιάδης, -ου, ὁ *Strepsiades*
στυγέω *loathe, hate*
στυγνός, -ή, -όν *hateful, loathsome*
σύ (pron.) *you* (s.) (4.1/2)
συγγενής, -ές *related to, relative*
συγγενής, -οῦς, ὁ *relation, kinsman*
συγγίγνομαι† *be with, have intercourse with, have dealings with* (+dat.)
συγγιγνώσκω† *pardon, forgive* (+dat.)
συγγνώμη, -ης, ἡ *pardon, forgiveness*
συγγνώμην ἔχω *forgive, pardon*
συγγραφαί, -ῶν, αἱ *contract, bond*
συγκομίζω† *bring/gather together*
συγκρίνω† *compare* (something with something, acc. and dat.)
συγχωρέω *agree to/with; concede, admit; yield to* (+dat.)
συλλαμβάνω† *collect; understand; seize, arrest*
συλλέγω† *collect, gather*
σύλλογος, -ου, ὁ *meeting*
Συμαῖθος, -ου, ὁ *Symaethus* (river in Sicily)
συμβαίνω† *happen, occur, result; correspond with, fit*
σύμβασις, -εως, ἡ *agreement, arrangement*
συμβουλεύω *advise, give advice* (+dat. and inf.); (mid.) *consult, discuss with* (+dat.)

συμμαχίᾱ, -ᾱς, ἡ alliance

συμμαχίς, -ίδος, ἡ alliance,
    confederacy

σύμμαχος, -ου, ὁ ally

συμμείγνῡμι mix together; (intr.)
    meet with (+dat.)

συμπάρειμι be present together

σύμπᾱς, σύμπᾱσα, σύμπαν
    (= πᾶς) all, all together, the
    whole

συμπληρόω fill up

συμπορεύομαι march in company
    with

συμπόσιον, -ου, τό drinking-party,
    symposium

συμπότης, -ου, ὁ drinking-
    companion

συμφέρει (impers.) it is useful/
    expedient (+dat. and inf.,
    21.1/4a)

συμφορᾱ́, -ᾶς, ἡ event; disaster,
    mishap

σύν (prep.+dat.) together with;
    with the help of

συναγορεύω (aor. συνεῖπον, 18.1/4
    note 2) advocate (a course of
    action) with (someone)

συναιρέω† to bring together
    ὡς συνελόντι εἰπεῖν to speak
    concisely, in a word

συναμφότερος, -ᾱ, -ον both
    together

συνδόξαν (acc. absol.) it having
    seemed good also (21.1/5)

σύνειμι be with, be joined with
    (+dat.)

συνεκπονέω assist (+dat.)

συνελών see συναιρέω

συνέρχομαι† come together,
    assemble

συνετός, -ή, -όν intelligent

συνήθεια, -ᾱς, ἡ acquaintance,
    intimacy

σύνθημα, -ατος, τό sign

συνθηράω hunt with (+dat.)

συνίημι† understand

συνίστημι† (mid. and intr. tenses of
    act.) conspire (+dat.)

#συννεάζω be young with (+dat.)

συντάττω arrange, draw up in
    battle-order

συντίθημι† put together; (mid.)
    arrange, agree upon

σύντομος, -ον concise, brief

συντρίβω smash, gash

συντυγχάνω† meet with (+dat.)

Συρᾱκόσιος, -ᾱ, -ον Syracusan

Συρᾱκοῦσαι, -ῶν, αἱ Syracuse

συσκευάζομαι pack up; contrive,
    concoct

σύστασις, -εως, ἡ composition,
    constitution

συστρατεύω join an expedition,
    fight alongside

σφαγή, -ῆς, ἡ slaughter,
    slaughtering

σφάζω slaughter, sacrifice

σφαῖρα, -ᾱς, ἡ ball

σφαλερός, -ᾱ́, -όν perilous,
    precarious

†σφάλλω trip up, make to fall;
    (pass.) be tripped up,
    stumble, fall; be baffled /
    disappointed

σφᾶς (σφῶν, σφίσι) see ἑ (9.1/4a)

#σφε (dat. σφι(ν)) (pron. acc. s. or
    pl.) him, her, them

σφέτερος, -ᾱ, -ον (poss. adj.,
    strengthened by αὐτῶν, 25.2.3
    l. 7) their own

σφόδρα (adv.) very much,
    exceedingly

σφοδρός, -ᾱ́, -όν impetuous

σφώ, σφῶν (pron.) you two (dual
    of σύ, 24.1/4)

σχ- aor. act./mid. stem of ἔχω

σχεδόν (adv.) nearly, near, almost

#σχεθεῖν poet. aor. act. inf. of ἔχω

Σχερίᾱ, -ᾱς, ἡ   Scheria (land of the
    Phaeacians)
σχῆμα, -ατος, τό   form, shape,
    appearance; character
σχήσω fut. of ἔχω
σχοινίον, -ου, τό   little rope
σχολή, -ῆς, ἡ   leisure, rest
    σχολῇ   in a leisurely way, tardily
†σῴζω   save, keep safe
Σωκράτης, -ους, ὁ   Socrates
    (philosopher)
Σωκρατίδιον, -ου, τό
    (diminutive)   dear little
    Socrates
σῶμα, -ατος, τό   body, person
Σωσιγένης, -ους, ὁ   Sosigenes
σωτήρ, -ῆρος, ὁ   saviour
σωτηρίᾱ, -ᾱς, ἡ   safety
σωφρονέω   be discreet/prudent
σωφροσύνη, -ης, ἡ   good sense,
    moderation
σώφρων, -ον   sensible, temperate,
    reasonable, moderate, discreet

ταλαιπωρίᾱ, -ᾱς, ἡ   hardship,
    distress
τάλαντον, -ου, τό   talent (= 6,000
    drachmas)
#τάλᾱς, -αινα, -αν   miserable,
    wretched, unhappy (10.1/3
    note 2)
τἆλλα (or τἄλλα) crasis for τὰ ἄλλα
ταμιεῖον, -ου, τό   storeroom
Ταμώς, -ῶ, ὁ   Tamos (13.1/1a)
Τάνταλος, -ου, ὁ   Tantalus
ταξίαρχος, -ου, ὁ   taxiarch,
    brigadier
τάξις, -εως, ἡ   arrangement, rank,
    battle-array
#τάραγμα, -ατος, τό   confusion
Τάρᾱς, -αντος, ὁ   Tarentum (town
    in southern Italy)
ταράττω   trouble, disturb
ταρβέω   be terrified

ταριχεύω   embalm, mummify
ταρρός, -οῦ, ὁ   mat
#Τάρταρος, -ου, ὁ   Tartarus; the
    underworld
τάττω   station, draw up; appoint,
    place in order; order, instruct
ταύτῃ   here; by this route; in this
    way
ταφή, -ῆς, ἡ   burial
τάφος, -ου, ὁ   grave, tomb
τάχα (adv.)   quickly
ταχέως (adv.)   quickly, soon
τάχιστος, -η, -ον   quickest (supl. of
    ταχύς)
    τὴν ταχίστην   the quickest way
    ἐπειδὴ τάχιστα   as soon as
τάχος, -ους, τό   speed
ταχύς, -εῖα, -ύ   quick, fast
τε*   and
τε* ... καί/τε*   both ... and
τέθνηκα   I am dead (perf. of [ἀπο]
    θνῄσκω 19.1/3a)
τείνω   stretch; lead (a life)
#τείρω   oppress, distress
τείχισμα, -ατος, τό   wall, fort
τειχομαχέω   fight against walls/
    fortifications
τεῖχος, -ους, τό   wall
τεκ- aor. stem of τίκτω
τεκμαίρομαι   conclude, infer
τεκμήριον, -ου, τό   evidence, proof
τέκνον, -ου, τό   child
τεκνόομαι   beget, produce
τελευταῖος, -ᾱ, -ον   last
τελευτάω   end, finish; die
τελευτή, -ῆς, ἡ   end, death
†τελέω   accomplish, fulfil,
    complete; conduct
τέλος, -ους, τό   end,
    consummation, fulfilment
    τέλος (adv. acc., 20.1/5)   in the
    end, finally
    διὰ τέλους   through to the end,
    throughout

†τέμνω cut; ravage
#τέος = σός
#τέρμα, -ατος, τό end
  τερπνός, -ή, -όν delightful,
    pleasant
  τέρπομαι enjoy oneself
  Τερψίων, -ωνος, ὁ Terpsion
  τέταρτος, -η, -ον fourth
  τέτοκα perf. of τίκτω
#τετράπαλαι (adv.) long, long ago
  τετταράκοντα (indecl.
    numeral) forty
  τέτταρες, -α four (7.1/5)
  τέττιξ, -ῑγος, ὁ cicada, grasshopper
  Τευθρανίᾱ, -ᾱς, ἡ Teuthrania
  τέχνη, -ης, ἡ skill, art, expertise;
    way, manner, means; trick,
    wile
  τῇδε (adv.) here
  τηλικοῦτος, -αύτη, -οῦτον so great,
    so important
#τηλουρός, -όν distant
  τήμερον (adv.) today
  τηρέω watch, guard; watch for,
    observe
  τί; what? why? (10.1/1 note 1); in
    what respect?
  Τιγράνης, -ου, ὁ Tigranes
†τίθημι put, place; make, render
    (act. and mid.) (18.1/2)
  νόμους τίθημι lay down laws
  νόμους τίθεμαι make/adopt
    laws
†τίκτω bear, beget, give birth to
  τῑμάω honour; value, reckon;
    (+dat.) fine
  τῑμή, -ῆς, ἡ honour, privilege,
    respect
  ἐν τῑμῇ ἔχω respect, honour
  τίμιος, -ᾱ, -ον held in honour
  Τῑμόκριτος, -ου, ὁ Timocritus
  τῑμωρέω avenge (+dat.); (act. and
    mid.) take vengeance on,
    punish (+acc.)

  τῑμωρίᾱ, -ᾱς, ἡ revenge, vengeance
  Τιρίβαζος, -ου, ὁ Tiribazus
  τις, τι* (indef. pron.) a certain,
    someone, something (10.1/1)
    τι (adv. acc., 20.1/5) to some
      extent
  τίς; τί; (interrog. pron.) who?
    which? what? (10.1/1)
  Τισσαφέρνης, -ους, ὁ Tissaphernes
    (Persian satrap)
  τίτλος, -ου, ὁ title, inscription
†τιτρώσκω wound
  Τιτυός, -οῦ, ὁ Tityus
#τλάω (aor. ἔτλην) venture, bring
    oneself to do something
  τλήμων, -ον wretched,
    unfortunate; patient, resolute
  τοι* (particle) in truth, be assured
  τοίνυν* (particle) now then, well
    now (13.1/3a)
#τοῖος, -ᾱ, -ον = τοιοῦτος
  τοιόσδε, -άδε, -όνδε of this sort, of
    such a sort, such (21.1/3)
  τοιοῦτος, -αύτη, -οῦτο(ν) of this
    sort, of such a sort (21.1/3)
  τόκος, -ου, ὁ offspring
  τόλμα, -ης, ἡ daring
  τολμάω dare, be daring; undertake
  τόξον, -ου, τό bow (also in plur.
    τόξα, bow [and arrows]);
    (poetry) ray/shaft (of
    sunshine)
  τοξότης, -ου, ὁ archer
  τόπος, -ου, ὁ place, region; topic
#τόσος, -η, -ον = τοσοῦτος
  τοσόσδε, -ήδε, -όνδε so much, so
    large, so great (pl. so many)
    (21.1/3)
  τοσοῦτος, -αύτη, -οῦτο(ν) so much,
    so large, so great (pl. so many)
    (21.1/3)
  τότε (adv.) then, at that time
  του = τινος of someone/something
  τοῦ can = τίνος; of whom/what?

τοὔνομα crasis for τὸ ὄνομα
τούτῳ dat. of οὗτος
    ἐν τούτῳ   *meanwhile*
τράπεζα, -ης, ἡ   *table; bank*
τραῦμα, -ατος, τό   *wound*
τράχηλος, -ου, ὁ   *neck, throat*
τραχύς, -εῖα, -ύ   *rough, prickly*
τραχύτης, -ητος, ἡ   *roughness*
τρεῖς, τρία   *three* (7.1/5)
†τρέπω   *cause to turn, put to flight*
†τρέφω   *rear, raise, feed, nourish*
†τρέχω   *run*
τριάκοντα (indecl. numeral)   *thirty*
τριᾱκόντερος, -ου, ἡ (sc.
    ναῦς)   *thirty-oared ship*
τριᾱκόσιοι, -αι, -α   *300*
τρίβω   *rub*
τριηραρχέω   *serve as trierarch*
τριήραρχος, -ου, ὁ   *trierarch*
τριήρης, -ους, ἡ   *trireme*
τρίς (adv.)   *three times*
τρισχίλιοι, -αι, -α   *3,000*
#τρίτατος = τρίτος
τρίτος, -η, -ον   *third*
τρίχες, αἱ nom. pl. of θρίξ
Τροίᾱ, -ᾱς, ἡ   *Troy*
τροπαῖον, -ου, τό   *trophy*
τρόπος, -ου, ὁ   *way, manner, way
    of life;* (in pl.) *ways, habits,
    character*
    τίνα τρόπον; (adv. acc.,
      20.1/5)   *in what way?,
      how?*
    τοῦτον τὸν τρόπον (adv. acc.)   *in
      this way*
    τούτῳ τῷ τρόπῳ   *in this way*
τροφή, -ῆς, ἡ   *food, nourishment*
τρύω   *wear out, distress*
Τρῳάς, -άδος, ἡ   *Trojan woman*
Τρῶες, -ων, οἱ   *Trojans*
    (13.1/1b(i))
Τρωικός, -ή, -όν   *Trojan*
    τὰ Τρωικά (sc. πράγματα)   *the
    Trojan War*

†τυγχάνω (+gen., 13.1/2a(iv))   *hit
    (the mark), succeed; chance/
    happen upon, obtain;* (+pple.)
    happen to -, be actually -
    (15.1/2e)
#τύκισμα, -ατος, τό   *working* or
    chiselling in stone
τύλη, -ης, ἡ   *cushion*
τύμβος, -ου, ὁ   *tomb*
τυπείς aor. pass. pple. of τύπτω
τύπτω   *strike, hit, beat*
τυραννεύω   *be tyrant*
τυραννίς, -ίδος, ἡ   *sovereignty;
    tyranny*
τύραννος, -ου, ὁ   *absolute ruler,
    sovereign; tyrant*
τῡρός, -οῦ, ὁ   *cheese*
τυφλός, -ή, -όν   *blind*
τυχ- aor. stem of τυγχάνω
τύχη, -ης, ἡ   *chance, luck, good* or
    bad fortune; (personified, with
    cap.) *Chance, Fortune*
τῳ = τινι   *to/for someone/
    something*
τῷ can = τίνι;   *to/for whom/what?*
τῷ ὄντι   *in fact, really*

ὑβρίζω   *treat violently/
    disgracefully; humiliate*
ὕβρις, -εως, ἡ   *aggression, violence,
    insolence, insult, humiliation*
ὑβριστής, -οῦ, ὁ   *violent/ insolent
    person*
ὑγίεια, -ᾱς, ἡ   *health*
ὕδρᾱ, -ᾱς, ἡ   *hydra* (water serpent)
ὕδωρ, -ατος, τό   *water*
ὕει (impers.)   *it is raining* (21.1/4c)
ὕειος, -ᾱ, -ον   *of pigs, pork*
υἱός, -οῦ, ὁ   *son* (13.1/1c)
ὕλη, -ης, ἡ   *wood, forest*
ὑλοτόμος, -ου, ὁ   *woodcutter*
ὑμεῖς (pron.)   *you* (pl., 4.1/2)
ὑμέτερος, -ᾱ, -ον (poss. adj.)
    your (pl.)

ὑπάρχω† _be; begin_ (+gen.)
ὕπειμι _be beneath_ (+dat.)
ὑπέρ (prep.) (+acc.) _beyond;_
(+gen.) _for, on behalf of_
ὑπερβαίνω† _step over, cross_
(mountains)
ὑπερβάλλω† _pass over, cross_
Ὑπέρεια, -ᾱς, ἡ _Hypereia_ (a
spring)
ὑπερέχω† _be above, stick out_
above
Ὑπερίων, -ωνος, ὁ _Hyperion_ (the
Sun-god)
#ὑπερμαχέω _fight for_
#ὑπέρπικρος, -ον _exceedingly bitter_
ὑπερύψηλος, -ον _very high_
ὑπερφρονέω _be overproud, look_
down on
ὑπέρχυσις, -εως, ἡ _overflow_
ὑπηρετέω _perform a service_
ὑπηρέτης, -ου, ὁ _servant_
†ὑπισχνέομαι _promise_
ὕπνος, -ου, ὁ _sleep_
ὑπό (prep.) (+acc.) _under, along_
under, up under; (+gen.)
from under; by, at the hand
_of;_ (+dat.) _under, beneath;_
(Homeric) _at the hand(s) of_
ὑπόδημα, -ατος, τό _sandal_
ὑποζύγιον, -ου, τό _beast of burden,_
draught animal
ὑπόθεσις, -εως, ἡ _proposal,_
supposition
ὑποκαταβαίνω† _descend gradually_
ὑπολαμβάνω† _take up, answer,_
reply; assume
ὑπολείπω† _leave behind_
ὑπόλοιπος, -ον _remaining_
ὑποπέμπω† _send secretly_
ὑποπτεύω _suspect, be suspicious_
ὑποπτήττω _cower before_ (+acc.)
#ὑπορρήγνῡμι† _burst beneath_
ὑποτελέω† _pay_ (tribute)
ὑποτίθημι† _place under_

ὑποφαίνω† _dawn, begin to break_
ὗς, ὑός, ὁ/ἡ _pig_
Ὑστάσπης, -ου, ὁ _Hystaspes_
ὑσταραῖος, -ᾱ, -ον _following, next_
τῇ ὑστεραίᾳ _on the following_
day
ὕστερον (adv.) _later, afterwards_
ὕστερος, -ᾱ, -ον _later, last_ (of two)
ὑφ᾽ = ὑπό
ὑφαίνω _weave_
ὑφαιρέομαι† (aor. act./ mid. stem
ὑφελ-) _steal, take by stealth_
ὑφίημι† _send;_ (mid. and intr.
tenses of act.) _submit, yield_
#ὑψηλόκρημνος, -ον _with lofty cliffs_
ὑψηλός, -ή, -όν _high_
ὕψος, -ους, τό _height_

φαγ- aor. stem of ἐσθίω
#φαεινός, -ή, -όν _shining, radiant,_
bright
φαεσφόρος, -ον _light-bringing;_
(personified, with cap.) _the_
Light-Bringer, i.e the Morning
Star
†φαίνω _reveal, declare;_ (pass.)
appear, be seen, seem; (+pple.)
obviously be; (+inf.) _seem to_
_be_ (15.1/2d)
Φάληρον, -ου, τό _Phalerum_ (a port
of Athens)
Φαληροῖ _at Phalerum_
φάναι inf. of φημί
φανερός, -ά, -όν _clear, obvious,_
visible
φάος, -ους, τό _light, daylight_
φάραγξ, -αγγος, ἡ _chasm, ravine_
φάρμακον, -ου, τό _poison; drug;_
remedy; potion
φάσκω _allege, state, declare, claim_
φαῦλος, -ον (also -η, -ον) _mean,_
poor, low; trivial, ordinary,
indifferent, cheap
Φειδιππίδης, -ου, ὁ _Pheidippides_

Φειδιππίδιον, -ου, τό (diminutive) dear little Pheidippides
φείδομαι   spare (+gen.)
φέρε (2nd s. imp. of φέρω)   come!
†φέρω   carry, bring; bear, endure; produce; lead (of a road)
    ἄγω καὶ φέρω   plunder
    χαλεπῶς φέρω   be annoyed at (+acc.)
φεῦ (interjection)   alas!; ah, oh! (+gen.)
†φεύγω   flee, flee from, escape (+acc.); be a defendant, be on trial; be proscribed, be banished, be in exile (17.1/5)
†φημί   say (7.1/2)
†φθάνω   anticipate (15.1/2f)
φθέγγομαι   speak, say, utter
†φθείρω   destroy, ruin
#φθίμενος, -η, -ον   dead
φθονέω   feel ill-will/envy/jealousy against, grudge (+dat.,13.1/2b(i))
φθόνος, -ου, ὁ   envy, jealousy
φιλάνθρωπος, -ον   loving mankind, man-loving, humane
φιλάργυρος, -ον   avaricious, miserly
φιλέω   love, like, be a friend of; kiss; be accustomed to (+inf.)
φιλητέον   one must love (24.1/5)
φιλίᾱ, -ᾱς, ἡ   friendship
Φιλιππισμός, -οῦ, ὁ   siding with Philip
Φίλιππος, -ου, ὁ   Philip (father of Alexander the Great)
φιλόκαλος, -ον   loving beauty, fond of elegance
Φιλοκράτης, -ους, ὁ   Philocrates
φίλος, -η, -ον   dear, friendly; pleasing to (+dat.)
φίλος, -ου, ὁ   friend
φιλοσοφέω   pursue/study philosophy

φιλοσοφίᾱ, -ᾱς, ἡ   philosophy
φιλόσοφος, -ου, ὁ   philosopher
φιλότης, -ητος, ἡ   love, friendship; sexual intercourse
φιλότῑμος, -ον   loving distinction, ambitious
φιλοφροσύνη, -ης, ἡ   love, affection
φίλτατος, -η, -ον   most dear (supl. of φίλος)
#φίλυμνος, -ον   loving song
φλόξ, -ογός, ἡ   flame
φλυᾱρέω   talk nonsense
φλυᾱρίᾱ, -ᾱς, ἡ   nonsense
†φοβέομαι   fear, be afraid of; φοβέομαι μή fear lest/that (14.1/4c(ii))
φοβερός, -ά, -όν   terrible, frightening
φόβος, -ου, ὁ   fear, panic
#φοῖβος, -η, -ον   pure, bright, radiant
Φοῖβος, -ου, ὁ   Phoebus (Apollo)
#Φοινῑκογενής, -ές   Phoenician-born
Φοῖνιξ, -ῑκος, ὁ   Phoenician
#φοίνιος, -ᾱ, -ον   bloody
φοιτάω   go regularly to, frequent, resort to (a person as a teacher)
φονεύς, -έως, ὁ   murderer
φονεύω   murder, slay
φόνος, -ου, ὁ   murder, slaughter, homicide
φορέω   carry, bring
φόρος, -ου, ὁ   tribute
φορτίον, -ου, τό   load, burden
φράζω   explain, tell, declare
#φρήν, φρενός, ἡ   heart, mind (pl. is used in the same sense)
φρονέω   think, consider; be wise, sensible
    εὖ φρονέω   be sane
    μέγα φρονέω   be proud, have high thoughts

φρόνημα, -ατος, τό arrogance, pride

φρόνιμος, -ον sensible, wise

φροντίζω think, ponder, consider, worry; pay heed to (+gen.)

φροντίς, -ίδος, ἡ thought, care, concern

Φροντιστήριον, -ου, τό Think Tank, Thinking shop

φροντιστής, -οῦ, ὁ deep thinker

φρούριον, -ου, τό fort

φρύγανα, -ων, τά dry wood, firewood

φυγάς, -άδος, ὁ exile; runaway; fugitive

φυγή, -ῆς, ἡ flight

φυλακή, -ῆς, ἡ guard, guarding, garrison

  ἐν φυλακῇ εἰμι be on guard

φύλαξ, -ακος, ὁ guard

φυλάττω (perf. πεφύλαχα) guard, watch; (mid.) take care, be on one's guard against (+acc.)

φύρω spoil, defile, mar

φύσις, -εως, ἡ nature, character, temperament

†φύω cause to grow, produce

  ἔφῦν was born; am naturally

  πέφῦκα am naturally, am inclined by nature

Φώκαια, -ᾱς, ἡ Phocaea (city in Asia Minor)

φωνέω speak

φωνή, -ῆς, ἡ voice, language, speech

φῶς, φωτός, τό light

Χαιρεφῶν, -ῶντος, ὁ Chaerephon (disciple of Socrates)

†χαίρω rejoice

  χαῖρε greetings! hello! farewell! (17.1/1 note 7)

χαλεπαίνω be angry/annoyed at (+dat.)

χαλεπός, -ή, -όν difficult, hard

  χαλεπῶς ἔχω be in a bad way

  χαλεπῶς φέρω be angry/displeased at (+acc.)

χαλινός, -οῦ, ὁ bit (for a horse's bridle)

#χάλκευμα, -ατος, τό anything bronze; (pl.) brazen bonds

χαλκός, -οῦ, ὁ bronze

χαλκοῦς, -ῆ, -οῦν of bronze

#χαλκοχίτων, -ωνος bronze-clad

Χάονες, -ων, οἱ the Chaonians (tribe in Epirus)

χάος, -ους, τό chaos

χαρακτήρ, -ῆρος, ὁ engraved mark; characteristic, character

χαρίεις, -εσσα, -εν graceful, elegant, charming, nice

χαριεντίζομαι jest, joke

χαρίζομαι, oblige, do a favour to (+dat.); give graciously

χάρις, -ιτος (acc. χάριν), ἡ grace, charm; favour; recompense, thanks

  χάριν οἶδα / ἔχω be grateful to (+dat.)

Χάρυβδις, -εως, ἡ Charybdis (a whirlpool)

χεῖλος, -ους, τό lip

χειμών, -ῶνος, ὁ storm; winter

χείρ, χειρός, ἡ hand

Χειρίσοφος, ου, ὁ Cheirisophus (Lacedaemonian general of Cyrus)

χείριστος, -η, -ον worst (supl. of κακός)

χειροτέχνης, -ου, ὁ craftsman

χείρων, -ον worse (compar. of κακός)

χελῑδών, -όνος, ἡ swallow

χελώνη, -ης, ἡ tortoise

Χερρόνησος, -ου, ἡ the Chersonese (the Gallipoli peninsula)

χἠ crasis for καὶ ἡ

χῆτος, -ους, τό *want, lack, need*
χθές *yesterday*
#χθών, χθονός, ἡ *earth, land*
χίλιοι, -αι, -α *thousand*
Χίος, -ου, ἡ *Chios (island and city in the Aegean)*
χιτών, -ῶνος, ὁ *tunic, shirt*
χιών, -όνος, ἡ snow
χολή, -ῆς, ἡ *bile, gall; anger*
χορεύω *dance*
†χράομαι *deal with, associate with, treat, use* (+dat., 13.1/2b(iii))
χρείᾱ, -ᾱς, ἡ *use, serviceability*
†χρή *it is necessary* (+acc. and inf.)
χρήζω *desire, want, need* (+gen.)
χρῆμα, -ατος, τό *thing;* (pl.) *money, goods*
χρηματίζω *deal with business* (in the Council or Assembly)
χρῆσθαι inf. of χράομαι
χρήσιμος, -η, -ον *profitable, useful*
χρησμός, -οῦ, ὁ *oracle*
χρηστήριον, -ου, τό *oracle*
χρηστός, -ή, -όν *good, fine, serviceable*
χρῆται 3rd s. pres. of χράομαι
χρῑστός, -ή, -όν *anointed*
χροιά, -ᾱς, ἡ *skin*
χρόνος, -ου, ὁ *time*
διὰ χρόνου *after a time*
χρῡσίον, -ου, τό *a piece of gold, gold*
χρῡσός, -οῦ, ὁ *gold*
χρῡσοῦς, -ῆ, -οῦν *golden*
#χρώς, -ωτός (also χρόα, χροός, χροῖ), ὁ *skin, flesh*
χυτός, -ή, -όν *poured; melted* (with λίθινος, *made of glass*); *piled, heaped up*
χύτρᾱ, -ᾱς, ἡ *pot*
χὠ crasis for καὶ ὁ
χώρᾱ, -ᾱς, ἡ *land, country*
χωρέω *go, come; be in motion*
χωρίζω *separate*

χωρίον, -ου, τό *place, space; region; farm*
χωρίς *without, apart, separately (from)* (+gen.)

ψάλια, -ων, τά *curb-chain of bridle, bridle*
ψάμμος, -ου, ἡ *sand*
ψέγω *blame, censure*
ψευδής, -ές *false, lying*
ψεύδομαι *lie, tell lies; cheat, deceive*
ψεῦδος, -ους, τό *falsehood, lie*
ψευδῶς (adv.) *falsely*
ψηφίζομαι *vote*
ψήφισμα, -ατος, τό *decree*
ψῆφος, -ου, ἡ *voting-pebble, vote*
ψῑλοί, -ῶν, οἱ *light-armed troops*
ψόγος, -ου, ὁ *blame*
ψόφος, -ου, ὁ *noise*
ψύλλα, -ης, ἡ *flea*
ψῡχή, -ῆς, ἡ *soul, life, spirit*
ψῡχοπομπός, -οῦ, ὁ *conductor of souls*
ψῦχος, -ους, τό *cold, period of cold weather*
ψῡχρός, ά, -όν *cold*
ψύχω *breathe*

ὤ *what!* (+gen.)
ὦ *O (addressing someone); ah! (exclamation of surprise)*
Ὠγυγίᾱ, -ᾱς, ἡ *Ogygia (island of Calypso)*
ὧδε (adv.) *thus, as follows;* (poet.) *to here, hither*
ὠδῑνω *be in labour (of childbirth)*
ὠή (exclamation) *help!*
Ὠκεανός, -οῦ, ὁ *Ocean (son of Heaven and Earth)*
#ὠκύς, -εῖα, -ύ *swift, quick*
ὠλόμην aor. of ὄλλυμαι
ᾤμην impf. of οἶμαι

438

ὤμοι (exclamation) *ah me, woe is me, alas*

#ὠμοφάγος, -ον *eating raw flesh, where raw flesh is eaten*

ὤν, οὖσα, ὄν pres. pple. of εἰμί
τὸ ὄν *reality*
τῷ ὄντι *in fact, really*

†ὠνέομαι (aor. ἐπριάμην) *buy*

ᾠόν, -οῦ, τό *egg*

ὥρᾱ, -ᾱς, ἡ *season* (of the year); *time; hour; beauty*

ὡρμισμένος, -η, -ον perf. mid./pass. pple. of ὁρμίζω

ὡς (for a summary of uses see 22.1/1)
(adv.) *as; like*
(exclamatory) *how!* (+adj. or adv.)
(+numerals) *about, nearly*
(+pples.) *on the grounds that, under the impression that; with the intention of* (fut. pple.) (12.1/2a(ii) and (v))
(restrictive) *for, considering that* (+supl.) *as . . . as possible*
(conj.) *that* (= ὅτι); *in order that* (= ἵνα, ὅπως); *when, as* (ὡς τάχιστα *as soon as*, lit. *when quickest,* but if this expression is used adverbially it means *as quickly as possible,* 17.1/4d); *since*
(prep.) *to, towards, to the house of*

ὥς (adv.) *thus, so*

ὡσαύτως (also ὡς αὔτως) (adv.) *in the same way, just so*

ὥσπερ (adv./conj.) *like, as, as if*

ὥστε (conj.) *so that, that, with the result that, consequently* (+inf. or ind., 16.1/1)

ὠτ- stem of οὖς *ear*

ᾧτε see ἐφ᾽

ὠφελέω *help, assist, be of use to, benefit*

ὠφελητέον *one must help* (24.1/5)

Index